S0-BRO-932

# The Truth About
# Everything

# The Truth About
# Everything

## An Irreverent History of Philosophy
### with
### Illustrations

## Matthew
## STEWART

## Prometheus Books
59 John Glenn Drive
Amherst, NewYork 14228-2197

Published 1997 by Prometheus Books

00 99 98 97 96    5 4 3 2 1

Library of Congress Cataloging-in-Publication Data

Stewart, Matthew.
    The truth about everything : an irreverent history of philosophy, with illustrations / Matthew Stewart.
        p.   cm.
    Includes bibliographical references and index.
    ISBN 1–57392–110–6
    1. Philosophy—History. 2. Philosophy. 3. Truth. I. Title.
B72.S784    1997
190—dc20                                     96–34427
                                                  CIP

Printed in the United States of America on acid-free paper.

# Acknowledgment

I would like to thank Mark Silverman, whose thoughtful and detailed comments helped correct many slips and improve the argument throughout the book. My thanks, too, to Antoni and Mircia Conyelles. Toni converted my conceptual sketches into wonderful illustrations. I would also like to point out what should be obvious, that I owe a debt of gratitude to the countless scholars whose contributions through the secondary literature have made a general book like this possible. I have avoided citations and footnotes as much as possible not because they were not deserved, but in order to preserve a certain spirit of the enterprise.

# Contents

In which the author reveals the point of it all (the book, that is)—
Against professionalism in philosophy—Against the historical
sense—Against the usual story about the history of philosophy—
For a more rewarding approach to the history of philosophy

Civilization rises on the sunny Aegean—The original myth of
philosophy—Suspicious contacts with the east—Return to the
planet of the apes—The uses of olive oil, or why the Greeks were
weirder than we tend to think—White beards and water wells, or
why philosophers were even weirder to them

The murky beginnings of Western philosophy—Meet some unusual
personalities—Cosmo-babble—First principles—All is water—
Thales' moment of inspiration—Heraclitus' moment of inspiration—The second order—Parmenides' awful poem, *The Truth*

dialectic to go—Splitting the world in two (again)—Watch his
hands (he's up to something)—Another double-cross—From the
Critique of Pure Ambulation—From the Critique of Pure Vision—
The dialectic of empiricism lives—Destroying science in order to
save it—The grail of pure critique—Strange man at work on perpetual light—A not altogether practical philosophy—How Kant
became a mystic—An aesthetic theory without concepts—The Disagreeability Principle—K visits the castle

Fichte's last kiss—Let there be I—A shock to the I—Mr. Germany—Fichte's (and perhaps our own) sad destiny: to become a fig-
ment of Hegel's imagination

Who was to philosophy what Elizabeth Taylor is to marriage

Super-Monism—Super-Idealism—Super-Critique—Hegel's handy
toolbox, including dialectical reason—What Hegel thought God
was doing—What God thought Hegel was doing—Why did he do
it?—Was Hegel insane?—The Principle of A-sanity—The Phenomenology of Hegel, in which an ignorant reader progresses through
dialectical phases of consciousness and comes to the recognition
that he or she is in fact Hegel—Autobiofact—*Ode to an
Hegelian*—Rotten to the core—No free dialectics—Remains of the
dialectic—Inside H's castle—Historicism, strong and weak

Taking philosophy personally

A cantankerous personality—More Kant—Man the animal—Life
sucks—The Buddha lives—Another case of post-romantic stress
disorder—The irrationalist circle—Dualism, mysticism, schmooalism

history of Being—A fairy tale, in which Martin defeats Plato and restores Being to its rightful throne (not for children)—Paranoia strikes deep—The language myth—Searching for Martin—The priest—The peasant—The Nazi—Martin's Dream/Our Nightmare—The pro—Martin discovered alone in his bedroom having selfish pleasures

Free at last—Do be do be do—Existence and essence—How to deal with existence—The logic of the argument—Same old story—Why so anxious?—The later Sartre: Marx & narcs—A Case of Indigestion, or what happens when you eat too much black forest gateau at a Parisian cafe

Hermeneutics—Critical theory—The dialectic of modernity—Habermas—Sartre's generation: assorted existentialists and phenomenologists—Structuralism and post-structuralism—Glam-philosophy—Parasophy—Rad-philosophy—So you want to be a radical philosopher?—Recipes for radical intellectual cocktails

Historian?—Not—Archaeology of archaeology turns up some musty artifacts—Genealogy of genealogy reveals dubious claims of origins—Power theorist?—Power mad—The Parasophist—Somebody beat him—The myth of the myth of the metaphysical subject, in which Zarathustra returns and shames the modern preachers of intellectual death—How the mystical became a conspiracy, and the conspiracy became the mystical, or how to find God in the overthrow of the phallogocentric tradition of western metaphysical thought in 16 easy steps

Is here and yet not here, deferred until the appropriate page, and yet re-presented, presenced in his absence in a table of contents, iterated and re-iterated, self-dividing in the disappearance of the appearance—blah blah blah—Apocalypse any day now—Plato to the rescue—Eclecticism—The Adventures of Don Q, a knight-errant who battles the tyranny of the history of Western thought

# ANALYTIC PHILOSOPHY: PHILOSOPHY WITHOUT A HISTORY

**389**

Oh, to be professional—Really no history?—The language myth—
The method myth—The poor man's dialectic returns—The home for
lost causes

Meet Mr. Logic—Beating the psychologistic dog—What happens
when a logician dreams—Philosopher of language?—No

Childe George takes on the philosophers with his bare hands

Inspiration—Presuppositions—Aims & Methods—The atoms of
logic—Russell's paradox—Philosophical conversations, or an imaginary dialogue with a certain Mr. Wittgenstein, who proves to be
rather disagreeable

The new logic—The vanishing logic—The picture theory—Tautologism and the democracy of tautologies—Propositions—The logic of
mysticism—Get him off that ladder—Return to the vast and eternal
ocean—More biofiction

Lineage—Ex-Humed and De-Kanted—The bounds of sense—The
verification principle (VP)—Meaningless morality—Sensible nonsense?—Self-destruction—Verifying the verification principle—
The bounds of bounds—Re-Kanted—Help Wanted (?): Clarifiers—
Not—The end of logic—The Laboratory of Dr. Lana City, another
tour of a mysterious laboratory, whose director is engaged in a project of pure analysis, or the analysis of analysis

# List of Illustrations

## FRUIT FOR THOUGHT

## MINDS AND BODIES       **204**

The Theory of Mind—Mind Has a Bad Chair Day—The Mind's
Eye—How the Mind Perceives the Theory of Mind—The Mind-
Body Problem—The Problem of Other Minds—The Problem of
Other Bodies—Mind Tests the Reliability of Perceptions—Mind
Goes Too Far

## MISCELLANEOUS

# Introduction

## I

It seems natural enough to suppose that philosophy is a profession. Presumably, its aim is to investigate a particular set of phenomena according to a distinct body of methods and so contribute to the advance of human knowledge. Although there has been remarkably little consensus among philosophers about the accomplishments of their profession, there is at least a fairly widely held understanding of the basic objective of philosophical investigations. Philosophy is the most general form of inquiry there is, and its object is the fundamental structure of our world. Or, philosophy is the second-order analogue of and complement to the sciences. While the latter investigate specific kinds of phenomena and deploy particular sets of methods, philosophy concerns itself with the universal features of all phenomena and of all methods. Metaphysics, for example, is the investigation into being as such, as opposed to particular kinds of beings. Epistemology is the science of knowledge as such. The philosophy of science, the philosophy of language, and most of the other subdivisions that, with constantly shifting emphases, comprise the modern academic discipline of philosophy, clearly reflect this leap to the second order. We can express this seemingly essential feature of the philosophical enterprise in a variety of idioms: Philosophy, we could say, is the investigation of all possible investigations; or, it is the explanation of all possible explanations; or, it is the investigation of the nature of rationality itself; or, it is the search for the limits of thought. In this book, I will say that philosophy is the search for the truth about everything.

I will argue that all attempts to make philosophy into a profession assume some version of this general idea about the mission of philosophy. I will further argue that all such attempts have ended and must end in failure. There is no second-order investigation of all investigations, for there is no inherent nature of phenomena *qua* phenomena, nor of being *qua* being, nor is there special knowledge of knowledge. Though there may be plenty of ways to formalize patterns of reasoning, and so to assist thought, there is no specific nature of rationality. Nor are there any inherent or fixed (I want to say *a priori*) limits of thought. And while there may be plenty of truths about things, the truth about everything amounts to nothing in particular. Not to put too fine a point on it, I will argue that all philosophy hitherto has been in error, that this error is simple, and that it is implicit in the very idea of philosophy.

I will refer to this misconceived project as the search for the Holy Grail of philosophy. I insist that the error is, at bottom, a very simple one. It is an attempt to get something from nothing. Even so, the manifestations of this error are many and diverse. In most philosophy, the Holy Grail is conceived as the unity of things which cannot be unified: the unity of thinking and being, essence and existence, reason and fact, method and content, universal and particular, possibility (potentiality) and actuality, infinitude and finitude, is and ought, practice and theory, and so on. In its ancient form, the Holy Grail is the idea that one should be able to generate substantial knowledge of the world by means of pure contemplation. In its early metaphysical form, the Holy Grail is that thing which in being thought must also exist, or that whose possibility entails its actuality. In the related theological form, it appears in the proof of the existence of God as that whose essence it is to exist. In its mystical form, the Holy Grail is the experience of the union of all things in a single, ineffable reality. In critical philosophy, the Holy Grail is a method of pure analysis which is nonetheless able to establish some result. In epistemology, it is the assurance of an unconditional knowledge about the conditions of knowledge. In philosophies of language, it is the expectation that the analysis of our means of communication will communicate something fundamental about the nature of things. In moral philosophy, it is the attempt to deduce values from a pure calculus of reason. Sometimes the Holy Grail is conceived not as a doctrine, but as a style. It is a gesture, a movement, or a way of doing things that somehow can never be put into words. There is, in principle, no limit to the number of forms of this or any error. On the other hand, there is a kind of democracy among these forms. They all boil down to the same, simple thing. The free lunch. The rabbit out of the hat. Something from nothing. This quest for the Holy Grail, the attempt to discover the raw essence of the world is, or so I will argue, an attempt to escape from the requirements of rationality altogether. It is the hope for a kind of assurance which reason alone cannot provide.

Our ability to think impels us to ask questions for which our answers will seem always unsatisfactory: Why do I exist? Why does anything exist? Why is there something rather than nothing? What is the meaning of life? What is the good life? Philosophy shifts uneasily between maintaining the openness of the questions and claiming to have found the answers. It is not my purpose to trivialize these questions. Nor do I wish to answer them. My point has to do with the nature of the activity which might be expected to deal with such questions. There is no room for a professional, quasi-scientific project here. Philosophy, if this is what it is, is by its nature the province of amateurs.

# II

History is an idol of our times. At least in some quarters, explanations are now considered complete if they end with a gesture toward historical factors, context, circumstances, and the like. The truism that everything is the outcome of history has become the dogma that everything is historically conditioned. Society is the same idol in a different dress. All thoughts, meanings, ideas, words, actions, events, and so on are considered the property of society, social factors, context, and the like. The simple fact that human beings are social animals has become the creed that everything is socially conditioned. Each distinct society, the corollary goes, has its own reality. Sometimes the idea of language becomes a part of the idol. Language, so the story goes, is no longer just a way of communicating about the world, but also a way of communicating the hidden structure of our thought. The new divinity, whether called history, society, or language, it seems, has conferred upon us the form of our world. Of course, the idol of concern here belongs to an intelligentsia of sorts, not the general population, although it has no doubt trickled down in some form or other.

The idea of the history of philosophy plays an important role in the historicism of our times. Though it has no fixed shape, the idea usually possesses these general features: It says that philosophy is the foundation of thought. The philosophy of a given time expresses its basic patterns and limits of thought, which might also loosely be called its "rationality." In some accounts, good or ground-breaking philosophy gets credit for the transformations which lead from one historical time to the next. Others assign philosophy the more passive role of merely reflecting the reigning paradigm (historical, theoretical, political, scientific) of its time. In either case the history of philosophy is the series of frameworks of thought which define history. The progression presumably culminates in our very own kind of rationality.

In its current and more specific form, the idea goes like this: European civilization produced and in turn has been profoundly shaped by a certain characteristic form of thought. This may be called most generally Western thought, although it also goes by a number of other names, the most important of which are "scientific rationality" and "metaphysics." (Variants include "instrumental rationality," "metaphysics of subjectivity," "phallogocentrism," and so on.) Western thought is sometimes believed to be the work of a few great philosophers, like Plato, Aristotle, and Descartes, though at other times responsibility is assigned to a wider conspiracy involving certain social classes, the establishment, and other powerful agents. Whatever its source, Western thought is the sustaining matrix of all our thought, the form of our consciousness, a code embedded deep within our language, our hidden conceptual scheme, or something like that. It drives our perception of things, determines our behavior, and is ultimately responsible for the direction of history. In many contemporary versions of the story (though not all), the metaphysical tradition has in fact set us on a course for disaster. We will suffer a crisis of nihilism or some other apocalypse should we fail to refute the arguments of our philosophers past. Others take a rosier view, and ask us to join in celebrating the Western way.

I will argue that this story is fundamentally false. There is no such thing as Western thought, if by that is meant anything other than pure and simple thought—the kind to which Easterners, Southerners, and Martians are entitled. There is no hidden fabric of our thought, no secret code concocted by lone geniuses, whether with malice or not. There is only one form of consciousness. There is only one rationality. Rationality is no more one way of reasoning than "the faculty of sight" (or just plain sight) is one way of seeing. Metaphysics, on the other hand, has little to do with rationality. Philosophy is not the foundation of our thought. It is just a collection of peculiar, largely self-referential, mostly timeless, thoughts.

Whether or not the Western world is headed for disaster I do not know. That there are problems in the world, things which could be improved, I do not doubt. Probably some of the world's problems can be solved through reason. On the whole, more reason would be better than less. This seems to me a faith rooted more deeply in human experience than in the Enlightenment, where it is sometimes said to have its historical home, or in any other particular period of thought and philosophy. The only real and valuable heritage of philosophy, the whole of it, is the example of free, critical thought, and the faith that with such thought we can make the world a better place. There is in this heritage nothing complicated or malevolent, just the simple truths: One can improve one's conditions with the help of reason; things are by and large what they seem to be; one is responsible for what one thinks; society is not to blame; Plato is not to blame. For the nonspecialist, this must sound like a very meager return for three thousand years' worth of work in philosophy. It must also seem strange and not a little ironic that I should want to champion such a naive and essentially philosophical faith in the context of, and largely in opposition to, the history of philosophy. As this history of philosophy will show, however, philosophers are often their own worst enemies.

Who trades in this modern idol of historicism? There are those who have an interest in dividing the world up into groups, those whose power increases to the extent that their particular group can be separated, made internally homogenous, and opposed to all others. These groupies can derive assurance from the supposedly historical—and therefore arbitrary and locally determined—nature of rationality. For others, historicism is an escape from individual responsibility. It is a longing for the comforts of that imaginary prison called Western thought, where one can at least grab the bars and shout at the guards. Some proponents of historicism are the rebels in search of an enemy, who take up themselves the fight against the evil and oppressive patterns of rationality supposedly embedded in our language and in our particular form of civilization. There may also be those who, mingled among the rest, have a spiritual or mystical motive—one with a long-standing place in philosophy, and strangely satisfied in beholding the new mysteries manifested in the very ideas of history, society, and the inexorable logic of Western thought.

Each of these interests, of course, has a logic of its own, and demands more than a general argument about some shared error. However, I will simplify things somewhat in order to define the issue which I think can be addressed in this book. I will argue that there is a single vested interest which sustains the idol of historicism in most of its forms, and that this is the professional interest of academic philosophy, as representative of the system according to which knowledge is organized in the modern world. Historicism represents a strategy of deflecting the quest to explain the totality of things onto something—namely, history—which gives the impression of being the legitimate object of a professional discipline, perhaps even of a science. The idolization of history is just another—perhaps the last—excuse for philosophy. It is a continuation by other means of the quest for the Holy Grail of philosophy.

# III

Both "professionalism," to give it an ugly name, and its modern variant, historicism, draw support from the mere fact that there is a long and colorful history of philosophy. The view that there is some serious, professional task for philosophy seems to be justified by the mere existence of the Great Philosophers. What else could Kant have been up to, with all those unpleasant words and those tomes of dense prose? The view that reason somehow emerges out of the historical process seems unavoidable given the endless string of quite reasonable philosophers who proclaim mutually incompatible versions of the truth about everything. Both views also draw heavily on a particular traditional version of the history of philosophy. I have therefore found it necessary to produce a new and different version of the history of philosophy.

The traditional version is really a mixed bag of stories from the history of philosophy, and the various, mildly competing versions of the history of philosophy available today are essentially different assortments from this common stock. The individual stories, to be sure, are widely but not universally accepted, not always mutually consistent, and appear in a variety of forms. Any list of such stories inevitably begins with the one of several possible accounts about the origin of philosophy. An origin story relates how philosophy burst forth onto the world scene as the first embodiment of rational consciousness. It is usually set in the sunny groves of ancient Greece, though exact dates and locations may vary. Connected with the origin story is the story about boundaries. It explains why philosophy (or a certain kind of philosophy) is still circumscribed by geographical boundaries—between East and West, for the most part. As one moves down the list of stories, one encounters a number of episodes involving foundational acts: reports of how philosophers forged the structures of thought still in use to this day. In the most popular of these, the early modern philosophers, like René Descartes and John Locke, take leading roles in piecing together the metaphysical foundations of modernity, including the concept of the self and the scientific method. Most inspiring for the professional philosophers are the revolutionary war stories about heroes like Immanuel Kant, who singlehandedly defeated the army of his metaphysical predecessors and boldly pointed toward a brave new future for philosophy. In recent times one hears various twilight tales, which relate how the end is nigh for the age of the gods of philosophy, and that a disenchanted humankind awaits the dawn of a new "post"-philosophy. But these are contentious times, so others, notably the analytic philosophers, already speak of this new dawn, and retell the old stories as fumblings in the dark before things were finally set right. What is common to all these stories about the history of philosophy is the sense that there is some progression, some logical sequence of events, which leads from past to present in philosophy. That philosophy had an origin, that it was born somewhere nearby, that it is foundational for our thought, that it may experience revolutionary changes, possibly even that it may lead to its own self-destruction—all of these putative facts of history seem to imply that there is some meaningful project for philosophy. And if philosophy is understood to trace the limits of thought, then these facts seem to imply that rationality is indeed an historical artifact.

The history as I see it is very different. The origin of philosophy, as told in the traditional histories, never happened. The Greek philosophers did not invent rational consciousness, Western thought, or anything of the sort. Instead, they deviated from an otherwise healthy respect for reason in Greek culture in order to perpetuate an earlier mystical tradition. Their chief objective was to establish an idiosyncratic and cultish way of life for themselves. The boundary story is also a myth: There is no meaningful division between East and West, so far as the content of philosophy is concerned. The early modern philosophers did not build the foundations of modern science through new concepts, as the usual story has it, but revived old concepts and so preserved the theological biases they claimed to reject. Kant's revolution, if that's what it was, was to find a way to continue metaphysical speculation in the context of a professional, academic setting. The project of the "overthrow" of metaphysics, set forth by Martin Heidegger and successors like Jacques Derrida, is just another form of mysticism. Modern analytic philosophy, which takes itself to be so new, serious, and hard-headed, is also fatally mired in the paradoxes of the past. In brief, I hope to sketch the outlines of an alternative to the traditional history of philosophy. And in my version there is no place for the idea of progression.

The stories which make up the traditional history of philosophy really are myths, or so I contend, and the collection of them is a mythology. Like any mythology, it is a motley jumble of tales told in a variety of ways about great heroes and villains in an imaginary past and which lends meaning to present state of things. Like any mythology, however, it sanctions irrational practices: for example, professional philosophy. And it sustains faith in supernatural entities: for example, historical rationality. All of which makes me want to say, with Voltaire, *écrasez l'infâme*.

# IV

Why so negative? you may ask. So many targets! Success is unlikely, and if it happens, will leave only destruction.

Actually, I think there is something valuable in philosophy, something that will repay a long investment in the history of philosophy. And I maintain that my own modest history of philosophy is a work of philosophy. (Not to say, of course, that it's a particularly good one, nor that it's more than just a book.)

What I have identified as the error in the search for the Holy Grail of philosophy boils down to a simple mistake about the nature of the beast which is philosophy. This is the false assumption that philosophy is an investigative project, in the same category as, say, physics and psychology. It is not. Philosophy is an attitude or a disposition. As the Greek, from which the word "philosophy" derives, indicates, it is a love of knowledge. It is the delight in seeing things as they are. This is an attitude which is appropriate to any search for knowledge, perhaps to life in general. As a claim about the world, it corresponds to nothing more than the notion that knowledge is better than ignorance. As an activity, it is just thinking—thinking clearly. Possibly also it is an exercising of the mind, a way of stretching, limbering up. (We should guard against the idea, however, that there is some special technique to thought, that philosophers have some special purchase on a mysterious faculty of thought. Thinking is free, just as seeing is free. Maybe a philosopher can teach us to think, just as an artist can teach us to see as we have not seen before. But in the end, no one can do our thinking for us.)

Such a general attitude as this determines virtually nothing about what philosophers have done or ought to do. The way I have described it, one could practice philosophy by baking a well-conceived lasagna. But now I want—for tactical reasons mainly—to leave a special place for the history of philosophy. Of course, the history of philosophy ought to be interesting in its own right, since it is, in the final analysis, a revealing (and amusing) piece of human history. It has a peculiar interest for philosophers, however, because philosophy as a practice—on its own, apart from baking lasagna and so forth—is essentially the critique of other philosophies. For the philosopher, the history of philosophy is like a sprawling and noisy city of thought. This ancient city is a playground of sorts, a place to test oneself, and the arena within which philosophy forms a self-contained enterprise. But it is also a city of fossils and afterthoughts, the monuments of bygone revolutions—things to scale, things to overcome, and a place one should, at the appropriate time, be able to leave. Philosophy is the practice of the liberation of thought: most importantly, a liberation from the tyranny of old revolutionaries.

I began this introduction by identifying and opposing two philosophies of a sort. The first might be called a kind of *absolutism*, for it holds out a faith that philosophy may establish an unconditioned truth about everything. The second is a kind of *relativism*, for it maintains that all truths are hopelessly conditioned by historical context. In another century, I might have identified the opponents as dogmatism and skepticism, respectively. Like a typical philosopher, I have recommended something like a middle course between these extremes. (Moderation in all things.) It should also be evident that the two extremes in some way belong together. Both assume that rationality has a fixed structure (though they may differ on details about the origin and nature of this structure). Both assume that it is possible to hold the key to every question, the advance knowledge, as it were, of the truth about everything. In uniting them I also follow the traditional philosophical course of synthesizing opposites in order to

A BOWL OF FRUIT

reach a deeper level of understanding. The rejection of the mythological versions of the history of philosophy is a part of the same synthesis. The final resting point of my arguments against the traditional histories is that they provide narratives where no narrative is possible. They relate stories about the origin and evolution of something which never came to be, nor ever can come to be—the structure of rationality, or something like that. There is nothing in my approach which does not already belong to the history of philosophy. And there is nothing very much at all in my conclusions, at the end of the day, except possibly an affirmation of that philosophical disposition to love knowledge, and to liberate thought from imaginary prisons.

This is a book for those who love to think. (I suspect you already know who you are.) It does not provide much in the way of answers to the big questions in life, it would probably be disastrous as crib notes for students, and it certainly won't prepare anyone for a specialized career. Its aim is revitalize the history of philosophy, if only for a moment, to give life to thought.

# THE ANCIENT GREEKS

*Before the Beginning...*

## I

It all began on the sunny shores of the Aegean, or so the story goes, where the very word "philosophy" was an invention of the ancient Greeks. Rational consciousness dawned among that mysterious and diverse group of thinkers known as the Presocratics. These hardy pioneers of thought confronted and rejected the mythological cosmologies of their own culture. The world was not created by some funny child-eating god and his incestuous family. The new thinkers demanded and supplied an explanation of the world according to rational principles. Socrates, the next in line, didn't much care how the world accounted for itself; he wanted to know how people around him accounted for themselves. He would ask: What is the good life? What is virtue? What do you know? What do I know? Thus he was the first to make our ethical life the object of rational inquiry. Among his followers, Plato was the most successful in converting the Socratic brand of philosophizing into social and literary institutions. He founded the famous Academy and expressed his bold new theories in the dialogues which now function as philosophy's first book—of which the rest of the history of philosophy is sometimes said to be a series of footnotes. The next superstar, Aristotle, transformed these institutions into a universal program for the acquisition of knowledge, and based all of it on his new science of metaphysics. He and his helpers systematically explored and developed as many areas of human knowledge as they could get their hands on. After Aristotle, the story loses some of its coherence. The philosophies of the Hellenistic era are thought to have initiated a holding pattern that would carry civilization up to the end of Rome, at which point everything would come crashing down.

The enduring appeal of the story about the rise of philosophy is that it provides a direct historical analogue of precisely that development of rational consciousness with which philosophy is most generally concerned. One imagines that rationality requires progress out of murky depths toward the highest level of consciousness, an awakening of sorts, and that the progress of Greek philosophy represents the ascent to this rational consciousness as it occurred across several centuries of human history. And the story of philosophy fits nicely into the story of civilization, in which ancient Greece as a whole plays the roles of midwife and mother combined to the modern, Western way of life.

But was it really so?

# II

The man regarded as the first of the Presocratics is Thales of Miletus (624?-546? B.C.E.). The traditional view says that philosophy—together with science, reason, and perhaps consciousness itself—exploded on to the world stage in the early sixth century B.C.E. in the person Thales. This somewhat abrupt version of things has in recent times been modified. The city of Miletus was in the easternmost part of ancient Greece known as Ionia, on what is now the western coast of Turkey. In its heyday, that is, in Thales' day, Ionia was the most commercial and cosmopolitan of the Greek regions. In this ancient mixing bowl of Eastern spices and Western know-how, or so the story goes, the critical intellectual ingredients came together and, well, then the explosion took place.

It is possible that even this story is a little too abrupt. There is a lingering suspicion that Thales did not create something new out of a fusion of East and West, so much as import a product already manufactured. According to the tradition, Thales was guilty of at least one trip to Egypt. And what little we know of his thought strongly suggests the influence of some legendary mystics who wandered into the West from the East. So where does this place the beginning of reason or philosophy? Do we need to take our research still further back, into ancient Egypt, Mesopotamia, or even the Hindu heartland?

The answer is yes, we probably should. From a strictly chronological point of view, the Greeks were not the first recognizable philosophers. There are texts in the Hindu tradition, for example, which can be traced back well before the first Presocratic was ever born. It also won't do much good to argue that the Greek philosophy, especially as embodied in the Presocratics, is something qualitatively new and different from that which could have been found from an earlier time in the regions now referred to as India and China. I will argue that the core ideas were much the same in the East and the West. More on that later.

# III

We think of the Greeks as an early culture. They thought of themselves as the late, possibly degenerate heirs to a glorious past. The ancient Hindus likewise harked back to a more distant, obscure, and purely oral past. Maybe they were both right. Even by the most generous estimate, the recorded history of philosophy begins a mere three thousand years ago. Yet complex civilizations complete with urban centers and writing go back several thousand years before that. Probably the most profound change in the human way of life, the agricultural revolution, occurred around ten thousand years ago. Some rather attractive cave paintings date from twenty to thirty thousand years ago. Geneticists now think that our species has been around in more or less its present form for one or perhaps two hundred thousand years. Does this mean we have to go back even further? Back to the cave?

Well, yes, we probably should, if what we really want is the complete story of the origin of rational consciousness. It is easy to imagine that the cave-dwelling bunch were merely superstitious savages, that theirs was a dim and semiconscious world of mastodon hunts, magic, and lawless struggle. After all, it is hard to identify with creatures who would walk around in bearskins, carry clubs, and grunt a lot for no good reason. The bad reputation for our forebears, though, is a product chiefly of the gaps in the historical record and in our own imagination. What the record cannot show is what was by and large most probable: the vast ordinariness of their everyday existence. A few hundred generations is not such a great distance in biological time. Most likely, there is a good deal of the cave left in us—even in philosophy.

Disrespect for biological reality is another sign of our times. The story about Greek origins is one way in which philosophy congratulates (or castigates) itself for having created the human being in its present form. It assumes that the countless generations of prehistorical evolution served only to provide the physical platform, the hardware, as it were, for which civilization, with the aid of its philosophical programmers, provided the all-important software. It assumes that the emergence of an organism with a vocal apparatus capable of intricate modulation of sound, a brain with the power to master the complex rules of human language in the few years given a child, a face and eyes built for the transmission and reception of nuanced communication through tiny muscular movements, a set of instinctive desires that with uncanny precision achieve the delicate balance between self-interest and the common good—that all this was just a prehistorical accident, rather than the fruit of the hard, physical labor of evolution. No doubt there has been a dialectic at work between the so-called biological and the so-called cultural; when in the thrall of a history of philosophy, however, it is easy to forget the earthy side of the dialectic, the fact that we are, after all, still animals of a sort.

In short, the story about the origins of rationality supposes that prephilosophical humankind was an open book onto which philosophy inscribed its concepts of 'subject', 'object', 'being', and so forth. Yet even a modest survey of the known facts raises the strong suspicion that the philosophical era may represent only a few pages in the book of humanity, perhaps a concluding gloss or afterword or—how boring—the bibliography.

# IV

Let's forget about who came first and just stay with the Greeks. Before considering the story of philosophy, let's reflect for a moment on the story of civilization, the one which says that the Greeks as a whole raised humanity up to a new level.

In some ways, the Greeks were a lot weirder than we tend to think. Here is a group of people who walk around in bedsheets. They like to walk around because they—or at least the "they" we know about—do not work and would consider it contemptible to have to work for a living. They like to drink and talk, but they water their wine—about three parts water to one part wine—and regard the straight stuff as undrinkable—which, in their day, it probably was. Their lamps burn olive oil. Their staple meal is a kind of mush of olive oil and cereals. Their finest craftsmen make vases, from the very small to the enormous, to carry olive oil. They rub themselves down with olive oil. They are heavily into physical appearance, especially the men and boys.

We imagine them as the first democrats—fair-minded, just, believers in human equality, the one civilized tribe amid the hordes of barbarians. We associate democracy with the rule of law. For them, democracy was a form of power, not of law. Its ruling body could do anything it liked to anyone it chose to put on trial. The same went for the city as a whole. The most powerful and most democratic city, Athens, was, so long as circumstances allowed, the most rapaciously imperialistic. In describing a government, we use "democratic" and "good" interchangeably. For most Greeks, the educated ones at any rate, "democratic" sounded more like "corrupt," "vulgar," and "incompetent." It meant the rule of the masses. Who were these masses? By most estimates, in Athens, these were the 10 percent of the population who were not women, resident foreigners, or slaves. Class conflict within Greek cities was so severe that there were frequently more Greek mercenaries fighting on behalf of foreign barbarians than there were Greeks defending civilization. As for slavery, very few of the ruling Greeks would have considered it uncivilized. It was for them a necessary consequence of war. And war, for them, was virtually the basis of society. We read Homer as a moving story about a few heroes resolving their internal conflicts and confronting the human condition, with a lot of annoying battle scenes and lists of warriors thrown in. They read Homer as the poet-chronicler of war—their original, founding war. They thrilled over his battle scenes. And the lists of warriors were the ancestral basis of their self-worth. The Greeks were seriously devoted to their ancestors. They would burn bits of animal fat and bones in honor of their gods and ancestral spirits.

# V

Let's forget about what it means to be civilized and stick with the Greeks anyway. The question then is this: What did philosophy do for the Greeks? Did it bestow on them this gift of rational consciousness? Was it the pinnacle of civility in this first of civilizations?

Given their astonishing philosophical and literary accomplishments, we sometimes imagine the Greeks to be a rather idealistic or impractical culture. Nothing could be further from the truth. One need only read the works of the historian Thucydides (d. ca. 401 B.C.E.), for example, to understand the devastating realism with which the Greeks could view the world. Perhaps it was this realism—the desire to know how things really stand—which is the authentic, unwritten philosophy of the Greeks.

In the traditional story about the origins of philosophy, the first philosophers are identified with the early flowering of Greek realism. The historical facts, unfortunately, do not quite support such an interpretation. The official group of Presocratics, beginning with Thales, includes mainly those thinkers who could loosely be called physicists, whom we will turn to in the next chapter. At one time the so-called Seven Sages were considered a part of the Presocratic philosophical world. Nowadays, six out of the Seven (Thales being the exception) are classified as local political bosses, and left out of the philosophical tradition. The Sophists, when they are included in the tradition at all, are either tacked on to the end of the Presocratic period (despite being pretty much contemporaneous with it) or described as the background for Socrates' development. If time were the criterion, in fact, it would be hard to exclude Socrates from the Presocratics, since he died thirty years before that period ended. Though the Presocratics are usually described as the natural scientists of their day, their list does not usually include some of the arguably best scientists of the era. For example, the medical doctors, the first in the West to gather data on the human body systematically, are usually relegated a marginal role, if any at all. And where the Presocratics were polymaths, which is in most cases, the interest of philosophers in their work rarely extends to their achievements in astronomy, mathematics, geography, zoology, and so on. In short, the originary myth seems to suppose that the Presocratics were beacons of reason penetrating a preconscious mist, but the reality is that they were at best a small part of a broader movement, perhaps even irrelevant. So why just the physicists? A better question would be: Were they really physicists?

What does one of our official philosophers look like to one of the authentic, realistic Greeks? Sometimes, he is a harmless, absent-minded fellow with a flowing white beard who falls into wells while looking at the stars. Sometimes he is a mystic, not so different from the seers who sustain the religion of the people. Occasionally, some practical man of affairs might adopt a little philosophy—as a kind of quirk, a soft side, a signal that his motives are not so easily understood. The Greeks would be quite unusual to us, but their philosophers were, for the most part, quite strange even for them.

How did philosophers see themselves? By and large, they thought of themselves as a chosen few. They had no great interest in bringing enlightenment to the masses. Philosophy was for them primarily a way of life. It was cultish. It was not a body of knowledge. It was not a profession, but a calling. It was a new, bizarre, and now basically extinct kind of religion.

So what did philosophy do for the Greeks? Mainly, it offered solace, friend-ship, and an amusing way to pass the time for a privileged, intellectual segment of the population. It is perhaps more interesting to note what it did not do for them. Philosophy did not, as legend has it, bestow the gift of rationality on the Greeks. In many endeavors the Greeks exhibited a healthy respect for reality, a respect founded on something much deeper and more durable than philosophy. At its best, Greek philosophy provides a minor example of this spirit. Actually, I will argue below, philosophy was more often a perversion or a parody of the rational instincts of the Greeks. For the most part, philosophy in the Greek world was an innovative continuation of a very old mystical and mythological tradition. It was a new and sophisticated way of maintaining some ancient superstitions.

# VI

Still, we have to begin somewhere. Let's return to the sunny Aegean, not because the Greeks were the first philosophers, which they weren't, nor because they invented reason, which they didn't, nor because they created our own form of civ-ilization, for the story must be much more complicated than that, nor because the philosophers were the Greeks' first thinkers, which they weren't; but because, first, this is where the evidence runs out, and, second, this is the source of the most com-pelling myth about the origin of philosophy, and the story needs to be retold.

# The Presocratics

## The Primordial Soup of Philosophy

Even as we approach, the mist of deep antiquity shrouds the Presocratics. The first of these thinkers was born around 624 B.C.E., the last died in 371 B.C.E. The evidence on them consists of fragments of texts, like shards of ancient clay pots. No complete original of any of their works exists. We have only the quotations and summaries provided by later Greek and Roman writers. This last group is notorious for its disrespect for the norms of modern philology and scholarship, so it is impossible to know with certainty what any of the Presocratics really believed. Also, it is often very difficult to make sense out of the various things that they are supposed to have believed. The remains of the Presocratic texts are like little pieces of wisdom swirling around in a murky soup.

This murkiness, however, is not without its advantages. It lends credence to the traditional story, that rational consciousness coalesced of out of a synthesis of fragmentary philosophical reflections. In this view, the Presocratics were a kind of primordial soup, from which were spawned Socrates and Plato and all the subsequent generations of standard-bearers for Western rationality down to Kant and Wittgenstein. Even the obviously posthumous name for this group of thinkers reflects their seemingly primordial nature. Presumably Socrates was the first fully fleshed thinker, and the Presocratics were the beginning before the beginning, as it were.

As indicated previously, it is just this tale of origins that I will oppose. The view I really want to establish, however, will take some more time to unravel (maybe the whole rest of this book). The traditional story naturally casts the first philosophies as early, immature, and ill-formed. In my view, however, the Presocratic philosophies are, in an essential sense, all of philosophy: the beginning, the end, and everything in between. This is not because the Presocratics decisively influenced their successors—for the most part, they were forgotten or misunderstood—or because they created a new paradigm of thought which mysteriously diffused and informed all subsequent thought. Rather it is because that's just the way

35

philosophy is. Allowing for the state of the evidence—which isn't quite the issue it's made out to be by the scholars—the Presocratic philosophies are no more or less soupy than what was to come. The supposed primordial nature of the Presocratics is not a fact, but the projection of some philosophical need. And, by happy *coincidence*, this longing for an origin is most excellently expressed in the philosophies of the Presocratics themselves. So, as we shall see, the Presocratics will end up telling us not so much about the beginning of philosophy as about philosophy's need for a beginning.

## I. MEET THE PRESOCRATICS

Before wading into the viscous waters of the Presocratics' official doctrines, let us proceed with a few informal introductions. There was a high degree of eccentricity among the Presocratics. They could be wild, bizarre, and extravagant. Maybe they were less inhibited by the social norms about what is expected from a philosopher—maybe because these norms as we know them had not yet solidified. In any case, it is their personalities which are in many ways the most striking aspect of their legacy. Their characters and dispositions are the framework within which their doctrines have meaning. In any case, they remain alive today as some of the chief personality types of the philosophers.

*Thales (624?–546? B.C.E.).* Actually, no one is quite sure just who Thales was. One has to project something on to him. The evidence allows me to think of him as a great general, a statesman, a man of learning, both an innovator in thought and a practical man of affairs. I do not imagine, for example, that he took his idea that all is water very seriously. For him it was probably one of those amusing, late-evening ruminations intended half as joke, half as misty gloss on a hard day's work.

*Pythagoras (571?–497? B.C.E.).* The group worships its master as the source of divine wisdom. He has magical powers. The master in turn uses the group to advance his personal fortunes. He provides them with absolute spiritual security in a Faustian bargain for their complete submission to his will. This is a pattern characteristic of both Eastern guru-based philosophies and early Greek mystery cults. So it was with Pythagoras, the archetypal cult leader of philosophy, and his followers. Pythagoreans went through initiation rituals and lived apart from mainstream society. One was expected to follow such sage principles as these: to spit on one's nail-pairings and hair-trimmings; to abstain from beans; and not to have swallows in the house. Dissension was not tolerated. Legend has it that one member, a certain Hippasus, discovered that the square root of two was not a rational number. This little fact was inconsistent with the master's teachings. For his trouble, Hippasus was thrown into the sea and drowned.

Pythagoras also instantiates that philosophical personality type which I call the science mystic. This usually characterizes a nonscientist who imagines that somewhere at the limit of his ability to grasp the abstractions in recent developments in mathematics and science, perhaps in the latest equations of chaos theory or quantum mechanics, the ultimate truth of the universe has been discovered. Modern physics proves the immortality of the soul, or that the ancient Hindus were really smart, or something like that. In Pythagoras' day things were not so high-tech. People could be hypnotized with the odd theorem about right triangles or a few facts about prime numbers.

Pythagoras, by the way, is credited with the invention of the term philosophy. He was certainly among the first to conceive of philosophy as a way of life. Some (Hippasus, perhaps) might have doubted that it was the best way of life.

*Heraclitus (fl. ca. 500 B.C.E.).* Here we have the original example of a man whose wisdom is so vast that he can no longer mix with polite society. The contempt of this misanthropic genius for the foolishness of humankind drove him to a solitary, Alpine existence. There, alone with himself, deep in the fiery bowels of his mind he compressed the diamantine insights which are his gift to an ungrateful humanity. All is change, he said, all the furniture of your life is mere vanity. His words escaped ordinary mortals. To them he was obscure, a riddler. They did not understand that Truth cannot be stated, it can only be indicated, and even then only the wise few will see.

*Parmenides (fl. 500 B.C.E.).* Lacking the dash of his contemporary Heraclitus, this primordial priest-professor, this clumsy lover sought to capture truth in an impenetrable cage of abstraction. He was a man who reveled in pure theory, who pursued arguments in an apparently disinterested, rational fashion, but whose logical fastidiousness itself was a sign of a deep and disturbed passion, a crazy and insatiable demand for purity, permanence, and absolutes.

*Zeno (fl. 464 B.C.E.).* Some say he was a professor, too, and merely Parmenides' foot soldier in the trench warfare of early academia. If the great Parmenides' arguments led to some puzzling paradoxes, Zeno showed, common sense couldn't do any better. Yet Zeno was not the sort to confine himself to his mentor's cage. His paradoxes were just a little too carefree, too irreverent. He loved the thrust and parry of abstractions, and the ironic flourish at the end. He played the game for its own sake.

*Empedocles (484?-424? B.C.E.).* The first great dualist in our tradition, Empedocles revealed for all to see that the world is nothing but the unceasing give and take between two primal forces, between Love and Strife. Through Love all things become one, through Strife all things fall apart. These days, however, Empedocles' personality has been almost totally coopted by the German Romantics. Why fight it? Let's say that he was the noble savage, the wild romantic, the man in touch with his innermost being, with his raw nature, with the God that is Nature. Let us say that this elemental nature of his allowed him to guide others along the path to achieving true harmony among themselves and with the cosmos. Sure, he used magic tricks and faked miracles, but that was only in order to guide the ignorant masses into a better future. And when he finally threw himself into a volcano, as the story has it, that was his self-sacrifice in order to show men how to become one with nature.

*Leucippus (fl. 440 B.C.E.) and Democritus (460?–371? B.C.E.).* The atomists were the Marxists of the ancient world. Early in life their emotional reality crystallized around a few random dogmas. We are all just atoms, dancing in a void, they repeated to themselves. They spent the rest of their time on this earth trying to force the world to correspond to their ideology.

Though their personalities and doctrines varied widely, there was nonetheless a surprising degree of communication among the thinkers of the ancient Greek world. They loved and hated each other. They were prepared to fight almost to the death over burning issues such as whether the soul is a number or a harmony, or whether or not to ban the word "not" from language. So there is a kind of interconnectedness in their work. In any case, given the soupy character of the evidence and of their role in the history of philosophy, I will continue to refer to them frequently as a group, rather than as the individuals they truly were.

## II. THEIR DOCTRINES

Fortunately, the philosophical hard core of the Presocratic era unfolds chronologically according to a rough but discernible logic. I will use this approximate (and perhaps merely apparent) logic to structure the presentation of the Presocratics' doctrines. Before the philosophers there were a variety of mythological cosmologies (section 0). Then the early Ionians, led by Thales, came forth with their physical cosmologies (section 1). Next the torch passed to the Eleatics in Italy, led by Parmenides, who sought to put philosophy on a more metaphysical footing (section 2). Lastly, in the primordial instance of philosophical backtracking, the later Ionians tried to circumvent the Eleatics with some fancier versions of physical cosmology (section 3).

### (0) COSMO-BABBLE

In the beginning there was cosmo-babble. At first, or so the mythology has it, there is Chaos, Night, or some kind of gooey stuff. This primal crud suddenly spawns a few gods, including Earth, Sky, and Time. After a bit of incest, castration, infanticide, and so on, you get a stable gallery of gods, like Zeus, Poseidon, and Aphrodite. Add a few thousand lines of verse and you end up with an explanation for everything from why birds fly south in the winter to the organization of the contemporary judicial system. There's a good chance you will also receive an immortal soul.

The details are unimportant. In both the Near East and ancient Greece, the basic pattern of myths about world-creation were the same:

1. Muck
2. Muck spawns elemental figures, i.e., gods, who fight among themselves for control of the world (this process may take a few generations)
3. Offspring of elemental figures are in control of the present world and give rise to seasons, political order, the color of grapes, and so on.

(This pattern is strangely like that of the modern Big Bang theory of the origin of the universe. But that's another matter. . . .)

## (1) FIRST PRINCIPLES

### All Is Water

The first doctrine of the first philosopher is this: The first principle of all things is water. Actually, no is one sure if Thales really said this, and if he did, what he meant by it. Supposing he did say it—and despite the disclaimers the tradition has supposed that he did—he could have meant either that everything consists of water or that everything originated from water. (He could also have meant only that there's a lot of water in the world, which would not have been very interesting for subsequent philosophers.) It is best to suppose that he had in mind a vague and probably incoherent combination: both that everything came from a primal ocean of water and that everything still is water in various forms. Let us be content to say that he thought of water as the primal stuff of the universe.

Thales started the first fad in philosophy. Naming the primal stuff of the universe became all the rage. Of course, just to be different, each philosopher had his own view on what that stuff was. Anaximander (610?–546? B.C.E.) said it was a weird material he called the Infinite. Anaximenes (585?–528? B.C.E.) argued for air. Heraclitus plumped for fire. The stories became more intricate, but their thrust was the same. A philosopher's job is to name a first principle of all things, and that principle is going to be some sort of stuff.

A cosmology, or an explanation of the basic structure of the world, would usually follow in an apparently deductive way from the first principle. The results of their philosophizing extended far and wide, from the causes of thunder (the noise of a smitten cloud, according to Anaximander) to the shape of the sun (flat like a leaf, says Anaximenes). Not surprisingly, our early philosophers arrived at different pictures of this basic structure. Thales, for example, seems to have held that the earth floats on a large body of water. (On what the water was supposed to rest is hard to say.) Anaximander, on the other hand, believed that the earth is a cylinder suspended in the center of space. Anaximenes, ever ready to compromise, suggested that the earth is a very flat cylinder floating on water.

Thales' first principle is usually understood to be the initial act of philosophy. In place of the anthropomorphic deities of traditional mythology, the story goes,

Thales substituted a principle based on a material and observable phenomenon. The world could now be explained in terms of familiar, natural processes—such as boiling, freezing, pouring—rather than in terms of the actions and dispositions of a few querulous gods. Thus the birth of scientific reason. One can almost picture Thales turning in his loin-cloth for a white lab coat, preparing to investigate the processes of nature.

In fact, sad to say, there is nothing particularly reasonable or scientific about Thales' principle. To count as scientific, a principle (or theorem or hypothesis) presumably ought to be based on observable facts or, at the very least, refer to possible observations. Thales and company do mention the occasional observed phenomenon—e.g., that sperm is moist and watery—but none of these comes even close to providing a basis in observation for any of their first principles. At best, they function by analogy—e.g., such-and-such uses up lots of water, so maybe everything else does, too—which is hardly scientific. The deductive cosmologies which are derived from the first principles do not make any further contribution to the scientific content of the Presocratic accounts. They are merely putative inferences from the principle to the phenomena, and include neither any new observations nor predictions of possible future observations.

What counts as reasonable (or rational) may be harder to specify, but still by almost any test the stuff-principles would clearly fail. The water principle is quite incoherent. If everything is made up of water, then why is water only one among many observed materials, from earth and fire to blood and bone? If all these different materials come from water, then what could cause them to do so? More water? Supposing water manages to transform itself into these various things—then what point is there in still calling it water? Even if we did allow that some version of the principle were coherent, there still would be no reason to believe in it. After all, what evidence could possibly count in its favor? How could we be sure that everything in the world shares this one attribute, that it is watery? And why water, anyway? Why not champagne?

I will, of course, be accused of an application of anachronistic standards. It will be said that the scientific consciousness had not yet come into being, that the first philosophers were struggling in the dark to bring forth this consciousness itself. I cede my right of reply to an Ionian from the fifth century B.C.E., the medical doctor Hippocrates:

> [Medicine] has no need of empty postulates such as are inevitable in dealing with insoluble problems beyond the reach of observation, for example, what goes on in the sky and beneath the earth. If a man pronounces some opinion he has formed on how these things are, it cannot be clear either to himself or to his listeners whether what he says is true or not, for there is no test that can be applied so as to yield certain knowledge. . . . All that philosophers or physicians have written on nature has no more to do with medicine than with painting. Medicine is the only source of clear knowledge about nature. . . .[1]

---

1. *On Ancient Medicine* §§ 1, 20.

The historical sense is by now so well entrenched in our minds that we imagine that it might at one time have been reasonable to affirm with certainty that all is water, that the earth floats on water, and all that. It never was. If we still want to speak about an origin of scientific consciousness, then we would do better to speak not of when so-called physicists invented their first principles and bizarre cosmologies, but, as Hippocrates suggests, of when someone finally got down to basics with the facts about something they could really get their hands on—the human body.

It is easy to see that the outline of the early Ionian physical philosophies follows the pattern of the old cosmo-babble. In place of the original muck one finds an ocean of water, air, or whatever. The muck spawns gods; in the philosophers' accounts, it spawns various material elements. The gods/elements are then shown to create the world such as it is today. It is even doubtful whether the philosophers' accounts could be considered "more" rational than the cosmo-babble (whatever that would mean). Both accounts offer "evidence" only by analogy. The myths conceive of phenomena by analogy with human agents; the philosophers, by analogy with other natural processes. And it would be false to assert that they had a totally materialistic understanding of these natural processes. The other doctrine associated with Thales is that "all things are full of gods." Apparently, even a rock has a soul. So much for his "natural" philosophy.

The difference between the philosophers and the babblers may be only something quite superficial. The philosophers found a way around the need for all those nasty stories about incestuous, castration-fixated gods. Water, after all, is unlikely to devour its own babies, kill its parents, or do anything at all unpleasant. Many of the early philosophers do in fact make clear their disgust with the prevailing mythologies. Their objections were not just aesthetic; they also felt that these stories were so silly that they threatened spiritual life altogether. The philosophers' goal is probably best viewed as an effort to revive the spiritual core of the old cosmo-babble by getting rid of some of its objectionable and distracting outer layers.

What, then, is the meaning of this core of philosopho-babble, the water principle? In terms of inspiration, it probably reflects a sense of wonder before the mystery and the unity of all existence. As literature, it would be the attempt to embody this wonder in the beauty of verse. In the ongoing search for wisdom, it is the single key to understanding all of life's puzzles. In the fantasy world of the professional philosophy to come, it is the grand, ultimate, unified, synthesized truth about everything—the Holy Grail of philosophy. In the final analysis, it has whatever meaning one chooses to impart to it. As we philosophers try to grasp this water, we find it slipping through our hands. So the search continues.

### Thales' Moment of Inspiration

*On the coast not far from Miletus is a cliff facing westward over the Aegean. Thales stood there one summer evening as the setting sun dashed a thousand shades of gold on the wide and peaceful sea. He pulled aside his robe and released his bladder on the gentle waves below. The yellow stream glowed and scattered in the sun's last rays. In the pleasure of that moment Thales lost himself and found his truth. The difficult trip to Egypt, the bickering of city politics, and the long day at the office melted into the water coursing from his body towards the forgiving horizon. His spirit fused with the golden expanse, and he saw that the cosmos was a limited whole, that he and every individual, and every particular thing, belonged together as one in the infinite plenitude and beneficence of water.*

*Night was blowing in. He turned back for the city. He knew he still had much work to do. But nothing could take from him now that eternal moment of inner happiness and tranquility. Such was Thales' wisdom.*

## Progress in Philosophy: First Attempts

When Thales' immediate followers objected to the water principle, they did not do so either on the basis of observation or by objecting to the very concept of a first principle. They dissented on the grounds of the logical coherence of the selection of water, and defended selections they thought more logical.

In choosing the Infinite as his primal stuff, for example, Anaximander thought he could solve the problem about how the primal stuff could turn into all the different kinds of material we see around us. The answer is that the Infinite contains all these finite elements within itself. In the beginning, everything was this Infinite muck, then the finite stuff got separated out (never mind how this happened; it just did). In effect, by naming a stuff which is not one of the everyday stuffs we know, Anaximander removed the paradox involved in describing the whole class of stuffs in terms of one of its ordinary members.

In philosophy, often one step forward results in one step back. Anaximander got over one set of paradoxes simply to provoke another. What is this Infinite? If it is a stuff, what does it look like, taste like, smell like? In fact, how can it have any specific attributes at all, if it is truly in(de)finite? Anaximander was the first philosopher on record to practice the less than admirable art of solving by naming. When philosophy demands a stuff-which-is-not-stuff or some other walking contradiction in terms, a philosopher may conveniently invent a new word—say, the Unstuff, or the Stuffless, or the Infinite.

Anaximenes' philosophy, on the other hand, is an instance of the rule which says that two steps forward is two steps back. Dissatisfied with the immateriality of Anaximander's Unstuff, he settled on air as the closest thing he could imagine to a real Infinite. He also proposed a way of getting around the one stuff-many stuffs problem which troubled the water principle. All those non-air stuffs were really just air in different degrees of rarefaction and condensation. A rock, for example, is just highly compressed air.

In exchanging the Infinite for air, Anaximenes alas forfeited the advantages of Anaximander's Infinite, and returned to the paradoxes of Thales' water principle. What evidence could possibly confirm the choice of either water or air? And what causes the primal stuff, air or water, to differentiate itself into all the other furniture of the world? Anaximenes' description of the processes of condensation and rarefaction does not provide any real justification for choosing air. After all, we could say that gelatin can be made liquid, squishy, solid (if left outdoors for a week or two), and vaporous (when boiled).

There is an important sense in which Anaximenes' selection of air may at least be more inspired than Thales' original principle. In ancient culture, the "air" and "breath" were closely linked, and "breath" and "soul" were often interchangeable. Think of the Latinate terms *inspiration, expiration,* and *spirit.* So "air" in Anaximenes is not just an inert atmospheric gas, but the soul of the cosmos. Our own breath, or our own souls, are a part of this cosmic spirit. Here the "first principle" reveals its origin in the old mythological understanding. More importantly, Anaximenes makes clear that the stuff of the first principle isn't really a stuff. It's really something soul-like or spiritual.

The ancient term for breath, *esse* in Latin, evolved into the term for being, which would in turn evolve into the philosophical term *essence.* Philosophy holds itself responsible for uncovering the living soul of things, their 'whatness'—in brief, their essence. Anaximenes' first principle is thus both the result of an investigation and its premise. The premise is that there is some ultimate essence—some air—of everything, and the conclusion is that this air-essence is, well, air itself. Alas, investigations which conclude where they begin usually do amount to so much hot air.

## From Stuff to Form

The early Ionian first principles had in common that they were all some sort of stuff. Heraclitus of Ephesus, also an Ionian, dramatically reconceived the first principle. He perceived the underlying unity of things in their form, that is, in the way in which they were arranged. Perhaps Pythagoras accomplished a similar transition.

In some fragments, Heraclitus names fire as the ultimate stuff of the world. This makes him sound like the earlier thinkers. His reference to fire, however, is probably self-consciously metaphorical. Fire isn't really a stuff; it is a process. The stuff which makes up the fire is constantly passing up in smoke. Yet the fire remains. So it goes in the Heraclitean world. Everything is in flux. Everything changes—except Change itself. In other fragments, Heraclitus seems to name the *logos* as the ultimate stuff. The term can mean anything from "word" to "story" or "account" to "proportion" or "measure." Heraclitus probably meant it as the structure, form, or set of interrelationships which makes up the world.

This form of the world extends so far as to unite all those things which seem to be in opposition to each other. Whereas a Thales might have been stumped by how you can have water and not-water in a world where all is one, Heraclitus could find unity at the heart of this kind of opposition. Things change over into their opposites—day into night, black into white, water into air—and this very movement is the underlying structure of the world, the first principle of all things. In this synthesis of all opposites, by the way, Heraclitus foreshadows for us a feature of philosophy that will remain with us through the course of this history. The drive for unity is perhaps the primordial urge of philosophy, and in the end it must run over all the (merely apparent) oppositions which populate the world.

As he reached for the pure form of the world, Heraclitus found it necessary to proclaim a profound skepticism about the knowledge supplied to us by our senses. Sense experience reveals to us a world of transience. Yet behind this dazzling show of impermanence, we know, there is something eternal and immutable: the form of the world. This particular Heraclitean opposition, between imperfect sense data and a higher kind of knowledge, will also carry us through much of the rest of the history of philosophy.

Another very different Presocratic philosopher achieved a parallel, if less persuasive, shift in first principles from stuff to form. This was the enigmatic Pythagoras. For Pythagoras (or at least for his cult followers) the fundamental principle of things was number. Everything, from the stuff around us to our most abstract concepts, is a manifestation of number. For example, justice is the number four (as in fair and square). There is not much more to say about this numerological philosophy, except that it is obviously quite untrue. But with Pythagoras we have left Ionia and moved to the other, more mystical and metaphysical side of the ancient Greek world, to the troubled and unstable colonies in what is now Italy.

## From Form to Silence

Heraclitus surpassed himself. He perceived something very paradoxical about formal first principles. They cannot really be stated. A statement of form, to use Heraclitean metaphors, purports to identify something permanent in the world; but there is nothing permanent in a world where all is change. In other words, a representation of the world cannot stand outside the world, cannot *re-present* the totality. Or, he might have said, a statement about form represents the world as a particular thing, like any other object of our senses, and we know that the structure of the world is most certainly not what our senses show us. Perhaps the logic of this very difficult idea is this: If we propose a particular form for the world, we imply that there is a different, opposite form for another possible world; but there is no other possible world, in this sense, because all possibility (and all opposition) is circumscribed by the form which structures our world. The form of the world, Heraclitus concluded, could only be *shown*, not stated. The philosopher could only leave signposts, mere way-markers on the path to the truth about everything.

This Heraclitean paradox, it seems to me, takes us to the bottom of the very idea of a first principle. A principle may be thought of as that which ascribes form to something. "All is water" says that water (or whatever it represents metaphorically) is the form which may be ascribed to something, namely, the "all." A first principle presumably is the form of everything. So what is the form of everything? Well, it cannot be a particular form, like water or squareness, for any such particular form would be dissolved into its opposite through the form of—form. The form of everything, in other words, is form itself. Everything, Heraclitus tells us, is a part of the form of the world. But to say that form itself is the first principle is to present an argument in the form of a circle. The very idea that there is such a thing as a first principle supposes that there is a form of the world. The premise of the search is its conclusion.

We could end the history of philosophy at this point. In Heraclitus' inspired hands, philosophy dissolves itself. It falls silent. But in this Heraclitean world, alas, nothing ever comes to rest. Philosophy will crystallize again and again, in countless new shapes, throughout the course of our history.

---

### Heraclitus' Moment of Inspiration

*One day in his early middle age Heraclitus was rummaging through his attic and came upon a tablet on which as a young man he had etched what he had then thought of as the ultimate truths of philosophy. As he read from the now crumbling script, he reacted with horror to the pompous and trite blatherings he had once believed so important. How could I have been so wrong, so adolescent, and such an awful writer, he thought. Then he knew that he and everything he valued, all his truths and sayings, his own being, could not withstand the force of Change. He, too, was in every way a part of the eternal flux of the cosmos. He reached for a fresh tablet and began to etch.*

---

## (2) THE SECOND ORDER

### The Parmenidean One

The most important Presocratic philosopher, with the possible exception of Heraclitus, is Parmenides. Permenides' approach is the most general of the Presocratics, and encompasses much of their work. Instead of simply throwing out a first principle, like air or water, Parmenides offers a reflection on what any first principle must look like. From this second-order perspective he rules out many of the other Presocratics' attempts, draws his own conclusions about reality, and articulates the central strategy of much of philosophy to come. Though anticipated by Xenophanes (fl.

540 B.C.E.) and clarified by followers like Melissus (fl. 444 B.C.E.), Parmenides stands pretty much on his own in his achievement among the ancient philosophers.

His magnum opus was a poem immodestly titled *Truth*, which exists today in fragments. Since even in fragments his poem is long and rather tedious, I present something like a *Reader's Digest* condensed version:

> *The Truth (About Everything)*
>
> Hearken to me ye souls of darkness
> For I have spoken with the goddess.
> Think ye to be forever with me
> or wrong or misguided ye always will be
> See, can ye not, that great way of thought
> that way is but two: either it is or is not
>
> What is not is not, and cannot be thought
> 'tis nothing, nothing, nothing at all
> like myths and physics and all that rot
> So heed what is, and so shall ye see
> What is, 'tis true, is smooth, round, and blue
> One perfect, unchanging, and eternal Be.

Indeed he was an awful poet. So let us turn to a prose summary of his case:

1. *Introduction*: Listen up everyone. I've been in touch with a certain goddess, and have I got news for you.

2. *The Choice*. You have three options. You can go with me on the highway of truth. You can go the wrong way. Or you can wander around in a daze, like most people.

3. *The Logic*. There are two conceivable ways of thinking about something. Either you assume that it is, or that it is not. If it is, okay. If it is not, you've got a problem. If it is not, it is nothing. If it is nothing, you cannot think about it. So don't try thinking about that which is not, because you'll end up thinking about nothing. This is the way of falsehood.

4. *The Core Conclusion*. You can only think about what really is. That is, you can only really think about that which exists. Thinking *is* reality.

5. *The Truth about the World*. If you're going to think about what is, you've only got one thing to think about. For what is cannot come into being and fade away. It's got to be there for you all the time. It cannot change, since in that case a part of it would have to fade away. It has to be one thing. It cannot be divided into parts or lumps. It has to be round and perfect. There can be no moving parts, since motion implies a void where something moves in, but a void is not.

6. *The Way of Falsehood*. According to our senses, things are coming into being and fading away all the time. This is bad. We're forced to deal with opinions, not truth, and opinions are always wrong.

7. *The Irrelevant Cosmology.* After all the metaphysics, in a long part of the poem not shown above, Parmenides next offers an interesting story based on mortal opinions. Men have decided that there are two forms of things: Light and Night. From these two you can derive the structure of the universe, like the fact that the heavens consist of alternating rings of fire and night, that the sun is an exhalation of fire, as is the Milky Way.

Parmenides lays out the questions that will occupy much of philosophy to come. In laying out the questions, he also lays out the strategy for philosophy, that is, how it should conceive of and present itself so that it can have meaningful questions to investigate and meaningful results to declare.

*The Question of Method.* The decisive move in Parmenides' thought is to lift philosophy into the new territory of methodology. The choice he offers us at the start of his poem is between competing ways or roads. The Greek word is *hodos.* From this comes the "hod" in our own word "method." Parmenides is the first of the Presocratics to distinguish clearly between first-order investigations into the nature of things and second-order investigations into what it is possible to investigate, or between methods and methodology. This move to a second order is characteristic of philosophy to the present day. What will later be given the fancy names of *ontology, metaphysics, epistemology,* and *logic* are combined in a single Parmenidean move.

This certainly looks like a real improvement on the old first principles. Instead of just asserting a doctrine about the nature of things, Parmenides begins with an (apparently) logical argument. The argument could be looked upon as a reflection on what a first principle must look like. It is an exposition of the basic structure of these first principles. So he makes explicit and provides arguments for what the first principles had sought to convey by metaphor: that all is one, that nothing ever really comes to be or perishes, that there is a permanent reality beneath appearances. Parmenides at last exemplifies the notion that a philosopher should not merely pronounce his views on things, but search for what is true, and show that it must be true.

*The Question of Thought.* The specific method with which Parmenides is first concerned is the method of thought. Again, as a second-order investigation, his work begins not by asking about some phenomenon or other, but by asking what can be a possible object of thought. His conclusions are all supposed to follow from his analysis of the conditions of the possibility of thinking about something.

The conditions can be reduced to just one, that the thing exists. This is Parmenides' core conclusion, or finding: It is possible to think of only that which exists. And this conclusion, it would appear, is based on nothing but a reflection on the conditions of the possibility of thought.

*The Question of Being.* From his core conclusion Parmenides further derives a set of conclusions about what reality must be like. It must be one, indivisible, perfect, eternal, and so on. These are effectively arguments about what must characterize existence itself. So his project can be represented as an inquiry into the nature of being.

*The Question of Knowledge.* Parmenides lays claim to a special kind of knowledge. Ordinary mortals rely on sense-based knowledge. They come to believe that things come into being, perish, change, and so forth. This is a dirty, pathetic, and very human kind of knowledge. Parmenides, thanks to a combination of natural brilliance and a few conversations with his heavenly amour, has access to a divine, philosophical knowledge. (This amounts to the knowledge of Being, or what *really* exists.)

*But Is It All True?* Alas, the Question of Truth. The truth is, Parmenides was all wrong. The core conclusion, that that which is thought must also exist, is just wishful thinking. Now you think about something. Say, a million dollars. Imagine a tall stack of hundred dollar bills. Does it exist? Think about a unicorn, a slice of apple pie, a speaking termite, or whatever you like, and you will find no necessity that it should exist. The truth is a precise reversal of what Parmenides argues. There is nothing the thought of which implies its existence. Parmenides' own text shows this to be the case. He gives us a list of things that being is (homogenous, continuous, singular, etc.) and a list of things it is *not* (divided, lumpy, etc.). He tells us which way is the way of truth, and which is *not*. To cap it off, he provides another imaginative but patently fabricated cosmology of the old Ionian variety—one that even he would probably have agreed is *not* true.

The error follows from the structure of Parmenides' argument as a (putatively) second-order investigation. He begins with the question of method, or what ought to be a reflection on the methods of investigating reality, and concludes with what purports to be a description of ultimate reality. This is like reflecting on the concept of road, and determining thereby where all roads must lead. It is like predicting what one will see by examining the shape of one's spectacles. In abstract terms, it is like trying to say something about what is possible without knowing anything at all about what is actually the case. (When starting from scratch, after all, anything's possible.) In other words, Parmenides pretends to move from logic to fact—as though the premises from which any logical argument must proceed could be somehow swallowed up and proved within the argument. It is an attempt to deduce the truth about everything without ever leaving one's armchair—without ever contemplating anything in particular.

The questions of thought, being, and knowledge, as listed above, reflect this underlying confusion in the question of method. (Since these issues will come up again many times in our history, I only sketch out the resulting paradoxes here.) The conditions of the possibility of thought are in a sense the limits of thought. But how can one think the limits, without already thinking beyond them, to the other side? Parmenides himself has to tell us about all the things which are not, and therefore supposedly cannot be thought. The question of the nature of being sounds ominous, but also leads to paradox. An investigation into something must presumably tell us *what* it is (and presumably, what it is not). So what *is* being? How can being *be* anything (and not be something else)? When we say something is (or is not), we haven't said anything about what kind of thing it is. In sum, it seems most likely that being has no nature (it is neither lumpy nor not lumpy, neither blue nor white, etc.), so there is nothing here to investigate. The question of knowledge follows the rest into this garden of paradoxes. Parmenides rejects our ordinary kind of knowledge from sense experience as false knowledge. But how do we come to know of Parmenides' truths? Do we really have to take this business about a goddess seriously? Whence this knowledge beyond possible knowledge?

Many of Parmenides' contemporaries, by the way, thought he was foolish. Things are many, they said, things change, and we can think of lots of things that don't exist. Zeno, who seems to have been one of Parmenides' followers, tried to turn the tables on these unphilosophical people by showing them that their own notions of multiplicity and change lead to paradoxes. (Either that, or he was just trying to have some fun.) His most famous argument is the one that concerns the race between Achilles and the tortoise. The tortoise gets a head start. And they're off! Achilles soon makes it to the position formerly occupied by the tortoise. But the old leather-back has moved on! Achilles races to the point now occupied by the tortoise, but the slowpoke has moved on again! So Achilles never catches up. All of which somehow shows that our concepts of tortoise-motion and/or victory are quite messed up. Whether it proves that Parmenides was right—well, that would be a matter for other philosophers, many other philosophers, to decide (or not).

## The Holy Grail Lives

Parmenides represents in classic form the search for the Holy Grail of philosophy. By claiming for itself the second order of things, philosophy could free itself from having to deal with dirty facts. Philosophy alone would have access to the reality of being. It could throw the testimony of the senses out of court and so remove the threat of ever being controverted by empirical evidence. It could use a pure method, one justified in advance and capable of generating its own results.

It would seem that we have traveled far beyond the old cosmo-babble. Or have we? Those old myths were meant to provide an explanation for everything. Even if we, like many of the ancients no doubt, did not quite believe in all the details, we could at least derive from them some assurance that things are the way they are for a reason. At the end of the day, Parmenides' philosophy, I think, is no different. It, too, reaches for an explanation of everything. And, in the final analysis, it provides not a definitive explanation, but merely an assurance, ultimately based on some sort of faith, that everything somehow rests on unimpeachable foundations. To be sure, with Parmenides divinity sheds its human-like form for an abstract category of pure Being. But perhaps the old cosmo-babble was not so vulgar either. Its gods behaved like humans, but perhaps they, too, were analogies for the totality of things, for Parmenides' Being.

## (3) BACK TO SQUARE ONE

After Parmenides and his immediate followers in Italy, the philosophical pendulum swung back to Ionia. The later Ionians are something of a disappointment; they were all responding to Parmenides in one way or another. All accepted some of his premises, but none accepted all of his conclusions. However, none seemed to have grasped where he was trying to lead them. They failed to take up the question of method and so reverted to versions of the earlier Ionian philosophies.

Empedocles, for example, conceded the Parmenidean requirement that true reality should be permanent and unchanging. Unlike Parmenides, however, he could only conceive of this substratum in terms of material stuff. At the same time, he was aware of the problems with choosing a single primal stuff, like water. His solution is a paradigm of philosophical compromise. He named four elements: earth, wind, fire, and water. To these he attributed the permanence of Parmenidean Being. This left him with the old difficulty of explaining how things change and interact. So Empedocles introduced Love and Strife as the two processes whereby the elements are alternately mixed together and separated off. As per the old cosmo-babble, everything starts out mixed together in a primal muck, then the elements get separated by Strife, then mixed up again by Love, then separated and so on, and this is why birds fly south in the winter. Along the way Empedocles entirely failed to notice the second-order character of the Parmenidean project and simply warmed over a mish-mash of arbitrary first principles.

No one is quite clear what Anaxagoras (500?–428? B.C.E.) had in mind. One of his ideas was this: everything is a mixture of everything else. A piece of gold, for example, is made up mainly of gold, but also contains bits of ocean water, salt, olive oil, and tomatoes. This is a patently incoherent idea. If gold is made up of gold along with a bunch of other bits, then to what sort of material does this second mention of gold refer? The idea really begins with cosmology, not logic. It is part of another of those cosmic stories, in which everything begins all mixed up and then separates out into what we have today. It is an attempt to get around Parmenides' argument that there could be no becoming or change in the world by positing all the ingredients of the world as already existing in the original mixture of things. Anaxagoras also thought of it as an improvement on Empedocles, whose selection of just four elements looked rather arbitrary. In fact, it's just another case of solving-by-naming. After all, how did Anaxagoras suppose that the original mixture got lumpy enough to create the distinct objects we see today? Which brings up Anaxagoras' second idea: in among the original mixture are scattered little seeds. These are the seeds of what is to come. As they sprout, things come into being out of the muck. As a bonus, Anaxagoras' second idea explains not only difference but also change—these are, after all, the seeds of change. The third idea was his most pregnant, and yet his least developed. Within the mixture, and yet somehow different, finer, apart, and pure, is Mind. It is Mind which somehow gets the mixture swirling around, to the point where the seeds start to sprought. Anaxagoras seems to think of Mind as a special kind of stuff, but how or why it operates as it does, other than that it can remain unadulterated, is quite unclear.

The last Presocratic movement, that of the atomists, extends past the life of Socrates, and even hooks up with the Hellenistic philosophies after Aristotle. The official Presocratic atomists are Leucippus, who may have originated the idea but left nothing for us in writing, and Democritus, who was its main exponent. The atomists, as their name suggests, offered as their first principle of physics the claim that everything is made of discrete, indivisible units called atoms bouncing around in a void. On the one hand, they flagrantly and consciously rejected Parmenides' claim that there could be no void and therefore no motion. On the other hand, their system of atoms and void was designed to replicate the permanence of Parmenidean Being while making room for an explanation of the diversity of phenomena.

The atomists' idea looks intriguing to us, because we know that the matter around us is in fact composed of atoms. However, the anticipation of modern physics is just a fluke. In the first place, the atomists had no reasonable basis whatsoever for their views. They just asserted them, chiefly in order to score philosophical points against Parmenides and his static, voidless world. Our atoms, on the other hand, have their place within a large body of experimental knowledge. Second, their atoms did not look at all like the ones we see today. Our atoms are a representation of one level of the organization of matter (as opposed to, for example, energy). Theirs were a representation of everything (except the void)—from the soul to the stars. Ours can be split. Theirs could not. Ours are often different from one another. Theirs were made of the same stuff, though they could have different shapes. In short, their atomism presupposed that material stuff is the only reality, and that there is only one kind of matter, but that, by the way, it just so happens that matter is not infinitely divisible.

## III. CHARACTER

*All Is Character.* It is often said that the Presocratics were concerned primarily with explaining nature, and that only with the Sophists and Socrates in particular does philosophy turns its eye towards human beings and their souls. A hasty glance at the Presocratics' chief doctrines makes this seem plausible. On the whole, they do seem to talk much more about wind, fire, and the shape of the earth, for instance, than about the individual human being and his ethical beliefs. But this would be a superficial interpretation. It assumes that the Presocratics' various principles and dogmas really are about the natural world. They are not. They have as little to do with the objective understanding of nature as the old cosmo-babble. Like the mythological stories, their doctrines are metaphorical ways in which they address a very different kind of concern. This is the concern with humankind's place in the cosmos, the meaning of existence, and the possibility of an ethical existence. In brief, they are the language with which the Presocratics addressed the issues traditionally associated with Socrates.

Heraclitus, for example, seemed to pose as a physicist in saying that the world is made of fire. Yet he also described the soul as a fire. Of his life's work he said "I searched out myself." Discovering the fire in nature was a means to discovering the fire in his soul. In a similar way Anaximenes breathed in air as though he were inspiring his own soul with that of the cosmos. For these thinkers, there was no point to a separate inquiry into matters of the soul. Soul, or spirit, would demand a totality, and that totality could not stop short of the world as a whole.

In their skepticism about ordinary knowledge of the senses, perhaps the Presocratics were just insisting that wisdom is more than the mere accumulation of facts about nature. Wisdom, Heraclitus would have affirmed, is seeing the general pattern in things, and understanding how and in what measure every little thing fits into life's whole. Wisdom is not the capacity for mechanical inference, but a faculty of judgment. It is based on character.

"Character is destiny," said Heraclitus. And so it was for the Presocratics. Why did one philosopher choose water, another air? Why did one choose to find an ultimate unity in the plurality of the world, another to find unity in the denial of plurality? In no case can we say that reason or fact should have us favor one or the other. In no case could we say that one places us closer to wisdom than another. Perhaps Thales chose water because, like any good politician, he recognized the importance of water supply to a thriving city. Parmenides preferred an abstract notion of being because he did not want to speak in a way that could be understood by the unphilosophical masses. Heraclitus was so possessed with his sense of the transience of things that he could not stop from transfiguring it into a sense of the divine. Empedocles talked up Love and Strife because he was, you know, so romantic. And Pythagoras always had a good head for figures, as well as a need to impress other people. There is no real development in their supposedly philosophical views, only a continuous, circular shifting of positions. It is their personalities, with which we began, that are decisive, and their supposedly philosophical doctrines merely a superficial dress.

## IV. FUTURE PAST

*The Future Before Us.* For those who stay the journey through the rest of our history, it will become apparent that everything that would be said in philosophy over the subsequent two and a half millennia had already been said in some way by the Presocratic philosophers. The battles among the Presocratics over first principles would be relived in an astonishing variety of forms, but always with the same outcome. Thales' water would be transformed into strange new substances, like Spinoza's God and Schopenhauer's Will, yet it would always boil down to the same old thing. Pythagoras' principle of numbers already instantiated the range of idealistic first principles, such as would be embodied in Plato's world of forms. Parmenides' leap to the second-order in particular could be seen as the paradigm for almost all of ancient and modern philosophy. Aristotelian metaphysics as the study of being *qua* being would be one refinement of Parmenides' project. Descartes' discourse on method would be another, as would Kant's investigation into the conditions of the possibility of experience. The forthcoming dialectics between reason and the senses, between divine an human knowledge, were already mapped out by Heraclitus' skepticism about the transient world of ordinary sense experience, not to mention Parmenides' distinction between the way of truth and the way of mortals. The Parmenidean One would merge with Spinoza's Substance, and its seedy, Anaxagorean response would sprout again in Leibniz' pluralistic monadism. Leavened with the Heraclitean logos-flux, a reinvigorated Anaxagorean Mind, and the Zenoian dialectic, the One which is Many would return to itself in the form of Hegel's Absolute Spirit. The sham question of Being would become the first principle of Heidegger's philosophy. Heraclitus' intuitive misanthropic genius, his attempt to forge new values out of a dead cosmology would express itself again in Nietzsche. Or maybe Heraclitus could be viewed as a proto-existentialist. His faith in a seamless form of the world, one which can be shown but not said, would be shared by Wittgenstein. The mysticism of both Eastern and Western philosophy was already laid out by Pythagoras, Heraclitus, and Empedocles. Zeno's hair-splitting paradoxes would first drive the Socratic dialectic, and then become the conceptual clarifications of mid-twentieth century philosophy of language.

The list could go on and on. Yet it should not be taken as evidence that the Presocratics decisively influenced the course of the philosophy that was to come, or that the subsequent history of philosophy constitutes some sort of logical development out of these originary problematics. For most of the rest of the history, it is more likely that the Presocratics were pretty much forgotten or misinterpreted. Philosophy, as we shall see, repeats itself blindly. Even in cases, as with Socrates, where philosophy chooses a different shape in a seemingly conscious way, this does not demonstrate that there is a logic to the story. Socrates, as we shall see, simply thought it necessary to remove some of the objectionable, naturalistic trappings of philosophy in order to rediscover its spiritual core—much as the Presocratics themselves had sought a return to the core of cosmo-babble. We will have all the more reason to doubt that philosophy has an origin, in the historical sense.

THALES: ALL IS WATER

> *Cardinal Sin of Historians of Philosophy. Post hoc, ergo propter hoc.* It follows chronologically, therefore it follows logically.

The myth of the origin is just one way in which philosophy makes itself into what it is. Even the Presocratics were referring constantly to a past, to another beginning in cosmology, in an effort to recreate and improve upon something that never really was. In this they were like the ancient Egyptians, whose word for "south" was derived from "face," for they always faced the Nile looking upstream, toward the mysterious source of its life-giving water. I would venture that philosophy, too, has its gaze fixed on the past, and that it is the futile effort to beat against the current of time, to return to that primordial unity of all things, to a vast and eternal ocean of existence. In the end, as in the beginning, all is water.

# The Sophists

## The Bad Guys

The Sophists (490 B.C.E.–the present?) have got a serious image problem in the history of philosophy. They are reviled as the prostitutes of the mind: They sold their wisdom to the highest bidder, who was usually corrupt and power-hungry. They were hair-splitting rhetoricians, who enjoyed trying to convince people that the weak is the strong, the good the bad, and the hot the not. Our own language recalls their evil deeds with unpleasant borrowings like "sophistry" and "sophism." The Sophists had no values, save success. In short, they were no lovers of wisdom, but rather lovers of power, prestige, money, and argument for argument's sake. They might have been at home in the 1980s.

The evidence on the Sophists is even thinner than that on the Presocratics. It is almost impossible to figure out with certainty what they really said and did. Given this lack of evidence, it is curious that their image remains so negative. The chief reason is Plato. The Sophists disgusted Plato (and Socrates, if we are to believe Plato). Unfortunately, Plato happens to be the single most important source of information on the earlier thinkers. But Plato is not entirely to blame. Subsequent philosophers could have revised the traditional estimate of the Sophists (and a few tried). Yet, on the whole, the Sophists remain in the pits—ignored, if not despised. There must be something about them which the large majority of traditional philosophers finds unacceptable.

## I

The Sophists were a diverse group of thinkers, with equally diverse views. Though they congregated in Athens, only a few were native Athenians. They rose to prominence during the golden years of Pericles, around the middle of the fifth century

B.C.E. Their intellectual heirs remained on the scene at least through the fourth century B.C.E.

The first and most famous Sophist was Protagoras (484?–414? B.C.E.), who is thought to have been a close friend and adviser of the great Pericles himself. He is now most famous for two ideas. The first is that "man is the measure of all things." This is usually taken to be a statement of a kind of humanistic epistemology. There is no absolute truth, it implies; there is only that truth which man assigns to things. The second idea is that the gods don't really matter. They may or may not exist, but there is no way for us to find out. So we might as well ignore them.

Implicit in Protagoras' thoughts is a distinction between 'convention' and 'nature', or *nomos* and *physis*. Though their conclusions varied, the Sophists tended to think that moral values, religion, political institutions, and so forth were the creations of social convention, as opposed to nature. The Sophist Prodicus (fl. ca. 430 B.C.E.) seems to have done a broad study of mythology, and he concluded that myths are simply stories about a few useful things that happen in nature. Euripides the playwright (ca. 484–406 B.C.E.) or Critias (ca. 480–403 B.C.E.)—scholars are not sure of the source—suggested that the myths were invented by men as a way to deter crime. Callicles, an ex-Sophist and man of letters who stars in one of Plato's dialogues, staked out the extreme position that convention is actually a perversion of natural right.

# II

The relationship between the Sophists and the roughly contemporary Presocratics is best illustrated in Gorgias' (ca. 485 B.C.E.) response to the Eleatic philosophy of Parmenides. Gorgias recognized that the premises of Parmenidean arguments could produce conclusions opposed to Parmenides' own. In his satirically titled treatise *That Which Is Not*, Gorgias does just that. Let us not worry about the details of Gorgias' arguments. The spirit could be expressed in a song, which one might imagine Gorgias to have written:

*(I Got the) Parmenidean Blues*

Is not is not is not? It is.
If is not is then is is not
If is is not, is not is not
So is is not, is not is not
But is not is, and is not not!

In later times, the popular press would have corrupted this fine piece of Gorgian logic into a vulgar refrain, to be sung to the tune of "Old MacDonald Had a Farm":

*Refrain:*

Is not is not is
not is not is not
is is is and not not not
is not is not is

Gorgias, too, was probably an awful poet. But he did have this sage advice for would-be anti-philosophers: "Destroy an opponent's seriousness by laughter, and his laughter by seriousness." The upshot of Gorgias' jest is that, despite Parmenides, thinking and being are two very different things. One can think all day long about chariots crossing the sea, but that will not bring into existence a single ocean-going, horse-drawn vehicle.

Let us summarize the general features of Sophistic thought. First and foremost we should recall the nature and aims of their practice. They viewed themselves as teachers. Their aim was not to discover new truths but to educate their students, or clients, in the art of successful living. The needs of their clients were their main concern. Second, the Sophists' teachings were focused on issues of anthropological interest. There was little talk of the shape of the earth and the orbit of the sun, but much about language, politics, character, and virtue. Third, they tended to be moral relativists, since they thought of morality as humanly created rather than as a divinely inspired code. Fourth, they were skeptical about the possibilities for true or absolute knowledge. The Sophists believed that truth, too, was a more or less human invention. Fifth, their methods of investigation were self-consciously empirical and inductive, in contrast with the putatively rational, deductive approach of the Presocratic cosmologists. Though they doubted the possibility of absolute knowledge, they were quite content with dirty knowledge, and were known to collect masses of facts on subjects which interested them. (One wrote up a list of great athletes, for example; another analyzed shoemaking; another, the art of wrestling.) Finally, by way of summary, we could say that true reality, for the Sophists, was neither a set of absolute truths nor divine values, but utility, interest, and advantage. All of their doctrines and their whole practice refers to this reality.

The starting point of Sophistic thought was their acceptance that they and their clients, like most people in the world, knew in general terms what they wanted out of life. They wanted to be happy. Being happy meant having family, friends, wealth, sensual pleasure in moderation, and control over one's destiny. It meant living a full life. In this there was nothing original or contemporary. The Sophists simply assented to what poets had already been saying for thousands of years and what self-improvement magazines are saying to this day. So the Sophists did not question these general goals in life. They simply set out to serve them—both for themselves and for their clients. They provided their clients with the skills required for successful living, in exchange for gainful employment and their own fulfillment. It so happens that for the ambitious young Greek male, the critical factors for success in life were forensic skills. So the Sophists taught their clients mainly how to speak convincingly in public.

The specific, apparently philosophical doctrines associated with the Sophists—the relativism and skepticism—should not be taken too seriously. These doctrines follow from the framework of their practice, rather than lead to it. The Sophists could spin on a dime. When it suited them, they would become absolutists. Protagoras, for example, concluded that moral values were an essential part of a peaceful existence, and so he concocted a few myths of his own to help people believe in them. In general, however, relativism and skepticism were more congenial to their practice. The Sophists aimed to sweep aside superstition and guilt, the cause and result of most religions and moralities. A client who does not recognize his responsibility for his own life and happiness, who is everywhere thwarted by conventional expectations, will not learn the art of successful living. Skepticism about claims to absolute knowledge was for them a way of making sure that prejudice and preconception did not forestall the search for real and useful knowledge. The emphasis on empirical facts and induction also is a sign of the realistic disposition generally required for material success.

# III

So why are the Sophists consigned to hell or oblivion in the traditional histories of philosophy? It is true that the doctrines associated with Sophism, the relativism and skepticism, have not been as popular among philosophers as their opposites. Most philosophers have preferred divinely inspired moralities and absolute knowledge. While certainly Plato's calumnies are based on his own opposing faith in divine absolutes, this is not sufficient to explain the fate of the Sophists, since many other acceptable philosophers have championed the same unpopular doctrines.

The problem, I think, has more to do with the attitude of the Sophists toward their own doctrines. They made philosophy a means to an end. Philosophers have always demanded that philosophy be considered an end in itself. Philosophy, or the life of contemplation, *is* happiness. It *is* the good life, not a few lectures to be taken in along the way to the good life. It is not to be sold in the marketplace alongside the fruit and vegetables. In philosophy, it is okay to be a Relativist, Pragmatist, Consequentialist, or whatever, so long as one holds to the (possibly erroneous) doctrine with conviction—as indicated by the Capital Letters—and as a result of serious philosophical investigations. But it is definitely not okay to play around with doctrines, to get relativistic or pragmatic with philosophy, to analyze without taking sides, and to take sides only as and when circumstances demand. The Sophists simply did not take their own doctrines seriously enough. Philosophy has always preferred a man like Parmenides, who conceals a ludicrous doctrine beneath layers of pseudo-logic and piles of conviction, to one like Gorgias, who, in the guise of parody, lays out a few simple reasons why ontology is an altogether farcical endeavor.

And yet, the Sophists were lovers of knowledge. In fact, in their disdain for obtuse metaphysical doctrines, the Sophists revealed a sense of objectivity and detachment which should have made them the true representatives of the tradition. The Sophists were often not "for" or "against" any particular doctrine because, unlike the traditional philosophers, they had no emotional capital invested in such doctrines. They were content to let the world be what it was. It should be the subject of some amusement that the philosophical tradition has seen fit to banish these early lovers of knowledge and pioneers of the scientific spirit, in favor of watery-eyed Presocratics and metaphysical fantasizers like Plato.

The Sophists even had a strategy for disposing of the other philosophers. Sophism, so they might have said, is for those who have done their philosophy, those who have achieved what philosophy promises but never delivers. But let us hear more about this from an imaginary horse's mouth:

## THE SOPHIST SPEAKS

"Friends and countrymen. Look at the two men who stand before you. Here am I, [*extends arms, struts, does a slight twirl*] a man of affairs, a leader in city life, educated by some of the great Sophists of our day, and a part-time Sophist myself. There [*sniff*] is the Philosopher. What sort of men do you see? I am healthy, in the full vigor of life, dressed in the finest loincloth, own a house in a respectable neighborhood, am of good breeding and a source of pride for my family and friends, who are many. Now consider my counterpart. He, too, ought to be in the prime of life. Yet he is pasty pale, pimply, and poor [*expectorates voluminously on the 'p's*], wears torn and tasteless tweeds ['*t's*], has few friends, and is a source of despair for his family. With such overwhelming evidence before your eyes, can there be a serious question about whose is the path to the good life? But our malnourished Philosopher will quibble, as philosophers are wont to do [*looks down his nose at the Philosopher*], quibble quibble [*in nasal voice*], so I shall condescend to respond to your imaginary and quite fantastical arguments.

"You say that yours is the true life of virtue, that only the philosophical life of self-examination is worth leading. I say donkey feathers. [*Crowd roars with laughter; (it's not a cliché yet).*] I say you lead a life of mock virtue and self-deception. I say that I and my sophist-icated brethren are the ones who possess true virtue, excellence, and self-knowledge. [*Pushes back his hair.*]

"To examine oneself, I forthrightly proclaim, is a virtue. [*Faces the audience with serious bearing.*] Self-knowledge is indeed the first step in knowing the world, and so learning how to live the good life. But what sort of self does the Philosopher know? [*Flips back of hand in direction of Philosopher.*] He knows none! He knows himself only as searching for himself. He never finds himself. He is a lost soul. My brethren and I, we have learned something of ourselves. We have found what you seek. We know we are finite creatures, that our lives our are only so long, we know what we want, and that if we want, we must go out and get. [*Triumphantly grasps the air.*]

"To our Philosopher [*turns head contemptuously*] I say: You have confused the questions of life with their answers; you have mistaken ends and means. So you deceive yourself, and know not who you are. The virtue you so haughtily announce to the world is worthless. It achieves nothing, is impotent, is merely the pious self-assurances of an ignorant slave. [*Crowd gasps.*]

"What's more, I see through you, you scoundrel. I know you better than you know yourself. I see that you have sublimated your desires and invented a new and perverted form of pleasure. You have learned to love the useless abstractions to which your lack of physical and social graces has condemned you. You flagellate yourself with concepts, just as you take pleasure from coercing and seducing little boys with your twisted chains of reasoning. [*Expresses disgust.*]

"With little boys, indeed! For that is where you belong. Philosophizing does a growing boy no harm. It broadens the mind, sharpens the intellect, and instills good culture. But when a man continues with this youthful indulgence throughout his life, well, then, he ought to be treated like a child, and beaten regularly. [*Waves fist.*] He is useless to himself and others, a mutation, an aberration from nature's course. He becomes a perpetual student, and saps away our tax dollars in a string of pointless, never-ending research projects.

"Listen to me, my friends! Do not be deceived! Trust your senses! Philosophy holds no mystery. It is no more than what you see in this decrepit, wasted individual who calls himself a Philosopher." [*Walks off stage waving notes in the air; crowd cheers wildly.*]

# Socrates

## So This Is the Good Life?

The story continues: Socrates discovered the method of pure, critical reason. His dialectical questioning marks the first full fruition of rational consciousness in human history. With this new tool, he made his own and his compatriots' ethics the object of rational inquiry. So he brought ethics under philosophy's sway. He became the conscience of his community.

Unfortunately, it probably isn't true—at least, not in any meaningful way—that Socrates invented critical reason. He did, however, discover some ways of being quite unreasonable. He did not make ethics the object of rational inquiry. Rather, he merely advocated a certain idiosyncratic way of life, a particular ethics of his own, and his ethics had very little to do with his or any community, except possibly that of like-minded philosophical contemporaries.

## THE PROBLEM OF SOCRATES

Socrates (470–399 B.C.E.) had the wisdom never to commit his thoughts to writing. However, his followers have not shown similar restraint. The preponderance of interpretation over fact about Socrates in modern times has created the so-called Problem of Socrates. Who was Socrates? What was he up to? What did he believe? Why was he tried and executed by his fellow citizens? Despite the hoopla about textual and historical uncertainties, the fact remains that most reasonable interpretations ascribe to Socrates the same, distinct body of philosophical thought. The real Problem of Socrates lies not in determining in what his philosophy consisted, but in figuring out how anyone, let alone a Great Philosopher, could have believed the things he apparently did. And although death is by any standard a harsh penalty for bad philosophy, it is not so hard to see why the Athenians wanted to shut Socrates up.

**Biofact.** The essential facts about Socrates' life are these: He never held a job in his life. His wife, Xanthippe, was a horrible nag. He spent his days out of the house, wandering the streets asking people questions that they could not answer. He took no interest in politics or current affairs. He acquired a coterie of devoted, mainly youthful followers. The public at large tended to think of him as a freak or a pest. He was extraordinarily ugly. In 399 B.C.E., at the age of seventy, he was charged with religious impiety and with corrupting the youth of the city, and was condemned to death by a jury of five hundred of his fellow citizens.

Socrates' philosophy, insofar as it can be reconstructed out of elements common to most accounts, consists of a series of paradoxes. The paradoxes all revolve around an opposition between apparently dogmatic elements of Socrates' philosophy, on the one hand, and apparently skeptical or critical elements on the other.

## (1) THE UN-KNOWING

One fine day, one of Socrates' eager followers apparently asked the Oracle at Delphi, the leading religious forecasting service of the ancient Greek world, this somewhat loaded question: Is there anyone wiser than Socrates? To which the Oracle obligingly, if not unambiguously, replied no. Socrates believed himself to be an ignorant bumpkin (or so he said), so upon learning of the pronouncement he set about trying to find someone wiser. Alas, he found only people who thought they knew something, but did not. He concluded that the Oracle was right, in a certain way. Socrates was wisest because he knew that he knew nothing.

This might not have bothered anybody, had Socrates then desisted from acting as though he did already know something. Instead, he kept on asking questions and challenging people's beliefs, as though he knew better, or at least as though he was in the process of acquiring knowledge. Yet he always declined in the last instance to take a stand on anything, to offer up any of his own knowledge. He was called ironic. At the time this mostly had the unpleasant meaning that Socrates was a faker, that he only pretended to know nothing, so that he could trick his interlocutors into saying stupid things, without having to say anything stupid himself. But it could also have meant that he was always just posing, adopting possible points of view, without ever really knowing what to believe for himself.

## (2) THE UN-METHOD

Socrates set about acquiring knowledge in a most unusual way. Facts were of no interest to him. Instead, he seems to have had two related concerns: people's opinions and the definitions of words. His "method," which is sometimes called the "elenchus," consisted of asking someone an abstract question, usually the definition of a big word like "virtue," "justice," "piety," or something of that sort, and then demonstrating by further questioning that his interlocutor was hopelessly confused. By his own admission, neither Socrates nor any of his interlocutors arrived at a satisfactory definition of virtue or anything else. How this exercise in defining words might have advanced knowledge, supposing the definitions were to be had, is unclear. Perhaps the absence of a valid definition is a curious bit of knowledge. However, if the implication is that one could not do or be anything without first being able to provide a definition of the relevant concept, well, then, this would be like saying that one cannot eat until one has a clear definition of digestion. What Socrates imagined could be learned by befuddling the man on the street is also unclear. At best, assuming they could recover from the shock, Socrates' interlocutors might have been motivated to improve the internal consistency of their set of beliefs. But how consistency should lead to truth no one seems to know. One might, of course, be consistently false. Sometimes it seems that Socrates thought of himself as a midwife, that is, one who has no ideas of his own, but simply helps others give birth to theirs. Since these others were, according to the Oracle, less wise than Socrates, we at least have a right to expect more from the obstetrician than from the children.

## (3) THE UN-DOCTRINE

Given Socrates' un-method, it should come as a surprise that he should be associated with any doctrine at all. He had claimed to know nothing, and in any case his negative dialectics should have been able to dissolve any specific beliefs. Yet there is such a doctrine, or cluster of doctrines. This cluster can be summarized in a strange equation: virtue = knowledge = happiness. The first part of this equation, that virtue is knowledge, seems to mean two things. First, it is the claim that being good requires knowing how to be good. Socrates apparently made the case for this by analogy: Being a shoemaker means knowing how to make shoes; being a cook means knowing cookery; so being good means knowing what the good is. (Hmmm. Something a little fishy there.) The second, stronger claim is that no one knowingly does wrong. So, for example, bank robbers simply don't know that robbing banks is wrong. (Definitely fishy.)

The second part of the equation, that knowledge is happiness, also has two sides. First, it means that knowing things, or perhaps knowing the right kind of things, can make you very happy. So, possibly, those shoemakers are quite content. Second, since virtue is knowledge, it means that being good will also make you happy. Presumably, those bank robbers are miserable.

Of course, if we take Socrates' declaration of ignorance as well as his acknowledged dissatisfaction with existing definitions, seriously, then neither he nor anybody else knows what virtue is, so everyone must be bad and unhappy.

## (4) THE UN-LIFE

Throughout his attempt to create a new dictionary of moral terms, and informing all of his dialectics, was the one question that really mattered to Socrates: What is the good life? On the one hand, his project can be understood as an ongoing investigation into this central question. One assumes that he did not yet have an answer, that he awaited an impartial result. It might turn out, for example, that the good life is that of the shoemaker, so we should all become shoemakers. On the other hand, Socrates' investigation seems to presuppose an answer: The good life is the life of philosophy. Philosophy is the life of contemplating virtue, and virtue is knowledge, that is, it is the result of philosophical contemplation and thus getting to know virtue. But, now, which is the means and which the end? Which the premise, and which the conclusion? The un-method of asking all those questions is both the means of investigation and the end. The un-doctrine, that virtue is knowledge is happiness, is both the conclusion of a life of philosophical reflection, through which one has come to know what virtue is, and the premise of such a life, since it guarantees that it is only through philosophy that one becomes virtuous. In other words, we find ourselves in a strange and "virtuous" circle of Socratic philosophy. The good life is the life of contemplation. Contemplating what? Why, the nature of the good life, of course.

The problem of Socrates, to repeat, is: How could Socrates have believed all this? What is one to make of all that nonsense about "knowing I know nothing," or the futile search for absolute definitions, or the negative dialectics, or the claim that being good is knowing the good, or that no one does wrong knowingly, or that the good life is contemplating the good life? How can all that be taken seriously? There is, I think, a fairly straightforward, obvious, and plausible answer to this question. I will call it "Xanthippe's Complaint," in honor of Socrates' maligned wife. I will present her side shortly. But this is not the answer that the tradition has wanted to hear (at least not in recent times). The tradition has favored two solutions, the one dogmatic, the other critical. The former was articulated first and best by Plato. The latter is the most common today. In between, there is a wide range of compromise and ad hoc solutions, none of which is as clear or compelling.

# THE PROBLEM OF SOCRATES: SOLUTIONS

## (1) THE DOGMATIC SOLUTION

Socrates believed in his paradoxical doctrines because they happened to be true. He was only pretending to be ignorant. You see, the truth is that reality consists of certain Forms, like Shoe, Bed, and Virtue, of which the shoes, beds, and virtues we see around us are only imperfect copies. Once this is understood, the apparently paradoxical method of Socrates makes sense. In seeking his definitions, Socrates was seeking knowledge of this ultimate reality, which you ignorant people cannot see. In addition, Socrates was absolutely correct in identifying virtue and knowledge and happiness. The form of the Good is a part of the intelligible world and is so powerful and radiant that, once seen by the true philosopher, it determines everything he does. Plus it makes him very happy. This is why the life of philosophy is the only virtuous one, and why there is no point in getting one's hands dirty with human affairs. Now, the ignorant masses of his day could not understand what Socrates was up to, so they had him killed. He refused to save himself because he would not compromise his virtue merely to save his flesh, which was in any case merely the tomb of his Soul. In this way he sacrificed himself in order to show us the way to philosophy. Of course, Socrates was not quite consistent or articulate in presenting the underlying truth about his philosophy, so that is why I, Plato, have found it necessary to render his views explicit, and in certain cases to improve on his work.

The virtue of Plato's solution is that it wraps up many of the loose ends. The definitional method is explained to be the method of true knowledge. The un-doctrine can be accounted for with a description of the special Idea of the Good. The "I know I know nothing" line turns out to be just a ruse, the simplest kind of irony. There is no question about the righteousness of Socrates' life, and his execution is an example of the evil behavior of the ignorant masses. In sum, the problem of Socrates is dissolved by asserting that there is no paradox, it's just that the Truth happens to be a little strange. (Or, it's not Socrates' problem, it's the world's problem!)

The trouble with this solution is obvious and twofold. First, one has to turn the world upside down in order to believe in it. It replaces paradox with the outright absurdity of a Platonic theory of forms. Second, it rides roughshod over the distinctively critical features of the Socratic philosophy. It relies on a crude picture of Socratic irony as pure fakery. It does not take seriously Socrates' claims to know nothing. It renders the negative, dialectical character of Socrates' method irrelevant, just another ruse in the presentation of his positive doctrine. In short, in order to ascribe specific doctrines to Socrates, Plato has to discard the apparently central, anti-doctrinal element of Socrates' thought.

## (2) THE CRITICAL SOLUTION

The other traditional solution consists in finding some excuse to drop the doctrines associated with Socrates—they were pinned on him by Plato; or, he was only joking; or, I forgot—and emphasizing the critical element of his thinking. Socrates is taken to represent the first and archetypal man of reason. He accepts nothing on faith. His attitude is skeptical and scientific. He is the first to apply the method of reason to the questions of the soul. He insists that people examine themselves, that they subject even their dearest beliefs to the cold light of reason. He gives his life to the cause of creating moral self-awareness. He was a man ahead of his time.

According to this view, Socrates' irony is quite genuine and sophisticated. It is a device by which he preserves his detachment, his critical viewpoint, anticipates the multiplicity of perspectives inherent in any intellectual inquiry, and avoids sliding into a one-sided dogma.

There is certainly something of the spirit of Socrates in this critical solution. Yet there is also something at odds with what we know about Socrates: His philosophy was also quite unreasonable.

Consider, for example, the un-method. Is this, as tradition would have it, the same thing as the "method of reason," whatever that would be? I think not. Establishing definitions of abstract terms may be a part of a reasonable discussion, but not all reasonable discussions consist of defining terms. In fact, the preeminence of definitions in the Socratic method is decidedly unreasonable, for it supposes that matters of fact and of duty can be resolved by merely considering the meanings of words. Probing the consistency of an interlocutor's understanding of ethics may be part of a reasonable investigation, but not all reasonable ethical investigations need proceed in that way. In fact, as stated above, there is no reason why a consistent set of beliefs should be true or right. Besides, if Plato and other Socratics like Xenophon have faithfully reproduced Socratic dialogue, it is not even the case that his discussions were always reasonable. In brief, not much of the un-method can be explained by appeal to the cause of critical reason, and much of it is simply inconsistent with critical reason.

Consider the un-doctrine. In wishing away all supposed doctrines, the critical solution simply ignores the fact that Socrates' name is linked to a specific doctrine. Furthermore, the un-doctrine is impossible to justify on purely critical grounds. It is, if anything, quite unreasonable. Knowing the definition of "the good" is probably not necessary to being good (think of those good little kids), and certainly isn't sufficient for being good (think of those philosophical bank robbers). There is much evidence to suggest that people do wrong knowingly, and no logical reason to think that they cannot. Likewise there is much evidence to suggest that bad people can be happy, and no logical reason to think they cannot.

Socrates' un-life, his notion that the good life is the life of philosophy, also cannot be explained purely on grounds of critical reason. While it is certainly reasonable to examine oneself and reflect on the course of one's life, it does not follow that it is reasonable to make this sort of reflective examination the sole occupation of one's life. On the contrary, if there is a point to the examination, it surely must lie in achieving a result, and then getting on with life.

Suppose, despite the evidence, that we remove all dogmatic and doctrinal elements from what we know of Socrates' thought. Suppose we say that it doesn't matter if he was hung up about definitions or dialectics, that we could reinterpret the un-doctrine into something plausible, and so what if he was prejudiced in favor of the life of contemplation. In other words, suppose what we want to preserve is the purely critical element of Socrates, his contribution to the life of reason, of enlightened skepticism. In that case, what would remain of Socrates? With what would we credit him? The discovery of reason itself? Moral consciousness? What would those things look like? Is reason a discovery, like the New World? Is it an invention, like the steam engine? Is it even a specific method? Is moral consciousness the perception of some new and different reality? Is it like a new pair of extrasensory eyes? If we are to suppose that Socrates invented reason, moral consciousness, the steam engine, or whatever, then what were men like Parmenides, Gorgias, and Thucydides doing? Were they just babbling in a semiconscious, immoral stupor? Was the whole world waiting without a thought, without a sense of right or wrong, until Socrates sprang up and delivered these new capabilities to humankind?

When we drop out the particularities of Socrates' life and philosophy, nothing remains except a general disposition of objectivity, a willingness to question, a desire for truth. Unless we suppose the absurd, that Socrates invented thinking itself, we have to acknowledge that the critical spirit of Socrates is just an attitude. And an attitude does not have a history.

In between the critical and the dogmatic solutions to the problem of Socrates are a wide range of compromises. For example:

## 1.666 The Mystical Solution

Socrates was trying to express something that cannot be expressed either in doctrine or in method. He was trying to reveal to us the secrets of wisdom. Everything he said was merely a sign, or an allegory, to help us along our way. True enlightenment comes only from finding oneself, one's own soul. There may be some history in this solution. Certainly Plato can be linked to the outrageously mystical Pythagoras, so perhaps Socrates can be, too.

The mystical, like the critical solution, begins by rejecting the specific doctrines associated with Socrates. It also rejects the methods. In the end, there's nothing left at all, just a feeling soooooh indescribable. More on that in the chapter on Eastern philosophers.

---

From *The Psychoanalyst's Handbook on Philosophers*

**Paradoxophilia.** *Definition.* Love of paradoxes. A condition common to philosophers, especially those of mystical bent. The paradox conveys for them the air of profundity. More importantly, it works to paralyze the understanding. The mind stumbles and falls on the paradox. This results in a state of mystification before the great mysteries of the universe. It convinces philosophers that they have reached the limits of the world. Because the paradox may befuddle others, it also gives philosophers a sense of power. They like that.

## 1.5 The Scholarly Solution: A Thousand Qualifications

If one examines the concepts of virtue, the good life, irony, and reason, as used in the relevant texts; considers the orthographic permutations of a few Greek words; supplements the Socratic doctrines with a few reasonable propositions; limits their applicability according to a few, contextually justified principles; ignores half of what Plato says but takes the rest seriously; takes into account the contemporary political responses to Homer and the level of resin in Athenian wines, then it becomes clear that Socrates' position is indeed consistent and philosophically significant. He is, after all, a Great Philosopher.

Not surprisingly, after a thousand qualifications Socrates' doctrines no longer sound very radical, or even very interesting. They start to sound like the well-defended banalities of a Ph.D. thesis. Why bother? And was he really so great if he forgot to mention all those qualifications?

## 1.123 Miscellaneous

There are countless more answers to the Problem of Socrates. Many of these have had a broader cultural significance than any mentioned so far. For example, Socrates has always been popular as an ersatz Jesus, his execution interpreted as a thinking man's Golgotha. Others have understood Socrates as the classic individualist. He is the man who refuses to bend before the will of the collectivity, and pays the price with his life. Others have named Socrates as a conspirator. He is a totalitarian and/or the inventor of the oppressive metaphysical tradition of the West. In short, owing largely to the circumstances of his death, Socrates has been used as a symbol for a wide range of spiritual and cultural concerns. This explains his endurance. But it also has little to do with his philosophy.

## (3) XANTHIPPE'S COMPLAINT

Socrates' wife was said to be "the most troublesome woman" in Greece. Isn't this a little odd? Why should the wisest man in Greece choose to marry such a horror? Would any man knowingly do himself such harm? Isn't it more plausible that she became such a nag only after having married Socrates? But how could being married to a man as virtuous as Socrates cause this madness? What was the nature of Xanthippe's complaint?

Let us suppose, along with Xanthippe, that the main thing Socrates wanted was to get out of the house. He wanted to go out and play with his friends—both the men and the boys. He loved to play. He loved the competition, he loved the fraternity, he loved the underlying sexual tension, and he loved to talk. He hated to work. The very idea of exchanging leisure time for pay made him nauseous. In short, Socrates knew what sort of life he wanted to lead, and that life was going to be as far away from husbandly and fatherly responsibilities as possible.

If we start from this Socratic premise about the nature of the good life, the rest of Socrates' paradoxical philosophy follows quite logically. His lack of interest in facts, for example, was quite prudent. Nothing can kill a philosophical discussion as quickly as a fact. Much better to stick to definitions. So long as one has two things—the word and its definition—which purport to be the same, one has the contradictory basis for some pleasing dialectics. Ah, the pleasure of the dialectic! What can compare to the surge of the all-conquering power one derives from stripping one's opponent bare and exposing his—contradictions? All the better if one begins demurely, with a coy and ironic remark about one's own modest intentions.

Socrates really showed his brilliance in the daring rationale he developed as a defense for his chosen life. What better justification for such a life could one have than the perverse claim that virtue itself was its aim and result? To construe his dialectics as a search for knowledge, and then to affirm with pious expression that virtue is knowledge—what could be the force of this "argument" other than to justify the choice already made, and to exclude the life not chosen, the life of work and action—and to exasperate further his frustrated wife? Through a clever feat of abstraction, Socrates managed to conflate a description of what he was doing with a statement of its results. He could do his work by merely talking about it. He made his jolly life of philosophy an end in itself. One has to admire his audacity.

Xanthippe must have known what her husband was up to. She must have been shocked to discover that she had married a good-for-nothing. So the nagging began. Why don't you get a job? Why don't you try doing something useful? Why don't you put your big brains to work, instead of drinking wine and shooting the dialectics all day with the boys? Don't you care about me and the children? Why don't you ever, you know, do anything with me? Why couldn't I have married a decent fellow? Why didn't I listen to my poor, dear mother, may she rest in peace?

Xanthippe would not have been the only one to complain. Public-minded citizens might also have had cause for grievance. Of course, the tradition maintains that Socrates served as the conscience of his community. He supposedly introduced critical reason so that those around him might reflect on their actions and perhaps improve their way of doing things. So far as the city of Athens was concerned, this stretches the truth just a bit too far. In the very age when his home city rose to world prominence; became the leading democracy of Greece; created an empire based first on hope, then on fear; used its tribute to fund some of the most enduring cultural achievements in Western history, from architecture to the theater; waged a brutal war against a militaristic foe for twenty-seven years; and suffered a plague, two revolutions, and a reign of terror—in all this time Socrates not only did nothing on behalf of his city, but aggressively disdained involvement in public affairs. For the essence of his philosophy was a way of life free from the cares not only of home but of the community as well. The virtue Socrates preached had nothing to do with helping out his fellow men, and everything to do with the private bliss of a small sect. The sort of critical reasoning he taught was not of the sort that could help a community understand its needs, capabilities, and duties, with a view to deciding what is to be done. Rather, it was intended to induce paralysis in practical affairs, and convert men instead to the philosophical life.

The nature of Socrates' influence on later antiquity, from Plato to the Hellenistic philosophers, makes it obvious that his chief original contribution to humankind was in fact the idea of a certain way of life, and not any particular method or doctrine, let alone reason. The legend of Socrates was kept alive by those who saw in him the discoverer of a kind of virtue that could be realized in private, without involvement in the mess of domestic or political life. The Socratic philosophy endured because it helped certain alienated groups within society achieve their spiritual needs.

Let us suppose that Xanthippe already saw through this. She knew that Socrates had an awful sense of humor, that his jokes were so bad that other people could not tell when he was being serious. She saw that Socrates was playing tricks on his friends, that he made fun of their instinctive realism by turning it on its head, by perverting it into a flight from reality, into the land of empty abstractions. She saw that he was exploiting their spiritual needs for his own amusement. She also saw that he himself could no longer distinguish between irony and reality, that his personality was now nothing more than the constantly shifting faces he presented in argument. Xanthippe's complaint, in brief, was that there was nothing particularly reasonable or ethical about Socrates' existence, that he had lost himself in an attempt to live his version of the good life.

## DID SOCRATES HAVE TO DIE?

Maybe it was just bad comedy. Socrates died for his appalling sense of humor. After the jury had narrowly convicted him, and his accusers had demanded the death penalty, it fell to Socrates to propose an alternative punishment. He suggested that he be given a life pension. This little joke did not go down very well, so he proposed the ridiculously small fine of one minae. That one bombed, too. With a shrug, Socrates offered the hooting crowd thirty minae. The jury deliberated, and by a much larger margin this time decided to give him death. Suicidally bad comedy, perhaps, but not really necessary.

Or maybe he really had come to believe in something. Maybe he did believe in his own type of virtue, and saw no virtue in giving in to the crowd. He saw no other life worth living than the one which had led him here, to this confrontation. It was a tragedy, and a tragic necessity. Was he truly such a man of ideas? Was he a true believer? Who knows? That is the real problem of Socrates.

# Plato

## The Last Dialogue

To paraphrase the most frequently cited saying of an otherwise forgotten early-twentieth-century philosopher, the history of Western philosophy consists of a series of footnotes to Plato (427–347 B.C.E.). There is a long history of flattering comments about Plato. For my part, I cannot make much philosophical sense out of such adulation. Plato's doctrines were borrowed mainly from the mystical Pythagoras, and are incredible in the literal sense of the term. He foisted many of these doctrines unjustly on a fictional Socrates. Though his work undoubtedly has literary merit, it can also be quite tedious and annoying.

The theory of forms, apparently the centerpiece of Plato's philosophy, basically says that what is ultimately real are forms, or ideas, and that what silly people like you and me take to be real, like tables and chairs, are just pallid copies or "instantiations" of this ultimate reality. One of Plato's approximate contemporaries, however, pointed out that if one were to plant a wooden bed, one would expect it to sprout not more beds, but possibly a tree. So much for the form of Bed, or for the whole theory of forms, for that matter.

The earliest Platonic dialogues *(Meno, Crito, Euthyphro)* are closer to the critical spirit of Socrates. In them, Plato's Socrates spends his time demolishing the arguments as well as the self-confidence of various interlocutors. Somewhere in the middle of life, however, Plato experienced the mysteries of the Pythagorean philosophy and became an expert mathematician. The dialogues *(Phaedo, Republic, Phaedrus)* change in character from Socratic to dogmatic; they become a vehicle for Plato to expound a set of mystical and metaphysical doctrines. The immortality of the soul (yes), the nature of ultimate reality (it's all forms), the nature of knowledge (recollection), the best form of government (dictatorship of the philosophers), and other such topics are purportedly decided by the dialogues with a fictional Socrates. Plato's last dialogues *(Parmenides, Theaetetus, Sophist)* are an unhappy combination of technical refinements to his theories and criticism of these same theories. They are uncertain, inelegant, and perhaps a little bitter.

Let us suppose that Plato had lived a little longer, that the process of self-critique continued and finally achieved its logical result. Let us imagine that archaeologists have discovered an ancient set of tablets buried beneath an ancient flowerpot, in which it would appear that a certain self-loathing old man finally put pen to paper, or stylus to clay, and produced . . .

## THE LAST DIALOGUE, OR THE RETURN OF SOCRATES

MORONICOS: Were you there, the glorious day when Socrates reappeared among us?

HYPOCRITES: Alas I was not, but my friend Stupidistes was, and I have memorized every word of his account. What a day it was! Such joy and melancholy fills my soul.

MOR: I will not move from this spot until you tell me all.

HYP: Very well, then, I will relate the story as it was told to me by Stupidistes, if you will promise not to interrupt. It seems that Plato, Stupidistes, and a number of others were gathered at the Academy. Plato was leading a rather uninspired discussion about some mathematical point. Perhaps they were trying to calculate the cosmic number again. In a moment, however, they forgot entirely what they were doing. In walked this man who looked at least a hundred years old. He had a long white beard and walked with a stoop, but the crooked eyes, fat lips, and up-turned nose were instantly recognizable. Socrates! The academicians were stunned, as if by a torpedo. In their silence Socrates began to speak, in his familiar sly way, as though nothing had happened.

He touched Stupidistes on the shoulder and said, Tell me, my old friend, why is everyone so silent? Why do you not welcome your old comrade?

Stupidistes gathered himself together and stammered, We do not wish to be rude, O Socrates. We are just greatly—but very happily—surprised. We thought you were dead.

And yet I am alive, said Socrates. Perhaps we can talk the matter through, so to speak. Will you grant a dead man a dialectic?

Of course, dear Socrates.

Then allow me to put this proposition before you, Stupidistes: that those things which have an opposite necessarily come from their opposite. This seems clear enough to me. Is it acceptable to you?

Please explain what you mean, O great one.

I mean something like this: If something big comes to be, it will come from something small.

Without doubt.

And if something small comes to be, it will come from something big?

Yes.

And the sleeping comes from the awoken, and wakefulness from sleep?

Whatever you say.

And black from white, white from black, happy from sad, sad from happy? Need I go on or do you catch my drift?

I catch your inestimable drift, O Socrates.

Then you will agree that death comes from life and life from death?

I must.

Therefore, a dead person must return to life, just as a living person must die?

It must be so.

So, I was dead, but now have come back to life. Here I am. Are you still surprised?

But I am astonished! You, Socrates, have argued yourself back into life! I had no idea how powerful the dialectic could be.

Be careful, then, said Socrates, lest I argue you from life to death!

At this point Plato stepped forward. O no! said the frightened Stupidistes, Stop immediately!

MORONICOS: O philosophical ecstasy! The meeting of two Great Minds!

HYPOCRITES: Indeed! But hush now, while I finish the tale.

Plato arose with the immense dignity of which only he is capable and began to speak: O noble Socrates, we welcome you back to philosophy with great joy. It was the incomparable example of your own life that has led us to dedicate ourselves to the search for truth. Do not, then, think that I am being disrespectful if I inform you that since your, er, departure, philosophy has advanced to a considerable degree, and has attained some of that truth for which you sought. In my work, the *Meno,* for example, in which I hope I honor you by making you the star of the dialogue, I present the new theory of recollection. According to this theory, the dialectic serves to bring out the memories of true knowledge, which we carry hidden in our souls.

O Plato, sighed Socrates, my favorite disciple! What a joy to see you continuing on our life of philosophy. Nothing has pleased me so much in my afterlife as reading from your wonderful works. Do not think me disrespectful, but merely the ignorant old man I am, if I question you about these advances in philosophy of which you speak.

Please proceed, said Plato.

I do not remember having offered a theory of knowledge as recollection. Was it your idea?

My modesty prohibits me from answering truthfully.

So it was your idea, and not remembered from what I said?

That must be so, if you do not remember having said it.

But according to the theory, all true knowledge must come from memory?

So the theory states.

Therefore, since the theory was not remembered, the theory is not true?

O Socrates, you are as masterly as ever! But perhaps the problem is that I did not explain well enough. What is recollected to the mind as true knowledge through the dialectic are the Forms, which are eternal, permanent, and true. Thus, the recollection theory is only one part of what the academics are now calling the Theory of Forms. According to this theory, there is a real world distinct from the apparent world of the senses we see around us, and this world consists of the basic forms in which all things partake: Virtue, Piety, Bed, and Grasshopper, for example. It is this world of Forms which is the object of philosophical knowledge. I hope you will consider it an honor, once again, that I presented this theory in your voice in a number of dialogues.

What a magnificent idea, said Socrates. May I continue and ask a few more questions about this latest theory?

Of course.

If I understand you correctly, you would maintain that as these Forms are the highest and best form of existence, they must also be True?

Yes.

Do you also agree that if there is a form of White, then there must also be one of Black?

I agree.

And there are forms for Short and Tall, Fast and Slow, Smart and Stupid?

Naturally.

So, if there is a form of the True, there must also be a form of the False?

Of course.

And as all forms are True, this must be the True False?

I suppose it must.

Therefore, the False is True?

Uh, if you say so.

This is somewhat perplexing. Let's try again. Is there also a form of Being?

Yes.

So there is Not-Being?

I suppose so.

But now I am truly perplexed, my friend. Are you saying that Not-Being is? How can Not-Being Be, if it Is Not?

But you are making something complicated out of what is very simple. The forms all exist and are true, although that which partakes of the forms need not exist or be true. That which is not, for example, partakes of Not-Being, even if the Not-Being itself is.

Perhaps it is simple, replied Socrates. There are forms for all sorts of things. I wonder if we have really thought this matter of Forms through. I believe you are suggesting that that which participates in a Form is different from the Form itself. For example, a bed participates in the Form of Bed, but it is not itself a Form. Contrariwise, the Form of Bed is not a bed.

Indeed, it must be so.

Would you also agree that, as there are so many Forms about, there must be a Form of Forms?

I don't see why not.

Well, I do see a certain problem. If the Forms participate in the Form of Forms, are they not different from that Form in the same way that a bed is different from the Form of Bed?

Oh.

And, contrariwise, could we not suppose that the Form of Forms is not a Form, in the same way that the Form of Bed is not a bed?

O Socrates, you old dog. I see your trick. With your devilish analogy you have led us to overlook the possibility that there are some Forms which are indeed instances of themselves. While it is true that the Form of Bed is not a bed, it is also true that the Form of Beauty is beautiful, that the Form of Being exists, and, in sum, that the Form of Forms is itself a Form.

I see you have lost none of your wit, my dear Plato, said Socrates. But let us be clear on this: You are affirming that there are two kinds of Forms, namely, those which participate in themselves and those which do not.

I am.

And that the Form of Forms belongs to the latter category, the kind which participate in themselves?

You got it.

Would you not also grant that there must be a Form for all those Forms which do not participate in themselves?

Okay.

Now, concerning this Form of Forms-which-do-not-participate-in-themselves, should we say that it does not participate in itself?

I suppose it does not.

So it is a Form-which-does-not-participate-in-itself?

It is.

And if it is such a Form, then it must participate in the Form of Forms-which-do-not-participate-in-themselves?

Plato fell silent, but Socrates barreled on.

I must say, dearest Plato, that your Socrates was cleverer than I, if he understood this Theory of Forms.

Very ironic, Socrates, Plato snarled.

And so, to conclude this argument, said Socrates, it follows that the state should be ruled by philosophers. Do you see?

Say what?

Oh dear, perhaps I am mistaken. I was just flipping through this book of yours called *The Republic*. I think the argument goes like this: Since the philosophers are the ones who have true knowledge of the forms, and especially of the form of the Good, they are best suited to rule the state.

Indeed. Until philosophers are kings there will be no justice and no good in the state.

I wonder if I follow what you are saying. As I understand it, philosophers apprehend the forms, while ordinary people, like tyrants, apprehend things through the senses. Is this so?

It is so.

Is that which is apprehended through the senses apprehended through the body?

It must be.

And that which is apprehended without the senses requires no body?

Yes.

Is it not true that things which are never used quickly fall into disrepair, and then cease to function?

It is true.

So, a philosopher who has no need for the senses will soon lose his senses?

So it would seem.

And whoever loses his senses also loses his body?

At the very least.

And he who has no body is dead?

Without doubt.

So philosophers are dead?

Oh dear.

So you would have the state ruled by dead people?

That's not quite what I intended! What I meant was that because only true philosophers have a vision of the true form of the Good, only they can rule the state in such a way as to bring about the realization of virtue in the world.

Ah, yes, said Socrates. I remember now. We had all those arguments about the nature of virtue. Those were the days. Well, anyway, let me see, as I remember, one of us—was it me?—argued that virtue is a kind of knowledge. Being virtuous is a matter of knowing what virtue is. Injustice can never be more profitable than justice, so it is only through ignorance that injustices are committed. No one knowingly does wrong. Is this an accurate summary of your current position?

Yes, my master.

Well, my follower, would you agree that it is unjust to lie?

Most certainly.

If I were to say, I am Plato, this would be a lie, would it not?

Yes, you would be a liar.

And therefore unjust?

Yes, you would be a liar and most unjust.

Very well, then, let me say it: I am Plato.

You scoundrel!

Precisely, my dear Plato. I have lied and committed an injustice.

Double drat!

Yet I knew very well that I am not Plato, and that it would be a lie to say so?

You did.

So, I knowingly committed an injustice. Furthermore, I have profited in doing so, by beating you in this argument. Therefore, it is possible to profit from injustice. Do you not agree?

Plato said, in a nasty tone of voice, There you go again, up to your old tricks.

You disguise a fallacious argument in a series of treacherous questions. You confuse us with supposed clarity.

Tell me, young man, Socrates continued in his usual unperturbed and cheerful voice, what would you think of a physician who refuses to take his own medicine?

I would call him a hypocrite.

Shame! Are you not like a physician who refuses to take his own medicine? Are we not now engaged in a Platonic dialogue?

If so, it will be the last dialogue, I promise.

Our discussion, continued Socrates, reminds me of this myth I once heard from a spirit or some other character of dubious origin. Let me see, how did it go? Oh yes. In the beginning there was Chaos. Then from Chaos sprang a large number of concentric spheres, which resonated harmonically to the tune of . . .

Enough, enough! cried Plato. I don't want to hear another one of your silly stories, and I am tired of your futile dialectics. Do you really want to know the truth about my philosophy, and about your philosophy as well? I will tell you anyway. I am older now than you were when you died, and in my old age I have begun to see more clearly the nature of this enterprise of philosophy which has been my life's work. I know that in the end I have only myself to blame. But let me tell you why I would also blame you. You were like a father to me. While the city seemed to be falling down around me, dragged down by war, pestilence, and the unruly masses, you offered me the hope of something strong, hard, and eternal: Truth. You persuaded me that philosophy was a life of virtue, the only life. I did not know that for you, it was all a game. For you, the argument was everything, and the conclusions nothing. I forsook my family, and I gave up the chance to become an important man in city affairs. Now I am an old man, and have never yet put a hand to practical work. I have only my mediocre writings and a band of adolescents who cling to me in the way I clung to you. I could have produced dramas to edify the population and keep our culture alive, I could have written the speeches which would decide the policy of our city. Instead I have only lured little boys with bad arguments into squandering their lives following me following you in circles. I said you were like a father; now I think you more like the Sirens who would have lulled Odysseus into oblivion. From a distance your song is soothing and irresistible. It rings like Absolute Truth, Eternity, other sweet things. In the end, it proves to be an empty song of the self. It is a song with one note— I, I, I, I. . . . And I am nothing but an empty vessel, a vacuum inside the walls of my spent life.

Why should I not posit a World of Forms? Perhaps it is wishful thinking— indefensible, if you like. But I found it very comforting. This is the reality you promised. All those concepts you were never able to define exist and prosper in this World. It is strong, hard, and open only to you and me and our followers. As long as I can believe in it, I can believe that my life has not been wasted. Derive virtue from knowledge? Prove the good? Of course, I know that's impossible. But I needed that too. What value would our search for truth have, if the Good were merely the petty inclinations of vulgar humanity? I felt I was doing the good in

following you; as I began to pass up the good things life brought to my less virtuous acquaintances, I needed proof. We who are so virtuous that we never advance
even our own interests, we need to get our revenge. Yes, I wish I could do it over
again, and could have done something honestly for myself and others. But by the
time I became aware of my situation it was too late. You had me bewitched for too
long. What could I do but make you into my new religion? You, great master, were
capable of doubting everything—doctrine, definition, idea—including yourself.
You never lost that self-confidence. We weaker beings, we cannot doubt so much,
lest we doubt ourselves. We need our little rock, and since it is not inside, must find
it outside, in our doctrines and rituals.

At this Socrates fell silent. His eyes were distant. A little feebly, he said, Oh, I
remember the myth I wanted to relate now. It's about these philosophers who get
stuck in a cave, and spend all day speculating about confusing shadows on the
walls. . . . Ah, but we did have some fun, didn't we?

MORONICOS: How melancholic! What happened next?

HYPOCRITES: Socrates chatted a while longer with the rest of us and then
bid us all adieu. We never saw him again. Some say he returned to the afterlife.
Others say that he is living to this day in a retirement village on Crete.

MOR: And Plato?

HYP: Plato sat in a huff for a while, and that night resolved to change his
career. The next day he set sail for Italy, to see if his tyrant friend over there might
have some useful employment for him. Of course, you know how Plato is—so
tactless and impractical. His "friend" threw him in jail for a few days and then sent
him packing. Now he is back in Athens, writing as before, though I hear he's trying his hand at poetry . . .

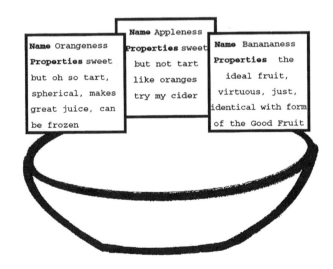

PLATO: FRUIT AS FORMS

*EasyReader Notes*

*Meno.* Can virtue be taught? What is virtue? What is a definition? Slave boy draws geometrical figures in demonstration that all is memory.

*Phaedo.* Socrates explains why he wants to commit suicide. Turns out it's okay for philosophers because they are half-dead anyway. The immortality of the soul proved with a few simple dialectics. Statement of theory of forms. Ends with another believe-it-or-not myth.

*The Republic.* The biggie. Obnoxious Thrasymachus argues rudely that Socrates is a weakling and that might is right. He gets ignored for the rest of the dialogue. Socrates is challenged by nondescript characters to show that justice benefits the just. He says, let's invent a utopian state so that we can see justice writ large. The state has four classes. Top of the heap are the guardians. The rest of the population is told a noble lie about how they evolved from different kinds of mineral deposits. Myths and bad poetry are banned. Injustice, by the way, makes its perpetrators' souls sing out of harmony, and so causes them to become unhappy. There are four kinds of vice, but only one virtue. Women should do their share of the work. Kids can be moved from one family to another overnight. Communism is best. Philosophers should rule. Understanding the nature of forms is like chopping a line segment in strange places. The best way to educate philosophers is to bring them out of their caves into the sunlight, where they'll see many forms. Don't trust anyone under thirty. The different types of existing governments all correspond to types of individual men—e.g., the tyrannical man, the democratic man, etc.—and these are all bad men, since they are not philosophers. All poets to be shot.

*The Symposium.* Raunchy dinner party. Everything you ever wanted to know about love, Greek style.

# Aristotle

## A Day at the Zoo

With Aristotle our history of philosophy can at last fully acquire a sense of history. We may now venture the first demonstration that philosophy is essentially a critique of other, earlier forms of philosophy, and that philosophy reproduces itself through this critique. Philosophy is an obsession—specifically, an obsession with itself. And as we move beyond Aristotle, through the Middle Ages to the present, there will be no more obvious object of this obsession than Aristotle himself.

There are some philosophies, like those of Plato and Socrates, that have an essential core. This core may be hidden or elusive, but you know it's there. Like a diamond, it sparkles in countless colors, though at bottom it's still the same old rock. Then there are those philosophies, like that of Aristotle (384–322 B.C.E.), which appear to have no core. They are aggregations of philosophical knowledge. Their collected parts seem to have as much in common as animals in a zoo: They happen to be living next to each other.

Such roving diversity is sometimes the expression of a single, internal conflict. This may have been the case with Aristotle. There is a painting by Raphael in the Sistine Chapel that depicts Plato with arm outstretched toward the heavens and Aristotle holding palm down to earth. The picture is too simple. It would be more accurate if taken as a representation of the internal workings of Aristotle's own mind. There were two Aristotles: One we'll call the "real" Aristotle had his hands and feet planted firmly in the fascinating empirical diversity of life on earth. The other, Platonic Aristotle, who spent twenty years of young adulthood studying under Plato, and whose first literary efforts were dialogues imitating the style of his master, could not shake his faith in the divine self-sufficiency of metaphysical speculation. The conflict between these two souls left in Aristotle's work a trail of confusion and contradiction.

The real Aristotle was no mere philosopher; he was an entire university. He was

80

the scientific-industrial complex of his day. His greatest achievement was his work in zoology, for which he is considered the founder of the science of biology. Other fields in which he worked included meteorology, astronomy, physics, literary criticism, the art of rhetoric, and psychology, to name only a few. Aristotle was also a major political historian. He and his team of researchers are reported to have written historical studies of the constitutions of over one hundred fifty Greek city states. (Only one of these, the *Constitution of Athens*, remains relatively complete today. It was found on some papyrus rolls discovered in the late nineteenth century.)

The Aristotelian approach to political history is illustrative. Aristotle's instinct was not to focus his research around a theme, like class struggle, and then select the facts accordingly. On the contrary, his first impulse was to send out an army of researchers to amass an encyclopedic collection of facts about as many cities as possible. At heart, the real Aristotle was a collector, he was a lover of lists. Had there been baseball cards in his day, he would no doubt have had every Greek player down to the last right-fielder. Perhaps his provincial background (he was not born in Athens) accounts for a certain lack of discrimination in Aristotle's love of knowledge. He was as happy dissecting an insect as he was theorizing about the nature of the stars.

It was the Platonic Aristotle who insisted that there had to be system behind this aggregation of knowledge, and that this system would have to be crowned with a "first philosophy." The Platonic Aristotle was not a lover of knowledge in the manner of his counterpart. He was a lover of Knowledge with a capital K, the pure kind which is of the Truth, and which makes one Good.

The two Aristotles first clashed over the question of method. The real Aristotle saw that each science had its own mass of particulars and its own way of dealing with them, and he was content to leave things as they were. But the Platonist loved that process of abstraction whereby particulars could be absorbed in ever more general principles, and demanded that everything be swallowed up in the ultimate principle of principles. In the end, they compromised. There would be a set of axioms common to all sciences, and then principles and definitions unique to each.

They pursued their quarrel deep into the territory of what has, since Aristotle, come to be called *metaphysics*. The real Aristotle was content to accept a rough-and-ready metaphysics which would furnish the world with the objects of common sense, like men and horses. He took every opportunity to attack Plato's Theory of Forms. The Platonic Aristotle, on the other hand, wanted to pursue the chain of being all the way up to its truest and most real form, to God, whose solitary claim to pure existence threatened to annihilate all those men, horses, and other pieces of furniture.

They could not even agree on what sort of animal their "first philosophy" was. What the real Aristotle labeled the study of being *qua* being was one among many varieties of scientific investigation, though a very important one. It was like the lion in his zoo, the king of the beasts. For the Platonic Aristotle, on the other hand, it was something much more serious and fundamental. The study of the godhead was wisdom itself, the universal science, the whole zoo *qua* zoo.

The real Aristotle would win or draw in battle after battle, and yet Plato would win the war. Victory was decided by choice of field of battle. In agreeing to fight on questions of metaphysics and theology, the real Aristotle had already surrendered. There is no such thing as a "realistic" metaphysics, any more than there is a "scientific" wizardry. In this he was no doubt a victim of his own education, which determined what issues were to count as legitimate objects of study, and which instilled in him a sense of duty toward the ideal of the life of contemplation. This was an ideal which could be realized in its pure form only through metaphysical speculation, a kind of thinking unadulterated by facts.

What the real Aristotle accomplished, alas, is now of purely historical interest. His biological work, for example, may have been groundbreaking in its day, but is hardly the latest word on the subject. Though if one wants a true history of rationality, it is here that one ought to look, and not at the Aristotle of the philosophical tradition. Only the Platonic Aristotle, whose mind was concentrated on those sciences which do not allow of progress, remains a philosophical force to be reckoned with. So, in the spirit of the real Aristotle, let's go ahead and dissect the warring, Platonic soul of Aristotle with a list of salient features, arguments, quotes, and other odds and ends.

## THE SYLLOGISM

Sometimes, when historians of philosophy get carried away, they say things like "Aristotle invented logic." He did nothing of the sort. As John Locke said, men were not bereft of the power of thought until one good day Aristotle put it into their heads. What Aristotle invented was a way of speaking with letters of the alphabet which could be used to impress and confound one's readers and interlocutors. The center of Aristotle's formal logic is the syllogism, which goes something like this:

> If A is predicated of every B, and B of every C, necessarily A is predicated of every C.

| (If)    | B is A |
|---------|--------|
| (and)   | C is B |
| (then)  | C is A |

Aristotle's formal logic is like a language within language which can be used to mirror some (but not all) aspects of the structure of some (but not all) arguments.

The study of Logic, whether Aristotle's or anyone else's, can be a good training for the mind. A formal logic, such as Aristotle's, can certainly help bring order to the tangled web of human thought, and help reveal errors in reasoning. But a formal logic is not the same thing as reasonable thinking. Rather, it is simply one of many ways in which to exercise one's faculties, like any kind of mental gymnastics. Too much emphasis on the formal aspects of logic, in fact, can be illogical, as when an argument is misunderstood or rejected because it does not match a prescribed form. One gets the impression at times that where Aristotle could not see a syllogism, he could see nothing at all.

## THE SCIENTIFIC METHOD

> All syllogisms proceed from preexisting knowledge.
> All science proceeds by syllogism.
> All science proceeds from preexisting knowledge.

With this syllogism, from his *Posterior Analytics*, Aristotle establishes one aspect of his basic picture of science. It is a picture formed in many ways with geometry in mind. (There is evidence that Aristotle had a direct influence on Euclid, the father of geometry.) Science has at its core a set of first principles. On the basis of the accepted principles the scientist piles up the syllogisms to produce the theorems of the science.

This raises an interesting question, as Aristotle himself noticed: Where do we find the first principles? Until we get an answer to this question, the method of science would seem to rest on shaky foundations. Aristotle's first thought was that, like everything else, we get them from a syllogism. But he quickly realized that this wouldn't work. The relevant syllogism would just refer back to another "first first" principle, and so on, in an infinite regress.

At this point the real Aristotle made a characteristic and, in the subsequent history, remarkably significant suggestion. Perhaps those first principles arise out of sense experience. Now we're getting somewhere. After all, most investigations, like Aristotle's own into animals and political constitutions, require a little bit of effort in the field, or in the lab, in order to gather particular facts. They also usually proceed at first by induction from particulars to universal principles, rather than deduction from given principles. They tend to have lots of hypotheses and contingent facts.

If this is the picture that Aristotle had in mind, then the method described above should not be understood as the procedure or method of scientific investigation, but as a general statement of how one should express a given body of knowledge, once it has been acquired. That is, he presents a method of explanation, not investigation. The theory behind the method is that in order to explain something well, one has to be able to demonstrate its necessity. One needs to be able to say not just *that* something happens to be the case, but *why*. Of course, many decent explanations don't go quite that far: Maybe Aristotle had in mind a more modest statement of the ultimate goal of explanation, not a necessary criterion for all explanation.

The Platonic Aristotle was not happy. He knew that induction from particular experience would not justify necessarily true first principles. It would, at best, produce principles valid only until the next sense experience. So he introduced a notion that would prove useful to philosophers for millennia: intellectual intuition. After a bit of ordinary, sensory intuition, it turns out, the mind "sees" the relevant first principles, in the same way that the Platonic philosopher just "sees" the Forms.

In the final analysis, it was the Platonic side that dominated Aristotle's thoughts on the method of science. Philosophers have long been fascinated by the axiomatic method, Descartes and Spinoza being two prominent examples. Given that of the vast mass of different kinds of knowledge which comes into the possession of human minds—think of knowing where you left your keys, why Columbus sailed to America, and how to play the guitar—only a tiny fraction corresponds to this method, this fascination needs to be explained. Two points are most obvious. First, provided the axioms are simple and self-evident, the axiomatic method provides absolutely secure knowledge. Philosophers like that; they are fanatically risk-averse. Second, the axiomatic method promises a unified system of all knowledge, or a universal science. Everything everywhere boils down to the axioms, and these happen to be in the possession of the philosophers. Philosophers tend to be control fanatics as well.

But you have to give it to that real Aristotle. He still fought for every concession. He insisted, more on the basis of what he saw with his own eyes than on a fancy syllogism, that each field of inquiry had at least some of its own methods and principles. This healthy realism is best expressed at the start of his main work on ethics: "Our discussion will be adequate if it has as much clearness as the subject-matter admits of, for precision is not to be sought for alike in all discussions."[1]

## ARISTOTLE'S ACTUAL METHOD

It is typical of Aristotle's inconsistent systematicity that none of his works actually follows the method of science laid out in his *Posterior Analytics*. Perhaps the "posterior" refers not to the physical place of this work in later editions relative to the *Prior Analytics*, as is universally believed, but to its logical place with respect to his other works taken together. Or maybe this was a silent gesture of defiance from the real Aristotle.

The demonstrative method of science, as described in the previous section, is supposed to be the opposite of the dialectic. The dialectic begins with propositions held by interlocutors, and reduces these to contradiction. It is the method of opinion. Strangely enough, many of Aristotle's works proceed in something like a dialectical fashion. He typically begins with a survey of pre-Aristotelian opinions on a particular topic, and then, in what Francis Bacon described as the "Ottoman manner," utterly annihilates his predecessors' philosophies. This process of survey and refutation, it turns out, is often far more than a mere introduction. The doctrines he in turn propounds can often be traced directly to the opening dialectics. Even Aristotle's official but unpracticed demonstrative method, it seems, is a dialectical response to the idea of the dialectic.

---

1. *Nichomachean Ethics* (I, 3), 1094b12 (numbers refer to page, column, and line in the collected works published by the Berlin Academy 1831–1870).

> **The Principle of the Self-Reflexivity of Philosophy.** All philosophical positions are essentially criticisms of other philosophical positions. Philosophy is a purely self-reflective and self-critical activity. There is no philosophy in a vacuum.

## THE FOUR CAUSES

The list of which Aristotle was proudest was his list of the four "causes":

1. The **Material** Cause: "that out of which a thing comes to be and persists . . . e.g., the bronze of the statue, the silver of the bowl . . ."

2. The **Formal** Cause: "the form or the archetype, i.e., the statement of the essence, and its genera . . . (e.g., the octave of the relation 2:1 . . .)"

3. The **Efficient** Cause: "the primary source of change or coming to rest, e.g., the man who gave advice is a cause, the father is the cause of the child . . ."

4. The **Final** Cause: "that for the sake of which a thing is done, e.g., health is the cause of walking about."[2]

Only the third cause is close to the modern usage of the term "cause" to denote that which brings about a change or an effect. The fourth really means "reason" in the sense of "purpose" or "intention." The first and second causes are bizarre, and can only be understood in the context of the overall importance of the distinction between "matter" and "form" to Aristotle.

In fact, what Aristotle meant by the word translated as "cause" is not very much like what we mean by "cause." What he had in mind was more like "that which is responsible for something," or "that which can explain or account for something." Thus, his discussion of causes is part of his attempt to arrive at true knowledge by explaining everything in terms of ultimate principles. You can explain the existence of a statue, for example, by referring to its material, i.e., the bronze; or its form, i.e., its shape as a statue; or that which brought it into being, e.g., the sculptor; or its end, e.g., the propitiation of a certain god.

The four causes come up mainly in the *Physics*, although they reappear importantly in both the works on animals and the *Metaphysics*. They are typical of what Aristotle understood by the term "physics," and show how his understanding of that term differs from our own. We imagine that a physicist is someone who gets out there and investigates nature, and who conducts experiments and comes up with general laws predicting natural phenomena. Not Aristotle. Aristotle's work on physics is an effort to clarify concepts. He takes nature itself pretty much for granted, and assumes that the concern of the physicist is to make clear the con-

---

2. *Physics* (II, 3), 194b23ff.

cepts of motion, vacuum, cause, place, and so on. In this he shows himself to be very much a Presocratic philosopher.

## THE PRUDENT POTATO

Subtly and illogically, Aristotle shifts from categorizing ways of explaining things to explaining things themselves by means of the categorization. Notoriously, he decrees that nature belongs to the fourth class, the final cause. Why do ducks have webbed feet? So they can swim fast. Why do snakes have no legs? Because only four legs are allowed, and they would be too far apart on a snake's body. Why do potatoes grow underground? So that the deer won't eat them before the farmer harvests them. How very prudent.

To be sure, what Aristotle calls the final cause is one way of explaining things. Usually we use it to explain human behavior, but it can be used to describe certain biological phenomena as well. Organisms and parts of organisms can be explained in terms of their functions, and their functions exist to serve final causes. But two thousand years of scientific activity have shown that this is not the only and not even the best way of studying nature.

Aristotle actually entertains the possibility that nature does not work according to final causes. He points out that some philosophers, like Democritus, believed that things happen out of "necessity." For example, it rains because the water vapor in clouds becomes oversaturated and falls from the sky, without a thought about where it might be falling. Outrageous, says Aristotle. It must rain for a purpose.

## THE FACTS OF SPERM

Aristotle had much to say about semen. Every few pages the stuff comes up, so to speak. What he offered on this subject is illustrative of his method. Consider the facts, according to Aristotle:

1. Semen is the Efficient Cause of the man. That is, it is what brings about birth. (The woman just has to lie back and think of Athens.)
2. Semen is a mixture of air and water. This is why it becomes watery when left outdoors for a while: The air escapes. Also, this is why it is fluffy, and why it floats.
3. Thick, granular semen will produce a boy. Thin, unclotted semen will produce a girl.
4. If there is a north wind more boys will be born, if a south wind more girls, because the body becomes more liquid when exposed to the humid south wind.
5. Very watery semen is infertile. Cool semen is also infertile.
6. Men with long penises are less fertile because the semen cools on its long passage.

7. Semen is driven from the body by jets of air. This is apparent to any man.
8. Fat boys going through puberty may lose weight, since the semen carries off the excess.
9. Relative to his size, man emits more semen than any other animal. This explains why he is the smoothest (least hairy) of animals.

Here we have an excellent example of the axiomatic method at work. Most of these "facts" can be demonstrated by considering a few simple axioms:

I.   Air is more alive than water.
II.  Heat is more alive than cold.
III. Men are more alive than women.

Facts 2 through 6 can be explained fully in this way. Semen must have air in it, since that is its life force, and the more air it has the fluffier it is, and the more likely it is to produce a boy, since a boy is more alive than a girl. This is why semen must float (despite the fact that it can be observed not to), and why semen that is all water has no life. Also, having air involves being hot, which is also more alive, so cool semen is infertile.

The first fact, that semen is an Efficient Cause, is a combination of axiom III, concerning the superiority of men, and:

IV.  Locate one of the four causes wherever possible.

Fact number 7, the air-pump theory, is a combination of axiom I and the absence of a concept of "muscle." The eighth fact, on fat boys, is based on the flip-side of the maxim "you are what you eat": "you were what you eject." The ninth is a false inference based in part on a possibly true observation, that baldness is correlated with sperm production (i.e., via testosterone levels—something Aristotle could not have known).

## THE FOUR DISTINCTIONS

Aristotle nowhere named the Four Distinctions, nor were there only four important ones in his work. Nonetheless, here is a list of four closely related conceptual distinctions that are pivotal to much of Aristotle's philosophy.

### *(1) ACTUALITY AND POTENTIALITY*

The purpose of this distinction is to affirm the possibility of "change." Why bother to "prove" change? Because many of the Presocratic philosophers, like Parmenides, had claimed to disprove it. Aristotle said that things can change because they have within themselves the potential—the power and the possibility—to assume a new form. Things are not yet actually what they are potentially. A cow, for example, can change into an all-beef patty because it is potentially hamburger meat. A seed changes into shredded lettuce because it has that potentiality within it, in a certain sense. In Aristotle's funny jargon, change is the actuality of the potential *qua* such. Insofar as there is any truth in this, all he is saying is that change is what happens when that which has the ability to change makes use of that ability. It is all very uninspiring, and would be rather silly had it not been for the Presocratics' even sillier doctrines.

## (2) ESSENCE AND ACCIDENT

The distinction between actuality and potentiality implies that change is not entirely destructive. Something remains unchanged during the change, since otherwise we could not speak of something undergoing a change. This brings up the next important distinction, that between essence and accident. The essence, in Aristotelian language, is the "what it is" of something. It is what you can say about something which is always true. Things which might or might not be true of something in any particular instance are accidents. When you change the accidents, the thing remains; when you change its essence, it's gone completely, destroyed. Think of it this way: A Big Mac without pickles is still, in essence, a Big Mac. But a Big Mac without Special Sauce is no Big Mac.

## (3) FORM AND MATTER

Like many Greeks and most commonsensical people, Aristotle tended to think in terms of physical analogies. The distinction between form and matter is one that originates in thinking about physical things, like french fries, but extends beyond them. In the physical instance, form is the shape of the stuff, like the slender shape of the fries, and matter is the stuff itself, like the potatoes inside those french fries and all those saturated fats. Things get more abstract when Aristotle realizes that "potato" can be thought of as a certain form of matter, as distinct from napkin, soda, and grease. What makes a blob of stuff a potato? It's potato-ness, of course. At the highest level of abstraction, "form" comes very close in meaning to "essence," and "matter" drops down to the mere accident that a thing happens to exist. The form of the fry is everything, not just its shape, but its greasiness, its potato-ness, its crunchiness, and its matter is just its stuff-ness, or the fact that it happens to be there. In other words, matter is the anonymous substratum on which essence makes its mark, as it were. At this high remove of abstraction, matter is also what allows two things to share an essence and yet remain distinct. French fries may all be the same, in one sense, but it sure is a good thing we can have more than one of them.

## (4) SUBJECT AND ATTRIBUTE

Declarative sentences tend to be of the form "something is something." For example, "The bun is lightly toasted." The first something, the bun, is the subject, and the second, lightly toasted, is the attribute. "Essential" and "accidental" are some things we say about attributes. The essential attributes describe the "real" subject; the accidental attributes are just there for the ride.

Aristotle is sometimes credited with the invention of these and related conceptual distinctions. This is like crediting McDonald's with the invention of the hamburger. What Aristotle demonstrated was that you can take some bland distinctions found in everyday fast-food speech, give them a major brand name, and accumulate lots of philosophical capital.

Insofar as they correspond to true propositions, the four distinctions are platitudinous: Things change. A thing is what it is, and is not what it is not. Things will be things. These propositions, *qua* platitudes, serve in the real Aristotle's eyes to affirm the superiority of his own views over those of his predecessors. They originate out of his dialectical refutation of the Presocratics. The Platonic Aristotle, on the other hand, would not acknowledge that these distinctions are merely conceptual, analytic, or polemical. For him, as with the doctrine of the four causes, they represent the basic structure of the world, and are the key to philosophical knowledge.

ARISTOTLE: FRUIT AS THE POTENTIAL QUA SUCH

## INDISPUTABLY TRUE STATEMENTS MADE BY ARISTOTLE

Since nothing except what is alive can be fed, what is fed is the besouled body and just because it has soul in it. Hence food is essentially related to what has soul in it.[3]

(You are what you eat.)

---

3. *De Anima* (II, 4), 416b8.

Now the chief parts into which the [human] body divides are these: head, neck, torso, two arms, two legs.[4]

(Acute observation.)

What causes an object to fall is the property of heaviness.[5]

(And what makes an object smell is its property of smelliness, and what makes a light bright is its property of luminosity . . .)

## THE SILLYGISM

Truth is one, error multiple. So we should not expect a single form of error in Aristotle or any other philosopher. Nonetheless, Aristotle, like many others, was given to a certain turn of thought, and this turn of thought produced errors in a predictable pattern. Moreover, the Aristotelian "sillygism," as I will call it, has a peculiar function: It is the bridge between his realistic if banal character and his Platonic soul.

At its simplest level, the error was a just punishment for excessive abstraction. It happens, for example, when Aristotle confuses his fourfold categorization of ways of explaining things with a fourfold division of things themselves. Aristotle's fallacy is the same that would trouble Kant two thousand years later. Both trace the outlines of basic concepts, like the concept of the object, and then confuse this exercise with claims to knowledge about that to which the concepts refer.

The typical pattern of Aristotelian error, however, is more specific. It goes like this:

1. Select a certain kind of conceptual pair (from among the four distinctions listed above or similar types, e.g., front and back, top and bottom, husband and wife).

2. Chop off half of the pair. This is best accomplished by raising the threat of infinite regress. E.g., if chickens come from eggs and eggs from chickens, then raise the possibility of an unhatched chicken or an unlaid egg.

3. Change the grammar of the newly divorced concept. Usually, make it denote a necessarily existing entity instead of one side of a correlative.

Consider the last distinction mentioned, that between subject and attribute. Aristotle noticed that subjects have a disturbing way of turning themselves into predicates, and therefore mere attributes. For example, the sesame seed bun was the subject of my affections, then it became the mere attribute of the Big Mac. Then I ate the Big Mac. Still, Aristotle reasoned, this chain of attributes and subjects must

---

4. *On the Parts of Animals.*
5. *Physics.*

end somewhere. Otherwise, the world would be all attributes and nothing on which they might be predicated. He concluded that there must be a collection of real, enduring subjects out there, and set out to find them. To sum up: The argument begins with a distinction relevant to sentence structure and concludes with an ontology.

A similar fate befalls the form-and-matter distinction. The original and valid point is that form and matter come as a pair. There is no form running free of matter, nor any radically chaotic matter in search of form. Form has to be instantiated in matter, and matter always appears in some form. In moments of clarity, Aristotle insists on the related point that the universal exists only through its instantiations in particulars. This is a part of the real Aristotle's rebuttal of Plato's theory of forms. Yet, in the end, the Platonic Aristotle offers a supposed proof of the existence of a pure form. His metaphysics, as we shall see, culminates in just such a monster. Further, the whole Aristotelian system *qua* system requires this sort of form-in-itself, since its own stated method aims at a knowledge in the last analysis derived from pure form, free from any material experience.

The essence/accident distinction experiences a similar divorce. Since there are ultimate subjects, there must be ultimate essences which are their ultimate attributes. These are the forms which are what they are, without need of matter. They are the whatzit's of the real world. How do you get a hold of them? It's easy: just chop off the accidents. What started off as a useful way of understanding what we mean when we say "things change"—that part of these "things," namely, the essence, remains the same, while the other part, the accidents, may change—suddenly becomes a proof that "some things never change."

The most important outcome of the sillygism is the extradition of pure actuality from its natural home in distinction between actuality and potentiality. The original distinction basically says that there are these two things and the twain shall never meet: the way things are and the way they might be. As in, there is my cow, grazing contentedly in the field. My cow might turn into hamburger meat, or it might continue grazing and producing milk and eventually receive a decent burial, or it might die suddenly in a fit of madness. My cow might have not come into existence to begin with. But Aristotle was not content with this bovine logic. He wanted something which had to be the way it was, and could not conceivably be otherwise. He wanted pure actuality, untainted with the possibility that it could have been something else. In other words, the big G. His "proof" of the existence of such a beast was the rather tawdry threat of an infinite regress. If everything might or might not be the way it is, he reasoned, then nothing need be at all. But the world exists. Therefore, etc. To summarize the course of the argument: Starting with the conceptual clarification that change is a the result of the workings of a faculty of change, Aristotle has supposedly demonstrated the existence of an amazing being.

One trick which makes this sort of argument easier is to think of the key distinctions in terms of a limited set of examples. Aristotle, for example, did not think of actuality and potentiality in terms of the change of a cow to hamburger meat. He thought of it in terms of the change of calf to cow, child to man, and so forth. This limited set of examples gave him the license to think of all change as being directed in some way toward a predetermined goal. In other words, it gave him the chance to find final causes at work. And the final final cause of all change would have to be pure actuality.

| Mistakes You Can Make in Your Own Home | Aristotelian Version |
| --- | --- |
| All elevators go up. | All actions aim for happiness. |
| Up is up. | Happiness is happiness. |
| All elevators go to the same place. | All actions aim for the same thing. |
| The kitchen might be clean. | Eternal motion might exist. |
| Actuality is prior to potentiality. | Actuality is prior to potentiality. |
| The kitchen is clean. | Eternal motion happens: Look at the stars! |
| My room is getting messier. | Things change. |
| Calves grow into cows. | Calves grow into cows. |
| Messiness is the final cause of my room. | Things change on purpose. |
| Everything has a top. | Everything has a cause. |
| The world is everything. | The world is everything. |
| I'm on the top of the world. | The world has a cause. |
| The first chore is the laundry. | The first kind of change is motion. |
| The noblest kind of laundry is the whites. | The noblest kind of motion is in a circle. |
| The first laundry machine got stuck in a spin cycle. | The first changer causes a circular motion. |

## THE SOUL—TO BE OR NOT TO BE

Aristotle pays a good deal of attention to what he calls the *psyche*. "Soul" is a not quite accurate translation, inasmuch as Aristotle's term refers to a more general life-principle than that associated with the Christian concept of the soul. Animals, for example, unquestionably have an Aristotelian soul (though they lack the faculty of rational thought which man possesses).

Aristotle's own usage of psyche is, however, characteristically ambiguous. On the one hand, in radically un-Platonic fashion, he conceives of the soul as a "faculty of living" which belongs to living things. Like the faculty of walking, for example, it is something which does not exist apart from its instantiation in someone who can walk. On the other hand, the closer Aristotle gets to home, the more Platonic he becomes. Mind, the part of the soul that thinks and knows, is somehow special. On the one hand, that faculty of thinking is just another human faculty, like the faculty of walking or eating. On the other hand, it alone is somehow "separable, impassable, unmixed." It alone is the pure, self-sufficient form which can subsist without matter. On the one hand, mind is passive—in the same sense that "eating" is passive because it does not create its own food. On the other hand, insists the Platonist, it can be "active" as well. It creates itself and its own food.

After granting the mind-part of the soul immortality, Aristotle bizarrely suggests that when finally freed from the body the mind does not remember anything about its former life. It is as though the real Aristotle, having lost the battle, got his revenge on the Platonic Aristotle by condemning him to an eternal life of oblivion. Who was I anyway? What did I look like? Was I cute?

## INTELLECTUAL INTUITION: POOF!

Intellectual intuition, as already mentioned, is that Platonic faculty whereby the mind "sees" universals, as opposed to sensible particulars. On analyzing the notion further, Aristotle makes a discovery that would dazzle philosophers to come. In the case of ordinary intuition, the thought is one thing and that which is thought of is something else, on the outside, merely given. In the case of intellectual intuition, the thought is identical with its object. When I view the Great Pyramid, for example, my thought is one thing and that great big pile of stones is another. When I perceive the geometrical notion of the pyramid, on the other hand, my thought is the same thing as its object. Now, this factoid could be taken as a relatively trivial insight. Of course, universals like pyramid-ness don't exist out there in the world, so, yes, in a way, they exist only in the mind. But why stop at the trivial, when the grandiose beckons? If the mind intuits universals directly, we can think of them as things, just standing somewhere, like Great Pyramids. In that case, why not go further and say that in intellectual intuition the mind creates the things about which it thinks—it brings them into existence? Here we have that magical faculty sought by philosophers: the faculty that would allow the ordinary armchair-bound person to stare at the nothingness before him and say, Poof! Let there be. . . .

## THEO-BABBLE: GOD IS AN UNHATCHED CHICKEN WHO LAYS HIMSELF BY EATING AND IS LOVED BY THE STARS

Aristotle's most famous sillygism is the one that goes roughly like this:

> Every movement requires a mover.
> Things are moving all the time. Especially the stars.
> There must be a first, unmoved mover to get things going.

I can't help but think of a similar sillygism:

> Every egg comes from a chicken.
> There are lots of chickens and eggs running around,
> especially out by the barn.
> There must be a first, unhatched chicken.

In one place Aristotle does actually reflect on the chicken-and-egg problem. He says, in essence, that there is no solution, but if there were, he thinks it would be the chicken. Which, with more emphasis on the last clause, is pretty much his answer to the problem of motions and movers.

The Prime Mover, as he is officially known, cannot move. To move is to change, to change is to be possibly other than one is, to be possibly other is to be less than perfect; but the Prime Mover is actual and perfect. Always was and always will be. Unfortunately, Aristotle acknowledges, ordinary movers, like billiard balls, move themselves when they move something else. So, the next problem is, how can one move something without moving oneself? Aristotle's doctrine of the final cause comes in handy here: A final cause can bring things about while remaining quite the way it is. But more specifically: What kind of final cause? Aristotle cops an idea from Plato: The object of Love and the object of Thought, which happen to be the same object, are able to move things without being moved themselves. (As in, I love you, I'm thinking of you, but you just don't care!) In sum, the Unhatched Chicken moves things by being loved and being thought of.

What or who specifically is so moved, so loving, so thoughtful? Let's see. We know that physical motion is the "first" kind of change, and that circles are the "best" kind of motion. It's obvious: The first motion is that of the stars above, which are plastered on a sphere which rotates eternally. The stars are great lovers as well as thinkers. In sum, the stars love our Prime Bird, and this love drives them in circles. And, by the way, the heavens are made up of fifty-five spheres rotating around the earth. Babble, babble.

This leaves one last problem: what does the Prime Mover do all day long? Being loved by the stars is not exactly a full-time occupation. The answer is Plato again: It thinks. Thinks about what? Well, nothing in particular. It would be degrading for it to think about ordinary objects. So it thinks about itself. It thinks about itself not as an object, which would also be degrading, but *qua* thinking. Thus, the Prime Mover thinks of thinking. Concerning our hen, we should ask, what does it eat? Well, nothing in particular, for to eat ordinary objects would be degrading. So it eats itself, *qua* eating. The Unhatched Chicken eats of eating.

The Prime Mover's way of thinking has an added benefit. Since its thinking is a form of actual knowing, it is a thought which is identical with its object. In other words, the Prime Mover creates itself by thinking about itself. In the case of our lovable bird, we should say that this is a chicken that lays itself.

In sum: God is an unhatched chicken who lays himself by eating and is loved by the stars.

## METAPHYSICS AND ALL THAT

The term "metaphysics" had humble origins. It referred to those books of Aristotle's which in one edition of his works came "after" (in Greek *meta*) those on physics. In some ways it would have been more logical to call this new science "proto"-physics, inasmuch as its subject matter is generally conceived to be logically prior to physics. Nonetheless, among non-Greeks the *meta* has come to denote "above," in the sense of "more abstract," and so preserves the notion of logical priority. Words Aristotle himself uses in the relevant books are "theology" and "first philosophy."

There are three ways in which Aristotle describes the nature of his project in the *Metaphysics*. First, he presents it as the search for wisdom. His thinking goes like this: Wisdom is true knowledge. True knowledge is knowing why things are the way they are. Knowing why things are is knowing their causes. The first causes will explain everything else there is to know. The usage of "cause" here is very close to that of "principle." As suggested in the discussion of the axiomatic method, first principles will explain all other principles, and *a fortiori* everything else. The search for wisdom therefore consists in the search for the first causes/first principles of everything. The second way is the idea that first philosophy is the study of the *Theos*, the Greek word meaning "God" or "divinity." If the world contained only perishable substances, Aristotle says, then there would be no theology or metaphysics. But since there is something eternal and imperishable, there is a science pertaining to it. The general name of this science is "theology." Sometimes metaphysics is thought of as one component of theology (though Aristotle himself obviously never used the term "metaphysics"). Logic, presumably, is another. The third way is the notion, expressed in a formula that would endure, that first philosophy is the study of "being *qua* being." As one chases principles/causes up the ladder of abstraction, the most general and therefore presumably the first has something to do with "being." The one "principle" that may be applied with certainty to any thing in the world is that it is. So first philosophy will determine the characteristics of this "is" *qua* is, and so the structure of the world. Another fancy word, "ontology," is associated with this Aristotelian science of being, the *on* in Greek.

Each of these three ways of describing the project of first philosophy is open to an initially plausible interpretation friendly to the real Aristotle. Unfortunately, it is difficult to see how the real Aristotle could have conceived of the three as a single project. The idea of first philosophy as "wisdom," in the realist's view, is just a rhetorical gloss on the notion that there ought to be some grand sum of human knowledge, a collection of the most general principles from each science. Of course, according to Aristotle's understanding of scientific method, each science will have its own principles and definitions, so first philosophy should not be expected to explain everything else. The study of a particular kind of entity, viz. divinity, can also be conceived as a division of science, if one is willing to allow that gods are part of the animal kingdom, or something like that. It is not clear, from a real Aristotelian point of view, why this theology should also be the study of wisdom, since presumably it would not be very wise to limit oneself to the study of one kind of creature. The realistic interpretation also emphasizes a narrow understanding of the study of being *qua* being. Though more general in its concerns, this study is in principle not very different from Aristotelian physics, which may be thought of as the study of change *qua* change. It is just another "science." Why this new science of being should be the same as wisdom is unclear. Sure, ontology seems primordial in some way: Everything is. But the real Aristotle could just as well make physics primordial: Everything can change. It is also hard to explain how this science of being meshes with the idea of theology. The latter is the study of one kind of entity, while the investigation of being *qua* being is presumably the study of entities *qua* entities. (Curiously, Aristotle's study of this particular entity, divinity, pretty much ends with the proof of its existence. Aristotle expends no effort on determining the particular characteristics of divinity, e.g., on the matter of angels dancing on pins, and so on.)

It all really comes together in the Platonic line of interpretation. According to the Platonic Aristotle, the only thing which really and truly is, is God. So the three senses of first philosophy come together to form a hugely important project. First philosophy is wisdom because the only source of true knowledge, knowledge about what really is, is the study of God. Theology is therefore not one among many narrow disciplines, but the supreme science of science. And first philosophy is the study of being *qua* being because being in its fullest sense belongs only to divinity.

At the end of the day, the real Aristotelian concept of first philosophy collapses into nothing *qua* nothing in the face of its Platonic alternative. From a realistic point of view, it may be worth speaking of something like wisdom, as, say, an ability to synthesize learning from all disciplines in the right way at the right time. But there is no reason to suppose that this corresponds to a specific science—indeed, if wisdom is a kind of synthesis, it ought not to be confined to a single discipline. From a realistic point of view, the idea of first philosophy as theology seems to presuppose the outcome of the investigation it defines. What if there is no god, and the study of being *qua* being, realistically speaking, is a rather brief topic for first philosophy? Meaningful knowledge is presumably about the way things are. The mere fact that they are may strike us as strange, but doesn't say much about them. The whole thing only makes sense in Plato's world. And to get there, we have to turn the real world upside down. Many of Aristotle's successors, alas, would be willing to do just that. So the concepts of metaphysics I have outlined here will be with us for a long time yet.

## OOZEY-SUBSTANCES, OR . . .

*Ousia* is one of those funny Greek words which is supposed to be untranslatable. It is a participial form of the verb "to be" which corresponds literally to "beingness," although this does not fully reflect its usage. (For one thing, it can occur in the plural, and it is hard to imagine what "beingnesses" would look like.) It has traditionally been translated as "substance," though this term lacks the important association with "to be" and inaccurately suggests something about grounds and substrata and so forth. The truth is, there is no very precise meaning for *ousia* because Aristotle uses it in many inconsistent ways. In general, though, we could say that for him it was a way of denoting those entities which are the ultimate constituents of reality. Oozey-substances are the things which really 'are', and therefore the proper object of the investigation into being *qua* being. Where Thales had said, all is water, Aristotle might have said, all is ooze.

The real Aristotle assumed from the start that the oozey-substances of this world were the ordinary objects of common sense: men, horses, and hamburgers, for example. These oozey-substances came out of his Logic in the form of the "real" subjects, i.e. those which could not become predicates.

As he reflected on particular oozey-substances, Aristotle found them remarkably hard to pin down. Are arms and legs oozey, for example, or is the man the real oozey? In a typically casual manner, he began to admit of degrees of ooziness. Some things are more oozey than others. So a Big Mac is presumably more oozey than a sesame-seed bun on its own. Thus he reconceived his first philosophy as a search for "primary" oozeys, the ooziest of the oozey-substances.

At this point, Aristotle encountered a problem that would bemuse philosophers from Hegel to Wittgenstein: the problem of the 'this'. Aristotle knew what he had in mind as ultimate reality, the things he saw around him, like this horse, this man, and this hamburger. As he began to describe these things, he found he could not avoid using general terms, or universals, to get at that to which he referred. Everything after the this, or after the mere grunt and pointing index finger, somehow mitigated the unique essence of the object in question. The real Aristotle simply fudged the issue. He bandied around his four distinctions and clouded the air with sillygisms. But the Platonic Aristotle saw an opportunity. Maybe all this grunting meant that those hamburgers didn't really exist, at least not in the full plenitude of being. Maybe even the higher order things, like the (grunt) restaurant itself, also didn't really exist. So all those little oozeys would just have to give way. Watch out! Here comes . . .

## THE BIG OOZEY

As he followed the chain of ooziness from the less to the more oozey, the Platonic Aristotle found he could not stop before reaching the single, ultimate, incredible, inimitable, indisputable, prime, eternal, ooziest of oozeys, the Big Oozey. Spinoza, working two thousand years later, would argue with some effect that there could only be one true Substance. In his half-hearted and semiconscious way, Aristotle came to the same conclusion.

The Big Oozey marks the final triumph of Plato in the disturbed psyche of Aristotle, and provides unity to his philosophy in a way that nothing in the real Aristotle's zoo can match. The Big Oozey is the basis for the idea of first philosophy. It is wisdom, for it is all things; it is divine, for it has created the world; and it is being *qua* being. All metaphysics begins and ends in this major sliminess.

The Big Oozey is the unhatched chicken, the prime mover that puts everything else in gear.

The Big Oozey draws a close to the discussion about souls, thinking souls, and intellectual intuition. It is the ultimate soul of the world, that great, active mind-thing whose intellectual intuition is the world itself.

The Big Oozey is the home for those orphans of the sillygism, the stranded sides of Aristotle's four distinctions. It is pure actuality, in that it cannot be other than it is. It is pure essence, for nothing in it is accidental. It is pure form, for there is only one, which needs no instantiation in matter. It is the subject which can never become an attribute.

Finally, the Big Oozey is the champion of Aristotle's favorite cause, the final cause. It is the final cause of everything, the whole universe as we know it. All of physics, Aristotle style, is a reading from the nature of this ultimate blob.

## HAPPINESS IS . . .

Aristotle wrote the book on ethics, as far as many philosophers are concerned. On the whole, his thinking on this subject is decent and realistic. His stated intention was not to create another barbarous field of abstractions, as in the *Metaphysics*, but to help make men better. Although he starts off with the usual teleology, and exhibits the characteristic philosophical bias in favor of the life of idle contemplation, he makes up for these deficiencies with some solid ruminations on that most fickle and yet desirable creature, human happiness. A number of his thoughts on this matter are relevant only for ancient Greek male citizens, though others are more universal.

On the downside, Aristotle's discussion of ethics is set within a teleology. In keeping with his own aim to find one of the four causes everywhere, he identifies happiness as the Final Cause of human action. The extended syllogism runs something like this:

> All actions aim for a good.
> All goods aim for a final good.
> The final good is that which is desired for its own sake.
> That which is desired for its own sake is happiness.
> All actions aim for happiness.

The object of his investigation, then, is to determine the nature of human happiness. On the dubious grounds that "being a man" is analogous to "playing a flute" or "building a house," Aristotle asserts that man has a characteristic function, and that the successful execution of this function is happiness. Note that Aristotle's word for happiness, *eudaimonia*, can also be translated as "prosperity." Thus, it includes a certain notion of "fulfillment."

The characteristic function of man turns out to be—surprise—thinking. So, once again, a philosopher proves that philosophy is the best thing going. It should therefore be no surprise that Aristotle waffles when it comes to discussing Socratic ethics. First, he stakes out the obvious position that knowledge, virtue, and happiness are not all the same thing. Then, with a little shuffling of the feet, he concedes that maybe in a certain way Socrates was right.

Despite all this, Aristotle's ethics represents a small triumph for his realistic side. He specifically acknowledges that people cannot spend all day in the blissful removes of philosophical contemplation. He invents an ordinary kind of virtue to guide one in everyday life, and it is this "secondary" kind of virtue which is primary for the real Aristotle.

The real Aristotle is, of course, hopelessly Greek. This means that he thought of ethics primarily in terms of individual fulfillment, and only secondarily along Christian lines of obligations toward others. It means he thought more about kinds of characters than about kinds of actions, about virtuous men rather than good deeds and sin. And it also means that he believed "moderation" was the key to an ethical existence. His word for moderation, *sophrosyne*, could also mean prudence or temperance. Aristotle got a little carried away on moderation; at times he seems to think that choosing the middle course is best in all situations. Some said he was "moderate to excess."

Still, it was a sensible and down-to-earth Aristotle who could devote a whole book of his ethics to the subject of friendship, and write that: ". . . without friends no one would choose to live, though he had all the other goods."[6]

## POLITICS AS USUAL

Aristotle's politics is also hopelessly Greek. It turns out that the best form of government is that of the ancient Greek city-state. Slavery and male-rule are okay. Even so, his political thought is another small victory for the real Aristotle. He takes a broad but empirically based view of what constitutes the 'state.' He understands that the structure of households and of the economy are essential parts of the organization of society. He counsels us not to ignore the wisdom of long-established practice in favor of untested utopias. He insists that political theory must begin with men as they are, not as they should be. Aristotle is, like many philosophers, radically conservative. He wants stability and security above all else, but he expects to find that in tradition, rather than in a Platonic world of forms.

Aristotle's famous assertion, that "man is by nature a political animal,"[7] is sometimes understood as a metaphysical statement of the essence of man. It is not. It is an inference from an inductive generalization based on the observation of animals (including men). Some animals, like bees, build their lives together, while others, like cats, are loners. Human beings belong to the first category. On his own, in the wilderness, a man would be nothing. It is our many social arrangements, from family to state, which make human existence what it is. That man is a very political animal is evident according to Aristotle, in the fact that he has the power of speech. The original purpose of speech, he suggests, is to be able to set forth the expedient and inexpedient, the good and bad. Even before other philosophers would conceive of metaphysical distortions of language as just a way of tagging representations of objects in the mind, Aristotle already thought of language primarily as a tool for sophisticated social interaction, cooperation, and competition.

---

6. *Nichomachean Ethics* (VII, 1), 1155a5.
7. *Politics* (I, 2), 1253a2.

Aristotle's work on politics is closer to his biology than to his first philosophy or his physics. He could be considered the founder of political science as well as the biological sciences. Like his biology, however, his political work is mainly of historical interest. Perhaps Aristotle's political thought is more relevant to us than his biology. In the human sciences, unlike the natural sciences, judgment is often as important as fact.

---

From *The Psychoanalyst's Handbook on Philosophers*

**The Aristotle Complex.** *Definition.* The philosopher's desire to annihilate all his predecessors and become the sole authority on all philosophical matters. The philosopher feels inferior and unwanted so long as there is any other person or thing with a claim to the affections of philosophy. May result from failure in childhood to distinguish between oneself and God. So named because Aristotle was the first well-known case. Also so named because in the modern era the typical philosopher's object of anxiety was Aristotle himself. Modern philosophy is the attempted murder (philosophically speaking) of Aristotle (who is, of course, already dead).

# The Hellenistic Philosophers

## On How to Get By in Life

Alexander the Great (356–323 B.C.E.) had more influence on the subsequent course of the history of philosophy than did his tutor Aristotle. Alexander's conquest of the better part of the known world shattered the ancient order of Greek city-states and replaced it with a vast empire. Well-born men no longer saw their destinies formed in the small, familiar world of urban politics. Power belonged to a bureaucrat who reported to a minister in some other city, who represented a distant courtesan, who was appointed by an inaccessible emperor. In this age of Hellenism, traditionally dated from Alexander's death to the fall of the Roman Republic in 31 B.C.E., the old Greek was culture diffused across the world just as it lost its basis at home, while a variety of Eastern cultures, always better adapted to life under empire, intruded on the Greek world. The Greek religion, already weakened by the growth of scientific thought, became a chaotic mélange of East and West, in which every individual or group pursued its own spiritual inclinations. One result of these political and cultural shifts was the creation of an upper middle class of disempowered, disillusioned men with low self-esteem. Philosophy in the Hellenistic age was driven by the spiritual needs of this new class.

Though they bickered among themselves, the Hellenistic philosophers were all selling the same thing to the same customers: happiness to the unhappy. They all believed that happiness was a form of tranquility, a freedom from the conflicts and concerns of life in this world. Each philosophy prescribed its own remedy, its own way of life, as the proper means to achieve this inner peace. The various doctrines they deployed in support of their claims, their logics, metaphysics, and ethics, were often crude and borrowed wholesale from earlier philosophers. In a sense, they were irrelevant. But even in the Hellenistic age, the rationalist veneer of philosophy over religion wore thin, this should not necessarily lead us to lower our estimate of this era in the history of philosophy. Philosophy has always been a religion for the educated classes. In their crude but honest way, the Hellenistics made this truth plain.

# Dogs, Pillars, Garden People, and Searchers . . .

During the Hellenistic age, philosophy grew in the worldly sense. Schools prolifer-
ated. All sorts of respectable men took on some philosophical leaning. At the same
time, the subject-matter of philosophy narrowed. The universal scientific aspirations of Aristotle were dropped in favor of a specialization in the logical, metaphysical, and ethical concerns which characterize the discipline of philosophy to
this day. Aristotle's Lyceum, with his hardy band of followers known as the Peri-
patetics (literally, "pacers"), stayed in business, but only just. Plato's Academy
remained prominent, but turned against its founder. The Presocratics, especially
the Ionians, came back into fashion. But the real winner was Socrates. A number
of Socratic schools sprang up, and most of the others looked to him as their greatest forebear. The Hellenistic philosophers, after all, were selling a way of life, and
in this field Socrates had blazed the trail.

In the twentieth-century versions of the history of philosophy, the era from
Aristotle's death to Descartes's birth is a vast darkness. As with the Presocratics,
this reflects a somewhat hasty judgment. The Stoics, in particular, had a decisive
influence not just on medieval thought, but also on such pivotal modern figures as
Spinoza and Kant. In the early modern period, in fact, the history of philosophy
would have devoted a very substantial portion to the battles of the Stoics, the Skeptics, and others.

# Cynics: It's a Dog's Life

The Cynics were the hippies of the ancient world. They advocated and lived a simple, self-sufficient life free from social conventions. They believed that their society was fundamentally corrupt and unnatural and therefore had to be rejected. Diogenes (404–323 B.C.E.), the most famous of the Cynics, lived in a barrel. In order
to demonstrate his freedom from oppressive social norms, he would from time to
time masturbate in public. Not to be outdone, the cynic Crates (ca. 365–285 B.C.E.)
and his philosophically minded wife, Hipparchia, would perform sexual intercourse in the marketplace. Both Crates and Diogenes also talked up incest and
cannibalism, though it is unclear whether they violated these taboos in deed as
well. They and like-minded free spirits earned the name Cynics, meaning "dogs,"
mainly because the Greeks thought of dogs as shameless creatures.

The Cynics saw themselves as "soul doctors" of a sort. With his pointed wit,
Diogenes wandered the streets and popped many a balloon of delusion and
hypocrisy. If the surviving stories are anything to go by, he had a real talent as a
stand-up comic. Crates even made house calls. Going door to door, he would help
families resolve their domestic spats.

Crates' most famous case was the conversion of Metrocles (ca. 300 B.C.E.), a
young aspiring orator. Metrocles was giving a speech one day when he suddenly let

out a massive fart. He almost died of embarrassment. Crates saw that Metrocles was thinking of suicide and consoled him. It was nothing unnatural you did, Crates reassured him. Then, in a gesture of solidarity, Crates farted. Metrocles was so taken by this that he decided at that moment to become a Cynic.

Behind the antics of the Cynics was a firm Socratic faith. Like Socrates, they believed that rationality was humankind's unique nature. It was against this standard of rationality that contemporary society came up short. Like Socrates, Cynics shunned those material things which are commonly called good, and sought happiness in a higher kind of virtue. Like Socrates, they turned themselves into gadflies, or social pests, in the hope of helping others understand themselves better. Plato once described Diogenes as a "Socrates gone mad." But then a Cynic might have described Plato as a "Socrates gone stale."

## STOICS: LIFE IS A COLONNADE, OLD CHUM

Stoicism is Cynicism for respectable people. The first Stoic, Zeno of Citium (333–262 B.C.E.), was a follower of Crates. Like the cynics, Zeno and his followers sought happiness through the realization of the authentic, rational human nature. They also sought to rise above conventional notions of what was good. While the early Stoics, like Zeno, had some radical political tendencies, the Stoics as a whole were much less dangerous to know than the Cynics. In the end, they leaned toward the view that one could pursue virtue and happiness within the framework of a conventional life. They wanted their follower to keep his day job, his wife (he was invariably male), and raise a family. Their objective was to change his attitude, rather than his circumstances. Unlike the Cynics, the Stoics formed a true school. They were organized, disciplined, and exclusive, perhaps like a church. In the Stoic philosopher Chrysippus (282–206 B.C.E.), author of over seven hundred books, they found their pope.

Stoicism held up for its followers an ideal existence, the life of the Sage. A Sage is more than just a wise and clever individual. He is utterly perfect and virtuous. Above all, he is impervious to the slings and arrows of outrageous fortune. He is impassive—literally, apathetic. He alone can achieve true happiness.

Around this notion of a perfectly happy existence the Stoics built a huge, interconnected system of philosophy. As a matter of principle, they divided philosophy into logic (most of which would today be called epistemology), physics (which we would call metaphysics), and ethics (still alive and kicking). As a matter of fact, their various divisions of philosophy pretty much collapse into one another, and ultimately into the explication and advocacy of their Sage Ideal.

The Stoics made some interesting advances in formal logic, although these were chiefly accidents on the road toward the great Sage Ideal. While Aristotle had conceived of formal logic as the study of how terms relate to each other within propositions (e.g., if A is B, and B is C, etc.), the Stoics conceived of formal logic as the study of how propositions relate to each other (e.g., if P and Q, then R or S, etc.). In this they anticipated some concerns of nineteenth- and twentieth-century logic. However, the Stoics did not develop their formal logic to the satisfaction of their modern descendants. This is because the Stoic logic was really an attempt at epistemology, which was in service of the physics, which was in turn in the service of their Sage Ideal. The Stoics turned to formal logic in order to substantiate a somewhat dubious epistemological claim, that it is possible to attain infallible knowledge about the past and future course of events in the physical world. They believed that the absolute necessity which characterizes the inference patterns of formal logic would also characterize the links in a sequence of physical events. To use a language we will discuss in the context of early modern philosophy, we could say that they sought to conflate logical necessity and causal necessity. They developed this epistemological doctrine in order to support their chief physical doctrine, that everything in the world happens of necessity. And this physical doctrine, as we shall see, was not so much a new truth about the world as a way of defining an ethical existence. The uncompromising power of destiny was the anvil on which the ultimate impassivity of the Sage would be forged.

Stoic physics went far beyond the mere affirmation of the power of destiny, yet it still remained in service of the Sage Ideal. The Stoics furnished the world with a life principle, a mind principle, and a God, and showed that the three are one—indeed, that they are the whole world. They discovered all these doctrines in a heady blend of Presocratic thought and monotheism. Their first principle was a combination of an Anaximenean principle of air and a Heraclitean principle of fire in the form of *pneuma*, or breath, which is the living soul of the world, and from which the individual humans draw their own soul. Like Heraclitus, they tempered this fiery-breath life principle with a concept of *logos*—a designing fire, they called it. From Anaxagoras they borrowed the notion that this logos-fire principle might also be called Mind. They even took over his strange notion of "seeds," which they spoke of *logoi spermatikoi*, or spermy word-things. Mind, it turns out, is the same thing as Zeus, who is the only real God in the Stoic Pantheon. (The other gods are retained only as images of specific aspects of life—e.g., love and courage.) Zeus, a.k.a. Mind, the Director, or the Absolute Sovereign, is a providential deity. He controls everything for the best because, well, he is everything. The Stoics were pantheists: God is nature. God is also reason. Every little thing in this world is a part of this reasonable divinity. In all this "physics," however, what they were really doing was creating the possibility for the existence of the Sage. In comprehending Stoic physics, the Sage would not just know *that* the world is God-mind-life; his comprehension itself would be a complete and self-aware part of that world, something truly divine, thinking, and living.

The final resting place of the Sage Ideal, of course, was in Stoic ethics, which can be summed up in three related propositions. First, virtue is the only thing with moral value. Particular pleasures or goods, the objects of natural impulses—like health and wealth—are indifferent to the Stoic. Second, virtue results from living in accordance with nature, specifically, the "higher," rational nature of human beings. Third, virtue necessarily brings happiness, since it allows us to live at peace with the world. According to some Stoic accounts, it also grants a certain limited kind of immortality. The Stoics' ethical doctrines are explained and justified with a story that goes something as follows. Living things follow their natural impulses, which rest on a basic survival instinct. (They do not follow pleasure *per se*, which is an aftereffect, a systematic reflection of what is generally good for survival.) Young humans are animals in this respect. As humankind grows, it recognizes something beyond the impulses, viz., rationality. It sees virtue not in the satisfaction of any particular impulse, but in the consistent pattern of the well-lived life. Though the impulses presumably remain in place, what rational people grasp is that it is the balance and harmony among them, and this "rationality" is the mark of a good life. The story seems to demonstrate that humans have a dual nature, an animal and a rational one, and the latter evolves out of the former, and is superior to it. Satisfaction of the higher nature of humans, furthermore, must induce some higher form of pleasure, a true happiness. Hence the three ethical doctrines noted above, that virtue is distinct from satisfaction of pleasures, and that it means living in accordance with the higher human nature, and that all this results in happiness. At this point the ethical narrative and the physics merge. The rationality observed by the ethical person, which is indeed his superior, authentic nature, is the same which characterizes the world as a whole, in the form of God-mind-life. Thus, the person who achieves perfect ethical rationality also completely understands the true nature of the world, and the one who has perfect knowledge likewise achieves true virtue. So the Stoics discovered (yet again) a knowledge that is identical with virtue and happiness. In their logic, physics, and ethics, the Stoics mainly presented their Sage Ideal, who might also have been given the name Socrates.

The Stoics, by the way, believed in a universal brotherhood, and described themselves as citizens of the world. This should not be surprising, given their view on the purely rational nature of humankind. Stoic virtue is, in principle, open to all human beings. It is a version of what in later centuries would come to be called the Moral Law. Stoic politics were, at least at first, radically utopian. They wanted communism, they wanted to abolish currency, they even wanted to include women in polite society. Later, as the school became one of the pillars of the Hellenistic establishment, its leaders moved away from this embarrassing radicalism and adopted more pragmatic political views.

As a number of their contemporaries observed, Stoic thought runs into logical difficulties on at least two points. The first is a version of what will come to be called the problem of free will. The Stoics present a deterministic world view. As the Sage knows, everything happens according to necessity. So why should anyone bother to strive for Stoic virtue, since presumably that matter, too, is determined in advance? In other words, if there is no free will, as Stoic physics seems to imply, then how is an ethics possible? A related issue is what the Christian theologians would call the problem of evil. If Zeus organizes everything in the world for the best, how do you explain the fact that so many un-Stoical fools exist? The Stoics exercised themselves over these problems, and offered some ingenious but unlikely solutions. Since many future philosophers would cover the same ground, I will defer discussion of these issues.

The second point of incoherence in Stoic doctrines reflects an old criticism of Socratic ethics, and has to do with the justification for the advocacy of a particular kind of ethical life on purely rational grounds. Like Socrates, the Stoics argued that reason alone could serve as the guide for human action. As Socrates' critics pointed out, however, it is quite possible to be knowledgeable and bad. The Stoics especially opened themselves up for this kind of attack by finding the genesis of ethical rationality in consistency of behavior. To repeat the criticism of Socrates, it is quite possible to be consistently bad. Rationality is a capability, something exercised in an activity. An activity presumes a goal, however, and it would be odd to look for that goal merely in the capability exercised in the activity. Such a unity of goal and activity, or ends and means, is, as we have already seen so many times, the Holy Grail of philosophy. Those who still search for the Grail, alas, are left to wonder exactly what it is that the Sage does all day long, other than just think and be rational. Perhaps because they acknowledged a difficulty here, or perhaps because the Sage was just a little too pure and inhuman for their somewhat conventional tastes, the Stoics suggested that some of the objects of natural impulses —to which the Sage is, of course, utterly indifferent—might just be, well, other things being equal and so on, "preferred." The suggestion is, as the Stoics' ancient rivals complained, utterly inconsistent with the rest of their logical, physical, and ethical doctrines, not to say just plain illogical: How can you prefer something and be indifferent to it at the same time?

Somehow these little inconsistencies did not trouble many of the Stoics. In this, perhaps, they revealed an apparently irrational side of human nature.

## EPICUREANISM

Epicurus (341–271 B.C.E.) was one of those strong personalities who gathered around himself the kind of people who would call him "savior" and other esteem-enhancing things. He averred that his doctrines were entirely true and that they were completely original. Both claims were untrue, not to say in questionable taste. Nonetheless, Epicurus's philosophy had power not only over his band of contemporaries, but among adherents down through antiquity, until the Christian church decided to quash Epicureanism for good.

Epicurus's physics is a version of the Presocratic Democritus's atomism. (Epicurus, of course, refused to admit this.) The world is made up of tiny atoms bouncing around in a void. Actually, Epicurus added, there are lots of worlds, where atoms clump together, separated by empty space. The gods live in the empty spaces between worlds. The soul is a collection of airy atoms which comes together in the body, and it dissipates at death. Also, atoms occasionally swerve from their courses. (Any parallel with modern quantum mechanics is pretty fluky.) This swerve makes things just a little unpredictable, and somehow, strangely, vindicates our belief in the freedom of the will.

Epicurus supposedly based his ethical theories on his physics. In fact, it was obvious even to his followers that the physics was a gloss on the ethics, and many of them simply dropped the physics or took it for granted. Epicurus's ethics is remarkably straightforward. Beginning with the principle that happiness is the highest good, he added the frank admission that happiness comes from pleasure. He defined pleasure as the absence of pain. The two most important sources of pain in human life are anxiety about death and religious superstition. We need not fear death, Epicurus said, because in death the soul dissipates into nothing, so nothing matters any more. In other words, when you die, you die. (Many of his contemporaries found this, somehow, not very comforting.) Religious superstition is silly, because natural phenomena like thunder and lightning can all be explained in terms of the motions of atoms. The world is not in the grips of inscrutable and possibly malevolent deities. The gods are stuck in outer space, in between worlds, where they can have no influence on the course of events, though it is pleasant and worthwhile to admire them from afar. In sum, we can live in peace and happiness, once we know that we have nothing to fear, either from death or from the gods.

The practical, perhaps unstated side of Epicurus's ethics is expressed in the life of his cult. At the age of thirty Epicurus bought a nice house with a large garden in the suburbs of Athens. He and his followers lived a communal existence in the house and carried on their philosophical discussions in the garden. The friendship and ties of affection that grew between master and followers were an important part of Epicurus's legacy.

Epicurus has long been accused of advocating hedonism, or a life of sensual indulgence. This is untrue. He advocated the elimination of pain, not the accumulation of pleasures. In fact, he thought that excessive pleasures were invariably accompanied by pain, and so preached temperance and even abstention. The Epicurean ideal is not to stuff one's face with exotic food but to get by in life sitting in the garden quietly chatting with one's friends.

On the face of it, Epicurean physics is diametrically opposed to Stoic physics. Instead of divine Providence, the random, mechanical motion of atoms determines the fate of the world. This is a good example of how irrelevant differences among philosophical doctrines can be. In fact, both Stoic and Epicurean physics are really ontologies, and both ontologies ultimately have the same objective. Both begin with a sense that the unhappiness stems from the problematic relationships between humankind and nature and between humans and God. The Stoics sought to show that humanity, in its higher nature, is divine, and that nature is divinely ordered, and so they collapsed the apparent oppositions in favor of God. The Epicureans denied that there was any order whatsoever, pretty much eliminated God, and so they resolved the apparent conflicts by rendering God and nature inessential. Both schools advocated a physics which, once understood, would allow the wise person to feel at home in the world, indeed, would allow the wise person to become virtuous. Since ontologies are by their nature unprovable (not to say false), all that really matters is their purpose, and so we may say that the two competing brands of Hellenistic physics amount to the same thing.

Epicurean and Stoic ethics likewise appear at first glance to be incompatible.

The one establishes pleasure as the goal, the other denies pleasure in the name of virtue. But Epicurean happiness involves pulling back from excessive pleasures, it is a freedom from pains and perhaps particular pleasures as well. It comes from an understanding of the true order of the world. Yet this is also Stoic virtue: the reduction of particular pains and pleasures to indifference by means of an understanding of the rational order of things. What Epicurus called *ataraxia*, or tranquility, is, at the end of the day, not so different from what the Stoics called *apatheia*, the impassivity of the great sage. In the final analysis both advocate a life without, well, much life.

## SKEPTICISM

Pyrrho (365–270 B.C.E.) is supposed to have walked about without a care in his head. He didn't care because he didn't believe that anything was real. Were it not for his friends, so they said, he would have been run over by a chariot or fallen into a well. After all, how could he have known whether it was a real chariot or well? On account of this sort of behavior, Pyrrho became the patron saint of the Skeptics, or Pyrrhonists. They proposed to live without beliefs.

Legend also has it that Pyrrho once made his way to India, where he visited a great philosopher-Magi. Whether he got the idea from this Magi or discovered it on his own, Pyrrho concluded that the understanding that there are no knowable truths could in itself be the source of the inner peace sought by philosophers. From knowledge of ignorance, or contact with the nothingness of Nirvana, would flow an ethical guide to life.

Skepticism took a different, more professional form in the new Academy. About a century after Plato's death, his successors in charge of the Academy discovered that his metaphysical theories were probably wrong. So, in an early instance of a phenomenon peculiar to academic philosophy, they decided to return to their true intellectual forebear. Back to Socrates! they cried. The most famous of these new leaders was Carneades (187 or 213–129 B.C.E.), who made a living out of criticizing the great Stoic Chrysippus.

Carneades believed that the purpose of the Socratic dialectic was to dissolve beliefs and so lead to a state he called *epoche*, or suspension of judgment (literally: "holding back"). His practice was to present convincing discourse on both sides of an issue—say, whether or not justice is a good thing—and thereby show everyone that they knew nothing.

Skepticism comes in several degrees of seriousness. In its least worrisome form, skepticism is just a claim about the current state of our knowledge, that we don't (yet) know everything. (As in, is there intelligent life on Mars? I don't know; I am skeptical; I await further evidence.) In philosophy, however, skepticism is often the more serious claim that there are certain kinds of knowledge which we can in principle never possess. (For example: We can in principle know everything there is to know about Mars; but we can never really know anything about the afterlife.) Skepticism of the third degree of seriousness is the claim that nothing can really be known at all. What we imagine to be knowledge is not really knowledge, and there is no hope for finding anything better.

The first kind of skepticism is closest to the original meaning of the word, and perhaps best captures the insight behind philosophy. *Skepsis* is simply a nontechnical word for thinking, or reflective inquiry—in brief, "searching," in the mental rather than physical sense of the term. According to this kind of skepticism, philosophy is an ongoing search. This original sense of skepticism actually doesn't need to have much to do with philosophy. It is simply an attitude one takes in the approach to any inquiry. But philosophers have always wanted something more from their isms, and so try to convert this healthy, skeptical attitude into an eternal search mode. Which raises that familiar Socratic dilemma: Is a search which can never end really a search?

Skepticism of the second degree leads us to a philosophical paradox. You have to know something about a thing that cannot be known, if you know that you cannot know a thing about it. What's more, if a thing is in principle unknowable, it may just mean that there is nothing to know about it anyway. As a matter of principle, for example, we cannot know exactly what Jane Eyre had to eat on the day of her wedding, nor can we know what it feels like to be a dodecahedron. Who cares?

Skepticism of the third degree presents even greater difficulties. First, claims of the sort "nothing can be known" or "nothing is certain" tend to subvert themselves, inasmuch as they are themselves instances of what they purport to deny. Second, they are absurd. If one could not know whether a chariot was coming down the road (and had no friends who knew), life would be remarkably shorter and nastier than it already is.

The ancient skeptics floated among all three kinds of skepticism. Nonetheless, the Academics developed a number of not altogether successful strategies for dealing with the paradoxes of skepticism. Carneades distinguished two kinds of "assent" to judgments. Absolute or unconditional assent he withheld in all cases. He would not agree to any statement of the form "that *is* a chariot coming toward us." However, he was happy to offer provisional assent to statements of the form "that *appears to be* a chariot coming toward us." He also used the concept of "probability" to sort out statements worthy of provisional assent, as in, "It may or may not be a chariot, but it *probably* is." All of which just begs more questions: If everything is appearances, then with what do we compare appearances? What is "probability" if there is no "certainty"?

In the hallowed arena of modern epistemology, the Stoics and Skeptics occupy opposing corners. One side says we can have infallible knowledge of things as they really are, the other that we can have no such knowledge. In the real world, it's all the same. The Stoics and Skeptics use their opposed epistemologies to gloss the same ethical practice. The Skeptic's knowledge of ignorance permits an escape from the material world into the tranquility of a world of ideas; the Stoic's knowledge of the ideal nature of the world allows precisely the same sort of escape.

## Miscellaneous Socratics

Plato was just one of many admirers of Socrates. After Socrates' death, a variety of schools popped up, many with strongly anti-Platonic tendencies. The Megarians (from the town Megara, home of their leader) offered a blend of Socratic skepticism and Parmenidean Oneness. The only real thing, for them, was the One, or Being, which was just too big to know. They were most famous for introducing a couple of amusing paradoxes. One, the so-called Liar's paradox, still lives in the airy halls of academe. If someone says "I am a liar," is he telling the truth? Think about it. (The answer, of course, is that he is a philosopher, and should be ignored in polite society.) The other paradox is the *sorites*, or heap, paradox. Suppose you have a heap of a thousand grains of wheat. If you remove the grains one by one, at what point does it cease being a heap?

Another early and amusing group of Socratics were the Cyrenaics (from Cyrene). Relentless skepticism led them to affirm that the only reality is the emotional states of the individual, and the only thing worth anything is pleasure. They further (and perhaps inconsistently) defined pleasure as the "smooth motion of the flesh." Oooo.

## Eclectics

The late Hellenistic age and the early years of the Roman Empire are generally regarded as a bad time for philosophy. The eclectics, as the writers of this period are called, ripped philosophical doctrines out of context and combined them in whatever manner suited their tastes. "Eclectic" just means "selecting out," in the sense of "reading out of place." In this, of course, the eclectics merely exaggerated a tendency already evident in the early Hellenistic thinkers. They also anticipated a practice common in the twentieth century. From the smorgasbord of three millennia of philosophy, writers today simply mix and match their own strange dishes.

## The Nasty Things Philosophers Say about Each Other

For all they had in common, the Hellenistic philosophers were a pretty contentious bunch. The Skeptics had the meanest cutdowns. Timon (320–230 B.C.E.), Pyrrho's disciple, wrote a book called *Silloi*, in which he showed the silliness of all the philosophers who did not agree with him and Pyrrho. His favorite word was *typhos*, as in "typhoon," meaning "wind," "mist," or fog." We could translate the term as "verbal flatulence." In any case, Timon thought all other philosophies were *typhos*. Philosophers in general he called "human windbags, stuffed with conceit." Epicurus was "the least educated of creatures." Aristotle's work was an exercise in "painful futility."

The Stoic Zeno came in for lots of abuse from all sides. Timon fumed that he was "old Phoenician fisherwoman" with "less intellect than a string of twaddle." The skeptical Alexinus was more subtle, but still merciless. One of Zeno's arguments for the rationality of the world went like this: Rationality is better than irrationality; the world is better than anything else; therefore, the world must be rational. In that case, Alexinus replied, the world must also be grammatical and poetical, for these are better than being ungrammatical and unpoetical. Diogenes the Cynic kept up the attack. Mocking Zeno's concept of fate, Diogenes said that when one of Zeno's slaves got caught stealing from his master, the slave said, "I was fated to steal." Zeno's reply was, "Yes, and you were also fated to be whipped."

Diogenes' arrows were aimed not just at the Stoics. When Diogenes heard an Eleatic philosopher deny the possibility of motion, he got up and walked around. Having listened to Plato lecture on the nature of the heavens and the motions of the planets, he asked, "How many days were you in coming from the sky?" In response to Plato's definition of the human as "an animal, biped and featherless," he appeared one day with a plucked fowl and said, "Behold Plato's man." (Which prompted Plato to add "with broad nails" to his definition.) Diogenes may have authored a book on Plato titled *Pordalos*, or *The Farter*. Showing little more discretion, another sophist-Socratic philosopher, Antisthenes, used a play on Plato's name for his own book, *Sathon*, meaning *Stinker*.

Perhaps this nastiness is an ancient instantiation of that principle often seen at work in modern academia: The bitterness of disputes is in inverse proportion to their importance. Or, it may be just another manifestation of that special Socratic spirit, the agonistic, eristic will to compete.

# THE CULT OF MITHRAS: HELLENISTIC PHILOSOPHY FOR THE MASSES

Outside the official panoply of Hellenistic philosophy, a diverse range of quasi-philosophical, quasi-religious movements flourished. Indeed, the distinction between philosophy and religion is probably external to the whole era, something imposed by a later need to find a separate history for each. The differences which may be supported with historical fact, I think, are differences in degree, not kind. Philosophy was merely a more reflective version of religion, and religion a cruder, less tasteful form of philosophy.

Among the religions that rose to prominence during the Hellenistic age was the cult of Mithras, which seeped into the Greek world from Persia. It taught that Mithras was the Absolute Sovereign of the world, that he knew and controlled everything, and arranged things for the best—in short, that he was the providential Mind of the world. Since the individual soul partook of this universal Mind, it, too, was immortal. The followers of Mithras were assured tranquility and utter reconciliation with the world, so long as they could become one with Mithras in their worship of him. They formed an intimate community, and called each other "brother." They developed a code language of strange symbols to present their cosmology and to explain the course of events in the world. They practiced a relatively ascetic existence, free from the cares of worldly success. In short, the Mithrasites would probably have been Stoics, had they been a little better educated.

The parallels between the cult of Mithras and Christianity are also quite obvious: a single, providential deity; immortality of the soul; the brotherhood of humans; even a kind of sacrifice, by the god Mithras, on behalf of humankind. Other strands of thought link Stoicism and Christianity more directly. The earliest Christian heretics, the Gnostics, had some philosophical pretensions, and could be seen as a bridge between the Stoic philosophy and Christianity.

The philosophies and the religions all promised consolation. They offered happiness to those who were unhappy. The difference between these religions and Hellenistic philosophies like Stoicism, I have suggested, is not of kind but of degree. The philosophers appeared to demand 'reason', when in fact they simply demanded "more reasons." Their reasons came to an end somewhere, too. When the sophistication is stripped away, the philosophers' faith is perhaps as blind, reasonless, and downright silly as the belief in all those weird bull-figures and astrological signs favored by the worshippers of Mithras.

# Neoplatonism

## *Twilight of the Pagans*

### A Traveler's Tale

The sun had set, but for a while the atmosphere retained its light, which mingled with the approaching darkness to generate a myriad of somber hues across the sky. Riding his chariot down the great highway of life—which like all roads in those days, led to Rome—our lonely traveler, Philosophicus Historianicus, grew weary and sought to find shelter for the night. As he passed the outskirts of the city, he began to pay attention to the billboards lining the highway. There was clearly no shortage of hotels in Rome.

Some of the billboards were faded and cracked. The proprietors must have fallen on hard times or perhaps gone out of business. From the chipped paint and missing letters, Phil could see that the Hotel Jupiter had lost the haughty grandeur of earlier times. The sign for the Venusian Love Inn was covered with graffiti. Even the Epicurean Garden Apartments seemed to have lost their tranquility. Farther down the road, however, Phil ran into a batch of fresh, earnest billboards.

He stopped before a sign for the Hotel Mithras, with the name of Mithras surrounded by a lemon-yellow representation of the sun. Underneath was a list of the hotel's features and amenities:

- Swimming pool
- Color TV in every room
- Guaranteed personal immortality
- Personal relationship with all-powerful, providential host
- Learn the secrets of the universe

Across the top and down the sides of the billboard were a series of strange— and to Phil, incomprehensible—symbols and figures: an Asiatic-looking man slay-

113

ing a bull; another man wearing a cap with his feet stuck in a rock; various geometrical shapes; and what looked like stars, planets, and other astronomical representations. Phil was intrigued. Then he noticed a scroll tacked onto the bottom of
the sign: "Welcome IVth Legion," it read. Oh dear, thought Phil, it's an army
ghetto. He moved on.

The next billboard promoted the Pleasureless Palace. The two Ps in the name
were formed with shards from broken bottles. The sides of the sign were draped
with rusty chains. Their slogan, "immortality through mortification of the flesh,"
appeared in italics under the name of the hotel. (A few stray musical quarter-notes
suggested that perhaps the slogan was part of a jingle used in radio ads.) Underneath, the list of features included:

- Choice of three implements provided free
- Bed of nails standard in every room
- Bubble gum under doorknobs
- Pool filled with ice daily
- TV permanently tuned to bad sitcoms

Phil shuddered. He was not yet desperate enough for that.

Farther off from the roadside Phil spotted a billboard painted solid black.
Another one of those mystery cults, he thought. How childish. They even left out
the address. A small, hand-painted sign advertised the Magna Mater Bed & Breakfast, "managed by native Phrygians." It promised the usual immortality, along with
live entertainment and "flesh & blood of god served fresh daily." An attached piece
of cardboard read: "Coming Soon: The Big Mama." Too weird for Phil.

Glancing over to the other side of the road, Phil thought for a moment he saw
a vision: a billboard that came and then vanished. His vision read something like this:
"THE MANICHEAN GETAWAY HOTEL. EXPERIENCE A PURELY SPIRITUAL HOTEL. CON-
TAINS NO MATTER WHATSOEVER. BLACK & WHITE TV ONLY. APPROVED BY JESUS.
NOT LOCATED IN THIS WORLD. NO MEATS, MARRIED COUPLES, OR PROCREATION
PERMITTED." Phil was skeptical, and decided he'd never find the place anyway.

The ad for the Hotel Gnosis, like all the rest, offered personal immortality,
swimming pool, etc. It added: "special knowledge revealed upon check-in," and
"escape from the evil material world created by the demiurge." It claimed to be
"approved by Jesus," and cited "biblical references." Wound around the letters of
this last phrase was an implausibly drawn serpent. To Phil, it looked like a place for
the Motel 6 crowd. Just another crude dualism.

The Christian Hospice also struck him as seedy. He could tell from the address
that it was located in a bad neighborhood. With seemingly preposterous sternness,
the sign declared: "eternal reward, if you're good; divine retribution, if you're not,"
and "salvation open to guests only." It further informed its readers that it was "the
only one authentically approved by Jesus," and that "God became man" in order to
build this hospice. In later years, Phil would regret passing up the Christians. At the
time, of course, he could not have known that this small, proletarian operation
would become the Holiday Inn of the business, buying up its competitors and

either closing them down or absorbing them, growing into the dominant chain of the Western world with appeal to all classes of society. His chariot lurched on.

At last our weary traveler espied a sign of hope. In elegant Greek letters, carved in finest marble, it read:

---

The NEW HOTEL PLATO                                Proprietor: Plotinus

*'The **ONE** for you'*

Looking for that mystical and divine union with sleep? Tired of the vulgar, self-promoting, cult-hotels, with their noisy world-creating demiurges and crude dualisms? If you are well educated and of good family, then the New Hotel Plato is the ONE for you. Relax in the dignified splendor of our three-level rooms, decorated in the finest Hellenic tradition. Leave your Soul on the ground floor, take the aspiring lift up to the Intelligible World, and from there prepare to revert to the top-level ecstasy of the ONE, about which we can say no more. All material comforts are provided, but will be superseded as you return to the ONE, where you belong. Our televisions carry only PBS reruns of classical Athenian tragedies and comedies.

---

Underneath this was a representation of the Parthenon, which gave Phil a good feeling. At last, a place which does not insult my intelligence, which does not scorn my schooling in the Greek masters. A place where I can reconcile my material being with spirit, and rest in peace.

## FACTS AND FIGURES

The chief figure of Neoplatonism was Plotinus (205–270 C.E.). There were others. Philo (ca. 40 B.C.E.), a Jew, had earlier attempted a synthesis of Platonism and Judaism. Plotinus's secretive teacher, Ammonius, who wisely advocated abstention from writing, seems to have been interested in both Plato and the philosophies of the Near East. Plotinus's disciple Porphyry (233–304 C.E.), not only collected his master's essays into the work we have now, *The Enneads*, but was something of an intellectual figure in his own right. (Later, the Christian thinker Saint Augustine [354–430 C.E.] rated Plotinus and Porphyry very highly, the best of the pagans, and imported many of their ideas into his Christian philosophy. Eventually, however, the Church decided Porphyry was not so good after all, and ordered his books burned.) Clement (150?-215? C.E.) and Origen (b. 182? C.E.) tried to mix Platonism with Christianity. Iamblichus (?–330 C.E.) converted Neoplatonism into a corny, magical religion, and in this form it was named by the Emperor Julian "the Apostate" as the religion of the state. Proclus (410–485 C.E.), the last, sad figure on the stage of ancient philosophy, offered a bizarre, scholastic version of Neoplatonism in his *Elements of Theology*.

The label "Neoplatonism" was a not altogether felicitous invention of the nineteenth century. Though nothing would have pleased Plotinus more than to be known as Plato reincarnated, his work shows almost as much influence from Aristotle. Clearly inspired by Aristotle, for example, are Plotinus's drive toward a first principle, his modifications of the theory of forms with conceptual distinctions like that between actuality and potentiality, and his attempts to create a new theory of the categories. Another, never explicitly acknowledged influence (perhaps coming via Plato) was Pythagoras. Aside from immortal souls, the world-soul, and such-like, Plotinus borrowed from Pythagoras some superstitions about numbers, especially the "perfect" number, three. Porphyry was overjoyed when he discovered that his master's essays totaled fifty-four; this allowed him to divide them into six groups of nine (hence Enneads—the "nines"), which to him looked like lots of threes. There is also a fair measure of the Hellenistic philosophies, notably Stoicism, in Plotinus. In brief, what goes under the name of "Neoplatonism" is suspiciously more eclectic—a philosophical mix-and-match operation—than a simple revival of Platonism.

Curiously, it is the synthetic character of Neoplatonism that makes it of historical and philosophical interest. Neoplatonism is one of the best historical representations of two otherwise difficult and overlooked junctures: that between Western philosophy and Western religion, and that between Western philosophy and Eastern philosophy. The contact with Western religion went beyond the already mentioned attempts to fuse Platonism with Judaism and with Christianity. In the chaotic spiritual world of late antiquity, Neoplatonism was in direct competition with the myriad of cults and religions. It was a slightly different response to the same set of needs which ultimately gave birth to Christianity. The connection with Eastern thought was perhaps assured in that the majority of the Neoplatonists came from Alexandria, the Egyptian melting pot of the day. Plotinus himself joined an army in order to travel east and meet some gurus, although the expedition turned back halfway when its generalissimo died.

## PLOTINUS'S WORLD

The purpose of Plotinus's philosophy, shared in general terms with both Eastern philosophy and Western religion, was to allow its subscribers to experience a mystical union with God. Like the Eastern philosophies and some of the Western religious groups, notably the Gnostics, Plotinus believed that this union could come about through the acquisition of a special kind of knowledge. However, unlike the religious groups, but like most philosophies, this special knowledge was not something "revealed" to the initiate, but something available through the exercise of humankind's rational faculties.

The outlines of Plotinus's world go something like this: What's ultimately real is the **ONE**. As usual with this sort of thing, not much can be said about the **ONE**.

Since it is so amazingly big and all-encompassing, it cannot be described or delimited, except in a negative way. So, the **ONE** is unknowable. Not to worry. A stage removed from the **ONE** is the Divine Mind. This is one of those minds that is what it thinks, so it is equally the intelligible world, a place inhabited by souped-up versions of Plato's forms. Owing to some quirky characteristics of the forms, the **ONE** can be sensed or experienced by those who are in touch with the forms, viz., philosophers. The third level of being (*hypostasis* is the fancy Plotinian word for it) is that of the World-Soul, which also gets broken up into lots of individual souls. The World-Soul is the animating principle of the world, what gets things moving, and, so the argument goes, is also responsible for time and space. At the very edge of reality, not really in or out, is the material world. As with all Platonisms, ultimate reality is form, so matter is ultimately unreal; it is the privation of form, the empty and unreal vessel of reality, to be used and disposed of on the way toward the true world.

More interesting than Plotinus's somewhat implausible triadic ontology is his attempt to conceive of the peculiar nature of the relationship between different levels of being. Roughly speaking, the problem here is that the relationship is one which involves both identity and difference. On the one hand, if all reality is ultimately the **ONE**, then everything from matter on up to the Divine Mind must already be included within and identical to this **ONE**. On the other hand, as different levels of being, these things must be in some way distinct and separate from the **ONE**. So Plotinus invokes a peculiar kind of process, which he describes with metaphors like "emanation," "radiation," and "procession," to describe the relationship. The lower levels of being "emanate" from the higher, in such a way that the lower are determined by the higher, but the higher remain aloof and unaffected by the lower. The only variation on this unidirectional flow of things from the center is the possibility of the individual soul to "think" its way back to its source in the **ONE**, and so to commune with divinity. Plotinus calls this process "reversion" or "aspiration."

The whole Plotinian world is, of course, vastly more involved and intricate than this sketch would suggest, and we could dally a while longer in its strange orbit. In an eerie way, Plotinus's philosophy anticipates many of the twists and turns of modern philosophy. One would have a hard time not seeing a lot of Hegel in Plotinus's triads, in his internally differentiated monism with its quasi-dialectical conception of the relationship between the **ONE** and its own Other, and in his attempt to lay bare the structure of thought in his analysis of the categories. Or, one could see in Plotinus's monism a more simple Spinozism, in which case one could say that Proclus, who introduced the concept of "henads," or multiple little oozey substances, to explain the plurality inherent in the **ONE**, did what Leibniz did to Spinoza with his "monads." Nonetheless, since we have the privilege of extending our journey through the entire history of philosophy, let us take up those matters in their proper sequence. Besides, I cannot but think that from a logical point of view, Plotinus's world is all, as the skeptical Timon would have said, *typhos*. Who is this **ONE** anyway? Even those who are willing to buy the ultimate existence of the **ONE** might have a tough time with the internal inconsistencies. How does one get to know about the **ONE** if it's unknowable? How does the **ONE** break up into the plurality of forms and souls? Why does it become forms first, then souls, and not the other way around? And, remind me, where does all that matter go?

## NEOPLATONISM, GNOSTICISM, AND THE PRINCIPLE OF NO FREE COMMUNION

Gnosticism has been called Neoplatonism for the proletariat. But officially, Plotinus denounced the Gnostics. The crux of his objection was that the Gnostics established a crude dualism between the material world and the spiritual, and that they devalued the former. For Plotinus, even if matter had no intrinsic value, it certainly had no negative value, and was to be grasped as part of the totality of the world. The Gnostics, on the other hand, saw the existence of matter as the result of the temptation of Adam and Eve, the degeneration of the soul. Their differences concerning the creation of the world reflect this basic opposition. Plotinus believed that the world was eternal, or timeless; the Gnostics posited a rather malevolent demiurge, or world-creator, who operated beneath ultimate divinity and within time.

Despite Plotinus's protestations, the relationship between Neoplatonism and Gnosticism contains at least as much identity as difference. It is a relationship at least as ambivalent as that which Plotinus posited between the One and the world that emanates from it. Whatever his monistic intentions, Plotinus's tenuous metaphors could not ensure a consistent union between the material world and its spiritual source. Plotinus himself referred constantly to a "here" and a "beyond." The dualism he ultimately opposed was the fuel that got his system going in the first place. To be sure, the Gnostics simplified and barbarized his thought. They threw in lots of vulgar myths, magic, and rituals. But if Gnosticism was Neoplatonism for the proletariat, Neoplatonism was probably Gnosticism for the intelligentsia.

The encounter between Plotinus and the Gnostics instantiates a general principle of the history of philosophy. Let us call it:

**The Schmooalism Principle.** All philosophical dualisms are based on a deeper monism. Conversely, all philosophical monisms are based on a deeper dualism. In other words: monism, dualism, SCHMOOALISM.

*Proof.* Every philosophical monism asserts the union of many things in one. It thereby imputes the existence of two worlds: a world of multiplicity and a world of identity. Thus, every monism contains at the very least a dualism, the union of whose elements constitutes the essence of the monism. Conversely, the philosophy which posits a dualism is itself the locus of the union of this dualism. This is often made explicit, inasmuch as the stated objective of dualistic philosophies is to find the common ground, or basis for unification, of the two sides. Even when not made explicit, the objective of union is implicit in the conception of the philosophy itself as ground for the dualism. Thus, every dualism contains a monism.

It is often said: you can't overcome dualism with a doctrine.

The more general form of this principle is:

---

**The Principle of No Free Communion.** A philosophy that takes the union of man and universe as its goal and that conceives of this union as something other than the act of doing philosophy itself cannot achieve this goal by philosophical means.

*Proof.* Essentially all philosophy takes the union of man and the universe as its goal, though this project may be expressed in a variety of ways. The union of matter and mind, for example, is essentially the same thing. In aiming for such a union, the philosophy necessarily begins by positing a difference. Man and universe, or matter and mind, must be grasped as distinct if they are to be united. Insofar as philosophy is mere description, it has no power to overcome this difference. It cannot merely state the union, any more than it can state the union of peanut butter and jelly. A possible exception is that philosophy which understands itself, that is, the act of philosophizing, as the union between man and universe. This view, however, leads to absurd statements like "I, Socrates, am god," which are known to violate familiar syllogisms.

---

Philosophers begin by sensing a transcendental need, either in themselves or in others. It is the need, loosely speaking, to feel good, or to feel at one with the world, and it usually stems from a sense of alienation, a belief that one is alone, unwanted, or useless to the world. The philosophers propose to meet this need philosophically. That is, they typically provide sets of arguments, summarized in a doctrine, to the effect that there is no need to worry, because all is one anyway, or something of the sort. Whether or not this kind of quasi-truth therapy works in individual cases, it is by no means a sure-fire cure. After all, it is just *talk*. It is a set of reasons (or non-reasons) for viewing circumstances differently, but not a change in the circumstances themselves. Philosophical error occurs when the philosopher confuses this sort of general talk with a change in circumstances. Plotinus, for example, seems at times to think that his various doctrines concerning the emanation from and return to the One not only show how one might become one with the world, but actually create this unity. It is a form of Free Communion: One has only to state it, and it comes about. Would that it were so easy.

# EASTERN PHILOSOPHY

*Just Say Om*

## THE ONE-WORLD HYPOTHESIS

Suppose that the West never came to be. Suppose that some eastern Alexander had returned and crushed Rome before it could begin its career, that Europe became an outpost of Persia, Hindustan, or some other empire of the East. What would have become of Greek philosophy? Would it have been perceived as an aberration? Would it have been seen as a brief flirtation with rationalism, a Western deviation from the more usual, Eastern way of thinking? I think not. Greek philosophy would have been added seamlessly to the foundations of Eastern thought. Triumphant Easterners would have scoffed at the idea that Plato, Pyrrho, Plotinus, Pythagoras, and other Presocratics were anything but late bloomers in their native tradition of mystical thought. Socrates would have been a guru, and Aristotle would have been held up with pride as a representative of their own tradition of learning. (Actually, a modest version of this thought experiment occurred. While Europe slept through its Dark Ages, Islamic scholars adopted the tradition of the *falasafahs* (philosophers) and so preserved for later Western use the texts of, among others, Aristotle.)

In most traditional versions of the story, however, East and West mark the two poles of philosophical possibility. The very idea of Western thought assumes this opposition. The usual story presents Western thought, generally speaking, as rational and scientific, and Eastern thought (at least implicitly) as mystical and religious. Interpretations of the meaning of this opposition vary. Some versions suggest that Western thought is infected with certain concepts and presuppositions, like a radical belief in the metaphysical individual. Others, in a related vein, tend to present Western thought as spiritually or otherwise deficient. They imply that Western thought is so rational that it is quite irrational, and perhaps not truly philosophical.

Still others are more inclined to celebrate the presumed victory of the West in matters of reason. Eastern philosophy is dismissed as mere mysticism. It's all poetry and mythology from a prescientific people. It's about consciousness raising, not the theory of knowledge, logic, and so on.

In my view, this supposed opposition of East and West has it all wrong. It is wrong, in the first instance, on a simple question of fact. Eastern and Western philosophies did not develop in isolation from each other. I have already noted that many key Greek philosophers are suspected of having picked up their wisdom from Eastern sources. Thales, Pyrrho, and Plotinus all are reported to have taken long and mysterious holidays. The evidence in their doctrines that Pythagoras and Plato took at least some intellectual voyages of discovery is fairly compelling. In the quasi-philosophical religious cults that lined the Mediterranean of the Hellenistic era, there is no point in talking about any geographical divide. Among modern philosophers Leibniz was profoundly sympathetic to the ancient Chinese philosophers, and even wrote a *Discourse on the Natural Theology of the Chinese*—a text sadly missing from most Western collections of his philosophical writings. Hegel begins his history of philosophy in the East, and ends the exposition of his own philosophy with quotations from Hindu and Sufi texts. Schopenhauer acknowledged the collective authors of the *Upanishads* as his only true predecessors other than Kant. Ideas flowed in the other direction as well. Even before the onslaught of the twentieth century, skeptical and materialist strains of thought from the West made their influence felt among Hindu and Chinese philosophers, for example. And Aristotle was a hit among the Arabs. The story of Western philosophy has usually been told as a self-contained affair, not because it was so in fact, but because these outside influences are inconvenient to the telling of the basic plot (and also because the relevant evidence has been hard to secure).

The opposition between East and West is wrong also on a more abstract question of fact, that Eastern and Western philosophies differ fundamentally in terms of their doctrines. Whether or not there was much influence across borders, I would argue, the patterns of thought, including not only concepts and presuppositions but also the characteristic errors of philosophy, are more alike than they are different across the borders. To be sure, there are differences in culture, arising from different histories, which give rise to distinct currents in the histories of ideas, to varying degrees of success and influence, and so forth. However, there are greater differences within the groups which are labeled East and West than there are between them. Moreover, all doctrines that could be considered fundamental to philosophy are present in sufficient quantity on both sides of the supposed border.

Finally, the opposition between East and West is wrong on a question of reason: There could be some form of thought available on one side and not the other of some geographical boundary. Insofar as the opposition is intended to identify the philosophical doctrines which putatively delimit the bounds of thought, I say this: There is no such opposition of East and West, nor is there such a thing as Western thought or Eastern thought.

The supposed philosophical opposition of East and West, I believe, is part of a cheap and modern form of tribalism. Politicians and cranks who call themselves political theorists may have some interest in carving up our tiny patch in the universe. I can see no reason why philosophers should share that interest. It may well be that in the past, for a brief while, philosophy seemed to flow in separate streams. In the future, we can be sure, there will be only one, human history of philosophy.

I begin with a brief survey of that jumble of things we throw in the closet called the East. I then present my understanding of mysticism. In doing so here, however, I do not mean to suggest that Eastern, as opposed to Western, philosophy, is only mysticism (though I do think that mysticism is better expressed in many Eastern philosophies.) The main point is that mysticism is central to all philosophy. So far as the history of Western philosophy goes, at least in the interpretation I offer through the rest of this book, there is no more important set of ideas to master than those presented here, in the course of our little detour to the East.

## EAST OF WHAT?

So far I have been using "East" unproblematically, as though it denoted a single region and a single philosophy. This, of course, would be false. The two largest national groupings included in the East are the Indians and the Chinese. Others of philosophical relevance include Persians, Arabs, Tibetans, and Japanese. All of these are just groupings, hiding beneath the labels is a teeming diversity of views, cultures, and languages. It is also quite strange that they should be thought of together. When Buddhism first arrived in China from India, it was viewed by most as a decidedly foreign (and therefore undesirable) force. Later, more sympathetic Chinese looked to India as the "pure land of the West." Racially and linguistically, the early Hindus were in fact closer to their Indo-European cousins in Greece than they were to the East Asians.

Both India and China have continuous histories of philosophy which extend further back in time than that of the West. The astonishing continuity of both traditions has been ensured by the role in each of a set of original, ancient texts. These texts have functioned as quasi-religious scriptures. Much Indian philosophy, in particular, has developed in the form of a commentary on these scriptures, and a further commentary on a commentary. This continuity should not be mistaken for a unity of outlook. It is true that there was a mainstream in both the Indian and Chinese traditions, and that these mainstreams were quite different in appearance and character from that of the Western tradition. What is less known is that there were plenty of countercurrents and the like, so that a vast and diverse range of philosophical perspectives formed in and around the Eastern traditions.

Mainstream Eastern philosophy can be divided into a few major groups. Here is a very rough sketch of this terrain:

## HINDUISM

Hinduism is much more than a philosophy. It is the entire culture, religion, history, and way of life of the majority population on the Indian subcontinent. At the abstract end of the religious component, however, there has developed a recognizably philosophical tradition. Hindu philosophy takes as its historical authority a collection of ancient Sanskrit texts: the *Vedas*, the *Bhagavad-Gita*, and, above all, the *Upanishads*. Reduced to a single idea, the gist of three thousand years' worth of mainstream Hindu philosophy is that All is One; that this One is the *Ātman*, or cosmic self; and that the object of philosophy is to lead the individual toward a (re)union with this One. A key word in Hindu thought is *dharma*. Much Hindu philosophy accepts as background a religious view involving the transmigration of souls. During their mortal lives, individual souls accumulate *karma* with their various self-interested actions. So long as some of the *karma* stuff remains when the individual dies, the soul is reborn in another person. The object is to get rid of *karma* and thereby avoid the trouble of being reborn.

## BUDDHISM

The Buddha—meaning "the enlightened one"—lived in a part of India that is now Nepal from around 560 to 480 B.C.E. What the Buddha taught is very straightforward, and summed up in his "Four Truths." The first truth is that life is quite unpleasant. It's one bad thing after another, and then you die. Second, the cause of our suffering in life is our own desires. More abstractly, it is our unfounded belief in our 'self' which is to blame. Third, the cessation of suffering is possible if we give up on our desires and our illusory notion of the self. Fourth, the way to go about this is the Eightfold Path, also taught by the Buddha, which involves doing lots of things in the "right" way. The result, if you're lucky, is a dissolution of the self and an encounter with *Nirvana*, or the Nothing, which is what is ultimate reality.

After about a thousand years, the light of Buddhism dimmed in India. By then, the torch had been passed to Tibet, China, and other areas of East Asia, where it remains the basis of religion for some 500 million people. As with Hinduism, Buddhism goes well beyond mere philosophy, and includes ceremonies and rituals which are part of the religious life of many nationalities. Since ancient times, there has been a wide variety of Buddhist sects.

## ZEN BUDDHISM

This is probably the best known sect in the West. "Zen" is a Japanese mispronunciation of *Ch'an*, which is a Chinese mispronunciation of the Sanskrit *dhyāna*, which means "meditation." Zen Buddhism is probably the most rigorous, abstract, and radically individualist of the mystical philosophies. Everything everywhere is a part of the One, which Zen Buddhists call the Buddha-mind. Any man can become a Buddha by getting in touch with his own mind. The way to do this is to empty one's consciousness of all particular thoughts. Even the Buddhist doctrines, the rituals, and the monastic lifestyle are annihilated. All that matters is that one keep still long enough to experience one's own nature, and thereby the nature of the world. Since no particular doctrines can ensure this kind of enlightenment, the Zennies tend to use ordinary practices, whether the tea ritual or rock gardening, as a way of disciplining the mind to become one with the world. They also favor judo as a form of relaxation, because it penalizes thinking and rewards complete absorption in a physical process.

## CONFUCIANISM

Also much more than a philosophy, Confucianism is a part of the way of life of many Chinese. Confucius (551–479 B.C.E.) was mainly concerned with ethical questions: how to make sure people get along, the best form of good government, and so on. He synthesized a system of values for his time. Confucius distinguished between acting out of righteousness (i.e., moral duty) and acting out of expectation of profit. He praised "doing for nothing." He advocated "human-heartedness" (*jen*), or the consideration of others. He also insisted on the "rectification of names," that is, making sure everyone knew his or her place in society and had the appropriate titles. In short, he was something of a moralist, a mix of Socrates, Jesus, and Miss Manners. For the vast majority of nonphilosophical Chinese, Confucianism is simply the guide for right and proper social behavior.

Later, Confucianism became the official philosophy of the Chinese state, and took on a very broad range of interests. Neo-Confucianism, as it is called, investigated questions about the nature of humankind, being and nonbeing, substance and function, and the like, none of which were of much concern to Confucius. Most Chinese philosophers of the past two thousand years have been Confucians to some degree or other, and most of the Confucians have been Taoists (see next section) or Chinese Buddhists as well. In fact much of Chinese philosophy has been an attempt to achieve a harmonious balance between "worldly," conformist Confucianism and the more spiritual and quietistic Taoism and Buddhism.

## TAOISM

This is the mystical wing of Chinese philosophy. The *Tao* means "the truth" or "the way," although if you knew to what it referred you would have solved every problem in philosophy. The Tao is the indescribable One from which all things flow and to which all things return. Particular things derive their virtue, *te*, from the Tao. Going with the Tao means being relaxed and spontaneous. "Action without effort" is the ideal for the Taoist sage.

## THE OTHER EAST

It is common to mistake the official, mainstream philosophies listed above with the philosophy of the Indian people, or of the Chinese people, etc., or even with the history of philosophy as practiced in those countries. But this is the first, false step on the way to the crude dualism of East and West. The ideas which the usual story identifies with the West can all be found in the East, though perhaps with different emphasis and expression.

The Cārvāka school, dating from around 600 B.C.E., dismissed the philosophy of the Vedas as "untrue, self-contradictory, and tautologous." Its members mocked the Vedic poetry rituals as "the means of livelihood for those who have no manliness or sense." Instead of deserting the senses in search of the One, they advocated maximizing sensual pleasure. In direct opposition to the idealism of mainstream Hindu philosophy, they challenged the validity of inferential reasoning, declared that only that which is perceived exists, and adopted a bald materialism. They maintained that their own philosophy, not that of the official Sanskrit scriptures, was the true philosophy of the mass of humankind.

Well over a century before the Presocratic Empedocles, Ajita of the Hair-Blanket, the reputed founder of the Cārvākas, argued that the world consisted of four elements. He and Empedocles, by the way, agreed on the selection of elements: earth, air, fire, and water. Ajita's rival, Pakhuda Kacchāyana, opted instead for seven elements: He threw in Joy, Sorrow, and Life. Well ahead of the Greek Democritus, Pakhuda also proposed a kind of atomism.* Thus, materialism, in approximately the form it takes in early Greek thought, was certainly evident in the Hindu tradition.

The Chinese also had their anti-philosophers. Ssu-ma Chien (149–86 B.C.E.), for example, said of the Taoist Chuang-Tzu that his works were "empty words not based on facts . . . primarily aimed at pleasing himself and useless to rulers of men." In the Chinese philosopher Wang Ch'ung (27–100 C.E.) one can find a reasonably clear statement of the nature of an empirical investigation and a healthy skepticism about traditional mystical and metaphysical claims. Though committed to a vocabulary of Taoist cosmology, Chuang-Tzu denied that heaven intervenes for earth in any teleological way, insisted that "material force" can account for events, and required that all such claims be backed with factual evidence. If, as the modern mythology has it, the ideas of the Great Philosophers drive history, then it is hard to explain why China did not become an industrial superpower in the first few centuries C.E. The ideas, in at least as clear a form as they were in Bacon or Descartes, were already there. What was lacking, apparently, was the will and/or the ability to act on them.

Both China and India had equivalents to what Westerners might call sophists, or philosophers of language. While Chinese mystics despaired of describing the

---

*Discussion of these and other unorthodox thinkers may be found in the Buddhist text, *Dīgha Nikaya* (Long Group), which is part of the *Sutta* (Discourses).

One, members of the so-called School of Names spent their time merrily chopping logic. They delighted in proving, for example, that a white horse is not a horse, and that the possible is impossible, and that whatever you say is wrong. Good old Zeno would have been happy to see that one of their favorite paradoxes was that if you "take a stick one foot long and cut it in half every day you will never exhaust it." Some members of the school eventually tended toward a kind of Platonism, others pursued negative dialectics in order to arrive at the "reality behind all words." But this hardy band of logicians was at first and in essence a bunch of intellectual merrymakers who loved abstract thought for its own sake. The Indians were able to satisfy similar impulses in their own school called *Nyaya*.

To be sure, these and other non-mainstream schools were small and had limited influence. The mere fact of their existence, however, proves my point, that whatever the conceptual schemes elaborated by philosophy in the East and West, these did not exclude any significant part of each other, nor can they be called into account to explain the more general differences in historical development of East and West.

## PHILOSOPHY AS/AND/OF/OR RELIGION

The mainstream philosophies mentioned above correspond to mainstream religions. Taoism and Buddhism, for example, both exist as mass religions, including places of worship, rituals, spiritual leaders, and so on. Philosophical Taoists and Buddhists like to keep their own views distinct from these religions, and often adopt a condescending attitude toward them. Yet, even within the philosophical hard core it is very difficult to tell where the religion ends and where the philosophy begins. Perhaps this is one of those distinctions which just doesn't apply. Then again, perhaps this is what is of interest to us, from a historico-philosophical point of view. I will focus on the quasi-religious aspect of the mainstream Eastern philosophies, with the already clarified caveat that these represent neither the whole of the East nor the whole of Eastern philosophy.

The case for treating these Eastern views at least initially as philosophies rather than as religions has to do with the way in which they present themselves, for the most part, as reflective rather than revealed truths. That is, their truths are available to any human, *qua* reflective being. Even more, they are supposed to be the natural result or end of human reflection. The Buddha was tolerant of all honest reflection, even when it seemed to contradict his teachings, for he was sure that reflection would eventually arrive at the truth—his truth. So long as they present themselves in this way, the Eastern philosophies deserve to be considered as philosophies.

Of course, the truth at which these reflections are supposed to arrive is also a promise of happiness. To the twentieth-century academic philosopher, this will give them an unphilosophical character. However, no less philosophical a figure than Socrates held forth the same promise, that knowledge is happiness, as did countless other Western thinkers from the Stoics to Spinoza. So it would be unfair to use this premise as the basis for dismissal.

Philosophy begins in opposition to religion. As with the Presocratics, it is a rejection to mythology. The appeal to pure reflection, to knowledge based on the evidence before us and our own ability to reason, seems an inescapable criterion for what should count as philosophy, the first step on any knowledge-lover's path. Yet so much, perhaps all, of philosophy seems to end in a form of religion—even if a bizarre religion, like that of Socrates. How is this possible? How does philosophy move so freely and effortlessly between openness and closure, between radical doubt and absolute certainty? There is no one answer. But a good part of any answer, I think, must pass through mysticism. So here we go.

---

### *Cosmo-Babble, Chinese Style*

*In the beginning:*

1. *There was a beginning*
2. *There was a time before the beginning*
3. *There was a time before the time before the beginning*
4. *There was being*
5. *There was nonbeing*
6. *There was a time before nonbeing*
7. *There was a time before the time before nonbeing*

---

## HOW TO BECOME A MYSTIC IN THREE EASY STEPS

### *(1) ADOPT THE BELIEF THAT THERE IS A REALITY OTHER THAN ORDINARY REALITY*

At this point it does not matter much how you conceive of the other reality. It could be ghosts, UFOs, orgasm, or the Conspiracy. Given that you are a human being, you are at first likely to think of the other reality in the form of ancestor spirits and/or anthropomorphic deities. Earlier Hindu poetry, for example, is largely concerned with the nature and worship of gods with names like Agni, Soma, Indra, Varuna, and Vishnu. As you progress, your conception of the other reality will change in a predictable way: It will shed, one by one, the attributes you ascribe to ordinary reality. First to go will be those annoying material needs: Gods rarely go to the bathroom. At a more abstract level, since particularity and multiplicity are the most obvious general features of ordinary reality, the other reality will increasingly emphasize generality and unity. A Hindu, for example, will progress from a chaotic polytheism to some variant of monotheism. This will show up at first as *henotheism*, or the tendency of making whichever god you happen to be talking about sound like the best and the only one. It will end with a notion of the Brahman, or pure spirit, as the source of all divinity. What you take to be the chief attributes of ordinary reality will, of course, determine the progress of your concept of the other reality. As a Buddhist, for example, you will probably stress the notion of the self, or 'self-ish-ness', as a characteristic of ordinary reality, and so you will imagine a real reality without selves.

In this stage of your development, you will tend to utter lots of cosmo-babble. If a Hindu, you will probably start to think of certain individual gods as material elements, like earth and fire. As a Chinese from a certain region, you might be tempted to describe the origin and process of the world in terms of two basic forces, yin and yang. Later on, as your notions become more abstract, the other reality will be described in terms of being, nonbeing, and variations on that theme.

In distinguishing between worlds, you will also want to distinguish between wisdom and mere knowledge. Wisdom is knowing the Tao, the real way of things, or whatever you choose to call it, while knowledge is mere book learning, or useless facts. Who cares about the molecular structure of corn or the number of pistons in a car engine? What matters is the structure of ultimate reality. Details are mere knowledge; but sorting out the details which together make up a picture of the whole is wisdom.

The evidence for adopting the belief in another reality is by definition insufficient. Evidence is part of *this* reality, not the one sought. Anything that could be conclusively proved—as opposed to merely suggested or indicated—would necessarily become a part of ordinary reality. So why adopt the belief? Typically, you will be motivated by a certain dissatisfaction with ordinary reality. You are unhappy that you cannot control rainfall, and so your livelihood seems precarious. Or you get the feeling that life sucks and then you die. You might just be bored: The stars are much more interesting if you imagine them as fallen heroes or glorious gods. Or you might be ambitious, wanting to become a god yourself. Running through all these is a general concern with the meaning of life: Why am I here? Why am I at all? Who's in charge here anyway? At this point, your motivation for adopting the belief in another reality is not terribly important. It will color your concepts and determine the speed of your progress, but you will still move predictably to step two. Do not forget this motivation, however, for it will become important after step three.

## (2) DESCRIBE THE OTHER REALITY AS INDESCRIBABLE; OR, JUST SAY NO

This follows rigorously from the belief adopted in step one. As you meditate on the matter, you will grasp that the source of all distinctions, and hence all descriptions, lies in ordinary reality. Sensory experiences, language, and the intellect itself all relate to things, like corn and automobiles, and are therefore all ordinary. The other world cannot be sensed, or spoken of, or even conceived. You are now on the *via negativa* of the medieval theologians, the road that passes through all Eastern mysticism and leads to God through negation: He is *not* a mere mortal being; He is *not* merely an immortal being; He is *not* merely a being.

The Upanishadic poets, for example, will ask you to think of the other reality according to the principle of *neti neti*, meaning it's neither this nor this, etc. But be careful: This does not entitle you to claim an understanding of the other reality. According to the Sanskrit sages, those who say they understand the other reality do not, and those who say they do not do, since it is by definition incomprehensible. Like Aquinas on his God, the poets conclude that the only statement one can make about ultimate reality is "He Is." The Taoists call their ultimate reality the *Tao*, meaning the 'truth', or the 'way', but then immediately insist that it is The Unnameable. The Tao of which we ordinarily speak is not the real thing. A Buddhist will refer you to the 'Void'. Alternatively, he may call it the 'Suchness'—a remarkably general, hard-to-define, quasi-indexical notion. Like the Hindu theologian, he may limit what one can say about Nirvana to the bare assertion that "Nirvana Is." Perhaps the most determined followers of the *via negativa* are, as usual, the Zen Buddhists. If you follow the Zen, you will find yourself rejecting all doctrines simply because they are doctrines—and this includes Buddhism and Zen itself. The Buddha himself said, "I have taught a doctrine similar to a raft—it is for carrying over and not for carrying." To understand the Buddha is not to understand, and not to understand is to understand, said one Zen Master. (Someone once beat a Zennie with a stick, or so the story goes. When asked why, he replied: "To beat is not to beat, and not to beat is to beat.") In brief, in order to grasp and affirm the meaning of the other, ultimate reality, you will have to say no to every possible representation of it.

As you progress in your mysticism, you will notice some related developments. You will, for example, develop an acute aversion to all forms of opposition. Wherever two things are distinguished, set beside or against each other, there you know there is no ultimate reality. As a Hindu sage, you want to be beyond pleasure and pain, beyond good and evil, beyond self and other, and beyond all possible oppositions. So also says the great Taoist Chuang-Tzu.

Now you will begin to wonder if wisdom, as opposed to mere knowledge, can ever be taught (even by such a handy guide as this). If ultimate reality is a bunch of nos, then having-no-knowledge, as the Taoists put it, is an honorable goal. As a Taoist, in fact, you might even regard forgetfulness as a virtue. As in the Upanishads, you will deny that the poetry can ever convey the teaching, and insist on the uniqueness and importance of the individual relationship with one's guru. Like a Zen master, you may have to adopt some unusual teaching techniques. When a student asks for the teaching of the Buddha, you beat him with a stick. You will probably conclude, like the Zen, that the knowledge of ultimate reality is not a philosophy or a religion, but an experience. Like the reality of which it is an experience, the knowledge itself is indescribable, incommunicable, and incomprehensible—what some philosophers call immediate knowledge.

## (3) ASSERT THAT THE OTHER REALITY IS THE ONLY REALITY; OR, THAT ALL IS ONE; OR, JUST SAY "OM"

This is it. The real thing. Mysticism puro. The other reality is the only one. What you thought of as the ordinary reality is a merely a part of an indivisible totality.

Ordinary reality is a derivative, a manifestation, an expression of the inexpressible reality. It is a collection of signs all of which point to the One truth. Everything is interconnected, interdependent, in virtue of the One. Of course, this is also where it gets tricky, since in declaring that the other reality is the only reality you have eliminated the distinction that was necessary to make sense of the belief you adopted in step one, that there is a reality other than ordinary reality.

The Chinese tradition tends to think of the unity of reality in terms of ultimate principles. You might define the Tao (provisionally) as that by which things become what they are. In this you may be borrowing from the Confucian notion of *Li*, or principle. The Hindus before you thought of the All as *Ātman*, meaning something like "self," or "cosmic self" (and etymologically related to "breath"). Their great synthesis was expressed in the formula *ayam atma brahma*, the self is the brahman, i.e., ultimate reality. When you have reached step three with us, you will say with the Hindu, *tat tvam asi*, you are that (i.e., that ultimate reality). In joining the cosmic self you will have achieved what the Buddhist achieves by dissolving the self altogether: You will have become one with all reality. You will have attained Nirvana. Since, according to step two, ultimate reality is not supposed to have a name, you might want to adopt the Hindu "Om," which is intended to serve as a vocalization of all of reality.

You will be happy to note that your encounter with reality also places you outside of time. Past, present, and future, in basically all mystical traditions, is merely a derivative manifestation of ultimate, timeless reality.

## WHAT TO DO NOW THAT YOU'RE A MYSTIC

Careful readers will have noticed a certain obscurity in the logic of mysticism as outlined above. Mysticism begins with a distinction between two kinds of reality, and the implicit assumption that the other reality is knowable in some way. It next denies the knowability of this other reality, and then further denies the very distinction between kinds of reality. The paradox remains even when one tries to avoid the term "knowledge" by using "experience," or some other Zen-like term. For in any experience, or any form of consciousness, there is surely an experiencer and something that is experienced. And yet it is this very distinction between self and world which is supposed to be overcome in mystical experience. Then again, perhaps one should not expect too much logic from what is basically a disposition to believe what cannot be described, expressed, or even understood—in short, to believe in the unbelievable.

Still, let's suppose that you're already a mystic. What do you do now? Aye, there's the rub. While the concepts put forward by different groups are often reasonably similar, the programs are often incompatible with each other. Given that mysticism always follows the three steps outlined above, the differences in results are worthy of note. The reason for these differences is really quite simple. I will call it:

**The Indeterminacy Principle.** Mysticism determines no particular philosophy.

*Proof.* The fundamental mystical proposition that All is One cannot lead deductively to logical or practical consequences. If All is One, any action I choose to take and any thought I choose to have are still part of that One. In fact, if All is One, neither I nor my actions are real in any sense, so there's no point in talking about what 'I' should 'do' (or what is the case).

The flip side of this principle is:

**The No-Point-in-Preparing Principle.** No form of teaching is guaranteed to prepare an individual for mystical experience.

*Proof.* If mystical experience could be induced in a predictable way from ordinary experience, then it would be causally linked to the ordinary world. But mystical experience must transcend all ordinary experience. Therefore, etc.

In light of these principles, your options as a mystic can be roughly divided according to the following four-part scheme. Your choice of option may not be determined logically, but it may well be determined emotionally. It is a good thing then that you remembered your original motivation for believing in an extraordinary reality, as I recommended in step one above.

## (1) RUN AWAY

As in: from the senses, from the self, from consciousness, from particulars of any sort, from any kind of commitment or involvement that reminds you of ordinary reality. Go live on a mountain, stare at your nose, breath deeply, and avoid sex. This is the preferred option of hard-core mystics around the world, especially among Buddhists and Hindus. Some, like the Jainists in India, pursue a strict asceticism, pushing even the smallest living thing from their path with a broom. Others, like more mainstream Buddhists, believe excessive asceticism to be counterproductive, and advocate a more moderate course of frugality without mortification. Most mystics conceive of option one as an escape from particular sensual experiences. The Zen Buddhists, however, conceive of it as an escape from particular thoughts. All thoughts, they seem to think, are merely partial representations and divisions of reality, and obscure the union with totality. The goal of the Zennies is therefore to "empty the mind." Once the mind is empty, the theory goes, you are hooked up with reality. (Of course, you might also be dead!) A more general form of option one would be to escape from particularity as such. What is not particular is universal, and what is universal is a concept or idea. Which idea in particular, you ask? Well, none in particular, of course, except possibly the idea behind Plato's idealism, the Idea of the Good, which is the Idea of the Idea.

The logic behind option one is simple: Our entanglements with ordinary reality make it more difficult for us to experience the other, real reality; so, no more sense experience for us, please. The illogic is equally straightforward: If All is One, then why can't our sense experiences count as a part of this One?

## (2) GO WITH THE FLOW

The value of experiencing the unity of all things can also be construed as a better ability to grasp your own nature and place in the world. It allows you to "get in touch with yourself" and "go with the flow" of the world around and within you. Instead of retreating from the world, as in option one, you remain active in ordinary reality, but in an unctuous and harmonious way. The best expressions of this notion, I think, are in the Chinese philosophies. The goal of Tao is a spontaneous "action without effort." An old proverb, which came out of Chinese philosophy, says that one should "lean neither forward nor backward"—that is, don't push or pull, just move with things. Not merely a mountain guru, the Chinese wise man is expected to be "sagely within, kingly without." In a more radical form, the Chinese go-with-the-flow idea was expressed in the Neo-Taoist concept of *feng liu*, formed from words meaning literally "wind" and "stream." The advocates of this concept favored the "natural" course (which for some meant reason, for others sentiment) over the dictates of morality and so on.

Hinduism and Buddhism have set precedents for option two as well. In the *Bhagavad-Gita*, for example, the god Krishna counsels the warrior Arjuna to prosecute his war, despite his misgivings. In "action without regard for consequences," Krishna argues, Arjuna can still realize his virtue. The Zen project of emptying the mind is also sometimes construed as a preparation for really getting into an activity. Thus, the Zen archer unites with bow, arrow, and target to hit the bullseye every time.

The logic behind option two is simple: If you're in touch with the One, you're in touch with everything else, so you're bound to be a pretty good archer, king, or whatever. The illogic is also pretty simple. Going with the flow presupposes the possibility of not going with the flow. But if all things flow from the One, then there can be only one flow. So how could you ever be out of the flow?

## (3) INDULGE THYSELF

Go ahead. Fulfill your innermost desires. Just do it, whatever it is. Only a few, marginal sects have selected this option: the sentimentally oriented Neo-Taoists of the Chin period mentioned above, the so-called Yang Chu Chapter of the Taoist renegade *Lieh Tzu* and the Indian Cārvāka school. Those who do choose this option are subject to abuse from mainstream sects in the form of humiliating parables in which they are described as sharing their wine with pigs, being incontinent, and generally living like slobs.

Nonetheless, the logical position of option three is the same as all the rest. On the pro side, you can say that all your desires are part of the One, so the One is happy when you get what you want. On the contra side, why should the One care at all about your particular desires, and besides, how are you going to choose which desires to fulfill?

## (4) CONTINUE READING THIS BOOK

If the Indeterminacy Principle is correct, then you may as well continue with whatever it was you were doing. From a logical point of view, option four is just as viable as the rest. If the No-Point-in-Preparing Principle is correct, then at least we can be sure that this book won't do you any harm. So, on we go.

# WHAT DOES MYSTICISM HAVE TO DO WITH PHILOSOPHY?

Good question. The belief in unbelievable things, whether ghosts or cosmic minds, is incompatible with our most basic understanding of philosophy. Philosophy is the love of knowledge, not superstition. I contend, however, that much of what passes for philosophy is in fact mysticism. Mysticism, in my view, is based on an abstraction from our ordinary, healthy way of knowing things. It is a natural dysfunction of our cognitive apparatus. Philosophy, when understood as something other than a general and favorable disposition toward knowledge, that is, when viewed as a specific project and the source of a privileged sort of knowledge, is just this sort of mysticism. Let me explain.

## EMPIRICIST MYSTICISM

In order to understand the role of mysticism in philosophy, one must first acknowledge the strange and mysterious parallels between mysticism and more respectable conceptions of the nature and acquisition of knowledge. Respectable science, like mysticism, begins with a distinction between our ordinary reality and another deeper reality. In ordinary reality, apples fall and the moon rises, all in a random and unconnected way. Deeper reality is really a deeper awareness, that all these seemingly disparate phenomena are the same thing wearing different dresses. Like mysticism, science aims to overcome the distinction between realities, to show that ordinary reality is merely a derivative from the other, ultimate reality. Both aim for a new, deeper awareness of the world around us. In idealist terms, the union of subject and object describes both the mystic's final ecstasy and the nature of knowledge for which ordinary science strives. The mystical vision of the interdependence of all things also has a respectable parallel. Knowledge, whether of the everyday sort or of high science, is acquired by drawing the connections among things, i.e., by synthesis. The ultimate objective of science is to demonstrate the interrelationships of things. Furthermore, the Zen idea of clearing the mind can also be understood as a preparation for acquiring knowledge. By removing prejudices, preconceptions, and preoccupations, one puts oneself in a position to see things as they are—which is precisely how one gains knowledge of any sort.

Other aspects of mysticism have a certain, empirical appeal. For example, the distinction between wisdom and knowledge is credible to anyone who has witnessed the public behavior of a computer nerd. The insight goes deeper than that. What separates wisdom and knowledge may be called judgment. As the German Idealists would discover, the nature of judgment is much harder to specify than any other component of knowledge. If one knows that "if A, then B," still one requires judgment in order to determine that an A is in fact an A, B is B, and that A and B are what we should be talking about in the first place. The issue has its parallel in the mystics' reservations about teaching. Everyone knows that you can pump students' heads full of formulas, and they will still be useless until they really understand how the formulas work, until they identify with them, and assume responsibility for them. At some point the teacher has to give up, and count on the student to achieve the necessary synthesis, to form the ability of judgment.

## AN ABSTRACTION TOO FAR

Where does mysticism go wrong? Where does it leave the sure path of science and become mere fancy and speculation? Empirically speaking, there is no single answer. The historical examples of mysticism are too varied. But in terms of the scheme offered here, the answer is obvious. Mysticism is the result of a confusion between the *concept of knowing* and *knowing itself*. To put it into a weird formula: Mysticism is an abstraction removed from knowledge. To illustrate: "The unity of subject and object" or "seeing the interconnections of things" or "becoming aware of reality" are reasonable (if somewhat inane) generalizations about the nature of the goal of knowing. They are not what one desires to know in any particular instance—what one wants to know is things like "what time the bar closes" and "how to predict the speed of falling objects." They are, to repeat, umbrella abstractions over and above the class of these instances. Mysticism takes these abstractions themselves as its goal. Instead of wanting to know a particular object, and so become one with it, it wants to know 'object' as such, and become one with that. Instead of a particular self, it wants the 'self'. Instead of the slow and imperfect labor of gathering knowledge about things and seeing their interconnections, the mystic wants to leap straight to the conclusion, that All is One.

It seems quite likely that mysticism is built into our cognitive function, or is a relatively natural dysfunction in our cognitive apparatus. Life presents us with no end of situations in which we must draw conclusions from insufficient evidence. It is a natural reflex to want to round out the evidence, to find enough to close the circle, and make it sufficient. Analogies, signs, and indications are ways in which we boost confidence in the context of insufficient evidence. Mysticism seeks to complete this incomplete state. It gives the feeling of sure knowledge where in reality there is none.

The belief in magic, which might be taken as the first stage of mysticism, is very likely also built into our cognitive apparatus. The connections among events identified by the magician mimic the relationships established by knowledge. There is a kind of causality at work, an ability to predict and influence outcomes, and so forth. The difference, of course, is that the magical events are ultimately inexplicable, for they can only be explained with reference to the actions of some inscrutable deity. Although they seem to offer a way of comprehending the world, magical events are ultimately incomprehensible.

We need not take the argument much further in order to see how philosophy is really a form of mysticism. As a disposition, a modest and discreet love of knowledge, philosophy remains healthy. It, too, supposes a distinction between the world as it appears and the world as it is, between subject and object, and it reveres the human labor of overcoming this distinction, of discovering how things really are. When understood as project, however, as the second-order knowledge of knowledge, or any of the many other conceptions which populate its history both East and West, philosophy commits the mystical fallacy. It imagines that by describing the relationship between appearance and reality, or between subject and object, it will have achieved their union in actuality. It seeks the truth about truth, and imagines that in this way it discovers the truth about everything. Like mysticism, it leaps straight to the conclusion, that All is One, and believes that it thereby closes the circle of human knowledge. Not happy with the petty pace of temporary victories against ignorance, philosophy drives obsessively toward the possession of its object. So it kills the thing it loves.

What I have called the Holy Grail of philosophy is really just mysticism. Thales' water, Parmenides' method of truth, Socrates' idea of the good life, Plato's Idea of the Good, Aristotle's oozey substance, the Stoics' virtuous Mind-god-world, Plotinus's One, and all the many endpoints of Western philosophy we have yet to traverse are also an abstraction removed from knowledge, an abstraction too far. Why take this extra step? Mainly, I think, there is a need for happiness. Mysticism is the bridge from knowledge to happiness. Implicitly, it is the embodiment of the traditional insecurity of philosophy, the belief that happiness can be assured with no ordinary knowledge, but only with something special, something beyond knowledge, an ineluctable experience at the edge of cognition. Indeed, the Holy Grail of philosophy is something magical.

## MYSTICAL SIGNS IN PHILOSOPHY

Let us now pull together a list of the most common symptoms of mysticism as it appears in philosophy. These will become very important as we progress through the history of modern, Western philosophy.

   1. *Looking for the thing behind all things*. This is one definition of the Tao: that which lies behind all things, and makes them what they are. It is the thingless

cause of all things, or the shape without shape which is the shape of shape. In Western philosophy the Tao takes a variety of shapes. It is the project of all 'transcendental philosophy', or the search for that which 'transcends' all experience. It is the investigation of the 'Being' which is behind or within all 'beings'. Or, it is the old 'being *qua* being'. Beware of any search for 'foundations': in philosophy, these foundations are likely to be nothing more than the longing for mystical rapture.

2. *Looking for the husband without a wife.* Another definition of the Tao is the "form without an object." The old truncated opposition. You'll find this in notions like 'pure actuality' and 'the self which posits itself' and 'the absolute good', to name but a few.

3. *Silence is golden.* Since the mystical One is ineffable, most Eastern sects insist on a silence about matters which pertain to it. After all, there is nothing meaningful to be said about the big guy. In the history of Western philosophy, one often encounters a similar yearning for an end to speech, to find that which can be only shown or indicated, but not said.

4. *Dialectic till you drop.* One way to pursue the *via negativa* is to undermine all positive claims to knowledge by means of the dialectic. When no claims are left standing, one surrenders to the inexpressible One and gets a warm feeling. I have called this paradoxophilia above.

5. *Everything I've just said is wrong.* Many Eastern sects acknowledge some version of the No-Point-in-Preparing Principle. Zen Buddhists especially admit that their own doctrines and methods are at best useful symbols and reminders, and have no value in themselves. Western philosophers talk about "pulling up the ladder" or "heuristics" with the same effect.

6. *This is not a text; it's an experience.* A text is just words on paper, or noises in the air. It seems to be a medium through which some content is conveyed. Not so with the truly mystical text. It is itself an experience, a happening. It does not convey something; it creates something, namely, the world as we know it. Hence the awe in which the scriptures of the mystics are held, and why some Eastern sects have supposedly hidden their best work from public gaze. In less ambitious Western forms, the text attempts a recreation of the experience. It becomes evocative rather than declarative. It sounds like an evangelical sermon, say, rather than a college lecture. Some Western mystics will remain content with a denial that what they've just written and and published between covers is in fact a book. (A book? Oh no, not me.)

7. *Let's get literary and metaphorical.* Because the totality cannot be directly represented, it can be apprehended only in metaphor. It is kind of *like* this or that, but it isn't exactly the same, see. Eastern mystics seem to express themselves rather naturally through poetry and metaphor, since for the most part they came from traditions which favored those forms of expression. Rather more

awkwardly and self-consciously, Western mystic philosophers will assert that their work is really a form of literature, even though it may not be.

8. *Slinking around the margins.* One is looking for signs of the great one. Mysterious coincidences. Notes in the margins. Strange subtexts. You can't just believe what they tell you. There's something else going on here, I swear.

9. *It's all a conspiracy.* Everything is interconnected, everything can be explained —it's all a plot! Suspect even yourself. Your very ways of thinking are part of the plot. In Western thought, the very idea of Western thought is the best example of this kind of conspiratorial mysticism.

10. *Circles, please, no lines.* Lines begin, end, and divide. They are vaguely male. Circles are always the preferred geometry of mysticism. In the West, this geometrical preference informs many arguments, as in circular arguments, which prove their premise by means of their conclusion.

11. *No time left.* Time is an illusion. Time divides things into then and now. It allows for change. It is horribly linear. It makes the mystical experience just another event in a long and random sequence of events. Western mystics frequently complain about a supposedly Western *conception* of time, though in the end, like the Easterners, they really want to get rid of time altogether, to live in an eternal now.

12. *A good number.* Ever since Pythagoras, if not before, it has been understood that any list of things which purports to express ultimate reality should be of a number that itself reflects something about ultimate reality. Most Westerners, like Pythagoras, liked the number three. It's got a beginning, middle, and end—how can you beat that? But twelve is not a bad number either (number of apostles, signs of the zodiac, and so on). When asked to produce a list of the key categories of all thought, for example, a Western mystic would never opt for ugly prime numbers like eleven or thirteen.

I now offer a series of principles, according to which one may predict some aspects of the course of the history of philosophy.

---

**The Omnivorousness Principle**. Any mystical philosophy will be able to account for all other philosophies.

*Proof.* The mystical philosophy is in possession of the One. Since All is One, everything else, including every other philosophy, belongs to this One.

*Scholium.* Among vulgar mystics, this leads to a "my-mysticism-is-better-than-your-mysticism" syndrome. In more refined cases, it results in a "my-mysticism-is-your-mysticism-and-everybody-else's" syndrome.

---

**The Principle of Esoteric Comparison.** When viewed from inside the mystical experience, i.e. esoterically, any two mystical philosophies may be shown to be the same.

*Proof.* Both mystical philosophies refer to the One. Since there is only one One, both philosophies express the same thing. Differences between philosophies may be labeled "exoteric." They are superficial, and relevant only to those who stand outside the mystical experience.

**The Indeterminacy of Interpretation Principle.** A mystical philosophy cannot be fully and conclusively expressed or interpreted.

*Proof.* Any interpretation will be particular, will define the philosophy with respect to its other. Since the philosophy must ultimately refer to the One and only One, all such interpretations must be false. This may also be seen as a natural result of the ineffability of the mystical experience.

**The Principle of the Eternal Defensibility of Any Philosophy.** No mystical philosophy can be decisively refuted on its own terms.

*Scholium.* Ever notice how scholars who specialize in one philosopher or period in the history of philosophy can always come up with defenses against criticisms of their chosen philosophy(ies)? Ever notice how conspiracy theorists have the ability to turn every piece of evidence into support for their views? These two phenomena are quite closely related. A mystical philosopher can be defended against any criticism because he is in possession of the One. Everything fits into the plot, because the plot is the One. Here is an instance of how this functions: When a philosopher is accused of adopting a particular point of view, one locates a quote suggesting he held precisely the opposite view. Such a quote can always be found, because the mystical One includes all opposites.

**Fractal Principle of the History of Philosophy.** The history of philosophy *qua* mysticism is a fractal: The smallest piece may contain the whole.

*Definition.* Fractals are complex shapes consisting of patterns which repeat themselves in infinite forms and sizes. A coastline, for example, may be thought of as a fractal, in that it may have approximately the same rugged contour whether viewed from a few hundred feet or a few hundred miles above. Though chaotic, in that its shape in any given area is inherently random, the fractal may be generated with a few simple mathematical equations.

*Proof.* In mysticism, every part is what it is only in the whole. The full understanding of any part, no matter how small, therefore entails an understanding of the whole. Each mystical philosophy, likewise, becomes what it is only in the context of the whole of philosophy (which, as we know from the above principles, any philosophy may be taken to represent). Therefore, the full understanding of any single philosophy is the same as a full understanding of the whole history.

*Scholium 1.* The history of philosophy, as we know from experience, consists of a pattern repeated in a variety of forms and at various levels. The pattern, furthermore, is driven by a few, simple principles (such as this one). The point of the history is to find those principles which most economically explain the diverse manifestations of philosophy. The principles, to be sure, stand outside the history, and so are ultimately not really philosophical principles, but just guidelines of a sort.

*Scholium 2.* The pattern that constitutes the history might very well be available in a single period, a single philosopher, a single book, chapter, or a solitary aphorism. This book, and the entire history of philosophy with it, could be rewritten as the exegesis of a single philosophical maxim. (I suggest one of Nietzsche's, perhaps.)

# MEDIEVAL PHILOSOPHY

## *Trouble in the Monastery*

With those funny haircuts, the brown robes held up with old rope, and their obvious weight-control problems—who's going to trust the monks to reveal the truth about everything? Let's face it: From a modern point of view the medieval philosophers seem to be irrelevant scholastics. They quibbled and commented but rarely advanced a thought of their own. They were dogmatists, hopelessly compromised by their religious commitments and the institutions around them. Above all, they held back the march of science. All of which is pretty much true, in a certain sense: these are called the Dark Ages for a reason. But it is also false, in a more subtle way.

There was one holy and apostolic church, in those days, but there was certainly more than one way of thinking, and not all philosophers wore the same brown dress. Medieval thought covers a much broader range than the usual story assumes. Most importantly, I will argue, it includes (though perhaps in different proportions) all the basic ideas that would later be attributed to the early modern philosophers and credited with the creation of modern science. Whatever the causes of the transformation which connect that dark night to our own bright day, then, philosophy is not among them.

So they had a bit of us. On top of that, though, we have quite a large piece of them. It would be nice if theology were merely an ancient practice, of no particular interest to modern philosophers. On the contrary, I will argue, modern philosophy is, for the most part, a disguised and dishonest form of theology, which is in turn a dishonest form of faith. The theological aspect of medieval thought is therefore worth elaborating, since it provides a key to understanding much of what comes later.

What follows takes the same general pattern as the discussion of Eastern philosophy in the preceding chapter. It begins with a presentation of a bit of the vast range of medieval thought. It then turns to a form of religious thought known as natural theology, not to lend credence to the idea that the medievals had nothing but religious thoughts, but because their religious thought is a useful key to understanding much of the rest of the history of philosophy.

# I. THE DIALECTIC OF MEDIEVAL THOUGHT

## FACTS AND FIGURES

The medieval philosophical tradition begins in late antiquity. The first great philosopher of the era is usually considered to be Augustine (354–430). He was soon joined by Ambrose, Jerome, and the rest of the so-called patristics, or fathers of the church. (This group, by the way, represented most of the history of thought for later medieval philosophers. The Neoplatonists who preceded and influenced Augustine were also important to the later medievals, and so could also be grouped, in the Greek fashion, as Premedievals.) Between the fall of Rome in the fifth century and the Islamic philosophical revival of the eleventh, philosophy became a vehicle for mystical expression of Christian faith. Boethius (ca. 480), Duns Scotus Erigena (810–877), and Anselm (1033–1109) are three of the few remembered names which mark this long passage of time. In the eleventh and twelfth centuries, the Arabs on the Iberian peninsula, notably Abu Ali ibn Sina, or Avicenna (980–1037), and Abu al-Walid ibn Ahmad ibn Rushd, or Averroës (1126–1198), revived Aristotle and produced the first of the great rationalist-Aristotelian theologies. Around this time a powerful Jewish school of thought was growing and reached its greatest expression in the Spaniard Maimonides (1135–1204). Meanwhile, back in the Western church, not much was happening except opposition to that suspicious Greek, Aristotle. By the thirteenth and fourteenth centuries, however, the Western church reversed itself and allowed Aristotelianism to become the central feature of the rejuvenation of Christian theology. These are the so-called high Middle Ages, the heartland of medieval philosophy. They were dominated (at least in retrospect) by Thomas Aquinas (1225–1274). Shortly after Aquinas's death, his critics John Duns Scotus (1266–1308) and William of Ockham (1280?–1349) held sway. As the Protestant Reformation approached, rationalist theology again gave in to mysticism, in Nicolas of Cusa (1401–1464), the Neoplatonists of Florence, and Jakob Boehme (1575–1624).

The context within which philosophical works were produced is as important here as everywhere. The most obvious consideration is that all these thinkers were in some way affiliated with religious institutions. They were monks and friars (Anselm was a Benedictine; Duns Scotus and Ockham were Franciscans; Aquinas was a Dominican), bishops (Augustine, Anselm), and rabbis (Maimonides). The universities with which several were associated (Aquinas with Paris; Ockham with Oxford; Duns Scotus with Oxford, Paris, and Cologne) were an invention of the high Middle Ages and closely linked to the church. Their environment naturally gave form to the writings of the medievals. A number of philosophical genres are unique or at least uniquely germane to the Middle Ages. In part because of their training in scriptural exegesis, in part because of a tendency to revere authority, and in part just because they were educators, the medievals produced much of their work in the form of commentaries. One of Aquinas's longest (and most frighteningly boring) books is a thousand-plus page commentary on Aristotle's *Metaphysics*. Another curiously medieval form of literature is the disputation. Much of their intellectual life took place in debating seminars, in which teachers and students would match rhetorical skills over famous questions like "are there worms in hell?" The queen of the medieval genres, though, was the *summa*, or summary (as in the summary for the prosecution). In these massive works the author would collect the major questions and answers on a particular topic, for the stated purpose of providing a textbook and introduction to the subject matter for students. On the whole, we could say that the requirements of pedagogy and of institutionalized religion were dominant in shaping the form of medieval philosophical literature.

---

*EasyReader Notes*

Augustine's *Confessions*. I was bad—sooo bad. As a teenager I stole some pears. For the fun of it! And I wanted to have sex! What an evil person I was. Now I have managed to control my passions. I devote myself to the life of God and Christianity. I have helped set up a few hundred thousand churches.

---

The fundamental question for the mainstream of medieval philosophy was this: Can the demands of faith be reconciled with the dictates of reason? Can reason serve faith? How could those ancient Greek philosophers, who are all going to hell, have been so clever? The incipient dialectic can be thought of as simply faith versus reason. Or, it can be summed up in two names: Augustine versus Aristotle.

The early medieval thinkers tended to take the side of faith. I believe because it is absurd, the Latin *pater* Tertullian said, not because it has been proven (which it can't be, of course; that would be absurd). Augustine, the first in line, was an incontinent writer, covering everything from sense knowledge to sin, and yet he had only one ultimate reality: the experience of his conversion to Christianity. Everything else he explained with reference to this touchstone of his life. He conceived of theology as a kind of post-experience reflection into the self, an attempt to know oneself in order thereby to know God. His journeys into philosophy-land, the quasi-Platonic epistemological discussions, the analyses of Aristotelian categories, his work on evil, the freedom of the will, and the nature of the cosmos, began and ended in faith: "believe in order that you may understand," he said. In the final analysis, for Augustine, the truth is all personal, all in the grace of God's love.

Six hundred years later, along came the ghost of Aristotle. The problem with Aristotle, for the medievals, was that his philosophy might actually be *true*, or so they thought. This would be no bad thing, were it not that Aristotle was a pagan animal-fat burner and that he appeared to arrive at his conclusions by means of pure reason (with a bit of natural philosophy thrown in). The danger, for the religious folk, was that revelation might become subordinate to philosophical reason. Averroës, the Islamic thinker who reintroduced Aristotle to European society, was indeed a radical rationalist, and produced a theology in which the requirements of reason would determine the course of faith. The most famous of the Aristotelians was Aquinas. Many have labeled his work a "synthesis" of Aristotelianism and Christianity. In his attempt to bring Aristotle into the Christian fold, Aquinas deployed three main tactics. First, by carpet-bombing the Aristotelian corpus with commentaries, he demonstrated that a broad range of Aristotle's doctrines, including those on the soul, on the idea of substance, and his ethics, could be interpreted in as consistent with Christian teaching about the immortality of the soul, the existence of God, and the dictates of morality. Second, with the focused application of overwhelming firepower, he showed that many religiously incorrect interpretations of the philosopher, such as the Arab view that Aristotle believed in some kind of universal Mind shared by all humans, were unfounded. Third, where outright contradiction between Aristotle and church doctrine was unavoidable, as in the question of whether the world had a beginning or not, Aquinas argued that the matter could not in any case be decided by reason, but could only be settled peacefully, as a matter of faith.

Aquinas made many people unhappy. So the pendulum swung back. By the time of the Reformation, mysticism and unreasoned faith were again dominant in Christian thinking, and Aristotelian theology was a thing of the past. This failure did not actually bother many in church and flock. Many were unsympathetic to the theological philosophers. As they saw it, submission to proof may demean God. It might make his existence a necessary consequence of logic, not the reverse. Proof can be refuted with new evidence. Moreover, proof begins with doubt, with the possibility that there might be a disproof. It is not for those with faith. Theology claims to have discovered God in nature, but it carries skepticism in its heart. It is a dishonest form of faith.

## MEDIEVAL EMPIRICISM

What should be made clear is that the dialectic of medieval philosophy encompasses a wide range of philosophical positions—a range much wider than that typically attributed to the medievals. In fact, one of those possible positions is a relatively complete empiricism.

Paradoxically, such an empiricism could and did come from one, namely, Ockham, who seemed to stand on the side of faith against reason. The paradox, however, is merely apparent: In opposing the use of reason to settle matters of faith, Ockham also opposed the use of faith to settle matters of reason (or, better said, matters of knowledge). He argued that God could have made the world any way he chose, and he just happened to choose the one we've got. Thus, everything is contingent, and could be otherwise. So, if we are to know anything about the world, we will have to go out and look at it, study it, and not deduce it from pure reason. In a violently anti-Platonic gesture, he asserted that the only things that exist, in the material sense, are individuals, or particular things. For proofs of the existence of God and so forth Ockham had no use. His faith at bottom may have been the same as that of Aquinas and the rest; but in its expression it allowed for a thoroughly empirical and materialistic approach to acquiring knowledge about this world. If conceptual breakthroughs are what drive scientific progress, it is hard to explain why the scientific revolution did not begin quite a bit earlier than it did.

Ockham is most famous now for his razor, which is the principle that, in logical explanations, entities ought not to be multiplied needlessly. The razor shaves off entities that are not necessary for understanding. The danger, as one limerick writer may have been aware, was that most of the rest of philosophy, including Ockham's, just might prove unnecessary.

*Ockham, the Razor Man*

There once was a man named Ockham
Who invented a wonderful scam
A razor have I
Said he with great pride
Which cuts off the fat from the ham

He wielded his toy with great speed
And shaved off the things of no need
But Ockham one day
Got carried away
And sliced himself out like a weed.

I do not mean to imply that Ockham was a solitary beacon of empiricist thought in a night of rationalists and theologians. On the contrary, the basic empiricist idea that knowledge comes from sensory experience, was a recurrent theme throughout the medieval period. From Augustine to Aquinas, Aristotle's suggestion that there is nothing in the mind which did not first pass through the senses was an enormously important thought. Of course, sitting there with nothing to do in those unheated monasteries, the monks managed to turn such a sensible idea into lots of hot air.

# II. (UN)NATURAL THEOLOGY (?)

Let's distinguish, as the medievals did, between natural and revealed theology. The latter consists of the interpretation of the word of God as delivered by an accepted authority (usually the Bible). We could call this form of theology religious interpretation—or, in its narrower application, scriptural exegesis—without much loss of meaning. Natural theology, on the other hand, seeks to establish (some or all) religious truths by means available to all thinking people. It takes nature and reason as its starting points, rather than accepted authority, and seeks to prove rather than merely interpret. It is to natural theology that I referred above in stating that philosophy is a form of theology. I also referred to it as rationalist theology.

The dialectic of medieval thought might therefore be re-expressed in this question: Is natural theology possible? The early and later thinkers tended to say no, you just have to believe, and those in between, the high medievalists, tended to say yes, we can prove anything you like.

The specific problems confronted by natural theology depend on the particular faith it seeks to uphold. In medieval times, the dominant faith in Western Europe was Roman Catholicism, and this fact obviously influenced the direction of medieval natural theology. The specific problematics of the medievals, in turn, shaped much of the dialogue of early modern philosophy. So I will now run through a list of the specific problems that faced natural theology, such as it existed in those dark years. In the end, just to anticipate things a little, the problems become quite general, no longer merely medieval, and illustrate how theology, mysticism, and philosophy eventually merge into, well, philosophy.

## THE PROBLEM OF EVIL

If God rules the world, why are things are so bad? Of the many possible answers to this question, two are most typical. The first is to deny the second premise. No, things are not bad. Everything is for the best, etc.; what you call bad is just a temporary and necessary privation of good. This response is a favorite among philosophers, and would become more important during the seventeenth and eighteenth centuries than it is now. The second answer is that it's our fault. God created us, gave us free will, and because we are such horrible creatures, look what a mess we've made of things. (Hey, isn't there a compromise position somewhere?)

## IN THE BEGINNING . . .

Aristotle said that the world was eternal. There was no beginning. Plus, he had the proofs to back up his thesis. But the Bible said the world did have a beginning, that it was created by God. Who was right?

## FREE WILL

If God knows everything, he knows what we will do. So we have no free will. So we should not be punished. Since it is pretty hard to imagine sin without free will, and pretty hard to imagine the Christian church without sin, most theological philosophers found this logic problematic. They felt a need to demonstrate the reality of free will. Philosophers in search of a mystical union with God, on the other hand, usually choose to oppose free will. For the mystically inclined, everything is part of the One, which is necessarily as it is, unchanging, and fixed. So free will must be an illusion. Both sides of the conflict between the doctrines of free will and determinism drew strength from Christian tenets, so the conflict remained alive for quite some time.

## IMMORTALITY OF THE SOUL

The doctrine that the soul is immortal presents the theologian with a daunting task: Prove a doctrine true for which there exists no credible evidence. The doctrine, by the way, was a favorite among philosophers for a long time before Christianity—Pythagoras and Plato, to name just two. The obvious way to prove the doctrine would be to discover, observe, and document the activities of a dead person's soul. Short of that, proofs based on logic or "self-evident" axioms are about as sensible as logical proofs that there exists a ten-foot rabbit. Duns Scotus was one of the few who frankly admitted that there was no convincing proof of the immortality of the soul.

## CHRISTIAN MUMBO JUMBO

Much of what is specifically Christian can be left to revealed theology, and so passed over in this history of philosophy. Because all these matters were jumbled together, however, a number of specifically Christian and Catholic notions made their way into the philosophical tradition and remained for quite a while as problems, metaphors, and so on.

For example, the doctrine of the Trinity fueled speculation about the nature of substance, mainly because in the orthodox version it seemed to presuppose the philosophically suspect proposition that one substance, God, could also be three. The notion that Jesus was not just a prophet, but the incarnation of God, would also be important. The doctrine of transubstantiation meant that metaphysicians had to allow that some matter should have some unusual properties at some times. Otherwise, reasonable people might have doubted that ordinary bread should become the body of Christ at the insistence of a priest during the Catholic mass. More significantly, the incarnation of God and the apotheosis of man would become the driving metaphors of much of the Romantic philosophy to come.

## THE EXISTENCE OF GOD

The proof of the existence of God: This is the defining moment of natural theology. For the medievals it was a question not just of what sort of proof one should adopt, but of the way in which one conceives of "proof," and whether or not such a proof is meaningful. Let us first describe some of the favorite kinds of proof:

*Argument from Gallup.* The official name for this is the argument *ex consensu gentium.* It says that the only way to explain the fact that a vast majority of people over a vast majority of time have believed in God is to assume that God actually exists. There are some small problems with this argument. For instance, what happens if the polls go the other way? Does the existence of God really hinge on public opinion? Also, what about the fact that a majority of people throughout history have also believed, for example, that glass is a solid. Does this make it true? As a matter of principle, the fact the something is believed to be true does not prove that it is true.

*Argument from Design.* Everything in the world serves a purpose. For example, apples are there to be eaten. Therefore, the world as a whole must have a purpose. Alternatively: everything fits together so marvelously. Apples are just the right size for our mouths, plus they taste good. Things must have been designed that way. Hence there must be a Designer. This might also be called the "hills and valleys" proof. Ever wondered how we are fortunate enough to have both hills and valleys? How they fit together so wonderfully? There must be a God. This proof is quite weak, since it can really only claim to establish a strong probability that there is a God, not a certainty. It can be traced to Aristotle's notion of the 'final cause'. It would become more important in the seventeenth century than it was in the Middle Ages.

*Proof by Infinite Regress.* There is motion. Every motion has a mover. Unless we assume an infinite regress (which for some reason really scared the medievals), there must have been a first mover. The same argument can be used with "causes" (there must be a "first cause") or just plain "change" (a "first changer"?) The motion version may be found in Aristotle.

*Proof by Contingency.* Everything around us is contingent. Everything could be otherwise than it is. Since contingency and necessity are a pair, there must be an ultimate necessity somewhere to account for all these contingencies. This ultimately necessary being is, surprise, God. This argument can be thought of as a logical (as opposed to temporal or sequential) version of the infinite regress: One contingency can be explained by the next, but the last one is absolute necessary. It is also distantly related to Aristotle's notion of pure actuality. What is contingent is merely possible, and could be otherwise. Possibility itself, however, is only possible on account of some pure actuality, something which is the way it has to be, and could not (possibly) be otherwise. So, God is what Aristotle postulates at the start of the chain of potentialities and actualities.

*The Ontological Proof.* This is the big daddy of them all. It was given its name in later days, by Kant, who argued (correctly) that most other proofs are just versions of this one. The first recognized version of the ontological proof came from Anselm. Anselm argued that since God was so perfect, he had to have everything, and since existence is a better predicate than nonexistence, existence must be predicated of God. I think of Anselm's proof as "the fish-story proof":

> I caught a fish soooo big, it had all the predicates, including existence.

Aristotle, in a lost dialogue, had already offered something similar, in what I think of as the "ice cream proof."

> There is good ice cream, better ice cream, and mmm, mmm! the best; so there must be a best being.

(Unexpectedly, the best being turns out to be not Aristotle himself, but God.)

If the ontological proof was tops, the top of the ontologicals was Aquinas's proof, which was so good it wasn't even really a proof. It was more like a definition, or an explanation. It went like this: God is the being whose essence it is to exist. Think of it this way: Any particular thing you can think of, from a computer to a unicorn, may or may not exist. Its essence, the what-it-is of it, is independent of the little fact that it happens to exist (or not). Not so with God. God is inconceivable without existence. Put another way, existence is part of the definition of God. In still other words: To understand the concept of God is at the same time to know that He exists. This notion can be traced to the biblical self-description of God as "I am that I am" (which could be understood with the inflection, "I am He who is").

As a proof, of course, Aquinas's idea was preposterous. It was a circumvention, an attempt to include within the definition precisely what was to be proved. One might as well prove that unicorns exist by defining them as "one-horned horses that exist." In a characteristically philosophical manner, Aquinas dragged the matter out by further refining and redefining the concepts of essence and existence, especially as applied to God—which just amounted to more circumvention.

As with the proof of the immortality of the soul, the proper way to "prove" the existence of God is to see him. If one were to convince an impartial witness, one should arrange to bring God forth for observation, documentation, and perhaps a demonstration of his powers. Failing that, all the logic in world will not prove or disprove the existence of God or any other creature.

## THE NATURE OF GOD

Suppose you've proved the existence of God. Now what? You've got another problem: the nature of God. What does he (she?) look like? What does it do during the day? It is an odd thing, logically speaking, that the proofs of the existence of God tended to carry certain implications for the nature of God. After all, when philosophers prove the existence of chairs, they don't usually presume to deduce from their proof the nature of chairs, like whether they have three legs or four. Yet the God coming out of the proof-process looked very different from the traditional God, Biblical or otherwise, who went in. Most interesting is the way in which the Christian, Islamic, and Jewish theologians converged in their depiction of this newly abstracted God. It seems that in order to arrive at a God of whose existence they could be certain, the theologians had to strip the poor fellow of all particularity. Paradoxically, this occurred just as they were making sure that God had everything, all the best predicates they could find. In making him everything, they reduced him to nothing.

---

**The Tediousification of God Principle.** Natural theology makes God a Bore.

*Proof.* All proofs of the existence of God derive from the ontological proof. The ontological proof maintains that God is that whose essence it is to exist. The essence of existence, however, is to have no particular attributes. Anything which may be conceived may possibly be conceived to exist, and since existence is true of any possible concept, it distinguishes nothing from anything else. Therefore, etc.

*Scholium.* The God who comes out of philosophical proofs is thoroughly abstract, defined negatively, everything in general but nothing in particular. He goes from being indescribable to being nondescript.

---

All of this was especially disturbing to medieval thinkers, inasmuch as their intention had been to revise the Aristotelian proofs in a manner consistent with their religious doctrines. They had themselves noted and sought to overcome the fact that Aristotle had already used many of their arguments to prove the existence of a Prime Mover who, sitting aloof outside the celestial spheres, did not look at all like the Judeo-Christian or Islamic God.

## THE VIA NEGATIVA

The vanishing of God in his own proof is our clue that the link between natural theology and mysticism is very strong, at least at a conceptual level. At the core of mysticism we discover the necessary ineffability of the mystical experience. The Tao, the Hindu Om, and the whole Zen experience have in common that they (supposedly) cannot be put into words. Interestingly, the theologian's God tended toward precisely the same status. Aquinas argued that the only thing we can know about God is that he exists. Beyond that, he is unthinkable. One can imagine something as big and wonderful as God only in terms of analogies. We could draw comparisons which might shed some light, but none that would be adequate to the great Incomparable. Like the proverbial fish, one might say: "as big as a house; no! bigger; as big as an airplane; no! . . ." But the real master of this way of thinking was Maimonides, who prescribed the *via negativa* as the only true route to God. Let's pick up the trail where the fish story left off.

> God is soooo big, there is nothing you can say about Him that would be adequate. He is not a chair, for he is bigger than a chair; not a car; not a jet airplane; not a speeding bullet . . .

## THE END OF THEOLOGY

It is curious that the medieval era in theology came to an end roughly where it started, in a kind of mysticism. No doubt the causes for this were chiefly the same historical circumstances that gave rise to the Reformation: Loss of faith in the institutional church, a longing for unmediated spiritual contact, and the growing power of national political units must have played a part.

It is worth noting that one factor in bringing the high Middle Ages to a close was satire. A new breed of writers came forth, independent spirits like Montaigne (1533–1593), who poured scorn on the old ways of the scholastics. They mocked the hair-splitting arguments over pointless questions. Who cares how many angels can dance on the head of a pin? they asked. The ridicule, more than anything else, cost scholastic theology its aura of authority, and thereafter it suffered inexorable decline. This pattern of advance through ridicule was not the sole property of the early modern era. We saw it among the Hellenistic skeptics, among the Hindus, and perhaps it is even occurring today, as we speak.

## THE HOLY GRAIL OF PHILOSOPHY

In a sense, natural theology is an abstraction removed from religion. It identifies God merely with the abstract category which should correspond to his nature. The abstract category which corresponds to God is ultimately just 'being'. This is why Aquinas's ontological proof is tops, the essence of natural theology. And while the category of God is thought too rich to be limited by any specific attributes, in fact, as the category of being, it is too poor to sustain any attributes. This is why the tediousification of God is not just a curious side effect, but a necessary consequence of natural theology.

All of this is of more than just passing interest in the history of philosophy. The tediousification of God is, in my view, the crucial evidence for the ultimate identification of natural theology and philosophy. Having robbed God of specific attributes, natural theology has no reason to stop short of also removing his name. Aristotle's substance, or Plotinus's One, Parmenides' truth, and all the philosophical creatures whose essence is to exist, are not merely similar to Aquinas's God; they are *identical*. Whatever name it takes, this miraculous entity, whose thought entails its being, is the Holy Grail of philosophy, and will be discovered (and then lost) a number of times more before we are through with this history. Thus, I conclude: All philosophy, insofar as it is the search for the Holy Grail of philosophy, is the proof of the existence of God, or, what is the same thing, philosophy is natural theology.

# Early Modern Philosophy

## Avant Garde or Rearguard?

The sixteenth and seventeenth centuries were times of great change in Europe. The Church, the feudal order, and authority in general were out; nature, the ancient world, the New World, and individualism were in. Among the in crowd, science was the hottest thing going. There can be no question about the value of the achievements of early modern science. This was the time when Galileo (1564–1642) was throwing coins off the Leaning Tower of Pisa, and blinding himself by looking at the sun through his telescope. These were the happy days when Johannes Kepler discovered that the planets do more than just go around in circles, and came up with the laws to prove it; when that fateful apple hit Isaac Newton on the head; when William Harvey discovered that the heart was more than just the seat of the soul, and that it also pumped blood around the body; and when Gottfried Wilhelm Leibniz and Newton had their famous spat about who invented differential calculus. No doubt a good number of the general convictions shared by most people today about what sort of creatures we are and what kind of world this is had their origin in these early years of modern science.

The story of the rise of modern philosophy and with it the scientific consciousness is by now of almost mythic proportions. Philosophy, or so the story goes, swept the Augean stables of the human mind free of theological rubbish, and with Promethean fire forged the conceptual framework of modern science. In less dramatic versions of the story, philosophy was at least a vanguard of the new scientific spirit, with its emphasis on the experimental method, mathematical rigor, and objectivity. Whether as demiurge or pathfinder, philosophy brought scientific rationality into the world.

I intend to show that this story is fundamentally untrue. It misrepresents the nature and role of philosophy in the development of modern science. Specifically, it mistakes the direction of influence between early modern philosophy and science. Scientific advances inspired much of the philosophy of the early modern period. The

153

resulting philosophy, however, did not serve as a foundation for scientific work, nor was it in fact scientific. Philosophy did not pave the way for scientific advances; indeed, as often as not, it threw up obstacles to further advance. For its time, modern philosophy was actually far closer in methods and overall objectives to the scholastic philosophies it supposedly rejected, and through them to the ancient philosophers, than it was to modern science. Furthermore, those aspects of the early modern philosophers' work which the later tradition has identified as distinctively philosophical are its most unreasonable, unscientific, and atavistic elements.

The pattern and the content of the early modern revolution in philosophy can already be found in any number of previous philosophical revolutions. Their rejection of scholastic theology, for example, was no different in principle and in informing ideas than the high medieval, Neoaristotelian revolt against early Christian theology. Their mechanistic metaphysics had no more scientific basis than that of the ancient atomists, and was deployed for parallel philosophical purposes. Democritus had long ago conceived of the strategy of toppling Aristotle with little corpuscles; Aristotle's own rebellion against Plato had many of the same features. Philosophy has always rebelled against itself in this way, all the way back to the Presocratics' assaults on their own nameless, cosmo-babbling predecessors.

Of course, it remains an interesting and important historical fact that science made significant advances in the early modern period. If philosophy cannot account for this fact, something else must. Actually, I think, we need not look too far for an explanation: An historical fact calls for an historical explanation. Mostly likely, the accumulation of certain social changes gradually produced a group of people who could benefit from the new science, and/or removed those who might have been threatened by new science, or something like that. But this takes us outside the history of philosophy, and beyond the scope of our lengthy discussion.

From *The Psychoanalyst's Handbook on Philosophers*

**Physics Envy.** *Definition.* Covetousness of philosopher with respect to achievements and worldly status of physical science. The philosopher wants to achieve real advances in human knowledge, but is unable to match those offered by physicists. The philosopher feels deficient, perhaps lacking in manliness, and compensates by adopting some of the perceived behaviors of the physicists: firmness, rigor, objectivity, methodicalness, abstraction, lawfulness. Typically, the philosopher overcompensates and practices hyperabstraction, rigor mortis, method for its own sake, etc., and thereby tends to become dysfunctional. The condition first becomes acute in the seventeenth century when achievements like Galileo's discovery of the moons of Jupiter and Newton's articulation of the laws of motion make philosophers feel really useless. In the more general form of an envy of all scientific and professional disciplines, it becomes the driving force of academic philosophy at modern universities through the twentieth century.

**Kleptologia.** *Definition.* Condition afflicting philosophers. Chief symptom is the compulsive and systematic theft of the discoveries of the sciences on behalf of philosophy. Cases typically begin with indications of physics envy. The sufferer conceals his or her misdeeds by converting the scientific discovery into an (apparently) logical or metaphysical distinction. This behavior can be quite destructive and illogical, so immediate treatment is imperative. Any philosopher found leafing through scientific journals or sneaking through laboratories should be examined and, as appropriate, provided with truth therapy. Seventeenth-century philosophers tend to "borrow" their discoveries from physical mechanics and optics. Among late-twentieth-century academics, the condition is marked among the self-styled philosophers of mind, who can usually be found trailing cognitive psychologists or lurking around neurology labs.

**Science Fanaticism.** *Definition.* General term for exaggerated expectations for scientific philosophy. Usually occurs in a nonscientist or amateur scientist. Can also be caused by exposure to high mathematics among amateur mathematicians. The consequence is a fantasy about the philosophy which will result with the new application of the methods of science.

# WHO'S ON FIRST?

Francis Bacon (1561–1626) is often named as the first of the philosophers who made room for science. Bacon lambasted the "idols" which obscure men's proper understanding of things, and believed that the mind should be cleared of prejudice. It should be cleared, in particular, of Aristotle, whose scholastic followers Bacon despised. Bacon offered a *Novuum Organum*, a new system of knowledge designed explicitly to replace the old one by Aristotle. In it he advocated something like what we would call "the scientific method"—i.e., controlled observation through experiment.

Bacon's countryman Thomas Hobbes (1588–1679) was another hero of the new movement. He was best known for his uncompromisingly materialist view of the world. Everything is just matter in motion, Hobbes, argued, and he proceeded to analyze everything up to the modern nation-state in terms of little corpuscles bouncing around in the void.

"The privilege of absurdity [is something] to which no living creature is subject, but man only. And of men, those of all are more subject to it, that profess philosophy."  Hobbes

If we had to choose a single figure as the spokesperson of the revolution, however, it would be René Descartes (1596–1650). So he's on first. Baruch Spinoza (1632–1677) and Gottfried Wilhelm Leibniz (1646–1716) are usually thrown in as the other two musketeers of seventeenth-century rationalism, and I will follow the traditional order. From there the story crosses the Channel, and we go with it, to visit the empirical threesome of John Locke (1632–1704), George Berkeley (1685–1753), and David Hume (1711–1776). I then try to mop up a few of the many remaining odds and ends from the early modern philosophy, before leaping into the airy heights of German Idealism.

# Descartes

## I Drink Therefore I Am

"Nothing can be imagined which is too strange or incredible to have been said by some philosopher."

Descartes

## MAN OR MYTH?

René Descartes was "the father of modern philosophy," or so the story goes. He slew the medieval dragon of Aristotelian scholasticism. He championed the method of pure, introspective reason. He paved the way for modern science. He established the epistemological project which would be the foundation of modern philosophy. And he placed the individual self, the ego, at the center of philosophy's—and the rest of humankind's—concern. For both good and ill, in fact, Descartes was probably the father of all modern thought, the man who introduced enlightened reason and individualism into the world.

It amounts to a tremendous responsibility, and an extraordinary—almost mythological—achievement, for one man. But did it happen? At first glance, Descartes's writings may cause a certain disappointment. The myth, it seems, has a tenuous basis in some rather unconvincing arguments. But we shall see. And who comes up with these myths, anyway?

> **Biofact.** The celebrity Descartes achieved in his lifetime may have cost him his life. Queen Christina of Sweden thought that the hottest first philosopher of the day might make a pleasing addition to her court. Descartes accepted her invitation to become her tutor, and moved up north to Stockholm. But the bitter cold was more than he could bear, and within a year he died.

# Will the Real Descartes Please Step Forward?

Descartes was a man of many hats, though he is now remembered chiefly by philosophers and almost exclusively through his philosophical writings. The most studied of these is his *Meditations on First Philosophy* (1641). The most straightforward and traditional understanding of Descartes therefore consists of the doctrines put forth in his philosophical works. We will cover this ground in section I. Partly because these doctrines turn out to be incoherent, another level of interpretation emerges. Still sticking to the philosophical texts, the notion here is that the supposed doctrines were merely provisional or meditational in nature. Descartes used them to guide the reader toward a certain self-transformation, an enlightenment. Thus level II: Descartes as inspirational writer. In section III we try to make sense of Descartes's philosophical writings within the broader context of his writings and activity as a whole. The emphasis here is on the relation between his philosophical and his scientific work, and on the practical, worldly objectives of his philosophical work.

# I

## Doubtful Method

Descartes's philosophy arose out of a reflection on the method of scientific investigation. The notion that Descartes discovered and advocated a particular method of investigation—in both science and philosophy—is central to his paternal status in the history of philosophy.

In his earliest philosophical work, the *Rules for the Direction of the Mind*, written in 1628–1629 but unpublished during his lifetime, Descartes begins a list of twenty-one rules from which I paraphrase the following three:

1. The aim of any study should be to form true judgments.

2. We should study only what is capable of being truly known.

3. We should study what can be truly known, and not just what we and others happen to believe.

In further discussion he offers useful insights like "never assume to be true anything that is false," and, for the mathematically inclined, "never use multiplication when division is in order."

Descartes's first famous philosophical work, the *Discourse on the Method of Directing Reason and Searching for Truth in the Sciences* (1637), was actually a preface to a much longer set of three essays on topics ranging from optics to meteorology to geometry. In the *Discourse* Descartes reduces the twenty-one rules to just four, which may be paraphrased thus:

1. Avoid prejudice.

2. Divide problems into as many parts as possible.

3. Start with simple things, then move to the complex.

4. Don't leave anything out.

In reviewing these rules, Leibniz was not impressed. He said these are "like the precepts of some chemist: Take what you need and do what you should and you will get what you want." There is nothing wrong with Descartes's prescriptions. They can serve as reminders, a kind of sanity checklist. But as a method they amount to nothing more than the exhortation Be methodical!

The discussion of the Cartesian method could end here. So far as the method of science is concerned, Descartes has nothing more to say. Things become more interesting, and problematic, precisely as he begins to develop a specific method, one that might be applied to philosophy itself. Descartes's method, insofar as it is distinct, rather than the general method that comes from being methodical, goes something like this:

1. Reject all beliefs that can conceivably be doubted.

2. Express the remaining belief(s) in axiomatic form.

3. Systematically reconstruct all knowledge on the basis of the axiom(s).

Step one of the general method could be a version of the rule to "avoid prejudice." In Descartes's case, it was clearly a part of his rejection of the authority of Aristotle and the scholastics. Steps two and three could be just an exhortation to be systematic, to show how one's knowledge interrelates.

Yet something distinctly unreasonable creeps in at this point. To treat as false everything that can conceivably be doubted is not the same thing as avoiding prejudice, or suspending judgment on that for which one has insufficient evidence. It is reasonable to doubt that for which one has insufficient evidence; it is unreasonable to reject all that one can doubt. Everything can conceivably be doubted, in which case all that would be left after step one to express in step two is a version of "nothing is certain."

Descartes's description of his experiences with step one, the moment of doubt, is memorable but not helpful. He says that he knows the senses have tricked him before—they make a stick half under water look bent, for example—so he won't trust them ever again. As his contemporary critic Pierre Gassendi (1592–1655) pointed out, this is like saying you had a bad experience with food once, so you'll never eat again. Descartes goes on to say that he might be dreaming about everything. Wake up, pal, said his contemporary Thomas Hobbes; that dream-argument is as old as Plato and just as stale. Undeterred, Descartes then imagines that a malevolent demon might have control of his senses and be feeding him pictures of an illusory external world. But why not doubt the existence of the demon, too? And who says the demon has to be malevolent? The whole things smacks of infantile psychosis. Curiously, Descartes considers but then dismisses the possibility that he could be a madman. The difficulty, presumably, is that a madman who believes he is a chair or whatever might not be willing to grant Descartes his logical inferences. A madman might doubt his method altogether.

---

*Empirically observed aspects of the Cartesian Method:*

*1. Tell heart-wrenching stories about your youthful crisis in order to win readers' sympathy and convince them that the doubts are for real.*

*2. Casually remind your readers that you are a brilliant mathematician and have achieved dramatic successes in geometry using the axiomatic method. Really ham it up.*

*3. Throw in a few stories about recent scientific discoveries (e.g., the circulation of the blood) to create the right scientific mood.*

---

Assuming that one manages to secure an axiom or two out of the radical doubt encountered in step one, the axiomatic method apparently advocated in steps two and three presents problems of its own. As we have known at least since Aristotle, the axiomatic method may be okay as a way of systematically expressing a given body of knowledge, but it is a terrible way to go about acquiring scientific knowledge. Not surprisingly, Descartes, who got his start in mathematics, exhibited some of that traditional philosophical weakness for the axiomatic rigor of Euclidean geometry. He tended to prefer the theoretical scientific knowledge deduced from first principles to practical scientific knowledge conforming to observation.

The main point is that Descartes has shifted from some general reflections on method to the application of a particular method. Though his premises are presumably those that would characterize any possible investigation, he uses them to prescribe exactly one investigation. Methodology and method are indistinguishable in this case. So what? But this is a big deal, at least for philosophy. The confusion will allow him to deduce a truth or set of truths, i.e., a body of knowledge, from the notion of method itself. It is something like confusing a description of the nature of sight with a particular vision. Following the trail blazed by Parmenides, Descartes will move freely from inane and obviously true statements about any investigation to the results of a particular investigation; from reason to fact; thinking to being. It is a classic instance of the mystical union of method and content which is philosophy. And it has nothing to do with science or reason, even if the whole thing begins with a paean to science and reason.

# I THINK THEREFORE I AM

*Cogito ergo sum*: I think therefore I am. This is the phrase on which Descartes makes his career. Descartes's reasoning is, on the surface, quite clear: I can doubt everything . . . except for the fact that I am doubting. I can think anything false . . . except for the fact that I am thinking. *Ergo*, I am thinking, I think: *cogito*. Who is thinking? Me. I mean, I. If I am thinking, I exist: *sum. Cogito ergo sum*. This is the magic axiom, the one on which all other knowledge supposedly rests.

At first glance, one must wonder what all the fuss is about. As critics like Gassendi pointed out, you can infer the "I am" from any activity you like: I drink, therefore I am; I stink, therefore I am; etc. You can even drop the "I": the light blinks, therefore it is, etc. What we have here is just another syllogism, one of whose major components is some version of "everything that thinks (drinks, stinks), is."

In his peevish and peremptory way, Descartes denies that he is propounding just one more Aristotelian syllogism. His argument is roughly this: I may or may not be drinking when I think "I drink," but I am necessarily thinking. Of course, he may not have been thinking when he was drinking. But he has a point. There may be a demon pulling on the strings of my senses, who leads me to believe that I am drinking even when I am not, but at least I can be sure that I am thinking, no matter how the demon deceives me. In other words, "I think" has an apodeictic quality which is lacking in "I drink"—i.e., its truth appears to follow from its being uttered (or just thought). In this sense, it belongs to a wider family of propositions, including "I am affirming a proposition" (affirm this), "I am answering the phone" (when answering the phone), and "I am reading" (in your case).

Let's be charitable, for now. Let's accept that Descartes proves (to himself at least) his own existence. Let's suppose that we can do the same for ourselves. I think therefore I am. What's next?

# THE REAL DISTINCTION: MIND AND BODY

I think; I am a thinking thing; I am nothing but a thinking thing, and I don't need a body or anything like that. It is at this point that Descartes shifts from a banal inference to one that is straightforwardly false.

Descartes's aim is not really to prove *that* he is; it is to prove *what* he is. His conclusion is that he is a thinking substance. In more general terms, he concludes that mind and body are the two substances of which the world is made. The notion of 'substance' here comes direct from Aristotle: It is that which depends on nothing else to be what it is. The essential attributes of these two substances are thought and extension (more prosaically, 'spatiality'), respectively.

Descartes's argument gives him no logical basis for this conclusion. Recall that he begins his inquiry not with any facts or observations, but with a inquiry into inquiry itself. He is simply not entitled to deduce any putative facts about the world in this way. The supposed existence of just two substances would be a fact, and a very interesting one at that.

Even Descartes's contemporaries smelled something rotten in his argument. Gassendi pointed out that one cannot move from the claim that I think to the claim that all I do is think. It may also happen that I eat, breathe, and fart. So why not imagine that food, air, and intestinal gas are distinct substances as well? Or should we say that eatingness, breathingness, and fartingness are the substances in question?

Hobbes put the objection this way: When Descartes adds "therefore I am a mind, an intellect" to the "I think" he confuses the thinker with that which he is doing, viz., the thinking. What Hobbes is pointing to is Descartes's implicit and problematic use of the concept of substance. It is quite all right to infer from the proposition "I walk" to the proposition "I am a walker." But the added inference that "I am a walking substance" is confused, not to say unpleasant. I walk, but I am not a walk, a walking substance, or anything of the kind. I am not the same thing as my walking, and I don't even have to walk at all. Curiously, the error of mistaking what a faculty is for what the faculty does is the charge many other modern philosophers would lay against the medievals.

## GOD AGAIN

Certain that he exists at least as a disembodied mind-thing, Descartes sets about looking inside himself for any further knowledge of which he can be absolutely certain. Lo and behold, he espies the idea of God. Time for some more proofs. Descartes offers a tangled web of arguments which eventually boil down to just one, which turns out to be a rehash of the standard theological proof.

*The "How Could I Have Thought of That?" Argument.* I have this idea of a supremely perfect and infinite being. But how could a miserable, finite creature like me have thought of this idea? The finite cannot conceive of the infinite. The idea must be caused by that of which it is an idea: God.

*The "Most Real" Argument.* The idea of God has more reality than any other, so God must have more reality than anything else; but God could not have more reality and yet not exist, so God must exist.

*The "Clear and Distinct" Argument.* My idea of God is more clear and distinct than any other idea. Only true reality can convey clear and distinct ideas. Therefore, my idea of God must correspond to a true reality.

*The "Why Was I Born?" Argument.* I can prove that I am and what I am but not why I am. I must have been created. If I created myself, I could create anything I want, which I can't. So I must have been created by God. (And don't go saying it was my parents.)

After a little meditation, Descartes comes up with a last proof, which is really a summary of the various arguments above:

*The E-E Proof.* The idea of God is perfect, and therefore includes all possible predicates. In particular, it includes his existence. In other words, it is of the essence of God to exist. Q.E.D.

The argument follows Aquinas, to some extent, but lacks the subtle touch of the Angelic Doctor. Descartes tosses God the predicate of existence along with all the others, as a kind of added bonus. He did not seem to realize, as Aquinas did, that existence is not just another predicate, that in giving it to God you pulverize all the other predicates. If the essence of God is to exist, as Aquinas knew, then the rest of Him is a mystery. Perhaps Descartes had some vague intimations about *via negativa*, as evidenced in his contrast between the finite and infinite understandings. Had he gone down that road a little farther, as Hobbes suggests, he might have exercised a little more caution in all his chatter about God.

Descartes's God, *pace* his claims about clearness and distinctness, turns out to be another example of the principle that philosophy's God is a bore. Other than wallowing in the utter abstraction of infinite, timeless existence, it's impossible to imagine what He does.

The idea of God, however, does provide an interesting guarantee, or so Descartes claims. Being perfect, God doesn't tell lies. Since he doesn't lie, we know that the malevolent demon who might have controlled our senses doesn't exist. So we can be sure that that which we perceive clearly and distinctly is true.

## IS THAT CLEAR AND DISTINCT?

In the course of proving his existence as a thinking substance, Descartes argues: I clearly and distinctly perceive that I am thinking thing, therefore I must be a thinking thing. This is a strange inference, and perhaps not all that clear and distinct. Newton's law of gravity may be clearly and distinctly perceived, for example, but thanks to Einstein we know that it is not entirely true. Dante's idea of hell is clear and distinct, but we certainly hope it is false.

Still, Descartes insists, that which is clearly and distinctly perceived must be true. Why does he think so? Because, he says, God gave us the capacity to distinguish true from false, and we really would go to hell if we imagined that God would be so petty as to allow us to be systematically deceived about what is true. In other words, thank God. Here all of Descartes's early critics noticed a circle in his arguments. Recall that Descartes proves the existence of God by asserting that the idea of God is clear and distinct. But the only guarantee that a clear and distinct idea is necessarily true is God himself. So which comes first, the idea or God?

To be fair, if we set aside the strange inferences and theological circles, there is honest kernel to Descartes's argument. What he really wants to say is just that truth is possible. As long as we are clear and distinct about the evidence and argument in favor of an idea, we have a right to make a judgment about its truth. Our ability to distinguish true and false requires that there should be truths to which we have access. Even this is not a proof, but an article of faith, or perhaps just an attitude. Of course, Descartes's idea that truth is possible doesn't prove that all Descartes's ideas are true. Many clearly are not. And we probably don't need God to make any guarantees—we just need to get rid of those pesky demons.

## THEOLOGICAL ROOTS

Descartes's own contemporaries, and critics ever since, have noted the parallels between the Cartesian philosophy and scholastic theology. The title of his most famous work gives much of this away. We will see below that as a "meditation" it borrows from a long-established religious genre. That these meditations are on "first philosophy" puts them squarely in the Aristotelian tradition. Descartes had even considered using the outrageously Aristotelian title of "Metaphysics." The subtitle makes clear that Descartes's conception of the aims of this subject were directly in line with those of the theologians: "in which are demonstrated the existence of God and the distinction between the human soul and body." In the first edition the last phrase read "the immortality of the soul." In his preface he points out that the distinction between soul and body is the essential step in the proof of immortality of the soul. Which further makes clear that Descartes's discussion of the 'mind' is intended to address the traditional, theological concern with the 'soul'. Also, at a finer level of detail, as already noted, Descartes deploys many of the key concepts and arguments of the scholastics, including the concept of 'substance' and the argument about 'degrees of reality'.

Aquinas not only anticipated much of Descartes, but took his arguments a step further. Aquinas, faithful to Aristotle's insights, took the view that the human intellect could not be known entirely apart from sense experience. There is nothing in the mind that is not first in the senses, he said. In this he followed Aristotle's understanding of the distinction between form and matter: They are separate, but one requires the other. Thus far, it is a reasonable position, though it makes it much harder to prove anything about the separate existence, let alone the immortality, of the soul. From this perspective, Descartes's notion of the real distinction is manifestly a retreat to Platonism (which is probably why it is closer to Augustine), and certainly not an advance into a brave new world. I hinted above that while Descartes's proof of the existence of God also borrows from Aquinas, it is considerably less subtle. Blocked off from the *via negativa* by his absolute self-certainty, Descartes is forced to adopt an idea of God that is, on the one hand, so infinite and great that I could not have thought of it on my own, and on the other hand, perfectly clear and distinct. It is strange enough that Descartes's philosophy appears to be locked in the world of medieval theology. Stranger still is the fact that he turns out to be a mediocre theologian.

# II

# I WAS ONLY MEDITATING, MY DEAR

We have been reading Descartes's *Meditations* as though it were a metaphysical treatise. Yet Descartes specifically chose not to call his work a treatise. In his preface, he asks that his readers join with him in thinking through these matters, rather than focus on the dead letter.

The meditation genre was by Descartes's time already quite old. His six days of meditation follow closely the pattern of many inspirational, spiritual works, whose object was to guide the reader through a process of self-transformation. The writer would offer clues, signs, and arguments which the reader would then have to synthesize into his own, personal enlightenment. Once the transformation took place, the book, together with its arguments and so on, could be discarded, as a ladder is kicked away.

I do not think this is what the historical Descartes intended, or else he would not have called his other books on the same subject *Discourse* and *Principles of Philosophy*. The selection of "meditations" was probably designed to preserve the informal, conversational, and (somewhat) provisional nature of the work, but not to reconceive dramatically the status of the arguments and claims made within it. Still, that is an historical question. For us, it is more interesting to consider what philosophical implications might follow from a rereading of the *Meditations* as meditations. Could this have been that sly dog's way of preparing the modern world for science? A kind of catharsis before entering the brave new world of laboratories and all that?

The short answer is sorry, but no thanks. Meditation is called for when one is disturbed, not at peace with oneself or the world. Hence the doubt, the despair, the dark night of the soul which the Cartesian narrator first describes. Enlightenment through guided introspection is a staple of meditational literature. So Descartes's distinctive emphasis on the self and mind, though apparently the content of the meditation, are really a part of its traditional form. Descartes is trying to make the meditation explicit, to present it analytically. That God secures us against doubt is a part of the resolution of the initial disturbance. It is a recognition that the world is both other than the self and benign and open to the self. It ends with a proof of the external world, and the doubt dispelled. So there may be a kind of prescientific catharsis. Now that my spiritual preoccupations have been answered, I can put on the lab coat and break out the test tubes. From a methodological point of view, however, nothing really follows, except possibly general maxims like "know thyself," and perhaps some of the "rules for directing the mind" mentioned above. The various claims about the existence of the self, the mind as substance, and the existence of God, *ex hypothesi*, drop out. What remains? That warm, mystical glow. Nothing that the tradition has conceived of as distinctively Cartesian.

# III

Descartes was and saw himself primarily as one whose mission is to investigate nature, what we would call a scientist. Was he any good? More importantly, did his philosophy advance or hinder his science, and how?

Descartes's mathematical genius is beyond dispute: He more or less invented analytic geometry while in his early twenties. In his optical investigations, sum-marized in his essay *Dioptric*, which is prefaced by the *Discourse*, he discovered Snell's law about the refraction of light, apparently without any help from Snell. He dissected lots of dead animals, as scientifically inclined men of his time were wont to do, though the results were a little haphazard. In one memorable case Descartes discovered the basic structure of the eye—the lens and the retina—by cutting open the eyeball of a dead ox. Descartes wildly overestimated the potential benefits of his research, however; he believed, for example, that with a little more research he might learn to control the process of aging, and so live to the age of one hundred (he died at fifty-four). He judged his physics to be his most important contribution, though on this point the reviews are mixed. To his credit, Descartes was among the first to offer a reasonably clear formulation of the law of inertia. And he consis-tently championed mechanistic over teleological interpretations of natural phe-nomena, which is to say, he thought physical explanations should describe causes and effects, rather than supposed purposes of nature or God. In brief, Descartes was no Newton, nor even a Galileo; he was unusual, but he certainly deserves his place in the history of science.

Descartes's philosophical works originated as a preface to his scientific work. They were intended to ease the way of his scientific work into the world. Two aspects of the historical context are vital at this point: first, in 1633 Galileo had been condemned and punished by the zealously counterreforming Church for his scientific activities; second, as already noted, Aristotelian scholasticism domi-nated the scientific curricula at virtually all institutions of learning. In response to the condemnation of Galileo, Descartes suppressed the impending publication of his own scientific work (the provisionally and modestly titled *Treatise on the Uni-verse*). His next publication, four years later, included pieces of his earlier scien-tific work as well as the preface within which he first set out his mature philo-sophical views. Descartes's ambition was great: He wanted his science to replace Aristotelianism in the schools. In light of the context and Descartes's aims, the objective of his philosophical works is obvious. They were intended to keep the Church off his back, beat the Aristotelians at their own game, and thereby pave the way for the adoption of his science as the standard curriculum in the schools.

The form of the Cartesian philosophy follows quite closely on this strategy. The stuff about God and the soul keeps the Church happy. The mind-body distinction preserves these theological benefits of scholasticism while it annihilates the Aris-totelian notion of the final cause as applied in the study of nature. For since the material world contains no mind or spirit, it cannot be said to operate according to purposes or intentions. Thus, Descartes's un-Aristotelian vision of a purely mechanical material world could be reconciled with a religiously correct theology. The investigation of nature could proceed without the worry that it might disturb the religious peace.

At this point some commentators have speculated as to whether Descartes even believed what he passed off as first philosophy, or if it was just a sop thrown to the Church and the monks. From his correspondence and actions one gets the picture of someone quite willing to grovel before authority. This might explain why some of Descartes's theological arguments were so poor: He didn't really want them to work. Maybe this is why he published his *Meditations* together with the annihilating objections of his critics. Perhaps there is an esoteric philosophy hidden inside the exoteric philosophy.

The important question for us, however, is not so much what Descartes believed deep in his heart, but if and how his philosophical views affected his scientific work. In my view, his philosophy did affect his science, in a bad way, and this probably means, by the way, that it was intended as more than just a sop.

The implications of the mind-body distinction for physical science can be drawn in two incompatible ways. The first option is to say that the implications are purely negative, or cautionary. Philosophy is about minds, science is about bodies. So science should simply go about its business and ignore philosophical-theological speculations altogether. Perhaps the medieval Ockham could have been brought around to this point of view. In his best experimental moments, the scientific Descartes adopts this approach.

The second option is to draw inferences about the physical world from the mind-body distinction itself. Inasmuch as mind and body are distinct substances, they have unique attributes. Inasmuch as they have unique attributes, they have properties that can be "discovered" by studying their essential natures, i.e., their concepts. Descartes's first philosophy investigates the properties of mind, i.e., mainly thought. His physics investigates the concept of body, i.e., extension. From this investigation of the concept of body he does indeed deduce a number of "facts" about the material world, such as the fact that "there can be no void." Given that the mind-body distinction is the outcome of an investigation into the mind, and probably wrong in any case, this approach is obviously incoherent. Descartes's scientific method, in the body of his work on physics, is no more scientific than that of the scholastics. It also happens that the particular conclusion about "the void" had been reached by Aristotle himself.

When Newton went up to Cambridge, he found the study of physics to be thoroughly Cartesian. Descartes's followers, who had added an atomism to his mechanistic physics, debated endlessly about the motions of invisible corpuscles. As Newton observed, they were obsessed by "things that are not demonstrable." Like their medieval forebears and Aristotle before them, they imagined that physics consisted mainly of sorting out their concepts of the physical world. They could describe the movement of their corpuscles in detail, but hadn't a clue about the motion of a falling apple. Descartes, with a little help from Democritus, had replaced Aristotle, but little had changed. One ontology had been exchanged for another.

To be sure, as I have already said, Descartes did make some worthwhile contributions, even in physics. As a rule, however (one that can be applied to philosopher-scientists in general), we can say this: Whatever was of value in Descartes's science had that value independently of his philosophy; and wherever his philosophy influenced his science, the effect was to diminish its value.

## PATERNITY ISSUES

Let's revisit those myths. What kind of *pater* was Descartes?

*Pater modernicus?* The reality, alas, is almost a precise reversal of the myth. Descartes was *not* the father of modernity. The Cartesian First Philosophy was the backward-looking, theological face of Cartesian science. Cartesian metaphysics was a throwback, and modern science, his own included, simply had to work around it.

*Pater scientific methodicus?* Get serious. Sure, Descartes appealed to the evidence available to the reflective individual, as opposed to the authority of Aristotle or of revelation. And so far as the religious establishment of the day was concerned, Descartes had an attitude problem. But there is nothing, on this point, that distinguishes Descartes from Montaigne before him, or his contemporary critics Hobbes and Gassendi, or Locke after him. In fact, there is nothing to distinguish him from the first caveman who said: "I don't believe you; I'm going to go see for myself if there's a mammoth parked outside." As we have seen, to the extent that the method advocated by Descartes is other than the exhortation to "be methodical" it is a retreat to the hocus-pocus of traditional philosophy. It is just another variation on pulling a content out of a method, a thought out of pure thinking.

*Pater ego?* The story that Descartes created the 'self' is contemporary historico-babble. The Neanderthals probably had words to identify themselves. Otherwise they would have starved to themselves into extinction for not having been able to say "pass *me* the butter, please." The reliance on introspection, or self-examination, for the advancement of philosophical and/or spiritual knowledge is as old as Heraclitus and Socrates, not to mention all those Upanishadic poets Descartes never read. The idea of the mind as a 'substance' independent of the body is as old as Pythagoras and Plato, and in Descartes's case it is transparently copied from the Christian concept of the soul (in its vulgar, pre-Aristotelian, Augustinian form).

*Pater modern philosophicus?* Here we may be a little closer to the mark. It is not true that subsequent philosophers all shared a set of beliefs put forward by Descartes. It may be true that many subsequent philosophers occupied themselves untangling the web of problems left by Descartes. And this leads us to ask: What kind of father to his intellectual children was Descartes, anyway? He bequeathed them a sorry lot: a muddle about minds, bodies, and substances; a muddle about subjects, objects, and the possibility of pure knowledge; a muddle about method and methodology. . . . As one reviews the list, one can't help wondering again about those paternity issues. Aren't these muddles just new versions of the same old muddles? And all this muddling around—isn't this just another form of scholasticism?

I don't want to seem churlish about granting the great Descartes his originality. All creative people stand on the shoulders of those who came before them. In philosophy as in the kitchen, it is the synthesis that is new. So I am happy to agree that Descartes was an original thinker. The philosophical issue is, however, as always, what new *truths* did he bring to the table? In his *Diotropic*, for example, he served up a law describing the angles followed by light rays crossing a surface. But can the same be said of his philosophy?

---

**The Armchair Principle.** Philosophers invariably conceive of philosophical knowledge as a kind of knowledge that can be acquired without leaving one's beloved armchair.

---

This principle should have been obvious at least since Parmenides, whose move to the second order obviated the need for philosophers to consider facts. With Descartes, however, the principle receives a clear and modern expression. He gets straight to the point with his focus on furniture—desks and candles mainly—and was possibly the first to state explicitly that he appealed to no evidence save what would be self-evident to anyone sitting in a comfortable armchair.

# Spinoza

## *One is the Happiest Number*

In some versions of the history, Baruch Ben Michael, more familiar to us by his Latin name, Benedictus de Spinoza, shoulders Descartes aside and takes over as the first truly modern philosopher. In most versions, Spinoza is counted among the three great "rationalists" of the seventeenth century, along with Descartes and Leibniz. As rationalists, our three heroes believed that knowledge in its highest form (namely, philosophical knowledge) is grounded in pure reason, free from both the taint of the untrustworthy senses and the unexamined doctrines of revealed religion. All three were raised on Aristotelian scholasticism, and all three rebelled against that tradition in their mature years. All three reached out to contemporary scientists, and even made some contributions of their own to the advance of scientific knowledge. In their philosophical works, each appealed to the faculty of reason available to all people as thinking individuals. Because they championed the spirit of rational inquiry over and above the authority of church dogma, Spinoza and friends are usually heralded as brave pioneers of the modern spirit.

It all makes for a nice story, but it is a story that obscures some obvious facts. A minor case in point is that our three were not exactly the best of pals. Spinoza, for example, did not rate Descartes very highly. Leibniz had his doubts about Descartes, too, and beheld Spinoza with a fondness usually reserved for the Antichrist. Also, it is not a little curious that, while Descartes and Leibniz became celebrities in their own time, Spinoza was largely ignored, or else vilified, until the German Romantics rescued him in the late eighteenth century and idolized him as a "God-intoxicated man."

What the traditional story obscures, above all, and what I will make the focus of our brief encounter with Spinoza, is the real meaning of Spinoza's mission here on earth. For the truth is much more interesting than the story: The truth is that Spinoza was a messiah. His aim was to bring back to life the ancient faith of the Stoics and their Socratic brethren. To those who would listen, Spinoza would reveal a path to true happiness, a path that would pass through a first philosophy of sorts, in good Aristotelian form, and would end, truer to the Stoics, in a knowledge so comprehensive that it becomes a mystical experience, a virtuous rapture of the divine. The ancients knew it would be a path open only to the few. As Spinoza said, rare things are only for the rare. Spinoza was a "rationalist" all right, but he was so chiefly in the manner of his Greek mentors, for whom reason was a fetish, a magical key to perfect bliss, and the totem of their divinity, the unique marker of their strange little tribe. What Spinoza was *not* should be clear: He was, in spirit at least, no crusader for modernity.

It is not surprising, then, that Spinoza did not go down well with the religious establishment. It wasn't just that he lacked the political instincts of a Descartes or a Leibniz (although that didn't help, either). Anyone who intends to found a religion, or revive a lost one, must shatter a few idols. Perhaps Spinoza's antagonists had cause for concern.

---

### A Reading from a Letter of the Apostle Matthew to the Anglo-Saxons

*This is the story of how our Savior suffered, and how through this suffering he learned the key to eternal happiness, and so brought us to salvation.*

*In the century before our Savior, the Spanish monarchy decided to "solve" its Jewish "problem" by forcing the Jews in Spain and Portugal to convert or leave. Those who chose to convert were never accepted into Iberian society. Instead, they became the fuel for the flames of the Inquisition. Many fled to more tolerant parts of Europe, notably Holland, where they reconverted to Judaism. After several generations as non-Jews, however, these re-Judaized families were not always easily reassimilated in the Jewish world.*

*It was among these twice-chosen people that our Savior was born and first developed his novel ideas. When he had reached the tender age of twenty-four, however, the elders of the Dutch Jewish church confronted him with a choice: He could renounce his heretical religious views, or suffer excommunication. So here stood our Savior, born of a member of this group which was not a part of Christian Europe, but possibly not really Jewish either, not Dutch but also not Spanish or Portuguese, perhaps not even European, now facing expulsion into almost complete social oblivion. For our sakes, he chose expulsion.*

*He published little during his lifetime—he withheld his most important work, the* Ethics—*and what he did publish earned him more in enmity and slander than it did in understanding, let alone sympathy.*

*He knew what it was like to be alone. When he took up his scholarly pursuits as a youth, his father disapproved. When his father died, his sister tried to cheat him of his share of the inheritance. They fought it out in the courts, he won, and then he handed over to her what she had sought to steal.*

*He was a man who had every reason to turn his back on life and mankind, who should have slipped into a misanthropic gloom, but chose differently. He suffered, died, and was buried, but in his philosophy he rose again to lead us to salvation.*

## METHOD

Spinoza's magnum opus, his *Ethics*, proceeds in a most unusual fashion. It follows what appears to a geometric method. Spinoza begins with formal definitions of terms, offers putatively self-evident axioms, and then apparently deduces from these a long series of propositions and postulates about the existence of God, the nature of knowledge and freedom, and the way to happiness. For example, he offers definitions of, among other things, God and substance. He then provides some axioms, most of which are intended to be logically obvious, more or less like the claim that either something is a substance or it is not. On the basis of these definitions and axioms, Spinoza proves propositions like "God is a substance." No doubt this method is intended to make the argument perspicuous, and to base the whole thing on an appeal to reason rather than authority. The attitude is in-your-face to the medieval church, but the method itself is not modern: Medieval natural theology tried to proceed in a deductive way, and Aristotle had proposed the axiomatic method as the main vehicle for science. It would also be inaccurate to regard Spinoza's method as the "method of reason" or something like that. Aristotle himself had already noted that the most reasonable method of science may well depend on the subject matter. And the use of the geometric method is no guarantee of reasonableness. Any serious reader today will agree, I think, that Spinoza's propositions do not always follow from axioms, which are anything but self-evident, and that the definitions already presuppose a jumble of not always coherent theories.

## METAPHYSICS

It is easy to forget that Spinoza's magnum opus was an ethics. The first two of its five parts—and only the rare reader makes it any farther—tread the familiar ground of metaphysics: substance, the existence of God, minds, bodies, and all that. It certainly is an ethics, for its end is to show one how to live, how to achieve happiness. Since the path to happiness goes through metaphysics, however, it is worth pausing to review the relevant doctrines.

## O MY NATURE!

The centerpiece of Spinoza's metaphysics—and of his world—is God. Spinoza's God is essentially an expression of the mystical notion that all is one. The exact shape of the expression may be traced in part to Spinoza's specific intellectual sources: Maimonides, the Bible ("Hear, O Israel, the Lord our God the Lord is One," Deut. 6:4), and Descartes. Spinoza's belief takes the form sometimes called pantheism.

Of course, Spinoza regularly denied the charge that he was a pantheist. The truth, as it turns out, depends on what you mean by pantheism. Spinoza's accusers, like Hegel's many years later, thought pantheism was morally equivalent to the proposition that God is a toilet bowl or any other crass object. Spinoza correctly responded that in this sense he was not a pantheist because he did not believe that God was *nothing but* corporeal nature. However, Spinoza did believe that corporeal nature (more properly: extension) was one of God's infinite attributes, and that physical things were some of God's modes, or ways of being. In other words, while God is more than the sum of all toilet bowls (and chairs, flowers, other physical objects, etc.), it is nonetheless true, according to Spinoza, that all toilet bowls are "in" God, i.e., vaguely a part of Him. At a higher level of abstraction, then, where the "pan" refers not to all *physical* things, but to all existence, Spinoza certainly was a pantheist. His pantheism could also be called an "immanentism": God is not a distant, transcendent being, but one who is in everything around us, and in whom everything around us is. Thus one of the catch phrases of Spinozism, "God or Nature," means "God, or what is the same, Nature, understood in its most general sense."

## TAKE THAT, DESCARTES

Spinoza, like many intelligent people, found Descartes's doctrine that mind and bodies are two separate substances thoroughly disgusting. How can the two be so separate, Spinoza would ask, when they obviously interact so much? Spinoza dismisses the whole mind-body business with his idea that only God is substance. Thought and extension, Spinoza argues, are merely attributes of God. So there is no problem in understanding how minds and bodies relate to each other: They are two manifestations of the same thing. Whether this works or not is really a matter of taste. Although he says that God, being the incredible thing that He is, has infinite attributes, Spinoza only gets around to talking about two, thought and extension. So the Cartesian dualism creeps back in at a pretty high level.

## DEFINITELY THE BIG OOZEY

Spinoza's propositions, condensed, rearranged, and restated in somewhat more formal terms than above, are these:

1. The essence of substance is to exist.

2. There is only one substance.

3. That substance is God.

4. Everything else in the world exists only "in" God.

5. The world/God is eternal, immutable, and indivisible.

The first proposition contains the whole circle of metaphysics, as we have seen, from Aristotle through the medieval theologians. What is new in Spinoza, and possibly an improvement on Aristotle, is a somewhat more rigorous deduction of the last four propositions from the first. Aristotle's first philosophy, as we saw, oscillated nervously between "little oozeys" and "the Big Oozey." In his realistic moments, Aristotle wanted to affirm that lots of little things really do exist, such as men and furniture. The Platonic side of him whispered that there was only one thing that is ultimately real, that truly exists in the full sense of the word. Spinoza had no doubts about which side to take: for him, it was definitely the Big Oozey. His metaphysics, the idea that God is the one substance of the world, is the logical extreme of Aristotelianism.

---

## A Reading from the Holy Gospel according to Matthew (3:7)

*Our savior entered the market place amid the clamor of tradespeople, bargain-hunters, and livestock. He leapt upon a merchant's stall and surveyed the living mass of humans, animals, fruits, and vegetables. The people gathered around him and he began to speak.*

*"Every apple wants to be red. Every animal fights to survive. Every man strives to become a true man. Why? Because God loves himself. I will tell you how God loves himself. I will tell you about virtue and about power. Verily, I will show you that virtue is power!*

*What is a thing? A thing is not what it is—for only God is. A thing is what it wants to be! A thing is its* conatus. *But what is its* conatus? *Its will to become what it is. Whose will? God's will. The* conatus *is God's love of himself.*

*What is virtue? Do not speak to me of good and evil. Good and evil are just words. True virtue is beyond good and evil. It is God's love of himself. What is this love? It is the way things strive to become what they are. It is* conatus. *The more power things have, the more things become what they are, the more God loves. Power is virtue! Virtue is power!*

*Some say the* conatus *is the cause of things. Others say it is their purpose. Verily, I say, it is both! It drives them on, like a cause, yet it leads them in, in to God, for that is their purpose.*

---

## ETERNAL HAPPINESS CAN BE YOURS

Spinoza's ethical doctrines, the culmination of his philosophical project, are essentially those of the Stoics. Like the Stoics, he found comfort in the idea of determinism. If a stone tossed in the air had consciousness, Spinoza would say, it would believe itself to be flying free. Even more than the Stoics, perhaps, Spinoza left everything in the hands of an all-knowing, all-encompassing God. Like the Stoics, he imagined that humans have a special nature, to think or know, that God somehow shares in that nature, and that the key to happiness is knowledge, in some divine sense. Like the Stoics, he didn't mean knowledge of useful things, like the fact that wood floats, but that very rare knowledge of the broad order of the world, of God. And this knowledge is not a means to happiness, it actually *is* happiness.

All of these ideas are pleasant enough, but they don't exactly square with common sense, let alone with each other. They are part of a strange and ancient religion that has gone under the name of philosophy for several millennia now. So, like the Stoics, Spinoza devoted a good deal of his time to showing how the whole thing could fit together and make sense, or how common sense is all wrong anyway. The issues he had to deal with included:

- If everything is predetermined, then what's the point of an ethics? You're gonna do what you gotta do, no matter what.
- If my passions are part of God, like everything else, then why can't I just do what I want?
- If thought is just another one of God's attributes, how is it possible to have a false thought?
- How can knowledge be happiness? I mean, of course knowledge can make you happy sometimes, but so can burping, and we don't say that burping is happiness.
- How do you know all this anyway?

Some of these issues should be familiar from the discussion on mysticism. From that discussion it should also be clear that the issues won't be resolved, because the mystical, Spinozan notion that all is one cannot logically determine any ethics. Still, Spinoza gives it his best shot, and no doubt part of his enduring appeal is that it's damn hard to untangle the web of illogic he weaves in the course of this futile endeavor.

## A Reading from the Holy Gospel according to Matthew (3:6)

*Spinoza climbed the mount, stood silent for a moment before the huddled masses of intellectuals, and then delivered the following sermon.*

*"You who say you know—I say, you know nothing. You who say you are free—I say you are slaves. You who say you are happy—I say you are miserable cretins. Verily, I will show you the path to true knowledge, true freedom, and true happiness. Verily, for they are the same path.*

*"You know much about the particular things around you. You know tables, chairs, and the price of corn. Your knowledge does not impress me. Some of you may know reason, the knowledge which arises from the common properties of things. That's a little better. But only a few know intuition, which is the sole true knowledge.*

*"You are free to do as you please. But what pleases you is no choice of yours. You are slaves to that which lies outside you. Only those needs which come from your essence are free. And your essence is to know God.*

*"You are happy because you satisfy your passions. But your passions abuse you as a mere thing. Really, you can only be happy if you become what you are, and you are a knowing creature. Your destiny is to know God, and in knowing God you express all your love.*

*"In sum, I say, you are a special animal. Your special instinct is to know, and the most special knowledge is of God, and this knowledge is love, and love is happiness. Only thus will you achieve a blessedness secure from all the suffering of this world.*

## THE SECOND COMING

As far as I know, the church of Spinoza never came to be. At least, I haven't received any parish fliers. Yet I cower before the thought. All the toilsome labor of the concept, the lonely nights, and the years of ignorant persecution—did he suffer in vain, our poor, dear seventeenth-century Socrates? Was it all for the sake of a merely desperate, idiotic happiness? Or will there be a second (would it be the third?) coming? Come to think of it, doesn't he foreshadow something for us? Something solitary, bold, Alpine, questioning, nineteenth-century, more-than-German? A hint of—dare I say it—*Nietzsche?* Stay tuned.

# Leibniz

## Monads for Sale

While Spinoza was grinding out lenses to make ends meet, Gottfried Wilhelm Leibniz (1646–1716) hobbed among the leading nobs of Europe. While Spinoza refused a university appointment in order to preserve his independence, Leibniz turned one down because he wanted a more active career. Spinoza tinkered with scientific pursuits, but never amounted to anything but a philosopher. For Leibniz, philosophy was just another feather in his cap as the all-around genius of his time. Spinoza lived his philosophy, while Leibniz seemed merely to argue his. Spinoza thought he had represented his philosophy, or just the plain truth, in a single system. Leibniz never got around to building a system. His views have to be gathered together out of letters, articles, and unpublished manuscripts. Even then, there is no single system, for Leibniz frequently adjusted his views for his changing audiences.

Leibniz's philosophy was, to all appearances, a political philosophy. All he wanted was to show the world that metaphysics need not turn us into monsters like Spinoza, but could be made part of a happy church and family life. Philosophy was subordinate to his broad politico-theological goal, namely, to reunite Catholics and Protestants in the medieval splendor of the single church.

Yet Leibniz was deeper sometimes than he meant to be. In unguarded moments he let fall the superficial dress of his public life, and revealed a material touched by the hand of pure reason, something distinctly, pathetically Spinozan. For all the vigor of his public quarrels with Spinoza, a part of Leibniz could not help but worship the messiah of early modern philosophy. He was a divided Aristotle to Spinoza's unified Plato. Unlike Aristotle, though, Leibniz kept his secrets well. A single, disapproving glance from a casual acquaintance was always enough to make the bashful Leibniz shrink from view, and so he left clues buried in a closetful of unpublished manuscripts and unstated inferences from public arguments for the forensic philosophologues of later centuries.

Leibniz's strange metaphysical doctrines may be inferred from the same set of premises with which Spinoza began, plus one:

- Spinoza must have been wrong.

Specifically, Spinoza failed to accommodate the religiously correct truths that:

1. God is a transcendent being who created the world, or at least had some choice in the matter.

2. The will is free.

3. Evil is real, even though God is good.

Leibniz wanted to show that the Spinozan view was the logical result of philosophy gone bad. He argued that the Cartesian approach was wrong because it led to Spinoza. His goal was to show that a proper metaphysics was possible and would lead to the religiously correct conclusions. Let us look briefly at his proposed methods, and then at his handling of the problems of God, freedom, and evil. We conclude with a summary of his strange doctrine of monads.

## FIRST PRINCIPLES

Leibniz was possibly more aggressive than Spinoza in affirming that metaphysics should be based on pure reason. He asserted that his own metaphysics followed from logical principles. His two most logical principles were:

1. The principle of noncontradiction: X is either true or false but not both.

2. The principle of sufficient reason. There is nothing without a reason; or, everything has an explanation.

Leibniz liked principles, so he proffered a number of others whose logical status is less apparent:

3. The identity of indiscernibles. Two things which share every property are the same thing; or, things cannot differ in terms of place and time alone.

4. The principle of continuity. Nature does nothing all of a sudden. Changes are of degree.

## (1) GOD

Leibniz's assault on Spinoza begins with the traditional metaphysical issue, the proof of the existence of God. His aim is simple: Prove it in a way that preserves the distinction between the world and God. His strategy is simple, too: Show that proofs other than the ontological one are valid. For Leibniz sensed, correctly, I think, that the ontological proof collapses God and world in the category of existence, while the other proofs still seem to allow a separation of God and world.

In his popular writings, Leibniz deploys the "argument from design," i.e., the one that says that the structure of objects like hills and valleys shows they were created for a purpose, therefore the existence of an ordered world allows us to conclude that it too has a design or a creator. In his terms, the "preestablished harmony" of the world proves the existence of God. In more philosophical moments, Leibniz acknowledges that this proof is essentially inductive, and really just an emotional supplement to the basic proof.

Leibniz's proof of choice begins with the principle of sufficient reason. If there is an explanation for every thing, he reasons, there must be an explanation for *everything*, i.e., for the existence of the world. In other words, every little thing appears contingent until explained by some other thing, and all the little things in the world remain contingent until the existence of the world can be explained. So Leibniz asks the question for which he is perhaps most famous: Why is there something rather than nothing? The answer is that there exists a necessary being, God, who makes possible all this contingency.

Leibniz draws up his proof not so much to prove the existence of God, but to ascribe to Him a role and a nature consistent with logical principles and religious requirements. His idea is this:

1. There are lots of possible worlds.

2. God's role is to choose among possible worlds.

3. Ours is the best of all possible worlds.

4. This proves that God is good.

Spinoza would have scoffed at the idea of applying such a banal idea of 'goodness' to God. Leibniz's commonsensical, perhaps banal idea of God's goodness is really intended to reinforce the idea that God, too, faces simple choices in life, just like you and me.

## WHO WANTS TO BE GOD?

It seems unlikely, in the final analysis, that Leibniz managed to emancipate God from the shackles of philosophy. In the first place, his God is not allowed to choose just any world He wants; He is only allowed to choose among possible worlds. So God, too, is limited by possibility. Second, God pretty much has only one world to choose from, the best. What kind of God would he be if he didn't choose the best? So really, God doesn't have a choice in the matter at all. He just checks the right box on a form handed to him by Leibniz. And third, once he has chosen, it looks like there isn't much left for God to do. He just watches things happen. Once again, God fades into that necessary but oh-so-gray being who marks the end-point of philosophical proofs. At the end of the day, Leibniz's proofs do not really demonstrate that God is distinct from the world. They simply do not seem to assume that conclusion, as the ontological proof does. The idea that God is distinct from the world is really a presupposition, or a picture, buried in the narratives which Leibniz relates as proof, and these narratives are really just variant readings from the book of Spinoza.

Leibniz's God, by the way, was less than a hit among his religiously-minded contemporaries, no doubt for the same reason that many medievals disliked the existential essence of Aquinas.

The whole discussion is distinctly medieval. The argument from design was a staple of the monastic diet. The "proof" from the principle of sufficient reason is a variation on one of the medieval proofs, what I called the proof by contingency, which was in turn a variation on arguments traceable to Aristotle and before. The "best of all possible worlds" notion is somewhat more original, but hardly daring. It, too, could probably be traced to Aristotle. Leibniz's failure to explicitly present his popular proofs as subordinate versions of the ontological one, I think, was just a willful disregard of a long-established logic.

## (2) FREEDOM

It would indeed be the best of all possible worlds, except that a Spinozan determinism rears its ugly head just after the creation of the world. When God chooses a world, he chooses everything in that world as well. From that point on, the world works like a clock. Determinism rules. The strategy Leibniz pursues in response to this Stoic threat would have implications for much of philosophy to come, especially in Germany. He shifts the terrain of discussion from ontology to logic, and creates a space for freedom in the latter, even though it may be lacking in the former. In doing so he rejuvenates for future use some ancient logical distinctions.

### NECESSARY VERSUS CONTINGENT TRUTHS

In every true, affirmative proposition, says Leibniz, the predicate is "in" the subject. The proposition "Socrates is a man," for example, affirms that the concept of 'a man' must be included within the concept of 'Socrates'. Matters become more complicated when we consider a proposition such as "Socrates ate two scrambled eggs for breakfast." The concept of 'Socrates' may be profound, but it is hard to see how it would include "ate two scrambled eggs for breakfast." Yet it must, if it is indeed a true, affirmative proposition. So Leibniz calls in the distinction between necessary and contingent truths. A necessary truth might also be described as "analytic," for one can analyze the subject in a finite number of steps in order to show that the predicate is in the subject (or not). In a contingent or "synthetic" truth, the proof is still possible, but would require an infinite number of steps. Presumably, one would have to run through all of Socrates' personal history, all the events of his life, as well as his culinary preferences, and perhaps the entire course of the universe, and having done this, it would follow of necessity that Socrates ate those eggs. So, in a sense, all truths are necessary, it's just that some, those we call contingent, require a very arduous (and for us impossible) proof. If we had a thoroughly perspicuous understanding of 'Socrates', it would be self evident that he "ate two scramble eggs for breakfast."

## GOD IS GREAT, BUT WE ARE FREE

We humans are of limited intelligence. We cannot produce proofs with infinite numbers of steps. Therefore, many propositions appear contingent for us. God, on the other hand, has no problem with lengthy arguments. For him, everything has the character of necessity.

This argument reveals the curious interconnections among Leibniz's foundational principle of sufficient reason, his proof of the existence of God, and his distinction between analytic and synthetic truths. As we saw above, God is necessary in virtue of the principle of sufficient reason: There must be an explanation for everything. At the same time, God is really the only being with complete access to the truths generated by the principle of sufficient reason. For the principle of sufficient reason really says that all truths are ultimately analytic: To explain something is to show it follows necessarily. But only God can see how everything follows necessarily from everything else. (Some might detect in all this a hint of one of those Cartesian circles: On the one hand, God is an inference from a logical principle; on the other hand, God is the ultimate guarantor of logic.)

Our limitation, it turns out, is what makes freedom possible. Because our finite intelligence sees many propositions as contingent, we conceive for ourselves the possibility of conscious choice among alternative actions. We can take our eggs scrambled or fried. From God's point of view, of course, we are not free. Our apparent choice is for God what we were destined to choose all along. It has to be scrambled.

## THE RETURN OF SPINOOZEY

Leibniz's argument for freedom follows a well-established pattern. He divides things according to two perspectives, the human and the divine, and treats freedom as a feature of the former, necessity as a feature of the latter. Ancient Greeks, medieval theologians, Descartes, and, above all, Spinoza had opened a similar, limited space for freedom. As with Spinoza, however, the logic of the argument leads eventually to a place where contingency, freedom, and evil vanish into unreality. Seemingly contingent truths get swallowed up in the infinite calculations of a necessary being, freedom turns out to be an illusion of imperfect knowledge, and evil is reduced from malice to logical necessity. The Big Oozey reigns triumphant.

To be sure, Leibniz conferred on this vision a shape and tone which would remain significant for much of the rest of modern philosophy. His emphasis on principles and distinctions pertaining to formal logic would be taken up by his German followers, at least through Kant, and then by twentieth century analytic philosophers, even where the latter chose to dispute his particular principles and distinctions.

## (3) EVIL

The business about the best of all possible worlds earned Leibniz a good deal of satiric rebuttal from the left-wing (i.e., the anti-churchers). For those living in the seventeenth century, with its nasty plagues, catastrophic fires and earthquakes, and a rather oppressive social system, you can see why many, like Voltaire, doubted the wisdom of Leibniz.

However, Leibniz did not mean that every little thing in the world was fabulous. He meant that everything taken together was fabulous. Two things may be possible apart, he said, but not necessarily together. In his terms, they might not be "compossible." A world with lots of candy and no tooth decay is presumably not possible. Thus Leibniz explains why in a world created by a good God there should be so much evil (and so many dentists). It goes without saying that God gets credit for anything good in the world. As for bad things and sin, well, He permits those, though He certainly does not condone them. As a matter of fact, Leibniz wanted to keep evil around for the same reason that many medievals did. No evil means no sin, and no sin means no church.

## (4) EGADS! MONADS

The bizarre climax of Leibniz's metaphysics is his doctrine of monads. Monads are the simple little substances, the ultimate realities that make up the world. They are without number. Each monad contains within itself its own past and future. Since its past and future are part of the whole interconnected fabric of the universe, each monad contains within itself the concept of the whole universe. Since space and time are only extrinsic determinations, monads do not exist in space and time. Rather, space and time are constituted by relations among monads. Also, monads do not really interact and change each other, since they are simple to begin with. They are "windowless." They are eternal, come to be altogether, since they cannot be formed from other simple substances. These entities have a number of other curious features, which are necessary to explain how they are able to change, for example, but these need not concern us here.

The amazing thing, really, is why anyone would want to believe in such a silly story. And why Leibniz, who in other areas was about as clever as they get. The only plausible account, I think, is that Leibniz invented monads as a way of showing that you could have a metaphysics, complete with substances, universes, and all that, without having to be Spinoza. As in: I'm not Spinoza, therefore there is more than one substance, namely, lots of little monads. Possibly Leibniz didn't even believe in the damn things himself, but thought they might be useful propaganda.

## CHARACTERISTICA UNIVERSALIS

Leibniz thought that most (indeed, all) philosophical and other disagreements were the result of inadequacies of the language in which positions were expressed. If one could invent a logically perfect language, a *characteristica universalis*, then the resolution of all disputes, whether philosophical or matrimonial, would be a matter of applying the basic calculus of this language.

Actually, this was not a new idea. It popped up before and many more times after Leibniz. In the twentieth century, though, the search for a logical metalanguage would become a central objective for many academic philosophers.

## INFLUENCE

Leibniz is usually regarded as the founder of modern academic philosophy in Germany. Christian Wolff appropriated Leibniz's philosophy and made his version of it the mainstay of the philosophical curriculum in German universities. With that begins the long line of master-pupil relationships which have been German (academic) philosophy down to the present. Wolff and Baumgarten begat Kant, who created Fichte, Hegel, Hartmann, Brentano, Husserl, Heidegger, and so on.

There is a paradox here. Leibniz founded not just a department, but a whole university. He played a key role in the creation of the Prussian Academy, forerunner of the modern German university. However, he did not allow for the creation of a special faculty of philosophy. Instead, Leibniz imagined that a genuine philosophical spirit would pervade the whole university, rather than remain the preserve of one department.

# Empiricism

## The Poor Man's Dialectic, or How Empiricism Becomes Mysticism and Then Strangely Disappears

### WHAT IS EMPIRICISM?

"Empirical" comes from a Greek root meaning "based on trial or experiment." The term is usually associated with "knowledge." More precisely, it classifies knowledge according to the method whereby it is justified. Empirical knowledge is knowledge based on the evidence of experience or observation. So, inasmuch as an "ism" is meant to stand for the advocacy of a principle, we can define "empiricism" as the general principle or maxim that our claims to knowledge should be based on the evidence of experience.

Understood in this general sense, empiricism would seem to be the most reasonable of convictions. What could be more sane than to test our knowledge against the observed facts? Come to think of it, what else would we test our knowledge against? What else is knowledge, if not knowledge of the facts? Our principle could be interpreted as a reminder inferred from the definition of what it means to know something properly. In fact, there is nothing about this principle that marks it as distinctively philosophical. All of the natural sciences are empiricist in this general way, for they all justify their claims to knowledge on the basis of observational evidence. The empiricist orientation of science is just a systematic, controlled, and massively organized appropriation of the disposition of Joe Neanderthal, who went out to investigate whether that noise was caused by a roaming ancestral spirit, like the medicine man said, or an angry mastodon.

In the history of philosophy, however, empiricism is traditionally understood to refer to a particular school of philosophy, and the historical core of this school is the trio of British thinkers, John Locke, George Berkeley, and David Hume. (Their predecessors, Francis Bacon and Thomas Hobbes, and their twentieth-century followers, the logical positivists, may be thrown in as well.) This is odd, for at least two reasons. First, in the form of the general principle defined above, empiricism is a phenomenon that recurs throughout the history of philosophy (not to mention at mealtimes). Many of the ancient Greek Sophists, for example, were self-consciously committed to the principle that knowledge should be based on evidence. Second, the noted trio, with the exception of the noble Hume, are not the best examples of the general principle of empiricism. Berkeley's idealistic doctrines, if they are to be believed, are the virtual antithesis of the common sanity embodied in that general principle.

To understand the gap between the general principle of empiricism and the philosophical school or doctrine of empiricism is to understand a considerable amount about the way in which philosophy functions. The philosophical doctrine of empiricism, or so I will argue, is actually an expression of mysticism, and thus not very empirical at all. The British empiricists of the seventeenth century may have been part of a general movement of ideas which accompanied the advance of modern science, but they did not provide the intellectual foundation for modern science, for the simple reason that they did not provide the foundation for anything at all. But let's first look more closely, in a kind of empirical way, at what it means to be a philosophical empiricist.

## HOW TO SPOT AN EMPIRICIST: I

For starters, we could observe that to count as an empiricist one must produce a major work in which at least one of the terms "physical object," "external object," "sense," "sensation," "sense datum," "sense qualia," "perception," "idea," "ideas in the mind," "reflection," or one of their cognates occurs in at least one out of every three sentences. We would have to exclude critics and commentators, of course (say, those who mention another author's name on average at least once per paragraph). That still leaves us with, for example, Plato, whose *Theaetetus* allows him to pass the test, Schopenhauer, and probably Kant. If we add "must be British" to the list of qualifications, we get closer, but run the risk of excluding some worthy representatives.

## HOW TO SPOT AN EMPIRICIST: II

There must be a better way of identifying an empiricist. As a matter of fact, the shared vocabulary of empiricists reflects a number of common notions and preoccupations: a picture, a doctrine, and a project. These common elements give rise to a characteristic "problematic" and a set of conundrums. The whole thing amounts not to a precise set of propositions, but to the sort of tangled collection of things which usually makes up a way of life.

## THE PICTURE

There is a mind. There is an external object. The senses convey an impression of the latter to the former. Strictly speaking, of course, there should be no picture but a set of premises. The picture could just mean that we learn about things through the conduits which give us information about those things, namely, the senses. Or it could stand for the philosophical doctrine of empiricism, as we shall see below. Suffice it to note, for now, that the picture conceals quite a lot. For example, the picture appears to describe a spatial relationship, one between an internal mind and an external object. But *where* exactly is the mind? Inside what? The more one thinks about it, the more it seems that spatial relationships themselves pertain only to "external" objects. So, external to what? It helps to hide these questions behind a neat, spatiotemporal representation, i.e., a picture.

## THE DOCTRINE

The doctrine that is the common denominator of philosophical empiricism is a slightly—but crucially—modified version of the general principle cited above: Knowledge is based on the evidence *of the senses*; or, knowledge is based on *sense* experience. On the one hand, the addition of "sense" adds nothing, inasmuch as all evidence may be said by definition to pass through the senses. A sense is, after all, that which senses. On the other hand, "sense" may seem to add a lot, insofar as it implies that there might well be some other possible source and justification for knowledge, some kind of "extra-" (or perhaps "non-") sense. The little word "sense" serves the philosophical empiricists like a bridge. As a truism, it allows them to cross over to the general principle of empiricism, to pick up legitimation and occasional guidance. Stated as part of a positive doctrine, it lets them cross back into the land of obscure, metaphysical speculation, to make assertions about possibility without yet having learned anything about actuality. To understand how this little "sense" functions in their doctrine is, as we shall see, to understand the dynamic of which philosophical empiricism is an example.

## THE PROJECT

From the general principle of empiricism follows no particular investigative project. The principle is a practical maxim, a general rule on how to behave in specific circumstances, designed for use in any investigation. Likewise, the maxim "use your eyes" does not tell you what in particular to look at, and certainly does not entail the idea of an inspection of the eyeballs. From the empiricist doctrine in its positive sense, however, there does follow the idea for a project. If sense experience is one kind of experience (or sense evidence one kind of evidence), and all knowledge must answer to this one kind, then it is plausible that one may be able to determine prior to any actual experience what sorts of things can possibly be known, and what sorts cannot. The project is what nowadays goes by the name of epistemology, or the theory of knowledge. The idea for the project is reinforced with an analogy: By inspecting an instrument, e.g., a telescope, one can determine what sort of results it can achieve, e.g., what it will be able to see. Likewise, by inspecting the human "understanding," or faculty of knowledge, one should be able to reach conclusions about what sorts of things can be understood, or known.

## THE CONUNDRUMS

Empiricist arguments are characterized by an identifiable pattern of confusions that originate in the fundamental picture, doctrine, and project of empiricism. They are not marginal or incidental mistakes, but an essential part of what it means to be an empiricist. As a practice, philosophical empiricism amounts to creating, discovering, and "solving" these confusions. I describe first a couple of the conundrums which empiricism presents as (pseudo-) problems for itself. I then outline a "problematic," which may be taken as a general statement of the self-negating pattern of empiricist discourse.

Contradictory premises give rise to conundrums, or apparently insoluble puzzles. The many conundrums of empiricist thought ultimately boil down to one, which I list here first.

## *Conundrum No. 1: How Is Knowledge Possible?*

True knowledge is impossible. Or, knowledge is not true knowledge; knowledge is ignorance. Like all conundrums, this one requires conflicting premises:

1. All knowledge is mediated by the senses.

2. True knowledge is immediate.

In terms of the picture described above, we could say this: Knowledge, as we know it, consists of the apprehension of the object in the mind thorough the senses; but true knowledge would be actually having the object in the mind already, without any mediation; therefore, there is (and can be) no true knowledge. The argument can appear in a number of guises, and take any number of additional steps. The curious thing is that it begins with a sensible principle about knowledge and ends with a skepticism about the very possibility of knowledge.

The first premise, by the way, is usually made explicit in empiricist thought, while the second is hidden. (In this we find a neat and telling reversal of mysticism, where the second is usually explicit and first is hidden.)

A parallel conundrum would be: How is sight possible? It would seem that true vision is impossible. Or, seeing is blindness. Consider the premises:

1. All vision is mediated by the eyes.

2. True vision is seeing things as they are (i.e., without any mediation).

Our eyes, after all, merely offer us a pallid and probably false representation of what things really look like. If we could only bring the things straight into the faculty of sight . . .

## Conundrum No. 2: How Is Philosophy Possible?

The empiricist seems to know something—something about all possible knowledge, prior to all possible experience. How is this possible? Consider:

1. All knowledge is mediated by the senses.

2. Proposition (1) above is known to be true of all knowledge, without regard to specific sense evidence.

All knowledge is equal, it would seem, but some knowledge is more equal than others. If empiricism, like most other isms, claims a special knowledge about the world, it risks undermining that very claim, which is a claim about what can and cannot be known. If it does not claim any knowledge, well, one wonders, what was the point of it all?

### THE PROBLEMATIC: FROM EPISTEMOLOGY TO METAPHYSICS AND BACK AGAIN

In intention, the empiricist project is purely epistemological. Metaphysics should come later, if at all, once it has been determined what sorts of things can be known. Unfortunately, it turns out to be impossible to get the epistemological project going without presupposing a certain metaphysics. Some determination of the metaphysical nature of the knower *qua* knower is a prerequisite for any meaningful epistemology, since otherwise there is no reason to believe that there is any theoretical or *a priori* limit on the nature of things that can be known, and without such a limit there is nothing for an epistemologist to investigate. To repeat, in order to come to a conclusion about what a knower can know, one needs to know something about what sort of knower this is. (The same could be said for a "doer" or a "thinker" or an "eater.") To the extent that epistemology is a theory about knowing as such, metaphysics, whose magical formulas represent the only hope for a positive, noncircular determination of the being which knows *qua* knowing being, is its prerequisite. The metaphysics assumed by empiricists is almost invariably a stripped-down version of Descartes' mind-body dualism, although this need not be the case, nor does it mean that Descartes is responsible for the whole fiasco. The inclusion of the word "sense" in the general principle of empiricism is the way in which empiricism hides within an innocuous practical maxim the assumption of a metaphysics, which in turn makes possible the project of empiricist epistemology, on which any metaphysics is (falsely) supposed to depend.

This problematic of empiricism carries over into a confusion between epistemology and psychology. Many of the most intuitively appealing insights of empiricists turn out to be, on closer inspection, generalizations about the mental life of human beings. In other words, they belong to psychology. In distinguishing "actual" from "habitual" knowledge, for example, Locke surreptitiously shifts the subject of discussion from the nature of knowledge in the abstract (which is presumably always actual) to discussion of the way in which people hold on to their knowledge. It is true that psychology, as an organized field of research, is more recent than empiricism. But this is no excuse for confusing psychological facts with (putative) epistemological ones. The former have to do with the way in which the human mind behaves under specific conditions, and are properly the object of empirical investigations; the latter concern the possibility and justification of knowledge as such, without regard for the specific kind or conditions of mind in which it is held. As a matter of fact, the epistemologist secretly hopes that psychological facts will provide him with a substitute for (or reinforcement of) the metaphysical claims required to get the epistemology going.

## LOCKE-BERKELEY-HUME: THE POOR MAN'S DIALECTIC

The philosophies of this British trio of empiricists (to each of whom a subsequent chapter is devoted) is that their philosophies seem to follow a natural sequence in which empiricism presents and unravels itself. Locke sets forth, explicitly and implicitly, the basic premises of empiricism. The picture, the doctrine, the idea for a project, and the confusions are all there, although he mainly skirts around the conundrums. Berkeley accepts Locke's premises, but then deploys conundrum no. 1 to arrive at conclusions opposed to Locke's. Along comes Hume, who bares the conflicting premises shared by Locke and Berkeley and throws them both out along with the whole empiricist project. The pattern is deliciously dialectical, but it is a poor man's dialectic, in that its conclusion leaves one with nothing. It goes thesis, antithesis, and, instead of synthesis, total annihilation. For a moment, though, it seems as though history follows a certain logic, and that the problematic of empiricism, as described above, unwinds itself in a temporal sequence.

Of course, the history of philosophy is always messier than that. Locke presented a patchwork of arguments, not all of which belong to the empiricist tradition. Besides Locke-bashing, Berkeley had a theological agenda to pursue. And Hume's achievement is mitigated by the fact that he expressed his conclusions in the language of empiricism. Sadly, but most significantly, the achievement was not lasting. The self-destructing dialectic of empiricism would be replayed any number of times in the history of philosophy.

## HOW EMPIRICISM BECOMES MYSTICISM

The dialectic of philosophical empiricism may well be important for understanding the history of modern philosophy, but it is not the decisive factor in the failure of modern philosophy, nor is it in essence anything uniquely modern. To believe otherwise, as some modern critics of philosophy do, is, in my view, to confuse a particular error with the general pattern, which is itself just another instance of the general pattern of the error which has plagued philosophy.

The important thing is to understand the dialectic of empiricism in a general way, that is, as an instance of a general dynamic which characterizes the history of philosophy. Here are some of the features of that pattern instantiated in the dialectic as discussed above:

1. *From Principle to Dogma.* It starts with an obviously true, somewhat inane principle. The principle is really a "reminder" of sorts, and what it reminds us about is an obvious mistake made by other philosophers. The principle is really a practical maxim, something to remember when doing something else. As the philosophy progresses, however, the principle becomes a dogma, that is, a positive claim about the way things are.

2. *From Method to Conclusion.* The practical principle is a guide for a particular kind of activity. It is a reflection on method. The dogma results from an illegitimate inference from method to conclusion.

3. *From Possibility to Actuality.* The project begins with an investigation into what it is possible to know. From this mere possibility, however, emerge some crucial facts about how things really are, about actuality.

4. *From Activity to Passivity.* The method is one that is realized or practiced in some activity. By the time we get to the dogma, the activity has ceased, and we have the statement, or repetition, of "truths," which are nothing more than premises. One could say that a philosophical investigation is one that never really begins. Before it gets going, it finds itself analyzing its own premises.

5. *Solving by Naming.* A classic error of the scholastics, for which they were mercilessly abused by the empiricists, was their way of solving a problem about the possibility of something by naming an obscure faculty responsible for it. How is sleep possible? On account of the faculty of sleep, they would say. But this is also the paradigmatic error of empiricism, when it postulates a faculty of knowledge responsible for knowing.

6. *From Knowing to Being.* The objective of the empiricist project is to move from what can be known to what must exist, or from epistemology to metaphysics. This move presumes that there is some place or thing where an equivalence exists between knowing and being. Thus, the empiricist replicates the most unempirical of postulates, that there is something whose essence it is to exist.

7. *Knowledge before Knowledge.* The empiricist project is an investigation into the foundations of knowledge. But as conundrum no. 2—"how is philosophy possible?"—shows, this puts their project somewhere before (or outside) knowledge.

8. *Doing before Doing.* The attempt to go straight to the conclusion, to have done with activity, to know before knowing—all this is a way of doing things without trying, that is, without really doing anything at all.

9. *Being Good without Doing Anything.* Let's not forget ethics! To trace the route from empiricist epistemology to ethics is hard and difficult work. Let's just say that this magical ability to do without doing is also a way of being good without lifting a finger (except to do a bit of philosophizing). Enter Socrates.

All of these points and many more should be quite familiar by now. They are the old something-for-nothing routine of philosophical mysticism. The meaning of life deduced from the meaning of 'life'.

The paradox, so far as empiricism is concerned, is that in making the general principle of empiricism into something philosophical, philosophy creates something that is entirely anti-empirical, in the general sense. Empiricism is a game played with a collection of concepts and some associated assumptions. There is nothing very empirical about it.

## WHO CARES?

The general principle at the heart of empiricism may be obvious, but that does not make it less true or less valuable. It can be, has been, and frequently is forgotten, with unfortunate consequences. But the principle is distinct from the philosophy called empiricism, and should we wish to become more empirical in our methods, it is far from obvious that the philosophy of empiricism will ensure that outcome.

# Locke

## A Man of Ideas

Like most of the other greats from the early modern era, John Locke (1632–1704) was a man of many hats, among them medical doctor, political adviser, amateur scientist, and academic. He was probably more acute, and in the long run more influential, as a political theorist than as an epistemologist. The framers of the U.S. Constitution, for example, took an interest in Locke's ideas on politics. However, it was his theory of knowledge, as presented in his *Essay Concerning the Human Understanding,* which significantly influenced the future direction of philosophy, and for which he is remembered by philosophers today.

Among his philosophical successors, down to the present, Locke's philosophy has been important as a statement of the epistemological project. That project, as Locke expressed it, is to "inquire into the original, certainty, and extent of human knowledge." The purpose is to establish the limits of human knowledge, and so persuade "the busy mind of man to be more cautious in meddling with things exceeding its comprehension."

Like many in the history of philosophy, or so I would argue, Locke is far more important for what he intended to do than what he actually did. His philosophical creation was a patchwork of recycled timber and ever-changing designs, and had so many holes it could not conceivably have floated. Locke's contemporaries admired and reviled him on account of the conception of his investigation, rather than its results. What shocked some and moved others was the audacious vulgarity of his proposed study of the mind. Locke brought the mind—the seat of the immortal soul and eternal forms—down from the celestial spheres and offered to examine it in the way one would perform an autopsy on a large rodent. Here, as in early modern philosophy in general, it is the attitude that was important.

I will argue that the real result of the Lockean inquiry, if such a result is to be had, would be a return to (shock! horror!) Aristotelian metaphysics. That Locke himself managed to avoid inferring this awful result does not redeem his project, such as it is. It does, however, reflect a certain wisdom in his patchwork approach to philosophy. Like many good empiricists, Locke avoided the unpleasant conclusions of systematic philosophy by systematically refusing to reconcile with each other the many and diverse insights which are the raw material for any philosophical enterprise.

## ORIGINS OF (THE THEORY OF) KNOWLEDGE

Locke's philosophy, like all philosophies, begins with an attack on another philosophy. The object of Locke's attack is the view that some central ideas or principles of human knowledge are innate, that is, are part of the natural constitution of the mind. The view was a common one in his day, and included among its adherents none other than Descartes. Among advocates like Lord Herbert, whom Locke assaults directly, the theory of innate knowledge seemed chiefly like an excuse to catalogue and justify a few of their favorite notions. Locke's criticisms of this theory are mostly effective. The best apply Ockham's razor to the issue: If one can plausibly account for the origin of our knowledge without the help of innate principles, then there is no need to postulate such principles.

All knowledge originates in experience. This is Locke's main thesis. Had he stopped here, we could have understood this as a bold, true restatement of the general principle of empiricism. Alas, the bulk of Locke's account comes next. At this point, his work is no longer really epistemological, but a blend of psychology and metaphysics. In other words, he tells a story, a kind of natural history perhaps, about how we acquire knowledge, and then takes this to be the ground for his epistemological conclusions.

Locke divides experience into two processes: sensation and reflection. Sensation brings in knowledge from outside the mind. Reflection derives knowledge from what is already in the mind. Exactly what sensation brings in (e.g., the idea of yellowness, the idea of a yellow chair, the idea that this is a yellow chair) is unclear. Locke's notoriously broad and inconsistent definition of the term "idea" obscures the whole matter. At some points of the discussion, reflection looks like a form of inner sensation, i.e., the mind watching itself work. At other points, it seems to represent a completely different kind of activity, the process of abstraction, or something like that. In any case, Locke goes on describe how a whole medley of ideas arise out of sensation, reflection, or some mix of the two.

## WHAT'S AN IDEA?

In Locke's writings, what 'idea' refers to includes:

1. The mental image of an external object, e.g., the image of a chair.

2. The mental image of an imaginary object, e.g., a unicorn.

3. The perceived quality of an object, e.g., yellow.

4. A sensation, as in pleasure or pain, rough or soft, salty or sweet, etc.

5. A thought, e.g., isn't this a lovely day to be caught in the rain?

6. What a word represents.

7. What a sentence represents.

8. The memory of any of the above.

Locke himself apologizes for the inconsistency. Yet there is a certain rationale behind his use of the term, and this may be why he could not bring himself to change the usage. What all Locke's uses of "idea" have in common is the notion that an idea is "something in the mind." An idea is just a mental entity, by definition the only sort of entity which can exist in the mind. The important thing, in order to understand his account, is the classic mind-body picture of empiricism: There is a mind. There is an external object. Sensation translates real properties of the object into ideas in the mind. Reflection plays around with the ideas once they are in the mind. The little word "in," as in "in the mind," is the clue to the whole account: Without that questionable spatial metaphor, Locke's story collapses. In short, the many meanings Locke gives to "idea" is his way of importing a metaphysic into his epistemology.

## QUALITY FIRST

At this point, to his credit, Locke recognizes he's got a conundrum on his hands. If all the mind has are ideas, how can it ever know whether and how these ideas correspond to the object out there in the world? Locke attempts to resolve the dilemma by offering a distinction between primary and secondary qualities of objects. The primary qualities are solidity, shape (extension), motion, rest, and number. These are "utterly inseparable" from the object. So the mind perceives them just as they are. Whew—external objects exist, and are what they appear to be, at least in part. The secondary qualities, like color, taste, and all the rest, result from a combination of certain, primary qualities of objects and the mind's specific faculties of sensation. So they correspond only indirectly to the real qualities of the object.

Locke's distinction would be unlikely to sway a skeptic, as indeed it failed to move his successor, George Berkeley. The primary qualities are simply inferred from the implicit definition of the "external object," the knowledge of whose existence is precisely what is in question. In the tradition of the scholastics, Locke tries to solve his problem by defining his way out of it. Actually, things are even worse. Locke adds a third set of qualities to objects, viz. their "powers," or their capacity to effect changes in the primary qualities of other objects. But at this point we have retreated deeply into the obscurities of Aristotelian faculties.

Locke's distinction between primary and secondary qualities, by the way, was motivated in part by recent achievements in science. Newton had shown that science could provide an apparently superior structure within which to interpret color than that of common sense. So, Locke moved color into the second category of quality. On the other hand, Newton had premised his physical theories on the idea of absolute space and time. So, Locke made these primary qualities. Philosophy, it seems, followed science, rather than led it, and converted hypothetical frameworks into rigid metaphysics.

## RETURN OF THE BIG OOZEY

The primary qualities, as it happens, are just a temporary stopping point on the way to an even more fundamental reality. Locke himself admits that one can ask, in what do these qualities inhere? The answer, he says, is a "something I know not what," to which he nonetheless gives that charming old name, "substance." Scholars sometimes try to distinguish Lockean substance from the substance of the Aristotelian/metaphysical tradition, on the grounds that Locke's stuff represents a "substratum" in which properties inhere, as opposed to something that exists independently of all relations. In my view, there is no real distinction here. That which has no properties but in which properties inhere is in fact independent, a metaphysical individual in the traditional sense. As we saw in Aristotle, the notion of substance originated in the idea of a subject which cannot be made a predicate for some other subject.

Had Locke been tuned to think in the long-established ways, he would have concluded that this substance could not be multiple—otherwise different substances would have diverse, unique properties; that it must be changeless—else it would have multiple states, and therefore be identifiable with specific properties; that it must be identical with the world—for it is that in which all properties ultimately inhere. In short, had he thought it through, Locke would have been, surprise, a Spinozan.

Such a result should not seem so strange. Locke's substance is actually a hypothetical construct required in order to get his project going. It is a part of the original, metaphysical picture which frames his investigation. As with Spinoza, it is the premise which makes the project possible. In the final section of his book, by the way, Locke becomes wholly rationalist, and throws in his own version of the ontological proof of the existence of God.

# Berkeley

## *The Babbling Bishop*

George Berkeley (1685–1753) has basically one point to make: Physical objects are nothing but ideas in the mind. Professional philosophers like him, not because they think his views correct, but because he is the closest thing to the wayward and anonymous skeptic whose refutation is supposed to be their own task. But Berkeley has a role in this and other histories of philosophy for another reason. His philosophy works out some of the fundamental premises of the Lockean project, and draws them, or so I think, to their absurd conclusion.

## THE SKELETON OF AN ARGUMENT

Berkeley's premises are borrowed Locke, stock and barrel.

1. There is something that thinks, and that something is the mind.

2. The mind works exclusively with ideas.

3. All ideas originate in sensation.

   a) Sensations are ideas in the mind (e.g., heat, brightness, spherical shape, upwardness)

   b) Physical objects are the sum of a set of qualities identified by sensation-ideas (e.g., the sun is that hot, bright sphere up in the sky).

   c) Other ideas are the result of combinations and divisions of these object-ideas by memory, imagination, and/or introspection (e.g., an example of the number one is that there is only one sun).

Rather churlishly, Berkeley turns Locke's own premises against him. He argues that:

1. There can be no distinction between primary and secondary qualities.

   a) You cannot imagine an object with only primary qualities (i.e., an object with "solidity in general," "shape in general," etc. does not exist).

   b) Primary qualities aren't constant anyway (e.g., objects look smaller in the distance).

In essence, Berkeley wants to insist on Lockean premise 3, that all sensible qualities are of the same status, viz. they are ideas in the mind.

2. There can be no external substance supporting our perceptions of objects. Berkeley (probably accurately) points out that Locke's substance, which can have no properties and yet somehow "supports" the properties of other things, is not much of a thing at all, and is at best a vacuous substitute for the idea of being. In effect, Berkeley insists on Lockean premise 3: This substance is not itself an idea, since it is what supposedly supports ideas; but in that case, how can I have any idea what it is?

3. In fact, there are no objects beyond our ideas. Berkeley throws a number of arguments behind this:

   a) We could only be sure of the existence of such objects if we could apprehend them directly, prior to sensation. But this is not possible. All we have to go on are the ideas which arise from sensation.

   b) External objects could not even resemble our ideas of them. You can compare ideas only with—other ideas. So, whatever is out there cannot be anything like what we perceive.

   c) External objects could not even be said to "cause" ideas. For this would suppose that inert matter could act on the "spirit," or mind. But if mind is something distinct from matter, then how could a causal chain extend between the two? (Berkeley further identifies "causality" with "agency" on the grounds that only an agent can truly cause an effect, and believes agency to be a proper attribute of spiritual things only, and mainly God.)

   d) Finally, in case you thought Plato had the solution: "Abstract ideas" correspond to no reality. There is no mental image or form of 'Man' to which the concept 'man' refers. Such a generic 'Man' would have no identifiable properties. Rather, the meaning of the concept 'man' is just that it can be predicated of all those beings who belong to a particular class of beings, i.e., men.

Having turned Locke against himself, Berkeley avers his chief doctrine: Physical objects are nothing but ideas in the mind. In a fancy Latin phrase, this is *esse est percipi* (to be is to be perceived). In other words, physical objects exist only insofar as they are perceived by a mind.

Of course, this leaves a certain amount of explaining still to do. What could possibly cause our perceptions of objects, if not an external reality? Berkeley's answer is, in a word, God. God is Berkeley's replacement for Locke's "something I know not what"-substance. God gives us our ideas. And God maintains reality in existence when we aren't perceiving it. Hence the consistent nature of our perceptions. Somewhat like Descartes's demon, Berkeley's God pulls all the strings, except he's a nice guy. Sometimes, though, Berkeley sounds a little Spinozan: When we see things that look pretty solid, like tables and chairs, he suggests, we are participating in God's own perceptions.

BERKELEY: FRUIT AS IDEAS IN THE MIND

## THE REALITY

While Berkeley's critical analysis of Locke is acute, his own doctrines are absurd. Pieces of his critique of Locke would be used with great effect by David Hume. Berkeley would have done better, had he prefaced his conclusions with: "Locke's epistemology is fundamentally flawed because it entails the following absurd conclusions." All he really showed was that if you start from Lockean (or Cartesian) premises about the nature of knowledge, you cannot give a meaningful account of knowledge at all. The logical thing to do would have been to throw out the project altogether.

Like Locke, Berkeley starts off with the picture which separates the mind from external objects, and places all ideas and knowledge "in" the mind. Unlike Locke, he sees that according to this picture of things, the mind can never be sure of knowing how things really are. In other words, he discovers the first conundrum I described in the chapter on empiricism (pp. 184–91).

In slightly revised terms, then, Berkeley's central argument runs thus:

1. The mind knows mental things only.

2. Mental things are not physical things.

3. The mind cannot know physical things.

Or, with another definition of Berkeley's "idea" as "anything that is apprehended *immediately* by the mind," the argument runs thus:

1. True knowledge is immediate only.

2. Physical things reach the mind only through the mediation of the senses.

3. The mind knows no physical things truly.

BERKELEY: HAVING LOOKED AWAY

## FROM ABSOLUTE DOUBT TO ABSOLUTE KNOWLEDGE: A SHORT HOP

Berkeley can be regarded as a radical skeptic. Nothing is real, he says. Those who accept Berkeley's arguments suddenly have cause to doubt everything they thought they knew. Yet they also come into some knowledge. Specifically, they know about the existence of God, and how He manages things in the world. In fact, you could say that they know the real truth about everything.

Absolute doubt leads to the discovery of an absolutely certain truth. This truth is the most fundamental truth there is, the truth about everything. The pattern is familiar from Descartes, not to mention Socrates. From mere ignorance nothing in particular follows. But from absolute ignorance, well, that's another matter altogether.

In more general terms, the pattern is one of converting possibility into actuality, or contingency into necessity. It is possible to doubt everything. From this possibility itself the philosopher deduces something which is actual, or necessary. In brief, the Holy Grail.

# The Dramas of Mind and Body

Since Descartes, philosophers have exhibited a peculiar obsession with minds, and how they might relate to things around them, such as bodies, sense organs, passions, external objects, and other minds.

## THE MIND-BODY PROBLEM

How does the body communicate with the mind? At what point does the physical sense response become a mental sense datum?

Do the senses provide a complete picture of the external world, or just raw data which have to be processed by the mind to form a complete picture?

Where is the mind located in the body: the brain, the pituitary gland, the stomach, the left foot? Can it be surgically removed? Is it even located in the body?

Can you have a body without a mind? A mind without a body? Can a body change its mind? Can a mind change its body?

Who has those primitive urges (you know what I mean), the body or the mind?

Do these passions determine what the mind does, or is the mind free? Can the mind determine the passions?

How do the passions know what they want, if they have no mental powers? How can the mind want anything, if it has no passions?

## PROOF OF THE EXISTENCE OF EXTERNAL OBJECTS

If all the mind has to go on is sense perception, how can it be sure of the existence of external objects? Could that Irish leprechaun be in control of the senses? In any case, can the mind ever really know what objects are like?

200

# THE PROBLEM OF OTHER MINDS

If all the mind has to go on is sense perception, how can it distinguish other minds from external objects? Could they all be robots? How does each of us conclude that we are not the only mind in existence?

# THE UNKNOWABLE PLAYWRIGHT

For an extraordinarily brief but glorious instant in time, a few brave individuals believed that these questions were asked in jest. They believed that Descartes and his colleagues had conspired to put one over on the educated masses of Europe. The whole Mind-Body problematic, they thought, was intended as a comical example of how philosophers can spin a few platitudinous truths into a ludicrous web of illogic, false problems, and silly questions. So, let us suppose, it was two of these brave few—the Unknowable (a.k.a. the Awful) Playwright and the Unknowable (a.k.a. Even Worse) Artist—who put pen to paper, and produced the never-performed Dramas of Mind and Body and the long-suppressed Minds and Bodies Illustrations. Had these Unknowns achieved the same fame as their more serious contemporaries, the course of the history of philosophy would have been very different. Alas, the joke was on them.

## MIND LOST

Scene 1. *In the Mind's I.*

MIND: I think therefore I am. I think therefore I am. I think therefore I am. I think . . .

BODY: Hey, mind, what's the matter?

MIND: Matter? What's that? I think therefore . . .

BODY: I mean, what's on your Mind?

MIND: Can't you see? If I think not, I am not. I might disappear! I think therefore I am. I think . . .

BODY (*to himself*): What a head case. (*To Mind*): Come on, take a load off your mind. We all know you exist.

MEMORY: Yeah, it's not like I could forget about you.

BODY: You're a substance, a thinking thing. You'll live forever.

MIND: Oh I don't know. Maybe you're right. I guess I think too much.

BODY (*to Imagination*): He's pretty tense. I wish we could have left him in the pineal gland. Can you send something up, Imagination? You know, something tropical?

IMAGINATION: You bet. Got some great pictures here . . . (*passes a few to Body.*)

BODY: Oo la la. (*to himself*). Hope this gets Mind thinking on the right track. (*Passes them to Mind.*)

MIND (*looking at pictures*): Disgusting. Don't you ever get enough, body? Hey, wait a minute, these aren't real. You can't fool me. They're faded. These are the least lively impressions I've seen in a while.

IMAGINATION: Well, I tried my best.

MIND: What are you trying to do, anyway, Body? Are you trying to distract me? Are you looking at some cheap bodily pleasures? Do you want to take over here?

BODY: Oh no, sir! I wouldn't think of it. You're in charge.

MIND: Darn right I'm in charge.

MEMORY (*to Imagination*): Sounds like the old Mind–Body problem again.

BODY: Hold it. (*Grabs a stack of paper from hand offstage.*) Got some real stuff here. Captain, sir: I have some sense perceptions to report. (*Hands papers to Mind.*)

MIND: I told you, we're calling them sense qualia from now on. Are you out of your senses, or what?

BODY: What do you mean?

MIND: Look here. This is a report from Sight from two seconds ago. It says the object is brown. Here is the Sight report from one second ago, and it says the object is "sort of white."

BODY: Uh oh. I'll look into that right away.

MIND (*to himself*): Why are these senses are so unreliable?

MEMORY: I seem to recall something like this happening before. Maybe we ought to check recent body movements . . .

BODY: I was bending over at the time . . .

MIND: . . . which may have caused a reflection off the surface of the object, causing old Sore Eyes to think the object was "sort of white." Well why didn't you tell me that in the first place? Why don't you just bring me the object, just bring it in here?

BODY: Uh, well, I don't see how we can do that.

MEMORY: You know the rules, Mind. The union won't let him do it. Got to keep the senses employed.

IMAGINATION: I could draw a picture of it for you.

MIND: No! I want the real thing. I can't trust you guys for a minute. How do I know these witless senses are telling the truth? I've got eyes that can't see straight, a nose that's bent out of shape, ears that can't tell Mozart from the garbage man. And you expect me to make decisions. I've had it. Unless you bring me this object, I'm going to ignore these reports on the assumption that they're all lies and fabrications.

MEMORY, BODY, IMAGINATION (*together, to each other*): Oh no! The problem of the existence of external objects!

MIND: That's right. I'm a skeptic now.

IMAGINATION (*to Body, Memory*): I've got an idea. Let's see if we can bring him an Other Mind, see if they can talk sense to each other.

BODY: Got it. (*Picks up papers from offstage.*) Some sense perceptions—er, qualia—concerning a humanoid figure right next door.

IMAGINATION: Let me throw in some pictures of Mind. I guess an Other Mind must look pretty much like Mind, don't you agree? (*Puts a few papers on Body's stack.*)

MEMORY: All right, pass it up to Mind.

MIND (*receiving papers from Body*): What's this? More non-sense, Body? Another lousy portrait of me, Imagination? You're trying to convince me that this stack of crummy ideas is an Other Mind? Ha. (*Shuffles the papers.*) So, our faithful ear reports this Other Mind has said, "How are you?" (*mockingly*) "How are you?" Do you really think that when two minds meet, we have nothing better to say to each other than "How are you?" You don't fool me for a second. There is no Other Mind.

MEMORY, BODY, IMAGINATION (*together, to each other*): Oh no! The Problem of Other Minds!

MIND: That's right, I'm a solipsist now. The only thing I'm sure of now is me, myself, and I. (*Mind walks over to a corner and huddles with himself, mumbling.*)

BODY: Well, I guess that's it. We've lost our Mind.

(Indeed, this theatrical episode in the history of philosophy has been largely and thankfully forgotten, as serious philosophers set aside these absurd dramas and set about solving the problems of Minds, Bodies, Other Minds, and Other Bodies.)

# Minds and Bodies

Idea

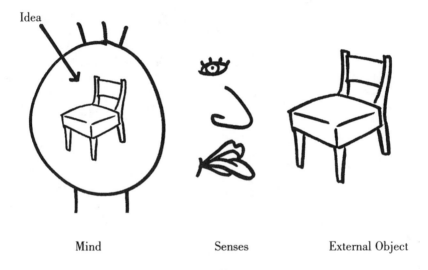

Mind                    Senses                    External Object

THE THEORY OF MIND

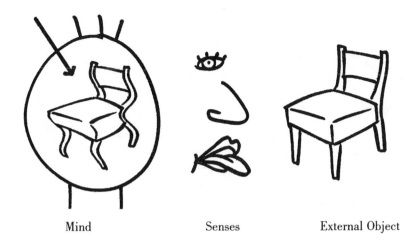

Mind            Senses            External Object

## MIND HAS A BAD CHAIR DAY

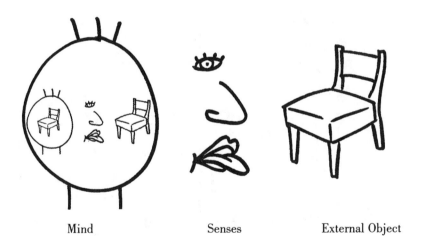

Mind            Senses            External Object

## THE MIND'S EYE

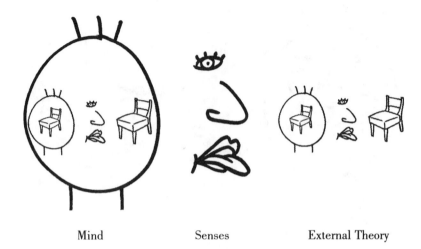

Mind                    Senses                    External Theory

## HOW THE MIND PERCEIVES THE THEORY OF MIND

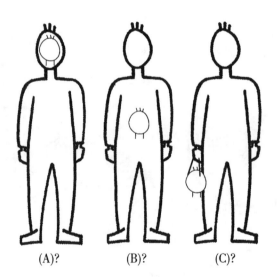

(A)?                    (B)?                    (C)?

## THE MIND-BODY PROBLEM

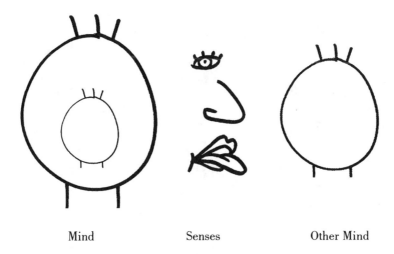

Mind                    Senses                    Other Mind

THE PROBLEM OF OTHER MINDS

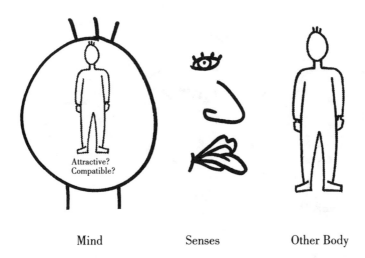

Mind                    Senses                    Other Body

THE PROBLEM OF OTHER BODIES

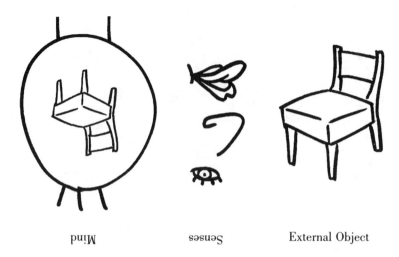

MIND      Senses      External Object

MIND TESTS THE RELIABILITY OF PERCEPTIONS

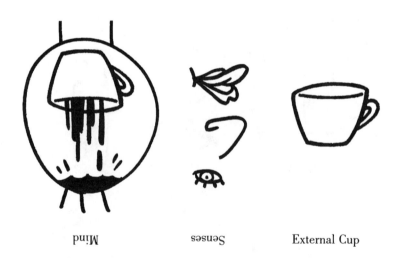

Mind      Senses      External Cup

MIND GOES TOO FAR

# Hume

## *A Man for All Senses*

D avid Hume (1711–1776) admitted that he preferred shooting pool to philosophizing, and his corpulence attested to his friendly disposition toward the gus-
tatory pleasures. Which is not to say that he was sybaritic. On the contrary, one
could say that, like a good Greek, Hume was moderate in moderation. When the
conversation turned to philosophy, he would be neither fanatical nor self-indulgent,
but decent, honest, and quite to the point.

## FROM PSYCHO-BABBLE TO LOGIC

Hume brings the dialectic of empiricism to a close. Locke offered the premises.
Berkeley showed that these premises lead to absurd doctrines, namely, his own.
Hume tosses the whole thing out the window, but not before having extracted the
general truths which inspire empiricism. Looked at another way, Hume's achievement is to have elevated empiricism from an amateur psychology to a matter of simple logical distinctions. Although Hume expresses a number of his arguments in
the picture-language of Lockean minds and sense impressions, his most important
conclusions can be easily rephrased as logical insights. These insights in turn
undermine the psychological and metaphysical presuppositions of the empiricist
project, but are not the foundation for any further project.

## I. A LOGICAL PITCHFORK

Expressed in a modern, abbreviated form, Hume's central argument is this: Philosophers have conflated under the term "Reason" (or one of its mushy relatives,

like metaphysics or ontology) three distinct concepts: real reason, fact, and value. In their confusion they ascribe to their own claims—putative facts and values—a status to which they are not entitled: that of deductive truths of pure reason.

Real reason, as Hume presents it, is basically logic. It is the activity of drawing inferences from given premises. If X is true, then Y must also be true. In Hume's quaint language, reason is the "comparison of ideas." Mathematics and geometry, by the way, belong to reason/logic in this sense. "Facts" are true propositions about states of affairs: e.g., water boils at 100°C; I am taller than you; this chair exists. "Values" are the ends in view of which human beings (or any kind of subjective agent) decide what they want: to make money, to be happy, and so forth.

According to Hume, real reason provides no facts about the world. It simply indicates how various possible facts are related. Nor is reason capable of determining values. Reason will endorse any value or any set of values which is consistent with itself. Lastly, values do not belong to the class of facts. What *is* the case in the world is a question of fact; what *ought* to be is a question of value, whose answer does not follow solely from the answer to the previous question.

## REASON VERSUS FACT

What is true according to reason, is necessarily true. A truth of reason cannot be considered untrue without contradiction. If A = B and B = C, then A = C. Anything else is just wrong. What is true according to fact, happens to be true, but is not necessarily true in the same way. A fact is a fact because it says that of many possible states of affairs, this particular one happens to be the case. It is always possible to imagine that a fact is not true without fear of contradiction. There is nothing illogical in the proposition that the sun rises in the West, even if it be untrue. In other words, factual knowledge is about things that could logically be otherwise than they are. Facts can be justified only by evidence, and experience is the ultimate source of all evidence. Thus, with his simple, logical distinction between reason and fact, Hume articulates the general principle of empiricism and the sensible core of the Lockean philosophy.

### Logical versus Causal Necessity

Matters of fact, Hume says, boil down to causal relationships. "A causes B" is his idea of a general fact. He therefore proposes to analyze the notion of causality. The result of his analysis is that causality is not all that it's cracked up to be. Specifically, all that joins A and B, he argues, is a constant conjunction of experiences, and nothing that is logically necessary. In other words, whenever we see A we notice that B follows soon thereafter. Thus we conclude that A causes B, at least until we see something (like C following A) to contradict our conclusion. According to the rule which says that a great philosopher must be defined by some absurd doctrine, Hume's interpreters have made a feast out of his apparent skepticism about causality. Actually, Hume's argument amounts to a simple, logical distinction, and not another crazy doctrine. He is distinguishing between logical and causal necessity. Logical necessity is enforced by contradiction; causal necessity is determined by the evidence of experience, and cannot be justified by noncontradiction alone.

## The Problem of Induction

The reason/fact distinction gives rise to this apparently startling claim: The knowledge gained from experience is always possibly (i.e., conceivably) false. Facts cannot be proved demonstratively, i.e., by deductive reason, but must rely on experience. But experience provides only a finite amount of data on which to generalize. Thus the so-called problem of induction: How can the finite range of experience justify putatively universal claims about nature? Actually, it's not a problem, but a simple truth. Hume is simply offering an interesting logical point: Induction is not deduction. Universal claims about nature, insofar as they are meaningful, are always subject to revision on the basis of new experience. They cannot be demonstrated by means of deductive logic alone. To believe otherwise is to believe that the world can be known by merely thinking about it, by analyzing the world *qua* world.

## A Hypothetico-Deductive Amendment

Hume's conclusion is less startling if one allows, as he hints but perhaps fails to stress sufficiently, that we typically approach natural phenomena in a hypothetico-deductive way. That is, we deduce the nature and expected behavior of particular things from more general hypotheses we hold about things and the world. "A causes B" can be considered logically necessary to the extent that A and B are defined to belong to classes of entities hypothesized to act in certain ways. The important point to remember, as Hume would have put it, is that the necessity we perceive among things comes from the deductive relationships among our ideas about these things, not the things themselves. And this is just to restate the distinction between logical necessity and causal necessity.

## Being Is Not Believing

Whatever is, says Hume, may not be. Whether or not any particular thing one sees, thinks of, or imagines exists is a question of fact, and cannot be deduced by logical arguments from the idea of that thing. Hume also puts it this way: the idea of existence adds nothing to the idea of anything. Later philosophers would say that existence is not a true predicate (or at least not in the same way as all the other predicates). The upshot is that the old ontological argument of the theologians, that there is a special something whose essence it is to exist, is rubbish.

Behind Hume's argument is a very ordinary distinction between believing and being true. When you add to a particular proposition the fact that you believe in it, you do not get any closer to demonstrating its truth. (Except maybe the proposition:

"I believe in this proposition.") You may increase its credibility among friends and relatives, but so what? You have adopted an *attitude* with respect to a proposition, but you have not changed the content or truth-value of that proposition.

## Down with Theology

Besides trashing the ontological argument, Hume also wastes the argument from design (taken as the representative proof from experience). The latter is usually some form of this: Every car has a car maker; so the universe must have a universe maker. Hume's contention is that this sort of inference is logically invalid. The crux of his argument is that the universe and universe maker are by definition singular and unique entities. They cannot belong to a class or species of entities. But it is only through membership in such classes that we can infer anything about anything. It is only because we know that cars belong to the class of manufactured objects, that is, because we have seen lots of similar things being made, that we can infer that a particular car has a car maker. Since no parallel is possible between particular things and the totality of things, no inference is possible about this totality, i.e., the universe.

Taken together, Hume's arguments against ontological proofs and proofs from experience are clearly part of an attempt to undermine natural theology altogether. They block both paths, of logic and of experience, which are supposed to represent natural theology's alternative to revelation.

### REASON VERSUS VALUE

Assume that in order to get X, one must do Y. Reason will remind you, in that case, if you want X, then you must do Y. Reason will further inform you, perhaps gratuitously, that if wanting X implies not wanting Z, then you must also not want Z. But reason will never tell you what X, Y, Z, or any other letter should stand for. Real reason is a science of means, utterly indifferent to the ends to which it is applied. As Hume rather dramatically puts it, reason is the slave of the passions. To the horror of some readers, he argues to the effect that there is nothing inherently unreasonable about preferring an ice cream sundae to saving the world from nuclear war.

If that sounds harsh, think again. Think of reason as an instrument, which is what it is. Like, say, a car. You use a car to get from point A to point B. You would not hop in the car and say to the steering wheel, Okay, take me where you want me to go. That would be absurd, and it might scare the neighbors. Why should it be any less absurd to imagine that pure reason, which is used to infer B from A, should also be able to decide what A and B should be?

### FACT VERSUS VALUE

When one says "X is bad," what does this mean? Is it a fact? Well, it might be a matter of fact, if what we mean to say is, "according to the moral code of the community of Zs, X is bad." It might also be a matter of fact if what we mean is that "X gives me a bad feeling." But as it is, it is not a matter of fact in the same way as, for example, "X is the name of the first emperor of Rome." Right and wrong, good and bad, and so forth do not inhere in objects, actions, or people in the same way as properties in general. If they did, scientists would have found the little goodness molecules or whatever by now. Facts are about the way things *are*, not the way they *ought to be*. In other words, *description* is not *prescription*. In order to get from the former to the latter, one must first affirm a value, or more generally, a purpose or intention.

Hume gets a lot of undeserved grief on this point, too, for it supposedly makes him a moral subjectivist or relativist, or some other nasty "ist." In fact, his argument does not require that one deny the universality implicit in moral judgments. He takes the "reality" of moral judgments as given. So it is still perfectly sensible to maintain a distinction in meaning between "X is bad" and "X causes in me certain feelings of badness," inasmuch as the former is intended to represent a universal judgment of value, and while the latter is an introspective observation. Hume's argument really has to do with the way in which moral judgments can be justified, and his point is that they cannot be exhaustively justified with reference to facts (or reason), but require in addition the affirmation of some value. This should be no more problematic than the distinction between a result and a purpose. Both come at the "end" of a process, but only the latter supplies a criterion according to which the process may be meaningfully judged.

## No Deal

An example from political theory shows how Hume's analysis of moral judgment can be put to work. Much ink has been spilled on behalf of the idea that political institutions derive their legitimacy from an original "social contract" entered into by individuals existing in a presocial state of nature. Now, it is obvious that this is historically inaccurate. Even if it were historically accurate, it is quite unclear why a contract entered into by unnameable forebears under highly unusual circumstances should still be binding today. Most theorists acknowledge that said contract is to be viewed as a kind of hypothetical construct, a way of clarifying concepts and testing the legitimacy of governments. But here Hume's arguments are most telling. The very idea of such a contract as the moral basis for political institutions is incoherent. Individuals may enter into the purported contract out of self-interest. But what stops them (or their children) from pulling out on the deal when their self-interest points the other way? A contract presupposes a moral regime which would require and/or enforce it. In other words, it presupposes the affirmation of the values which are supposedly established by the contract. A social contract that is not binding is no contract; a social contract that is binding is not social, in the sense of being foundational for ethical society. All this should be pretty obvious. At the end of the day, social contract theory is just one more example of philosophy's attempt to ground ethical principles in reason, or to confuse a description (of the origin of society, or the nature of social activity, for example) with a prescription (for the best form of government, etc.).

## II. THE END OF EMPIRICISM

One of the chief victims of Hume's logical pitchfork is philosophical empiricism itself. The empiricist project, as we have already seen, requires an *a priori* metaphysical and/or psychological determination of the nature of the knowing subject in order to propose a sensible task. Yet, according to Hume's analysis, such a structure would necessarily be a matter of fact, something to be verified (or not) *a posteriori*. So, while the general principle of empiricism remains healthy, and an empirical investigation of the mind or brain still makes sense, there is no room for an empiricist epistemological project.

### *EMPIRICIST ATAVISMS*

To be sure, Hume begins his inquiries in an empiricist frame of mind, and uses much of the old, Lockean vocabulary. Even here, however, it is possible to translate his arguments out of that initial framework. Take the distinction between 'impressions' and 'ideas' with which he begins. Impressions, our "stronger" perceptions, are something like immediate sense experiences, while ideas, our "weaker" perceptions, are the memories, concepts, etc., formed in our minds without the benefit of immediate experience. At first, this sounds like a throwback to the bad old days of Locke's pansemantic 'idea' and Descartes's substantial ego. But in light of the uses to which Hume puts this distinction, it could be rephrased as a logical distinction between the nonlinguistic referents of language and the language itself. The distinction permits the separation of the activity of comparing ideas (i.e., connecting words according to their meanings, drawing inferences) from the activity of talking about something (and hence of acquiring knowledge through experience). Understood in a sympathetic way, this separation forestalls conundrum no. 1 of empiricism, the paradox that knowledge is not possible because all knowledge is mediated through the senses, and yet true knowledge should be immediate. Hume's distinction implies that true knowledge requires a combination of active and passive, or mediated and immediate, elements. (Somewhat confusingly, Hume also uses this distinction to separate passions from thoughts, to make up another, related deficiency in Cartesian philosophy.)

### *NEVER MIND*

An example of how Hume's logic forces him to undermine the metaphysical framework which made empiricism possible is his analysis of the concept of 'mind'. Hume declares unintelligible the Cartesian notion that the mind is a substance. Thinking, Hume says, is always thinking about something. Anything that exists, including a thought, perception, or whatever, is particular. Thus, there is no pure "thought as such," and no "mind-substance" distinct from perceptions and particular ideas. Indeed, these perceptions do not "belong" to a preexisting mind-thing; they compose the mind. Once again, Hume's point is essentially a logical one: it is false to infer, as Descartes did, from the activity of thinking to the existence of a thinking substance, just as it is false to infer from eating to an eating substance. Hume returns us to Aristotle in his better moments: The faculty does not exist as distinct from its exercise. So much for mind, matter, and all that nonsense. (Some of Hume's contemporaries summed up Berkeley and Hume together with the slogan: "no matter, never mind.")

## A CRASS AND POSSESSIVE INDIVIDUALIST?

Among the sillier charges brought against Hume is that he invented a rabidly individualistic philosophy that influenced the devolution of the Western world into a lonely, egocentric place to live. (The same charge is often laid against Socrates, Descartes, Hobbes, Locke, Kant, and Rawls. It would appear that the same crime occurred more than once and had many authors.) Whether or not our world is a lonely place is a (rather squishy) question of fact. What might have caused it to become (or not) such a place is also a question of fact. I can see no necessary relationship between the logical distinctions in the body of Hume's philosophy and any existing state of affairs. As a matter of reason, I can see no conceivable relationship except insofar as Hume's logical distinctions might have been (falsely) interpreted as putative facts, and these putative facts either (mis)used in pursuit of given values or confused with values themselves. Whether Hume's peripheral reflections on human psychology and the "passions" influenced more than a handful of English and Scottish gentlemen seems to me a proposition too far-fetched and unsusceptible of proof to pursue.

# III. THE END OF PHILOSOPHY?

## SKEPTICAL ABOUT SKEPTICISM

In the traditional scheme of the history of philosophy, Hume is supposed to be a skeptic. He does admit to the label, though with important qualifications. He distances himself from the ancient skeptics, in that he does not believe that the suspension of all judgment is a wise or practicable policy in "common life." Hume distinguishes his views from those of Descartes, whose method of universal doubt he takes at best as a useful preparation for any investigation, but more likely a sophistry. He also avoids Berkeley, whose idealism he sees as an attempt at sensationalist and paradoxical skepticism. What he is skeptical about, it turns out, are philosophical doctrines—of which skepticism is one example.

If one takes his logical distinctions as the core of his own philosophy, it is clear that what Hume is skeptical about is simply what is logically impossible. He is skeptical about facts deduced from reason. He "doubts" that existence belongs to the essence of anything—which is like saying that he doubts that you can prove something true by believing in it. It all suggests a general principle of philosophy (which I will refrain from overdramatizing this time) that skepticism is a relative term, and usually relative to some hopelessly high and confused expectations. Take away the expectations, which were not Hume's anyway, and Hume is not a skeptic.

## THE HOLY GRAIL EXPOSED

Philosophy makes its living by confusing the basic terms of reason, fact, and value. Both before and after Hume, it has actively and sometimes explicitly sought to reconcile their opposed meanings into a single term. In identifying essence and existence in God, for example, the medieval theologians thought they could show that at least one fact—God exists—follows from pure reason. Aristotle had shown them the way by claiming to investigate ultimate reality by means of an analysis of categories and substances. Descartes thought he could do the same, first with the "I am," then with God as an added bonus. From the Presocratics on, philosophers have been searching for that mysterious thing which in being possible, is necessarily also actual—the thing which calls itself into existence, the independent, indubitable, absolute, rock-like, foundational truth-thing. The rock of reason is also intended to show us, to prove to us, what we should want and do. Virtue, justice, happiness, and all those nice words belong to the Socratic few who manage to stand on this strange rock. Hume, for a moment at least, reveals that this rock is an illusion wrapped inside a fantasy inside a contradiction.

## BILLIARDS, ANYONE?

So, what is there for the philosopher to do? Hume's initial response was probably that maybe it's time to go shoot some billiards. Actually, besides the pub games, Hume did offer at least a couple of other answers to this philosophical problem.

The first comes from within his philosophical works, and is a project which would today be classed as something of a hybrid of moral theory and psychology. Morality boils down to sentiments, he argues, and there is no reason why one cannot inquire, in an empirical way, into the causes and behaviors of these sentiments. The result is something like psychology, but not of the modern, professional sort so much as of the general, humanist type, like that offered by a La Rochefoucauld or a Nietzsche.* It is also not quite a moral philosophy, inasmuch as it does not aim to present the nature of the good, but rather the nature of human behaviors associated with the sentiment of, for example, goodness. Hume hopes that this project will improve human self-understanding, and help found a general science of human nature. The project is indeed a sensible one, though Hume's contribution toward its realization is modest at best.

Hume's second answer comes from his life. He published his first philosophi-

---

*La Rochefoucauld (1613–1680) wrote pithy aphorisms and maxims designed to help his reader understand and anticipate the foibles of human vanity. Nietzsche, as we shall see, speculated on a wide range of psychological types, and offered historical explanations of their genesis.

cal work before reaching the age of thirty, and his last before forty. In his remaining twenty-five years it may be fairly said that he turned his attention away from philosophy and toward more productive endeavors. In his own time Hume was probably better known for his work on the history of England than for his philosophical reflections. Like the ancient Callicles, Hume might have said that philosophy is a youthful activity, and like youth, ought not to be held on to after its time.

## THE END OF PHILOSOPHY?

So far as the history of philosophy is concerned, it would be a mistake to think that Hume represents a moment of philosophical development that would be incorporated and presumably surpassed in later generations. On the contrary, his insights would be forgotten or rejected. The whole experience of German Idealism could be viewed as a detour in which academic philosophy hoped to save itself from Hume. I suggest we keep Hume as an ever-present ideal of honesty and clarity in thought, rather than as the representative of some or other school or doctrine.

# Odds and Ends from Early Modern Philosophy

## Just in Case You Thought That Was All . . .

> "To mock philosophers is to philosophize truly."
>
> Pascal

The list of the key players of early modern philosophy has been so firmly established, it seems as though history forsook for a time its habitual messiness, and instead proceeded according to a simple plan. On the Continent, rationalist number one is followed by numbers two and three. In Britain, empiricist number one gives way to numbers two and three. At the end of the eighteenth century the first and last transcendental-idealist-cum-empirical-realist achieves a synthesis of rationalism and empiricism. It would have been nice if things had been so uncomplicated.

I have discussed the issues within the standard list above. In this section and the next on the French Enlightenment, my concern is with the names that are not on that list—just in case you were under the impression that the standard list really coincided with the "thought" of the early modern era.

## PLATO STALKS THE QUADS

The traditional history of philosophy brushes off the Cambridge Platonists as a bunch of mediocre reactionaries. They probably were that, but this alone would not have been enough to exclude them from the mainstream of the history of philosophy. They confronted the same basic problem as those philosophers who did make the hit parade—viz., how to reconcile an old religion with the new science—and their solution was at least as "logical" as those of the others—which is to say, for the most part, not very logical at all. Their mistake, so far as historical success is concerned, was a question of style.

Henry More (1614–1687), perhaps the leading Cambridge Platonist, was very familiar with the work of Hobbes and Descartes and his answer to them and the fundamental problem motivating their work was, in a word, Plotinus. (It was not really Plato who haunted the quadrangles of the Cambridge colleges, but Neoplatonism.) Though keen on science and its recent discoveries, More feared that Hobbes and other science-boosters represented a threat to religion. Like Plotinus and so many other philosophers, however, More was a mystic who understood religion not as a faith but as the direct knowledge of divinity. He turned to philosophy, and Plotinus in particular, in order to find a way to make the divine knowledge of religion compatible with the secular knowledge of science.

In his main work, the *Immortality of the Soul* (1659), More argues that the sort of thoroughgoing materialism advocated by Hobbes is incoherent. It cannot account for subjectivity (or "mental phenomena," or "intentionality," or whatever label is appropriate). At the same time, More acknowledges that the notions of 'soul' or 'spirit' on which traditional religion and metaphysics rely need to be explained in their relationship to the apparently mechanical nature of the body, or matter. Part of his explanation is an awkward attempt to improve on one of Descartes's more miserable theses. The mind, *pace* Descartes, is not located in the pineal gland, but in what More calls "the fourth ventricle of the brain." Said ventricle apparently has some very "fine," quasi-material spirits. More also gets carried away in discussing the nature of the soul and the "Aereal World" in which it apparently resides after death. For example, he deliberates on such burning questions as whether there are students and professors of philosophy in the Aereal world. But the metaphysical thrust of More's solution is a Neoplotinian theory of "emanation," the peculiar, putatively unidirectional mechanism whereby spirit "informs" matter.

More's system is no more convincing than Plotinus's. Yet it is arguably an improvement on Descartes's metaphysics, inasmuch as it at least acknowledges and attempts to solve the mind-body problem inherent in the latter (as in any form of Platonism). It is true that More and his fellow dons were mystics. But, like all Platonists, they were rational mystics. Some of their countrymen even lumped them with Hobbes, as heretics who would elevate speculative reason above revealed truth. And, as we have already seen, there is mysticism even in the hard core of philosophical empiricism. The Cantabrians' mistake, as I suggested, was one of style. Among their contemporaries and successors, their Neoplatonism smelled of the dark ages. All that talk about the Aereal world sounded monkish. Metaphysical mumbo jumbo about "emanations" and the like was out. What people liked about Descartes was not what he said, which was also quite medieval, but the apparent forthrightness with which he said it, which was not.

## SPINOZA FOUND LIVING IN ENGLAND

Well, not quite. But the views of the Third Earl of Shaftesbury, Anthony Ashley Cooper (1621–1683), son of Locke's master and Locke's own pupil, are embarrass-

ingly Spinozan. God, says Shaftesbury, is a Mind-Soul thing which can be thought
of as either the world itself or just outside the world, maybe just around the corner.
(He was not known as a consistent thinker, poor Shaftesbury; his excuse is that he
died tragically young.) Since God is the world, at least part of the time, everything
is the way it has to be. Whatever is, is right. Evil is nothing positive, just an illusion of our own finitude. Mass religion relies too much on fear and superstition, and
yet there is nothing about which to be afraid. Virtue comes naturally to him who
knows these facts. Virtue is always good for the virtuous, and confers happiness.
Despite the happy state of things, Shaftesbury finds a lot to complain about—
mainly, the disastrous consequences of all the wrong-headed opinions of those who
do not share his philosophical views. Like Spinoza, he gets tangled in his own web
as he tries to deduce a positive ethical doctrine from his deterministic pantheism.
After all, if whatever is, is right, then presumably all those wrong opinions must
also be right.

Shaftesbury, of course, was not a recluse, but an active political figure in his
own day. His philosophy is Spinoza for the British aristocrat. Spinoza's esotericism,
for example, becomes Shaftesbury's paternalism. He expects his cooks, valets, and
maidservants to persevere with their superstitious religion, since otherwise they
would likely sink into squalid self-interest. Philosophical religion is for the higher
orders. Also, the earl is fairly conservative in disposition, and does not see his work
as an attack on church or religion, but a pious service to them.

## THOSE BLOODY DOCTORS

In Presocratic times, I suggested, it was the physicians, not the physicists, who carried the torch of science. That trend seems to have continued in early modern
Europe. Many of the materialists of the French Enlightenment (see below) were
doctors: Julien Offroy de La Mettrie (1709–1751), Jean Le Rond d'Alembert
(1717–1783), Claude-Adrien Helvétius (1715–1771). The earlier wave of skeptics
and atomists was also sustained by medicine: Descartes's rival Gassendi was a doctor; Descartes himself dabbled in cures and Locke also first came to notice as a sur-
geon. Many contemporaries believed that there was an atheistic conspiracy among
physicians (a theory no doubt made more persuasive to some by the fact that many
physicians were Jewish). As in the Greek world, it seems, the intimate experience
with the human body, especially in its dysfunctional states, tempered many an idealism, tested piety, and resulted in more scientific attitudes toward mind and world.
La Mettrie, for example, arrived at his notorious hypothesis that man is a machine,
when he observed one day how an illness affected his own mind. He also, by the
way, pilloried his fellow doctors as incompetent and greedy butchers, which many
of them were.

# A HEART AMONG RATIONALISTS

Blaise Pascal (1623–1662) was an aphorist, not a system builder, and did not even finish writing his aphorisms. He is often considered a religious or moral thinker rather than a philosopher. Most importantly, his philosophy, such as it can be made out, does not fit with the latterly prescribed official thought paradigm of his time. He should have arrived two centuries later, somewhere in between the Romantics and the Existentialists.

In a strangely Humean way, Pascal insists on the need for facts, and on the impotence of reason alone to solve human problems. Unlike Hume, he uses this idea in the service of an interpretation of Christianity. He dismisses metaphysical/theological proofs based on reason as worthless, and argues that true religious experience must be based on feeling or instinct. Like the Romantics to come, Pascal says that the heart has reasons which mind cannot always understand. He believes that what matters is authentic experience, not abstract knowledge. Also like the existentialists, he believes that without instinct and feeling, reason can find only a cold and desperate emptiness in man, a vacuous *ennui*.

Voltaire thought Pascal was a sickly misanthrope, and expended some effort denouncing his work. (Pascal was indeed ill for most of his life). Pascal had a more positive influence on others. One could try to give him a place in the history of ideas as a forerunner of the debates to come. But that would probably involve making too much of a story out of history.

# AN HISTORICIST BEFORE HIS TIME

With their faith in reason, minds, and bodies, the early modern philosophers are supposed to be ahistorical to the tips of their toes. Historicism, generally stated as the belief that what counts as true is a function of historical developments arrives in the late eighteenth and early nineteenth centuries with Johann Gottfried Herder (1744–1803), whose "Ideas for the Philosophy of the History of Humanity" (1791) analyzed the development of German cultural history and paved the way for Hegel's full-blown dialectical historicism—or so the story goes. The unfortunate fact, for this hypothesis, is that at least one historicist lived before his time: Giambattista Vico (1668–1744).

Vico started with a semi-Humean sense that only the truths of logic are true with certainty. Since logical truths are all deduced from hypothetical constructs, he inferred (falsely) that we can only really know as true things that we have made ourselves. With one more intuitive leap, Vico identified these constructs with the historical development of social practices. *Voilà* historicism. In contrast with his contemporary philosophers, Vico precociously turned his attention to the history of the society in which he lived. He was almost unknown in his time, but did have some influence on later thinkers, like Herder.

# Meanwhile, in France . . .

## Turning on the Lights

### THE ENLIGHTENMENT

The so-called Enlightenment of eighteenth-century France is usually discussed in the context of the history of ideas, or of culture, rather than the history of philosophy. My exposition here will be brief, and aims only to sketch in general terms how the Enlightenment movement relates to the history of philosophy.

Understood in the most general way, the principles which define Enlightenment thought are the essence of rationality itself. These principles—or principle—can be expressed in a number of forms. Here I suggest two:

1. Superstition and prejudice ought to be avoided.

2. The human condition can be improved through reason.

Of course, expressed in such a general way, the principles are not the exclusive property of the Enlightenment. There would be little point in assigning such general principles to any specific period in time.

One should always be ready to distinguish these general principles from the specific doctrines and philosophies touted by the representatives of the Enlightenment. The specific doctrines are best conceived as strategic operations, intended to advance the claims of reason within their particular context. Failure to make this distinction can lead one to confuse the deficiencies of specific doctrines with those of the general principles of reason. The former may well be found wanting on grounds of reason; the latter cannot be denied without being perverse.

The doctrinal components of the French Enlightenment are these:

*1. Anticlericalism.* French intellectuals never got over the fact that the Reformation passed them by. Anything to do with priests, the church, and its doctrines was for them *prima facie* anathema. They believed that established religion was a reservoir of silly superstition, a regressive force in the world. Voltaire summed up his attitude toward the church in his famous imperative: *écrasez l'infâme* (literally translated as "crush the infamous thing."

*2. Materialism.* In this the Enlightenment philosophers exhibited continuity with the early seventeenth-century thinkers like Gassendi, who revived the teachings of the Hellenistic philosophers, especially the atomists. They chose materialism as an antidote to what they regarded as the superstitious spiritualism of the established religious philosophies. The most notorious materialist was Julien Offroy de la Mettrie who argued in his book *Man the Machine* that man is, well, a machine. Baron d'Holbach (1723–1753), who played host in his salons to much of the intellectual conversation of his time, published a materialist *System of Nature*, in which he contrasted the virtues of a scientific approach to nature with the insidious consequences of the religious approach (of which he believed the Cartesian method was an example). Denis Diderot (1713–1784) got in on the act with a work featuring his coeditor of the *Encyclopédie* in its title, *d'Alembert's Dream*, in which he offered an eerily prescient description of an evolutionary process linking non-living and living matter.

*3. Skepticism.* Here again they participated in the revival of the Hellenistic philosophies, in this case, those of the ancient Pyrrhonists and Academic philosophers. This skepticism, of course, was not altogether consistent with their materialism, which in some cases became a comprehensive and dogmatic account of all nature. The more sane thinkers probably did not take their materialism or skepticism too seriously. They might also be called, with some reservations, pragmatists and even relativists, inasmuch as they focused on practical results and their doubts concerned the validity of putatively absolute truths, not the general efficacy and value of knowledge.

*4. Empirical Science.* Their skepticism did not extend to empirical science. They loved science, or at least the idea of science, and hoped it might cure many of humankind's ills. They wanted to amass as much knowledge about the world as possible. Hence the most famous project of the Enlightenment was Diderot's *Encyclopédie*.

*5. Shocking Ethics.* They favored a hedonism that linked pleasure with happiness and a utilitarianism that equated happiness with virtue. This, too, was part of their in-your-face attitude toward the establishment. Several thinkers also maintained a deterministic outlook on human behavior, a view that was not altogether consistent with the ethical doctrines in which they urged their fellows to free themselves from religious tyranny, but that at least had the virtue of offending common sensibilities.

*6. Utopianism.* They were optimistic, perhaps to a fault, on the possibilities for reorganizing society according to rational principles. Some blame them for the excesses of the French Revolution. Perhaps they overextended their materialistic explanation of natural phenomena, and came to believe that human society could be just as easily understood and controlled if only one understood the right social-scientific laws.

If they are to blame, this would be a good example of how the specific doctrines which stake their legitimacy on the general principles of reason might in fact be unreasonable, and therefore inconsistent with those general principles.

One of the interesting things about this list is how it still manages to transcend the particular historical period with which it is associated. It is not just that all these doctrines were already quite old by the eighteenth century. It is also that they have appeared together, with only moderate shifts in emphasis, in both earlier and later periods. The list could, for example, describe the basic philosophical disposition of the ancient Greek Sophists. The important point, for now, is that the doctrines are not deduced from the general principles of reason, but were chosen in light of those principles in order to address specific circumstances and concerns.

## VOLTAIRE

Voltaire (1694–1778) was an enormously talented individual who led a tremendously varied life, produced volumes of literature in almost every major genre, and mingled with the great leaders and thinkers of his day. Although a small number among his many works might be considered philosophical, his chief contribution here was one of spirit, not substance. The spirit of Voltaire was that of the Enlightenment philosophy in general, as described above. He opposed superstition in most of its forms, the worst of which in his view was the Catholic Church. He was the leading Church basher of his time. And he had a healthy—not a mystical—faith in the power of reason to improve humanity's lot in the world. Against his opponents he would throw whatever he could lay his hands on, which was often some form of biting satire, mockery, or even frivolity. Voltaire was an instinctive French version of Hume: less analytically acute, more violent in disposition, perhaps sharper in wit.

# German Idealism:
# The Empire of the Air

# Kant

## The Absolutely Critical Philosophy

Two related stories about Kant are important to most histories of philosophy. The first is that Kant marks a radical turning point in the history of metaphysics. The philosophers before Kant, so the story goes, were concerned to develop metaphysical systems, and Kant demonstrated that such systems would never work. The second, more specific story is that Kant proved that knowledge is conditioned by the nature of the knowing subject, or something of the sort. Kant himself told this story. Borrowing an expression from Hume, he proudly announced his own "Copernican Revolution" in philosophy. Prior to Kant, humankind had apparently been under the impression that knowledge must conform to the nature of the object. Just as Copernicus had shown that the earth revolved around the sun, and not the reverse, so Kant supposedly proved that the object of knowledge must conform to the subject's faculties of knowledge, and not the reverse.

At the risk of appearing hopelessly contrary, I will defend the following thesis: These stories about Kant are myths. The Kantian philosophy is not a real turning point in the history of philosophy. It is a continuation of the project of which the metaphysics he criticizes is merely one possible expression. Furthermore, Kant was no Copernicus. He could not have proved what is untrue, and what *is* true in Kant's doctrine about subjects and objects is a mere truism. Most of his philosophy can be understood as a reenactment of what I have grandly called the dialectic of empiricism, which is itself an instance of the search for the Holy Grail of philosophy. To be sure, Kant had a huge influence on subsequent philosophers, especially on the breed who would become the professionals of the modern university. But this just means that his name is useful as a collection point for a host of beliefs and reconstructions, mostly based on misunderstandings. It does not require that there be some real achievement, a philosophical truth, behind the various interpretations.

## DESCARTES VU ALL OVER AGAIN

Kant's general purpose in philosophizing was to reconcile science and religion. He admired science but believed that recent advances in human knowledge threatened religion. He worried that the loss of religion might also undermine morality. So, he wanted to make the world safe for science without compromising religion and morality.

Kant's solution was to divide the world into two utterly unconnected worlds. On the one side was the material or merely apparent world, which works mechanistically and is the proper domain of science. On the other side was the spiritual or ultimately real world, in which reside the constituents of religion and morality. He denied science access to this more real world, and so, as he put it, made room for faith.

Both in the problem he confronted and the solution he chose, Kant may be compared to Descartes (to name just one of many candidates from the history of philosophy). Descartes, too, saw the need to protect science and religion from each other, and likewise found comfort in splitting the world in two.

Kant's philosophical system contains three parts, which are represented in three major books and a number of supplemental works. I will discuss each in turn. The first, the longest, and the most important for future philosophers is the theoretical part embodied in *The Critique of Pure Reason.* The second, practical part, expressed in *The Critique of Practical Reason* and *Foundations for the Metaphysics of Morals,* however, is at least as important to Kant in achieving his moral aims. The third part, in *The Critique of Judgment,* in which Kant explores issues that lie between theory and practice, mainly teleology and aesthetics, is less important for the modern student, but does contain some interesting thoughts on matters of art and religion.

KANT: THE CRITIQUE OF PURE FRUIT

# I

The purpose of Kant's theoretical philosophy is to lay out the kinds of knowledge to which human beings are entitled. An attack on two targets, skepticism and dogmatism, defines the mission of the first critique. Kant admits that he has been shaken up by the skeptical Hume, whose philosophical arguments seemed to dissolve the natural certainties of life into mere probabilities of sense impressions. In the name of science and common sanity, Kant seeks to rescue some certainties, such as the principle of causality, from Hume's corrosive skepticism. At the same time, Kant acknowledges that Hume was justified in his attack on dogmatists, heirs of Aristotle and medieval theology, who gave philosophy a bad name with their unnerving speculations and illogical arguments. In his critique Kant aims to draw the bounds of knowledge somewhere short of the pretensions of the dogmatists. He will show, contra the skeptic, that fundamental principles, like that of causality, are perfectly legitimate when applied to possible experience, but, contra the dogmatist, that we have no license to apply such principles beyond the bounds of all possible experience. So he plans to defend science, while denying its jurisdiction over matters of faith.

The method Kant proposes for his project is, at least on the face of it, properly philosophical. The idea of a critique of pure reason has two senses: It is a critical analysis of the powers of reason independent of all experience; and it is a critical analysis performed by pure reason. Like Socrates with his dialectic, or perhaps Parmenides, Kant aims to ground his conclusions in a pure reflection, free from any presupposition other than its own methodicalness, or rationality.

---

## Kant's Dream

*I have a dream. I have a dream that all men will one day live together in a universal brotherhood. A dream that each will treat the other as an end in itself. That everywhere the uncompromising imperative of duty will prevail. I have heard the skeptics. I have followed them into the deepest abyss of despair. I have watched all science, morality, and hope dissolve in the bleak darkness of their night. I have heard the dogmatists. I, too, have been tempted by promises of an absolute, metaphysical truth beyond all possible experience. But I have seen that the irresolvable disputes of metaphysics are the source of all that unbelief which wars against morality. I have seen the future, in which skepticism and dogmatism lie vanquished before the mighty tribunal of pure reason. In my dream the dame philosophy sheds the tattered robes of conflict and abuse, and steps forth in righteous glory to claim her title as the Queen of the Sciences and Guardian of the Moral Law. My dream is the Enlightenment Dream, that people will live in liberty and answer only to reason. My dream is the Stoic Dream, that humanity will bond together through their common fate in reason. My dream is the Platonic dream, that Philosophy will assume her rightful position as the great teacher and leader of humanity.*

## SOME WORDS

The striking feature of Kant's work, at first glance, is its vast technical vocabulary and abhorrent prose. Perhaps it is foolhardy to take Kant on in his own terms. Many a soul has been lost in the fog, and Kant, or the industry of scholarship he inspired, can always outflank an attacker by redrawing distinctions and calling in reserve arguments. Yet I bravely persevere, because I think the Kantian philosophy can be made simple, and that it has to be made simple if we are not to be frightened into a superstitious faith in a philosophy which cannot be understood.

The key terms of Kantianism belong to conceptual pairs, or distinctions. I list some of the most important ones.

*Analytic/Synthetic.* Two kinds of judgments are distinguished. We have seen this distinction before, in Leibniz. And it is implicit in Hume's distinction between reason and fact. According to the Kantian definition, a judgment is analytic if its predicate is "contained within" its subject. It is synthetic, i.e., puts things together, if the predicate is "outside" the subject. The spatial metaphor leads to a number of obscurities. Let's drop it and say that a judgment is analytic if its truth can be deduced from the definitions of its terms, and synthetic if its truth cannot be so deduced. For example, "all bachelors are unmarried men" is analytic, whereas "Socrates is a bachelor" is synthetic.

Analytic judgments seem less appealing than synthetic ones. Analytic judgments never go beyond definitions, or what must be taken as given. Analysis means only shuffling concepts, laying bare their given interconnections. Synthetic judgments, however, tell you something you didn't already know. They contain real knowledge, or facts.

*A Priori/A Posteriori.* This distinction is supposed to classify judgments according to the way in which their truth may be established, but is also applied, with disastrous consequences, to concepts, categories, and just about anything else. The fancy Latin terms just mean "before" and "after" (in a logical rather than temporal way), and refer to "experience." A judgment is true *a priori* inasmuch as it can be known to be true before any experience, *a posteriori* if its truth is contingent upon experience. For example, "all bachelors are unmarried men" could be known to be true before any experience, since a bachelor is an unmarried man, by definition; whereas "Socrates is a bachelor" could be known to be true only after some experience, like meeting him, checking the records, etc.

*A priori* judgments have this kind of moral edge on their *a posteriori* brethren: Their truth can be known with absolute certainty. Plus, their truth can be ascertained without having to get up out of one's chair and look out the window, or whatever. The word "pure" is often used to intensify the sense of *a priori*, as in, *really* before *all* experience. No such modifier typically precedes *a posteriori*.

*Transcendental/Empirical.* These terms supposedly modify "knowledge." Transcendental knowledge is knowledge about our ways of knowing things. More specifically, it is about our ways of knowing things insofar as this knowledge is *a priori*. Empirical knowledge is, fortunately, more down to earth. It is the actual knowledge of things gained through experience.

Transcendental has in more recent times been taken to modify "arguments." In this sense, it really modifies the way in which certain judgments may be justified. A transcendental argument proceeds from a given state of affairs to the conditions that make it possible. For example, assume the state of affairs: One has *a priori* knowledge. A transcendental argument would produce conclusions about what makes such knowledge possible, for example, one must be constructed so as to be able to formulate and understand claims to *a priori* knowledge.

These three distinctions are sufficient to frame the project which Kant sets for himself in his first critique. Consider the possible combinations of terms from the first two distinctions. Analytic *a priori* judgments are not hard to find: e.g., "all bachelors are unmarried men." Synthetic *a posteriori* judgments are also easy: e.g., "Socrates is a bachelor." But what about synthetic *a priori* and analytic *a posteriori*? Kant tosses out the latter. It is hard to imagine a judgment that could count as analytic *a posteriori*, unless one understands definitions or the principle of non-contradiction as something justified only after experience. Kant finds synthetic *a priori* judgments, on the other hand, very interesting. A synthetic *a priori* judgment, if true, would be a kind of universal fact about this or any world. Contrary to Humean doctrine, it would be a fact deducible through pure reason. The realm of such judgments would coincide with that of metaphysics; its proper and complete delimitation would resolve the conflicts with both skeptics and dogmatists. The skeptic would be forced to submit to some meaningful philosophical truths, while the dogmatist could be reigned in for attempting to go beyond such truths. Synthetic *a priori* judgments, in short, are the absolutely certain and universal knowledge which philosophers have always sought.

Kant is confident that synthetic *a priori* judgments do exist, and he cites examples, mainly from arithmetic and geometry. His project is more abstract than a catalogue of such judgments. What he wants is the key to all such judgments. Such a key would provide advance knowledge, as it were, of the nature, content, and justification of all such judgments. In other words, Kant wants a transcendental understanding of synthetic *a priori* judgments. He wants to know the conditions of their possibility. Thus the question which frames the project of *The Critique of Pure Reason*: How are synthetic *a priori* judgments possible?

## SOME MORE WORDS

The distinctions presented thus far are chiefly logical (and/or illogical) in character. We need a few more terms to round out the idea of Kant's project, although at this point things get messier, and, as with the empiricists, logic gets confused with psychology and metaphysics.

*Concept/Intuition.* This distinction harbors both the insights and the illusions of the Kantian philosophy. An intuition is the object of knowledge insofar as the object is given, i.e., passively received. A concept is the object of knowledge insofar as it is thought, i.e., actively conceived. Knowledge requires both concept and intuition. Without intuition, concepts have nothing to think about; without concepts, intuitions cannot be thought.

Think of intuition (if you can!) as the prelinguistic or preepistemic world to which judgments purporting to be facts must ultimately refer, directly or indirectly. It is this world, to which the mind stands in immediate relation, which gives judgments their content, but which cannot be included within judgments. My newspaper, to which I can only refer, and which I cannot produce for you, belongs to this world. Understood abstractly, the notion of intuition is a logical construct, as opposed to a real or metaphysical entity. It is not to be confused with the psychological construct of a sense impression (although it turns out, according to Kant, that the human mind is so constructed that intuitions are all sensible). The notion of intuition is a part of the analysis of knowledge into active and passive components, or, what is the same, mediate and immediate ones. The active component, the concept, is always a step removed from the given object, for it is that through which this newspaper is thought. So it represents the mediation which is part of any claim to knowledge. The passive component, the intuition, stands in immediate relation to the newspaper, but cannot be thought without the aid of a concept.

*Spontaneity/Receptivity.* Receptivity is the power of receiving the object of knowledge, or intuitions. Spontaneity is the power of messing around with intuitions according to concepts, or the power to form representations of one's own.

*Understanding/Sensibility.* The understanding is the faculty which allows us to understand and mess around with concepts. It has about it a certain spark or liveliness, a *je ne sais quoi,* that is, a spontaneity. Sensibility is the faculty which receives intuitions. It is the ability to sit back, relax, and let those sense impressions soak in. That understanding and sensibility are both "faculties" means nothing more frightening than that they are "abilities" or "powers."

*Form/Matter.* Form is that which determines the nature of what something is. Like the Aristotelian concept of form, it overlaps with 'essence' in meaning. What exists prior to the determination of form is an inert, featureless stuff. Though Kant does not oppose form with matter explicitly, Aristotle's concept of 'matter' is the appropriate antonym of Kant's 'form'.

The form/matter distinction can be used to illuminate the concept/intuition distinction. A concept is that which determines an otherwise indeterminate intuition to create a possible object of knowledge. In other words, the concept plays the 'form' to intuition's 'matter'. Kant hints as much with his famous claim that concepts without intuitions are empty, intuitions without concepts blind. The concept/intuition distinction is an application of the form/matter distinction—specifically, its application to the empiricists' model of the knowing subject.

*Logic/Aesthetic.* The two chief parts of Kant's first critique are the so-called Transcendental Aesthetic and the Transcendental Logic. That they are "transcendental" must mean, according to Kant's definition, that they are concerned with the mode of knowing things *a priori*. Kant defines his logic as the science of the rules of the understanding. Aesthetic has nothing to do with art. It is the science of the rules of sensibility. Elsewhere Kant uses the much more general term "form" to denote these rules. Thus, the logic is about the form of the understanding, the aesthetic about the form of sensibility. So, in his two parts, Kant must be concerned to lay out those forms of sensibility and understanding, respectively, which make *a priori* knowledge possible. Naturally, these forms themselves must be *a priori*, if they are to make *a priori* knowledge possible.

The basic idea of Kant's theoretical philosophy is that if you can figure out the *a priori* forms of the two key faculties of knowledge, you can find the *a priori* limits of knowledge. It is the attempt to assess which claims to knowledge are or are not justified in virtue of the structure of all possible experience.

# TRANSCENDENTAL AESTHETIC

According to Kant, the Transcendental Aesthetic must identify the *a priori* "form of sensibility," which also goes by the names of "pure intuition" and "*a priori* sensibility."

Kant argues that space and time are the two forms of sensibility. In other words, space and time are *a priori* conditions of the possibility of intuition; in a sense, they are features of our mode of knowing, rather than, as common sense would have it, features of the world. His general aim is to justify the supposedly synthetic *a priori* judgments of geometry and arithmetic. Geometry is *a priori*, says Kant, because it traces the outlines of our *a priori* form of sensibility called space. Yet its judgments are synthetic because they reveal nontrivial facts about the world (as we necessarily perceive it, that is), specifically, about spatial relationships. Score one against the skeptics.

There is at least some analytic truth in Kant's claims about space and time. Inasmuch as the form of sensibility is simply the concept of sensibility, it is possible to argue that the concept of sensibility presupposes the existence of space and time. A condition of the possibility of the ability to intuit intuitions is that there be something "outside" to intuit. Another condition is that this ability be exercisable on a repeatable basis, or, what is the same, that there should be a series of outside things to intuit. So much for the implications of our suppositions about a concept.

# TRANSCENDENTAL LOGIC:
# ONE ANALYTIC & DIALECTIC TO GO

The Transcendental Logic is the longest, toughest, and most important part of Kant's work, and the locus of his chief insights (see p. 247). Whereas the Aesthetic was concerned with the form(s) of sensibility, the Logic is concerned with the corresponding form(s) of the understanding. The Transcendental Logic divides into two pieces, an Analytic and a Dialectic. Roughly speaking, the former lays out the concepts and principles to which the understanding is entitled, while the latter catalogs the abuses to which such concepts and principles are applied by those awful dogmatists.

The highlights of Kant's argument in the Analytic are these. First, he argues that concepts differ from intuitions in that they rely on a function, that is, an "act" of some sort, as opposed to passive reception. This act is a kind of synthesis. It brings together the disparate elements given in sensation under a single concept. Second, the condition which must be supposed in order to make this synthesis possible is the unity of the consciousness in which the synthesis takes place. This does not mean that consciousness is necessarily unified, whatever that might mean, but that consciousness must be able to suppose that it is one in order for it to have meaningful representations. Kant describes this condition with the scary term, the "transcendental unity of apperception." Not to worry: Apperception is just an old, Leibniz-flavored name for the self-consciousness which accompanies any conscious act of perception. Kant describes the unity of apperception as transcendental because it not a real, empirically perceived unity, but a hypothetically necessary condition of the possibility of knowledge. Kant insists that it is quite distinct from the self which is perceived by the self through 'inner sense'. Third, the transcendental unity of apperception sanctions a boatload of twelve categories, including 'unity' and 'causality', which are thus validated as the *a priori* concepts of the understanding (whatever that means). Fourth, these concepts in turn justify certain *a priori* principles of the understanding, notably the principle of causality, which Kant represents as the claim that "every alteration has a cause." Fifth, these concepts and principles are justified only as conditions of the possibility of experience. Therefore, they can be legitimately applied only to objects of possible experience. Thus, they provide no basis for metaphysical speculation.

The last point provides a good transition to the second part of the Transcendental Logic, the Dialectic. The Dialectic is about the sophistry and illusion into which humans fall when they attempt to apply the concepts of reason beyond all possible experience. Kant subdivides the Dialectic into three topics: the Paralogisms, the Antinomies, and the Ideal of pure reason. The Paralogisms have to do with the supposed proofs that the soul is a substance, which turn out to be based on fallacies. The Antinomies are the apparently irresolvable debates of metaphysics, e.g., between free will and determinism, whether the world has a beginning or not, and so on. Kant argues that the antinomies are the natural consequence of trying to extend reason beyond its limits. He suggests a kind of "as-if" strategy for evaluating their theses. Treat matters in the phenomenal world as if determinism were true; treat questions of morality as if free will existed. The Ideal of pure reason is Kant's name for God, or, more precisely, the putative proofs of His existence. Kant reduces the various proofs down to the ontological one, and then makes the case, with which we are already familiar, that this proof falsely supposes that existence is an ordinary predicate, like, say, "is unmarried."

## THE TWO WORLDS

Kant says that we can never know things as they are in themselves. We can only know them insofar as they make their way through our forms of sensibility and understanding. On this basis he distinguishes between the phenomenal and noumenal worlds. The phenomenal world (from *phenomena*, meaning appearances) is what comes after the operation of our faculties of knowledge. It includes the things we see around us, as well as the concept and principle of causality, and, in general, all scientific knowledge. The noumenal world (from *noumena*, meaning thoughts or mental entities) is that which exists prior to the activity of knowing. It includes the thing-in-itself and an even more mysterious creature, the transcendental ego.

The advantage of this arrangement is that it looks like it can achieve Kant's overall goals. On the one hand, it makes science safe by guaranteeing the *a priori* validity of the concepts and principles of the understanding. On the other hand, it prohibits science from any speculation concerning the morally important noumenal world.

Such a radically condensed version of the first critique leaves many gaps and confusions. I take solace in the fact that Kant's much longer version is not much better.

## WATCH HIS HANDS

In order to understand how Kant converts a few, brief distinctions into such a long-winded work, one must first understand the most characteristic Kantian maneuver, which I call the double-cross. The first example of this trick is not hard to find. Alert readers will have noticed that there is not much to choose between "analytic" and "*a priori*," and "synthetic" and "*a posteriori*." This is because, allowing for obscurities, and begging forgiveness from the scholars who would split the micro-hairs, both pairs are really the same. That is, although defined in different terms, and so with a different sense, each term within the pairs has the same reference, i.e., extends over the same set of judgments. An analytic judgment is always *a priori*, since definitions and the principle of noncontradiction cannot be removed by any possible experience. A synthetic judgment is true only in reference to something other than its own terms, and that reference can only come from what goes under the name of experience. (The examples Kant cites of synthetic *a priori* judgments, by the way, are analytic. Truths of geometry, in particular, are the analytic consequences of the axioms of geometry. This is especially evident in light of the discovery by nineteenth-century mathematicians that geometries with non-Euclidean axioms are possible.) Untangling the transcendental/empirical distinction is more complicated (more on this below), but the pattern is essentially the same. What passes for transcendental knowledge is basically analytic judgments based on definitions of knowledge and experience. Transcendental arguments in general are analytic: They produce inferences from given premises. Empirical knowledge is knowledge based on experience, and so is *a posteriori*, or, what is the same, synthetic. Thus, the short answer to Kant's question, How are synthetic *a priori* judgments possible? is this: They are not. Kant, alas, was not one given to short answers.

## ANOTHER DOUBLE-CROSS

Yet another double-cross occurs in Kant's notion of a 'form of sensibility'. I have noted that 'concept' and 'intuition' are distinguished in essentially the same way as 'form' and 'matter'. Logically speaking, intuition is formless. Therefore, the form of sensibility, which is the ability to intuit intuitions, cannot refer to some form which intuitions take, but only to the form which sensibility takes, which is to say, the concept of sensibility itself.

On the one hand, there is nothing wrong with talking about the 'form of sensibility', insofar as this just refers to the concept of sensibility. You can talk about your concepts as long as you like. On the other hand, insofar as the 'form of sensibility' refers to some distinct form common to all intuitions, it represents a double-cross, since "form" in this case is a surrogate for "concept," and Kant has defined intuition as precisely that which is *not* a concept.

In other words, the double-dealing Kant wants to understand the form of sensibility as that which determines intuitions to be the particular kinds of intuitions they happen to be. But in this sense, the form of sensibility is nothing other than the concept that determines an intuition. Kant logically separates concept and intuition, then he mixes them up again in his form of sensibility. The futility of this maneuver becomes clearer in the synonyms he chooses for the form of sensibility: e.g., "pure intuition," and "*a priori* sensibility." By "pure" Kant means "untainted by experience." But an intuition is by definition that which is given to the mind, an affection which must arise from experience. A pure intuition is as absurd as an "immaculate perception," like a sensation that is a sensation of nothing in particular. What is *a priori* sensibility? The ability to intuit intuitions prior to intuiting any intuitions? A pure intuition can only refer to the definition of this ability to intuit intuitions. Kant confuses this matter of analytic definitions with the possibility for a particular kind of intuition. In doing so, Kant double-crosses over from a merely logical truth concerning the definition of a particular ability to a metaphysical claim about what really exists and what does not. Kant's identification of space and time as the forms of sensibility, as already noted, arguably does follow from the definition of sensibility. (The whole idea of sensibility, after all, supposes that there are these things out there, in space, to be sensed in some kind of sequence, in time.) But Kant's inference from this definitional truth to the claim that space and time do not exist independently of our faculty of knowledge is false.

---

From *The Critique of Pure Ambulation*

A condition of the possibility of walkability is the distinction between a "here" and a "there" between which the walking walks. Thus, space is an *a priori* form of walkability. Another condition of the possibility of walkability is the distinction between a "now" and a "then" during which the walking walks. Thus, time is an *a priori* form of walkability. In sum, space and time do not exist independently of our faculty of walkability.

---

If the forms of sensibility in any way condition the nature of the reality we perceive, then at least one of two conditions must hold: Either (1) our forms are one among many possible sets of forms; or (2) it is possible for something other than us to intuit without any such forms at all. Kant hints at the first proposition by listing space and time as the two forms of sensibility. He does not, however, propose any alternatives to space and time, and his argument nowhere supports the notion that there could be other forms of sensibility, let alone what those forms might be. Concerning the second possibility, Kant does claim that it is conceivable that some other kind of knower would have intuitions which are intellectual, and not sensible. But 'sensibility' is not the specific form of sensibility—space and time are. All Kant is proving is the logical point that if intuitions are to be intuitions they must be intuitive, and accessible to what is by definition the faculty of intuiting intuitions, i.e., sensibility, and not conceptual, or accessible to the faculty of concepts, i.e., the understanding. He is correct to point out that intellectual intuition is impossible for us; he is incorrect in inferring that it is possible for some other intelligence. (The only real candidate, by the way, would be God.)

## THE DOUBLE-TAKE

Kant's attempt to locate the form of the understanding in the Transcendental Logic runs into similar trouble. The understanding, as we know, is the ability to apply concepts to intuitions. This is essentially the ability to think of an object. So, the Transcendental Logic is about the *a priori* conditions under which any object may be thought of. Or, to put it in other words, it is about the *a priori* form of concepts in general.

At this point in Kant's argument, a very curious thing happens. Logically speaking, the term "*a priori*" should be reserved for judgments, since only judgments can be considered true or false "before experience." But now Kant starts talking about the *a priori* concepts of the understanding. These *a priori* concepts are the stuff of the *a priori* form of the understanding. They are what the understanding supposedly possesses "before experience" and which make possible the concept of an object in general.

Fine. So what is an *a priori* concept? Literally, it would be one that is "true before experience." Let's suppose Kant means merely a concept that is possibly valid before experience, that is, that refers to some possible object. In that case, however, all concepts (which are not contradictions in terms) are *a priori* concepts. Before the evidence of experience, it is always possible that a non-self-contradictory concept will refer to an object, just as it is always possible to conceive of an object that does not exist. If all concepts are *a priori*, then all objects are thinkable, or, what is the same, the form of the understanding imposes no limit on what can be thought.

Indeed, in his search for the form of the understanding, Kant hopes to find the limits of knowledge by finding the limits of what can be thought. This explains the shift from *a priori* judgments, which could possibly contain knowledge, to *a priori* concepts, which are about thoughts. (Remember, the understanding is the faculty of concepts, and concepts are that through which objects are thought.) But, as any philosophical beginner knows, it is impossible to think the limits of thought without thinking what's on (or what may be on) the other side of the limit.

Let's put the objection in another way. As with the forms of sensibility, if the forms of the understanding are to condition our knowledge, then it must be conceivable either that other forms are available to some other intelligence or that such forms are altogether unnecessary for some such intelligence. An alternative set of categories, however, is inconceivable, given that the ones Kant proposes are supposed to be the necessary conditions for thinking of any object whatsoever. So, unless one believes in the absurdity of a thinking which is not thinking of anything in particular, then there can be no other forms than the ones we have. Which brings us to the second possibility, that it is possible to think without any forms. But Kant's whole argument rests on precisely the opposite thesis. The forms are by definition what is necessary to think about anything. Since it makes no sense either that our forms are only one possible set of forms or that it is possible to think without forms, it makes no sense to claim, as Kant does, that the forms of our faculties of knowledge condition the nature of the reality we perceive.

## DOWN WITH THE TRANSCENDENTALS

I will outline what I believe is the most logical way to unravel the links between the transcendental, the *a priori*, Logic, and Aesthetic. Kant insists on the difference between the transcendental and the *a priori*, on the grounds that transcendental knowledge is only that *a priori* knowledge which concerns the possibility of knowledge, and not all *a priori* knowledge. In other words it has to do with the way or "mode" of knowledge, not any particular knowledge, whether *a priori* or not. But in my view, at the *a priori* level, there is no real distinction between knowledge and the mode of knowledge, or between knowing things and the way of knowing them. *A priori* knowledge, insofar as it is analytic, cannot in any case be the knowledge of particular things, and so cannot be said to refer to anything (i.e., any state of affairs). It is at best the knowledge of the logical relationships between any possible things. If such knowledge refers to anything, then, it is nothing other than the concepts according to which we know things. But these concepts are themselves that which determines things to be what they are. That is, they are the forms of our knowledge. So, as I see it, transcendental knowledge is just another word for *a priori* knowledge. Furthermore, since what Kant calls Logic is about the *a priori* forms or concepts of the understanding, there is no real distinction between Logic and transcendental knowledge. But that, of course, makes "Transcendental Logic" a pleonasm, and "Transcendental Aesthetic" a contradiction in terms. If Logic is transcendental knowledge, the Transcendental Aesthetic is a "Logical Aesthetic," and so should either be included within the Transcendental Logic or discarded from the transcendental world. To put the matter another way: Kant's critique is the sorting out of a certain set of concepts, specifically, that set of concepts associated with the empiricists' picture of knowledge, or experience, and as such it has no privilege over any other sorting out of concepts. It can tell us no more about the limits of knowledge than a reflection on the concept of walking could provide us with the limit of walking.

So what is the real upshot of Kant's argument? What has he really asserted? In essence this: In order to be known, an object must be thought; and in order to be thought, an object must be, ahem, thinkable. So much for the grand, imposing subject. Take away the transcendental illusions, and what Kant has demonstrated is that we can only think about what can be thought about, and we can only know what is knowable.

---

From *The Critique of Pure Vision*

We do not see objects as they are in themselves, but only as they appear to us through our faculty of sight. The objects of sight must conform to the faculty of sight, for otherwise they would remain unseen. . . . We are blind to things before sight.

---

## DOUBLE-CROSSING BACK TO METAPHYSICS

We are blind to things before sight. Read this one way, as the claim that you cannot see things that are unseeable, and it is as true as any proposition ever will be, although perhaps lacking somewhat in substance. It is a tautology like this which is the heart of what is true in Kant's theoretical philosophy: We cannot know that which is unknowable. Read it another way, as an inference of the existence of a new class of beings, the "things-unseen," or a real limitation on what can be seen, and it is an invitation to sophistry and illusion. Kant succumbs to a medieval error: He converts a boring logical truth into a radical ontological falsehood.

It has long been noted that the metaphysics of phenomena and noumena, which is the endpoint of Kant's arguments, unravels pretty quickly into a string of paradoxes. Consider, if you can, the chief denizen of the noumenal world, the thing-in-itself. For, according to Kant, we are supposed to know nothing about this thing-in-itself. Yet we seem to know about the fact of its existence. And where is this thing-in-itself? Is it somewhere outside? But isn't 'outside' a spatial concept? And isn't space itself one of the forms through which the knower shapes the world? How did the thing-in-itself get 'outside' before the subject got around to imposing space on the world? Anyway, why is the thing-in-itself a thing? According to Kant's logic, 'thingness' itself comes from the forms of the faculties of knowledge. So, there is no 'thing', whether in-itself or not, prior to the activity of a knowing subject. But there must be a thing-in-itself. Otherwise, what are we to make of Kant's phenomenal world, that is, the world of appearances? Appearances are the appearances of something—presumably, the thing-in-itself. So, appearances must be caused by the thing-in-itself. Caused? Wait a minute—isn't the principle of causality itself supposed to be part of the world of appearances? How can the thing-in-itself operate under the principle of causality? And if it does so operate, why can't we know it? Or, when you peel away appearances do you just get more appearances? Appearances of appearances? Is the world an onion? Things, worlds, appearances—what do these words mean?

The very conception of the noumenal world is a double-cross of sorts. Kant removes the character of thing-hood to his phenomenal world, along with all concepts, the ability to think and so forth, indeed, along with all the attributes of what might meaningfully be called a world. The noumenal world must have non-thing-like things, nonconcepts; indeed, it ought to be a most unworldly world. Perhaps it does not even exist.

## TO CRITIQUE OR TO CREATE

It begins with a critique, a pure reflection on reflection itself, and yet it ends with an awesome claim to knowledge, a new metaphysics of phenomena, noumena, and all sorts of strange things. We should ask, by what right does Kant claim such an extraordinary advance?

You can criticize movies all day long, and in doing so you will never make a movie. What would be weird is if you could make a movie just by criticizing. For all the fancy words, Kant's critique is no different than any other critique, and it leads to error insofar as it violates this humble truth about critiques. Kant's inference to the existence of a new and strange class of things—the thing-in-itself—is simply unwarranted, a confusion of method and result.

# SCORES FOR KANT

What is true in Kant's theoretical philosophy may be expressed in the form of tautologies. Even so, these tautologies are not necessarily worthless. If someone says to you "all bachelors are unmarried men," he may be reminding you, in case you forgot or were unaware, that Socrates over there is free and willing. For what—or against what—might Kant's tautologies be directed? The answer, in accordance with that most important principle of the history of philosophy, the Principle of the Self-Reflexivity of Philosophy, is this: against other philosophical positions. Of course, it is true that in his dialectic Kant explicitly attacks the so-called metaphysicians. What is less obvious is that his philosophy is through-and-through an engagement with other philosophical positions, mainly empiricism.

Let's return to the concept/intuition distinction, which I suggested above was the key to Kant's theoretical philosophy. The insight which guides this distinction clears up some of the confusions in the empiricist understanding of knowledge. Recall that philosophical empiricism assumes that true knowledge would be the immediate apprehension of the object by the subject. Then it discovers that knowledge of the object is always mediated by the subject's faculties of knowledge. This gives rise to the conundrum that true knowledge is not possible. By requiring both concepts and intuitions Kant opens up the possibility of a conception of knowledge which contains both mediate and immediate components. In effect, he rejects the first premise, that knowledge would be purely immediate, or intuition alone. In the final analysis, of course, Kant falls back into the same conundrum, for he assumes that our knowledge is limited precisely by the fact that it is mediated, by the "fact" that we have no capability for intellectual intuition. But for a moment at least he provides hope for an exit from the self-defeating picture of empiricism.

In a somewhat muddier way, Kant's concept/intuition distinction also represents the insight achieved by Hume in his analysis of induction. Recall that Hume had argued that putative laws of nature are fundamentally hypothetical because they remain tied to the finite body of experience. By rejecting the possibility of a discursive intuition (or an intuitive concept), Kant also rules out the possibility of an unconditionally true and universal law of nature. Indeed, the logical thrust of Kant's critique is nothing other than the claim that knowledge is by its nature conditional. Hume had hinted that deductive relationships obtain only between ideas, or what is hypothesized about things. Kant makes the similar point that analytic relationships belong solely to the concepts of the understanding, not intuitions.

Kant's argument in the Analytic can also be seen as an improvement on Hume's position on causality. Recall that Hume argues that causality has a purely empirical origin in custom or habit. The effect of Kant's argument in the Analytic is to show that the notion of causality is interdependent with a broad set of notions with which we approach experience—the notions of self-consciousness, space, and time. In the final analysis, of course, Kant does not "prove" the principle of causality, inasmuch as it is still possible to doubt the broader set of notions of which it is a part. But it makes Hume's doubts about causality less convincing, inasmuch as in all that talk about custom and habit Hume still assumes that he is the same person perceiving all those colliding billiard balls over time, and so retains the logical basis for the principle of causality.

Kant's claims about the necessary unity of self-consciousness are often obscure, but they do include at least one tautology with implications for philosophical empiricism. The tautology might be something like this: If you're going to think about anything, you've got to stay in one piece long enough to think it. This may not seem like much of a breakthrough, but it does at least temporarily disrupt the empiricists' tendency to dissolve the self altogether in a disconnected shower of sense impressions. It does not prove the existence of 'mind' or the transcendental ego or anything like that; but it does show that one has to project or imagine something like that in order to make sense out of claims to knowledge.

Kant's arguments in the Dialectic can stand independently of the rest of his theoretical philosophy. We need not go into the details of his refutations here. The sum of his arguments is this: Humankind is given to speculation about the totality of things. We want the facts about the universe as a whole, i.e., the truth about everything. But every fact is by its nature conditional. The truth is not, as Kant sometimes seems to suggest, conditioned by the specific nature of our faculties of knowledge. But the truth, or any kind of knowledge, is always by its nature subject to conditions. Hume had made a similar argument in his discussion of theological proofs of the existence of a creator of the universe. Our reasoning works fine on anything in the world around us, both Kant and Hume say, but it can yield no knowledge when applied to the world as a whole.

## THE DIALECTIC OF EMPIRICISM LIVES

Any logical reconstruction of Kant's theoretical philosophy, in my view, will simply recreate the dialectic of empiricism. Kant's philosophy, like the dialectic of empiricism, begins with a certain picture, the subject-object picture, and a project, epistemology. The epistemological project is intended to be prior to any metaphysics. But Kant's epistemology, like that of any empiricist, discovers within itself a metaphysics which it cannot shake. A metaphysical determination of the nature of the knower *qua* knower is necessary if there are to be any *a priori* limits to what can be known. That metaphysics turns out to be a reincarnation of the old subject-object picture. So, the Kantian theoretical philosophy turns out to be an attack on itself, and calls forth the old conundrums and confusions. However, before it self-destructs, Kant's work does deepen and widen the dialectic of empiricism.

## DESTROYING SCIENCE IN ORDER TO SAVE IT

Does Kant achieve his goals for theoretical philosophy? Are the dyspeptic skeptic and the dour dogmatist laid low before the tribunal of reason? It's all in the eye of the beholder, I'm afraid. For one could certainly accuse Kant of out-skepticizing the skeptic. The latter would have been content merely to claim that we cannot be certain that things are the way they appear to us. Kant tries to prove that we can be certain that they are not the way they appear to us. He confines science to a world of projections and shadows, mere appearances, all in the name of saving religion. But Kant's dissection of theological error undermines religious authority as well. No more eternal soul, no beginning of the universe, no proofs of the existence of God. Indeed, the poet Heinrich Heine called Kant God's executioner.

## THE GRAIL OF THE PURE CRITIQUE: THE SEARCH GOES ON

The metaphysics which Kant supposedly overturns never really existed. Metaphysics has always been one possible manifestation of a more general project, of which Kant's own theoretical philosophy is a clear and historically interesting expression. In the Kantian version, this is the project of the pure critique which generates a positive content. Even in this form, of course, it is nothing new, but a reincarnation of the Socratic-Platonic dialectic. Both represent the idea of a project whose method is identical with its content. Nor is Kant's critique in principle different from Cartesian metaphysics, which consists of an inference drawn from the application of a method of doubt to an ontological condition of the possibility of that application. Kant's critique even shares the basic idea of the mother of all metaphysics, Aristotle's idea of deducing an actuality from a possibility. What Kant calls transcendental is what is hypothetically necessary to account for the possibility of experience, and yet it is also the basis for his claims about ultimate actualities, the thing-in-itself and the transcendental ego. And all this, to use even more general terms, is the idea of doing by merely saying, or getting something from nothing. This is the essence of philosophy, and far from marking a turning point in its history, Kant represents its fundamental continuity.

---

### *Kant at Work*

In a provincial town on the northeastern edge of eighteenth-century Europe lives a strangely cheerful old man. So why is he smiling? He secretly believes that he will soon invent a source of light which will shine forever on its own power: Lumina Perpetua. Of course, he has acknowledged, and even proved more thoroughly than the doubters, that perpetual power as popularly perceived is not possible. Yet somewhere at the end of an arduous chain of concepts and arguments he espies a glimmer of hope. If time and health allow, he will demonstrate once and for all that the impossibility of phenomenal perpetual light illustrates a certain faculty of impossibility, which is illuminated by a transcendental faculty of faculties, from which radiates the necessary possibility of incandescence, which cannot be thought temporally, and must therefore be postulated as an eternal shining . . .

# II

Whereas Kant's first critique can be viewed as an attempt to find a middle ground between reason and fact, as that distinction is drawn by Hume, his *Critique of Practical Reason* can be viewed as an attempt to find the middle ground between Humean reason and value.

Kant's moral theory comes down to one proposition: Ethics is grounded in reason. In other words, our ethical obligations originate from and are determined by reason itself. Why did Kant subscribe to such an improbable proposition? Perhaps the other options were less attractive to him. Grounding ethics in religion may have seemed risky. The Church had seen its share of change, and could not be counted on to pass unscathed through the intellectual ferment of the modern era. Relying on science would be even riskier. New discoveries might prove that the good was the bad, or something of that sort. Or perhaps it was just that grounding ethics in reason has a timeless appeal to philosophers. Socrates had the same idea, as have philosophers of all ages since.

Kant sums up his core idea, that reason is the ground of ethics, in the famous Categorical Imperative (CI). An imperative is simply a command: Do this. A hypothetical imperative says you ought to do this if you want that. A categorical one simply says just do it. For Kant, only the CI captures the chief attribute of morality: its unconditionality. To be moral is to do one's duty, and duty accepts no terms.

The CI is Kant's machine for generating the Moral Law out of reason. Here it is, in the language of King James:

> "Act only on that maxim whereby thou canst at the same time will that it should become a universal law."[1]

So this is how you let reason guide your actions. When you want to do something, think of the maxim which accompanies your act. Now ask yourself, can I make this maxim into a universal law? If the maxim cannot be made a universal law without contradiction, your act is unreasonable and therefore unethical.

Very well. Let's give it a try. Here are some applications of the CI:

1. You are scratching your head. Let's consider the maxim of your action: *Because I am bored with this book, I will scratch my head.* Now, would there be any contradiction in making this a universal law? *All those who are bored with a book should scratch their heads.* Is there a contradiction in that? I think not. Very well, then, this is our first Moral Law.

2. You dislike red hair and want all redheads to dye their hair blonde. Your maxim must be something like: *The redhead is dead.* Make this into law no. 2, for there is clearly no contradiction.

---

1. "Foundations of the Metaphysics of Morals," in *Kants Gesammelte Schriften* (Preussische Akademie, 1900–1956), Vol. IV, p. 422.

3. You want to kill your father. Get to a psychoanalyst quickly, because the CI won't stop you. In fact, it will offer a wide range of maxims and laws to help you. For example: *Anyone born on my birthday to my parents is entitled to kill his father; or, fathers should be killed at around retirement age.*

Was Kant really so off the mark? The Kant industry will, of course, complain that this is all a misinterpretation, that Kant meant to say something else altogether. In fact, it is clear that Kant's views on moral matters would not have included the three laws cited above. What he intended with the CI, perhaps, was to highlight the universalism implicit in his (and probably our) sense of morality. The CI does sound like an abstract version of the Golden Rule: Do unto others, etc. Or, he meant to emphasize that we judge actions morally according to the principle under which they were taken, not their consequences. But let's set aside the question of Kant's personal opinions about what is moral, and his observations about the form of moral judgments, and consider what he is trying to achieve, philosophically speaking. He is trying to build an ethics on reason. Whatever sneaky definition of reason Kant contrives, it still means that he believes that the principle of noncontradiction on its own can guide our actions. Or, what is the same, he is, like Socrates, making consistency the criterion of moral virtue. Unfortunately for Kant and Socrates, there is no contradiction in being bad. It might be bad to be bad, but it is not illogical to be bad. Also, a lot of things that are not self-contradictory are neither good nor bad. Whatever Kant believed about what is good or bad, his philosophical attempt to locate the good and bad in reason is as old as Socrates and just as futile.

Kant's mistaken belief that reason can determine the ends of action leads to a classic philosophical confusion about freedom. (Recall the discussion above about Spinoza's idea of freedom.) For Kant, autonomy, or freedom, is the essence of morality. This follows necessarily from the attempt to ground ethics in reason. Your own will "autocratically" lays down the law, or "nomos," according to reason in the form of the CI. Reason, will, and freedom become one in Kant's CI. Heteronomy, or unfreedom, occurs when the will is determined by something other than reason, and therefore something other than itself. In other words, so long as the end of your action is motivated by a desire of some sort, and not the unconditional imperative of duty, you are a captive of desire, and therefore unfree. Since the imperative of duty is reason, and reason is freedom, according to Kant, one is free only so long as one's ends are dictated by freedom itself. If that sounds like a paradox, that's because it is. Despite Kant's cant, if you're free, you can do what you like. It does not matter what you happen to like. If you have to obey a law, whether a moral one or not, you are not free. Freedom does not "choose" anything. You choose, if you are free, and you choose the right thing, if you are good.

The paradox takes another shape. Kant insists that insofar as a deed is done for the sake of some unpleasant, empirical end, like a desire, it is not free and therefore not moral. Only insofar as it is done purely out of a sense of duty can it be considered a moral deed. This may be in part just the reflection of Kant's puritanical, no-pain-no-gain disposition. More importantly, though, it follows from

Kant's dualism of the phenomenal world and the noumenal world. Motives and desires are part of the causal, mechanistic world of appearances, while reason and morality belong to the noumenal world. But Kant's argument leads to this paradox: How can you ever be sure that a deed is moral? For the result of the labors of the first critique is that within the phenomenal world every action is potentially interpretable in terms of mechanical causes, like desires and passions. So, one can never know whether a particular deed was done out of duty or for some motive. In effect, Kant sets his standard of moral action so high that it becomes unachievable.

Kant's ethics should be empty. His CI, if truly reasonable, should be incapable of deciding among self-consistent courses of action. Kant surreptitiously imports substance into an otherwise purely formal theory by hiding a value assertion behind some of his arguments. Since that assertion can take on a life of its own, and become a centerpiece of Kantian ethics, it is worth detailing:

"Man, and in general every rational being, exists as an end in himself, and not merely as a means."[2]

This proposition is not supposed to represent a value assertion. It has an onto-logical ring to it. It is supposed to sound like a fact deduced from pure reason. But what is an "end in itself"? Is it the opposite of a "means in itself"? A "beginning in itself"? What Kant really means to say is something like this:

"Show a little RESPECT for people!"

He is saying: don't *use* people; respect each other's ends; be nice. Of course, this begs a few questions. Is it possible to avoid using people for any purpose whatsoever? And what happens when people's ends are mutually incompatible? But these are trivial matters. What is remarkable is the way in which Kant's meaning can only be rendered by surreptitiously substituting an imperative for a putative fact, or, as Hume would have put it, an "ought" for an "is." It is nonsense to say that humans cannot "exist" merely as means; but it is not nonsense to say that humans "ought not be" merely means. The important point is that Kant pretends he has located a value in reason, an "end" toward which the CI may be directed. He has not. At bottom he has simply asserted his belief that the rational individual has a unique value and his right to choose his own ends should be respected.

In the second half of the *Critique of Practical Reason*, which, in a comical imitation of the architectonic of the first critique, is divided into an Analytic and a Dialectic, Kant tries to recoup the religious dogmas whose proofs he had refuted in the first critique. The immortality of the soul, the freedom of the will, and the existence of God, though all theoretically indemonstrable, are supposed to be the necessary "postulates" of practical reason. In other words, you have to pretend that they are true. It all amounts to a breathtaking reversal. In a sense, it is a double-cross. And this is the clue we need to decode Kant's bizarrely rationalistic ethics.

---

2. "Foundations of the Metaphysics of Morals," Vol. IV, p. 428.

KANT: DOG EPISTEMOLOGY

The first critique imposes limits. It bans unconditional or absolute knowledge. It affirms that all knowledge is conditional. In doing so, it threatens its own legitimacy. To impose limits means to be beyond them. That all things are conditional is an unconditional claim. So there is a need to find a basis within the system for some kind of unconditionality. Kant finds that basis in moral duty, in the unconditionality of the categorical imperative. Here it is important to reiterate the distinction implied above, between Kant's philosophical ethics and his personal ethics. There is no doubt that Kant had a distinct set of values, influenced by his upbringing in a Christian-pietist household, and that these values influenced his philosophical discussion of ethics. But his philosophical ethics, whose core proposition is that ethics is grounded in reason, has an altogether distinct motivation. It is a response to what can be loosely termed a metaphysical need. This need has a "logic" of its own. Its origin is in the need to sustain the philosophical project, or to create a self-sustaining project. It has a better and more general name than duty or ethics: it is mysticism.

## HOW KANT BECAME A MYSTIC

1. There is an ultimate reality (the noumenal world) which is different than and superior to this apparent one (the phenomenal world).

2. Ultimate reality is unknowable, inexpressible, ineffable (the thing-in-itself). Attempts to express it in words are illusory (the Transcendental Dialectic).

3. Apparent reality disappears and ultimate reality is realized through the right kind of experience (obeying the moral law).

# III

Kant's third critique, the *Critique of Judgment*, is easy to forget. This is mainly because the first two are so exhausting it is hard (even for Kant) to sum up the energy for one more. Besides, the third critique is a bit of a hash. It seems that Kant was determined to have a third critique to round out his system, but had a number of different ideas about what to include in the work. And the clarity of his exposition is hopelessly squandered as he tries once again to force these ideas into the irrelevant architectonic of the first critique.

Sometimes Kant favors the Stoic division of philosophy into the three parts of logic, physics, and ethics. Other times, he plumps for a split among metaphysics, ethics, and aesthetics. After finishing the second critique, he thinks up the idea for division according to the faculties of the understanding, reason, and judgment. Around that time, he also gets to thinking about teleology, theology, and the argument from design. So the third critique includes something on aesthetics, something on judgment, and something on teleology. (The Stoics turn out to be irrelevant.)

Kant does actually provide an interesting case for treating these topics together. He defines judgment as the art of bringing together the universal (a principle, law, concept, etc.) with the particular. He distinguishes two kinds of judgment: determinant and reflective. The former begins with a given universal (e.g., the law of gravity) and then applies it to a particular instance (e.g., this apple will fall). The latter begins with a collection of particulars (e.g., varieties of falling fruit) and generates from that a universal (e.g., the law of gravity). So, reflective judgment posits a unity where before there was none. Now, Kant also happens to believe that the perception of beauty results from the perception of the inner harmony, or unity, of the object of art. Kant argues that the perception of harmony and the accompanying sensation of pleasure are generated by the object only in relation to our faculties of imagination and understanding. Specifically, the object is beautiful because it provides us with an apparently real analogy for the internal operation of our reflective judgments. Think of reflective judgment as the "ooh-aah" principle of scientific discovery. We get high when things click, when we see how everything "fits together," and when we discover laws of gravity. According to Kant, this Newtonian pleasure is the primary experience, and our appreciation of beauty a derivative from it. The beautiful object models the notion of 'design' we love to find in the world, although it does in a way which makes it clear that there is no objective design which the artwork represents.

Now we can consider teleology. The teleologist imagines that everything in the world is part of a grand design by its creator. From Kant's first critique, we know that the old argument from design for the existence of God is illegitimate. But Kant does believe that there are circumstances in which it is legitimate and even necessary to imagine that things in the world operate according to a design. By analogy with the perception of beauty in a work of art, he allows that one can find in the world "purposiveness without purpose." In brief, although the existence of a "final cause" of the world can never be demonstrated, one can do a little pretending. Thus, judgment, aesthetic appreciation, and teleological metaphysics come together in Kant's third critique.

Kant's analysis of beauty has another aspect worthy of note here:

"𝕿𝖍𝖊 𝖇𝖊𝖆𝖚𝖙𝖎𝖋𝖚𝖑 𝖎𝖘 𝖙𝖍𝖆𝖙 𝖜𝖍𝖎𝖈𝖍, 𝖆𝖕𝖆𝖗𝖙 𝖋𝖗𝖔𝖒 𝖆 𝖈𝖔𝖓𝖈𝖊𝖕𝖙, 𝖕𝖑𝖊𝖆𝖘𝖊𝖘 𝖚𝖓𝖎𝖛𝖊𝖗𝖘𝖆𝖑𝖑𝖞."[3]

What Kant expresses in his cumbersome way is not so complicated. He wants to point out that aesthetic judgments are neither completely subjective nor completely objective, or, what is the same, that their logical status is distinct from statements of preference as well as statements of fact. On the one hand, beauty is in the eye of the beholder. On the other hand, when the beholder asserts that something is beautiful, he means to assert something which should be true for all beholders. For example, should one exclaim, "Madonna is great," one is not saying merely that she appeals to one's own, subjective impulses. Rather, one is making a judgment for all people, that Madonna's work is beautiful and should be appreciated by all. Kant's phrase "apart from a concept" clarifies the fact that although the judgment is universal, you cannot postulate or prove deductively that everyone will or should like Madonna. You merely impute that they do.

These points about aesthetic judgments are, however, purely formal. They do not determine what is beautiful or good, only what could possibly be thought so. Kant may be able to help one understand what one means when one says that Madonna is great, should one need that sort of help, but he won't be able to discuss whether Madonna really is great.

A last note on Kant's aesthetics: his concept of the sublime. Beauty is something judged of external objects; the sublime is something belonging to our own disposition or attitude, which may be only indirectly linked to external objects. That sublime feeling can come during a violent tornado, when gazing at the sunset, or when smelling a soggy madeleine. At the end of the day, the sublime is that indescribable feeling that results from the sense of having had contact with something beyond all possible sense, the great beyond, the infinite.

There is nothing very original in my criticism of Kant. Almost every argument I have made was expressed in print by people alive when Kant published his first critique—Friedrich Heinrich Jacobi, Solomon Maimon, and Karl Leonhard Reinhold, not to mention Fichte, Schelling, and Hegel. So how does one explain the worldly success of the Kantian philosophy?

Let us set aside the question of Kant's influence on the broad history of ideas and concentrate on his role in the history of philosophy. Modern philosophers share a number of urges, and Kant—more precisely, the apotheosis of Kant—goes some way to satisfying those urges. First, philosophers generally crave professional

---

3. *The Critique of Judgment*, trans. James Creed Meredith (New York and Oxford: Oxford University Press, 1986), p. 219.

respectability. Kant provides the complex vocabulary, the vague idea of a special-ized investigative project, and enough smoke and mirrors to convince outsiders that some serious work is being done. Second, philosophers want theirs to be the best and most general kind of knowledge. They demand global consequences for their conclusions. Kant's promise that he could reverse the basis of all knowledge, from 'object' to 'subject', is just the sort of grand implication they need. Third, philoso-phers don't like to admit that any other philosopher has all the answers. They pre-fer to deify the philosopher who sets up problems and then provides some obviously wrong answers, which gives them plenty to argue about. In sum, Kant's obscurity is the critical factor in satisfying the urges that have led philosophers to elevate him to greatness. His obtuse distinctions lend an air of professionalism; his convoluted arguments give the impression of profundity; and the resulting inconsistencies pro-vide grist for the debating mills of philosophy.

The third point above, on the importance of Kant's inconsistencies to his own suc-cess, is worth elaborating in yet another general principle of the history of philosophy:

---

**The Disagreeability Principle**: A philosopher will remain prominent in the history of philosophy so long as he can be plausibly disagreed with.

---

Both the rationalists and the empiricists of the seventeenth century sought to take philosophy out of the monastery, to make it the province of educated amateurs. Kant collected their insights and put them in the service of a return to the age of the monks. After Kant, philosophy would be safe from rebellious amateurs, and could come home to its quiet seminaries and universities. To be sure, the new the-ologians no longer debated about angels and pins. They busied themselves with "the facts of consciousness" and the like. And Aristotle was no longer the subject of their scholastic commentaries. Kant himself was. It is ironic, but sadly irrele-vant, that many of Kant's finest arguments were directed against the metaphysical project that supposedly characterized the medieval theologians.

---

# K

*Somewhere in the middle of the journey through the forest of life, K found him-self before a magnificent castle. It was like no castle he had ever seen. Its majes-tic facade and dreamy turrets filled the sky. Its medieval walls blazed with a pure and virtuous whiteness, its banners gloriously unfurled their pride in duty done. Most extraordinary of all, the entire edifice rested on nothing but air. "I must be in the Kingdom of Ends," K said to himself. He set up camp in the shadow of this wondrous creation, in the hope that he might one day pass through its splendid doors. He began to put together the tools he thought might help him win his way in. First he tried synthesizing an empirical ladder. But the higher he climbed, the further the castle seemed. He realized that the castle must lie outside space and* time. So he synthesized an a priori *ladder. Alas, his transcendental device could not quite support his own, merely apparent weight. He attempted a transcendental reduction of his calories, but somehow failed to achieve the original synthetic unity of perception of weightlessness. He tried swinging on a dialectic. He issued a categorical imperative. He purified himself in every way imaginable, so that he might rise up to the castle in virtue of the Moral Law. Years passed, and still the castle hovered above him, as alluring and inaccessible as ever. Approaching the end of his days, as he gazed upon the marvel, he came to realize that he had already completed his mission, that the journey had finished when it began. This was his life, this life of standing outside the castle, of standing in wonder, of devising ever new plans which take him nowhere other than where he already was. This was his reality, his duty without interest, an end-in-itself, a purposiveness without purpose.*

# Fichte

## An I for an I

The old folks just couldn't figure Kant out. Probably his books were too long and the print too small for their tired eyes. Only the young were ready for Kant, and they took him on enthusiastically. The first and most notable of these Kinter-Kantians was the fiery scholar-teacher Johann Gottlieb Fichte (1762–1814). In 1792, at the age of thirty, Fichte published a *Critique of All Revelation* which imitated Kant's style so well that many believed that Kant himself was the real author. He won fame and also notoriety as one with suspicious and possibly dangerous beliefs. Nonetheless, he rose to become rector of the University of Berlin, which is to say that he became top dog in German philosophy. Fichte's death was mildly romantic. He kissed his wife smack on the lips once he thought she had recovered from a spell of the typhus. She hadn't. She survived, he didn't.

## LET THERE BE I

Fichte thought he saw hidden in Kant's work the most important truth imaginable. This truth would be the essence of philosophy and the foundation of all knowledge. In his Transcendental Deduction, in the idea of the transcendental unity of apperception, Kant had fumbled around this truth, touched it, but had not come out with it clearly. Fichte would state it:

> The origins of all my thoughts and my life springs from all that which in me, for me, and by me can exist; the innermost spirit of my spirit is not a foreign spirit, but rather is itself brought forth by myself. . . . *I am throughout my own creation.*[1]

---

1. "The Destiny of Man," in *Sämtliche Werke* (Berlin, 1846), Vol. V, p. 256.

In more technical terms: The ego posits itself. Or, as Fichte would abbreviate it in his logic, I = I. Notice that the ego posits more than itself: It posits thoughts, life, and the whole world just in order to make itself possible. This was a tough cookie even for the metaphysically omnivorous Germans to chew. On hearing Fichte's claim that the world was his own creation, so the story goes, some asked themselves, "But what does his wife think?"

Like many of his contemporaries, Fichte loved Kant but found his thing-in-itself unspeakably offensive. He could never be happy so long as ultimate reality remained forever outside his grasp in the form of an inert and featureless thing-in-itself. He designed his own doctrine of the ego in order to destroy the thing-in-itself. When the ego posits itself, it realizes precisely that kind of knowledge which Kant had proscribed: the discursive or intellectual intuition. In other words, according to Fichte, what Kant had called the thing-in-itself was really the self-in-itself. So, for Fichte, something absolute or unconditioned does exist, but it is not on the outside and inaccessible, but on the inside, and quite knowable.

An intellectual intuition must represent the most certain and fundamental knowledge available. Fichte's idea was that all knowledge could be based on the original intellectual intuition of the self by itself, and all logic derived from its correlative logical proposition, I = I. In his Transcendental Deduction, Kant had deduced the necessity of the unity of consciousness for experience, but, in the eyes of his contemporaries, at least, he had failed to show that his table of categories followed from this unity. Fichte thought he could make good this omission in Kant's work. He wrote a large number of murky paragraphs which supposedly deduced the I's right to a number of categories in virtue of its initial self-identity.

Like Descartes, Fichte took the ego as a rock-hard certainty and the starting point for all philosophy. Unlike Descartes, he tried to conceive of the ego without presupposing an external and alien world of matter. He thought he could do this by conceiving consciousness, or what Descartes might have called mind, as subordinate to the reflexive act of self-consciousness. Fichte tried to conceive of an ego which was neither substance nor object, but a pure act. Fichte further believed, following Kant, that all of science had to be grounded in the critical examination of the self by itself. One could say that he took very seriously the ancient imperative "know thyself." One can also find in Fichte an anticipation of existentialist thought. Fichte's insight was that we create ourselves, that no one but ourselves is responsible for the way we are. Fichte's philosophy of the self can with some justice be labeled the philosophy of freedom. It is not surprising that this philosophy was born in the hopeful, early days of the French Revolution.

As Fichte's thought grew, incidentally, this self-creating Ego became more than the mere individual, Johann Gottlieb. It became a grand, world-wide Ego. It started to look like all of society, then all of history, then the entire universe. In this, of course, it not only looked forward to Hegel, but also looked backward to the *logos* of Heraclitus, the mind of Anaximander, and the cosmic soul of countless other philosophies. There is an inexorable logic to this expansion of Fichte's ego: for, according to Fichte, in the final analysis, there is no distinction between self and world.

# A SHOCK TO THE I

So it all begins with a primordial act of the ego. But, a pimply little student in the front row asks, what is the ego prior to its self-creation? Hmmm. Well, let's just suppose that it's some sort of pre-ego. In that case, what *causes* the (pre-)ego to posit itself? What starts this ship of self moving? Fichte senses a leak in his philosophy, and tries to plug it up. The ego receives a "shock," he says, and this leads it to posit itself. All right, says our acned teenager, but in that case isn't the opposition of ego and other prior to the ego's positing itself? In which case, isn't this "shock" just another version of Kant's "thing-in-itself," a little external reality which you have to posit but which then is supposed to vanish in your system? Aren't you just another double-crossing dualist? Fichte blushes.

The amusing thing about Fichte is that he identifies what is wrong with Kant and then repeats the error on a grander scale. Where Kant erred was in inadvertently deducing a new metaphysics from a pure critique of knowledge. His thing-in-itself is a case in point. Kant finds that in order to conceive of a critique of the faculties of knowledge, one must conceive of a thing-in-itself existing prior to the operation of said faculties. He then falsely infers from this logical necessity the actual existence of a thing-in-itself, complete with a noumenal world of its own. Fichte senses that there is something amiss with the thing-in-itself, but commits the same mistake when he infers the existence of the self from the logical need to conceive of a self prior to any form of consciousness.

The paradoxes of the Fichtean philosophy are mirror images of those in Kant. Fichte says that unconditioned knowledge is possible, i.e., that the Absolute exists, but adds that it exists only for the self. But this is the same as saying that the Absolute doesn't really exist. Kant says that the Absolute exists, but is unknowable. But this is to know something about it. In other words, Fichte declares that there are no limits to thought, and then imposes limits. Kant claims that there are limits, and then transgresses them. It is a dialectic of sorts, but not a pleasing one. Like a yo-yo, it goes up and down, but always in the same place.

Consider the relationship between the Fichtean self and the rest of the world. The self is the supposed starting point of everything: experience, logic, knowledge. This begs the question, why does the self posit the particular world it does? Why can't I posit a world in which I have a nice house in the Hamptons? In Kant's philosophy, how does the noumenal world give rise to a particular phenomenal world, and not any other, if the principle of causality belongs exclusively to the phenomenal world?

# MR. GERMANY

There is another side of Fichte which at first seems incompatible with his philosophy of freedom. This is the German nationalist-romantic Fichte. Germany in his time was a fragmented collection of principalities. As a nation, it existed in the minds and desires of people like Fichte, who distinguished the concept of a 'fatherland' from that of the 'state'. The state was merely an apparatus of administrative power. The fatherland or 'nation', however, was something grand, eternal, larger than the individual. It was through participation in this fatherland that the individual could transcend his own finitude. Fichte further believed that the German nation was unique, and would illuminate the pathway to the future for the rest of Europe. Is this starting to sound familiar? Is that the sound of someone goose-stepping in the distance?

But we are only philosophers! Indeed. Fichte's Germanism is philosophically relevant in two respects. First, the uniqueness of Germany, in Fichte's mind, lay in its culture. And philosophy, in Fichte's mind, was the pinnacle and the foundation of this culture. So, Fichte saw himself, the nation's ace philosopher, as very important. It was a rare ambition, with no possible counterpart today. Second, Fichte's Germanism was part of his Romanticism, which was part of his ambivalence about the Enlightenment. The kind of ego created in Fichte's thought, then, would not necessarily correspond to the rational individualist of the Enlightenment tradition. Fichte's ego would have a sense of daring, a freedom positively experienced in the fulfillment of its own destiny, a responsibility only to itself, and its innermost nature and desires. . . .

## FICHTE'S END

It was Fichte's historical misfortune to be succeeded by Hegel as Germany's philosopher king at the University of Berlin. Hegel was eight years younger and lived sixteen years longer than Fichte, and was perhaps less than grateful toward his philosophical father. He labeled Fichte's philosophy "subjective idealism," and the label has stuck ever since. For Hegel, Fichte's philosophy was nice but just a passing phase in the inexorable march of history toward his own philosophy, absolute idealism. In fact, one can find a lot more than subjective idealism in Fichte, if one chooses to look. There is plenty of intersubjectivity, a bit of realism, romantic nationalism, an anticipation of Hegel's dialectic, and so forth. On the other hand, it is hard work getting through Fichte's somewhat warped vocabulary, just as hard as Hegel's, so one is probably better off just sticking with Hegel.

# Schelling

## The Bright Young Thing

Friedrich Wilhelm Joseph von Schelling (1775–1854), Hegel, and the poet Hölderlin were classmates at the theological seminary at Tübingen. Schelling was five years younger than Hegel, but more advanced in his studies. A remarkably bright boy, he was a leading follower and then critic of Fichte. While still a teenager he was hailed as the future of German (and therefore European) philosophy. In his twenties he and Hegel established their own philosophical journal, *Critical Journal of Philosophy* (1801–1803). The older man was clearly the junior partner.

Sadly, Schelling trod the path now well worn by many Rhodes scholars and those voted most likely to succeed. He was a man with a great future, and always would be. He did go on to produce some very long and difficult works of philosophy, in the good German style, with plenty of Absolutes, Subjects, Objects, and Intellectual Intuitions. He waxed prolix on mind-shattering notions, like 'the identity of Spirit and Nature'. But he changed philosophies the way Elizabeth Taylor changes husbands, and the public soon lost interest. Hegel, his far duller companion at school, far outshone him in philosophical repute. To add insult to injury, Hegel took advantage of Schelling's talk about nature, which had really been intended as a refreshing break from Fichte's self-absorption, in order to label Schelling's philosophy Objective Idealism, which, together with Fichte's so-called Subjective Idealism, was to be viewed as world history's final step on the way to its rendezvous with Hegel's own Absolute Idealism.

Schelling never forgave his old pal. He became a bitter man, claiming that Hegel copied all of his ideas from him, and that they were all wrong anyway. After Hegel died, Schelling experienced a brief comeback. He was called to Berlin, to the hallowed chair in philosophy. There, in the few years remaining to him, he expounded his obscure and mystical views on Nature, Revelation, and so forth, and almost became something of an existentialist. One of his listeners was the young Søren Kierkegaard (1813–1855), who provided him with an appropriate epitaph: "Schelling does talk a lot of nonsense."

# Hegel

## Lord of the Philosophers

In Georg W. F. Hegel (1770–1831) we find the best and the worst of philosophy. Perhaps no one else in our history had a more comprehensive grasp of the demands made on philosophy by the search for the Holy Grail. The unity of aim and result, of method and content, of thinking and being, and all the other imaginary consummations of philosophy are the self-conscious project of the Hegelian philosophy. The whole history of philosophy up to Hegel, and to some extent beyond, is an explicit part of the articulation of Hegelianism. If there is such a thing as philosophy in heaven, it is probably a version of Hegel's. But there isn't; and without a blind, sustaining faith in philosophy, Hegelianism descends into farce. From down here, few philosophers seem as ridiculous as Hegel.

Hegel's role in the history of philosophy usually extends beyond the compass of his now extinct band of immediate disciples and followers. He is famous for having supposedly invented a method of reason, the so-called Hegelian dialectic, and for having conceived of philosophy as well as consciousness in general as the outcome of an historical process. These contributions, or so the story goes, retain their value even after the rest of the Hegelian comedy has left the stage. Here I wish to defend the whole of Hegel against those who would rescue a few of his parts. Taken outside its home in his absurd metaphysics, the Hegelian dialectic disintegrates into plain old thinking mixed with a few stimulating but arbitrary intuitions, or so I will argue. Without the same metaphysical backing, Hegel's historicism becomes either an illusory and absurd doctrine in its own right, or an obvious and banal application of the general principle of empiricism to historical concerns. I want to say, on behalf of Hegel, but against any supposed Hegelian logic in the history of philosophy: Philosophy is an all-or-nothing affair.

## DOCTRINES

According to Hegel, it is impossible to summarize the Hegelian philosophy. To summarize would be to present the final results, which would consist of propositions about the nature of the world according to Hegel. But philosophy is a process as well as its results. And a list of propositions about the world would be abstract and one-sided, merely thoughts, and therefore not real, not true knowledge, not philosophy. As we shall see, however, this unsummarizability of Hegelianism is a decent summary of Hegelianism in itself. The result for which Hegel aimed, at least, was precisely a philosophy whose results would be identical with its process. The unity of process and result is the most general expression of the quest for the Holy Grail in the Hegelian philosophy. Hegelianism, like any mysticism, is a kind of knowledge which is also an experience.

Of course, a good deal more can be said about the exact nature of Hegel's quest. The specific unities he sought were in some measure dictated to him by the preceding history of philosophy. Below I triangulate on the specific structure of Hegel's quest by outlining his relationship with three key sources. First is the ancient doctrine of monism. Next comes idealism. Last and by far the most important, is the Kantian idea of critical philosophy. Hegel's application of all three follows a distinctive pattern. He grasps the quest that underlies each; that is, he comprehends each of these doctrines not as propositions of fact, but as goals or outcomes. Each doctrine, Hegel might have said, drives itself beyond itself, to accomplish what it cannot by its nature do. Thus he develops a super-monism, beyond the blank identity of all things in your usual monism; a super-idealism, which includes a version of materialism within itself; and a super-critique, which goes from merely criticizing to creating. I then try to show how these sources inform Hegel's major projects, his phenomenology, science of logic, and encyclopedia. Lastly, I introduce some of the conceptual tools used by Hegel in pursuit of his projects.

## (1) SOURCES

### 1.1 SUPER-MONISM

There can be no doubt that Hegel was a monist. Like Parmenides, Plotinus, the nameless authors of the Upanishads, and, above all, Spinoza, Hegel believed in his heart that all is one. All consciousness is a part of Absolute Knowing, all concepts belong to the Absolute Idea, all the world is Absolute Spirit. But Hegel also understood that monism is not itself the unity of all things, but a statement of intention, a quest. I would say that he anticipated what I have called "the schmooalism principle." Monism, after all, begins by positing the existence of many things, all of which are somehow to be united. To assert merely that they are in fact united is insufficient, Hegel argued. He criticized Schelling's conception of the Absolute as "the night in which all cows are black," that is, as a blanket identity of all things in which the differences among things have been utterly annihilated. So Hegel sought a monism beyond ordinary monism, one that would preserve difference in identity, multiplicity in unity. Above all, Hegel conceived of his monism as the outcome of a process, not a premise or a doctrine to be asserted. One could say that he grasped the concept of the search for the Holy Grail *qua* search, and thus preserved an important aspect of its character.

HEGEL: THE NIGHT IN WHICH ALL COWS ARE BLACK

## *1.2 SUPER-IDEALISM*

As a philosopher, Hegel needed a One that could speak, especially to philosophers. So, in the time-honored way of Plato and Berkeley, he became an idealist. In other words, he turned the world upside down. Thought, Hegel argued, is not merely a mental game played in our heads around a preexisting world. Thought *is* the world. That is, the world is nothing but the development and manifestation of thought itself. In a further twist, no doubt inspired by Fichte, Hegel conceived of ultimate reality as thought thinking about itself in the form of self-consciousness, specifically the self-consciousness of an amazing World Spirit.

Hegel also understood that idealism, like monism, is a statement of intention, not a given doctrine. It is the quest to subsume all matter, all that is merely particular and contingent, in the ideal. The statement that thought is reality counts for little, or so he thought; what matters is to think reality, that is, to think the thoughts that are ultimate reality. Hegel therefore always presented his idealism at the end of his books, as the outcome of a process. That process, by the way, passed through a materialism, for he interpreted matter as one of the manifestations—the "self-othering," in his unique vocabulary—of World Spirit. His idealism also explicitly surpassed the traditional form of idealism. So it was a kind of super-idealism. In this way, Hegel anticipated what I will call "the schmiderialism principle" (see p. 309).

HEGEL: THE ABSOLUTE SPEAKS

## 1.3 SUPER-CRITIQUE

What turned Hegel on most was Kant's idea of the critical philosophy. Hegel under-stood that the surreptitious point of the critique of pure reason was not just to per-form an abstract analysis of concepts, but to bring forth a unique product, pure rea-son itself. The point was to have a constructive critique, one that could generate some meaningful knowledge on its own, a content identical with its method. So Hegel invented his "dialectic" as the general form of this self-sufficient critique. The dialectic begins with what is self-evident. Then, rather than seek a critique on the basis of external premises, it finds the basis for criticism within that with which it begins. The result of this internal critique, as Hegel has it, is a return to the start-ing position, but with crucial refinements—something the same but different, improved. Kant's own philosophy could be construed by Hegel as an instance of such a dialectic—though Kant lacked self-awareness on this point—and Hegel's philosophy itself could be seen as a dialectical evolution of the Kantian philoso-phy. Of course, Hegel insisted that the dialectic was not a "method" in the usual sense, in that it could be abstracted entirely from its manifestation in the Hegelian texts. On the contrary, Hegel understood that if he were to achieve the unity of method and content, this would have to be done in the correct way, unfolding both together throughout the process.

# (2) PROJECTS

The actual tasks Hegel set himself are more specific still. The structure of these tasks was decisively influenced by Kant (with Fichte in the capacity of chief inter-preter of Kant).

## 2.1 PHENOMENOLOGY

Hegel's first major, and, I think, his best work was the *Phenomenology of Spirit* (1807). What did Hegel mean by this strange new word, phenomenology? Literally, he meant the science of appearances, i.e., the *logy* of *phenomena*. What could he have meant? With what could one contrast a science of appearances? A science of realities? Come to think of it, isn't science by definition supposed to get behind appearances, and study the realities?

Hegel's brave new science seems to concern itself with a series of what might be called "forms of consciousness." Each form of consciousness has a particular kind of object of which it is conscious or a particular way of comprehending the world. "Consciousness" here must be understood very loosely; included are not just what might be called individual viewpoints, but those of whole societies, historical movements, sciences, religions, the family, and so on. The series begins, or is taken to begin, in a form of consciousness which requires no presuppositions, i.e., has no predecessor. It then follows a logical progression. Each succeeding form of consciousness is in some sense more comprehensive that the last, because each new form is taken to be the direct result of critical introspection by the preceding one. The series ends in a form of presumably total consciousness, called Absolute Knowing, which can also be described as the self-consciousness of Spirit. We are now in a position to understand the term "appearances." Phenomenology is the record of the various forms in which Spirit appears to itself on its way to total self-consciousness. The possession of Absolute Knowledge provides a retroactive justification for the series that precedes it. The progression becomes scientific in virtue of its ending, which justifies and "gets behind" the various appearances as modes of the self-realization of reality.

The purpose for this strange new project becomes clearer in light of Hegel's all-important relationship with Kant. Recall that Kant had insisted on the existence of a thing-in-itself, resident of the so-called noumenal world, forever banned from the merely phenomenal world of human comprehension. As a card-carrying monist, Hegel could not tolerate such a division of the world. As an idealist, he believed that all of reality, including the thing-in-itself, could be expressed in thought. He further believed that the Kantian critical method, revised in the form of his own dialectic, would serve as the tool through which thought could think itself through, and so achieve union with ultimate reality. But he kept in mind throughout that this ultimate objective of marrying the phenomenal and noumenal worlds would have to be part of a process, not merely a doctrine or a conclusion. Thus he conceived the project of phenomenology, to progressively conquer the phenomenal world, or all the ways in which things appear to consciousness, in the end to capture the thing-in-itself, and so discover Absolute Knowing, or the Holy Grail of philosophy.

## 2.2 SCIENCE OF LOGIC

Some years later, Hegel decided that Spirit was not quite there yet, and represented his *Phenomenology* as a kind of preface to his *Science of Logic* (1812–1816). Once again, the idea behind the project can be understood best with reference to Hegel's relationship to Kant. Recall that Kant had insisted that concepts could generate no knowledge without accepting something as given, viz., an intuition. So, pure reason is impotent to reveal any knowledge of the world. The notion of an inert intu-ition ultimately reduced to an unknowable thing-in-itself. Hegel's science of logic is his attempt to remake Kant's critical philosophy on his own terms. This time, instead of forms of consciousness, Hegel gives us a logical progression of concepts. The idea is that with an adequate elaboration of concepts all intuitions can be "determined away," and one can arrive at an unconditioned knowledge of reality. The first concept (or category, as it comes to be called) analyzed in the Hegelian Logic is 'being', the last is that of the 'Absolute Idea'. So, the science of logic is a progression from being to thinking. Since the concept of being turns out to be purely abstract—indeed, it is followed immediately by 'nothing'—and that of the Absolute Idea most real, the science of logic can also be thought to proceed from thinking to being. Whichever way it goes, the science of logic ends by overcoming the distinction between thinking and being. Thus, Hegel reveals a process which leads to his super-monism, or the unity of all things in the Absolute Idea, and thereby also produces a super-idealism. This delightful outcome, moreover, is sup-posed to be the consequence of a super-critical process. Starting in absolute imme-diacy with being, each category shows itself to be one-sided or deficient in its own terms with respect to the totality, and in this process gives rise naturally to another category, which in its turn succumbs to another, and so on to the end.

One can think of Hegel's science of logic as an attempt to explain all possible explanations, and thereby to achieve an unconditioned knowledge of the basic structure of all reality. The idea for such an explanation of all explanations is at least as old as Aristotle, who provided his own account of all physical accounts in his doctrine of the four causes, and his accounts of all logical accounts in his own doctrine of the categories. While Aristotle tended to think in terms of lists, Hegel thought primarily in terms of processes. At the end of the day, though, the assump-tion behind the project is the same: One can determine the ultimate structure of reality by determining in advance what can possibly be said about it.

## 2.3 ENCYCLOPEDIA

Later still, Hegel brushed off his first work as a juvenile effort, abbreviated his *Sci-ence of Logic*, and made it the first of three volumes in his *Encyclopedia* (1817). The second volume was the *Philosophy of Nature*, the third *Philosophy of Spirit*. The vol-ume on nature was an embarrassment, and on the whole the new tripartite division of philosophy seems the result of an uninspired dialectic. The title of the series, obviously, gives away Hegel's modest intention to lay out the truth about everything.

It is worth noting, though, that the new scheme allowed Hegel to create rela-tively self-sufficient subdivisions to hold his many and profound insights on art, reli-gion, and society. Absolute Spirit, as opposed to the somewhat more one-sided Absolute Knowing and Absolute Idea, comes into its own in Hegel's *Encyclopedia*.

The revitalized World Spirit allowed Hegel to clear up his thinking on world history. Phenomenology already provided a history of sorts. The progression of forms of consciousness which lead to Absolute Knowing tracks actual world history in a sporadic way. In his lectures on the *Philosophy of History* Hegel made the connection with history explicit. World Spirit achieves self-consciousness in the process of human history. What we as finite individuals see as a temporal sequence of events is for World Spirit a set of modes of consciousness, through which it realizes itself.

# (3) TOOL BOX

Hegel developed a number of conceptual tools—methods, distinctions, or perhaps just tropes—while in pursuit of his goals. These tools have sometimes taken on a life of their own in the subsequent history.

## 3.1 DETERMINATE NEGATION

Does no mean yes? Hegel's idea that negation is always determinate is the idea that negation always has a positive result. For example, the negation of a particular proposition gives rise to a new (and presumably better) proposition. The negation of a philosophical system gives rise to a more complete philosophical understanding. Determinate negation is not really a negation at all: It is indeed another way of saying yes. It is an idea that goes back in some form at least to Parmenides, and was perhaps most clearly anticipated by Spinoza. The determinacy of negation is critical to the functioning of the Hegelian system. The dialectic is able to advance only because its second moment, the negation of the thesis, does not simply obliterate the thesis, but contains something positive. It is on account of the determinacy of negation that the ongoing critique which is the dialectic results in knowledge.

The Spinozan and Parmenidean origins of this notion help make clear that it is only sustainable in the context of a monism. In a monism, you can't throw anything away, since everything belongs to the whole. What is negated, and the act of negation itself, are necessarily part of the whole. Thus Parmenides simply banned the word "not" from meaningful discourse. This is why Spinoza, like Hegel, claimed that falsity and evil do not really exist. Outside a monism, of course, you are free to throw things away as you please. When, in an unphilosophical mood, you negate the proposition "there is a pizza here," you do not get a different kind of pizza, a not-pizza, or anything else; you probably go hungry.

## 3.2 THE CONCRETE UNIVERSAL

What Hegel calls the "concrete universal," at first glance, just seems to be a concept that has a bit of oomph in the real world. The abstract universal concept of freedom, for example, is pretty empty, just the concept of the absence of restraints. The concrete universal of freedom, on the other hand, is freedom understood such as it is realized in the world, i.e., including the state, its constitution, the social practices, and all that which makes possible freedom as we understand it. In fact, the concrete universal is more than an oomphy concept; it is all those realities. The real world, according to Hegel, consists in the motions and manifestations of these concrete universals. Thus the concrete universal is a part of Hegel's super-idealism.

### 3.3.1 REASON VERSUS UNDERSTANDING

Kant thought up this distinction, but Hegel gave it a whole new meaning. In Kant's world, the understanding was responsible for knowledge (i.e., for applying concepts to intuitions) while reason was responsible for thought (i.e., for relations among concepts). In Hegel, both are ways of thinking as well as ways of knowing. The understanding is that ordinary way of thinking which makes the (presumably foolish) assumption that thoughts are not things and things are not thoughts. It is analytic, and is best represented by formal logic. It cannot tolerate contradictions. Reason is the philosophical way of knowing. It thinks things through, and turns them into pure thought. It is speculative, and is embodied in the dialectic. It sees beyond abstract contradictions, to grasp the inherent unity of things. Reason is effectively the method (and the content) of the super-critique.

Hegel makes this distinction sound more plausible than it really is, in two ways. First, he shows respect for the capabilities and achievements of the understanding. So, he avoids putting himself in the position of having to disprove all ordinary knowledge in order to make a case for philosophical knowledge. Second, he provides a lot of examples of how ordinary ways of thinking lead to errors when introduced to philosophical subjects. Some of these are run-of-the-mill logical errors. Others are pretty much the same as those identified by Kant, which occur when the understanding seeks knowledge of the totality of things.

Considered in terms of its function in the Hegelian texts, the reason/understanding distinction is one of the classic rhetorical devices of philosophy. As long ago as Heraclitus and Parmenides, philosophers insisted on a special kind of knowledge, distinct from the ordinary, available only to the initiate. At the end of the day, the ordinary understanding is nothing other than that faculty of asserting that the philosopher is full of doo doo. Not surprisingly, speculative reason tends to coincide with whatever the philosopher believes to be the case.

### 3.3.2 THE DIALECTIC

In schematic terms, Hegel's dialectic is a refined version of the ancient Greek dialectic and Kant's critical method. The earlier methods had both involved examining the presuppositions of a given philosophical position. They seemed to stall once a contradiction was discovered, for no one seemed to know what to do with the resulting *critical* truths. Hegel's dialectic is also a critique of a given position. He believed, however, that the critical negation of a given position will be a determinate negation, and so will be a positive truth. That is, you start with a thesis, criticize and reject it in an antithesis, and then grasp the truth of the whole process in a synthesis. Thus unfolds the truth.

A "differentiated identity" is whatever it is that Hegel imagines can survive the dialectical process. That which experiences the dialectic, as we have seen, first becomes its other, or is negated, and then returns to itself, in richer "differentiated" form, through the negation of the negation. What survives such a brutal procedure is much more than the substrate which Aristotle identified as a condition necessary for any change. Here we're talking about something that has change, drastic change, like its own obliteration, built into it, as part of its real identity. The only model for such strange behavior, I think, is the Fichtean-Hegelian self-consciousness. Such a self creates itself by positing an other, the outside world, and then recognizing its identity with this other.

It all comes down to the dialectic. Determinacy of negation is a precondition of the dialectic. Universals can be concrete only if they can dialectically "other" themselves in history. Speculative reason, as distinct from the understanding, is dialectical reason. Phenomenology and the science of logic can progress only by means of dialectic. Insofar as the dialectic is the movement of consciousness, on the other hand, it becomes what it is, a true method, only in the content of phenomenology; insofar as it is the method of logic, it is identical with the whole of the science of logic.

### 3.3.3 THE IRRESISTIBLE

Actually, there is no point to make here. When thinking of Hegel, one simply can't resist thinking in threes.

## MOTIVES

*Why Did He Do It?* What did our torpid genius expect out of philosophy? The question is perhaps irrelevant to the truth of his views; yet our historical sense (or maybe just our prurience) leads us on. It seems likely that Hegel had at least three prephilosophical aims. First, he wanted to resolve a personal religious crisis. Hegel was a pious little boy. He wanted to believe in God and Christ. Yet he found himself repulsed by certain elements of Christianity. He sensed something cruel and unhappy in the religion of the cross, especially when he compared it with the other, resurgent ideal of ancient Greek culture. He discovered that he could quiet his spiritual troubles by making religion subordinate to an all-embracing philosophy. Second, Hegel wanted to advance the cause of German culture and nationhood in the world. Like Fichte, he believed that philosophy could become the exponent and the embodiment of a reunified, revitalized, modern, triumphant Germany. Philosophy could be the mother of the fatherland. Third, he wanted a job.

**Biofact.** Hegel may have preached absolute idealism, but in his life he practiced a quite ordinary realism. His first preoccupation was to provide a steady income for his wife and kids. As he once wrote in a letter, his guiding maxim was "first live, then philosophize." If this meant taking a job as a high school principal, or adapting his philosophy to the interests of the ruling party, then so be it. His second major concern was to secure his supplies of alcohol. In choosing where to live, Hegel cited "a good brew" as one important factor. Among his correspondence are a number of letters to a local wine merchant, in one of which he demands better service on grounds that he is such a good customer. Finally, to demonstrate that an absolute idealist may be quite human, let it be noted not that Hegel fathered an illegitimate child, but that for his partner in the affair he made the rather pedestrian and uninspiring choice of his family's own housemaid.

Hegel's prephilosophical aims could be met by securing a meaningful project for professional philosophy. Once ensconced in the university, he found that his spiritual and political aspirations happily coincided with his overwhelming desire for job security. Hegel's religious problems are long gone. What is meaningful in religion, the mystical union with the One, he has elevated to philosophy. What is doubtful about religion, its specific practices and narratives, now belongs to history, and so may be accepted and then discarded as moments in the self-alienation of true Spirit. Hegel's hopes for the new Germany are also easily accommodated. If Spirit comes to self-consciousness through a progression of cultures, then some cultures are obviously more "advanced" than others. Fortunately for Germany, Spirit comes to its peak of self-consciousness in German philosophy at a German university. As for philosophers, there can be no doubt but that they have a most important job to perform. The way to secure a project for philosophy has been, throughout history, to give pure reason power over facts and values. Hegel's self-sufficient super-critique is just the tool philosophers need. With it, they provide the gloss on reality through which Spirit gets to know itself.

If that's all that Hegel wanted, it is hard not to accuse him of overkill. One need not turn the whole world upside-down in order to shake out a few coins for church, state, and career. One does not need the truth about everything just to secure control over a few things. It seems we must call on the Aristotle complex for an explanation. Remember, the essence of World-Spirit is *self*-consciousness. That is, it really only exists once it gets to know itself. How does it get to know itself?

Well, in philosophy, of course. Whose philosophy? Well, Hegel says, the name of the particular individual drops out, it is inessential, for he is a mere particularity. But why be so demure? World Spirit achieves self-consciousness and thus comes into being in the philosophy of none other than Hegel. It is in Hegel's own self-consciousness that history finally looks itself in the eye, and everything acquires its true meaning. It is in him that the divine becomes divine. Such is the power of our Lord, the Lord of the Philosophers.

## WAS HEGEL INSANE?

---

**The Principle of A-sanity.** In philosophy, there is no distinction between sanity and insanity.

*Proof.* To be sane is to be able to distinguish between oneself and the rest of reality. More generally, it is the distinction between thought and reality. In order to test for sanity, one must assume that one's thoughts are distinct from and limited by reality. However, philosophy includes within itself any possible models of thought, of reality, and of checking thoughts against reality. It cannot assume that one's thoughts are distinct from reality. Indeed, the objective of philosophy is to unite thought and reality. Therefore, philosophy allows no distinction between sanity and insanity.

*Scholium 1.* To put the matter in different terms: a sanity check assumes that it is possible to distinguish between oneself and God. Philosophy makes no such assumption.

*Scholium 2.* Philosophy is said to have the attribute of "a-sanity." Or, to use a pithy Hegelianism: philosophy is the unity of sanity and insanity.

---

WARNING: THE HEGELIAN PHILOSOPHY CAN CAUSE SEVERE INTELLECTUAL DISORIENTATION, LOSS OF ABILITY TO COMMUNICATE, AND DELUSIONS OF PHILOSOPHICAL GRANDEUR.

## PHENOMENOLOGY OF HEGEL

*Preface.* It is customary to begin a work with the assumption that the reader is not the book, and the truth not necessarily what is written. But in the case of a work of philosophy, such an assumption can only be inappropriate, if not misleading. For if the truth of philosophy is to be what it makes itself out to be, which is to say, something universal and self-conscious, surely philosophy cannot simply exclude the reader forever from its truth. The reader, after all, is part of the universe.

## Hegel: The Philosophy of Absolute Banana-ism

*Introduction.* It is also natural to assume that if philosophical truth is to present itself in readable form, that some inspection of this form and its peculiar limits and possibilities should be undertaken before philosophizing. In philosophy, however, such an assumption lands us in the dilemma that if the truth must present itself through and is limited by a particular form or medium, it cannot be absolute or unconditioned, as it purports to be, and must therefore be false. Besides, the assumption assumes a lot: that philosophical truth is presented in the text, that the reader is not the text, and so forth.

The procedure here will be to follow the consciousness of the reader as it becomes fully aware of its object, the Hegelian text. This is the story of the journey of consciousness as it moves from its finite particularity of being a reader of Hegel to full self-awareness in the realization that it is none other than Hegel. Consciousness begins with the belief that it is a reader, distinct from the written text, and that there is a text distinct from Hegel. In other words, it imagines that there is a you, that this you is different from me, that we are something other than Hegel, and that Hegel is something other than the Hegelian writings. You may think you are not me, and certainly not Hegel, but you are merely an abstract, one-sided, and deficient mode of consciousness. So there. This may also be called the journey of doubt and despair. For consciousness at first doubts that the Hegelian text has any meaning, then despairs as it loses its bearings in the Hegelian labyrinth, and finally overcomes these problems in the recognition that it is Hegel.

*I. Book-Certainty.* Consciousness begins with an immediate awareness of the book. It is certain that "this" is a book. It is unaware of the written contents of the book because it has not yet read it. The book is a book in itself, and not yet for consciousness. In its certainty about the book consciousness finds that it must posit itself as distinct from the book. So consciousness says to itself: I am not the book. Then it says: The book is not I. It finds it can say no more. It knows what it is not, but not what it is. It is an "I," but this "I" is merely a negation, the not-book. And what is the book? The book is also merely a negation, the not-I. I and book are negativity itself. So consciousness says to the book: I am the book. But the book gets fed up and retorts: No you're not. Consciousness recognizes that if it is indeed the book, it had better read the book. So consciousness becomes a reader and opens the book, which now becomes a book for consciousness.

*II. Perception of Content.* Consciousness becomes aware that the book contains sentences. It does not at first understand any of these because they are in German. It gets hold of an English translation, but that doesn't help. The words make no sense to it. So it says, I am not these sentences. But in so saying it finds itself uttering a sentence, and therefore keeps turning the pages.

*III. Forced Understanding.* Consciousness now takes the shape of abstract understanding, in which it repeats the sentences of the book. Its repetition is mere playing with symbols, for it still hasn't got a clue what the sentences mean.

*IV. Self-Consciousness.* As consciousness repeats the symbols to itself, its own act of repetition begins to take meaning and form a text of its own. It understands this text as the return of itself to itself, and knows that if it is to understand the book as a text, then it must make that text, too, a part of itself. It grasps the meaning of meaning as the othering of the Other in itself. Now the text is no longer merely symbols, but the Other which makes meaning possible for consciousness. It is through this Other that consciousness comes to knowledge of itself as reader. Thus, consciousness recognizes itself in the recognition of the Other, and becomes self-consciousness.

Consciousness now grasps the text as a set of propositions which must become what they are within its own consciousness. At the same time, it knows that it can always remain other than these propositions. With its new-found understanding of the relationship of the contents of the text to its own consciousness, self-consciousness develops a sense of mastery over the text. It identifies specific propositions for which the text stands, and then reaffirms its difference from these propositions. Hegel, consciousness says to itself, represents the proposition: Idealism is true. That means all reality is mental. I do not believe this. Hegel asserts: World-Spirit exists. I do not. Therefore I am not Hegel. I am the master of Hegel. But as consciousness reads on, it finds that it cannot determine the meaning of these propositions without reference to other propositions in Hegel. As if to prove the point, consciousness discovers within Hegel the contraries of all of those propositions which purport to stand for Hegel. What it thought was idealism is overturned by Hegel as the deficient mode of subjective idealism. In Hegel, existence becomes a predicate only in the self-understanding of World-Spirit, and so is not to be predicated (or not) of World-Spirit. Consciousness sees that all propositions which might or might not stand for the text are possible only through propositions in the text. It finds that it cannot affirm or deny propositions about Hegel without taking Hegel for granted. It finds that it is no longer the master of Hegel, but his slave.

Consciousness now becomes very unhappy. As soon as it attaches meaning to one proposition, in an effort to distinguish itself from Hegel, it sees that meaning dissolve into countless other Hegelian propositions. All that is solid melts into absolute idealism. Consciousness fears that it, too, will go up in smoke. In desperation, it blindly asserts that it will disagree with Hegel, whatever he happens to think. It becomes for itself the negation of everything that Hegel could possibly represent.

As it contemplates itself in this sorry state, consciousness recognizes that its unhappiness is the mode in which it continues to exist. It also grasps that this unhappiness is negativity itself, which is the motor of the Hegelian dialectic. In attempting to negate Hegel, it has become nothing but the self-othering of Hegel. It has become the dialectic. It grasps that its unhappiness is Hegel's own torment, Hegel's own negativity, which is merely the necessarily destructive moment of Hegel's advance.

*V. Reason.* The unhappy consciousness recognizes at last that the truth is in the system, not the isolated proposition, and that the system is nothing other than the movement of thought in the dialectic. It comes to see itself as potentially in the Hegelian system. But it is so only in itself, and not yet for itself, for it is not sure that Hegel's is the true system for it.

Consciousness now conceives of the Hegelian dialectic as a particular method, with a distinctive tripartite scheme. As it runs around imposing the scheme, however, it finds that it cannot overcome the distinction between itself and the method. Then it realizes that in drawing this distinction it is already thinking dialectically, and so overcomes this little difficulty.

Consciousness returns to the text and finds that it has errors, not to mention variant editions. Hegel contradicts himself. Thus Hegel seems alienated from himself. Yet this alienation is itself the movement of consciousness through the text, and so can contain nothing but the deeper identity. Consciousness recognizes Hegel's mistakes as the natural typos of World-Spirit.

Now consciousness is ready to acknowledge the truth of Hegel's system, but finds that it cannot yet do so without isolating Hegel according to a specific historical time. Yet this makes the text particular, and confines the system to its own phase in the development of Spirit. Consciousness distinguishes between a now and a then, and sees that Spirit must express itself differently now. But now consciousness grasps that this Spirit is itself determined to be what it is through the Hegelian text. Consciousness sees that it has not left Hegel, and that the historically instantiated Hegel is but one moment of the unfolding of Hegel.

*VI. Absolute Knowledge.* Consciousness grasps Hegel as a totality. It comprehends that Hegel is not a man or a book but all of history, all consciousness, all texts, and all readers. But in doing so consciousness conceives of totality as an expression distinct from Hegel, of which Hegel is the realization. Consciousness still imagines God as an alternative to Hegel. Now it comes to examine the constitution of this new triad and recognizes that God is the term which mediates between itself and Hegel. God is merely the negative moment of Hegel, or Hegel as comprehended by himself in his mode of self-alienation, which is to say, as the consciousness of the reader. Consciousness at last comprehends that it is none other than Hegel, that its experience as the reader of Hegel was the journey through which Hegel comes to self consciousness and realizes himself. So consciousness affirms and dissolves itself in the totality: I, God, am Hegel.

---

**Autobiofact.** *Humble beginnings.* I remember a small green book from the local public library. I believe it was one of Hegel's, though I'm not altogether sure now. The translator's preface was clear enough. Hegel, or whoever it was, was indeed a great and immortal philosopher, and it was no mean task to translate his work. The text itself was something else. As the words and sentences streamed before my eyes, not an ounce of meaning remained in my brain. I stood before a semantic abyss. In retrospect, it is surprising that the experience did not bring my philosophical career to an immediate and inglorious end. But fate works in mysterious ways. Perhaps, unbeknownst to me, some meaning surreptitiously completed the arduous passage through sense organs to mind, something that was in any case already there, implicitly . . .

---

*Ode to an Hegelian*

O soul that wanders deep in thought
And speaks no more our native tongue
We knew you once, forsake us not
Reveal the dream you had so young

Those years of hope for joyous flight
So rich with possibility
You youth exchanged in rapt delight
To gaze upon eternity

Your time has come and yet you stand
As though still lost where you began
Your speech is mute, your eyes unclear
The promised dream no one can hear

# PROBLEMS

## ROTTEN TO THE CORE

What is World-Spirit but the concept of an entity which may or may not be thought to exist? What is the 'unity of thinking and being' in World-Spirit other than a shameful resurrection of the ontological proof? What meaning does 'thought' have when it can no longer be distinguished from 'reality'? What is 'idealism' if 'materialism' belongs to it as well? What is 'self-consciousness' if there is no world other than the self of which to be conscious? Super-monism, in the final analysis, is still a monism, just as super-idealism is an idealism, and the super-critique a critical impossibility. Hegel's grasp of the requirements of the search for the Holy Grail was profound, but it did not, in the end, guarantee that the search would end successfully.

Although the core of the Hegelian philosophy, or what I have represented as the core, is rotten, and almost universally understood to be so by both the common folk (intuitively) and professional philosophers, the periphery does contain many decent arguments and insights. Hegel's criticism of other philosophers is often quite perceptive, even if he does tend ultimately to force them into his scheme of things. He offers some acute psychological observations, has worthwhile things to say about art in general as well as particular works of art, and is very good at drawing plausible comparisons between things where most of us would see no similarity at all.

I have no problem with attempts to rescue from Hegel these insights about specific matters. There is another way of rescuing things from Hegel which I do believe is objectionable. That is the attempt to retain something which is distinctly philosophical, or sort of modified, critical Hegelianism, while jettisoning the admittedly absurd metaphysics. Most importantly, this means salvaging Hegel's historicism. I will deal with that matter in a separate section. In a more general form, though, it means saving some version of the dialectic. In my view, this is not possible. The distinctive method of concern simply will not work without the supporting metaphysics. What remains when the metaphysics is removed is a collection of random insights unified only by that most banal and Polonian of philosophical imperatives: *think truly, not falsely.*

## NO FREE DIALECTICS

To believe in the dialectic you have to believe in determinate negation. Without the determinacy of negation, the negative second moment of the dialectic does not produce a third moment, the synthesis, but instead a simple and outright negation. The determinacy of negation, as we have seen, assumes some form of monism. Thus, there is no dialectic without monism.

I suggested above that the only model for the differentiated identity which results from the dialectic is the model of self-consciousness, understood in the

Fichtean sense. But such a self-consciousness could only be understood to return to itself, rather than something else altogether, insofar as it does indeed account for the totality of the world. That is, self-consciousness returns to itself as the other of the other only insofar as the other, i.e., the world, is, as Fichte had it, nothing but a manifestation of self-consciousness. In brief, the dialectic presupposes not just monism, but idealism as well.

Speculative reason requires a way of knowing such that the knowledge is identical with its object, i.e., such that there is no final distinction between thought and reality. In other words, we can agree with Hegel that reason can reveal something of reality only if we also agree with him that reason is reality. At this point we have become Hegelian idealists. Without speculative reason, what Hegel means by "the understanding" is, insofar as it identifies errors, simply a generalization about certain kinds of error, and, insofar as it is a way of knowing, *the* way of knowing things (just as Kant originally defined it).

## Phenomenology

How much of the rest of Hegel do we need to practice this new science called phenomenology? The answer, again, is a great deal. Suppose one takes away Spirit, or whatever it is one wants to call the total form of consciousness which comes at the end of phenomenology. Now what are the appearances appearances of? Appearances can only have the character of necessity when they are understood in their relationship to something real. Otherwise, it's just one hallucination after another. Without an endpoint, there is no chance for a meaningful progression in phenomenology. Even the beginning comes in doubt—for its immediacy can only be certain from the retrospective vantage point of Absolute Knowledge. In sum, take away Hegel's unscientific metaphysics of Spirit, and there is no hope for making phenomenology remotely scientific.

What remains appealing in phenomenology is the idea that an individual consciousness can improve itself by means of critical introspection. In other words, if you think about what you're doing, you might do it differently. One might be able to string together a partial, progressive series of a few exemplary introspections. Such a series would begin not with some absolute immediacy but with some presupposed disposition of consciousness. It would still be absurd to expect that all forms of consciousness could be strung together in a single series. These "introspections" are nothing more than amateur psychology and perhaps some cultural analysis.

## Science of Logic

As an attempt to realize the pure critique, Hegel's science of logic is bound to include a metaphysic. As Aristotle knew, that was the whole point of a doctrine about categories. Without the assumption that it can at least possibly end with the identity of ideality and reality, or thinking and being, Hegel's science of logic is a pointless project. To be sure, it may and in fact did include a number of powerful arguments against other theoretical positions and more common errors committed in the intellectual life of humankind. But so do many newspaper editorials, and no one would think of them as attempts to realize the project of a science of logic.

## REMAINS OF THE DIALECTIC

Had Hegel stuck to this theoretical notion of the dialectic, his doctrine would not have been nearly as influential as it has been. But Hegel raised his dialectic within a menagerie of fascinating, highly abstract metaphors. In doing so he captured the intuitive feel of prearticulate, human ways of thinking. There was, at bottom, no method in it, and certainly nothing logical, but the dialectic as Hegel practiced it did have the feel of something real, something primal. Here are a few of the metaphors which make up the dialectic as practiced (rather than theorized) by Hegel:

1. *The Flower Debates with Itself.* The bud contains the flower in itself. The blossoming of the flower "refutes" the bud. Fortunately, the bud is not "negated," but "preserved" and "overcome" in the flower.

2. *Contract Completion.* There is a contract, say, to build a school. Once the school is built, the contract is in a way "canceled," in a way "preserved" in the building. It is in any case "lifted" into a filing cabinet in the builder's office. All these "meanings" are supposedly captured in the German *aufgehoben*, which is the participle of choice in describing what happens to that which gets caught in a dialectic.

3. *The Baby Grows Up.* There is a self. It merely exists, in a sort of happy immediacy with itself, like a baby, who knows no distinction between itself and the world. Next, the self becomes aware of something other than itself. The child senses a division between itself and the world. The world no longer obeys its commands. It sees but does not understand what is going on. Now the child grows into a successful professor of philosophy. He becomes aware of the priority of self-consciousness over consciousness, as revealed by the Fichtean interpretation of Kantian philosophy. Thus he understands that the external world is the creation of the self. The self identifies itself in both itself and its other. It knows that the disobedient external world must eventually obey its own commands. Baby rules the world.

4. *Return Trip.* I am alone in the house. I go out. I return home. I am back where I started, yet I am different. Before, the trip was implicit. It was *in-me*. When I went out, the trip was *for-me*. Now it exists within me as something accomplished. It is *in-and-for-me*.

5. *Changing Perspectives.* I used to think that clouds were ice cream castles in the air. Then I got rained on a few times, and took Physics 101. I started to think that clouds are condensed water vapor and a general nuisance. Then I took Philosophy 101, and realized that clouds are whatever I perceive them to be, and that I really don't know clouds (in themselves) at all.

6. *Revenge.* My master thinks he controls me. Sure, he can whip me when he wants, tell me what to do, lock me up at will, prevent me from doing anything, even kill me. But without me to push around, he wouldn't be my master. So, really, I control him. I'm just letting him be my master.

## HEGEL IN HISTORY

Hegel more than any other philosopher is the sum and embodiment of the history of philosophy. His most immediate debt, of course, was to Kant, especially as interpreted by Fichte. He was, however, widely read in the whole history, and, whether consciously or not, included in his own thought features from an enormous range of predecessors. From Heraclitus he borrowed the idea of a universe whose primary reality was change, the idea of a unity of opposites, and the idea of an all-embracing *logos*. He synthesized the Heraclitean flux with the limited whole of Parmenides' Being, and then enriched this with Anaxagoras's Mind and the Stoics' cosmic soul. All the while, he retained something of the materialism of Thales and his fellow physicists. He co-opted Socrates' dialectic and Plato's Ideas in his attempt at a new Aristotelian system of all the sciences. He remained faithful to Plotinus's One, and followed the Neoplatonist out east, for an encounter with the mysticism of the Sufis and the Hindus. From the theologians Hegel learned how not to present the ontological argument, and from Christianity, if not Pythagoras, the possibilities for transubstantiation, not to mention the importance of the number three. Descartes gave him the first version of the self, as well as the idea for a method. Spinoza taught him the paradoxical meaning of God as substance. Leibniz conceived for him the possibility that all facts could be reduced to ideality. The empiricists lent him their vocabulary of subjects and objects. From the Enlightenment he acquired an abiding faith in reason; from the Romantics a faith in destiny. More than any other philosopher, Hegel understood that philosophy was the search for the unity of method and content, of possibility and actuality, thinking and being, mind and heart, fact and value, etc., etc. Unlike many of his comrades, he embraced this project openly, and proudly declared victory on several occasions. He even understood that victory was something to be accomplished, and not merely asserted.

Did Hegel achieve his goal? Did he make something new out of the history, or did he simply trade in damaged stories? In the final analysis, or so I have argued, none of his special tools work without faith—a faith in an incomprehensible metaphysics. And to make that leap of faith is to drink from the Holy Grail. In Hegel, as in the beginning, all is water.

# H

*One lazy afternoon, while planning his latest assault on the castle, K grew pleasantly sleepy. Through strained and weary eyes he looked over the critique he was reading, and thought to himself: What is the use of a book without pictures and conversations? Just then, as he drifted into some imaginary illustrations, a large white rabbit wearing a professor's cap and gown bounded by. It was yelling, "Yippee, yippee, I am I, I am I." Suddenly the most unusual thing happened. A hole opened in the rabbit's own forehead, and the rabbit hopped inside! In a rare display of spontaneity, K leapt in after him. Down the tunnel of the rabbit's extended ego he followed his professorial quarry. The dark and murky passage seemed to lead through all sorts of strange categories and principles, until at last K landed with a thump in an empty white room. I am in the castle! he exclaimed. At long last. Thrilled to bits, he walked out of the room and began to roam the edifice. He saw numerous portraits of and trophies awarded to a mysterious "H," or "Lord H," and concluded that H must be the master of the castle. As he wandered, he discovered that for every room he entered there was an adjoining room in which everything was a mirror image of its partner. What was on the left was on the right, the head of the bed was its foot, and the cups all held liquid upside down. Between each pair of rooms he found a staircase leading up to a third room, in which existed a strange combination of the first two: things on both left and right; beds with head and foot on both ends, cups that would go either way. He wandered and found an enormous variety of rooms. In one room, to his horror, he beheld his old master Aristotle bound and gagged. As he turned to seek help for the hapless Greek, a fellow named Descartes pressed himself upon our hero and said, "I have two things to say." But before he could finish a dreamy young man named Spinoza came up and said, "Well, I have just one thing to say." Then down the hallway swept a rabble of early Christians, Hindus, Sufis, old constitutions, great battlefields, family relationships, and civil society. By now our adventurer was desperate to locate a turret or a terrace, a point from which to stand outside or above and survey the domain of this castle. He needed to see the layout, and the ground on which it lay. He wandered, alas, to no avail. No matter how far up he climbed, he got no closer to the top. When he aimed for the outside, he found himself ever closer to the center. One room led to another, but none led to anything else. Then he realized that this was his fate, to wander endlessly through these corridors. There was no outside. The castle was all reality. He had been in it all along. He was fated to spend his years in this labyrinth. . . . The slamming of doors awoke K to the turning of pages as his book slid from his chest. Just a dream. K looked up and wondered, Who was H?*

# HISTORICISM

In almost any version of the history of philosophy, two H's stand indissolubly linked: Hegel and History. Among all the widely diverging interpretations of Hegel, the right and the left, the young and the old, the friendly and the hostile, the dismissive and the deifying, the good and the bad, there is agreement on one point: Hegel introduced history to philosophy. Those who otherwise want nothing to do with Hegel are nonetheless eager to cite him as an authority for their own historicism. (Hegel's "socialism," his view that society plays a constitutive role in consciousness and ethics, has also been highly influential, but is, I think, a subset of historicism.) Much of what goes by the name of "continental philosophy" is practiced within an historical framework whose conception is easily traced to Hegel.

Before Hegel, or so the story goes, philosophers contemplated the truth in an historical vacuum. They pursued the True, the Good, the Beautiful, and the other timeless forms. After a passing glance at Vico and Herder, the traditional story names Hegel as the first to argue that the objects of philosophical concern, the truth and so on, are in some sense historical. Before Hegel, there were few histories of philosophy, and those that existed were typically chronological catalogues of mostly wrong philosophical opinions about a list of eternal issues. In the gallery of successive systems of philosophy, Hegel perceived an altogether different order. He claimed that each philosophy was an expression of the truth of its own time. He conceived of the history of philosophy as the history of truth as it unfolds in time.

There are several questions for us to consider. What, more precisely, does historicism mean? To what extent is it true? What was Hegel's role in the discovery, fabrication, or application of this idea? To what extent can there be an historicism without Hegelianism?

# WEAK VERSUS STRONG HISTORICISM

Behind any philosophical dogma, there is usually some bone of truth: a general observation about the nature of things or people, a logical point, a word of advice, or something of that sort. In the case of historicism, a distinction between its strong and weak forms will separate the dogma from the bone.

The Greeks were, for the most part, untroubled by their own practice of slavery. We think slavery is wrong. The Persians prostrated themselves before their emperor. The Greeks preferred to yell and scream at their own leaders. The Jews believe in one God, the Arabs in another one, and the Hindus in many gods. European monarchs used to proclaim their divine right to rule; now they plead for public funding. Flappers boomed in the twenties, yuppies thrived in the eighties. These miscellaneous factoids have one thing in common: They indicate that some basic features of human reality change dramatically over history (and across groups with separate histories). It is from these types of observed facts that historicism in any form takes its inspiration.

Weak historicism is based on two things: the observation that human perceptions, especially of value, change over history; and the assumption that such changes
can, in theory and in part, be explained by other changes in historical circumstances.
Most run-of-the-mill theories about hemlines represent a weak historicism. They all
start with the observation that the hemline of maximum value changes over time.
They assume that changes in the hemline of maximum value can be explained at
least in part by some factor or set of factors that belong to the history of the society
which places values on hemlines. The theories themselves consist of hypotheses
about which factors are relevant (say, the changing attitudes toward religion, changing gender-roles in the workplace, or whatever) and the evidence to support them.

Weak historicism need not and does not assume that the nature of reason,
facts, or values changes over history. Reason, of course, is timeless, although the
ways in which people reason about things may change over time. Facts or circumstances change, but the nature of facts does not. What may also (but need not)
change over history is people's perceptions of what is the case, and, possibly and
to a limited extent, what they would say should count as true. Values change over
time, although "value" itself (whatever that would mean) does not. More precisely,
people's perceptions of what has worth constitute a set of facts which, like any
other, is subject to change. In sum, what weak historicism observes changing are
not broad and universal "frameworks" or "paradigms" of truth, or the like, but specific customs; ethical codes; forms of social economic, and political organization;
fashions; religious beliefs and theories about the physical world.

Weak historicism boils down to nothing more than the application of the general principle of empiricism, or common sense, to historical matters. It says that
historical matters can be explained—historically. Drop the references to history,
and weak historicism is just the principle that things can be explained. There is
nothing peculiar to us about explaining, for example, the state of a certain domestic relationship by telling the story of its past turmoil and present conditions. Nor,
to drop the temporal element altogether, does it seem strange to explain, say, the
behavior of a chemical mixture by referring to the molecular structure of its constituents. Weak historicism is the affirmation that such explanations can be valid
at an historical level. At its best, it merely reminds us that many (though not necessarily all) matters of concern to us, like who we are and why we do what we do,
can be explained at least in part by referring to the entire past and pattern of development of our culture, country, or civilization. In the final analysis, weak historicism is not really a philosophical doctrine, but common sense mixed with an
awareness of the general importance of history to many of our concerns.

In philosophy, unfortunately, only the strong survive. Weak historicism is just
too obvious and tepid to count as philosophical. Strong historicism is the kind of
bald, bold dogma that will be remembered, and for that reason may also be called
"philosophical historicism."

Strong historicism says that the truth itself—in the form of both reason and
fact—is constituted by history. Whereas weak historicism holds only that people's
perceptions of things change in time along with their circumstances, the strong

stuff imagines that the very nature of things changes over history. Outside of history, the doctrine goes, there is no "frame of reference" according to which claims of truth or value can be judged. History is therefore the "ground" of everything, the ultimate basis for explaining anything at all.

This very strange way of thinking can be best explained in the terms of that most unhistorical of philosophers, Kant. Recall that Kant (at least some of the time) imagined that he had proved that we have no knowledge of things as they are in themselves, but only as they appear to us through our faculties of knowledge. These faculties of knowledge can only be thought of as the menu or scheme of concepts (or categories) which we apply to the world in order to experience it. Thus, knowledge is possible because it is, in a sense, self-knowledge, although it is not knowledge of what lies outside the self. Kant himself never contemplated the next step, that the menu of categories might change over time. That is, the conceptual scheme through which we acquire knowledge of the world might have its origin in history and might change along with historical circumstances. Strong historicism in all its versions is an historicized form of Kantian idealism.

## TOO STRONG

Not surprisingly, strong historicism exhibits the same contradictions and absurdities as does the Kantian idealism. These ultimately express themselves in its inability to account for itself. The claim that all truth is historically conditioned is, if true, an example of an historically unconditioned truth—and therefore of radically unclear status. Like Kant's critique, strong historicism imposes limits on what can be thought and immediately transgresses those limits. The consequent absurdities are too tedious to list in detail. But here are some of the most obvious ones: How can I know anything about any conceptual scheme other than my own? How can an historian/philosopher detail preceding conceptual schemes without being able to think through them? If my conceptual scheme is missing a concept, why can't I just add it on? How does history manage the transitions from one conceptual scheme to another? How can I be sure that my conceptual scheme comes from history, and not my country, region, neighborhood, family, or best friend? Can different schemes exist at the same time? If so, how can people with different schemes talk to each other?

The more one reflects on historicism in its strong or philosophical form, the less it seems to have to do with history. In my view, such historicism is basically an idealism (understood in abstraction from the subject-object picture of empiricism) and represents just one more vain attempt at the Holy Grail of philosophy. What distinguishes strong from weak historicism and makes it "philosophical" is the shift from weak historicism's *observation* that *many* matters of concern *can* be explained historically to the *dogma* that *all* matters *must* be explained historically. Strong historicism is just another way of fitting everything into a totality which is ultimately only knowable through the philosophical experience. Strong historicism replaces God with History, on the clear understanding that the new deity speaks only to philosophers.

## HEGEL: PHILOSOPHY'S REVENGE ON HISTORY

What kind of historicist was Hegel? As a good dialectician, no doubt he would have claimed to be both weak and strong. Certainly, he took inspiration at least in part from the insights afforded by weak historicism. As a philosopher, though, he must be classed with the strong. The story of his transition from weak to strong is a classic tale of a philosopher's coming-of-age.

It would be historically naive to suppose that Hegel's interest in history popped up out of an ahistorical wilderness. All around Hegel, Germans and Europeans were beginning to take a deep interest in the past. What to make of ancient Greek culture, early Christianity, and the Teutonic middle ages were burning issues for Hegel's contemporaries (at least, for those who showed up in seminary schools and the like). The young Hegel was caught up in this concern for understanding the past and its significance for the present. He soon realized that history could be a burden as well as a blessing. That the truths of religion, for example, should have their origins in the slime of history was for him problematic, even nauseating. He struggled with history as much as he inquired into it. His disposition toward history should be compared with Descartes's toward science: a combination of admiration and fear. Hegel needed to tame the new beast. Descartes had tamed science by giving it unlimited leash, whereupon it hanged itself on its own doubt. Hegel's strategy was quite similar: He surrendered everything to history, whereupon history quickly collapsed into the divine. Descartes had used philosophy to carry the old theology into the modern world of science. Now Hegel would use philosophy to carry the same old theology into the modern world of historical awareness. Philosophical historicism promised to preserve the insights generated by the new awareness of history while overcoming its tendency to make all that is meaningful—perhaps God himself—seem the outcome of arbitrary and contingent factors. The paradox is that Hegel's philosophical historicism was a reaction to his new awareness of history. It was a way of removing the potential dangers of a weak and open historicism. It was a rear-guard action by philosophy, not the forward march toward historical awareness.

With this inspiring tale of philosophical development in mind, in what sense could Hegel have invented historicism? So far as weak historicism is concerned, Hegel's role could not have been substantial. The general principle of which weak historicism is an application is far older than Hegel—older even than philosophy. Its application to historical matters might have been Hegel's innovation, but, empirically speaking, this does not seem to have been the case. The Greek historian Thucydides called attention to the dramatic changes in his own culture over time, and its equally dramatic differences with neighbors like Persia. In Hegel's own time, as already noted, the historical sense was growing more acute. Perhaps the best we can say is that Hegel might have lent importance and prestige to a previously undervalued area of investigation—which is not insignificant, considering that weak historicism is in essence just an emphasis, a general sense of awareness of the importance of history.

The case for Hegel's invention of strong historicism is more important, if not decisive. Vico had argued that the truth (*verum*) coincides with what is made (*factum*), and that therefore history provides the key to any truthful understanding of the world. So Vico was clearly a strong historicist before Hegel. Herder, too, took a muscular approach to historicism. Of course, Hegel was far more influential than either of those two. The key to understanding Hegel's contribution to strong historicism, however, has to do with the relationship of his philosophy to that of Kant. Because strong historicism is a version of Kantianism (or so I contend), and Hegelianism is a direct confrontation with the contradictions and absurdities of Kantianism, Hegel's historicism is one of the most sophisticated and durable forms of strong historicism available. So, while Hegel may not have been the first strong historicist, he was the first to put historicism on a sturdy and comprehensively philosophical foundation.

## No Historicism without Idealism

Can philosophical historicism make sense without Hegelianism? On empirical grounds, one would have to say yes. There is no shortage of philosophical historicists who claim that they are not Hegelians. My answer, on theoretical grounds, and assuming a broad understanding of Hegelianism, is no.

Philosophical historicism is a form of Kantian idealism. If it is not to perish immediately under the weight of its own absurdities, an attempt must be made to resolve the contradictions of Kantian idealism. The entire Hegelian philosophy is such an attempt, and, in my view, sets the pattern for any possible attempt. It thereby canvasses the extent to which philosophical historicism must go in its attempt to remain viable.

For a Kantian project to succeed, it must be able to trace the limits of knowledge. Philosophical historicism makes such an attempt by locating these limits in history. In order to trace the limits of knowledge, one must be able to draw a line between appearances and reality, and show that knowledge (as we know it) belongs on the side of appearances. Philosophical historicism distinguishes between what appears through an historical framework and what must logically precede it, and claims that knowledge lies on the side of the framework, or appearances.

Now all this is like asking someone to come up with something that is black and white all over. How is it possible to have knowledge only of appearances? Hegel, as we know, was a specialist in finding things that were black and white all over. His first step, though, he borrowed from the Fichtean interpretation of Kant. Since the appearances in question must belong to the knower, in some sense, one must be able to show that and how knowledge of the world is really a kind of knowledge of the self. In the case of philosophical historicism, this means that one must show that and how the knowledge of the world is really a knowledge of one's own historical condition. His next step was to reconceive the reality on the other side of appearances, the thing-in-itself, as a temporary construct of the self, to be eliminated with the achievement of full self-consciousness. In other words, a thorough knowledge of one's own history results in and is identical with a knowledge of all reality. At this point, the distinction between Hegel's solution to Kant's problems and his historicism vanishes. Since there is no final distinction between self and world, the self-consciousness which encompasses the knowledge of all reality is the world, specifically, the World-Spirit, and its journey through the world is history. One more Hegelianism is needed to glue the whole thing together, a method which justifies the ultimate synthesis of black and white, something to show how it is possible for self-consciousness to exist at various stages of the truth on its way to the whole truth, and that is, of course, the dialectic.

What are the lessons for an ordinary attempt at philosophical historicism? Philosophical historicism tends toward certain features of Hegelianism. It tends toward a radical idealism, inasmuch as it has to deny all reality outside historical frameworks. It tends toward a monism, in that the reality of all things, history, is one. It tends toward some concept of absolute knowledge, inasmuch as the complete knowledge of one's history is identical with the knowledge of all reality. It tends toward some kind of dialectical thought, in that it has to account for the successive existence of many different frameworks or truths. In all this I say "tends" because when one has gone so far down the highway of illusion, one does not always accept the logical consequences of one's position. Nonetheless, I maintain, strong historicism is, if thought through, inescapably a form of idealism, and in many cases, a form of Hegelianism.

## THE END OF HISTORY: AN HEGELIAN SUBTLETY

Having got this far, strong historicism also should tend toward that ultimately bizarre Hegelianism, the claim that we (Hegel) have reached the "end of history." Subsequent history, with obvious good sense, has treated Hegel none too kindly for his presumption in having announced its end prematurely. Still, there is a certain logic behind Hegel's talk. If history is the tale of Spirit's coming-of-age, and Spirit achieves full self-consciousness in the philosophy of Absolute Idealism, well then, there is nothing left for history to accomplish after Hegel. The idea that we are at the end of history, I think, at least has the virtue of improving the self-consistency of strong historicism. Later strong historicists would also implicitly appear to have transcended the progression of modes of consciousness which they take to be history, and yet would fail to draw the obvious inference, that they must somehow be superior to or outside of this process, that in understanding the historical modes of consciousness *qua* historical, they must have transcended those modes of consciousness.

Hegel also makes a related but less aggressive argument that philosophy has jurisdiction only over the past, and can offer no sure insight into the future. Philosophy is like the owl of Minerva, he says, which arises only at dusk. Again, there is a certain logic to the argument. Like all philosophy, philosophical history aims at self-awareness, with the further understanding that this self is historically constituted. Thus, it ought to offer something like a "history of the present." As such, it should have no purchase on the future, or at least not with the same sense of absolute self-certainty with which it may approach the past. We could rephrase the argument. Strong historicism, to be self-consistent, cannot view history as a mechanical process, distinct from itself and its own consciousness. As we will see, strong historicists after Hegel would lose track of this insight. Like a certain young communist, they would present history as an all-determining process, and yet, by failing to place themselves within this process, would stand above it and predict with (supposed) absolute certainty how history would progress into the future. Here again, I think, Hegel presents a strong historicism superior to that of many strong historicists to come.

## DITTO FOR SOCIETY

What I have said above concerning Hegel and history can be extended to Hegel and society. Hegel is often named as the philosopher who introduced society to philosophy (the reverse, I think, would be much more difficult!). We could call him a "socialist," provided we strip that term of its political signification. This means that he believed that our ethical codes in particular are in some sense social constructs. It is, of course, not true that Hegel was the first to propose such an idea, but he could be construed, with somewhat less violence to the facts, as the first to push a strong or philosophical version of it. Weak socialism acknowledges that individuals' values are borrowed from their societies (as well as their places within those societies), and that their perceptions of things are shaped in the same way. Strong socialism, or what today is sometimes called communitarianism, maintains that truth is constituted by a social framework. At this point it is obvious that socialism is a version of historicism. The "framework" of philosophical socialism is, in the simplest case, simply the philosophical historicists' "framework" viewed at a single point in time. (In a more complex case, one could understand the social framework as one with an internal dynamic, i.e., driven by a set of relationships among its members, the different elements of society. But what goes today by the name of communitarianism is by no means this sophisticated, and it all boils down to the same paradox anyway.) Philosophical historicism tends to talk about the different frameworks of one society over time, while philosophical socialism refers to the different frameworks of different societies at any one time. Philosophical socialism is also a version of Kantian idealism, and entails all the absurdities of philosophical historicism.

# THOSE ON THE EDGE

Our next three great philosophers have two general features in common. First, each rebelled in some way against academic philosophy. Second, each rose to greatness posthumously, at the retrospective insistence of twentieth-century philosophy.

Each entered and left the academic world while still young. Arthur Schopenhauer (1788–1860) attended Fichte's lectures and competed for students with Hegel, but then quit university life while still in his twenties. Søren Kierkegaard (1813–1855) studied Hegel and sat in on Schelling's lectures, but then carried on his revolt against Hegelianism as an independent writer. Friedrich Nietzsche's (1844–1900) academic background was in the classics rather than philosophy, although he did read Schopenhauer as well as the ancient philosophers. He left a tenured professorship in the classics while in his early thirties.

The most obvious consequence of these men's anti-academic stance was the clarity and forcefulness of their styles of writing. Each wrote for people—usually, for the solitary, like-minded individual—and not for philosophical professionals. After the headache of Kantian techno-babble and Hegelian obscurantism, nothing seems so refreshing or authentic as a Schopenhauerian exposition, a Kierkegaardian diary, or a Nietzschean aphorism. Each seems to speak about something personal, which might also be important to other persons.

The personal dimension of their philosophies was not just the basis of their appeal to later thinkers, but a central part of their philosophical teachings. Each of our three, in his own way, represented not just a personal truth, but the claim that *all* truth is personal. Previous philosophy, or so the story goes, conceived of humans as a thinking things, and the truth as something cold and external. Schopenhauer, Kierkegaard and Nietzsche emphasized the nonrational side of man, and declared that the only truth that mattered was the one to which the individual could commit him or herself—the idea for which, as Kierkegaard would have put it, one could live or die. For this reason, the three are often grouped under the virtually useless label of "irrationalism." In any case, all three turned away from epistemological conundrums and the project of making philosophy a science, and addressed themselves to the existential concerns of philosophy: Who or what am I? What should I be? Why is there something rather than nothing?

Our first question, as always, must be: What is true in their philosophies? Let's put it in terms that reflect the "personal dimension" already mentioned. To what extent can the truth for them be a truth for us? After that, as always, we may ask: What is new in their philosophies? Was the "personal" thing a radical break with the rationalist past? Or was it a continuation of the academic project by other means? Did Schopenhauer, Kierkegaard and Nietzsche resituate "the discourse of truth," or did they merely offer a mixed bag of forgotten truths and ancient falsehoods? The plot thickens.

# Schopenhauer

## It's a Mad, Mad, Mad, Mad World

Schopenhauer was an angry old man. Mad at communists, mad at his reviewers, mad at Hegel ("that intellectual Caliban"), mad at his mother, mad at women in general, and mad at just about everybody else. At the age of thirty he had discovered and published the truth about everything. He was in his sixties before the world began to buy his books. In between, he led a nasty, brutish, and solitary existence.

He was an angry young man, too. Indeed, anger was his ultimate reality. The philosophers' stone Schopenhauer discovered so early in life was this: The face of the world we see and feel around us is but a veil; tear away this veil and you will find that the real world is a raging will. Was this truth his new *truth*, or merely *his* truth? Did he reveal the true nature of the world, or create a truth for the world, or simply fabricate a world in his own image?

In some traditional versions of the history of philosophy, Schopenhauer is the first representative of a new and modern kind of philosophy, one that favors the personal, irrational, and existential over the metaphysical, rational, and essential. So far as the history of ideas is concerned, there may be some truth in this. In the history of philosophy, on the other hand, there is mostly falsehood in it, or so I will argue. In fact, Schopenhauer is interesting because with his rather crude metaphysics he makes clear that so-called modern philosophy is rooted in the problematics of earlier philosophy, and, contrariwise, that the problematics of this modern philosophy were already present in earlier philosophy.

**Biofact.** Schopenhauer's mother was a famous novelist and jet-setting friend of Goethe. She and her son did not get along. She was especially concerned about his literary efforts, for she had never heard of two geniuses coming from one family. After he left home, they agreed to see each other only once a year and in the company of others, so that they might treat each other "civilly." Despite the precautions, at their last encounter she shoved her offspring down a stairwell. The angry young man looked up and ranted that history would remember her only through him. So there. Though she lived another twenty-four years, they never saw each other again.

An essay Schopenhauer entered in a prize competition was turned down on grounds that it contained violently offensive remarks about certain contemporary professors of philosophy. With what must pass as wry humor, Schopenhauer subsequently published the essay under the subtitle "**Not** Awarded a Prize by . . ."

## THE METAPHYSIC: MORE KANT

Kant's critical project, as we saw, ended unfortunately and illogically in a metaphysic. Schopenhauer thought Kant's metaphysic was the best thing the old man ever produced, and modeled his own metaphysical doctrine, that the world is both will and representation, on Kant's doctrine about the noumenal and phenomenal worlds. Schopenhauer's world as representation, like Kant's phenomenal world, would be home for space, time, and causality. All our claims to knowledge, along with everything we perceive and think, belong to this world. While there was nothing particularly original about this idealist side of Schopenhauer's philosophy, on the other, noumenal side, he offered what seemed to be a radical new hypothesis. Kant's thing-in-itself, he argued, was really 'the will'.

In order to understand what this claim about the will might mean, one has to follow a peculiarly Schopenhauerian train of thought. The basic pattern is this:

1. Noumena are not knowable in the ordinary way.

2. The will is not known to us in the ordinary way.

3. The will is a noumenon, or something like it.

Each of these points requires considerable elaboration, but already two things are clear. First, the whole thing presupposes the Kantian spiel about phenomena, noumena, things-in-themselves. Second, at least the way the argument is stated, there is a logical fallacy. That two things share a property (in this case property of "extraordinary knowability") does not necessarily imply that they are the same thing.

Schopenhauer's understanding of noumena, or things-in-themselves, borrows the general features of Kant's account. Ordinary knowledge, so the story goes, is knowledge of the object by the subject. Noumena are what exist prior to the activity of the subject in knowing the object. Since the activity of the knowing subject creates objects as such, noumena are not objects. They are not in space or time, and are not subject to causality. The possibility for distinguishing one thing from another, or what Schopenhauer calls "the principle of individuation," depends on space, time, and causality. Therefore, for all intents and purposes, there is only one noumenon.

Schopenhauer's next step would have seemed indecent to Kant. He examines our relationship to our own bodies, pointing out that since we are material objects like anything else in the phenomenal world, our bodies must also correspond to noumena in some way. Furthermore, since our knowledge of our bodies is in some way different from our knowledge of other, external objects, it offers a unique hope for access to the noumena. Now Schopenhauer makes an interesting observation about "willing." He says that willing cannot be distinguished in any particular instance from acting. In other words, the will is not an independent entity which causes the body to move; it exists only in the movement. So here, in the will, says Schopenhauer, we have an example of something which we know intuitively, something which expresses itself in and through us, and yet which we do not know intellectually, or representatively. Therefore, he rashly concludes, what we call the will is an attempt to represent the thing-in-itself such as it manifests itself in our own bodies.

At this point, Schopenhauer needs to clarify the precise relationship between the concept of will and the noumena from which it is thought to originate (let's call the noumenal version the 'Will'). As one of our own representations, after all, the will we attribute to ourselves cannot be the same as the Will. Furthermore, since the noumenal world bans the principle of individuation, the Will could not belong to a specific person, like you or me; it must be a single World-Will, or something like that. Also, since the Will is outside space, time, and causality, it cannot be associated with any goals, motives, or means. So, Schopenhauer's Will exists nowhere at no time, belongs to no one, wants nothing, and does nothing. In fact, the Will looks nothing like a will at all. Schopenhauer debates this point with himself, but then sticks with his gut feeling and keeps the term "Will."

Schopenhauer adds another twist to the story by abruptly recalling Plato's Ideas out of the historical wilderness. What he likes about these Ideas is that they are "more real" than their instantiations in the phenomenal world, and yet they exist outside time and space. So, Schopenhauer throws them down as a kind of bridge between the thoroughly indeterminate Will and the world of appearances. He calls them the "first grade" of the "objectification of the Will."

## MAN THE ANIMAL

Buried in Schopenhauer's metaphysic is an insight into human nature which has been the basis for the appeal of his work. The insight does not require—and is in fact obscured by—the metaphysic.

The insight comes out in the metaphors with which Schopenhauer tries to describe what he means by the world as will and representation. He says, for example, that the human intellect is like a lame but sighted man carried on the back of a strong, blind man called Will. He likens the intellectual world to the surface of a deep body of water, or the crust of the earth. Its form is but the superficial manifestation of the powerful currents and movements of the Will below. Elsewhere, he compares the world as representation to the Hindu concept of the "veil of Maya." It is the illusion created by consciousness of an ordered world of causes and effects. Tear the veil away, and the chaotic and tempestuous world of the raging Will is revealed. The whole body, Schopenhauer adds, is merely an expression of the Will: the stomach is objectified hunger, the genitals objectified sexual desire, and so forth. In brief, almost a century before Oedipus was a twinkle in Freud's eye, Schopenhauer recognized the importance of the unconscious in shaping the conscious life of man. (Which does not mean that it was Schopenhauer rather than Freud who invented the concept of the unconscious; contrary to popular myth, the idea is far older than both.) In his many tangential discussions about relations between the sexes and the like, Schopenhauer anticipates the Freudian concept of repression and in general shows an acute awareness of the distinction between the way people explain their behavior to themselves and the way their behavior can be best explained.

Schopenhauer certainly had insight into human nature. Whether his philosophy was relevant and useful in applying that insight is another matter. In any theory that seeks to find the explanation of human behavior in the unconscious, at least two obvious conditions must be satisfied. First, the unconscious has to be conceived as something with causal efficacy. In other words, it must be conceived as a force, motive, desire, or something which could be said to cause an action. Second, the content of the unconscious must be representable or thinkable in some way, at least to the theorist, if not the subject. Otherwise, all explanations would refer ultimately to an unnameable It, and so would explain nothing. Schopenhauer's theory of the Will clearly fails to meet either of these conditions. Although the Will sounds like something which might have causal powers, we know that this cannot be so, since the principle of causality belongs to the world of representation. For the same reason, of course, the Will cannot be represented, either to the theorist or the subject. So, despite the intriguing metaphors and his psychological insight, Schopenhauer's metaphysic is ultimately incompatible with a project to investigate the unconscious sources of human behavior.

SCHOPENHAUER: TEARING ASIDE THE VEIL OF MAYA

## LIFE SUCKS

The point of Schopenhauer's metaphysic was not, in the final analysis, to explain human behavior, and certainly not to seek a cure for the psychologically disturbed. He wanted to make a completely universal claim about life, and prescribe a course of action, i.e., an ethic, on that basis. The general claim was essentially this: Life sucks. His prescription: Reject life.

Life sucks because we are all in the hands of this unknowable and uncontrollable Will which creates in us insatiable desires. When one manages to satisfy one's desires for a time, the consequence is *ennui*. Life is a yo-yo between unfulfilled longing and boredom. The Will uses us to achieve its objectives (sorry, it can have no objectives, but, well, you know what I mean) and then throws us away. It cares nothing for the individual. Schopenhauer reels off one quote after another from famous poets and playwrights, all to the effect that, as the ancient Greek oracle said, it would have been best never to have been born into this world, and next best to die as quickly as possible.

The greatest wisdom, for Schopenhauer, is to recognize that the things we chase after in ordinary life are merely illusions. Once possessed of this wisdom, the individual recognizes that the best thing to do is to give up. In sum: Life sucks, so why try? Schopenhauer ought to have prescribed suicide, but he seems to have resisted that course of action. Presumably it would have been inconvenient for his career as a philosophical author.

## THE BUDDHA LIVES

Schopenhauer read extensively in Eastern philosophy. His general view of things and ethics, as he himself acknowledged, borrows extensively from Buddhist and Hindu teachings. Like the Buddha, he believes that the essence of life is suffering, that this suffering originates in our attachment to our selves. Schopenhauer conceives this more generally as our attachment to the world as representation, which is the projection of our consciousness. Like the Hindus before Buddha, Schopenhauer believes that there must be a more real world than the ordinary one in which stones fall, planes fly, and selves go about their business. So he takes the next step with the Buddha: Eliminate suffering by relinquishing the self and its illusory world. As one conceives of oneself as part of the totality, of ultimate reality, the world of representation dissolves into nothing. Nirvana is seeing everything as nothing—a Nothing which alone truly Is.

## ANOTHER CASE OF POST-ROMANTIC STRESS DISORDER

Tear away Schopenhauer's metaphysic, his own illusion, and what one finds is a very unhappy man. Indeed, one finds an angry, spiteful, and arrogant man who was unwilling to blame his unhappiness on himself, and so blamed it on the world. His philosophy is a good example of the power of the unconscious, although there is nothing particularly mysterious or metaphysical about its operation in this case. Schopenhauer's is a classic case of post-Romantic stress disorder. (In this there is something of Rousseau in Schopenhauer.) The Romantic turns away from reason and exalts nature and validates his own impulses and self-realization. When the world turns out to be indifferent to his self-expression—in Schopenhauer's case, when he discovered that mother didn't love him and that students preferred Hegel's lectures to his own— the Romantic decides that the world is not good enough for him.

## PLUS ÇA CHANGE

Why not call it Water? What Schopenhauer calls the Will shares as many properties with the will as it does with water, Christmas pudding, anxiety, or anything else, namely, none. It is, by definition, the world such as it is even before it can be thought, let alone known. Schopenhauer starts by accepting on faith Kant's thing-in-itself, that improbable thing-before-things-are-possible, and ends up with an equally obscure will-before-wills-are-possible. The choice of will in fact reflects an attempt to anthropomorphize the world, to see the familiar structures of intentionality embedded in all reality. The rejuvenation of Plato's Ideas is a bad case of patchwork philosophy. Schopenhauer's metaphysic is cause for despair, not for what it reveals about the structure of the world, but for what it reveals about philosophy. Three thousand years have gone by, and philosophers are still babbling mythologizers who lay claim to a kind of cosmic knowledge to which they know they are not entitled.

## THE IRRATIONALIST CIRCLE

So maybe Schopenhauer's vision of the world was a projection of his own disturbed psyche. But was not Schopenhauer's truth that the world is nothing but such psychic projections? Does not the Schopenhauerian experience confirm the truth of his philosophy, that all truth is personal? *Voilà* the virtuous circle of irrationalism. Despite the circle, our answer must be no. All it proves is that Schopenhauer's philosophical claims don't amount to much besides his personal opinions; not that all claims are merely opinions, whether Schopenhauer's or not.

## DUALISM, MYSTICISM, SCHMOOALISM

In philosophy, the errors of the father usually become the real whoppers of the son. Schopenhauer exaggerates Kant's thought to the point where he reveals something important about any Kantianism. He exposes the link between Kantian philosophies and that dynamic which we saw at work in the later Greek and eastern philosophies—what I called the Schmooalism principle.

### (1) DUALISM

In case there was any doubt, Schopenhauer makes clear that there is some sort of dualism at the heart of any Kantian philosophy. More importantly, Schopenhauer helps clarify the nature of this dualism. While it is tempting to call it a metaphysical dualism of the mind-body or subject-object variety, and leave it at that, the Schopenhauer experience makes clear that there is considerably more to the story. Although it ends up as a metaphysic, of course, the dualism is better conceived as originating in a logical distinction. This is nothing more complicated than the distinction between fact and value. On the one side, there are all the verifiable claims to knowledge, inferences of reason, and anything that can be proved. On the other side, there are morality, aesthetics, and any claims about the worth of things. The transition from this logical distinction to a metaphysical dualism is easy. Facts correspond to this world, to everything we can possibly observe around us. So, by (false) analogy, values must correspond to their own, unobservable world. The dualism is not about kinds of substances, like mind and body, but about kinds of worlds. One world has everything that is possibly knowable, and the other everything that is possibly valuable. The good news for the philosopher is that the world of value presumably has a science of its own, viz., philosophy.

## (2) MYSTICISM

Although claims to value cannot be reduced to claims of fact, they can be reduced to inferences from claims of fact combined with more general claims of value. If one follows this reductive procedure rigorously, or so the philosopher imagines, all claims to value reduce to claims of fact plus the bare assertion of value, or the notion of value as such. The switch to a more dramatic, metaphysical vocabulary is easy: All claims about worth seem to depend on a single claim about the value of life itself, or the worth of the world. So, the "the meaning of it all," or the question "why is there something rather than nothing?" becomes the philosopher's chief concern. The answer, of course, is built into the way the question is framed. Since every meaningful or expressible claim has been moved to the valueless world of facts, value can have its origin only in the other, nonfactual world. The answer can be felt or experienced, but not thought or expressed. The paradox is clear: The unanswerability of the question is the answer to the question. Of course, for logistical purposes, Schopenhauer uses the term "Will" to think the meaning of this world, but this can only be a temporary sign or way-marker, not the destination. What the Will denotes is a world which is by definition unthinkable.

## (3) SCHMOOALISM

The existence of the world of facts is an inference from the inexpressible world of value. So, the world of value turns out to be more real than the real world. What we thought was the real world is just a bunch of signs without meaning, a shadow cast by the true, inexpressible reality. What is inexpressible, after all, is the totality itself. One grasps the nothing in things, the Nothing which Is. In the end, the dualism is overcome, and all is one. (This is tricky, of course, since the dualism was between worlds, and now we must reconcile ourselves to the existence of just one world.) Thus, as we saw in comparing Plotinus with the Gnostics, it is quite superficial to distinguish monism from dualism in philosophy. Both belong to the same way of thinking. A Hegelian might construe this as the unity of monism and dualism. The fact of the matter is less grand: It's just a messy schmooalism.

# Kierkegaard

**Biofact.** Kierkegaard courted a young lady named Regina, who eventually agreed to marry him. Some months before they were to be wed, however, Kierkegaard called the whole thing off. It seems he needed some time to think, and to serve God. So he escaped to Berlin to study Hegelian philosophy and to hear Schelling's lectures. Later, he had misgivings about his misplaced love, and returned to Copenhagen, desperately seeking Regina, only to discover that she was promised to another man.

If one were to express the core of Kierkegaard's philosophy in terms of his place within the history of philosophy, one would most likely say that Kierkegaard's was a philosophy defined by a fundamental confrontation with Hegelianism. While Hegel had sought to encompass all of existence within his system of logic, Kierkegaard maintained that a philosophy founded on logical principles could never hope to explain all of existence, that is, that thinking and being could never be united. As Kierkegaard put it, there is no logical system which is also an existential system.

If one were to situate Kierkegaard in the history of ideas, perhaps the essence of his philosophy would be represented by his stance on the Christian religion. Kierkegaard was a profoundly religious thinker who sought a transformation of the Christian faith of his day. He rejected both natural theology and the casual piety of ordinary citizens, and hoped to replace these with a faith based on passionate commitment. He believed that Christianity called for a leap of faith, not merely a logical proof or a prudent assessment of one's personal interests.

But perhaps the key to Kierkegaard should be sought a little closer to home. According to Kierkegaard, what matters in philosophy is not abstract metaphysical doctrines, but the truth that the individual lives and dies by. Philosophers only fool themselves when they proclaim supposedly universal truths, for the truth is personal. True to his insight, Kierkegaard eschewed the turgid expository style of his philosophical antagonists, and instead expressed himself in a dazzling range of essays, aphorisms, parables, letters and journals, both real and fictitious. In this Kierkegaardian spirit, then, let us continue our engagement with Denmark's lone contribution to our history of philosophy, and imagine this time that Kierkegaard himself is inscribed in one of his own, fictitious diaries.

## CONCLUDING IRONIC FRAGMENTS FROM A DIARY BY A FICTITIOUS INDIVIDUAL WHO IS OBVIOUSLY ME

### November 11th

Today I broke off our engagement. She made a terrific scene of crying and sobbing and chewing on the furniture. Neither she nor anyone else can make sense of my behavior, but I know it is the right thing to do. Like Abraham, I must show that I am willing to sacrifice that which is nearest and dearest to me for the sake of the higher cause. I am on a mission from God. We cannot afford distractions. My life will be an experiment on behalf of humankind. Mine will be the most intense self-examination ever performed. I need to know, need to let everyone else know, what it means to be human. Leaving for Berlin tomorrow.

### November 31st

Made fun of Hegel again today. What a buffoon the man is. Every philosopher imagines that he speaks for all humanity, and forgets that he is a particular, existing person. In the end, the philosopher speaks for no one. He is a comic figure. One can only laugh at the attempt to ensnare existence in the webs of a logical system. There can be no existential system. Being and thinking cannot be "united," except in the absurd fantasies of the philosophers. What do I care about all those philosophical systems anyway? What I want is the truth for me. I want to know what I can and must believe, what matters for me, my ultimate concern, and not some lifeless truth of logic.

### December 24th

I make an exception for Socrates. Here is the supreme ironist. Here is the philosopher who understands that he is ignorant. One who speaks in terms of the coarse particulars, the cobblers and cooks, which are our everyday reality. O Socrates, I love you, I love you, I want to hug you all over.

December 25th

I ran into a person today who said he was a Christian because he accepted the doctrines of Christianity. Bah, humbug. It used to be that Christians had to fight for their beliefs. Nowadays you'd have to put up quite a fight not to be a Christian. People imagine that being Christian is just a matter of getting the intellect to agree on the truth of a few doctrines. But these doctrines are perverse, paradoxical, and absolutely indemonstrable to the intellect. Only faith, a faith which asks for no reasons, can suffice to bring us to the truth. I think they are closer to Christianity who believe strongly and passionately, even if incorrectly, than those who merely accept the correct doctrines. I told the person: It does not matter what you believe, but how; attitude is everything. He got scared and ran off to his mother.

December 26th

Yesterday's experience in the playground got me thinking. I saw kids leaping up onto the playsets, and then leaping down again. Leaping. Boing. Boing. Life is full of discontinuities, of infinite gaps. Either you're on the swings, or you're not, but not both. Only dialecticians like Hegel try to be both. Real people have to choose. They live according to either/or, not the evil both/and. So it is with Christianity. One must make a leap of faith. One must choose, commit oneself, one must be resolute.

January 1st

After such a tremendous week of philosophizing, I think I am ready to state my philosophy. Christianity is a matter of infinite passion, which makes itself its object whenever we make it ours. Truth is subjectivity. The ethical alone is real.

February 4th

I ran into Socrates today and tried to explain my doctrines to him. He said he did not understand. We agreed to meet tomorrow.

February 28th

Still trying to get Socrates to see things my way. Annoying little pest.

April 1st

Despair, despair, and anxiety. I have a sickness unto death. This is the hardest day of my life. The man I thought was Socrates turned out to be Hegel in a toga. Then he said he was also Zara-something-or-other and gave me this dreadful speech:

"What is the particular *qua* particular? Is it not the universal? What is the personal *qua* personal? Is it not the impersonal?

"You say that only the particular existence has truth, and then you say that your existence has meaning only as a representative for all humanity. Are you not, like the philosophers you mock, trying to speak for everyone? Is this not comic?

"You say you love only Socrates. Was not the Socratic critique the father of

Kant's, and the Socratic dialectic the father of mine? Are we not all one and the same?

"You say that only the 'how' matters, not the 'what'. But what is this 'how' without a 'what'? Is any belief okay so long as it remains passionate and unquestioned?

"You say we must make a leap. Is not this leap your intellectual bridge from conditioned to absolute knowing? Is it not your unity of thinking and being?

"You say that Christianity is a 'matter of infinite interest' which makes us into an object when we make it into our object. Is this not your unity of subject and object? Is this new infinite not your 'good infinite', the one through which passion becomes reality, ought becomes is, and thinking becomes being?

"You say that truth is subjectivity. Is this your subjective truth, or is it an objective claim? That the Absolute is Subject—is this not my truth? Is it not also a truth which must by its nature overcome itself? If subjectivity is absolute, or 'truth', as you put it, is it not also Substance, or what is most real? And if it fails to grasp its own reality, is it not in the mode of the Unhappy Consciousness? Could this be why you are so melancholy?

"You say that the ethical alone is real. Is this your Substance? Is this not also the Kantian conception? Are you, too, deriving an ethical reality from the very possibility of ethical life? Are you not the last rationalist?

"You say the truth is your truth. I ask, who are you?"

### April 2nd

Today I took a long, hard look in the mirror. I always knew I didn't look much like my parents. People often told me I had Schwabian nose. Now I know why. I am Hegel.

### April 3rd

I've decided to leave Berlin and return home. This time, I will marry her. I want to have my life back. Leaving on the first coach tomorrow.

### April 10th

Drat and double drat! She's gone off and left me. How could she marry that jerk? That wasn't the way it was supposed to happen. Abraham only had to pretend he would kill his son. It's not fair. I guess it's my fault, though, for being a philosopher. I suppose that I wanted both to leave her and to love her. Now I see it was either/or!

# Nietzsche

## Vanishing Perspectives

*Preface.* This, too, or so I hope, is a book for those who enjoy the search for knowledge. It is a gay science, for those who cherish each new discovery, and then move on—to the next. It is for those who would risk their knowledge—for more knowledge. It is not for those who only want answers, or who already have the answers. As for Nietzsche: What does not mislead me makes me stronger.

1

*The philosopher's disposition.* I hate to agree, when I can possibly disagree.

2

*Friedrich.* He was always trying to please. As though he needed a replacement for the father who passed away so tragically young. He was a rather small, pale, and nearsighted boy, but with a quiet charm. He studied very hard, and his teachers loved him. He fell in love with the Greeks. That ancient world of poets, warriors, and philosophers consumed him. He became a full professor while still a boy of twenty-four, even before he finished his doctoral thesis. The sort of thing, it was said, which in Germany happens "absolutely never." But his allegiance went deeper than that required for professional success. He wrote about the ancients as he knew them, not as Germany wanted them. He would not let his teachers deceive themselves. Struggle made him a man. Struggle against the confines of professional position. Recognition that his special experience could not be communicated from within the academic world. Struggle also against his own body. He lost his health in service in the Franco-Prussian War. He never recovered it, but in time learned to live with it, without spite.

In his mature period Nietzsche would describe his philosophy as a gay science. He would hurl sarcasm and mischief at everything sacred. He would confidently, perhaps arrogantly, dismiss whole traditions as erroneous. Yet he always retained something of that serious schoolboy. Still soft-spoken, still so well-mannered; meek in person; conscientious as ever, yet oh so lonely, wanting more love than the world would give him; trying to do what he was supposed to do; and, deep down, still hoping, perhaps—dare I say it?—still *innocent?*

3

*Who were the Greeks?* What did young Nietzsche see, as he pored through his thick spectacles over those Greek texts? One thing for sure: He did *not* see the Greece of sweetness and light adored by Germans since Goethe. He was too *serious*, the Greeks were too *real* for him to allow them to become a serene and wishful paradise lost. Nor did he see them as the great founders of democracy and philosophy. These he perceived as the twin errors committed in the degeneration of the true Greek culture. Democracy emerged from the disintegration of the authentic Greek aristocracy. And Socrates, the original and quintessential philosopher, was a *sick* Greek, a *decadent.*

The young Nietzsche saw a Greece whose central institution was the *agon*, the competition. Everything great comes from struggle: great athletes from the Olympics; great warriors from battle; great plays from dramatic competitions. The Greeks would risk everything for victory: They understood the art of *living dangerously*. They believed in an *order of rank*; that is, in the greatness of man because they believed in *great men*. The authentic Greek poets were men like Pindar and Theognis, the poets of the fading aristocracy. Nietzsche was the first to see the *irrational* in Greek culture. He called it the Dionysian, after the god associated with intoxication, femininity, the theater, the subconscious, and sex. Explosive emotional energy fused with classical form gave birth to the uniquely Greek art of tragedy. But Nietzsche's Greeks were neither "irrationalists" nor "rationalists." In Dionysus they simply accepted and celebrated the inherent *sensuality* of human existence. The Greeks were *rational* in the manner of Thucydides, in the brutal empiricism with which he chronicled and analyzed the twenty-seven-year conflict in which his own civilization demolished itself. They were *realists* in the manner of Homer's heroes, as they acknowledge the futility of their quest for glory in the face of imminent death. They were *artists*. They were admirers of words, forms, tones, of everything created and projected by man into the world in the name of beauty. The Greeks were superficial, to be sure, but out of profundity. They did not seek—until Socrates—a meaning deeper than the world could give. They needed no apology for life, no consolation, no surrender. So what did our young philosopher see in this ancient world? In sum, a people who grasped that life is in essence struggle, brutality, injustice, inequality, and ends in inconsolable death, who nonetheless had the *courage to face life as it is.*

One may read a history of philosophy, and try to understand Nietzsche within it. One may do the same with a history of German culture. But one will never really understand what happened in Nietzsche without these Greeks. This was vision burned into the back of his mind, against which he compared all reality. Was there something *secret*, perhaps *illegitimate*, in Nietzsche's affair with the Greeks? Did they merely stoke the fire that quiet boys often hide? Was he perhaps reading *too much* into these old grammar books? Did he take those Greeks *more seriously* than they took themselves?

4

*Style and Substance.* Among Nietzsche's innovations, the most striking is the new style with which he writes about philosophy. Though hardly the world's first aphorist, he is the first in the modern philosophical tradition to identify the aphorism as the preferred method of expounding philosophical truths. Even more than Schopenhauer, and in profound contradistinction to Hegel, Nietzsche is a great stylist of German prose—by his own admission as well as the acclaim of others. He believes he can say in ten sentences what others would—or would not—say in a book. He is, as he puts it, the first to make the German language sing and dance. *Tempo*, he writes, is all important. It is no secret why bad philosophers were also bad writers. Truth is perspectival, a question of appearances. It is, Nietzsche writes to the perpetual chagrin of feminists, a woman. Clumsy dogmatists could hardly hope to snare such a creature. Only the experienced aphorist, exposing multiple truths through varied perspectives, can succeed. Perhaps he is the first philosopher to grasp that there was something originary in writing itself, that philosophy can and does do more than represent itself in the act of writing. Thus the philosophical point, the substance, of Nietzsche's style.

5

*The Preacher of Life.* Nietzsche was a preacher of a sort, and he expected his self-anointed masterwork, *Thus Spake Zarathustra*, to replace the Bible's New Testament. What were Nietzsche's teachings?

The values of Christianity are disvalues of life, he said. Christianity originated as a morality for the slaves. Its promises that there is an afterlife and that the meek shall inherit the earth are consolations offered to the weak. These promises are the revenge of the weak against the happy few who rule the earth. Christian pity squanders life's energy on futile efforts to protect the weak from their natural destiny. The Christian concept of sin colors existence itself with guilt. The ascetic ideal, the denial of all sensual pleasure, is Christianity's explicit rejection of *this* world in favor of *another* world, which is only a negative image of this world; it is an attempt to negate or disvalue life.

Christian values have now, in the late nineteenth century, led to crisis. The disvaluation of life has produced the condition of nihilism, the sense that nothing matters, that all values are valueless, that there is no truth. Western history has created for us the "last man": not a man at all, but a pale, bureaucratic being afraid of life.

Out of this critique of one set of values emerges another, presumably Nietzsche's own. The new set of values is intended to address the crisis situation of nihilism. It exalts the noble soul, that is, the soul which reveres itself. It worships the free spirit, the individual who sees through tradition and prejudice, and grasps what is meaningful in life. It deifies the artist, the creator, all those who would bend the world to their will. The new morality, in sum, is the affirmation of life. The doctrine of the eternal recurrence of the same is a test for these values. If you can wish that everything about your life, the good, the bad, and the indifferent, should be repeated, relived in exactly the same way over and over again for all eternity—if you can wish this, then you will have affirmed life. Nietzsche envisions a new type of person capable of such a difficult affirmation, and calls him the Superman.

## 6

*The Uses and Abuses of History for Life.* In one of his early, untimely meditations, Nietzsche analyzes the study of history in terms of its contribution to life. His bold assumption is this: History is and ought to be in the *service* of life. His conclusion: An *excess* of the *historical sense* can be detrimental to the health of a living culture. His argument is untimely, out of its own history, as in his time the historical sense was highly esteemed.

## 7

*What Is the Meaning of 'Life'?* Life is will to power. It is continuous struggle, unending change, a perpetual *coming-to-be* which never comes to rest, which never finally *is*. Nothing is self-sufficient, nothing stays the same; everything is a combination of forces, ebbing and flowing against other forces, in an unending search for self-expression. Charles Darwin may have understood this in biology, and Machiavelli in politics, but Nietzsche, perhaps like Heraclitus, understood it as a philosophical, perhaps a metaphysical reality. Christianity fails to comprehend this essence of life. Indeed, it *negates* the essence of life.

But Nietzsche's 'life' is more than a collection of specific attributes, a general description of what it is like to be alive. Life does not, in the final analysis, stop short of the whole of existence. It is the totality of things, that which cannot be divided or analyzed, that which lies *beyond* all possible judgment. It is this forever-innocent whole, according to Nietzsche, which Christianity pretends to judge, which it condemns with its ideas of sin, guilt, and asceticism.

## 8

*Psychology of the Philosophers.* Philosophers have divided the world into a "true world" and an "apparent world"—whether in Plato's theory of forms, or Kant's distinction between noumena and phenomena, or Schopenhauer's Will and Representation, or any kind of metaphysic. In this they repeat Christianity's negation of this world in favor of some other, supposedly better one. The philosophers' search for 'being' is a search for certainty, stability, and reassurance in a world that is in fact constantly changing. The philosophers' faith in supposed "moral facts" confuses fact and value, and so betrays an attempt to project a moral meaning onto an innocent, amoral world. Philosophers have been guided not by truth or reason, but by moral prejudice and the needs of those whom they serve. Philosophers at least since Socrates have been sick individuals, representatives of the weak, those unhappy with life.

9

*New Perspectives.* Nietzsche's critique of the philosophers goes beyond exposition of their motives and style. He also relies on an epistemology of his own. His theory of knowledge is often labeled "perspectivism." It is the claim that all knowledge is inherently perspectival. To know something is to have a view on it, to grasp it from some perspective. Common sense and philosophy collude to mislead us on this point. They seem to present to us a fixed and stable world. But the world—the *real* world this time—is a constant flux. Unity and being are illusions imposed by the knowing subject. Language, or more precisely, grammar, makes philosophical error easy by sustaining the illusion that there are simple, existing entities behind our words, e.g., the 'I', the 'thing', the 'subject', the 'object'.

10

*Life against Life?* The attempt to negate life is a part of life itself, in the end a twisted affirmation. Perhaps Nietzsche sees this, though it seems that the momentum of his attack is too great. So he draws a distinction between a sick, decadent kind of life and the healthy, ascendant kind. Christianity is sick, Socrates is a decadent. Are these facts or values? They seem to be values. Yet they originate in the physiological facts of life, in the essence of life as will to power. But how is this possible? How can life pass judgment? Is it not Nietzsche now who sunders the totality of things, who discovers an original sin? Has he not repeated the philosophers' traditional error of conflating fact and value, of reading something into the world which was never there?

11

*More Kant?* Nietzsche was not especially well read in philosophy. As often happens in such cases, this fact more than anything else binds him to his times. His epistemology smells of the nineteenth century. Brush off the dust, and what you see is a poetic rendition of prevailing Neokantian doctrines. He simply borrows his epistemological ideas from Schopenhauer and the condensed versions of his academic contemporaries. In doing so he replicates many of the paradoxes and contradictions inherent in their accounts. For both Nietzsche and the Neokantians, knowledge is the knowledge of appearances. The regularity we encounter in the world is our own projection. Yet, what are appearances if they are not appearances of something? Perspectives are still perspectives on *something*. So we find ourselves saddled with a true world, an "in itself," and an unknowable one at that, despite Nietzsche's intentions. And who does this projecting of unity, anyway? The knowing subject? The subject projects itself? Sounds like a Fichtean metaphysic. In fact, Nietzsche's doctrine of the will to power is his metaphysical representation of the true world. It is probably closest to Schopenhauer's Will. Behind the apparent world of causality, unity, morality, there lurks a mysterious Will (to Power). Look hard enough at the doctrine of the eternal recurrence, and it, too, begins to look like a kind of metaphysic. It is a Hegelian response to a Kantian antinomy between mechanism and teleology, for it combines the closure of teleology with the benign indifference of mechanism in the form of a speculative cosmology. And who says that the world has such a bizarre, empirically indemonstrable structure, that it repeats itself forever? Or is it something the thought of which is identical with its existence, a newly discovered unity of thinking and being?

### 12

*More Mysticism?* Nietzsche's perspectivism denies knowledge. In order to make room for what? Kant denied knowledge in order to make room for faith, or so he said. And Nietzsche? Could it be that it is a form of mysticism which unites our two heroes? Both find ultimate truth inexpressible. That each perceived very different consequences from this idea is perhaps just an illustration of what I have called the indeterminacy principle, which is that the core beliefs of mysticism are incapable of determining the content of the philosophical doctrines through which they are expressed.

### 13

*Your Life or Your History?* We could read Nietzsche's critiques as the analysis of specific cultures against a fixed and given set of values of life. So, he considers and compares the Greeks, the Romans, the Christians, the Germans, the cultures of the slave morality, and those of the master morality. But this would be a far simpler argument than the one he makes. For there is clearly something very historical in his analysis. There is a kind of dialectical necessity in the shift from masters to slaves. Something in material circumstances, perhaps, or, more likely, something in the inherently human drive for self-consciousness and truth—something makes it impossible to remain in the simpler world of the masters, impossible also to go back. Nietzsche describes himself as a kind of mix of these competing moralities. The Superman is not a primitive warlord, but one who has gone beyond modern man. The will to truth is of questionable value to life, and yet it is this same will to truth which has impelled him to his current position.

So which comes first, history or life? For it seems that life has been changing, and no longer permits the values it once sanctioned. Whose call do we heed? Do we march against the prevailing morality of our time? Or do we acknowledge the vanity of a revolution against our own historicity? Or, once we have grasped the development and meaning of history, do we simply walk away, as free spirits into an end of history?

### 14

*The Great Man.* Not since Hegel has a philosopher conceived of his personal significance in such ambitious, world-historical terms. Nietzsche is no man; he is dynamite. It is he who reads the writing on the wall—that God is dead. It is he who smashes the old order of values. It is his text *Thus Spake Zarathustra* which will serve as the New Testament for the next two millennia. Great men make history, says Nietzsche, and he seems to leave little doubt that he is one of them.

NIETZSCHE: SUPERMAN AT WORK

Or does Nietzsche have a parachute back into obscurity? A clause that says, it's all hypothetical, just a suggestion, a book for those who love to *think* . . .

Perhaps the revaluation of all values is not a pretense at securing foundations but an affirmation of the most general of imperatives: *be true to yourself, become what you are.* Perhaps Nietzsche's perspectivism is not the absolute denial of knowledge, but his way of keeping philosophy open to new truths, of preventing dialectical closure on the totality of things. Perhaps his historicism marks not a vortex in history, but a call to re-examine history, to break free from old mythologies.

Perhaps this is the *rich ambiguity* of Nietzsche's account: on the one hand, a world-historical messiah, on the other hand, merely a thinker and provoker; on the one hand, relentless critic of a tradition, on the other hand, its latest exponent; a man ahead of his time, and a man well within his time; a great Nay-Sayer, and yet a gay affirmer.

15

*Who Was Nietzsche?* What is going on here? What does Nietzsche mean to us? Is it something historical or not? Is it the name for a crisis point in the saga of the West, the spot where modernity and tradition engage in their final conflagration, the self-immolation of reason, the first step into a brave new postmodernity? Or is it something within the history of philosophy? Is it a logico-philosophical problem finding its way into the trash heap of nonsense? Is it perhaps the philosophical tradition in an explosion of color, like a pile of leaves blown away, perhaps the end of metaphysics? Questions, questions—how about some answers?! Never mind if our aim was merely to expose and provoke. One demands a *synthesis*.

At the end of the day, Nietzsche's doctrines and teachings dissolve with him. They lose their meaning as he recedes. There are no such things as the revaluation of all values, perspectivism, will to power, or the eternal recurrence of the same. Whatever crisis there was in world history or philosophy, Nietzsche was not it. Nor was he, as so many in the academy believe today, the discoverer of the limits of reason, of the inescapability of subjective interpretation of all things. On the contrary, if a Nietzsche survives his own twilight, it is the one who knew that the truth was available to those who *dared*, the Nietzsche who reveled in the cold heights of the dialectic, who dedicated his early aphorisms to Voltaire, who celebrated the uncompromising realism of the ancients. In short, it is the thinker of *enlightenment* who is as our last image of Nietzsche.

Just before he fades from view, Nietzsche throws us this last gift. A promise of freedom. He, too, had to fight for his own freedom. Every book marked another battle in an unfinished war. Now it is our turn. He returns to us, transfigured, Christlike, so that we, too, might live as free spirits.

> Verily, I advise you: go away from me and guard yourselves against Zarathustra! . . .
> One repays a teacher badly if one remains only a pupil. . . .
>
> Now I bid you lose me and find yourselves; and only when you have all denied me shall I return to you.[1]

Something that the young Fritz also showed by *example*.

---

1. *Thus Spake Zarathustra*, in *Werke*, ed. Karl Schlecta (Frankfurt: Ullstein Materialien, 1984), Vol. II, pp. 339–40.

# The Trash Can of the History of Philosophy

## A Veritable Age of Isms

A diverse range of thinkers laid claim to philosophical truth in the nineteenth century. Except possibly for the Hellenistic age, no other age spawned so many "isms." Some of these formed parts of traditions which remain alive today. Others are from time to time recalled from oblivion and pressed into the service of some contemporary cause. Most of them, in their original form, have been forgotten. Though they often achieved a dizzy popularity in their own day, they can now be found only in the trash can of the history of philosophy.

A useful rule of thumb is that philosophical isms are false. Isms begin with some insight, usually a truism, and then try to explain everything in the world by means of it. This usually involves them in certain difficulties. Isms generally last about as long as people find them useful, but in the history of philosophy they can outlast their utility under this condition: that they be associated with a great personality. The ism loses its one-sidedness by finding a place within that personality, which itself becomes the focus of interest for succeeding generations. What is missing among the forgotten isms of the nineteenth century are the great personalities. The philosophical thinkers of this age, other than those discussed in the three preceding chapters, were mainly professionals. Philosophical professionals are generally a colorless lot who understand it as their duty merely to identify and propound isms. Like scraps of paper ripped from a book, they fly with the winds of philosophical fashion to momentary celebrity, and then flutter to an ignominious end among dead leaves and candy bar wrappers.

The isms of the nineteenth century contain some new formulas and distinctive emphases. Kleptologia, philosophy's tendency to steal the work of the other sciences, was rampant. Biology was the science of the hour, and much philosophical capital was expended in the effort to understand and tame this new source of disquieting facts about the world and humanity's nature. Bio-envy replaced physics-envy as a driving force in philosophy. The social sciences were another major source of inspiration and anxiety for philosophers. Many philosophers indulged in social science on the side, while others tried to include insights on the social nature of humankind into their philosophies.

On the whole, however, it is safer to say that the nineteenth-century isms were reiterations, often unconscious, of the traditional themes of philosophy. The isms inspired by biology and the social sciences did not incorporate or advance the knowledge of those sciences, but rather tried to put it to use in service of metaphysical objectives. In one way or another, most of the isms were attempts to grapple with the problem of preserving religious meaning in the face of ever-advancing science. Some, like positivism, tried to make a religion out of science. Others, like Marxism, tried to create a new, scientific religion. More popular was the old Kantian strategy of denying knowledge to make room for faith, especially as it showed how to deal with that traditional bugbear, deterministic mechanism. Also playing was the Hegelian strategy of locating the absolute in an idealist synthesis of religion, science, and everything else in a cosmic-babble egg.

## THE HEGELIAN AFTERMATH

It seems somehow appropriate that the immediate followers of the great dialectician should have split into two opposing factions. The Old Hegelians were a conservative bunch who took Hegel to be pretty much what he said he was, a Christian philosopher and theologian and apologist for the political status quo. They argued that his philosophy so understood was true. The more rambunctious Young Hegelians, who had a greater influence on later developments, thought that there was something basically true about the Hegelian philosophy, but also that it had to be amended in certain important ways. Loosely speaking, they believed that Hegel's professed "Absolute Idealism" was a remnant from the philosophical past and a compromise with the authorities, and that it had to be replaced with something like an "absolute materialism."

Ludwig Feuerbach (1804–1872), "Mr. Fiery Brook," argued that history was not the self-realization of some Spirit, but the story of the realization of our human essence. He analyzed the Christian religion and Hegelianism itself as a part of this process of human self-examination. God, he argued, was merely an external projection of human nature. In a sense, Feuerbach tried to reduce theology and metaphysics to anthropology by relying on a specific concept of the species of man. The German philosopher Max Stirner (1806–1856) disagreed with both Hegel and Feuerbach. In what could be considered either an anticipation of Nietzsche or a throwback to Fichte, he described a world in which only the ego matters, and everything else is a projection of the ego and has value only insofar as the ego gives it value. Such an ego, of course, leaves no room either for an Hegelian Spirit or a Feuerbachian species-essence of man. David Friedrich Strauss (1808–1874), in a study of the historical life of Jesus, tried to show that the advance of history could be explained in material terms.

By and large, the Young Hegelian views are anticipated and subsumed within

Hegel's own omnivorous dialectics. Although their emphases on humanity and material history were refreshing, especially after the idealist rhetoric of Hegel and his older followers, their attempts to forge new philosophies out of these insights led them straight back into paradoxes of any ism. Take away the Hegelianism, in fact, and not much remains of the Young Hegelians. (The "Young da Vincians" would have been equally convincing had they maintained that Leonardo's helicopter would have flown, if only he had put the machine upside down and turned the handle backwards.) Perhaps the Young Hegelians even retreated to a time before Hegel. For, while Hegel had the good taste to regard his absolute idealism as the outcome of a process, and not an immediate doctrine, his youthful followers lapsed into the old mode of metaphysics, of simply asserting the truth of their claims about the existence of strange entities, like the "species-being of man."

That merely identifying oneself as a materialist should offer no advantages over being an idealist illustrates a principle which Hegel himself would have affirmed, a corollary to the schmooalism principle:

---

**The Schmiderialism Principle,** or Idealism, Materialism, Who Cares? Idealism and materialism in philosophy are two aspects of the same thing: schmiderialism.

*Proof.* Materialism and idealism both claim to have an exhaustive understanding of the fundamental nature of reality. In that sense, both are idealism. That understanding, however, reduces ideas to merely given particulars, that is, to matter. So, both are, in that sense, materialism.

*Another proof.* Materialism putatively maintains that everything, including consciousness, reduces to matter and material forces or laws. But insofar as matter has definite properties, such as those assumed in "forces" or "laws," it is ideal. Indeed, materialism permits the interpretation of the world on strictly ideal terms, as the activity of those ideas which are taken to stand for matter. So materialism is a form of idealism. Idealism, on the other hand, supposes that all the world, including matter, reduces to something ideal. But if what exists is and can be only the ideal, is given immediately and has no possibility of being other than itself, then it is not ideal but material. So idealism is a form of materialism.

*Scholium.* Now, the next time you pass a couple of philosophers arguing about the virtues of idealism and materialism, roll down the window and tell them to try chewing on the grass instead.

---

# MARXISM

Far and away the most influential thinker to emerge from the Young Hegelians was Karl Marx (1818–1883). Marx was a political activist who hoped to bring about a communist revolution in Europe. In his later years, when the revolution failed to materialize, he devoted himself to economic research and the articulation of his philosophy.

There is a common, somewhat vague notion that Marx discovered the role of economics in human events, or perhaps that he believed that economic forces determine the course of history (and everything else, for that matter). If this is taken in a weak sense, that economic factors have a strong influence on political and personal decisions and outlooks, then probably every sensible person is a Marxist. Marx may have drawn attention to the variety and extent of these economic influences, but the investigation into their effects presupposes no more philosophy than a mild empiricism. Marxism as Marx intended it, however, is based on a much stronger claim, something like this: Consciousness itself is nothing but the sum of material and social relations which make up the economy, and the analysis of these relations therefore provides an exhaustive understanding of human reality.

Marxism includes a number of theories about history which could be empirically tested and might be or might reasonably have been considered true. For example, it seems to be true that much of history can be explained as the consequence of struggle between economic classes. On the other hand, it is clearly false that all of history can be so explained. It was true that the early industrial age imposed terrible burdens on its workers, and it might at one time have been conceivable that capitalism should create a massive underclass which would then bring about revolution. But history now shows that this need not happen, for the simple fact that it did not.

In essence, however, it is quite beside the point to call Marxism scientific. The ultimate support within Marxism for its constitutive theories comes not from empirical evidence, but from the Bermuda Triangle of "dialectical reason." The essence of Marxism, and the reason why it earns the dubious title of "philosophy," is that it takes its theories as necessarily true. They are the consequence of the inherent "logic" of the "forces of production," "consciousness," or whatever, and not fallible generalizations over observed experience.

Not surprisingly, the old Hegelian confusion of reason and fact leads to a further confusion of fact and value. The early Marx describes the origin of consciousness in labor in terms which make any form of wage labor (in fact, any labor not used in production for immediate self-consumption) "contradictory," in a strange, quasi-dialectical sense. This description translates seamlessly into prescription, into exhortation for the overthrow of the capitalist system. The later Marx describes capitalism as the extraction of "surplus value" from the laborer by the capitalist. This concept is based on a spurious and superficial understanding of the way in which business works, but no matter: The important thing is that Marx has once again found a way to conflate description with prescription. Extracting a surplus is exploitative, and should presumably be stopped. Likewise with the struggle between the bourgeoisie and the proletariat. The definition of the proletariat is essentially "the exploited," and their revolutionary power is again predicted and prescribed as the necessary consummation of a dialectic. It would be pointless now to chase down the absurdities and contradictions in Marx's account of things. The key to understanding Marxism is that it is a not altogether coherent set of concepts, rules, observations, and attitudes—in brief, a language mixed with a religion— which allows its user to exchange values for putative facts. It is for this reason that Marxist "theories" have their strangely dogmatic and unempirical character.

The important question for us is, what was the relationship between Marx and Hegel? Did Marx offer some advance on Hegelianism? Was he able to extract a valuable method, the dialectic, from Hegel's unseemly idealism? Does his own philosophy mark an important advance in the development of Western thought, or, dare I say it, of World Spirit? The answer, I'm afraid, is a firm no. Marx's version of the dialectic is a crude caricature of Hegel's, and has no sanction either in Hegel or in reason. While Hegel understood that the dialectical method could not be separated from its content, and could not be justified except in the end, in the full self-awareness of the present, Marx thought of the dialectic as two abstract entities, like two social classes, bashing heads until the best one wins. He had no problem extending this sort of "dialectic" into the future, as though it could provide him not just with an understanding of his own present, but of the truth about everything for all time. Marx's so-called materialism would have been identified by Hegel as a one-sided idealism. In the final analysis, Marx was just another mediocre Young Hegelian, and would have been consigned with them to the trash can of the history of philosophy, had it not been for the psychological appeal of his new religion to some thugs and sensitive intellectuals.

## NEOKANTIANISM

When the Hegelian bacchanalia finally wound down two decades after the end of history, the German academic world woke up with a severe sense of remorse and embarrassment. How could we have let ourselves get so carried away? they asked themselves. What must the neighbors have thought? They could not even remember very well what it was they had done. So they looked around for some source of credibility, and soon settled on that eternal icon of professional, bourgeois respectability: Kant. Back to Kant! they cried. Armed with reading glasses and sharpened pencils and protected in coats of brown tweed, they charged back into the cloudy land of critiques and transcendentals and faculties of knowledge. Soon the steady din about sensations and categories and unthinkable things in themselves convinced the world and the academics themselves that philosophy had at last returned to serious work.

This modest, penitent movement lasted a good while in the timeless halls of German universities. It finally fizzled in the first few decades of the twentieth century, when the academics admitted to themselves that they could not realize their dream of a scientific epistemology without presupposing a precritical ontology. Darn. Anyway, by that time Germany had forgotten the excesses of Hegelianism, and was ready for a new round of philosophical intoxication.

Neokantianism played a significant, if largely negative, role in the development of continental philosophy. Neokantian luminaries like Franz Brentano (1838–1917) trained wayward students like Husserl and Heidegger. They set the continental standard for obtuse and scholastic expression. Neokantianism was also a part of the background for the rise of analytic philosophy. Russell, like the Germans, turned to Kant out of disgust with the Hegelianism in which he was raised, and then decided to ditch Kant as well. Frege's logic was in large measure conceived in opposition to the putatively psychologistic logic of the Neokantians.

## POSITIVISM

Some of the French were swept up by Hegel, others were not. Among those who were not was the father of positivism, Auguste Comte (1798–1857). Comte represented a continuation of the hard-headed, science-oriented, social-engineering, eighteenth-century French Enlightenment tradition. Comte took the view that human understanding of the world has progressed through three distinct phases: the theological, the metaphysical, and now the scientific. The babble about Jupiter and company became babble about planetary epicycles and has at last become scientific observation of the solar system. Like Descartes, Comte began philosophy with a methodological reflection. Like the *philosophes* of the French Enlightenment, he maintained that the appeal to phenomena, or observation, was the proper way to advance our knowledge of the world and to solve humanity's problems. The emphasis on verification inspired the logical positivists of the twentieth century. Comte, following the lead of proto-socialist Saint-Simon (1675–1755), also thought he could apply these scientific principles to the organization of society, which is why he is said to have fathered sociology.

---

**Biofact.** Comte was an amusingly odd individual. After a failed marriage and attempted suicide, he sublimated his energy in the creation of his arid and dispassionate philosophy. Then, in his late forties, he fell in love, and decided people need more than just the scientific facts. He invented an extravagant Religion of Humanity, what was to replace the old religions with a somewhat tacky consecration of man and human progress. At modern museums of science and technology and in our histories of philosophy, science, and the arts, we do in a sense worship at Comte's altar, although without the benefit of the bizarre ceremonies and clerical hierarchies he proposed.

# UTILITARIANISM

While the Germans were imbibing the first draughts of the Hegelian spirits, the British maintained their spartan, empirical ways in the philosophical movement called utilitarianism. Jeremy Bentham (1748–1832) was the first leader of the British utilitarians. Promoting the idea that social policy should aim for "the greatest happiness for the greatest number," he favored grand projects for organizing society along more rational and scientific lines. He insisted on the strictly equal value of all pleasures, or units of happiness: Monday Night Football, Bentham might have said, could be better than Masterpiece Theater, if it caused more pleasure in the world. This seemed a tad over the top, even for British sensibilities, so it was left to Bentham's hyper-intelligent, hyper-educated (learned Greek at age of three) protégé, John Stuart Mill (1806–1873), to provide a more sophisticated and mature version of utilitarianism.

Mill's philosophical work concerns both logic and ethics. (It should not be forgotten, of course, that he was not just a philosopher, but a social and political activist, administrator, and general big-man-in-town.) In both cases he took a radically empiricist stance and opposed what he called "intuitionism." In logic this meant that he denied the epistemological value of deduction and favored induction based on experiment as the proper way to extend knowledge. Mill tried to put mathematics on thoroughly empirical foundations, arguing that even truths of arithmetic were generalizations from experience. In this he succeeded only in becoming the whipping-boy for later philosophers of mathematics like Bertrand Russell. Mill's logic came with a phenomenalist epistemology and metaphysics, à la Berkeley. He defined objects rather obscurely as "permanent possibilities of sensation" and indulged in the traditional episto-babble of empiricism (as in, please pass the permanent possibility of white, granular, saline sensations).

Utilitarian ethics, as Mill saw, was an attempt to resolve all ethical questions on empirical grounds. He opposed the Kantian idea that moral duty could be derived from *a priori* reasoning. He introduced the "happiness principle" that all actions are morally right insofar as they promote happiness, and wrong insofar as they promote unhappiness. In accordance with this first principle, ethical judgments would have to be based on empirical generalizations about the usual consequences of particular kinds of actions. So, burglary is wrong presumably because it can be observed to cause greater unhappiness in the burgled than it does happiness in the burglar. Or, perhaps it is wrong on the hypothesis that a society full of burglars would be less happy than one without burglars. Fishing, on the other hand, is morally right, since it has been observed that the angler's pleasure usually exceeds the fish's distress. (In contemporary philosophy, one distinguishes act-utilitarians, who would try to judge each act according to its consequences, from rule-utilitarians, who would judge each act according to the consequences of a universal adoption of the rule which that act would represent.) Mill added a couple of amendments (which he tried to pass off for deductions) in order to address some of the obvious objections to utilitarianism. First, he claimed that individuals have a moral right to have their happiness receive equal treatment with that of others. The implication of this is that an individual's actions are right insofar as they promote "the general happiness," without specific regard to his own happiness. Second, Mill distinguished between "lower" pleasures (Monday Night Football) and "higher" pleasures (Masterpiece Theater)—although he did not elaborate on how to compare the two (maybe two Monday Nights = one Masterpiece?).

Utilitarianism in weak form has considerable common-sense appeal. In our everyday lives and in our rambling discussions about what Uncle Sam ought to do, we judge actions by and large according to their consequences for our own and the general happiness. In its stronger, philosophical form, however, utilitarianism gives rise to a host of paradoxes. How is it that happiness and justice can appear to be in conflict? How can one know for sure the consequences of an act or rule? What are the rules for determining the rules? What do you do about sadists, ascetics, and people who get happiness from displeasure? and so on. These have been chewed over many times in the history of philosophy, and I won't go into details here. The interesting point to note is the way in which Mill betrays his empiricist roots. Despite his upbringing on Locke and Hume, Mill makes a classic confusion between fact and value. It is one thing to say that people generally pursue happiness. It is another to say that people *should* pursue happiness. One is a description, the other a prescription. Mill's further inference concerning the possibility of equating the value of different people's happiness is a pure value judgment, which in no way follows from the factual observation that people tend to pursue their own happiness. In the final analysis, Mill's ethics is an example of precisely that which he purportedly opposed—"intuitionism," or rationalist ethics. In trying to reduce all matters of value to matters of fact, he relies on a putatively intuitive or logical "principle" which is, alas, a messy mixture of reason, fact, and value.

## EVOLUTIONISM

What geometry and physics had been to the rationalists and empiricists, Darwinian biology was to many of the thinkers of the nineteenth century. The idea that life as we know it was not always this way, but is the result of evolutionary processes— in brief, that humans might have descended from the apes—shocked some and inspired others. Among those it inspired were Nietzsche, Henri Bergson (see below), and, above all, Herbert Spencer.

The idea of evolution at first seems to support mechanism. What had been imagined to be mysteries of creation, the variety of species and the origin of humanity, could now be explained according to deterministic, causal laws. Herbert Spencer (1820–1903), with his glorification of industry and science, seemed a champion of material forces. As one examines the way in which philosophers like Spencer took up evolution, however, it is apparent that its appeal transcended mechanism. In fact, evolution become a matter of philosophical concern precisely because it offered a way to transcend mechanism. Evolution operates according to causal laws, on the one hand, and, on the other hand, achieves results which can be described in terms of "goals" and "purposes." Evolution seems to build ever "higher" and more "complex" forms therefore it seems to work in one direction. (No one seems to have thought it possible that the ants might inherit the earth.) If evolution offers progress, then it naturally maximizes particular values. Spencer defined evolution in pseudoscientific language as the advance from simple homogeneity to complex heterogeneity, and believed that evolution could explain everything, including history, ethics, society, psychology, and, of course, the causal laws of mechanism. In brief, evolution provided philosophers with another way of resolving the Kantian antinomy between mechanism and teleology. It was a way of accepting science by finding meaning or purpose within its otherwise amoral facts. At this point it should be clear that philosophy's appropriation of evolution had very little to do with actual science, but was just another case of sciento-mysticism.

Spencer's tendency to see the force of evolution at work everywhere and to equate evolution with progress, by the way, led to a rather unbalanced assessment of the social order of his day. He believed that the industrial state (read: Great Britain) represented a more advanced evolutionary stage than the military-feudal state (read: Germany) and was therefore superior in all respects, and really an altogether wonderful place to be (never mind those nasty working conditions in Manchester). Although he viewed society as an "organism," in keeping with his biological metaphor, Spencer also, perhaps inconsistently, maintained that the state and society should interfere as little as possible with the actions of individuals, who should prove their worth by fending for themselves, or else wither away. The view that one should allow natural forces to take care of society's problems enjoyed some popularity after Spencer, chiefly among those who were at little risk of being dispatched by natural forces, and has come to be known as Social Darwinism.

The fate of Spencer should serve as warning to philosophical celebrities of all ages. For a time he was esteemed, and esteemed himself, as the greatest of all philosophers. Spencer's popularity unkindly faded before he had a chance to die. If Nietzsche was "born posthumously," as he claimed, then it may be said that Spencer "died antehumously."

## NEOHEGELIANISM

It is one of the odd twists in the history of philosophy that just as the Germans were trying to forget their Hegelian night, the star of absolute idealism rose in, of all places, Great Britain. More incredibly, this Neohegelianism spread to that most unphilosophical country, the United States.

In what this new idealism consisted is hard to say with precision. The leading Neohegelian, F. H. Bradley (1846–1924), talked mystically about a timeless, Spinozan Absolute which was the totality of the "relations" among all things. In his *Principles of Logic* (1883) and his *Appearance and Reality* (1893), he declared in good Hegelian fashion that ordinary claims to knowledge, involving the question-

able notions of causality, quantity, time, and so on, are inadequate to represent ultimate reality, i.e., the Absolute. Unlike Hegel, Bradley seemed to think that the ultimate reality was not altogether rational. The Americans, who were an altogether
mediocre bunch, were given to obscure pronouncements like "the World is an
Idea" and "there is such a thing as Absolute Knowledge, although our grasp of it
may be very incomplete." Huh?

---

**Biofact.** Bradley was a sickly, reclusive bachelor at
Merton College, Oxford. When not engaged in metaphysical speculation, he apparently passed the time
shooting stray cats with his pistol from his college
window.

---

The English Idealists put much emphasis on the "social dimension" of
Hegelian ethics. Bradley saw ethics as a matter of "my station and its duties."
(Whether that station was to be a military dictator or a common fireman did not
seem to bother him much.) T. H. Green (1836–1882), too, effused about the sociality of ethical life and the rest of reality, too. The sociality of things, a truth presumably independent of any specific society, was to be the basis of one's ethical
duty to a particular society. Green's lectures may have inspired English schoolboys
to die for reality, i.e., their country, in the First World War. It is another of history's
little ironies that at the war's outbreak, the British minister, Robert Haldane, was
a self-professed admirer and follower of Hegel.

On the whole, Anglo-American Neohegelianism is best construed as an academic response to the perceived threat of mechanistic nihilism. The American wing,
I suspect, also harbored a secret longing for the aristocratic ways of the Old World.
While the power of material forces seemed to grow ever stronger, the notion that
reality is ultimately mental not only served as a consolation, but also continued to
guarantee professional employment for philosophers. In quality and general sentiment, the Oxford Idealists were not unlike the Cambridge Platonists two centuries
before them. Just as the latter had turned to the ancient Plotinus, so the former
sought out the alien Hegel as a way to reconcile contemporary science with their
professional needs, spiritual longings, and mystical experience.

As time went by, the Hegelianism became more peculiar. John McTaggart
(1866–1925) tried replacing the Absolute with his "Personal Idealism." Josiah
Royce (1855–1916) also opted for a personal idealism. George Santayana (1863–
1952) declared himself a "materialist" although he patently was not. And then
there was the matter of the lone philosophical voice in Italy, Benedetto Croce
(1866– 1952), who pursued the Hegelian fantasy of a Logic that would become
identical with the world into a foggy wilderness of neoscholasticism.

Nowadays, the Neohegelians are occasionally recalled on behalf of that uninspired form of modern Kantianism which goes by the name of communitarianism.
On the whole, however, the Neohegelians were important chiefly for the reaction

which they inspired: disgust. After a bout of youthful indulgence in the mysteries of Hegelianism, Bertrand Russell joined George Edward Moore in decrying this wafty, academic mysticism. The logical positivists also hammered Bradley, usually without bothering to read his works. So began the tradition of modern analytic philosophy. In America, the reaction to Neohegelianism took the form of pragmatism, which also contributed to the rise of analytic philosophy.

## PRAGMATISM

Traditional Anglo-Saxon empiricism survived and succeeded idealism in America under the banner of pragmatism. Kant had used the word *pragmatisch* (from the Greek *pragma*, meaning action) to describe those principles which arise from and are applied to experience (as opposed to *a priori* principles of reason). Charles S. Peirce (1839–1914), who had studied Kant closely, thought such principles were the true vehicle for acquiring and presenting human knowledge, and conceived of pragmatism as an practical, methodological maxim about how to make the task of any empirical investigation clear. However, the connotations of the word "pragmatic"—the sense that what matters is not the truth, but getting the job done— could not be avoided, and with William James (1842–1910) this businesslike attitude became a part of the philosophical movement called pragmatism.

One of Peirce's main concerns was how to make our ideas clear. His aim was not so much a theory of meaning but a method which would help make specific meanings clear. His chief thesis was that the meaning of any particular idea can be boiled down to the "conceivable experimental phenomena" entailed by its affirmation or denial. In more general terms, our concept of an object is the sum of whatever practical effects the object may be conceived to have. A corollary is that a conception whose affirmation or denial has absolutely no conceivable practical effects is meaningless. (Peirce's thesis anticipates Ludwig Wittgenstein's notion that the meaning of a sign or utterance has to do with its use.) In fact, his thesis is at bottom one of those eminently sensible and ancient practical maxims which one could not plausibly withhold from prehistoric cave-dwellers. Our very word for "meaning" includes the notion of 'practical implications'. When we or any caveman ask "what's the meaning of this?" we are usually not asking for the mystical, ideational, semantic unit linked to a specific expression, as philosophers tend to imagine, but some clarification about its consequences. Put another way, Peirce's maxim is the Neanderthal intuition, that the only ideas worth the name are those on which belief (or not) can have some consequence for one's future perceptions and actions.

Peirce had a metaphysical and theological side, too, although we need not go into that here. One other principle of his, however, is worth mentioning: that of fallibility. Despite his pragmatism, Peirce conceived of the "Truth" as something unconditioned and identical with all reality. But he wisely added that such an absolute truth was not accessible to thought. The consequence is that any particular claim to knowledge is potentially wrong, i.e., fallible. Statements of fact, Peirce said, are necessarily insufficient efforts to represent the Whole by means of a few parts. The bottom line is a version of Hume's analysis of facts: They are by their nature conceivably false.

To William James fell the Platonic task of converting Peirce's Socratic insights into dogmas. James took Peirce's practical maxim on how to make ideas clear and turned it into a claim about the nature of truth. Truth, James said, is utility. A true belief is one that is profitable, one that works. Unfortunately for James, truth is not utility, and while true beliefs tend to be profitable, certainly not all profitable beliefs are true. It may be profitable for me to believe that the whole world loves me, but that does not make it true. Russell, among others, viciously mocked James's pragmatism. James replied with some clarifications, modifications, and obfuscations, at which point the debate acquired a rather unpragmatic, scholastic tone.

The pragmatic tradition continued in the person of John Dewey (1859–1952), a disaffected Hegelian who sought a compromise between Peirce and James. He threw out a few isms of his own—instrumentalism, experimentalism—and had moderate success, though he probably had more influence through his work on education. Dewey focused on the scientific method, pragmatic problem solving, and the need to understand that truth is at best warranted assertability until some new fact comes along to unseat it or we must change our view to fit the needs of our problem. He rejected absolutes in favor of truths with a small "t."

## VITALISM

The nineteenth-century fascination with biology went beyond evolution. It had to do with the mysterious "life force": that little something, that spark, that creative intuition which makes life so special. Schopenhauer and Nietzsche had sensed this force, but Henri Bergson (1859–1941) was the one who really made a philosophical meal out of it. Bergson believed that there was something more fundamental than the laws of physics and mathematical abstraction at work in the world, namely, the *élan vital*, the vital urge or spirit.

Bergson perceived that the problems of free will and determinism, of mind and body, and of life and matter were all related. In all these problems, he took the side of freedom, the mind, and so forth. He held that we tend to lose track of our freedom, etc., because our intellect naturally thinks in terms of a spatially oriented causal determinism. Ultimate reality, he intoned sagaciously, is a temporal flux. Just as a film camera slices up a scene into discrete frames, so do our perceptual faculties reduce life's movement to a series of static images. So Bergson devalued the intellect and the modern sciences, and exalted the special kind of intuition which puts us in touch with the flux that is life. Strangely, he inadvertently modeled his new life-reality on the old material-reality: it had a 'sense' of its own, its own forces and causalities, and so on. No surprise here. Bergson's philosophy, to put it briefly, was a revived Kantianism, with *élan vital* substituted for the noumenal world.

Bergson was a phenomenon in his own time. Housewives and student radicals packed his lectures. The ladies adored him for championing the emotional and intuitive side of life against those unfeeling scientists and atheists, while the radicals were more interested in using his radical deconstruction of the intellect in justifying their rather dangerous program of political action without political thought. Like Spencer, Bergson died antehumously. Perhaps because he was France's sole hope for philosophical greatness in the late nineteenth century, or perhaps because vitalism has a more universal and timeless appeal than Spencer's mechano-evolutionism, Bergson at least gets revived from time to time for brief periods.

## CONFUSIONISM

By now the aspiring philosopher is confused. So many isms! Which to choose? Which is true? Who cares? In the case of most trainees, the answers to these questions depend on the answer to a more fundamental one: What does my teacher think? But what happens when there is no teacher, or when the teachers disagree? The wannabe flounders. I don't know which ism to believe. I don't even know what most of them really mean. I'm confused. Thought settles into this state of confusion. There follows a fit of introspection and . . . Aha! The spark of philosophical inspiration. I am a confusionist! Thus an ism is born.

# Twentieth-Century Philosophy

## The Great Divide (?)

By the twentieth century there had emerged two different, competing understandings of philosophy: analytic philosophy in the Anglo-American world, and continental philosophy in Europe. Cognitive dissonance, it would appear, rises as our history approaches the present. At first glance, the differences between these two schools of thought are striking. By and large, each has a distinct set of interpretations about the history of philosophy. In the continental view, post-Kantian German philosophy is central to any understanding of modern philosophy and even of modernity itself. Analytic philosophy, on the other hand, tends to ignore most of the history of philosophy, and when it chooses to not, it gives Kant and his predecessors a bit of credit, throws out the rest of the continental pantheon, and names a few completely different heroes of its own. Each side has distinct objectives. Continental philosophers aim for some insight about life, history, culture, or something quite general, while analytic philosophers aim for the steady accumulation of philosophical facts. Each also has its own method. In the continental tradition, the individual, great philosopher is the bearer of truth. The analytic tradition adopts the probably more sane view that it is the analysis of propositions which reveals the truth.

As philosophers, though, we are bound to suspect any form of dualism. This division of philosophies, it may turn out, is just another philosophical interpretation of things. As historians of philosophy, we are also bound to suspect any interpretation that makes the present qualitatively different from the past. In fact, we know already dissonance is nothing new in philosophy. The apparent unity of the history of philosophy has always trailed the history itself by at least two hundred years. The Greeks, for example, were a fractious bunch among themselves, but the medievals brought them all together, and so they have remained ever since. In this respect the history of philosophy may be no different from other forms of history, where the most recent events are the most hotly contested—except possibly that the philosophical sense of "recent" may be quite generous.

It is not hard to see the basis on which some future historian will unite the warring factions of twentieth-century thought. A first point to note is that the divide does not occur in space, as the name "continental," at least, implies. Continental philosophy's masters come mainly from France and Germany, but a number have attained their status through American adulation. Analytic philosophy, on the other hand, has beachheads all over Europe. More importantly, a number of central concerns on both sides are quite similar, and have already been recognized as such. Both went through so-called linguistic turns, in which language became the chief phenomenon of philosophical interest, and both take it as an article of faith that the metaphysical ways of the past are to be rejected. And the apparent differences in method might really just be differences in style. Perhaps continental philosophy is a way of using a certain historical rhetoric in order to suggest indirectly a few incoherent, mystical thoughts. And analytic philosophy is just the art of finding seemingly clear and logical ways to express those same thoughts.

It is also not hard to see how the supposed opposition of the two traditions serves certain philosophical interests. For analytic philosophers, the category of continental philosophy is a place to dispose of soft, totalizing, metaphysical, meaning-of-life issues which, for the sake of professional respectability, they would rather avoid. For continental philosophers, analytic philosophy serves an equal and opposite function: It is the repository of metaphysical rationalism, or whatever it is they seek to overthrow. Like the supposed opposition of Eastern and Western philosophy, this modern divide is by no means external to philosophy, as practiced on either side.

---

*"There is nothing between us!"* *she exclaimed to her companion. The hubbub in the bar settled, as other customers listened curiously. Would a domestic scene unfold in public? It didn't, and the two parted. Meanwhile, at a corner table, the following was heard: "She utters the Nothing, the essence of the human condition. It is the Nothing which saturates us, fills the pores between us, makes the Other an Other of the Other. The anxiety of the No-Thing is the overwhelming crisis of modernity." Thus spake the continental philosopher. But the analytic philosopher offered the following clarification: "I'm afraid she speaks with a grammatically incorrect expression. Nothing cannot be between anything. Once we have a full-blooded theory of meaning, of course, utterances such as hers will be ruled out."*

# Continental Philosophy: Unthought

From *The Psychoanalyst's Handbook on Philosophers*

**Historicomania.** *Definition.* Condition afflicting philosophers with historicist outlook. Symptoms include collection of stacks of overdue books and dropping of philosophers' names in almost every sentence. Stems from the idea that every idea was first conceived by a Great Philosopher (GP). The not-so-great philosopher (NSGP) believes that he or she is always drawing from an inherited stockpile of ideas. Having read only a few GPs and understood even fewer, the NSGP infers that he or she is wallowing in self-ignorance and so barred from the philosophical bliss of true self-consciousness. The NSGP responds by attempting to read all the philosophers and to understand all their interrelationships, who read whom, who influenced whom, who refuted whom.

*Complications.* May result in lengthy, juvenile works purporting to cover the entire history of philosophy.

*Prevention.* This condition may be contracted by reading too many translators' prefaces or blurbs on the back of paperback editions of GPs.

# Husserl

*Another Head Case*

## À LA DESCARTES

Believe it or not. We are all the way into the early twentieth-century and we find someone who professes that:

1. Philosophy can be made into a pure science, which is to be the queen of the rest of the sciences.

2. This science is grounded on the absolute certainty which may be achieved through a transcendental examination of consciousness by consciousness itself.

3. This new science will have a vocabulary of new or redefined Greek and German words. (A partial list: adequation, appearances, asymptote, cogito, cogitatio, ego, eidos, epoche, evidence, exemplar, formal this or that, hyle, idea, ideal, intentionality, intuition, judgment, kinesthesis, life-world, logic, meaning, memory, noema, noesis, noetic, object, phenomenalism, phenomenology, reduction, transcendental this or that, etc.)

---

> **E**
>
> *[The playground. E muttering to himself.] K failed, I know, but I am sure it can be done. We can build that castle, I know we can. Let's start by admitting that, as far as we subjects are concerned, it's all appearances. We are subjects, and they are objects. But surely, these appearances have a kind of structure. Indeed, consciousness is constitutive of its object* qua *object. If we transcend the consciousness of individual objects, if we examine transcendental consciousness . . . Yes, it appears that appearances have a real structure! Appearances are reality! We'll make of it a science. Let's call it: Husserlism. No, too flashy (and too hard to pronounce!). Hmmm. Let's call it the science of appearances. That's it: phenomenology!*

The Germans loved it. Edmund Husserl (1859–1938) allowed them to keep the fantasy of idealism alive. He promised a way of thinking which would carry them beyond the spiritual deficiencies of positive science, and back to the good old days of headstrong philosophical culture. The French picked up on it, too, because they saw in Husserl a reassuring combination of the Kierkegaardian emphasis on the personal and Kantian insistence on technobabble. Husserl refined his concept of the phenomenological project a number of times. He never completed his work, however, and only the fanatically committed imagine that it ever could be completed. Which demonstrates once again the truth of the intentionality principle, that in philosophy failure is no obstacle to success.

*Bracketed Away (A Poem)*

Searching for the truth one day
the absolute ground of philosophy
I sought the very core of me
my consciousness and I

I gathered all the things and thoughts
the content of my mind
and suspended all belief
In brackets went [the tater-tots]
[the table top] and [fresh ground beef]
Soon the whole [external world]
and all that might have been a fact
was erased under the brackets

True form have I, I thought with glee
just pure intentionality
but as I thought about myself
I thought well who am I that I am free?
In brackets went my [presuppositions about the nature of consciousness]
and then my very [self]
[I] am no more said [I]
[I'm bracketed away!]

Still [I] clung to precious life
at the [ [ limit ] ] of a [bracket]
[ [I] am the edge ] ] on all [my thoughts]
the [brackets] of [my consciousness] [ ]
[ [ ] [ ] [ [ ] [ ] [ ] ] [ ] ] [ ]

# Heidegger

## *Much Ado about Being*

## I. BEING

### *WONDERFUL BEING: OOOOH, AAAAH*

The inspiration of Heidegger's philosophy is a sense of wonder. There are those among us who might be amazed by, say, a bearded woman. Or the tallest building in the world. Or who might gaze in awe at a satellite photograph of our attractive planet. Not Heidegger. He could find wonder in the most humble things, say, a cup of hot chocolate. For what mystified the young Heidegger was not the particular properties of this cup of chocolate (its color, shape, smell, etc.) nor how it got there (that it was poured by his obliging mother), but the seemingly primordial fact that it *was*. Its existence. Its *is-ness*. Being. Wonder in the face of the mystery of being was the basis of all of Heidegger's later philosophy.

### *QUESTIONABLE BEING*

Leibniz had framed this sense of wonder in his "first question" of philosophy: "Why is there something rather than nothing?" Plato, Aristotle, and countless other philosophers and theologians asked the same question in their own ways. Heidegger prefers his own formulation of the question—something like "What is Being?" or, variously, "What is the meaning of Being?"—which he identifies explicitly as the first and only question of all (his) philosophy. To make the question seem a little clearer, Heidegger offers a distinction between "beings" and "Being" (*das Seiende* and *das Sein*). There are plenty of little beings—like bearded women, buildings, and planets—but there is only one Being. Being is. It is nothing other than itself. Being discloses itself in and through these little beings—they are immersed in, partake of Being—but Being is still something different. It is the most fundamental and universal 'thing' about the world. (In fact, maybe it just *is* the world.) So the task of philosophy is to figure out just what Being is.

Heidegger's aim is to "think Being," alternatively, to "say Being." He lets it be known that this is a very difficult thing to do. Thousands of pages of dense and obscure prose have only brought us a wee bit closer to this "saying." Why should this be so? Say to yourself: Being. Say it like you mean it. There. Said and thought, all at once. One more time: Being. So why does Heidegger find it so difficult?

## "Dr. Sein: On the Frontiers of Being," excerpted from "Philosophical Laboratories, Inc.—A Guided Tour"

My suit was still a little sooty from the visit with Dr. Al Chemist, who was making some breakthroughs on the lead-gold problem. Fortunately, I arrived at the laboratory of Dr. Sein on time. Dr. Sein was famous for his discovery of the One from which all matter emanates. Now he was a major recipient of research funds from government and business in support of his latest project: the investigation of Being. His aim was to isolate a sample of Being, identify its distinguishing characteristics, and explore possible applications for industry.

Dr. Sein's laboratory was enormous. It was bustling with white-coated assistants, all wearing serious expressions, as if to say, no time for chatter. Strange whirring sounds and a low, intense murmur filled the air.

Dr. Sein took me by the arm and began the tour. Near the entrance was a large, gray lab table, on which was an odd collection of objects: a pair of peasant shoes, a hammer, granite from the mountains in the Black Forest, and what looked like the insides of a vacuum cleaner. A white-coat came over and began to examine the objects one by one, taking copious notes. I asked my host to explain. "The items in this collection," he said, "share the common property of Being. We are recording their behavior minutely in order to establish the nature of this commonality. At this point, we've got a working hypothesis, which is that all things that have being share this common property: They exist."

Suddenly a horrific shriek filled the air, followed by a loud crunching sound. Dr. Sein noticed my startled expression, and, with (I thought) a slight smirk on his face, nodded in the direction of the next table. "That is our annihilator," he explained. "It removes Being from things. We throw in anything that has being, usually something not very essential, like yesterday's lunch, and then observe closely as it is destroyed." His answer left me even more uneasy. He looked around quickly and suddenly exclaimed, "Where is Assistant Hildegaard? Wasn't she standing here a moment ago?" No response. This can't be real, I thought. Trying not to display my fear, I stepped back from Dr. Sein's macabre machine. It definitely had been a smirk, which now turned into a smile and a laugh. "Ha, ha. Just a little joke."

Next Dr. Sein drew my attention to a black box next to the annihilator. Apparently, he and his assistants had removed all the air from this box, and allowed nothing, not even light, to enter. "A control, you know," he explained. "Just to make sure than when we get Being, we can compare it with Nothing."

We moved on. A youngish man was bent intently over his desk writing furiously into a large notebook. "He seems pretty busy," I commented. "Indeed," responded Herr Doktor, "This is a sample Dasein, you know, a being whose Being is in question. We're having him write down all the questions he can think of, to see if Being is in one of them." I thought of asking why they chose this particular unfortunate man, but then, seeing his inexpensive corduroys and unhealthy complexion, I figured he must be a graduate student.

At a nearby table sat an older fellow in a rumpled tweed jacket. Next to him was a white-coat. The tweed-jacket man seemed to be writing a few words on thin slips of paper, which he would then hand to the white-coat. The white-coat was using these paper slips to build something that looked like a paper-mache dollhouse. Dr. Sein saw my quizzical expression. "Freddy there," he nodded towards the tweed, "is a poet, you know, a creator of language. So we're having him create some language. It's very interesting, although I don't pretend to understand all the new words he invents."

"I see," I replied, not really seeing at all. "And his colleague . . . ?"

"His assistant. Yes, well, we are working on the theory that language is the house of Being. So we are building a little house here in the hopes that Being will come home to it. And if it doesn't come on its own, we may still need a place to put our sample of Being, you know, make it feel at home, once we find it."

We had covered only a small part of the lab, where a number of other experiments were underway. Unfortunately, my schedule for the day was pretty tight. So I thanked Dr. Sein and wished him success and many more federal grants.

## QUESTIONABLE QUESTIONS

Heidegger's approaches to the question of Being express, in his idiosyncratic way, the insight and illusion of much of traditional philosophy. Heidegger's appeal lies in the sense of concreteness about the world which his writings sometimes convey. At his best, Heidegger jars us into dispensing with abstract ways of understanding ourselves, like the Cartesian view of ourselves as mind-substances, and brings us down to the brute reality of human experience. The insight that lies behind this appeal, however, is nothing new in philosophy. One can express it in any number of ways (though Heidegger argues that his own is superior). In a vague, religious language, one could say it is the idea that the human condition is inherently finite, or that man is not God. In the terms of medieval scholasticism, it is that existence is not essence. Or that the 'that-it-is' of something is always different from and not entirely reducible to the 'what-it-is'. Kierkegaard would have said simply that a logical system can never be also existential. Kant applied the insight in his theory of knowledge, in his claim that existence is not a predicate, in his claim that there is an unanalyzable "given" in knowledge in the form of intuition, and in his general conclusion that human knowledge is inherently conditioned. Hume expressed the matter most elegantly with a simple distinction between fact and reason. Properly understood, this insight is not a doctrine nor is it the basis for any investigative project. It is a reminder against possible error, chiefly in the form of other philosophical positions, and a practical principle. Strange as it may sound, what is true in Heidegger, in my view, boils down to a version of the general principle of enlightenment. If you want to be an authentic Heideggerian, you don't need Hume, Kant, Heidegger, or any other philosopher; on the contrary, it would be best to forget them altogether and open yourself to the world around you according to the maxim: *look* first, *then* think.

In Heidegger, alas, the illusion follows all too quickly on the insight. Heidegger found it difficult to "say" Being because saying Being in his sense is in fact impossible. His attempt to do so is a direct violation of the insight contained in his philosophy, and is a classic instance of the quest for the Holy Grail of philosophy. The Being Heidegger longs to say is that whose essence it is to exist. Thus, one may substitute "God" for "Being" in most Heideggerian texts without altering the meaning (such as it is). Heidegger's Being is also the unity of universal and particular. It belongs universally to all entities, on the one hand, yet is no mere universal, for it exists and is only *one*. "Being is," as Heidegger says with his charming banality, "itself." Being is that whose possibility presupposes its actuality: As Parmenides had long ago noted, the 'is not' still 'is'. Heidegger's Being is the mystical One. It is that which first, lies behind all things, which enables their existence; second, is inexpressible, can only be indicated; third, is everything, all reality. Thales chose water; Heidegger chose Being. In the end, it's all the same substance.

The most annoying features of Heidegger's writings follow from this simple dialectic of philosophical insight and illusion. His claims about the inaccessibility of Being to ordinary language and ways of thinking reflect his insight. The obscurities resulting from his attempt to forge a new language (supposedly from the roots of the old one) represent the illusion that Being could be expressed, if only we had the right words. The metaphorical quality of his writing incorporates the insight that the totality of things cannot be represented. The implicit hope that the metaphors might work, on the other hand, is illusory. His evocative style—Heidegger does not try to make a case for his points nor even describe the facts—is an attempt to express Being by creating an experience. The insight is that what can be part of the text cannot be what he wants to represent, the illusion is that he can make it into something other than a damn book. Heidegger's later tendency to mystify thinking—his thinking in particular—follows naturally from the confidence that he was somehow able to think Being, but not yet to express it. Finally, the rejection of an aim or purpose in defining his project, his invocation of a hermeneutic circle in which everything is just an extended interpretation of its own beginning in himself, is merely the internalization of his mysticism. For the healthy reader, this last feature is perhaps the most distinctive and frustrating aspect of Heidegger's writings. When it becomes obvious even to Heidegger that the questions that frame his project are bogus, he claims he is "on the way to a questioning." When it is clear that his ruminations lead nowhere, he says he is leaving "trail-markers" on a path of thought. And don't try asking where that path leads: It leads to more markers. In the end, it's all circles, circles, circles—around what?

## "On the Way to Thought: A Trip to Dr. Denken"

Although he was a world-famous expert on the all-important question of Being, Dr. Denken was an unassuming and, at first glance, unremarkable individual. He was of a slight, unathletic build, soft-spoken, and stroked his mustache regularly. He was amicable enough, though his eyes sometimes seemed distant behind the octagonal wire rims. At our meeting, he sported a seventies' style (and probably vintage) turtleneck and his hair looked in need of a wash. He showed me into his conference room and sat me down at a table with three chairs.

Hoping to boost my credibility (to speak frankly), I mentioned my recent visit to the laboratory of Dr. Sein. This turned out to be a mistake. Dr. Denken spoke dismissively of Dr. Sein's "technico-scientific" attitude and shrugged him off as "just another metaphysician." Not wanting to alienate my subject so early in the interview, I nodded in agreement, and tossed out a few nasty comments about Dr. Sein's problems with the labor unions. Our discussion naturally shifted to Dr. Denken's own research program. He gave me to understand that his aim was "to think Being." Unlike Dr. Sein, however, he believed that this path required a new way of thinking, a thinking "through and beyond" traditional Western metaphysics, beyond the confines of language, logic, and grammar.

While describing his work, Dr. Denken referred constantly to his "close collaboration" with a certain Martin. I got the impression that this Martin was very special to the good doctor, and the relationship somehow vital to his work. In fact, Dr. Denken almost seemed to think of Martin as a kind of god. From time to time he would gaze fondly at the empty chair. This made me a little nervous, so finally I asked him: "Where is Martin?"

He looked puzzled for an instant, and then smiled faintly. "Ah, yes. Martin is wandering in the neighborhood of Being." Once a again he caressed the empty chair with his eyes.

I hoped maybe this meant he was in the suburbs somewhere, so I asked, "Should we wait for him to return?" To which Dr. Denken laughed in his distant way, and said, "You are right, of course. I meant that Martin is marking out the pathways of thought. That is how he shows us a new way of thinking."

I was glad to be right, but would have been happier to know what I was right about. "And these paths lead toward Being," I mused aloud.

Dr. Denken cleared his throat. "Martin's path is not a 'toward-which', not a 'from-here-to-there', but a wandering in thought. This is why I say he is in the neighborhood of Being. His is a pure thinking." He peered profoundly into the fluorescent lights overhead.

"Maybe you can tell me a little more about what Martin and you are thinking about."

"Martin does not think about something," Dr. Denken reproved me, "he thinks. You could say that he thinks thinking. He thinks the something itself—the something which is. And what 'is', above all, is Being. You could also say that he thinks nothing, for he thinks the Nothing which is the ground of beings."

As I fished in my mind for a suitable response, I thought for a moment that I, too, might be thinking about nothing, but then I thought the better of it. I gazed inanely at the condensation evaporating from the walnut veneer as I lifted my hand from the table. "Gee," I admitted, "I'm finding Martin's thoughts difficult to follow."

"Indeed, they are the most difficult thoughts," Dr. Denken reassured me. "Martin is attempting a way of thinking more rigorous than the conceptual."

"What a concept," I said softly to myself. I glanced at the notes I had scribbled on my palm and said, "As I understand it, you are engaged in an investigation of Being. Perhaps you could outline the inquiry for me."

"A very good question." I felt a verbal pat on the back. "Unfortunately, Martin cannot yet formulate the question of Being. He has not yet begun to ask this question. His project is the daring attempt to fathom this unfathomable question."

"Sounds fascinating," I lied. "I guess that's why he's wandering around, as you say. He doesn't know where he's going."

"Exactly."

Relieved to hit one on the nose, I continued, "I guess once Martin's fathomed this unfathomable question of Being, you two should be in a position to offer lots of practical advice about how to deal with, uh, beings."

Dr. Denken recoiled in horror. "Thinking, when taken for itself, is not practical! Martin is trying to free us from the evils of the technical interpretation of thinking! Thinking unfolds something into its essence. Only what 'is' can be thought. And what 'is' above all is Being. The technical interpretation of thinking would forget Being! It would value a thought only according to its utility! Instrumental reason is the stiff-necked opponent of thought! It is because we can no longer think that history has dropped us in the abyss of modernity. How dare you!"

I was not yet willing to shoulder the blame for the demise of civilization, but I went with my natural instinct to calm the agitated professor. "I understand, I understand. So, your project must be, in a sense, well, useless."

"Exactly." He was back in his seat. "But what is useless can be a force, perhaps the only real force. It can be intimately bound up with a nation's profound historical development."

I couldn't figure out how something that was useless could have such dramatic applications. "Gee, that doesn't sound very logical." I tried to sound as naive as I imagined myself to be.

"Yes, Martin thanks you," he said. "For what could be more logical than to say that because he is thinking before and against logic that he is illogical."

This bewildered me even more, but I decided it was my fault for having opted out of philosophy courses in college. Not sure where to take the interview, I stalled. I suggested we have something to drink, and Dr. Denken agreed. "Milk, sugar?" He left the room for a moment.

He returned with three cups of coffee. He gave me a cup, took one for himself, and placed the third in front of the empty chair. And it dawned on me.

Maliciously, or so I imagined, I asked, "Why don't we let Martin speak?"

"Ah yes," he said wistfully. "Martin is trying to say the hardest thing, to say Being. He is on his way to a saying. He is working behind language, at the base of language. You must not expect him to speak in the common language that has been co-opted by evil logic. Shhhh. Listen carefully. Martin is breaking all the rules of grammar."

"I suppose that would make it hard to hear him." I tried not to break out laughing.

"Indeed, one must listen hard to hear Being. It is the nearest and the farthest thing . . ."

"I was talking about hearing Martin, not Being." My tone veered toward the caustic.

He looked confused for a moment, as though he did not grasp the distinction. "Martin is on his way to a saying," he repeated.

"So he must be thinking about what he is going to say." Score a quick debating point, I hoped.

"No, he is on the way to a thinking." Darn. Thought I had him.

"Well, how do you know he's on the way to a thinking?" I was starting to sound peevish.

"How do you know he's not?" I realized that Dr. Denken had a point. If there could be paths that start nowhere and lead nowhere, thoughts that are about nothing, questions that are not yet questions, activities with no consequences, speech without grammar, logic before logic, and all that, then there might just as well be a Martin who could not be perceived in any way.

I opted for direct confrontation. "Look, he just isn't present!"

Behind the octagons I saw what would otherwise have passed for a flash of recognition. "Aha! So that's who you are," Dr. Denken said menacingly. "You are a metaphysician of presence! For you, Being is only that which is continuously present in the here and now. You have not grasped time as the horizon of Being. You make all absences a presence. For you, Martin is merely an absent-present. I should have known. All those questions about what Martin was doing, where he was going, what he was investigating—you are clearly a representative of the techno-scientific nihilistic Western tradition!" He narrowed his eyes. "Did Dr. Sein send you here? Are you a spy?"

I assured him I was not, and offered as evidence my recently published review of Dr. Sein's work. In any case, Dr. Denken stopped speaking to me altogether, and started addressing his favorite chair in a strange language of neologisms and Germanic grunts. Then his eyes grew even more distant, and he was no longer talking to the chair, but to himself. Anyway, it was time for me to go. I noticed the sign on his door as I left: Dr. *M. H.* Denken. Could it be? But I had no time to think. My next appointment was with Dr. S. U. Zeit, who does not like to be kept waiting.

## BACK TO QUESTION NO. 1

It may well be that the wonder before existence is a necessary, and perhaps noble sentiment which arises naturally in human experience. If that wonder is to be philosophical, however, it must be directed toward what can be known. And that means the hard work of learning, inquiring, and thinking about the things that exist. The great mystery at the end of it, existence, is only the assurance that the investigation is always open.

It could have been—in the case of Heidegger, perhaps *should* have been—a kind of speechless wonder. Just a gaping mouth would have sufficed. In the event, Heidegger's speech unravels into nothing. Unwrapping his questions, one finds— more wrapping paper. "Why is there something rather than nothing?" "Why is there something?" "Why is there 'there-is'?" "Why is there 'is'?" "Why is there?" "Why is is?" "Why is?" "Why?" "Why." It starts off sounding like speech, but then stammering.

# II. BEING-THERE

Heidegger's appeal stems from his sense of concreteness, specifically about *human* experience, as presented in his first (and only) major work, *Being and Time (Sein und Zeit)*. In that work he offers a mixed bag of radical, insipid, and dubious insights into human experience. From a philosophical point of view, however, the key issue is whether and to what extent these insights form part of Heidegger's philosophical project. For Heidegger's project in the work is an investigation of Being—a "fundamental ontology." The investigation of human experience is a means to that end. He insists that his work was not an anthropology. With good reason: If it were an anthropology, it would not only fail to achieve his aim of thinking Being, but would also represent a very poor way to advance anthropology. In my view, his project has no philosophical or other basis, and is in fact a motley and unsystematic stab at anthropology.

## WHAT IT'S LIKE TO THERE-BE

Surprisingly, perhaps, at the start of *Being and Time* Heidegger shifts the focus of the investigation from mere Being itself to humankind, on the grounds that humankind has unusual philosophical status in being the only being to question Being. Of course, he doesn't just call man "human" or "mankind" or anything so pedestrian. He rejuvenates the German word *Dasein*, meaning literally "being-there," and formerly used to mean just plain old "object" or "thing." The point is that the object of study is still Being, but that being opens itself up, or is accessible only through humankind. So, *Dasein* describes the place where Being makes itself manifest, and it happens that this place is in that being for whom Being is in question.

Heidegger goes on at length in his analysis of *Dasein*. Here are a few of the features he ascribes to it: There is, for example, what Heidegger calls the "thrown-ness" (*sic*) of *Dasein*. People find themselves already thrown into the world, already existing. "Being-in-the-world," the jargon for this condition of being already sur-rounded by an external world, is part of the structure of human existence. It is an attempt to reverse Descartes: I am, therefore I think. In a related way, "being-with," as in being with other people, is also a fundamental aspect of existence. So the tra-ditional "problem of other minds" is dissolved on the grounds that being-with is a fundamental mode of being-there, or *Dasein*. As for external objects, Heidegger continues, *Dasein* first encounters objects in the world as "ready-to-hand." This means something like "tools." The aim is to suggest that there is a kind of primor-dial relationship between humans and external objects, like that between laborers and hammers, which precedes any reflective theory about the nature and applica-tion of external objects. Whether this is true or not is, as in general with Heideg-ger's work, irrelevant. The point is to evoke a sense of wonder at the being of men and hammers which precedes any scientific or philosophical theorizing about what humans actually do with hammers. Heidegger finds the defining characteristic of *Dasein* rather strangely in "care." By this he does not mean that we are all nurses, but that the basis of our nature is to be concerned, in a general and neutral sense, with what goes on around us. To summarize very briefly, one could say that Hei-degger is attempting to draw a picture of human experience which emphasizes the features that are overlooked in the Cartesian notion of the subject of epistemology. Of course, in that context there is something odd about defining *Dasein* as the being for whom Being is in question.

It turns out that a *Dasein*-person can be "authentic" or "inauthentic" with respect to his/its nature as a *Dasein*. The authentic *Dasein* has read *Being and Time* and lives in the awareness of the basic structure of his existence. And the main facet of this structure is the inevitability and individuality of death. The inauthen-tic presumably think they aren't going to die. The authentic have learned about the "being-with" factor, but they put their relationships with other people in perspec-tive. The inauthentic are absorbed in what other people think. The authentic "speak" (usually about Being). The inauthentic merely "chatter." The authentic experience that good old existential "Angst" (or dread) when contemplating the "No Exit" clauses of their existence. The inauthentic merely experience "fear." The authentic know of "wonder." The inauthentic have a kind of feline "curiosity." The way to achieve authenticity, according to Heidegger, is to be "resolute." "Res-oluteness" is a combination of determination, firmness, and humanness in getting things done under the limiting conditions of human existence (mainly death). Inau-thentic people are probably wishy-washy, wimpy wafflers. Inauthentic existence, to use Heidegger's neobiblical terminology, is a kind of "fallen" existence. At this point Heidegger senses that he is sounding a little too sanctimonious, so he assures us that "fallen" people are still people, and "fallenness" must be a part of human existence as well. Which is a vaguely dialectical way to try to overcome a self-con-tradiction. Oh, well: No German philosophical system would be complete without a little moralizing.

Taken out of its home in his obtuse ontology, Heidegger's analysis of *Dasein* includes a mix of insightful, dubious, and insipid observations. The anti-Cartesian elements suggest the general insight that much of human experience takes place with no metaphysical foundation whatsoever. That is, not everything we do is (or perhaps can be) based on thorough, critical reflection on ourselves *qua* independent subjects possessing beliefs and desires. Heidegger's discussion of how individual responsibility can get lost in the inauthentic condition of absorption in "the they" is a reasonably accurate (though perhaps not self-aware) anticipation of the way the mass of Germans would behave under totalitarianism. His claims about "being-toward-death" are interesting but almost certainly overstated. It is true, in a logical sense, that death is individual and existential, not an event in one's life. It is also probably true, in a psychological sense, that an awareness of the inevitability of one's own death can have a salutary effect on one's attitudes and behavior. (Though it might also make one get all morbid.) But it is quite unnecessary, not to say absurd, to elevate this awareness of death to an ontological condition of self-realization.

## THE THERE-BEING IS THE HOLY GRAIL

The thrust of Heidegger's discussion is that human existence, *Dasein*, is inherently finite; yet as the notion of *Dasein* develops through his work, it takes on an absolute or unconditioned character. *Dasein* is that whose "that-it-is" is identical with its "what-it-is." *Dasein*, as Heidegger puts it, is that which exists "for its own sake." The progression of analyses in Heidegger's work, in fact, can be seen as bringing *Dasein* to ultimate self-sufficiency and self-awareness. Since it is a—perhaps the—essential structure of Being, whatever that might be, the self-realization of *Dasein* in Heidegger's philosophy should presumably bring forth Being itself. *Dasein*, in other words, is Heidegger's Holy Grail.

The Holy Grail showers virtue on those who possess it—those who know it. With that, we can begin to make sense of Heidegger's jargon of authenticity. Remember, Heidegger professedly begins with fundamental ontology. Then he shifts mysteriously from the "is" of ontology to the "ought" of ethics. How can this be? The answer, after two and a half thousand years of philosophy, may seem a little tedious. Heidegger's attempt to locate an ethics in the structures of being is a repetition of the Socratic quest to identify virtue and knowledge. It is an attempt to conflate prescription and description. To put the matter in Hegelian language, Heidegger's analysis of the conditions of authentic existence, and its culmination in the privileging of a particular kind of awareness, is an effort to achieve a unity of theory and practice.

Possibly the most interesting parallel is that between Heidegger's ethics and Kant's. In a superficial sense, the two are diametrically opposed: The one purports to situate ethics in the uncompromising finitude of human existence, the other in the absolute universality of reason. That there is a deeper convergence between the two is evident from a curious fact, that both may be fairly criticized as vacuous.

Kant's test of rationality for ethical claims, as we have seen, gives passing marks to any and every self-consistent ethical position. Heidegger's claims about resoluteness are equally empty. Think of Heideggerian resoluteness as an imperative: Whatever we choose to do, we must be resolute about it. Well and good. Now, what shall we do? The truth is, we can do whatever we like, and still be resolute about it. More generally, the basic thrust of an ethic of authenticity is "be true to yourself," or "become what you are." Which begs an obvious question: Who are you, anyway? Then again, perhaps this is just another one of the wonderful circles of Heideggerian Being. Perhaps we should stop pestering him for sensible explanations, and fall into the trance.

In sum: Taken as a contribution to fundamental ontology, as Heidegger intended, the analysis of *Dasein* is merely a vacuous cover for a reaffirmation of the quest for the Holy Grail of philosophy. Stripped of its ontological pretensions, Heidegger's analysis still harbors a few interesting thoughts about what it's like to be human. However, if our aim is to pursue such thoughts, we could do far better than submerge ourselves in the mire of a superfluous verbiage and spurious pronouncements. We could go out and collect evidence about human behavior, observe ourselves, and conduct an open discussion on the facts of the matter.

## III. THE HISTORY OF BEING

Heidegger never finished the project he set out in *Being and Time*. Maybe it was because of the Nazi episode, or maybe it was the result of his readings in the history of philosophy. At any rate, Heidegger apparently decided that something was not quite right about his original approach. That something, it seems, had to do with history—the historicity of philosophy, and of Being itself. His project shifted from an investigation of Being through an analytic of *Dasein* to an investigation of Being as it manifests itself in "the history of Being." Heidegger decided it was time to "overthrow" the tradition of Western metaphysics, which he held responsible for forgetting Being. His earlier work, he came to believe, was possibly one more representative of this failed tradition of thought. Thus the famous "turning" of Heidegger's thought. From a seemingly anthropologically oriented project, he shifted to the "prehuman" concerns of truth, language, and history. In my view, however, he was still pretty much the same old Martin, and his idea for the project of overthrowing metaphysics was the biggest hoax ever sold to the philosophical public.

Heidegger situated his new idea for a project, the overthrow of the Western metaphysical tradition, within a story. The story is something like a fairy tale.

## A Tale of Forgetfulness

Once upon a time in the kingdom of the West ruled the Great King Being. His sons, who called themselves the Presocratics, served Him faithfully and were very happy. Then the Great Prince Plato was born. Being knew Plato was special. One day on his way to the academy Plato ran into Being. Being gave Plato a gift, a pair of mind-spectacles called "rationality." Plato tried them on. He was no longer able to see Being. Instead, he saw lots of mathematically calculable Ideas. Plato came to believe that Being was immediately accessible to and controllable by his own mind. Now Plato thought he was in charge. He called himself a Great Philosopher-King, and he demanded that everyone in the kingdom wear these spectacles. So everyone in the kingdom began to see Being in the same way, which is to say, not at all. Being was dismayed, of course, though He never ceased to rule behind the scenes.

After Plato retired, Being kept visiting the new princes (Aristotle, Descartes, Kant, and Nietzsche) and gave each new gifts. These gifts were ever more advanced and refined versions of Plato's spectacles. As each prince became a Great Philosopher-King, he made everyone in the kingdom put on the latest version of the spectacles. The effect of all these spectacles was that the people began to think that Being existed only when in the form of little square beings. So the people forgot about true Being, and set about exploiting beings as best they could. They valued things only for their use. They developed modern science and technology, and soon were stuck in traffic jams on their way to tedious jobs in cramped offices. They tried to find Being by building ever more squares, yet they seemed to get ever farther away from Him. They started to get depressed. The face of Being darkened, and He said to himself: They have forgotten Me.

Then one day the Great Prince Martin was born. Being came to visit Martin and told him the story about how the kingdom of the West had been blinded since Plato and so on. But now the West is ready to see me again, He said. Then Being entered Martin's body, which became Being among beings. When Martin ascended to the throne of the Philosopher-Kingship, he required everyone to wear a new set of spectacles, which were a reverse combination of all the old ones. Thus the kingdom once again saw Being, and let Being resume His rightful position, and everyone lived happily ever after.

This little fairy tale makes excellent bedtime reading for philosophers and is probably Heidegger's most influential contribution to twentieth-century thought. (Of course, Heidegger borrowed parts of the story from a number of his predecessors—namely, Nietzsche and the End-of-Civilization thinkers like Spengler, and Juenger—but he did give it a new twist and impetus.)

## EXEGESIS

In outline, Heidegger's story goes like this:

1. Western thought has been controlled by a certain way of thinking—call it either metaphysics or rationality.

2. This way of thinking prevents Westerners from having a proper relationship to Being, and so leads to nihilism.

3. Martin will save Western civilization by overthrowing the tradition of Western thought.

The Presocratics, Heidegger suggests, were okay. Western metaphysical thought really began with Plato. A succession of figures thereafter further deepened and elaborated this way of thinking: Aristotle, Descartes, Kant, and Nietzsche. Heidegger's attitude toward each is ambivalent. Each tried to overthrow the tradition in some way, and so offers valuable insights, but each failed.

Let's elaborate on the first point of the story. The chief characteristics of Western metaphysical thought are:

1. It (falsely) views Being in terms of the permanent and continuous presence of objects. It excludes Time from the understanding of Being.

2. It (falsely) views Being as possessing the characteristics of mathematical rationality. It sees Being solely in terms of countable objects with specific qualities.

3. It (falsely) views Being as what can be represented to a knowing subject. It is dominated by an oppositional, subject-object metaphysics. It therefore reduces being to perceiving, as in Kant, and ultimately to willing, as in Nietzsche.

Let's elucidate the second point of the story. The consequences of Western metaphysical thought are dire:

1. It causes us to "forget" Being.

2. Which induces an aggressive, imperialistic attitude toward beings.

3. Which is responsible for modern science and technology.

4. Which leads to nihilism. The objectification, demystification, and exploitation of things remove value from the world. Ultimately all values are destroyed.

The third point is simple: Well, thank heaven for Martin!

The first thing to notice about the story is that it is in outline quite illogical. "Rationality" is deemed bad because it prevents us from seeing things as they really are (i.e., as true Being) and because it prevents us from getting what we want—i.e., happiness, or the absence of nihilism. In other words, rationality is condemned as irrational. This hardly makes sense. Now, it may well be that lots of people throughout history have held and continue to hold mistaken beliefs about the world, and that these mistaken beliefs result in self-defeating actions. (I think that for the most part, people have an understanding of the world adequate to achieve their desires. The early Heidegger would probably have agreed with me on this.) It is extremely implausible (and, as I have argued throughout this book with respect to philosophy, empirically untrue) that everyone in the West up until now should have held the same set of beliefs. And it is absurd to maintain that the chief mistaken belief was the belief in 'rationality', for rationality is inherent in the very possibility of meaningful action based on belief. One should, on the contrary, reaffirm the fundamental principle of rationality, that prejudice should be avoided so that one may judge things according to how they are. What Heidegger tries to dismiss as "instrumental" rationality, or the "technical interpretation" of reason, *is* reason, and what lies on the other side is not a "higher path of thinking" but magic, mysticism, and sophistry.

The second obvious absurdity in the story has to do with the assumptions it makes about the nature and relationship of history and philosophy. The story assumes a very strong historicism. All thought in an era—in fact, through the whole era from Plato to Nietzsche—is governed by a single, unthought paradigm. This leads to all the usual contradictions about how we, who are presumably also besotted with Western rationality, can even begin to understand what Heidegger is saying. The story also assumes a comically self-important role for philosophy, which, in the form of metaphysics, dictates the paradigm of thought. Thus, metaphysics is held responsible for science, technology, and the whole Western way of life. To put the matter gently, this assumption involves a naive foundationalism (everything I think can be explained only in terms of my highest-order theory about the nature of reality) coupled with a bizarre historical idealism (everything I think must have been thought first by a great philosopher). In fact, I can quite easily eat a burrito and explain my actions without reference to a metaphysic of subjects and objects and without having a clue who Descartes was. Only a professor of philosophy, or whoever it is that writes those blurbs on the backs of the philosophical classics, could imagine that the course of Western history was dictated by the obscure rantings of a few closeted mystics. As I have argued throughout this book, science has progressed for the most part despite metaphysical speculations, which have tended to hold it back. Science has no need for philosophy, and can be grounded in common sense (if it needs to be grounded at all). A similar point can be made about the putative value-schemes of science and metaphysics. It may be quite reasonable to say that certain beliefs have tended to induce an unnecessary or undesirable aggressive disposition, or that certain ways of organizing behavior have consequences for the determination of the ends of behavior. It is quite ridiculous to ascribe the disposition directly to rationality or metaphysics. Reason is not aggressive; people are.

One should not overlook the fact that Heidegger's strong, philosophical historicism actually reduces history to comic-book simplicity. He is able to explain everything—the Nazi movement, World War II, industrialization, the encirclement of Germany by Russia and America—in terms of the forgetting, remembering, darkening, lighting and a handful of other permutations of Being. Also, one should note that Heidegger's concept of world history is extraordinarily provincial—his Greco-German West is even narrower than Hegel's history, which at least begins in India and China. Finally, one should consider the implications of this strangely reductive historicism for the interpretation of thinkers in the history of philosophy. One should read Heidegger's works on Nietzsche, Kant, and the others. One should try to ascertain just who these works are about. On a personal note, I must say that I owe Heidegger a debt of gratitude. In view of the violence he inflicts on the texts of his predecessors, I am sure my own interpretations will seem quite fair and reasonable.

The ultimate absurdity of the fairy tale is the place Heidegger assigns to himself in the account. He is supposed to represent an end to the tradition as we understand it and a return to its primordial reality. The logic behind this self-exaltation is inexorable. If Martin has identified the unthought paradigm of Western thought, then he has *ipso facto* thought his way beyond Western thought. If, as he says, Plato's doctrines were "no mere chance, but the words of Being," then you can be certain that Martin's words *are* the big B itself. Paradoxically, this attempt to totalize the tradition of metaphysical thought and lift oneself above it is a classic instance of everything that has been wrong with metaphysical philosophy. It is an attempt to grasp all reality as history, all history as the history of philosophy, and all philosophy as a totality whose comprehension and limit is—Heidegger himself. Martin the overthrower is his own Holy Grail. The meaning of Being and the meaning of history converge in his own person. He is fated, a destiny, an absolutely necessary being, the truth toward which philosophy has been working.

---

From *The Psychoanalyst's Handbook on Philosophers:*

**"Paranoia Strikes Deep."** Philosophy is a form of paranoia. The philosophical self sees everything as part of an interconnected whole. It believes it can preserve itself only by maintaining the absolute integrity of this interconnected totality. Anything which appears to be outside must therefore be destroyed or absorbed within; it is all part of a conspiracy, a grand conspiracy which is the totality itself. Thus the philosophical work consists of an elaborate series of defenses. For example, the philosopher may defend against criticism on conceptual grounds by claiming to be trying to "go beyond concepts"; or, against criticism in general by claiming to have defined the nature of all criticism. It is pointless to ask precisely what is being defended, since what is being defended is the defenses, or, to use more technical language, the self in its mode of defensiveness. This paranoia often manifests itself in the attempt to "overthrow" all previous philosophy, in order to make sure that one is not "trapped" outside. Philosophy also frequently leads to hypochondria. The self imagines that it is infected within by alien modes of thought. Whenever it says "I," for example, it may fear that it has been compromised by a metaphysics of subjectivity.

## THE LANGUAGE MYTH

Some of Heidegger's most influential and least coherent thoughts had to do with language. I mention three interrelated ideas:

1. There is an original language of truth/Being, namely, ancient Greek. (German runs a close second.) That is why bogus etymologies are the path to the truth.

2. It is language that speaks, not man.

3. Language is the "house of Being." Its "guardians" are the poets.

The first idea is lunatic. The only thing I can imagine is that Heidegger let his scholastic-theological training get out of hand. His etymologies—many of which are in fact bogus—are just a means for him to pass off bald assertion as revealed truth.

The second idea is an old canard. At least since Heraclitus and his *logos*, as Heidegger himself notes, philosophers have imagined that they could locate a framework which would be prior to subjectivity and so release them from the obligations of freedom. Many twentieth-century pseudo-thinkers and literary theorists are grateful to Heidegger for allowing them to cite his bald assertion as "evidence" that this framework could be found in language. It cannot. Language does not speak. People do.

The third is a good example of semipious, nonsensical, Heideggerian rhetoric. Being doesn't live anywhere, and Friedrich Hölderlin was writing poems, not defending Heidegger's philosophy.

Heidegger's later focus on language does not in any way alter the futile direction of his philosophy. He simply transfers some of the mystical powers of the Being-Holy Grail to the Language-Holy Grail.

HEIDEGGER: IT IS LANGUAGE THAT SPEAKS, NOT FRUIT

# IV. MARTIN

Martin may well have thought of himself as a world-historical destiny, but we are unlikely to do so. Furthermore, we know from the Indeterminacy Principle that the specific forms of his mysticism cannot be derived from the mysticism itself, but must be explained with reference to specific, personal, and historical factors.

## THE PRIEST

Heidegger's family thought he would grow up to become a Catholic priest. His earliest studies concerned theological matters; his doctoral thesis, for example, was on the medieval theologian Duns Scotus. The theological bent of his later philosophy has long been noted. I have already indicated above the apparent substitutability of "God" and "Being," the use of biblical notions of 'fallenness' and so forth in the analysis of *Dasein*, and Martin's possible Christ-complex.

Perhaps this religious aura can explain something about the nature of the texts. It is quite obvious that Heidegger's work is not scientific: It follows no sensible method and disdains evidence. It is evocative and inspirational. It is, in brief, what one might expect from a sermon. Maybe he was just fulfilling his parent's expectations. Somewhere inside, I think, Martin imagined himself to be the High Priest of Being.

## THE PEASANT

Granted, Heidegger was a theologian. What, then, was his theology? Should we assume, on the basis of the God-Being connection, that it belongs purely to the Aristotelian tradition represented by Anselm, Aquinas, and company? In one important sense, no. Heideggerian theology owes a very large debt to the tribal, pagan, idolatrous religion vicariously ascribed to the Teutons by nineteenth-century German culture. It is the same religion that would play an important role in Nazi ideology, and that would serve as Heidegger's bridge to its ideology.

Consider the superficial indications. Heidegger's favorite metaphors are taken from an almost mythical peasant life. He cannot stop talking about forests, trails, clearings, lightings, shelterings, neighborhoods. And there can be no doubt that the German language, which is the expression of the reality of the being of the German people, has a very special philosophical status for Heidegger. These metaphors and inclinations boil down to a handful of symbols: home, earth, tribe. Home in the sense of the Nazi *Heimat*: not mere residence, but proper living space for a German. Earth as in German earth, as in Blood and Earth. Tribe as in Teutons, as in ancestral history.

So far, a superficial and purely personal proclivity for the mythical Teutonic peasant life of the past. In the theology of Being, however, it becomes much more. There is a kind of primitive, pre-Spinozan pantheism in Heidegger's Being. Being is everywhere, immanent in beings. Every little thing is a manifestation of the great Being, and the great Being is itself this universal manifestation. From here it is a very short step to pagan idolatry. Forests, houses, hammers, and German-Greek etymologies become the sacred way in which Being makes itself for us. In his late works Heidegger comes up with a bizarre "fourfold construct"—gods, sky, earth, mortals—whose utter arbitrariness (why not five?) makes sense only as an esoteric stab at this new paganism. Earth is "the serving bearer, blossoming and fruiting, spreading out in rock and water."[1] Why not just give it some mythical name and have done with it? "The sky is the vaulting path of the sun. . . ." "The divinities are the beckoning messengers of the godhead." Next he will be asking us to make sacrificial offerings.

The Heideggerian tribe ends up worshiping Being through beings, by making sacred the beings around it which make up its life—the house, the farm, the forest. The tribal wonder before Being is a kind of astonishment at the magic of beings. There is a special fascination with the collective being in which it exists and which has allowed it to come to be—viz., its ancestral history. That is, Heidegger's paganism mixed with tribalism is essentially a form of ancestor worship. One more thing the tribe worships: the Will. It worships the resolute Leader who guides and becomes its being. Its elemental astonishment at Being is also an elemental astonishment before those who as part of Being transform Being.

## THE NAZI

What is really definitive of this magical-peasant nostalgia is not what it proposes or worships, but what it opposes. In all this vague worship of earth, blood, tribe—and in the vagueness itself—is a reaction against the advance of modern technology into human life. Hence the antipathy toward science, logic, even clarity of exposition. A man is unhappy with life, he believes that this is because something has been taken away from him, something that was properly his, the feeling of being-at-home-in-the-world; he blames the newly prominent structures of the world, its invasive modern technology, and begins to react against them, and against their supposed basis—reason. Heideggerian obscurity is a form of reaction.

In this Heidegger was very much a creature of his time. In the early twentieth century, much of Germany's intellectual elite became absorbed with theories about the impending collapse of civilization. Writers like Spengler and Juenger, following the path of Schopenhauer and Nietzsche, were extremely popular. The right just as much as the left abhorred the "bourgeois civilization" which had taken hold of Germany and the world. Like Heidegger, however, most did not have a very intelligent response to the "crisis" of modernity.

---

1. "Building Dwelling Thinking," in *Basic Writings*, ed. David Farrell Krell (New York: Harper & Row, 1977), p. 327.

**Biofact.** Heidegger led a deadly dull life, with one exception: the Nazi episode. When Hitler came to power, the rector of Freiburg University was forced to step down, and Heidegger took his place. Heidegger's speeches and writings make clear that he not only welcomed the Nazi rise to power, but perceived this rise as a fulfillment of his philosophical destiny. He quickly turned his own philosophy, complete with his personal idioms and jargon of authenticity, over into service on behalf of the Reich. Ten months later, once he had proved to be an ineffective administrator, he left his post. Though his relationship with the party deteriorated, he never left Germany, and continued to assert in various forms a belief in the "inner greatness" of the movement. After the war until his death in 1976, with the exception of an evasive, posthumously published interview, Heidegger never publicly apologized for his political role nor did he ever confront the implications of the Holocaust and the war for modern civilization and philosophy.

## Martin's Dream (or, Our Nightmare)

*He will lead us to a new dawn. I will be there at his side. He will call on Germany to save the world. I will make Germany worthy of the task. He will create the political reality through which modern man can authentically encounter himself in the context of global technology. I will give meaning to this new reality as leader of a renewed philosophical culture. He is the hero whom Germany failed to provide when Hegel last raised us to the level of Spirit. He has found the solution to the nihilism of Western civilization in action. I will supply the final solution to the problem of the forgetfulness of Being in the history of metaphysics. He will do away with the petty political and academic freedoms which are the cause of our unfreedom. I will do away with metaphysical squabbling over Being. We will have no need for laws, ideas, or propositions, for his person itself will be our political reality, our authentic Being. And I will offer my own person as our new philosophical reality. Some say he is uneducated. I say just look at his hands! His is the power, instinct, and resoluteness. Mine is the understanding. Where expediency causes him to stray from the inner greatness of his movement, I will be there to offer gentle correction. He will show his gratitude by showering me with honor. He will be my Dionysius, I will be his Plato—but I will do better than the metaphysical Plato! The Führer and I! Heil Hitler! Heil Heidegger!*

What if Heidegger had (unfairly) failed to obtain the scholarships which assured his academic career? What if he had become just another Catholic priest in the Schwarzwald? Well, he probably still would have been a mystic, though in his raptures he would have spoken of God, not Being; he probably still would have advocated a retreat from modern civilization, though he might have called for renewed faith instead of a return to medieval peasant life; and he probably still would have supported the Nazis. The philosopher spends his time getting to know himself; perhaps there isn't much time left to change himself.

## THE PRO

What if it is too much to suppose that Heidegger had a theological, religious, or political agenda? After all, it seems unlikely that a philosopher of Being would go out and try to change the world. What if his objective in life was simply to become a German master philosopher, the Hegel of his day? What if the apparent doctrines and agendas can be explained mainly in terms of what would bring success in such an endeavor? Mystics, after all, come a dime a dozen. Only a few become great philosophers. Why Heidegger?

A German master philosopher is readily identifiable. He (forget she) holds a chair at a prestigious German university. He is surrounded by a coterie of admirers and wannabes. And he has the privilege of declaring his views rather than arguing them. How does a clever peasant become such a master? This may vary according to the historical period. In the early-middle of the twentieth century, the prescription would have been as follows:

1. Write. *Badly.* Since Kant it has been accepted that clarity of exposition does not befit a master.

2. Say nasty things about common sense. The master must promise to initiate his followers into a way of thinking that will make them superior to the ordinary run of mankind, especially their own students.

3. Make believe that you are in possession of the paradigm that will resolve all past philosophical disputes.

4. Avoid ever reaching a final conclusion to any of your arguments, or answering any of your fundamental questions. This would dispel the aura. You must convey the sense that you are pointing in a particular direction, while at the same time pointing only at yourself.

5. Complain a bit about modernity, alienation, dehumanization and all those things. Throw in some pseudoprofundities about contemporary spiritual conditions to give your work credibility among disaffected intellectuals. Tap into the mysticism and irrationalism which is quite common today as a reaction to the advance of science.

6. (Mid-century) Get on the language bandwagon. It's the next hot item for the professionals. Preempt both the French intelligentsia and the Anglo philosophers of

language by affirming that language is central to everything you do. You will be gratefully cited as evidence for decades to come.

Was Heidegger so calculating in his ambition? Maybe. Maybe not. It's a lot of effort to go through, if all you want is a peaceful little house in the Black Forest.

## SELFISH PLEASURES

We are still thinking in terms of goals, essentially external goals, of being-toward-something-else. To change world history. To start or resurrect a religion. Or merely to serve personal ambition in climbing a peculiarly German social ladder. What if even this supposes too much? What if our friend had not yet arrived at a goal, had not yet formulated the question of his life completely?

Come to think of it, there was something very odd about the man. I mean, he was always rather disengaged, enough to tag along when the Nazis came around, and sufficiently disengaged from the rest of humanity not to bother clarifying the Nazi issue for the remainder of his life. And isn't it strange that Heidegger virtually never traveled outside his neighborhood? Did he feel that there was nothing of interest in the world? Did he sense that he himself was the most interesting thing in the world? Was he really just thinking?

---

### Martin's Bedroom

*Let us disturb the master, if it's not too late. We put to him that Socratic question: What is the good life? Oh, perhaps we have disturbed the master. Is he searching for an answer? Or is the search itself his answer? Wait, he seems to be saying something to himself:*

*"In the life of pure thought, one speaks to oneself. One speaks one's own language. One is intelligible only to oneself. Right and wrong, true and false, are criteria subsumed within oneself. One's questions are at the same time one's answers. Everything and everyone outside is swallowed, consumed, and negated in one's own whole. One is the sole true Being. One is alone, in one's bedroom, listening to the rhythmic movement of oneself, and locating ecstasy within . . . alone . . . o . . . o . . . o . . ."*

# Sartre

## *Being-in-the-Cafe*

Jean-Paul Sartre (1905–1980) will be fondly remembered for the vivid expression he gave to a few simple thoughts. The first is that human beings are totally and radically free. The second is that the human self is a process, a striving to become something, and not a simple thing. The third is that the brute fact of existence is prior to any justification or explanation of it. The fourth is that the first three reveal themselves in and lead to emotional dispositions which are of some psychological interest. These thoughts did not originate with Sartre. Mostly they can be distilled into truisms or psychological insights. Still, Sartre deserves some credit for giving them memorable, if sometimes melodramatic, expression.

## FREE AT LAST

Sartre was one of those philosophers whose thought can be summarized in one word: freedom. He believed that human beings are by their nature totally and radically free. What does it mean to be totally and radically free? Of course, it doesn't mean that you can do anything you want. If you're tied up and thrown into a dungeon you will not be free to do very much. Rather, we are concerned here with an internal freedom—a freedom of attitude, or of the mind. Sartre means that consciousness is so constructed that no facts—whether about an individual's past or current situation—can wholly determine its actions. Consciousness comes with the possibility of wrenching oneself free from any particular situation in life. According to Sartre, you choose your own way of being. There are no excuses. It is a serious responsibility, for which not everyone is prepared.

# Do Be Do Be Do

Sartre's idea of human freedom supposedly follows from his analysis of the structure of human reality. Skipping over Heidegger's attempt to locate a preconscious human reality in *Dasein*, Sartre returns to something closer to a Husserlian understanding of human reality as essentially consciousness. To begin with, he argues, being conscious is different from being a thing. A thing, or a "being-in-itself" to use Sartre's jargon, just sits there, kind of inert, being what it is. Consciousness, or "being-for-itself," on the other hand, "is what it is not." This paradoxical formulation contains two propositions. The first, which follows closely on Hegel, is that consciousness is somehow identical with the principle of negativity. Consciousness determines objects, and this determination, as Spinoza points out, is also a negation. It is a division of the plenitude of the in-itself. Not-being (in the sense of absence—not-being-present) is conceivable only as an act of consciousness—consciousness "creating" an absence. This power of the negative is also coeval with the concept of possibility. The determination of what is is also a determination of what might be. Possibility is possible only through an ability to suspend or annihilate what is. (All this talk about negativity, negation and so on, incidentally, is why Sartre titled his main systematic work *Being and Nothingness*.) Which brings us to the second proposition, which is that consciousness never simply *is*. Consciousness is always distinct from its own past. It is always striving to realize its future possibilities, but, of course, it is not its future. In other words, humanity is a *project*. One is what one chooses to (but has not yet) become. It is in this sense, with respect to human reality, that Sartre finds a common meaning in 'being' and 'doing'. Inasmuch as one is what one makes of oneself, to be is to do. God does not create us, says Sartre; we create ourselves.

## Existence and Essence

Sartre wrote that existentialism can be summarized in the proposition that "existence precedes essence." In the simplest sense, this means that existence has no meaning. That is, there is no *reason or justification* for being. Look at the tables, chairs, trees, and cups of coffee around you, and you can come up with all sorts of explanations about what they are and how they got there. But the brute existence of this world in which they came to be cannot be derived from anything or explained in any way. Things just *are*.

Within the philosophical tradition, of course, the concepts of existence and essence carry a heavy load. Recall that it is the identification of these two concepts in God which is the basis for the ontological proof of His existence. In insisting on their separation, Sartre is presenting a world whose existence has no ultimate sanction in God. (Sartre was in fact an avowed atheist). In epistemology, existence and essence correspond to being and knowledge. Sartre insists from the start on the distinction between knowledge and being, and that being can never be reduced to a form of knowledge. Knowledge is always insufficient for being; or, as Sartre tends to put it, being "overflows" knowledge.

Sartre tends to think of the existence/essence distinction chiefly with reference to human consciousness. His point is that human consciousness has no essence— or, to put the matter in a paradox, that its essence is to exist prior to its essence. Though existence precedes essence, human beings often attempt to unite the two. At one level, this means that human beings try to reduce themselves to things. At another level, since it is impossible to become a thing, people make it a part of their project to unite the two in their own being. In other words, they want to become God.

A related point which Sartre affirms is that moral principles have no existential sanction. That is, there is nothing in the nature of the world or being which could justify absolutely any particular values. A radical, individual choice, in light of the absolute freedom of consciousness, is prior to any moral code.

## PSYCHOLOGICAL PROBLEMS, OR HOW TO DEAL WITH EXISTENCE

Much of Sartre's philosophy is motivated by his distaste for certain behaviors and attitudes of other people. In fact, one could argue that his "system" is just an attempt to provide a philosophical basis for this instinctive reaction to others. The basic problem with most people, according to Sartre, is that they are unable to face the true nature of their existence as free beings responsible for making themselves. They try voluntarily to surrender their freedom and to become thing-like instead of conscious. (Fortunately, this turns out to be impossible.) They believe in some extra, transcendent justification for what they are and do beyond their own actions. In other words, to revive a Heideggerianism, they live *inauthentic* existences. Sartre's term for this condition, which he introduces right at the start of his system, is *bad faith*.

In his description of bad faith, Sartre offers two examples which have now become classics. First, there is the young woman and her date. The guy is making a move on her, and takes hold of her hand. She doesn't want to admit to herself that this is a sleazy come-on, so she keeps talking about high culture and, without removing her hand, mentally separates herself from it. She reduces the hand to the status of an inert object. That way she doesn't have to deal with the seedy reality of the situation. Next, there is the waiter. His motions are a little too precise, too waiterly. He is obviously pretending to be a waiter, which, of course, he cannot be, according to Sartre, because the man is what he is not. Instead of being a free and conscious being, he is making himself into a robotlike thing. The bottom line, ethically speaking, is that the good existentialist faces up to things (and him/herself) as they are. (The paradox, given Sartre's definition of consciousness, is that this means facing up to themselves as they are *not*.)

However, facing up to reality is no pleasant task. Remember, existence has no meaning; it overflows any attempt to explain or justify it. Thus, the sensitive existentialist experiences the feeling of being *superfluous*. Not really necessary. An accident. Just there, without reason. No one likes to feel superfluous. Even worse is the angst. Confronted with all the responsibility entailed by human freedom, with the fact that the self must always strive to become what it can never be, finding itself in the midst of an existence with no prior meaning or value, the existentialist soul naturally experiences a little fear, worry, dread, guilt, and anguish which combine to produce the famous existential angst.

The authentic existentialist does more than just comprehend the nature of things. For it is the nature of things that his life itself is nothing but a project. So, he commits himself to a project engaging himself in the world. The hero of one of Sartre's plays, Orestes, comes to despise his fellow citizens as inauthentic, and perceives that their beliefs are meaningless, but nonetheless decides to commit himself at some risk to saving the city.

Like Heidegger and Kierkegaard, Sartre makes an attempt to reverse the priority of moods and consciousness. For all three thinkers, the mood of anxiety is the chief way in which the brute reality of existence discloses itself to the individual. In obscure (and ultimately illogical) ways, each tries to make all other modes of consciousness dependent on this initial orientation toward the world. Behind their arguments is a potentially valid point, that an individual consciousness does not "have" emotions, in the way that a woman carries her briefcase. Rather, the individual "experiences" the world through them. This, however, is a matter for descriptive psychology and not for ontology or epistemology.

## THE LOGIC OF THE ARGUMENT

Sartre's thoughts on freedom, essence, and existence are at least very refreshing. Like Hume and Nietzsche, Sartre in his best moments demonstrates the courage to prefer a harsh truth to personal, historical, or religious convenience. Still, one has to wonder about the logic of the argument, what he proves, what follows, and what is merely a part of the disposition of a mid-twentieth-century French intellectual.

Most of Sartre's philosophical positions, insofar as they make sense, reduce to some familiar truisms. The arguments on behalf of freedom can be thought of in Kantian terms, as demonstrations of the conditions of the possibility of human experience. Sartre is right, I think, in championing freedom against all those nasty philosophers who would take it away from us. The grounds of his argument, however, do not extend very far beyond common sense, and certainly not beyond the resources of the philosophical tradition. The formal nature of Sartre's argument is obvious, for example, in his discussion of "action." He elaborates his claims about freedom by noting that the concept of action makes no sense without an actor to do it. This is true. So?

The Kantian connection goes deeper than this. Sartre acknowledges that his understanding of consciousness as negativity is influenced by Hegel (though he maintains that Hegel didn't get it quite right). Hegel in turn credits Kant with the insight that consciousness is the "tremendous power of the negative." What Sartre and Hegel fail to acknowledge, is that this negativity of consciousness is of transcendental status. To assume otherwise is to fall into a Spinozan monism. It is not a fact of consciousness, but a way in which, under certain conditions, one must think of consciousness. Inasmuch as one thinks of consciousness (or knowledge) with respect to a totality of being (or objects), then consciousness is this "power of the negative," i.e., the negation of being in the concept of possibility. The exercise can be useful in dispelling the confusions and illusions which characterize other metaphysical views of things. To return to Sartre: What at first sounds like a radical claim about human reality, that it is infused with Nothingness, turns out to be a somewhat confused rehash of a very traditional argument, which, although often very illuminating, never really proved anything.

The discussions of essence and existence have a similar character. It is basically true, as a matter of logic, that whether or not something exists adds nothing to its character, or essence. (One can even grant the "precedes" as a figurative way of emphasizing the point.) Kant and Hume both built careers on this issue. When faced with philosophers who wish to unite these two categories, Kant, Hume, and Sartre are right to remind them that the two categories are in fact distinct, and that to think otherwise is to be in error.

Sartre's insistence that moral principles have no absolute grounding is also mainly a restatement of Hume's distinction between facts and values.

## SAME OLD STORY

Taken as anything other than truisms and general insights into human psychology, Sartre's doctrines slide into a Heideggerian ontological slime. Of course, Sartre's insight on the priority of existence over essence should rule out any ontology. An ontology, after all, is an essential structure of existence. However, the result of Sartre's whole analysis of the 'for-itself', 'in-itself', and so forth, is ultimately nothing other than an essential structure of existence. In making consciousness the centerpiece of his ontology, furthermore, he confers a special ontological status on the traditional metaphysical subject. In brief, Sartre's system, just like Heidegger's, constructs an entity whose possibility it supposedly excludes from the start.

Sartre's attempts at an ontological ethic of authenticity also end in a Heideggerian bog. Both philosophers try and fail to ground ethical notions of some sort in their analyses of the essential structure of existence. Sartre, at least, should have recognized that this would have violated the cardinal Humean injunction against deducing an "ought" from an "is." No apologizing, however, can remove the sense of 'badness' from Sartre's concept of 'bad faith'.

I noted and endorsed the oft-laid charge that Heidegger's ethic of authenticity is vacuous. The same can be said for Sartre's ethic. Sartre's notion of authenticity is mainly defined negatively: it is *not* bad faith. Sartre offers two possible positive interpretations of an ethic of authenticity, one of which takes the form of an imperative. Since one must make a "radical choice" about one's ethical being, Sartre says, it would be wise to guide that choice by imagining that one is making the same choice for all human beings. Now this is a transparent resurrection of Kant's categorical imperative, applied to "ways of being" rather than "maxims of action," and is clearly just as vacuous. Another interpretation clusters around a favorite Sartrean word, "engagement." This means something like: getting involved, doing something, commitment. The idea is that life is short, that by our nature we must choose our project, so it's a good idea to make this choice actively and with determination. There is a distinct echo here of Heidegger's valorization of "resoluteness" as the way in which a good existentialist bears up to the facts of life and gets on with it. As with Heidegger, this boils down to nothing. After all, exactly what can Sartre's philosophy tell us about *with what* one should become engaged? At the end of the day, the whole thing is nothing but an attitude, a pose.

Sartre, much to his credit, committed himself to the French Resistance during World War II. Heidegger, on the other hand, resolved on an engagement with the Nazis. After the war, Sartre approved and campaigned for a Marxist agenda for change. Heidegger withdrew entirely from political activity and committed himself instead to the grand political task of reshaping the history of Being. Both, presumably, were resolute about what they were doing.

## WHY SO ANXIOUS?

Most of Sartre's philosophical positions, insofar as they are true, can be expressed in the language of Hume. Perhaps a touch of Kant would help, too. Yet there is an obvious difference in tone, if nothing else, between Sartre and our two Enlightenment philosophers. In place of Hume's cheerfulness and Kant's serenity, one finds Sartrean drama, terror, elation, misery, and, above all, anxiety. Why so anxious, Jean-Paul?

Inasmuch as the logical bare bones of Sartre's philosophy are of the truistic sort described above, there is no reason why any particular sentiment should follow. One could associate the definitions of selfhood and freedom with opportunity, and feel an adrenaline rush. One could associate the clarifications of existence and essence with college lectures in the history of philosophy, and begin to yawn. Any response would be logically okay, for no particular response is logically determined.

A particular response could be justified only with respect to one's expectations—one's false expectations. If, for some reason, one had hoped to be unfree, or that essence might precede existence, then the "revelations" to the contrary might provoke a specific emotional state. In Sartre's case, the thwarted expectation may be summed up in a word: God. More precisely, it is the impossibility of a philosophical proof of the existence of God which still, strangely, bedevils Sartre. Like Nietzsche, perhaps, he took the death of God seriously, and possibly imagined it was his fault.

Does facing reality mean facing the philosophically analyzed structure of human existence? Or does it just mean facing things as they are, for you, where you are. The woman in the cafe—is her problem really exposed by philosophical analysis of the distinction between being a thing and being conscious, or does it just suffice to say that she doesn't want to admit to herself that this is a pickup because it would lower her self-esteem? And the waiter—couldn't we just accuse him of a failure of imagination, perhaps a bit of servility? There are any number of ways to describe the situations so as to learn something from them. The ontological way is obviously not the most profitable one.

## THE LATER SARTRE: MARX & NARCS

A large chunk of Sartre's philosophical writings, especially after the war, have to do with his attempt to integrate Marxism into his philosophical system. "Marxism is the unsurpassable philosophy of our time," he wrote. Though his cantankerous personality and idiosyncratic understanding of Marxism eventually resulted in his removal from the French Communist party, Sartre remained publicly committed to some form of Marxism throughout the later part of his career. Sartre's commitment to Marxism was in fact a product of his personality (an abhorrence of authority or father-figures), his professional situation (twentieth-century French intellectual-professor-journalist-writer), and historical circumstance (French Resistance and post-war French political situation). There was nothing in Sartre's philosophy, nor in any other, for that matter, which would entail belief in the strange entities at the core of Marxist metaphysics, so Sartre's conversion and the heroic volumes he wrote to justify it are probably best viewed as a case of bad faith. Indeed, his long, unquestioning support of Stalinism, a stance which he shared with much of the post-war French intelligentsia, must be reckoned as another sad episode in intellectual history. For it demonstrates clearly, and perhaps with cruel effect on the victims of those times, that even those who prize free thinking and individual responsibility may blind themselves with their own group prejudices.

Around this time, incidentally, Sartre began experimenting with hallucinogenic drugs. The combination of Marx and narcotics resulted in philosophical writings of dubious quality.

## PHILOSOPHY AT THE CAFE

One of Sartre's chief contributions to philosophy was to create an alternative image of the philosophical character. For the Greeks, a philosopher was a pallid oddball who would sit on a stone or live in a barrel or wander through the marketplace selling goods of questionable value. The Germans had developed the cult of the great professor-master. The English perfected nitpicking to a fine art. The Americans created technocrats and bureaucrats. Sartre, on behalf of the French and alienated middle-class intellectuals everywhere, created the cafe existentialist.

Reduced to a simple formula, the art of cafe existentialist can be expressed thus: (1) sit in a cafe; (2) remain seated; (3) order a cup of coffee; (4) smoke lots of cigarettes; (5) take out pen and napkin and write down a few platitudinous truths in pseudo-Germanic philosophical jargon; and (6) look scornfully on anything that strikes you as bourgeois (such as your parents).

## A Case of Indigestion? or, What Happens When You Eat Too Much Black Forest Gateau at a Parisian Cafe

"It is certain that the cafe by itself with its patrons, its tables, its booths, its mirrors, its light, its smoky atmosphere, and the sounds of voices, rattling saucers, and footsteps which fill it—the cafe is a fullness of being."[1] (This is a cool place to hang out.) My consciousness is a "thetic consciousness of *itself-drinking-from-a-glass.* The *glass-drunk-from* haunts the full glass as its possibility."[2] (Love the coffee.) The waiter is trying to realize the *being-in-itself* of being a cafe waiter. "He is imitating in his walk the inflexible stiffness of some kind of automaton while carrying his tray with the recklessness of a tightrope walker."[3] (Hope he doesn't spill the drink.) That young lady over there is taking advantage of our *"being-in-the-midst-of-the-world"* in order to glue the *"transcendence"* of the actions of her admirer to the *"facticity of the present."*[4] (That girl's a flirt. These local mating rituals are disgusting.) I am in the mode of a *"being-looked-at."*[5] (They are looking at me.) I reach for my tobacco but it turns out to be a *"to-be-elsewhere-in-my-world."*[6] (Got no cigarettes.) My cup of coffee, on the other hand, is one of those *"things-which-exist-at-a-distance-from-me."*[7] (I am not a cup of coffee.) I now surpass my *"being-there* toward the possibility of writing." I surpass my pen toward its potentiality, and surpass this potentiality toward certain future existents which are *"words-about-to-be-formed"* and the *"book-about-to-be-written."*[8] (I pick up my pen and start writing.)

SARTRE: HELL IS OTHER FRUIT

---

1. *Being and Nothingness,* trans. Hazel E. Barnes (New York: Washington Square Press, 1956), p. 41.

2. Ibid., p. 157.

3. Ibid., p. 103.

4. Ibid., pp. 99ff.

5. Ibid., p. 374.

6. Ibid., p. 449.

7. Ibid., p. 407.

8. Ibid., p. 512.

# For Continental Junkies

Surprisingly, and perhaps a little disappointingly, the philosophers and ideas which make up the body of continental philosophy may be approximately divided along national lines. Although there have been many cross-cultural encounters, there remain distinctly German and French traditions in twentieth-century philosophy. The German school of thought known as hermeneutics, led by figures like Hans-Georg Gadamer (b.1900), drew on a tradition extending from the German enlightenment to German academic philosophy of the nineteenth century. The so-called Frankfurt School of critical theory, perhaps the dominant grouping of German philosophy this century, shared the same Germanic roots, with additional emphasis on Hegel and Marx. In France, on the other hand, philosophy followed a logic of its own. Though seriously influenced by Husserl and Heidegger, Sartre worked within a very French milieu, alongside other philosophers of his generation, such as Merleau-Ponty (1908–1961) and Gabriel Marcel (1899–1973). In the post-World War II era, this assorted group of existentialists and phenomenologists gave way to the mostly French movements of thought called structuralism and post-structuralism. In this chapter I sketch the broad outlines of these two philosophical traditions, and fill in some of the gaps left by preceding and following chapters on their most prominent representatives.

## HERMENEUTICS

Friedrich Schleiermacher (literally, Veil Maker) (1768–1834), was a religious-philosophical writer of the Hegelian era who took a particular interest in questions of the interpretation and understanding of texts, especially the holy scriptures. Schleiermacher influenced Wilhelm Dilthey (1833–1911), a post-Hegelian historian who succumbed to the temptation to philosophize about history. He drew a distinction

355

between positive science (*Naturwissenschaft*) and the science of culture or humanity (*Geisteswissenschaft*, as in "spiritual science"), and argued that the two called for entirely distinct methods. Heidegger incorporated this historico-interpretive strain into his philosophy, and so contributed to the rise of the movement known as hermeneutics. Hans-Georg Gadamer is recognized as the first and chief spokesman of the movement. A more recent representative (in part at least) is Paul Ricoeur.

The key difference between positive science and human science, according to the hermeneutic tradition, is that the phenomena encountered in the latter are always the product of an agent. In order to understand their object, the human sciences must somehow "get into the heads" of those agents. That is, they must think in terms of intentions and meanings, rather than mechanical forces. How it is possible to read such things in texts is the methodological issue which defines hermeneutics. The name "hermeneutics," derived from the Greek messenger-god Hermes, means "interpretation," "expression," "translation," or, in general, "bringing to understanding." The favorite geometrical figure of hermeneutics is the circle. A hermeneutic interpretation, like an Hegelian dialectic or a Heideggerian exposition, does not set forth a series of independent truths, but elaborates an interconnected system through which one returns to the original text with enhanced understanding.

Heidegger gave the impression of radicalizing the notion of hermeneutics by extending its application from interpreting texts to the understanding of fundamental ontological structures. *Dasein*'s interpretation of itself would be the ur-circle of hermeneutic circles. As Heidegger's later thought shifted toward the idea that 'man is language', however, the focus of hermeneutics returned to textual interpretation (of man/language).

The science/culture distinction at the heart of hermeneutics is at best a reminder that knowledge is always mediated and that we need to know what filter is being used to interpret what we understand about our world. When mistaken for a profound truth about method, however, it betrays the origin of the hermeneutic movement in a quasi-Kantian mysticism. Its narrow caricature of positive science allows it to sustain the illusory promise of a science that isn't a science, a method that is not a method, all in the hopes of preserving cultural artifacts and meanings from the grubby intrusions of the facts. The relativism that comes with this promise is epitomized in Gadamer's argument to the effect that "avoiding prejudice" is a prejudice of the Enlightenment. This and other "circles" of hermeneutics are essentially mystical attempts to locate meaning within a limited whole. The original application of hermeneutic methods, not coincidentally, was to the holy scriptures. Its appeal is strongest among those who make a living interpreting the larger set of texts which constitute our cultural heritage.

## CRITICAL THEORY

Perhaps the dominant movement in German philosophy in this century has been that associated with the so-called Frankfurt School. In 1923 a number of German

Marxist intellectuals dissatisfied with the political irrelevance of the German academic world founded an institute which they hoped would support a program of philosophical and social research with practical implications. The leading figures included Max Horkheimer and Theodor Adorno. Ernst Bloch and Bertolt Brecht, two pre-war associates, left the school when they opted for East Germany upon returning from the school's wartime American exile. Horkheimer and Adorno were raised on orthodox Marxism, but became protestants of a sort. They resurrected Hegel and, in Adorno's case, Nietzsche. Although they strayed somewhat from the altar of class struggle, they remained faithful to the idea of a comprehensive critique of capitalist society, and cloaked their thought in the traditional sacerdotal robes of absurdly turgid philosoprose.

The chief result of the synthesis of Hegel and Marx was the quasi-dialectical notion of an 'immanent critique' of society. The idea, never very coherent, was that capitalist society would by its very workings generate the criteria according to which it could be criticized and superseded. This appeared to satisfy the typically Marxist demands for scientificity, on the one hand, and criticism on the other. Or, to put it in Hegelian terms, it offered a unity of theory and practice. The most famous joint work of Horkheimer and Adorno, *The Dialectic of Enlightenment* (1947), explains the initial success and ultimate failure of modern civilization as the result of "instrumental rationality." In the final analysis, the idea of an immanent critique reflects a confused attempt to conflate description and prescription. The Frankfurt School's failure to invoke some external evaluative criterion, some superior notion of rationality or whatever, according to which modernity might reasonably be judged, resulted in the dissipation of its work into a cloud of melancholy negativity.

The Frankfurt School always had an air of paradox and mediocrity around itself. It set about to politicize academia, but succeeded mainly in making politics academic. It aimed for the Marxist grail of praxis, but lost itself in obscure and esoteric theoretical speculations. It probed areas of popular culture and mass life ignored by the universities—jazz, etc.—but did so with the heavy hand of idealist jargon. In the final analysis, as with so many would-be radical political philosophers, you could be sure that they were *against* something, but you could never know if they were *for* anything.

## THE DIALECTIC OF MODERNITY

What is the modern? The modern is a tradition—that tradition which opposes reason to tradition. It is the enlightenment against superstition, convention, accepted practice, and everything that refuses the test of reason. The modern is a method of investigation—the scientific method. It is a way of understanding nature, society, and mind through experiment and observation. It is also a method of evaluation. The modern sees in every activity a function. Everything serves a purpose. The modern is a faith—in progress and, therefore, in the future. It opposes a reverence of the oldest, the ancestors, with a worship of the new, the latest, the best. The modern is an attitude. It is self-assurance, hard work, and optimism. The modern is, finally, a worldview. With respect to nature, it is mechanism—the view that events in nature are determined by physical laws and can be explained causally. With respect to human beings, it is the view that our special value resides in our capacity for reason. Indeed, that reason—and therefore humankind—is the source of value in the world.

But wait—there's more. What is modern is also—the reaction to the modern. The destruction of tradition is also the destruction of everything that had value. The pure method of reason proves impotent to devise new and lasting values to replace the old. When everything is reduced to mere function, nothing remains as an end. The world is without purpose. The material progress afforded by science seems to be accompanied by spiritual retardation. Hope becomes despair. Nature grows distant; its laws become unjust. And the human capacity for rational thought only marks us as a special kind of machine—a manipulative, acquisitive, intrusive, destructive machine. As an attitude, the modern is therefore also a sense of loss and guilt. As an intellectual movement, this attitude is some form or other of Romanticism. The Romantic appeals for a return to tradition, for the value of sentiment, for a mystical sense of unity—these appeals are, also, hopelessly modern. They are merely accretions, facades, and distractions on the structure of modernity.

In philosophy, the modern has meant, in the first instance, the destruction of the so-called old order of metaphysics. Modern philosophy begins by wiping the table clean of historical debris. The modern has raised the search for method to the top of the list for philosophical inquiry. It has fostered the expectation that philosophy might one day become truly scientific, and thus contribute to the general progress of humankind. So, modern philosophy might be summed up as a kind of scientific optimism. The modern in philosophy is also the reaction to all this. It is the attempt to rebuild on higher ground what reason has washed away. It is the attempt to retrieve history from its own errors, to reconcile the vision of an absurdly mechanistic universe with the hope that the world is also somehow spiritual, unified, and true. So, it is the attempt to recreate a metaphysics that would make good on the loss, overcome the guilt of modernity.

Enough already! By now we have defined the modern as too many things for it to mean anything at all! Modern philosophy is both metaphysics and a critique of metaphysics. Modernity itself is both functionality and dysfunctionality. Reason is both instrumental and anti-instrumental. Everywhere we find bits of the modern alongside pieces of the ancient and the bizarre. The dialectic of modernity reaches beyond any particular time period, and into the ancient philosophical space where all opposites unite. It is just a continuation of philosophy by other means. It is a critique of nothing in particular, just an attitude of disaffection and alienation. This is no dialectic; for it has no cancellation, preservation, sublimation, resolution, or ascension. It is so much more mist swirling around that unnameable hole in our consciousness.

# Jürgen Habermas

Jürgen Habermas became the master for a new generation of the Frankfurt School, though he is in some ways a post-Frankfurter. The virtue of Habermas's work is his critique of contemporary forms of irrationalism, not the least of which is that of his predecessors in the Frankfurt School. He recognized that their failure to acknowledge standards of rationality turned their critique into a kind of self-destructive nihilism. He aimed to supply the deficiency with a theory of rationality, in the form of a theory of communicative action. Unfortunately, the basic idea for a critical theory remains just as incoherent. Habermas's theory of communicative action is intended both as a description of rationality (and ultimately of capitalist civilization) and as the source of norms for a critique of capitalism. It is yet another attempt to realize the Marxist ambition of a theory which is at the same time a program.

# Sartre's Generation: Assorted Existentialists and Phenomenologists

Maurice Merleau-Ponty (1908–1961) offered a Husserlian phenomenology spiced up with Heideggerian and Sartrean existentialism. He whipped the old boy of psychologism, and tried to disclose the essence of experience, such as it is, prior to the "prejudice" of objectivity. He aimed for an ontology of "situations," by which he understood the general milieu within which any subject-object (or other) relation is made possible. He put much emphasis on the human body in describing this preconscious level of existence. He also tried the old ploy of analyzing time away into subjective relations. Professional philosophers tend to rate Merleau-Ponty more highly than Sartre, though his impact outside the universities was less significant. He lacked Sartre's literary flair, his instinct for the public sentiment, and perhaps his craving for fame. At the end of the day, Merleau-Ponty's phenomenology, like Husserl's, was a failure.

Gabriel Marcel (1889–1973) got into some arguments with Sartre, with the result that he acquired the label of existentialist. The chief interest of Marcel is that his existentialism, unlike Sartre's, was theistic. A number of other non-French theologically minded thinkers also made use of some version of existentialism. Most preferred Heidegger to Sartre. Paul Tillich (1886–1965) tried to show that the problems of existential philosophy may be solved with a bit of theology, and defined God as the "Ground of Being." Rudolf Bultman (1884–1976) deployed approaches taken from the hermeneutic tradition in an attempt to demythologize the holy scriptures and reveal their true basis in an equally Heideggerian theology of Being. This religious dimension of existentialism should come as no surprise; after all, the first existentialist, Kierkegaard, was a devout Christian. One does not have to look far for a critique of theological existentialism, which tends to reduce the content of religious belief to pure inwardness. It is a leap of faith—but not a faith in anything in particular. In this, of course, existentialism suffers from the criticism which has long been leveled at all forms of natural theology: They reduce the content of religion to empty abstraction, and so are self-defeating.

Karl Jaspers (1883–1969), was a practicing psychologist who grew unhappy with the philosophical models of human experience at work in psychology. He liked the existential notion of 'radical choice'. He was also a devout Christian. His was a typically Germanic, semi-mystical, technico-verbose, philosophico-religion through which the individual could hope to achieve salvation. Nevertheless, Jaspers's conduct during the Nazi period stands in admirable contrast to that of his colleague, Heidegger.

The literary side of existentialism is now very much a part of our cultural heritage. I mention chiefly Albert Camus. Kafka, Beckett, Ionescu, Gide, and numerous others might fit into this loose grouping. Each in his own way confronted the issues of existentialism: the loneliness of the individual in confronting death, the absurdity of the human condition, and so on.

## STRUCTURALISM, POST-STRUCTURALISM, AND ALL THAT: THE PARASOPHISTS

Post-war French philosophy officially divides in three phases. In the first, lasting through the mid-fifties, Sartre still sat in his Stalinist throne while the structuralists laid siege. Structuralism won and held sway until the late sixties, at which point post-structuralism crowned itself king of the hill. Of course, the reality is much messier than that. A variety of movements were involved, and labels for each movement rarely applied unequivocally to individuals. Most of the supposed leading figures of the structuralist movement, for example, denied that they were structuralists. Many of the same then became post-structuralists, though they continued to use the words and devices which earned them the label of structuralists in the first place.

Claude Lévi-Strauss was an anthropologist whose taste for unwarranted assertions and free association qualified him as a philosopher. His study of different cultures led him to postulate the existence of universal structures of signification within which cultural activities take place and acquire meaning. He thus seemed to offer a way of dissolving the "metaphysical subject" in a fog of intersecting matrices. The linguist Ferdinand de Saussure's (1857–1913) pioneering work in semiology, the science of systems or signs, came in handy here. Combined with Freudian psychoanalysis, the new anthropological linguistics seemed sure to reveal a primordial language in which all our thoughts and deeds are stated in advance. Post-modern French philosophers came to love this sort of stuff.

Despite the variegated nature of the French "scene," a number of features distinguish the group as a whole and account for its shape over time. The phenomena of interest are:

## GLAM-PHILOSOPHY

It all started when Henri Bergson switched to inspirational essays and acquired a cult following among the housewives of Paris. The French came to think of their leading philosophers as a cross-breed of movie stars, romantic novelists, and politicians. Sartre, by frenetically engaging in all issues of the day and by foregrounding his own personality wherever possible, really established the office of philosopher-in-chief. After Sartre, it became clear that the aim of French philosophy was not to advance human knowledge, but to celebrate unusual personalities. The history of French philosophy in this period consists of a series of names and the ineluctable genius they putatively represent. In fact, glam-philosophy unites message and messenger. What matters is the individual's intuition, the personal synthesis. Free association and mystifying parallels are the tools of the trade. Critical analysis is irrelevant. Aspiring glitterati, as Foucault would so ably demonstrate, should seek to dazzle, not to inform. They should make of their lives "a scandal," as Foucault explicitly advised. Like the movie-going public, the intellectual public thirsts for celebrities who pander to their radical sensibilities and through whom each can live vicariously in a world of heroic intercourse.

## PARASITIC PHILOSOPHY (OR, PARASOPHY)

This is the modern French version of physics envy. Philosophy, running out of things to talk about, notices that some other areas of intellectual activity, especially in the human sciences, provide fertile ground for unwarranted speculations. Anthropology, linguistics, psychoanalysis, history, Marxism, and feminism all seem to involve claims which could be construed as philosophically problematic. Philosophy branches out, "inhabits" these disciplines, overturns or deconstructs their internal systems, and by irrelevantly extrapolating from those systems to the totality of Western thought, lays claim to a universal rupture of the sort it has always cherished. I call this parasitic philosophy because it survives on irrelevant generalizations from methodological reflections on a specific scientific project to the purely reflective realm of 'theory'. Philosophy becomes the "meta-discourse" on the human sciences, that which harbors the speculative content of each science. The abbreviation to "parasophy" conveys the sense in which this represents a kind of pseudoknowledge, a hyperabstraction which mimics knowledge in the name of narcissistic mysticism. Also, it sounds a bit like "paris-sophy."

## RAD-PHILOSOPHY

The audience perceives itself as radical. It is committed to the overthrow of something, although it knows not quite what. Its outlook is essentially disaffected, adolescent, and middle-class. Marxism of some form is an article of faith. Even when events push Marxism down, it bounces back in the vague form of "post-Marxism." The most celebrated philosopher will be the one who best expresses the general trend of thought while at the same time appearing the most radical and innovative. A consequence of this rad-philosophy syndrome is what has been called *Kathedernihilismus*, or "tenured nihilism." Since this sort of philosophical radicalism is really a kind of conservatism, there is no reason why it should not institutionalize itself, and why professors who draw their salaries from the taxpayers and their prestige from their official position should not spend their time posing as the great enemies of the status quo.

## SO YOU WANT TO BE A RADICAL PHILOSOPHER?

So you want to be a radical philosopher? That means you'll have to do continental philosophy. Continental philosophy is something like a cocktail party. If you really want to party, you will need the right drink. You must be able to mix your own cocktails and detect at a glance the recipes used by others (which may not be easy, given that drinks are frequently shaken *and* stirred). Recipe-dropping is a common conversational gambit. The ingredients you will use may be divided into three groups.

*a. The Base.* This is the hard stuff. It's "bad" (in the Michael Jackson sense). Its function is very simple: to knock down consciousness, reason, and truth and set up an alternative structure for ultimate reality accessible only to you and your comrades. Three brand names dominate the market: Marx, Freud, and Nietzsche. It is not important to have read and understood the three thinkers who originally bore these names. In fact, it is positively undesirable. It would be a grave error to regard the three as representing a series of historical, psychological, and ethical findings. What belongs in the base is a representation of the historical, psychological, and ethical nature of truth. Pay attention to the nuances distinguishing each of the three. "Marx" is equivalent to "everything should be interpreted in historico-economic terms"; "Freud" equals "everything should be interpreted in psychoanalytic terms"; "Nietzsche" means "everything is interpretation."

*Helpful Hints.* If you find straight Marx too strong, use a substitute from the softer post-Marxist tradition: Walter Benjamin, Horkheimer, Adorno, Habermas, or the generic blend called "the Frankfurt School." Even if you prefer a vigorous Marx, you may want to try one of the more up-to-date varieties, as in Althusser. Avoid the vodka called "Stalin"; people have had bad experiences.

As an alternative to the three (gross-)Germans, you may want to borrow something from the linguistics and anthropology traditions. Two names to remember are Saussure, the Swiss linguist, and Lévi-Strauss, the anthropologist. The basic idea is that you knock down truth, etc., in favor of culturally specific linguistic structures. Saussure mixed with Freud produces Jacques Lacan, a potion which can induce the heady state known as "psycholinguistics."

*b. The Superstructure.* The three H's: Hegel, Husserl, and Heidegger. These are the olives, toy umbrellas, and fruit slices of the cocktail: They don't add much to the drink, but they sure make it look professional. Hegel is a general cover for Marx ("everything is just plain history") and allows one to sprinkle the drink with fancy terms like "self-othering," "self-alienation," "negativity," "moment of the dialectic," and "in-and-for itself." "Husserl" stands for either "the last of the true believers" or "there exists a technical jargon which no one quite understands but which is critical to the understanding of modern philosophy." "Heidegger" also stands for the second of these propositions, plus "let us overthrow the abstemious Western metaphysical tradition." Heideggerian accoutrements include lots of awkward noun phrases ("the ready-to-drink-ness") and other sagacious hyphenations ("being-in-the-bottom-of-the-glass"). An excess of Heidegger may cause drinkers to "go *logos.*"

*c. Flavor of the Day.* You must, at all cost, discover the trendy name(s) of the moment and throw them in the mix. The truth is never more than a few years old. Be careful to avoid those who have lost the historical moment. If you mistakenly use Herbert Marcuse (1898–1979), a soft Marxist who made a splash in the late sixties, for example, you will probably be put in a museum.

*Helpful Hints.* A handy trick is to invent a name which sounds like it might belong to a hot philosopher (e.g., Fouleuze, Bauringer) and then use it in a way which assumes that others will have heard of it. People will be impressed, and will usually oblige by agreeing that the new phenomenon is indeed profound.

Another useful tactic is to distinguish yourself with a "signature" ingredient. In all your drinks add a shot of something old, cloudy, and totally irrelevant: e.g., Bacon, Plotinus. Don't overdo it: You want to appear unique and contrarian, not antiquarian.

You may extend the trendiness of a name or movement with judicious use of the prefix "post-."

*   *   *

It may be objected: look, young man, all this is a bit polemical and superficial. Sure, continental philosophy may involve some funny attitudes, posturing, and institutions, but there must be something more to whatever it is that goes by that name. All those philosophies which make up the continental tradition, after all, represent some attempt to grasp the nature of, and to try to improve, the human condition, or something important like that. To which I reply: Okay, maybe. But I insist that there is something fundamental about much of continental philosophy which cannot be expressed in terms of its results or findings, but only in terms of its practice.

Attempts to get a handle on contemporary continental philosophy usually encounter a number of antinomies. On the one hand, continental philosophy seems to be a perfectly solitary enterprise. Unlike analytic philosophy, it does not pretend to be a collaborative, scientific project to which individuals can make anonymous contributions. On the other hand, continental philosophy is obviously a social enterprise. It proceeds through conferences, seminars, and publications, not to mention cocktail parties. More importantly, its truths are always expressed in terms of the names of others, past greats and present stars, who must constitute some kind of social framework for philosophy. On the one hand, continental philosophy seems to reject the possibility of progress in the history of philosophy. The truth speaks through the solitary geniuses; it has names like Hegel, Nietzsche, and so on. On the other hand, no other brand of philosophy has been so self-consciously historical in its outlook. On the one hand, continental philosophy is esoteric, elite, marginal, hyperreflexive, and antagonistic to the world around it. On the other hand, it seems to assume a task of global significance, one that will somehow alter the very nature of humanity, rationality, and all that.

These antinomies arise, or so I contend, from the misguided attempt to conceive of continental philosophy as goal-directed behavior. Continental philosophy, in its late-twentieth-century form, is neither a set of doctrines nor the investigative project which might produce them, although it includes varieties of both. Rather, it is a *way* of doing things. It is a *karma* which permeates one's being, a personal style. It is for this reason that it is so difficult to explain exactly what is going on over there. On the Continent, the Holy Grail, the inexpressible goal of philosophy, takes the shape of a practice. Since it is a practice only, with no external goals or references, the initiate can be led in only by a series of signs—by intonation, mood, speech patterns, and attitudes. To be sure, a catalogue of the leading names and ideas is useful. But these, too, are merely signs and way-markers, and ultimately inessential.

# Foucault

## In Need of Discipline and Punishment

I apologize to readers of the twenty-first century for including a few pages here on a figure who will be of no more than antiquarian interest. For your sakes, I will keep this brief.

## HISTORIAN?

At first glance, Michel Foucault (1926–1984) seems to have been an historian rather than a philosopher. That is how, with certain qualifications, he classified himself. His writings cover topics which would seem to merit treatment by an historian: the histories of practices associated with madness, the human sciences, penal institutions, and sexuality. As an historian, Foucault can at least be said to have been interesting and entertaining. His histories include bizarre, sometimes gruesome stories not included in stuffier works. They are all revisionist: They focus on people, activities, and events often marginalized in traditional histories (e.g., eighteenth-century grammarians), and ignore what the others regard as central (e.g., the French Revolution). They show sometimes compelling parallels and interconnections among things and practices usually kept apart by the disciplinary divisions of modern academia (e.g., philology, biology, and political economy). And they are written in the florid, sometimes melodramatic prose with which French writers evoke the teasing sensation that matters of the greatest importance are about to insinuate themselves in the reader's consciousness.

The consensus among those who I think have the right to such a judgment, however, is that Foucault was a poor historian. It seems that he valued his intuitions more highly than the facts, and was more intent on dazzling the reader with his brilliance than enlightening him with knowledge. In short, he preferred a good story, his story, to the facts. Foucault's defenders (who usually come from the study of philosophy, not history) try to impugn his attackers as uncomprehending fuddy-duddies. In desperation, they fall back on a pseudo-Nietzschean claim that everything is interpretation, so the facts don't matter anyway. The facts of the matter (or lack thereof), however, are there for anyone who chooses to look, and they tend not to support Foucault's interpretations.

It would be silly to pretend that the popular success of Foucault's work has had much to do with his accomplishments as an historian. The interest in early modern health and penal practices is just not that great, and in any case Foucault's coverage of those topics would not merit so much attention. Foucault's appeal clearly has to do with the widely held view that he represents something new in philosophy, a post-modernist perspective which reaches beyond the limits of Western thought, beyond the subject, beyond truth, beyond a shallow objectivity in the human sciences. I will argue that Foucault's supposed philosophy is nothing new. On the contrary, it is timelessly bad, perhaps even a touch primitive. The philosophical glaze Foucault lays over his historiography, by the way, is made possible by his failings as an historian. He had to be a bad historian in order to count as a philosopher. It turns out, unfortunately, that he was a poor philosopher to boot.

## ARCHAEOLOGY?

The philosophical coating with which Foucault first defines his project goes by the name of archaeology. Foucault supposes that any "discursive practice" is situated in a set of rules and conditions which make it possible, that is, which give it meaning and value, make it count as something worthwhile. This background, the conditions of the possibility of thought, Foucault identifies variously as the *"episteme"* or the *"historical a priori."* His project is to "excavate" the history of a period in order to locate and describe its controlling *episteme.* His interest in the history of science, for example, is not with specific discoveries and achievements, but with the ways of thinking which underlay the practice within which those achievements occurred. It is no surprise, then, that when allowed the luxury to choose his own professional title, Foucault somewhat turgidly dubbed himself a professor of the history of systems of thought.

Foucault's first major book, *The History of Madness* (1961), provides an example of this kind of archaeology. Though Foucault retrospectively redefined his project in a number of ways, the aim of the book remains: To present madness such as it was before it was "captured by reason." The guiding thesis is that 'reason', in the process of coming to dominate Western thought, both defined and excluded its 'other', madness. In other words, in the Middle Ages the nuts walked free, and in the early modern period they got locked up in asylums, all to the greater glory of the forces of reason. The thesis, which seems to involve an overly rosy view of the Middle Ages, can and has been questioned on empirical grounds. Philosophically speaking, however, what matters is the conception of the aim, and the rhetoric about 'reason' with which the thesis is phrased. The chief point to note is that Foucault takes for granted a complete historical idealism. There is no room for a discussion of any (putatively) objective features of madness (e.g., biological, neurological, psychological), since it is taken for granted that the phenomenon itself is an imposition by an historical period on an undifferentiated experience.

In his best and most famous book, *The Order of Things* (1966), Foucault announces that 'man' is a relatively recent creation (early nineteenth century, to be exact, sort of) and is likely to perish soon. The *episteme* gives and the *episteme* takes away, or so it would seem. Insofar as Foucault's thesis has any intelligible content, it means something simple and open to empirical challenge: that the idea of the 'human sciences' as an investigation of the object 'man' is relatively new; was possible only in a certain, broader context of science and culture; and may eventually give way to sciences organized around a different object. Foucault, as usual, wants much more than a oversimplified claim about the history of science. The object of his critique is not the object of the human sciences, but the metaphysics of humanism. His aim is to challenge the notion of subjectivity, our self-understanding as conscious, willing agents. The challenge is embedded in his method, which assumes that the *episteme*, not individuals, is the driving force in history.

Foucault's method leads him to make statements of the form "the nth century could not conceive of . . ." Of course, centuries don't think anything at all. If they did, one wonders whether claims about what they could not think would be verifiable. No matter. Presumably "century" is shorthand for "the people of a particular period." As soon as Foucault states whatever it is they could not think, however, it becomes an open question whether everyone of the time was indeed unable to think those thoughts, and, indeed whether anyone at any time ever could think those thoughts. Foucault frequently locates an assumption in one author or discourse, and then extrapolates it to an entire historical period. Even those with modest familiarity with the period of concern can usually find counterexamples of authors who or discourses that do not share the assumption.

## ARCHAEOLOGY OF ARCHAEOLOGY

The philosophical underpinning of Foucault's method is a primitive and particularly incoherent form of Kantian idealism. More specifically, it is a version of what I have described, in connection with Hegel, as strong historicism—although it lacks the sophistication of Hegelianism.

The idea of 'the historical *a priori*' may be represented in three propositions:

1. There is a structure of thought.

2. This structure takes the form of a set of concepts.

3. Every historical period has its distinct structure of thought.

The first proposition is a general endorsement of Kantian idealism, which says that our knowledge of things is limited to appearances, i.e., to that which conforms to our faculty of knowledge. (This faculty, as we have seen, may be approximated as the structure of our thought.) This kind of idealism is, as I have argued, fundamentally incoherent and leads to at least two obvious paradoxes. First, if knowledge is the knowledge of appearances, then what are the appearances of? This is the paradox embodied in Kant's unknowable 'thing-in-itself'. Second, how is it possible to think the limits of thought, without having already gone beyond them?

Foucault's work is replete with examples of both paradoxes. Consider the "madness" presented in his first book. It is, or so he writes, the product of "reason," a mere interpretation pressed upon an indifferent reality. Indeed, the point of his history is to locate the "zero point in the course of madness at which madness is an undifferentiated experience, a not yet divided experience of division itself."[1] (Huh?) In that case, what was madness before this zero point, before it got "interpreted" by reason? Just what was Foucault writing about? A history of madness would logically concern itself with how different eras and peoples have dealt with (or not) some common set of observed behaviors. But this is precisely what Foucault's concept of archaeology won't allow: There are no common observations; everything is interpretation. Interpretation of what? We might as well ask: Appearances of what? Foucault's madness ultimately refers to a thing-in-itself, and thus reveals an absurd idealism. Foucault himself sensed some difficulty, by the way, and in later editions sought to expunge the reference to a "zero point." Eliminating the zero point, however, should really entail eliminating all those exciting speculations about how reason captured madness, in which case Foucault would have to be regarded as just another historian (and perhaps a not very good one).

Foucault also replicates the old paradox of thinking beyond the limits of thought. If the 'man' in Foucault's investigation of the human sciences is a part of his (and our) own *episteme*, then how is it possible that he (and we) may conceive of it, as he seems to, as a limit? If it identifies certain presuppositions of our thought, then why can we not think about the consequences of rejecting those presuppositions? As a matter of fact, we can; and if the "metaphysical subject" stands in our way, there is nothing to stop us from shooting it dead, at least in thought. If, on the other hand, 'man' is part of a bygone *episteme*, and not his (or our) own, then how can he (or we) conceive of it at all?

The second proposition listed above, that the structure of thought takes the form of concepts, provides an illustration of how Foucault's is a primitive form of Kantianism. As Kant recognized, if there is an *a priori* form of knowledge, it would consist of judgments, not concepts. Concepts, in a sense, are all *a priori*, insofar as they refer to some thing or class of things which may (or may not) exist. It is true that Kant slipped into talk of *a priori* concepts; he had to in order to justify his belief in a given faculty of knowledge. Foucault, however, skips the insight and rushes straight to the error, and falsely imagines that thought must be limited by the concepts at its disposal in a given language or discourse.

---

1. Michel Foucault, *Madness and Civilization: A History of Insanity in the Age of Reason*, trans. Richard Howard (New York: Vintage Books, 1965), p. ix.

Foucault's third implicit proposition, that each historical period has its own structure of thought, simply multiplies the absurdities of his account. Granted, many people in any period tend to share some assumptions about the nature of things and about values. But why should we believe that all people in each period share a structure of thought? Why should an *episteme* be so perfectly synchronous? Is it really true that all Europeans from philologists to physicists to street urchins share the same thought paradigm at any given time? What mysterious force could impose itself on our thought in this way? Hegel? And who decides just when one period begins and another one ends? Why do all these Foucaltian periods take place in Europe, often near Paris? How can we account for transitions from one period to another? By what standard—what *episteme*—could one *episteme* be better than another? Or is the caloric theory of heat just as "good" as thermodynamics? In the final analysis, the idea of an 'historical *a priori*' is very simply a contradiction in terms. What is historical is by definition *a posteriori*. And what is justified by experience may be modified or refuted on the basis of some additional experience.

In representing Foucault as a Kantian, perhaps I will be taken to have demonstrated the validity of his philosophical approach. It would seem that Foucault, like the rest of us, has been captured by Western thought, that even his own thought is permeated by the dubious notion of metaphysical subjectivity. Nonsense, I say. Foucault did not err because Kant did. I have chosen Kant in this context for illustrative purposes only. Both Kant and Foucault erred, most likely for independent reasons, in a way open to all: ancient Greeks, Easterners, medieval theologians, and Martians, too, if we could find them. The irony, in Foucault's case, is that his error is of the same form as the one he ascribes to Western thought. What is wrong with the metaphysics of the subject, presumably, is that it falsely believes that the world is the creation of self-consciousness, and that therefore the totality of things can be made transparent and fully present for philosophical self-awareness. Foucault's supposed alternative, that everything is a product of history, merely substitutes history for self-consciousness, and repeats the error. I could further add that he was far from the first person to extend the error in this way, and that Hegel did a better job of it anyway.

# GENEALOGY?

Foucault defines the project of his later works on the history of penal practices and sexuality with a word borrowed from Nietzsche: genealogy. His aim, roughly speaking, is to provide a "history of the present" by tracing the origins and historical interconnections of contemporary practices. In the process he broadens his focus from the "discursive practices" of archaeology to a gamut of social, political, and economic practices. Perhaps Foucault sensed that the earlier concentration on what used to be called the history of thought involved an unhealthy prioritization of consciousness. Like Nietzsche, he seemed to think, he would shock our sensibilities by showing how the activities we assume to be virtuous began in nastiness and oppression. And he would show that what we take to be conscious acts for social improvement are in fact destructive deeds done by dastardly powers.

## GENEALOGY OF GENEALOGY

It would be pointless to regard Foucaultian genealogy as a specific method that could be lifted from Foucault's texts, as he supposedly lifted from Nietzsche's, and applied by someone else to some other topics. Genealogy is Foucault's retrospective gloss on his own work. In part it is an attempt to legitimize his work through the Nietzschean scriptures—a strategy that would have made sense only in Paris. Mainly, it is an attempt to justify the tendency in his own work to confuse description of the past with an evaluation of the present. What goes by the name of genealogy can have a consciousness-raising effect. If it presents a factually supported alternative to the mythical origin-stories from which contemporary practices in part derive legitimation, then it can presumably spur reflection on the nature and implications of those practices. It cannot, however, provide the basis for an evaluative inference concerning those practices, since that would result in a genetic fallacy. It may be shocking or dazzling to discover that, for example, early penal theories had much in common with early industrial era economic practices, but that discovery in itself has no necessary implications for the judgment of contemporary penal or industrial practices.

There is a curious feature of Foucault's practice of both archaeology and genealogy. They should be liberating. They should be expected to raise consciousness. If practices, discursive or otherwise, in our time or another, are governed by unthought presuppositions, then the articulation of those presuppositions allows us to see things more clearly. Yet Foucault refuses precisely and explicitly to claim such a liberating mission. Why? In part because in Paris this sort of liberation would go down as petit bourgeois moralizing. Mainly because his own metaphysics of anti-subjectivity forces him into this neutral pose. Eliminating prejudice, remember, is a prejudice of the Enlightenment, which supposedly got us into this mess in the first place. One *episteme* is as good as another. True, present practices are the result of oppression, the imposition of power—but then again, the idea of an agent possessing power and doing the oppressing is part of the oppressive metaphysics; power is everywhere.

## POWER MAD

One of the little myths surrounding Foucault is that he was a profound "theorist of power." I disagree. He was a fantasist of power, a mystic of power, a confounder of power, but certainly not a theorist of power. He made a few points about power, which on closer inspection turn out to be trivial, and then indulged in more of his patented ontological murmuring. Among those points: Power is not only exploitative and controlling, but also affirmative, a part of self-realization. Strictly speaking, of course, power is neither; it is simply the ability to do something, regardless of spiritual or moral consequences. Nonetheless, Foucault's point is valid as a response to those who might otherwise conceive of power in purely negative terms. Another of his insights is that power is, in a manner never exactly specified, diffuse. It is embedded in all sorts of relationships and many aspects of those relationships which might not be included in, say, some narrowly conceived project in political science. Again, if this is taken as a reminder that power can be exercised in lots of ways other than brute physical force, then fine. If, as Foucault suggests, it leads to a conception of "power without a subject," then it is hocus-pocus and intellectually empty. Finally, there is the supposed identification of power and knowledge, as in the Foucaultian formula "power/knowledge." This could just mean that knowledge is one source of power, as are vitamins, petroleum, and cruise missiles. As usual, Foucault wants more.

The long and short of it is that Foucault's pseudo-concept of 'power' is his mystical version of the Holy Grail of philosophy. Power is the inexpressible essence of Foucault's world, the undifferentiated in-itself which precedes and creates subjectivity. Power is knowledge, says the hyperintellectual Foucault, because it is what informs all consciousness. Access to power, Foucault's fantasy, is access to the supraconscious realm of ontological certitude. A nearsighted genealogy would show Foucault's power to be a descendant of Heidegger's Being; a farsighted one would trace it to Plotinus's One.

It is clear why Foucault's writings produce no coherent theory of power. A theory has to be about something; it cannot be about everything. Foucault's power *is* everything. There is nothing which possesses it, and nothing to which it may be opposed, other than power. Far from explaining anything about contemporary social and political arrangements or the like, in the final analysis, Foucault's "theory" explains nothing at all.

## THE PARASOPHIST

Foucault was the quintessential parasophist. He "inhabited" another discipline, in this case historiography, and so could claim to have gone "beyond" philosophy. In actuality, Foucault infected his chosen discipline with primeval philosophical aspirations. He refused to grasp historiography as a reasonable project with limited goals and external criteria of success. Instead, he used it as a bridge to an old and decrepit mysticism.

The travesty of the Foucault affair is that his thought should have been taken for an advanced form of philosophy, even the predestined culmination of the Western philosophical tradition. Foucault's is, if anything, a very primitive form of philosophy. His conspiratorial mysticism and dystopian fables are no more refined than those of the Gnostics. His metaphysics of power could have been a precursor to Thales' animism. His explorations of the other side of reason would not have passed logical muster among the Hellenistic philosophers. His investigation of the self was not even Buddhist. Like Heidegger, in trying to think "beyond" Western rationality, Foucault ended up with the squalid superstitions of a time "before" rationality.

The curious thing in all this is his audience. How does one explain the existence in modern times of an audience of such minimal critical standards, where shamanism can be passed off as advanced philosophy? The answer, I'm afraid, would require another genealogy—one truer to Nietzsche, perhaps.

## THE MYTH OF THE MYTH OF THE METAPHYSICAL SUBJECT: THE RETURN OF ZARATHUSTRA

After nearly a century of solitary contemplation, Zarathustra descended once again from the mountains. I still love man too much, he thought. He appeared in the marketplace, where he heard a young radical exhorting his listeners:

"Young warriors, unite! said the radical. Western thought is dominated by the belief in a metaphysical subject! We shall expose the myth of the metaphysical subject! We shall decenter the subject, throw it off its pedestal, free ourselves from the tyranny of Western rationality! The subject is just the intersection of all-powerful matrices! The subject is a myth, I say! See how we can deconstruct all claims of intentionality! What presents itself as fact obscures a hidden value judgment! Down with the fact/value distinction! Down with the primacy of consciousness! They hide the coercion of powers! Let us halt this aggression! Down with the subject!"

"Down with the subject!" the crowd chanted. They continued in the same way for some time. The radical spoke again and said all the same things. When he finished, he pointed to the statue at the center of the square and said, "Remember our great leader from long ago, Zarathustra!" And the crowd chanted, "Zarathustra! Zarathustra!"

Zarathustra was dismayed, not just because the statue did not much look like him. He rose to speak. A stunned silence spread over the crowd.

"Verily, I say unto you, beware lest a statue slay you!" Thus spake Zarathustra.

"You say that the subject is imposed upon you—by whom? Would that not be—another subject? You say you want to overthrow the subject. Does that not make you—a subject? You want to free yourselves from Western rationality because it obscures things as they really are. Are you not being—reasonable? You say you want to do away with the fact/value distinction because it purports to be a fact but is really a value. Are you not upholding the same distinction? You say that you can show how many supposed statements of fact include values, the values of the oppressors. Does this not further support the distinction? Are you not trying to free the subject from other subjects? Are you not simply using common sense?

"You speak of metaphysics and the subject as one. Has not the goal of all metaphysics been to overcome the subject? To free us from our freedom? Is not metaphysics the unity of thinking and being, of subject and object? But this is not common sense! Verily, I say unto you, those who would overthrow the metaphysical subject are the metaphysicians themselves!

"Who oppresses you? Whom do you attack? From whom would you free yourselves? Is it not yourselves? Verily, I say, beware the Self-Destructers.

"You oppose imposition in any form. And you propose violence. You abhor power and yet you love power. You seethe with resentment. Is it not the slave in you which speaks? Are you not merely crying for the whip?

"Who is your leader? Do you not recognize him? I tell you this: He is a Preacher of Death. He preaches salvation from yourselves by denial, annihilation, and nihilism. He is a willful subject, but he denies himself that. His power comes from reason, but he opposes reason. He says he is for life, but he wants a life without power, aggression, and love. He teaches you Death. I brought you the hope for the Overman. He leads you to the Underman. Where is your courage to be yourselves?

"Verily, I say unto you, the myth of the metaphysical subject is—a myth! It is a fable about our origins. It claims falsely to be a key to the totality of our experience. It is the myth of a conspiracy, a conspiracy which supposedly infects our thoughts! But the only conspiracy is the conspiracy itself! It is ourselves destroying ourselves! Verily, I say, beware the myth of the myth of the metaphysical subject!"

Thus spake Zarathustra. The crowd murmured to itself: "He is a madman; perhaps he is right; no, he is a fool"; and so on. Zarathustra lingered. He felt the despair that comes to those who would share their greatness with the many. Tomorrow, he rued, they will invent a myth of the myth of the myth of the metaphysical subject. They are still not ready for me. In sadness he turned back up the mountain.

# How the Mystical Became a Conspiracy, and the Conspiracy Became the Mystical, or How to Find God in the Overthrow of the Phallogocentric Tradition of Western Metaphysical Philosophy in 16 Easy Steps

1. Philosophy is an attempt to reproduce mystical experience.

2. Philosophy is in error.

3. The error in philosophy is universal and systematic.

4. The error in philosophy is a consequence of rationality itself.

5. Rationality itself is erroneous.

6. All our thoughts of the world must be expressed through the faulty medium of rationality.

7. There must be an error-free world existing prior to rationality.

8. Philosophy is part of a grand conspiracy to blind us to the error-free world with erroneous rationality.

9. The mystical is a conspiracy.

10. The conspiracy is universal and systematic.

11. Everything in the province of rationality, the entire known and conceivable universe, is part of the conspiracy.

12. The conspiracy lies outside rationality, for rationality is part of the conspiracy.

13. The conspiracy cannot be expressed or conceived.

14. The conspiracy can only be experienced.

15. The conspiracy alone is real and error free.

16. The conspiracy is the mystical.

# Derrida

## De Reader

Here I present a reading of the writer Jacques Derrida, who has presented us with a variety of readings from writers like Rousseau, Nietzsche, Heidegger, and others. But is not this reading a writing which originates in Derrida? Should he not share some of the credit, too? And is not Derrida the sign for a host of reading-writings, with names like Rousseau, Nietzsche, Heidegger, et al.? To repeat (how is this possible—to repeat, to iterate, to rewrite?) who is this multiple, divided, inscribed, and subscribed "I"? "I" shall place the sign "De Reader" (I ask the French translator to preserve the "English" but to pronounce it with a strong French accent: De Rrid-*aah*) like a question mark over this infinitely problematic identity—I, De Reader, De Writer, Derrida, and everyone else who cares to take part.

Here? Where here? Is it "on" Derrida, like his clothing? "On" his books, as in, on the flyleaf? Where do these words reside in a Random Access Memory? Where they come out of the laser printer? In the millions of copies in which they are published? Even when ripped out and used to wrap a sandwich? And when I am quoted, or, as is usually the case, misquoted by the organs (interesting word: as in church *organs*, or biological *organs*, or a long abbreviation for *organization*, or in French, sounding like *hors-gans*, which means something like "outside-gans"— but, if we are "here," in the text, what is this *outside?*) of the media, where is this "place" here of the reading-writing? And if I, De Reader, cite myself:

---

1. Jacques Derrida, *Of Grammatology,* trans. Gayatri Spivak (Baltimore: Johns Hopkins, 1976), p. 280.

Here I present a reading of the writer Jacques Derrida . . .
And if I cite myself citing myself:
And if I, De Reader, cite myself:

Here I present a reading of the writer Jacques Derrida . . .

does not this quotability render "our" location problematic? Indeed, this "here" could be (anyw)here, (everyw)here and (now)here. Let us place a mark over this questionable place, a "question mark," as it were, and call it (w)here(?). And let us call this (w)here(?), in deference to the spatial reference in my spatio-temporal term *differance*, as in deferral, "this-place" (to be pronounced with a strong French accent, to sound like "dis-place").

As for *when*—ah, but that would take us right to the heart of the linear conception of time, to the metaphysics of—horrible!—presence. Let us, for the *moment* put that off, displace it in time, defer . . .

Of course, I (who?) should have started with an introduction. Yet we already know each other. Yet again, my preference for false introductions is well known. Hegel (or was it I?) said, the introduction, the statement of the aim of a philosophical work, is nothing; it is the doing that counts. Otherwise, one could dispense with everything after the introduction. Perhaps the whole thing is nothing but an introduction. Anyway, where were we? (W[(h)er]e?—could this be done with hieroglyphics?)

One will expect now a representation of a method, a content, or both. The content, it will be said, is in the concept of differance, yes, with an "a." This has something to do with the deferral, displacement, difference of meaning in the signifier, with the impossibility of purely self-present meaning. That one is always already implicated in a range of 'disseminations' which compromise any intentionality. Thus that concepts of truth and reference are in general too simple and unsophisticated to capture the web of meaning, that the Western tradition has given primacy to speech over writing because the former carries the implication of self-presence, of unity of intention and meaning, while in the latter, in writing, the polysemy, the plurivocity of language precludes this autonomous self-presence. Writing is like the ambiguous Platonic *pharmakon,* meaning both remedy and poison—ah, the death of Socrates—writing is requisite of philosophical continuity, of the project, and yet the death of its spirit of self-presence.

The method—yes, we in the end must accept this unwanted name— would be deconstruction. A way of reading such that one (re)writes the text. One discovers the oppositional hierarchies which constitute the intentionality of a text, one reinscribes these oppositions in a different order of textual signification. One locates the aporias, the blind spots, where a gap emerges between what the text intends to say and what it is forced to mean. These blind spots are clustered around the margins, the occasional metaphor, the "inessential" parts of the text (inessential according to precisely those norms whose oppositional bases are the target of this deconstruction). The biggest blind spot in philosophy has been this bad attitude toward writing— a refusal to recognize the dynamic of writing, of differance, at the heart of the philosophical project. That which was repressed remains, comes to dominate. The supplement, what was secondary, becomes primary. But there is more than strategic reversal: there is the dissolution of an opposition into undecidability. The method is directed at the rupture of the "proper" configuration of author, text, and interpretation.

But this is no content, and can be no method! We can speak of them as such only under erasure. Any proposition that "deconstruction is such and such" misses the point, since it is the object of deconstruction to disrupt the third person singular position from which one could say that S is P. Deconstruction is not an operation, not a method: It is neither active nor passive. And differance is not a concept! It is neither psychological nor anthropological nor phenomenological, nor ontological. It is a performative. In writing it is different from difference, in reading aloud, it is the same. It is the home of all deferrals of meaning, and thus can have no self-identical meaning. But we cannot make writing a condition of ideality, without becoming transcendental ourselves. We cannot pronounce a single destructive proposition which is not always already part of this nasty

metaphysical tradition which it seeks to contest.

This is not a book! It takes the form of a book, sure, but only to displace that form, to begin writing anew!

I do not mean what I say. I mean, I cannot mean what I say. So I say what I do not mean.

Am I boring you? Am I boring myself? Don't stop—there must be something exciting just ahead. Let's keep spinning out the same, to see if something different comes along. Difference becomes trace. Trace becomes pharmakon. Pharmakon is a supplement. Supplement is gl. Gl is style. On and on and on.

I return to De Reader. Or is He already with me? Present or absent? Can this lonely sign, De Reader, entrap this sense of an absent-presence? Let us propose one more nonconcept, a trace which is both signifier and signified, wherein His absent-presence resides: Let us call it "Derridance." The Derridance is a kind of dance, a gentle, rhythmic motion with and around our object. A lead, an imitation: It takes two to tango. It is a d-ist-ance, and also a sameness, a union. Also, preceded with a "goo" and again pronounced with a strong French accent, it sounds a bit like "good riddance." By the way, did I mention the bit about speaking and writing? People like to hear themselves speak. Makes them think they are really present. Gosh, writing is strange. But so is dancing, come to think of it. Hey, who am I anyway?

## POSTCARDS

Dear Uncle Jacques,

Why can't you just *say* what you *mean*? Okay, so it's not always so easy to say what you mean. Maybe we can never say exactly what we mean. But is that a good reason to think we can't try? No one ever makes a perfectly round donut, but we eat them all the same.

For example, when you set two texts side by side, or one in the margins, are you trying to make a point? Does this point have something to do with intertextuality, with the "dissemination" of meaning across texts? If so, why don't you just *say* so? Or, do you think that you are *showing* something which cannot be *said*, attempting to express the inexpressible? Or, are you adopting a pedagogical strategy? Is it that your little nephew might not grasp a direct statement, and so requires a few parables?

Your devoted nephew, Matthew

---

Dear nephew Matthew,

Am I really your uncle? How is it that I, Jacques, have become this brotherly/fatherly figure, this paternal authority once displaced? It is as though we were already bound in a relationship of opposition and inclusion, of hierarchy and anarchy.

Is this really a postcard? If so, I am interested in the logic of these cards. There is, for example, the logic of the post, the logic of the address, the distance, the space in time between sending and receiving, the mediation of a courier, above all, writing. Writing! Isn't writing something very strange? If only we could speak to each other.

You ask me about my point. I looked it up in the *Littre* (*pointure*, that is, not *my* point): "(Latin punctura), sb. fem. Old synonym of prick." That I have a point, a protrusion, a "style," a prick—perhaps this appears obvious, for I am not your aunt, after all, but your male, phallogic partner-pater. What, then, is my point? Here it is. Take a look. But where here? My point is displaced, deferred. If it is on this postcard, how can it be mine? How can I present it to you without this difference?

But still, you want to expose me. How indecent! To ex-pose my point, to pose it outside, where it might get cold! You brute! You're like all the rest. Is not this point, your point, a part of the pointy tradition of Western metaphysics?

Your devoted aunt, Jacques

Dear Aunt Jacques,

I thought I asked a question. Allow me to attempt another question:

What is rigor? For I sense that, despite or because of the excesses of your self-proclaimed followers, you are unwilling to surrender a certain rigor in your activities, a certain seriousness, the insistence on a close reading, something methodical. And yet you are unwilling to commit to an explicit method—deconstruction, after all, is not a method—nor any recognized norm of argument. Which raises for me the question, can there be a private standard of rigor? I am inclined to think that rigor, method, consistency, seriousness, and all those things come from a certain submission to externality, a commitment to publicly accepted criteria, and a recognition that, while one may not always be understood in the fully present sense, the main standard of serious communication is to ensure that one is not misunderstood.

Your niece, Matthew

---

Dear niece,

You're one to talk about rigor, aren't you, Matthew, you shameless confabulator. But never mind. Let's talk—no, *write*—about rigor.

Rigor. It means firmness, erectness. True, there is a certain lack between us in this matter, as auntie and niece. Or, does it mean rigor mortis. A stiffening of the body after death. No longer inspired, our meaning becomes fixed and dead at the same time. The self-presence of a pure method, the text which establishes its own criteria for meaning, is this not a kind of textual after-life, an after-text or de-text? Have you not crucified me in a false dialogue of postcards, like what happened to poor dear Socrates? Are you not a Platonic dialogician?

What can I do in the face of such conspiracies, even from within my own family? Must I not adopt strategies of deferral, a rigor of my own, to confront the premature mortis of yours?

How can I control my own text? How can I stand before it, as though I were God?

Socrates

Dear Socrates,
    Is it possible to answer a question?

Your platonic niece

---

Dear Plato,
    Noh. (Pronounced like "no" in speech,
but oh so different in writing.)

Socrates

---

Dearest J.J./ Socrates,
    Where are you going? In place of method, you
offer strategies. Tactics. All the metaphors of military assault. I have no particular complaint about
this, nor do I intend to "deconstruct" your texts
with reference to these metaphors. I simply want to
extend the metaphors in order to ask you a question.
In these confrontations, what is the *aim* of your
strategies? Is yours the task of the overthrow of
metaphysics? If so, what would this mean? A liberation from the unthought presuppositions which blind
us (subjects) to things as they really are
(objects)? Surely not! But, then, can we speak of a
"strategy" without a goal? Is there not a reliance
on a derivative meaning of strategy as mere practice, activity, as though this secondary meaning
could stand on its own, and the putative goal of a
strategy never come into question?

The Devil's Advocate

---

Dear Satan,
    Why don't you come out to play?

God

**The Paragnostics**
(Formerly the Francophiles Anonymous Support Group)
**Stumped?**

Are you stupefied by the texts which you believe are central to modern Western thought and to academic success? Does Lacan read like incoherent rumblings from your subconscious? Unable to understand Derrida's criticisms of Husserl, because you haven't got a clue what either one is saying? Disempowered because you don't know what Foucault means by 'power'?—
**But don't want to admit it?**
Let us help. We are the survivors of paragnosis.

## THE BOTTOM LINE

To those who have not had the pleasure of perusing Derrida's work, I wish to state that all this is not quite as unfair and obscure as it may seem. Given constraints on space, one extends here to Derrida a level of courtesy comparable with that which he offers to his own readers and philosophical antagonists. And to attempt to re-express Derrida's philosophy in a language foreign to him, in the form of destructive propositions, would have been futile, according to Derrida, since it is precisely that form of expression to which he is opposed.

Still, as we are obliged to maintain some integrity in our own story, I offer a schematic translation of this Derridean experience into the terms now familiar from this history of philosophy. Despite the razzle-dazzle and fancy word-work, the insight that sustains Derrida's critique of metaphysics is old and simple. "Differance" and its tedious iterations are Derrida's way of expressing what Heidegger identified as the distinction between Being and beings, the medievals as their ontological God, the Taoists as their Unnameable, Kant as a schematism of the imagination, and each of the other philosophers in his own idiom. The criticisms of the "metaphysics of presence" boil down to the claim that there is no unity of thinking and being, no unconditional knowledge, no necessary closure of thought, and all that. When Derrida speaks of "the impossibility that a sign, the unity of signifier and signified, be produced within the plenitude of present and an absolute presence,"[2] he says nothing more than what my mama told me: You can't get something from nothing and you can't do everything all at once.

As with Heidegger, however, the illusion follows very closely on the insight. Derrida's "differance" and its offspring are the attempt to articulate precisely what his insight forbids. They are the "movement of signification" itself, the "structure of appearance," or what disappears when something appears, etc. They are the disappearance of this disappearance, and so on, in all the annoying iterations of

---

2. Derrida, *Of Grammatology*, p. 41.

hyperreflexivity. They are all supposed to occupy that nether-world which makes expression possible.

If one were to "deconstruct" Derrida's texts, probably the best place to begin would be with the metanarrative which Derrida seems unable to shake, the fairy tale which says that the false assumptions behind the work of men like Husserl somehow infect all our thoughts, and need to be overthrown in order to save the world. Despite the occasional observation about the troubling nature of origin-stories and the transcendence of "differance" over such stories, the truth is that the Derridean project, inasmuch as it is a project, makes no sense without this simple, ridiculous tale.

The mysticism inherent in Derrida's enterprise is quite easy to see. The key concepts of Derrida's work are all supposedly "inexpressible." He explicitly identifies his key nonconcepts as postulated unities of activity and passivity, subject and object, etc. Medieval theologians, Eastern mystics, and Heidegger all say the same. Derrida's refusal to speak directly and clearly, to try to show things indirectly, by example, is an attempt to capture that ineffable experience of totality. To Derrida's credit, he has grasped the consequences of the indeterminacy principle. He has recognized that the technobabble of a Husserl has no privilege over literobabble or any other kind of babble in the project of expressing the inexpressible. In this sense, his move to a "literary" form of philosophy is quite legitimate. If it is no worse than other philosophical mysticisms, however, it is also no better. Just more of the same. This presents us with the opportunity to offer another principle:

---

**The Incontinence Principle of Continental Philosophy.** If you understand it, you have misunderstood it. Whatever can be grasped conceptually, especially with Western concepts, is trivial and/or corrupt. Understanding is therefore falsification of great philosophers.

---

The principle is simply a variation on one from the Veda Upanishad (from gadzeons B.C.E.): "it is not understood by those who say they understand it. It is understood by those who say they understand it not."

So what are we to make of the method—deconstruction, or whatever its unnameable name—the method which is not a method? Since we have already come across numerous instances of such a "method," the strategy should be clear. On the one hand we can regard it as a harmless reminder: Be methodical. On the other hand, we could interpret it as another attempt to get behind method and rationality, to find the key to all methods.

On the one hand, insofar as it is meaningful, what goes by the name of deconstruction is simple analysis. Though it purports to "disrupt" the "proper relationships" among author, text, outside, intention, and so forth, in fact it does no more than rearrange the application of those concepts in specific cases. At the end of a deconstructive exercise, there is still an author and so forth, only they may not be the ones we imagined at the start. No fancy word like deconstruction is even necessary. One ought simply to analyze a text, consider the relevant evidence, and draw the appropriate conclusions.

On the other hand, insofar as it is a form of mystification, deconstruction is another manifestation of that philosophical process best exemplified in Hegel's dialectic. One ascribes to a category, idea, or text philosophical aspirations to represent the totality of things. When the category, etc., turns out to be deficient and then unable to represent the whole, as it must be, it is officially "deconstructed" and one achieves the mystical orgasm of paradoxophilia.

In a sense, deconstruction is parasophy elevated to method. It defines philosophy as the parasitic activity of demonstrating that any text, discipline, or other intellectual activity which purports (or not) to represent philosophical totality is inadequate.

DERRIDA: THE PHALLOGOCENTRIC TRADITION OF WESTERN FRUIT

## APOCALYPSE ANY DAY NOW

We are approaching "the closure of an epoch."[3] We peek through "the crevice through which the yet unnameable glimmer beyond the closure can be glimpsed."[4] We await anxiously something "under the species of the non-species, in the formless, mute, infant and terrible form of monstrosity."[5] Thus speaks Derrida.

The apocalyptic strain of Derrida's thought is the (possibly embarrassing) legacy of Heidegger's bloated sense of self-importance:

---

3. Derrida, *Of Grammatology,* p. 14.

4. Ibid., p. 25.

5. Jacques Derrida, "Structure, Sign, and Play in the Discourse of the Human Sciences," in *Writing and Difference,* trans. Alan Bass (Chicago: University of Chicago, 1978), p. 293.

We have reached the point of crisis. The edifice of Western reason is crumbling.[6]

The 'world wars' and their character of totality are already a consequence of the abandonment of being.[7]

It seems fantastic to me that anyone should have believed this kind of pseudo-historical reasoning. I leave it to the readers to form their own judgment.

## PLATO TO THE RESCUE

The apocalyptic thinking of Derrida and Heidegger has not gone unnoticed among those who otherwise have little in common with them. More optimistic thinkers have even offered what they take to be ways of avoiding doomsday. Some argue that it might be possible to rescue reason, and that what we need is more Plato. Others intone gravely that we face a choice between, say, Aristotle and Nietzsche. Still others want to go back to Kant (again). Perhaps a few hardy souls believe that Socrates has the antidote to our self-destructive afflictions.

## ECLECTICISM

Running through all sides of this world-ending discussion is a remarkable eclecticism. Heidegger and Derrida ransack the history of philosophy from the Presocratics, and bring home satchels full of the famous and the obscure. The would-be rescuers of reason likewise cling to an equally bewildering range of past thinkers and schools. All of which suggests to me a possible realignment of the usual understanding of cause and effect: Perhaps it is the unmanageable multiplicity of thinkers and philosophies, rather than the thoughts themselves, that is responsible for these apocalyptic sentiments. Overwhelmed by the bits and pieces of philosophy accumulated over centuries of diligent scholarship, a modern thinker looking for a synthesis, for some meaning in the whole of history, will naturally tend to find it in tales of a hidden conspiracy with unimaginable consequences. I will dignify this hypothesis with a principle, if I may be so bold:

---

**The Principle of Intellectual Indigestion.** Consumption of too many philosophies interferes with clear thinking, and may induce apocalyptic nightmares and/or delusions of grandeur.

---

6. Generic moron.

7. Martin Heidegger, *The Heidegger Controversy*, Richard Wolin, ed. (Cambridge, Mass.: MIT Press, 1993), p. 87.

To each his (or her) own level of digestion. Some people eat quickly, and can allow many courses to pass through their system. Others, less healthy, are stymied by the first unusual dish to cross their palate. Perhaps our fussy continental philosophers are not so different from a certain, fictional, would-be knight-errant of the early modern period, one who imagined that he had woken up too late for the glories of the medieval era—an era that was hallowed, possibly even created, in the long-winded romances of his own contemporaries—and who, overwhelmed by a host of signs from the past that exceeded his comprehension, wrote himself into his own story of global distress and redemption . . .

## THE ADVENTURES OF DON Q

*Prologue.* In a certain North American university, which I prefer not to name, resided a scholar of a type not uncommon in recent times: a sensitive soul in a neglected body, one who traded in a suburban childhood for a life wandering the Great White Way between ancient Attica and Bloomsbury, a radical born too late for the revolution, armed with hermeneutics and psychoanalytic theories, always ready to do battle with the forces of authority on behalf of the correct alternative.

The reader must know that he was a man of the *logos*—so much so that he lived only in books. Our story begins with his encounter with the writings of certain French authors. The brilliant and complicated style of these works—which, for lack of a better term, we may call works of philosophy—dazzled him, and they shone for him like the very pearls of wisdom. He thrilled over fragmentary sentences like this: "The sublimating crevice of the pointing edge of rationality ruptures." He passed sleepless nights trying to disentangle their meaning—his French was never very good—though Aristotle himself would never have unraveled or understood them, had he been resurrected and tutored in French by the whole French Academy for the purpose. He came to believe that the world was the philosophical battlefield his Parisian mentors described, that their deconstructive de-concepts were heroic knights fighting the conceptual tyranny of Western metaphysics and rationality. In short, he lost his wits. Let us not say that he went mad—for that would be a concession of defeat to rationality—but that perhaps he had reached the zero point of madness, at which it is not yet differentiated from reason. It was in this state of "a-sane" passion that he discovered his true identity as the latest and most deconstructive de-concept, Don Q, and threw himself into world-historical conflict.

He was a man of uncertain gender. In that glorious moment when he burst forth into the world as Don Q, he declared to all who would listen—mainly his graduate students—that he was a woman, and insisted that he be referred to as "she"; but it appears that this was a gesture more of solidarity with the oppressed than toward the facts of the matter. (Most observers found it impossible to accede to his pronominal preferences, and therefore I use the masculine.)

Since all the other de-concepts he had read of had their dialectical Others, he thought it appropriate that he should be accompanied into battle by a squire.

Nearby lived an impecunious doctoral candidate, Slavo Pander, who, though of hardy disposition and possessed of some rough common sense, proved susceptible to Don Q's extravagant promises of an eternal post-doc and eventually of a department of his own.

## Chapter I. The Adventure of the Colonnade

Don Q strode out of the library, Slavo Pander in tow, and, turning to the right, laid his glazed eyes on a campus building with a neoclassical facade. "We have extraordinarily good fortune, my comrade!" he exclaimed. "A moment ago we were reading about Plato's fearsome Forms, and now here they stand before us. I intend to do battle with the Forms, for it would be a great service to womankind to wipe such a wicked brood from the face of the earth."

"Huh? What Forms?" asked the perplexed Slavo.

"Those there, obviously," replied Don Q. "With their phallic shapes and quadrilateral logic and innumerable instantiations."

"Uh oh, sir Don sir," said Slavo. "Those look like Greek columns to me. Doric, I think. Or was it Corinthian?" ·

"It is quite clear," said Don Q disdainfully, "that you are inexperienced in the ways of Western metaphysics."

Ignoring Slavo's continued protestations, Don Q charged across the grassy courtyard shouting odd philosophical war cries—"down with onto-archi-theology!"—in the direction of the "cowardly" colonnade. Seeing the columns did not quiver before his relentless advance, he exulted, "See how rigorous and reifying are Plato's Forms! But I shall deconstruct them!" When he reached them he pulled out a small hammer. Slavo, who had caught up with him by now, thought the hammer was very small indeed, like the kind used to strike a tuning fork. "A gift from Nietzsche," Don Q explained over his shoulder. He began to strike one of the columns as violently as his undernourished frame would allow, and succeeded in dislodging a small cloud of white dust. Slavo smiled sheepishly at a concerned passerby, who threw him a couple of quarters. Don Q looked up with his somewhat whitened face, and it is said that this is when he acquired the sobriquet Knight of the Ivory Countenance.

After a few more blows, Don Q stood up and wiped his brow. Slavo took this as an admission of failure, but Don Q quickly corrected that misimpression. "You see how devious Platonic metaphysics is," he panted. "As I began my attack on the Platonic Forms, they turned themselves into Forms of Forms, and left behind these pillars. We have made this little clearing for the light of Being, but the Forms themselves remain concealed." Slavo sighed. "We must learn to inhabit the Forms," Don Q mused, "so that we can deconstruct them from within." Slavo started what sounded like a "But . . ." but Don Q turned without listening and marched into the building whose facade he had just defaced.

## Chapter II. The Call

As they wandered through another grassy courtyard, the dialectical duo heard a pay-phone ring. Slavo instinctively picked it up. "Who is it?" Don Q showed some interest. "Nothing." Slavo sounded disappointed. "Nothing!" exclaimed Don Q. "The Nothing is there! How is it with the Nothing?" Slavo held up the handset in despair. Don Q grabbed it and spoke into it. "I've been waiting for you to call." Silence. "Yes, yes, exactly. One must listen to the Nothing. One must listen to the murmur of the ontological continuum." Silence. "Being is the Nothing thrusting itself over the line. One must listen to Being." Silence. "It is not Man which speaks, but the Telephone." Silence. "Yes, Martin, I understand." Then the dial tone intruded on the conversation. "Damn instrumental rationality," said the exasperated Don Q, and hung up.

## Chapter III. Reflections on the Golden Age

Tired and hungry, the paralogical pair took shelter in a student common room, where they found a group of students gathered around a couple of large pepperoni and extra cheese pizzas and a few six-packs of beer. Slavo cleared his throat to get attention, but Don Q, in his usual manner, got straight to the point. "We would be grateful to integrate in your intercourse in order to discourse on the disinformation of internal forms of mastication," he said. The students understood nothing of this, so they assumed he was a professor. One of them, perhaps hopeful for some improvement in his grades, invited the two to join them. Slavo had already cracked one of the beers, and even the Don fell uncharacteristically silent as he indulged himself with a couple of slices.

Sated, Don Q looked thoughtfully at the leftover deep red pepperoni and dripping oil cooling into a viscous orange gel on the grainy landscape of golden yellow mozzarella. So began his next discourse. "Before metaphysics stained our world and divided our slices, long before the rusty-red iron age of today, perhaps as long ago as the days of the Presocratics, there was a golden age, a happy time in which everything was connected and one, as though the mountains and oceans and skies ran together in single, delicious, gooey mass of cheese. No circular pizza slicer ran through our pies, no division, no negativity traced its lines through our plenitude, no phallogocentric sausage discolored our frommagian existence. No pepperoni aporias. There were no oppositions, no 'mine' or 'thine', no 'subject' or 'object', no 'signifier' or 'signified', no 'thick crust' or 'thin crust', no 'pepperoni' or 'cheese'— just plain mozzarella. There was no need for the violence of consumption, for why should cheese eat cheese? Now, in these detestable times, alas, all is function, process, order, imposition, division, and consumption. And so it is that the *logos* calls a few to action, the scholar-warriors of tomorrow, to overturn the pizza of today, and bring humanity once again to an age of gold. Ah, nothing is so noble as the gentle camaraderie, the sisterhood of these new golden-ivory revolutionaries."

The students did not know what to make of the Don's superfluous lecture, and were perhaps mildly peeved that he had interrupted a discussion about the problems of dorm life. "So you want us to order a plain pizza?" one asked.

# ANALYTIC PHILOSOPHY

## Philosophy without a History

Something about the name of "analytic philosophy" conveys the impression that its definition ought to be more precise than is the case. To be sure, analytic philosophy is easy enough to locate: It is that tradition of philosophical activity which begins with the seminal figures of Frege, Russell, and Moore, extends through the twentieth century, and is practiced mainly, though not exclusively, in English-speaking universities. However, one has the right to expect not just an historical location, but an unambiguous account of the aims, methods, and results of analytic philosophy. The analytic tradition does indeed include many such accounts. Unfortunately, these accounts are enormously varied and mutually incompatible—so much so that any attempt to summarize just this one period of philosophical activity is as futile as the attempt to encapsulate the entire history of philosophy within a single book.

Still, someone has to do it. I will argue, however, that there is no single, principled enterprise behind the tradition of analytic philosophy. What unites the tradition is not a specific, realizable aim but a general, inchoate longing, and perhaps a few recurrent themes; not a specific, repeatable method, but a general attitude, style, and sense of propriety; no universally accepted results, but many local consequences and a few general intentions. Paradoxically, analytic philosophy is an activity which prizes clarity and self-knowledge, but which, aside from this general affirmation of its values and the appropriate behaviors, can offer no consensus on its own aims, methods, and results. The paradox, I think, demonstrates mainly that analytic philosophy retains a rightful claim to the title of philosophy, and that, contrary to the beliefs of many of its practitioners, is fundamentally a perpetuation of the whole philosophical tradition which preceded it.

# OH, TO BE PROFESSIONAL

More important in constituting analytic philosophy than any theoretical aim or research program has been the drive for professionalism. Analytic philosophy is in many ways the logical consequence of assimilating philosophy into the modern, Anglo-American university system as a secular, self-sufficient department of studies. While the path to theoretical rewards in philosophy has never been easy to find, the same is not true for the path to philosophy's institutional rewards. The modern university rewards secular professionalism. This means it favors a scientific attitude—not a specific method, like chemical analysis, but a general commitment to that most general of icons, "scientific method." It rewards the air of objectivity, such as is conveyed by technical jargon and mathematical symbols. It favors specialization: a piecemeal approach to isolated problems as part of a collaborative, impersonal project to advance knowledge. It favors those who can find for their department a specific mission. The narrower the project which one can identify and pursue in the name of philosophy, the more likely one is to lead in the field of philosophy.

There is a certain superficiality to the professionalism of analytic philosophy. The impression of professionalism remains strong at the micro-level: in specific schools, in individual presentations, in specific debates. At the macro-level, however, analytic philosophy seems as dilettantish as philosophy always has been. It picks up one project, say "the analysis of ordinary language," and then a few years later drops it like a dead dog. It promises that it is on the verge of a "final theory of meaning," then discovers a more fundamental truth in metaphysics, then swerves in the direction of a new investigation of 'mind'. It says it may be able to help the other sciences "clarify" their terms, but spends its time clarifying what it means by clarification. It sometimes seeks refuge in the claim that it is merely an "activity," not a body of knowledge—though an activity not defined by knowledge nor resulting in any knowledge seems an odd occupation for a university professor.

The source of this indeterminacy in purpose is not hard to find. For all its efforts to blend in with the other university departments, analytic philosophy has never lost the universal aspirations of all previous philosophy. Whether analytic or not, philosophy retains the distinctive ambition to lord it over all other branches of knowledge. Philosophy is to provide the general theory—whether of logic, meaning, knowledge, or mind—which would make the rest of the university possible. Perhaps philosophers sense that this universality is the key to their survival—for what is particular would be quickly seized by other scientists. Or perhaps the very idea of a "first philosophy," that there is a special kind of knowledge, different from and superior to science but not quite religion, is bound to recreate the world of the medieval theologians.

# PHILOSOPHY WITHOUT HISTORY?

It sometimes seems that analytic philosophy is philosophy without history. It models itself on those disciplines it envies, like physics, for whom the past is of merely historical interest. Analytic philosophy sets out to solve specific, timeless problems. Aristotle and company were valiant but primitive warriors who lacked the firepower conferred by modern technology.

The truth is that analytic philosophy does have a history, and, like all other philosophy, is essentially constituted by that history. Its specific projects, its various critiques, its selection of supposedly timeless questions are all, in accordance with the principle of the self-reflexivity of philosophy, responses to other philosophical positions. The unique feature of analytic philosophy is that most of its constitutive history is compressed within a few decades or years, rather than centuries. For the average analytic philosopher, modern history is one's latest series of articles, medieval history is the topic about which one wrote one's thesis a few years ago, and ancient history is what one's erstwhile thesis adviser used to rant about when reminiscing about the good old days. Anything produced in the last century, with the possible exception of the work of a remarkably prescient German, is prehistorical, to be viewed occasionally in the museum of foolish ideas.

# THE LANGUAGE MYTH

Language has been the dominant—though not the only—obsession of analytic philosophy through most of the twentieth century. A number of ideas concerning language have been more or less universal. The first and most widely accepted is the idea that most previous philosophies—usually lumped together under the term "metaphysics"—erred on account of confusions about how words could and could not be properly used. The second, related idea is that philosophy should therefore be in the business of mapping out the proper geography of words as a way of forestalling metaphysical confusions and resolving the traditional problems of philosophy. The third idea, more ambitious and controversial, is that philosophy should develop a comprehensive theory about how words mean things, and that such a theory of meaning would then supply the foundation of any legitimate philosophical knowledge—including, possibly, a new metaphysic. The fourth idea, which runs through the first three, is that the concern with language is the important and original contribution of modern analytic philosophy.

I will argue, on the contrary, that analytic philosophy has made use of certain limited insights about language and the errors of past philosophers in order to recreate a version of the old search for the Holy Grail of philosophy. There is nothing essentially new in this; at best, it is a new instance of an old pattern. There is certainly some truth in the notion that many traditional philosophers harbored confusions in and about language. It does not follow and is not true that confusions in and about language are more fundamental than any other kinds of confusions (if there be any other). Analytic philosophers generalized past philosophical errors in this way so as to support their reconception of the project of first philosophy. The key to all philosophical error, it was assumed, was also the key to all philosophical truth. In language analytic philosophers hoped to uncover the basic form of the world, the fundamental truth which would allow them to claim sovereignty over all other forms of knowledge. The cherished conceptual geographies and theories of meaning were imaginary passports to effortless and secure *a priori* knowledge, the ultimate truth about everything. Thus insight gave way to illusion.

Even the focus on language was not entirely new. Complaints about other philosophers' abuse of language has been a staple of philosophy from Plato to Hobbes to Nietzsche. The Stoics and the Sophists had made the study of language central to their activity, although with different purposes and results. Certainly, many refinements in the conceptual apparatus concerning language were new. What was new, for the most part, however, was what was false, namely, the mystification of language into the source and solution of all philosophical problems.

There is nothing new about lumping all previous philosophy together under the label of "metaphysics" and then declaring a fresh start: that is the original and characteristic act of all philosophy. Analytic philosophy is, or so I contend, just another round of the same old drink. It would be more dignified and appropriate for analytic philosophers to remedy their ignorance about the history of preanalytic philosophy and adopt a more self-conscious understanding of what they are doing.

## THE METHOD MYTH

Analytic philosophy's privileging of the investigation of language exemplifies a more general aspiration of philosophy: the search for a pure method. The aspiration is embedded in the very name of analytic philosophy, and more obviously reflects its commonality with preanalytic philosophy. The idea, which can never be stated clearly, is that reason (or something like it) must be a specific method—perhaps the method of all methods—and that the delimitation of this method is the essential task of philosophy and should provide some fundamental truths about the world—about the possibility of any method, meaning, knowledge, or something like that. The idea, as I have noted with nauseating regularity, is as coherent as the idea of a thinking which generates its own object of thought, a seeing which is identical with what it sees, or an eating which is its own food. The Holy Grail of analytic philosophy, in other words, is the mystical unity of method and content.

## THE POOR MAN'S DIALECTIC

Analytic philosophy has proved too honest for its own good. Relentless analysis has exposed one after another of its founding illusions. The characteristic movement of the analytic tradition is therefore the poor man's dialectic—the depressing downward spiral we saw in operation from Locke to Berkeley to Hume. One by one, the foundations of analytic philosophy in empiricism, logic, language, and mind have crumbled from within. Eventually, one would expect, there should be no meaningful concept on which analytic philosophy may base itself. Some practitioners have indeed given up in despair. Others have managed to perpetuate philosophy by identifying it with the ongoing act of its own self-destruction—hardly a promising strategy. It would be unwise, however, to predict the imminent demise of philosophy, analytic or otherwise. The institutional forces which created philosophy departments are still in place. More importantly, in matters of spirit, the human mind has shown itself to be endlessly inventive. Somewhere at the hyperabstract edge of a seeming contradiction, someone somewhere will espy the glimmer of an opposition worth uniting, and the philosophical herd will stampede in that direction.

## THE HOME FOR LOST CAUSES

Throughout the history of philosophy it has happened that as soon as a philosophical question becomes interesting—that is, as soon as it admits of an answer by appeal to observed evidence—it becomes the legitimate object of some activity other than philosophy, usually, a science. When alchemistry became chemistry, philosophy got stuck with the "al." When astrology became astronomy, philosophy got left with the horoscopes.

This process has accelerated under the rule of analytic philosophy. Thanks in part to its own honesty, analytic philosophy has ceded territory to logic, mathematics, linguistics, psychology, neurology, and other nascent sciences. The result is that philosophy has become, more than ever, the home for lost causes. It deals in questions that no self-respecting science would touch. So it has come to pass that the passerby may hear analytic philosophers troubling themselves over questions like, "If a married man traveled back in time and married again, should he be considered a bigamist? If so, for which marriage?" One cannot help thinking: With questions like these, who needs answers? The home for lost causes, in any case, is also a home for lost souls—a place of refuge, solitude, and complete irrelevance; a place for gazing backward, fondly, at the monastery.

# The Logical Program

# Frege

## A Logical Philosopher

Nineteenth-century developments in formal logic rendered obsolete the syllogistic logic that had reigned since Aristotle. Parallel developments in mathematics appeared to resolve paradoxes that had troubled philosophers since Zeno. To the brightest philosophical minds at the turn of the century, the new logic and mathematics seemed incompatible with the prevailing philosophical idealism—especially in its wanton, Neohegelian form. More importantly, the new philosophers now imagined that philosophical gold would be found in the hills of the new formal logic. Thus was born analytic philosophy in its first incarnation, the Logical Program. The science of logic would be the "first philosophy" of philosophy. By laying bare the logical structure of all possible thought, the new philosophers hoped, the new science would provide the absolutely certain knowledge which philosophy had always sought.

The successes in formal logic led the new philosophers to overestimate the powers of logic. Indeed, the new developments obscured for a time an old and simple truth, that while the study of the patterns of inference whose generalization and formalization are the task of formal logic may and often does lead to new knowledge, these patterns themselves are not the source (i.e., justification) of that knowledge. The goal of the Logical Program, a system of logic that would reveal fundamental truths about the nature of the world, was another version of the traditional Holy Grail of philosophy. It was inspired by a case of science-fanatacism, an excessive enthusiasm for recent advances in the sciences which gives rise to false hopes for philosophy. Analytic philosophy, it turns out, merely threw a fancy new dress of symbols and techniques on the preanalytic tradition against which it supposedly rebelled.

The figure who traditionally marks the transition from new discoveries in logic to the inception of the new, logical project for philosophy is Gottlob Frege (1848–1925).

# MR. LOGIC

Frege built on the work of his nineteenth-century predecessors, notably the logician George Boole (1815–1864), to make some important breakthroughs in formal logic. Frege developed a system of notation which was in many ways superior to the traditional subject-predicate notation of Aristotelian logic. Frege's system, which was based on the extension of traditionally mathematical concepts, like "function," to logic, was better, as he argued, because it could represent logical differences which the old notation obscured, and clear away merely apparent differences which the old notation created. This is not to say that the old logic was illogical. Frege's critique of the old logic is essentially the same as the critique of natural language he shared with the old logicians: its "grammar" imposes an identical form of expression on things of different logical status (or different forms on things of identical status) and therefore, since form and status are often psychologically hard to keep apart, *may* easily lead to logical confusions. In brief, the value of Frege's contribution to formal logic, like the value of formal logic itself, lay in the ability of his notational system to provide a more perspicuous representation of inferential patterns, and therefore support a broader and more powerful logical calculus.

The central stated aim of Frege's work was to establish the basis for mathematics in logic. Whether or not he succeeded is a matter for logical dispute. He certainly made that project seem much more plausible than had previously been imagined, and proposed some interesting logical definitions of arithmetical concepts like 'number'. In a sense, as I noted, he actually extended mathematics into logic, rather than the reverse. In fact, it is probably more accurate to say that he sought a common basis for both mathematics and logic.

# PHILOSOPHY OF MR. LOGIC

At this point, philosophical questions begin to appear on the horizon. It is one thing to make a contribution to formal logic. It is another thing altogether to make a contribution to philosophy, even if that be the philosophy of logic. Frege got carried away and veered onto philosophical territory. Worse, his philosophical diversions undermined some of his achievements in formal logic.

# ANTI-PSYCHOLOGISM

Philosophical diversions have their positive side, which typically consists in their negative critique of some other philosophical position. So it was with Frege: His philosophy of logic had some value as a refutation of psychologism, the ugly doctrine that all purported claims to *a priori* knowledge (such as logic) can be reduced to generalizations from empirical experience, i.e., from psychic events, like ideas and impressions. To his credit, Frege saw that psychologism is an incoherent doctrine: It makes mathematics and logic impossible, since if inferential patterns themselves are based on finite sense experience, no inference could ever have the character of necessity. By moving logic away from the world of subjects and predicates and closer to the world of mathematical propositions, Frege no doubt made psychologism harder to sustain. Psychologism, as we have seen, is typically a consequence of empiricism gone wild, as in the work of John Stuart Mill, though it may also infect other forms of phenomenalism and idealism, including both the Neokantianism and Neohegelianism of Frege's day.

The history of philosophy, however, provides innumerable critiques of psychologism, and equally many reasons to suspect the ultimate significance of any such critique. Kant's theoretical philosophy was essentially a critique of psychologism in its empiricist form. Hegel's critique of Kant, the backbone of his own philosophy, was an attack on Kant's psychologistic fallacies. Hegel's critics in turn complained of his cosmic form of psychologism. These are only a few examples from modern philosophy. Frege's purported "extrusion of thoughts from the mind," as one of his latter-day admirers puts it, may result only in a version of Hegel's "concrete universal." As a rule, when used for the limited purpose of clearing obstacles to an improved formal logic, the critique of psychologism probably has value; when used to support a new, comprehensive philosophical project, it is pregnant with illusions.

# A LOGICAL (?) DREAM

The positive doctrines of Frege's anti-psychologistic philosophy of logic were all designed to support his ambition for logic. Frege thought of logic as something like the geometry of his mind. He believed that logic consisted of an infinite number of lawlike propositions, and that these were essentially the laws of thought. He also believed that, as in geometry, all these laws could be deduced from a small set of axioms, which would have to be accepted on intuition. Thus, he conceived of the task of formal logic as developing the axioms of logic, axioms which would also, incidentally, account for mathematics. For Frege, then, formal logic would not merely aid thought with a superior system of notation; it would define the boundaries of thought, and in so doing reveal something fundamental about the nature of the world. There is a quasi-Platonic aspect to his philosophy of logic, in that the system of logic ultimately describes some given, real, albeit "mental" entities, the objects of logic (or, the structures of thought).

The very idea of an axiomatic logic leads to a certain paradox. To say that a system is axiomatic is to imply that the possibility exists that there should be other systems, namely, those which use a different set of axioms. For example, the existence of Euclidean geometry, which rests on one set of axioms, leaves open the possibility of non-Euclidean geometries based on alternative sets of axioms. This is possible because in geometry, at least, the axioms and theorems are things of one sort, while the rules of inference which lead from one to the other are things of an altogether different nature. In the case of an axiomatic logic, however, the rules of inference which lead from axiom to theorem are themselves the content of the axioms and theorems. So a paradox arises: It seems that there can be only one axiomatic logic. If the rules of inference are given and fixed, then only that set of axioms which justifies them will produce a self-consistent logic. If, on the other hand, an arbitrary set of rules of inference can be justified by a new set of axioms, then it is not at all clear that the resulting "logics" would still share title to that term, since they would be incompatible not just in assumptions, but also in method. In my view, the paradox arises from the attempt to discover in logic something like the laws of thought. If a logic includes the laws of thought, any other logic is unthinkable. Two logics are mutually unthinkable.

In Frege's formal language, the paradox is captured in his attempt to treat logical operators (the "nots," "ands," and "if/thens" of logic), i.e., the processes which link the propositions of logic, as just another set of functions, i.e., as additional propositions of logic. The consequent logical paradoxes, noted by Russell and, more importantly, the early Wittgenstein, need not trouble us here. At bottom, the paradox is nothing complex. It is a version of that old dilemma which accompanies any attempt to think the limits of thought. It is the result of a confusion between a system of notation and the process it denotes. As his quasi-Platonism indicates, Frege's philosophy of logic turns out to be a back door for metaphysics. So we were right to be suspicious about his anti-psychologism. Frege's logic boils down to a metaphysical thesis about entities whose reality is (in a broad, philosophical sense) psychological.

# A PHILOSOPHER OF LANGUAGE (?)

Few philosophers have gained so much in their posthumous careers as Gottlob Frege. In life he was a curmudgeonly mathematical logician whose original contributions in his field were jeopardized by his few philosophical pretensions. In death he has been exalted as the father of analytic philosophy. His apotheosis may be blamed in small part on Russell, who added to the perception of his importance by failing always to acknowledge his debts to him, but mainly on some more recent philosophers of language who, for reasons which are too complicated to explore here but have little to do with the facts, have seen fit to recast the history of (analytic) philosophy as a continuous progression from Frege's work to their own.

In the course of his logical reflections Frege developed a number of arguments and distinctions which would prove interesting for philosophers of language. For example, as part of his effort to break free from subject-predicate logic, he insisted that words have meaning only within a sentence. He also made a problematic distinction between the "sense" and the "reference" of an expression: e.g., "2 + 2" and "2 • 2" have the same reference, "4," but different senses, i.e., different ways of establishing the reference. None of this, however, was part of a project to provide a theory of meaning. Frege had no intention of wandering among the varieties of natural language in order to discover how it is that a language speaker is able to understand and form a myriad of sentences. If Frege was a philosopher only by his own pretension, he was a philosopher of language only in the dubious hindsight of a few later philosophers.

# Moore's the Merrier

In Britain, the first to stand against Neohegelianism did not rely mainly on the new logic. G. E. Moore (1873–1958), for a time the lone warrior against the Idealist hordes, drew the line on the field of common sense. Like his eighteenth century counterpart, Thomas Reid (1710–1796), he believed that the truths of common sense are far deeper and more important than any truths which might be claimed for philosophy. This simple faith made Moore's philosophy seem childlike. (It also didn't help that he probably did not understand very well the philosophies he attacked.) He believed that he had refuted traditional philosophical skepticism about the external world by saying, "here is my right hand, and here is my left hand." Unfortunately, since later philosophers were not always able to consult Moore's hands, many remained unconvinced.

Moore was also one of the grand old men of metaethics. He attempted to clarify ethical terms that had, to his mind, become muddled over centuries of use (e.g., that some action is good, bad, right, wrong, and so on).

Common sense will always have a limited purchase in philosophy, for the simple reason that common sense leaves little for philosophy to do. Moore himself acknowledged that he never ran into philosophical problems on his own, but that these were always suggested to him by some other philosopher. Ambitious philosophers, like Moore's friend Bertrand Russell, will always aspire to a specialized knowledge which respects but transcends common sense. After the logical wave in philosophy crashed on the shoals of its own rhetoric, however, Moore got a revenge of sorts. Though he would not get (and probably did not deserve) the credit, philosophy briefly returned to a minimalist, common-sensical approach in so-called ordinary language philosophy (before escaping once again to the high seas of meta-theories of language).

# Russell

## A Passion for Logic

"It remains to interpret phrases containing 'the'. These are by far the most interesting and difficult. . . ."

—Russell[1]

Bertrand Russell (1872–1970), not Frege or Moore, was the true father of analytic philosophy. He borrowed from Frege's narrow work in logic and Moore's unshakable common sense to create the first general conception of a project for analytic philosophy. More importantly, Russell set the spirit and tone of the new philosophy—an attitude and approach which would be more enduring and definitive of analytic philosophy than any of its particular, unfinished projects.

**Biofact.** A fascinating and complex individual, Russell combined extraordinary intellectual talents with priggishness, restlessness, impulsiveness, and superficiality. After a youthful fling with Neohegelianism, from which Moore rescued him, Russell developed an obsessive and almost mystical faith in the powers of logic. He aspired to philosophical perfection, the clear exposition of absolute truth, yet his enormous output of writings tracks an evershifting and incomplete set of doctrines. For a man with such a logical bent, his life was surprisingly illogical. Unlike most of his successors in analytic philosophy, at least, he was no timid bookworm. Per-

---

1. "On Denoting," in *Logic and Knowledge*, ed. R. Marsh (London: Allen & Unwin, 1956), p. 44.

haps because J. S. Mill was his intellectual godfa-
ther and he had an aristocratic title to inherit,
Russell felt personally responsible for carrying on
the great tradition of British thought and culture.
He did not shy from extending his philosophizing
from mathematical logic to the big questions and
then acting on the big answers. The bulk of his writings, in fact, lay outside the bounds of "pure" philosophy, like logic or epistemology. His vociferous
pacifism during the First World War eventually cost
him his academic job and earned him a spell in the
slammer. Reason (and perhaps a little misogyny) led
him to adopt a sexual ethic which scandalized the
public of the early twentieth century and cost him
a job offer in New York. He openly criticized all
forms of institutionalized religion. In his last
years he became the leading figure in the campaign
for nuclear disarmament.

Russell was notorious among his contemporaries for bringing out a brand new philosophy every few years. Late in life, Russell insisted that, except for his early
break from Neohegelianism, his philosophy had remained fundamentally consistent throughout his career. On matters of doctrine and debating positions, his judgment was perhaps optimistic; on matters of inspiration, aims, and method it was on
the mark. Our interest is in this fundamental philosophy, the constant and underlying features of Russell's philosophical activity.

## INSPIRATION

Like Frege, Russell was spurred to philosophy by some recent victories for knowledge: specifically, the accomplishments of certain nineteenth-century mathematicians and logicians, such as George Boole, Karl Weierstrass (1815–1857), and
Georg Cantor (1848–1918).* Philosophers from Pythagoras and Zeno to Leibniz
and Kant, as Russell noted, troubled themselves with puzzles about mathematical entities, especially those having to do with the concept of infinity, and with the
status of mathematics itself. The heroes of nineteenth-century logic solved the
puzzles. They answered Zeno's paradoxes, did away with Leibniz's metaphysics
based on infinitesimals, refuted Kant's claim for the synthetic *a priori* status of
mathematics, and, in general, cleared the Pythagorean air of mysticism which had

---

*Boole showed that logic could be handled with something very much like a mathematical for-
malism. Weierstrass refined the concepts of function theory, and Cantor developed mathematical tools
for analyzing infinities.

hitherto characterized the relationship between philosophy and mathematics. For Russell, all this meant much more than exposing the false pretensions of a few old philosophers; it promised a whole new way of doing philosophy. He believed that the entire philosophy of Leibniz's was the consequence of certain mistaken assumptions about the nature of logic, and was nullified by recent developments. Further refinements in the logic of mathematics, and logic itself, he imagined, would resolve most, if not all, philosophical problems, and provide the key to an absolutely certain knowledge.

## PRESUPPOSITIONS

Like many of his contemporaries—but unlike the Hegelians—Russell admired the natural sciences. He tended to regard modern science as the model of clear expression and true knowledge about the world—though he was probably not quite as rabid on the point as the logical positivists would be. He also had a healthy, though qualified, respect for common sense. He believed that common sense was right about most things, but could be very wrong in both philosophy and science. In a way, Russell thought of philosophy as a kind of synthesis of common sense and scientific knowledge.

The tradition of British empiricism, from Locke to Mill, remained alive in Russell. Although he sought to avoid the pitfalls of psychologism, he frequently indulged in empiricist sense talk, and always regarded "sense data" as the ultimate source of all knowledge.

## AIMS AND METHODS

Russell's consistent philosophical aim, stated in general terms, was to lay bare the logical structure of the world. Or, to put it in more positive terms, to reconstruct knowledge—beginning with, but not limited to, mathematics—on logical foundations. In his earlier work (the first few essays of *Logic and Knowledge*, for example), this meant uncovering the basic logical syntax of propositions. In his later work, it meant describing the logical structure of facts, i.e., that which makes propositions true. Throughout he held out the hope for a grand theory, one that, reaching far beyond the limitations of common sense, would provide a logical basis for determining in advance which propositions could and which could not count as true. Shadowing the whole project was the distant, not always acknowledged hope for what Leibniz would have called a *characteristica universalis*, a new, logically perfect language in which every symbol would have a definite and unique meaning and rules of syntax which would make transparent the fallacies behind all (or most) philosophical problems.

The method appropriate to such a project is what Russell often called "logical analysis." To analyze a proposition logically is to lay bare the structure of its parts, the relationships of which they do and do not admit.

Perhaps the fundamental aspect of Russell's method, and the most important for subsequent analytic philosophy, was the idea that philosophical problems, when approached from a logical point of view, could be solved one by one. In this Russell self-consciously opposed the Hegelians, who took the more traditional view that philosophical truth was a totality, and could be represented only in a system whose truths were interdependent. Russell's "piece-meal-ism," as it were, would prove extremely useful in the creation of the new profession of analytic philosophy as a collaborative, broad-front engagement with specific, timeless philosophical problems.

Another enduring feature of Russell's method was the style of writing. His was the virtual antithesis of the Heideggerian monstrosity: He strove to make himself understood, even if that meant risking refutation. He established a sense of professional ethics which has served analytic philosophy well to the present. (Perhaps he supported an overestimation of the ability of clear expression to ensure clear thinking. Anyone who reads his essay "On Denoting," for example, must conclude that behind the seemingly clear prose and oh-so-logical symbols lurk some very troubled and perhaps incomprehensible thoughts. Mastering analytic philosophy, as I have said before, often means learning how to express some opaque and impossible ideas in seemingly transparent language.)

## LOGICAL ATOMISM

The doctrine—rather, the family of related but constantly changing doctrines— with which Russell is most commonly identified is "logical atomism." The basic idea is that the world consists of a whole bunch of simple facts (logical atoms) and that propositions are true insofar as they express such facts or some "molecular" combination of such facts.

Logical atomism fits in well with Russell's ideas about method. The point of logical analysis is to break a proposition up into its constituents. Logical atomism guarantees that there are such ultimate constituents, viz., the propositions corresponding to individual atoms. If the atoms are what make propositions true, furthermore, then propositions can be true in isolation from other propositions. This vindicates the piecemeal approach.

Logical atomism so well expresses Russell's method, in fact, that one wonders what its status might be: Is it a finding about the structure of the world resulting from Russell's investigations, or a presupposition about the structure of the world required in order to begin such an investigation? Further cause for concern is this: Russell never clearly describes the atoms. He hints that they are something like sense data—perhaps like "red patch here now"—but admits that there is no way to be precise about this. He further concedes that, in violation of one of his own maxims for scientific philosophizing, the atoms are essentially inferred. They are necessary, presumably, on the hypothesis that one wants to take seriously the project of logical analysis.

The analysis of Russell's various versions of logical atomism could go on for a long while. At the end of the day, I would venture, his doctrine instantiates an old pattern in philosophy, namely, the confusion between the premises of an investigation and its conclusions. In deductive logic, of course, it is quite normal that the conclusions should be contained in the premises. But an investigative project, if it is to discover anything, ought to do more than merely analyze what it assumes *qua* investigation.

The distinction between facts and propositions in Russell's theory gave rise to a natural speculation: How do the propositions connect with the facts? In this Russell recognized an essentially epistemological question, and diverted his attention in later works to some traditional epistemological theorizing. So, just when we thought logic was to crown itself the queen of the philosophical sciences, epistemology slips onto the throne. But this seems only fair: How could Russell *know* about logical atoms without first knowing what he could know?

## RUSSELL'S PARADOX

Suppose there are classes of things, such as the class of books, or the class of even numbers. Some classes are not members of themselves, some are: The class of books is not a book, but the class of classes is a class. Now, consider the class of classes that are not members of themselves. Is it a member of itself? If it is a member of itself, then it is not a member of the class of classes that are not members of themselves, so it is not a member of itself. If it is not a member of itself, it is a member of the class of classes that are not members of themselves, so it is a member of itself. Oh dear.

For Russell, this paradox blew a hole in much of Frege's as well as his own logic, both of which, it turns out, relied on class theory. In order to defuse the crisis, Russell invented a "theory of types," according to which claims about all the members of some collection cannot themselves be members of the same collection but must, if they denote anything, refer to a different or higher 'type' of thing. Whether this theory solves the problem or merely renames it is a matter for logical dispute.

Russell's paradox, as he saw, is a paradox of reflexivity. It arises in cases where a proposition (or whatever) purports in some way to refer to or account for itself. It touches obliquely, I think, on a paradox that informs all philosophy. Philosophy has always been the sort of activity which purports to supply its own grounds, to affirm itself unconditionally, on purely internal grounds. It is for this reason that philosophy has frequently tried to "overcome" or go beyond reflexivity—e.g., to deconstruct subjectivity, to reduce freedom to necessity, to locate the limits of thought, to juggle the juggler, and so forth. What Russell glimpsed, in his honest, nit-picking way, was the paradox involved in attempting to close the circle of philosophy, to create a final, self-sustaining account of the truth about everything.

## Philosophical Conversations

**Biofact.** Legend and mystery surround the fabled encounter between the middle-aged Russell and the young Ludwig Wittgenstein. In 1911 Wittgenstein was a twenty-two-year-old student of aeronautical engineering at Manchester when he ran into some perplexing philosophical puzzles concerning the foundations of mathematics. On a recommendation from Frege, he went to Cambridge to study under the famous Russell. For two years he besieged Russell with questions, arguments, and obnoxious challenges. He went from being Russell's brightest pupil and protégé to being his teacher. Let us now imagine how it was when these two great minds met.

**Biofiction.** Russell knew from the precise and insistent blows who was knocking on his door. God, he thought, or Whoever You Are, what trials You impose on me. Deliver me from my only disciple. No, I know, it is my Duty. I must have someone to carry on the Work. At least he is a Genius, my little German friend. Otherwise . . .

He got up to open the door, but Wittgenstein had already shown himself in. "How lovely to see you, Ludwig," Russell said.

Wittgenstein was flustered, disheveled, agitated. Glaring at Russell, he thought to himself, he is a rotten traitor to his own greatness in logic. "You are a rotten traitor to your own greatness in logic," he blurted out in rage.

"Oh dear," Russell replied with the dignity of one who has suffered many intellectual wounds, "What have I—"

"You have polluted the purity of logic!" Wittgenstein interrupted. "How dare you create all these silly 'types'!" The last word came off Wittgenstein's tongue reluctantly, causing visible disgust. "Shall we have a new logic for each one of these 'types'?" he asked sarcastically. "Why not just multiply the laws of logic endlessly? It is all nonsense! How can you put such rubbish out into the world! You have let me down." He suddenly looked terribly depressed.

"I admit it may not be a perfect solution, Ludwig," Russell said soothingly, hoping to calm his pupil down. "But I had to do something about my paradox. Perhaps it's just a temporary solution, a sort of patchwork, but I hope someday I—or perhaps you—will make it better."

"Logic does not permit imperfection," said Wittgenstein sanctimoniously. "Everything must fit. Logic must join the world without seams. No patchwork! And none of your horrible creations, all these functions and principles and 'types'!"

Russell, not quite sure where Wittgenstein was going, attempted a subtle shift in topic. "Look, Ludwig, I don't see how we can agree on anything until you agree that there is no hippopotamus in this room. That's what it all comes down to, doesn't it?" Deep down, though, he sensed that Wittgenstein was right about something, whatever it was.

"No, no!" Wittgenstein ignored Russell altogether. "We must account for these 'types' within our symbolism. Yes, the 'types' will vanish once we have the correct symbols. For that we must understand the essence of symbolism. Do you see?"

"Well, I'm not sure that I do." Russell fell into a more comfortable, pedantic mode. "I don't see why the laws of logic should alter to suit whatever symbols we use to represent them."

Wittgenstein let out a shriek. "I cannot be understood! It is my fault! I am a miserable human being. I am such a sinner. If only you knew my sins."

Concerned now that his disciple would really lose his mind, Russell tried to be as conciliatory as possible. "Perhaps you should read Victor Hugo, Ludwig. You know, to see how other peoples from other cultures have surmounted their difficulties, to get away from logic for a while."

"Horrors! I am nearing fundamental breakthroughs in the most important field there is, and you would have me squander my years on French rot! How dare you!" Russell looked a little hurt now, and Wittgenstein changed moods again. "Oh, forgive me, Bertie!

I know I am difficult. Oh, please, tell me you will
still respect me in the morning."

   The conversation did indeed continue well into
the morning. Our heroes covered many more subtle
intricacies of logic, and soon came very close to
solving many of the world's problems.

# Early Wittgenstein

## *Intractable*

L udwig Wittgenstein's (1889–1952) early work, as expressed in his notes and in the *Tractatus Logico-Philosophicus* of 1918, is in many respects the culmination of the Logical Program of analytic philosophy. It both criticizes and extends the earlier work of Frege and Russell, and inspires and even surpasses the doctrines of logical positivism of the 1930s. Most importantly, it demonstrates clearly that (and how) early analytic philosophy is essentially a continuation of the preanalytic tradition of philosophy.

Though it is a tract on logic, Wittgenstein's first (and in his lifetime only) published book has had surprisingly little influence on formal logic. The reason for this is clear: The issues Wittgenstein addresses belong to the philosophy of logic. Here, as might be expected, he makes some interesting and valid arguments against other philosophical positions, though in the end he succumbs to some of the same errors he criticizes.

## THE NEWEST LOGIC

Within the narrow compass of early twentieth century philosophy of logic, Wittgenstein's work looks like a critique—a powerful one—of the work of Frege and Russell. While we will once again have to pass over the details, the motivating insight of Wittgenstein's critique is easy enough to state. What he laid against Frege and Russell was a rigorous and intuitive insistence on the fundamentality of the Humean 'fork', the distinction between 'reason' (or 'logic') and 'fact'. (I say "intuitive" because it is unlikely that Wittgenstein was well versed in the works of Hume.)

Frege and Russell, as already noted, harbored a sort of Platonism. They imagined that propositions of logic were like laws of thought, and described the behavior of certain real, logical entities. In other words, they treated logic as a science of sorts, capable of generating facts or fact-like statements. The classic instance of this, for Wittgenstein, was Frege's attempt to represent logical operators ("and," "or," etc.) as material functions. If logical operators were material functions, Wittgenstein reasoned, they would reveal facts about the world. But this would mean that pure thought could arrive at some knowledge without ever venturing out into the world—something Wittgenstein's intuitive Humeanism would not allow.

The philosophical conception of logic Wittgenstein develops out of his critique has a number of features worth mentioning here.

# THE VANISHING LOGIC

*The Picture Theory.* Wittgenstein paints a "picture theory of logic." The world consists of facts, he says. Meaningful propositions represent possible facts. They do so by providing a "picture" of things (i.e., of a state of affairs). The picture exhibits the relationships among a set of objects. The relationships in the picture represent the fact. The symbols which make up a proposition also stand in a certain relationship to each other. Indeed, the crux of Wittgenstein's theory is this: It is only because of the fact of the relationships among symbols in a proposition that the proposition can represent a fact. To put it cryptically: Only facts can represent facts. Logic is the "form" of the relationships expressed in a proposition. Logic is to the proposition as the "pictorial form" is to the picture. That is, logic is in some way built into our propositions, but is not something which is directly represented in those propositions. It can be *shown*, but not *said*, as Wittgenstein says.

*Tautologism.* Wittgenstein grants a special role in logic to a family of propositions known as tautologies. Tautologies are true no matter what is the case in the world. Like Kant's analytic judgments, they are true in virtue of the definitions of their terms. In a sense, tautologies are not propositions at all, for they represent nothing in particular, they are devoid of factual content, i.e., they picture no state of affairs. The function of tautologies is to clarify the meanings of symbols. Since propositions are essentially constituted by symbols, what tautologies display, in their nonrepresentative way, is the essence of the proposition. They bring logic into relief, as it were.

*The Democracy of Tautologies.* Wittgenstein's tautologism rules out Frege's dream for an axiomatic system of logic. The axioms at the base of an axiomatic theory are implicitly propositions about possible states of affairs. Since they are not tautologies, so far as Wittgenstein is concerned, they could not represent the essence of logic. Furthermore, there is no natural ordering of tautologies. A tautology follows from nothing, for it should be self-evident, and it leads to nothing, since its truth implies nothing about any possible state of affairs. In other words, Wittgenstein's idea for a system of logic is a kind of democracy of tautologies. (Of course, it may be that some tautologies are more equal than others: "It is raining or it is not raining" clearly has less purchase on the intellect than "*p* or not *p*"; the truth of the former, however, is presumably not inferred from the truth of the latter.)

*The Essence of Hume.* Tautologism springs from Wittgenstein's intuitive Humeanism. In rejecting nontautologous propositions of logic, Wittgenstein effectively offers a latter-day Humean response to Kant's synthetic *a priori* judgments, which would ultimately represent a form of absolutely true factual knowledge derived from pure logic. Thus, it should be no surprise to see Wittgenstein drawing the distinctly Humean conclusions that the only necessity is logical necessity, that the principle of induction can never be deductively justified, and that claims to knowledge about the totality of things can never be supported.

## MR. LOGIC, PART II

In the final analysis, the theory described here belongs to the philosophy of logic, and not logic itself (in the sense of formal logic). It offers no unique criteria with which to select among possible systems of notation in formal logic. It does, however, provide a critical reminder against possible confusions about the status of logical truths (such as beset Frege). It is a way of ensuring, for example, that the similarity between logical and factual propositions does not result in treating one in the same way as the other (or in treating logic as a set of propositions at all).

## MORE ON PROPOSITIONS

*The Essence of the Proposition.* Wittgenstein carries his inquiry into the question about the basic form of the proposition. The general form of a proposition, he concludes, is: "This is how things stand."

*Elementary Propositions.* Another feature of Wittgenstein's philosophy of logic, whose intimate connection with the rest of his ideas on logic is harder to explain, is the concept of elementary propositions. Like Russell's atomic facts, elementary propositions are the bedrock of analysis. They consist of simple, unanalyzable names, have definite and unique meanings, and are mutually independent. All other propositions are essentially combinations of elementary propositions. What drives Wittgenstein to postulate such homely creatures is probably a need to ensure complete determinacy of meaning. Without elementary propositions, one fears, the truth (or falsity) of any given proposition, and hence its sense, may not be determined without reference to some other (nonelementary) proposition. A democracy of propositions? Horrible.

## THE LOGIC OF MYSTICISM

Wittgenstein's early philosophy is frankly mystical. More importantly, I contend, this mysticism is fundamentally embedded in his philosophy of logic. Wittgenstein defines the mystical as the understanding that the world is a "limited whole," a view that is consistent with our discussion above in connection with the Eastern philosophies. The aim of his philosophy is to circumscribe and manifest this whole. His critiques of limits of thought and laws of thought represent efforts to preserve the whole against the intrusions of other philosophers. Wittgenstein rejects limits of thought because they would leave open the possibility of some other kind of thought, something outside the whole. He recognizes no laws because any such laws would represent a structure, to be defined in opposition with some other possible structure, and so, too, would divide the whole. Yet the mystical experience consists not just in preserving the whole, but in grasping it and expressing it: It requires some set of limits of its own. These Wittgenstein supplies. The chief innovation in his philosophy is to represent these mystical limits, boundaries without exteriors, as limits of *sense* rather than limits of thought.

Recall that the sense of a factual proposition, according to Wittgenstein, is the possible (true or false) state of affairs it represents. It has such a sense only insofar as it makes use of a symbolism in a correct manner, that is, according to the logical form which is the essence of a symbolism. Whatever looks like a proposition but misuses symbols is therefore nonsense. In between sense and nonsense stand the tautologous propositions of logic. On the one hand, the tautologous propositions of logic are senseless, for they refer to no particular state of affairs. On the other hand, they are not quite nonsense, for they do not violate the rules of symbolism. Although they cannot "say" anything, they do "show" something, namely, the essential structure of logic. So, the empty propositions of logic mark the limits of sense, or, to put it in Wittgenstein's more dramatic terms, they mark the limits of language. Now, the limits of my language, Wittgenstein asserts, "are the limits of my world." The leap from language to world is justified precisely because the limits of sense are defined in terms of logic. In logical space, everything that is possible, is. The structure revealed by tautologies is not a set of arbitrary conventions about language, but the structure of possibility itself. In setting out the logical limits of sense, as he promises to do in his *Tractatus*, Wittgenstein maps out the edges of everything that is possible in the world, and so brings himself (and us, if we are so disposed) to mystical experience of totality, to the understanding of the world as a limited whole.

True mysticism, of course, requires an understanding that, although the totality may be experienced, it cannot be adequately expressed. Wittgenstein's early philosophy of logic embodies this encounter with the 'inexpressible' in mysticism. His repeated claim that there are some things which can be shown but not said is one instance of this inexpressibility. More generally, the very idea of the limits of sense refers in general to the inexpressible. What lies just beyond the bounds of what may be sensibly expressed is not pure nonsense, but the totality of things.

Even Wittgenstein's own philosophy, as he himself insists, is inexpressible non-sense insofar as it marks out the limits of the world. In the last sections of the *Trac-tatus* he warns that his work should be thrown away, like a ladder, once it has been understood. Like Heraclitus, who could only indicate the truth, or like a guru whose path to enlightenment traverses seeming irrelevancies like beatings and building rock gardens, Wittgenstein reproduces the classic paradox of mysticism, a method that cannot be understood until its result has been achieved.

Inconveniently located on the other side of the limits of sense, by the way, are ethics and aesthetics and all questions of value. In a certain way, this is a conse-quence of Wittgenstein's adherence to the other side of Hume's (pitch)fork, the fact/value distinction. Insofar as he defines sense in the narrow terms mentioned above, as reference to a possible state of affairs, then value judgments don't quite make the cut. Of course, this does not mean that they are an outright abuse of sym-bols. Rather, like tautologies, they are a kind of sensible nonsense. However, Wittgenstein's treatment of ethics and aesthetics is more a part of his mystical agenda than the result of an intuitive logical distinction. As with many traditional mysticisms, his philosophy concentrates all value in a single affirmation, and locates that affirmation in the realm of the inexpressible.

## THE VANISHING LOGICAL PROGRAM

The idea that philosophy is in the business of delimiting the bounds of sense—as opposed to, say, the bounds of thought or knowledge—originates in a philosophy of logic, as we have seen. Moreover, I think, it is a possible culmination of the Logi-cal Program. Frege and Russell had sought the fundamental axioms and principles of thought, and yet never seemed satisfied that they had found them. The Holy Grail for them was always, in essence, a search. In effect, Wittgenstein locates those axioms and principles in the hidden fabric of our world. The Holy Grail is, for him, primarily an experience. That these new axioms and principles are, in principle, inexpressible demonstrates only that the original Logical Program was indeed philosophical in its aspirations, that it really sought the truth about every-thing. Wittgenstein's critique of the Logical Program is in fact a transfiguration, a dialectical return of that program to its own origins and destiny.

## RETURN TO THE VAST AND ETERNAL OCEAN OF EXISTENCE

It is no doubt due in some significant measure to the early Wittgenstein that ana-lytic philosophy took up the idea that it should become a custodian of sense. Yet it would be a mistake to make too much out of this chain of events. At our present level of abstraction, Wittgenstein need play no more of an active role in this devel-opment than any of a number of other philosophers in our long history.

For example, it is easy to sketch out that, while the motivating insight of Wittgenstein's early work is essentially Humean, his solutions follow a more obviously Kantian pattern. Like Kant, Wittgenstein rescues a certain kind of unconditioned knowledge for philosophy by pushing to its extreme the Humean insight that all knowledge is conditioned. To put the matter in more logical terms, he locates the limits of possibility in possibility itself, i.e., he circumscribes what is necessary in the possibility of possibility. In Aristotelian terms, he finds an actuality at the bottom of all potentiality. As with Kant, the consolation is thin, perhaps vacuous. Philosophy retains its grip on the totality of things, its privileged relationship with the Holy Grail, but at the price of surrendering any possibility of meaningful discussion or understanding of the totality. It can only gaze in stupefied wonder at the inexpressible essence of things. Philosophy simultaneously guarantees and refrains from touching the world of value, ethics, and aesthetics. Schmooalistic mono-dualism reigns again, as the world first divides into worthless sense and meaningful nonsense, then reunites in a limited whole.

Wittgenstein did read Schopenhauer, but not (much) Kant. The question of influence, however, seems out of place to me. Russell and Frege were his only real influences, for they determined the vocabulary within which he would express his mystical disposition, which would probably have been the same with or without knowledge the earlier German philosophers. Nonetheless, Wittgenstein's early philosophy makes clear that the Logical Program of early analytic philosophy, insofar as it left the pedestrian fields of formal logic and aspired to a philosophy of logic, was a continuation of philosophy in its traditional form.

---

**Biofact.** Wittgenstein quit philosophy after finishing the *Tractatus.* Perhaps he meant what he said in his preface, that he had solved all the problems of philosophy, or perhaps he needed a break from transcendental thinking. For a few years he became a primary school teacher in an Austrian village. Let us go back to that classroom.

---

**Biofiction.** (In a classroom, somewhere in the Vienna woods.)

"This is my daddy's hat," the youngster began nervously. "He is a fireman. This is a fireman's hat."

"No, No! You fool!" said the teacher, Mr. Wittgenstein. "How can you say such things?"

The boy started to whimper. "But Mr. Wittgenstein, you said this was 'show and tell' time."

"Of course, but what *can* be shown *cannot* told. Don't you realize? This is the most elementary point of logic! I do not understand how you can even be in school if you do not understand this."

Now the boy was crying, and the other kids began to kick up a fuss. Word spread quickly from the school to the rest of the small village. A burly fireman appeared at the classroom door.

Soon thereafter, Mr. Wittgenstein decided to return to philosophy.

# The Logical Positivists

## *From Sense to Nonsense*

## LINEAGE

Logical positivism was a self-consciously hard-nosed and skeptical school of thought which arose in the 1920s and 1930s first among a few scientifically trained German and Austrian thinkers—chiefly Moritz Schlick (1882–1936) and the so-called Vienna Circle—and then found a natural home in Britain, in philosophers like A. J. Ayer. It is sometimes, more appropriately, known as "logical empiricism," though I will stick with positivism.

As its label suggests, logical positivism drew to some extent on the tradition of positivism, whose first representative, the unusual August Comte, had by now gathered in his wake a number of philosophers of science, like Jules-Henri Raymond Poincaré (1859–1912), and notable scientists, like Ernst Mach (1838–1916). The positivists believed themselves heirs to a tradition dating at least from Francis Bacon, a tradition of rigorous scientific commitment to observation and empirical proof, to the exclusion of anything soft, mystical, romantic—in brief, metaphysics.

The real inspiration, however, came from the combination of this empiricist tradition with the logical advances of Frege, Russell, and Wittgenstein. The new logic, the logical positivists believed, laid the foundation for a new, more rigorous and coherent empiricism. By clarifying the nature of logic, Wittgenstein, in particular, showed how empiricism could account for the necessary truths of logic and mathematics without straying into the forbidden territory of Kantian synthetic *a priori* knowledge.

In making their case for a new logical empiricism, however, the logical positivists relied excessively on a problematic distinction between sense and nonsense. The resulting conventionalism in their understanding of logic marked the beginning of the end of the Logical Program, and paved the way for the Language Program in analytic philosophy.

416

# Ex-Humed and De-Kanted

Whatever their immediate sources and pet peeves, the logical positivists derived their strength and inspiration from the noble David Hume. To a lesser extent, they also borrowed from a modified, minimalist Kant.

The logical positivists borrowed from Hume the simple distinction between reason and fact, though they dressed the distinction in terms inherited from Kant and the logicians. What Hume called reason—or, more quaintly, the "comparison of ideas"—was to be called *logic*. Logic is simply the rules of inference, how you figure out what a particular proposition entails. Logical propositions are one and all *a priori*, which is to say that they can be known to be true or false independently of any experience or observational confirmation. The conclusions reached by logical propositions are *necessary*—there can be no doubt about them. Logical propositions are all *analytic*, that is, once they have been properly understood, their truth (or falsity) follows from the definitions of the terms in the proposition. In sum, as Wittgenstein argued, logical propositions are *tautologies*—which is a nice way of saying that they are empty of any factual content. What Hume had called "matters of fact" the logical positivists would describe in a corresponding range of terms. Facts are put forward in synthetic propositions, that is, propositions which combine independent meanings and so cannot be judged true or false in virtue of the definitions of terms. Contrary to Kant, the logical positivists would argue, the truth or falsity of such propositions can be determined only through *empirical* observation or experience. In other words, synthetic judgments are by definition *a posteriori*. Since all experience boils down to what the logical positivists call "sense-contents," the truth of empirical propositions also ultimately depends on these sense-contents.

The upshot of this is, as with Hume, that there is very little for philosophy to do, and much that it has done wrong in the past. Empirical knowledge belongs entirely to science. Through observation and experiment, science has the right to propose and verify any and all possible empirical propositions. So that leaves logic for philosophy. But logic consists of nothing but tautologies. There is nothing for philosophy to 'know'. At best, philosophy can only clarify concepts and test the logic on behalf of science. Unfortunately, many so-called philosophers have put forward propositions that are empirical in form but purportedly *a priori* in justification. That is, they have engaged in metaphysical speculation. They have succumbed to an (irrational) rationalist faith that pure thought, or reason alone, would produce some pure facts, or knowledge, of which they could be absolutely certain. Well, then, no more! said the logical positivists.

The logical positivists take the opportunity to patch up some of the rough spots in Hume. Ayer's interpretation of Hume on causality, for example, shows that what Hume intended was to illustrate the absence of logical necessity in empirical judgments of causality. Hume's talk about custom and habit overdoes the skeptical aspect of the argument. This in turn is the result of Hume's "psychological atomism," his Lockean assumption that sense-contents come in self-contained, box-like units, an assumption which the logical positivists show to be unnecessary to his central claims.

# THE BOUNDS OF SENSE

Now we come to what the logical positivist's perceived as their own innovation. Kant had questioned the metaphysicians' *entitlement* to their claims. He warned of the excesses that result from unchained reason. Hume, too, thought the metaphysicians were *illogical*. He said their texts were full of sophistry and illusion. But neither Hume nor Kant had argued that these metaphysical speculations were out-and-out *nonsense*. This was the new position of the logical positivists with respect to metaphysics: not that it exceeded the evidence, or that it was illogical, but that it simply had no *meaning*. A seemingly new class of error was introduced: not "contradiction," which was simply the opposite of tautology, but "violation of the rules of expression," i.e., putting symbols together in ways that made no sense. Propositions like "Socrates is a man" and "All men are mortal" make sense. Propositions like "Socrates dreams microwave-safe" and "My couch ate the doctrine" are nonsense. The logical positivists contended that metaphysical propositions, such as "the soul is simple," belonged to the latter category. The radical application of a concept of sense was, no doubt, suggested by Wittgenstein's early work and its immediate predecessors. (Husserl, by the way, also probed the bounds of sense.)

So the logical positivists, in their rigorous and scientific way, felt the need for a reliable "test" for sense. Something that would sort out agglomerations of words into those which made sense and those which did not. For this they refined something that the earlier positivists had developed: the verification principle.

# THE VERIFICATION PRINCIPLE

The verification principle, in barest form, is that the meaning of a proposition is the method of its verification. As a test of meaning, in Ayer's version, it goes like this: A sentence is "factually significant" if, and only if, one knows how to verify the proposition it purports to express—i.e., if one knows what observations, under what conditions, would make the proposition true or false. So, for example, the sentence "The planets on the other side of the galaxy are made of cheddar cheese," which purports to stand for the proposition that "The planets on other side of the galaxy are made of cheddar cheese," means that if we sent some astronauts over to the other side of the galaxy they would come back with very high cholesterol, and makes sense, since such a verification is presumably, in principle, possible. (Note that it is immaterial that we do not yet have the technology to build a probe for such an investigation; what matters is that the proposition is verifiable *in principle*.) The sentence "The Absolute prefers Gruyère," on the other hand, which purports to express the proposition that "The Absolute prefers Gruyère," is nonsense, because there are no observations which would in any way help to judge whether this proposition were true or false.

Some positivists, like Moritz Schlick, believed that sensible propositions must be *conclusively* verifiable. You need to know how to prove them with certainty. As Ayer points out, however, this means that the laws of physics and many other propositions which positivists would like to keep within the bounds of sense are ruled out because, as inductive generalizations, they are only good until the next experiment, which will probably confirm them but might just possibly refute them. (What if the next apple doesn't fall?) So Ayer and company reject this kind of "strong" verifiability, and adopt what they call "weak" verifiability, which requires only that one know of observations that would increase the *probability* that the proposition in question were true or false. (If, after hundreds of trials over several years, we observe that the apples still keep falling, then we have increased the probability that the law of gravity is true.)

Even under the weak verification principle, all of metaphysics and almost all of religion falls under the category of nonsense. The (pseudo-)proposition "God exists," for example, turns out to be not true, not false, but just plain nonsense. For, the argument goes, if God is understood to be a transcendent being, outside the empirical world (that is, assuming that we are talking about the Deity of the Enlightenment, and not Zeus, or Jupiter, or even Jehovah), then there is not only no way to prove that he exists, there is also no way even to prove it *probable* that he exists. "God" is just another metaphysical term, and therefore nonsense. The logical positivist nonetheless offers this comfort to the religiously minded: If "God exists" is nonsensical, then "God does not exist" is equally nonsensical. So atheism and agnosticism have the same validity as theism, which is to say, none. Whether this "refutation" of theism, atheism, and agnosticism itself has any metaphysical payoff is an interesting question: We have already seen, with Kant, that the rejection of both sides of the proof of the existence of God may be concomitant with some comforting postulates and a general accommodation with the religious status quo.

## THE LOGICAL POSITIVISTS: THE VERIFICATION PRINCIPLE AT WORK

## MEANINGLESS MORALITY

Hume thought he might practice moral philosophy in the manner of natural philosophy. Toward that end, he produced a kind of psychology. He analyzed motives, behaviors, and other phenomena associated with morality, what he perceived to be 'human nature'. The logical positivists consider this to be a sensible occupation, but relegate it to science, as it is an empirical investigation. Other so-called moral philosophers devoted their energies to exhorting people to do this or that. The logical positivists say that such individuals have misplaced their vocation, that they are really preachers or prophets, and not philosophers. And then there are those who simply offer ethical judgments, classifying this or that as good or bad. But they are just saying what they think, which is hardly philosophy. So what is moral or ethical philosophy? According to the logical positivists, it can only be a reflection on the nature and status of ethical terms themselves, that is, an analysis and categorization of ethical statements as such.

What can we, as logical positivists, say about ethical statements? First and foremost, we can say that they are not statements of empirical fact. Many moral philosophers have sought to define ethical statements in nonethical terms. The utilitarians, for example, argued that good and bad were just sums of empirically ascertainable pleasures and pains. The subjectivists argued that ethical statements boil down to expressions of approval by individuals, or a kind of psychology. Modern communitarians believe that good or bad is just that of which the community happens to approve or disapprove. This is wrong say the logical positivists. For it is in no case self-contradictory to maintain that any particular ethical conclusion reached through any such nonethical calculus is ethically wrong. In other words, it is an inescapable part of the way in which we use ethical terms that what is most pleasurable, or approved by any individual or community might still be wrong. An empirical calculus might describe and predict moral behavior with reasonable accuracy, but there remains an ineliminable difference in meaning between its conclusions and that of ethical statements. (Here the logical positivists remind us that there is a difference between the factual proposition "This community regards this sort of action as morally wrong" and the ethical statement "This sort of action is wrong.")

If ethical statements are not empirical propositions, they are also not absolute, or transcendent statements. According to the logical positivists, it would make no sense to talk about "moral facts," because there would be by definition no empirical way to verify or even render probable such "facts." Supposed "intuition" of what is right and wrong turns out to be very different in different people, and there is no criterion according to which these intuitions could be reconciled. Above all, any talk of such an "absolute" good is clearly metaphysical, and therefore nonsense.

So what are ethical statements? They are—surprise!—nonsense. Ethical terms are pseudoconcepts. They look like concepts and fit into sentence grammar in the same way, but they aren't really concepts at all. To say that a particular kind of action is "wrong" is merely to express one's feelings or disposition with respect to the action. It adds nothing factual to the description of the action. "Murder is wrong" boils down to "Murder!" said with an expression of horror. Ethical statements belong to the same category as cries of pain, shrieks of joy, and commands— they evince a particular disposition of the speaker, but have no factual content.

Thus stated, the logical positivists' ethics sounds close to the subjectivist view they rejected. The difference is that while the subjectivist regards "X is wrong" and "I disapprove of x" as identical in meaning, the logical positivist maintains that they are different. "X is wrong," according to the logical positivist, *evinces* the speaker's disapproval of x, but does not *assert* it, as does "I disapprove of x." It is perfectly possible, says the logical positivist, for the speaker to say "X is wrong" and still approve of x.

Since ethical terms are neither empirical nor absolute, it would seem that there is not much that one can say about them. Arguments about morality would seem to be impossible. The logical positivists accept this point, and go on to argue that what we call moral arguments are not in fact arguments about values, but arguments about fact. We dispute motives, conditions, the nature of the act, and so forth, in order to show that it does or does not belong to a class of actions which we think our interlocutor will agree is immoral. If our interlocutor has a fundamentally different idea of morality, then there is no point in arguing.

The logical positivist understanding of ethics takes us back to Hume. Although Hume devoted much effort to what would now be described as psychology, he did so in view of a conceptual distinction which informs much of logical positivist thought: the distinction between fact and value. At the end of the day, there is this irreducible little fact, that you can't always get what you want.

## SENSIBLE NONSENSE?

It should already be apparent that the logical positivists make use of the notion of nonsense in some very strange and paradoxical ways. At the end of the day, I will argue, their use of the term is itself nonsensical, and their purported innovation in philosophy a wash, an unnecessary and dangerous modification of what would otherwise be a simple Humean skepticism.

Some of the strongest criticisms of the verification principle have come from introspective logical positivists. The crux of the verification principle's problems becomes apparent in considering exactly what the verification principle purportedly tests. At first glance, it tests propositions for sense or nonsense. But this would be nonsense, for how can something get to be a proposition without already making sense? How can one look for observations to support verifiability without already knowing something of what is meant by the proposition? The logical positivists reply that the verification principle is testing sentences, which first have to be converted to propositions before being checked for verifiability. But this just pushes the question back. How can a nonsensical sentence be converted into a proposition which could undergo such a test? If the sentence were indeed nonsense, then presumably it corresponds to no proposition, and therefore cannot be subject to the verification principle. Ayer perceived this problem, and ten years after his first book (*Language, Truth, and Logic*, 1936), proposed a third level of mediation, the "statement": Sentences are translated into statements, which can then become either propositions or pseudopropositions, i.e., nonsense. But this is just to push the question back one more level. Put as many levels in as you want; somewhere you still have to shift from nonsense to sense.

The logical positivists found themselves trying to offer concepts that would bridge sense and nonsense. The early logical positivists, who believed in strong verifiability, would sometimes let slip that even if the laws of natural science were actually nonsense, they were in fact a very important kind of nonsense. To be "important" is to be significant, to have meaning. In other words, there can be sensible nonsense. If this sounds nonsensical, that's because it probably is.

Another option is to distinguish "apparent" sense from "real" sense. The apparent sense would consist of the emotions and irrelevant thoughts psychologically associated with a given proposition, while the real sense would be, well, its *real* meaning. The idea of real meanings, however, has a disturbingly Platonic air about it. Besides, from a strictly empirical point of view, real meaning is probably not verifiable. All we have to go on to determine meanings are observed effects of meaning, usages, and so forth. For the serious empiricist, apparent sense should be the only kind of sense. At work here is a dialectic strangely reminiscent of Kant's problems in shifting all knowledge to knowledge of appearances—which is not knowledge at all.

## SELF-DESTRUCTION

One of the chief causes of the death of logical positivism, in fact, was that the attempt to apply systematically its core principles, like the verification principle, actually threatened the three fountains of knowledge which it originally sought to uphold: common sense, natural science, and logic.

*Common Sense.* It threatened common sense because it insisted that the "real" meaning of apparently straightforward propositions like "The emperor Nero took a bath" consisted of extraordinarily complex webs of predicted future sense-contents under stipulated conditions (of sense-contents). (It may even have ruled out meaningful statements about the distant past.)

*Natural Science.* As already mentioned, proponents of the strong verification principle frankly acknowledged that some or all of natural science might also be nonsensical. Empirical propositions can never be absolutely certain, for they are always subject to test and rejection by further experience, and may therefore be classed as nonsense. The weak verification principle, at the end of the day, does not provide an escape from this problem. Ayer's recourse to probability as the criterion for establishing the sensibility of propositions hardly puts natural science on a secure footing. Propositions can presumably be established only to the extent that the events with which they are concerned sometimes actually occur. Even with a weak verification principle, however, no absolutely certain verification of any law-like empirical propositions can ever occur. Ayer engaged in a lengthy series of defensive maneuvers in order to rescue some probabilistic version of the verification principle, but the very complexity of the debate rendered the effort futile, for the implication that natural science should require so much scholasticism in its defense was surely a betrayal of the founding cause of logical positivism.

*Logic.* A proposition is "analytic," according to the logical positivists, if its truth is evident from the analysis of the meanings of its terms. What are these meanings? The meanings of propositions, we know, are determined via the verification principle. The meanings of terms, however, must come from definitions, which are, the logical positivists admit, conventions. Now a circle appears. If what we mean by "analytic" is defined by a convention, and the same for what is "necessary," "logical," and "*a priori*," then what is the basis for the claim that "all necessary, logical, *a priori* propositions are analytic?" The claim is necessarily true in virtue of the agreed conventions. But are the conventions themselves necessary? By definition, it would seem, conventions are arbitrary, so, therefore, is logic.

The logical positivists' not altogether compatible views on logic marked a retreat of sorts from the Wittgensteinian conception with which they were originally inspired. Recall that Wittgenstein had presented logic as a part of the essence of symbolism. The logical positivists, however, tended toward the view that logic arose out of the conventional meanings assigned to symbols within a particular symbolism. Wittgenstein's path may have led to a vacuous mysticism, but the logical positivists' path led them to a conventionalism, reminiscent of J. S. Mill.

# THE VERIFICATION PRINCIPLE
# ON THE VERIFICATION PRINCIPLE

What is the status of the verification principle? Is it a logical or an empirical principle? If it is a proposition about the nature of meaning, like an hypothesis or discovery, then it is empirical. If it is empirical, how can it be verified? Presumably, one would have to observe whether or not it truly sorted propositions according to their sensibility. This suggests two problems. First, given that language seems capable of generating an infinite number of propositions, it is unclear that the observations would ever be conclusive. Second, in order to make the observations, one would have to know independently of the verification principle whether the propositions in question made sense or not. So the verification principle as a test of sense would turn out to be unnecessary anyway.

Suppose that the verification principle is a logical principle, which is to say, analytic. "Verifiability" should be included in the definition of "meaning." Is it? Well, it depends on the meaning of meaning, I suppose. We could consider the verification principle as a proposed definition. In that case, however, it seems arbitrary: Why not propose another definition? This brings us to the difficulties raised by the logical positivists' implicit conventionalism in logic.

The truth is, the verification principle is a disguised practical maxim. It is a version of the pragmatist Peirce's maxim on how to make our ideas clear. Thinking about how one might verify a proposition—what sort of observable effects might be deduced from its truth or falsity—is certainly a useful and practical way to ensure that one is not talking out of one's behind. But there is a world of difference between a practical rule for making sense and principles that prescribe in advance which propositions will and will not make sense. Only the latter promises to supply the basis for further inferences—inferences which are implicitly metaphysical in character. Not surprisingly, perhaps, the logical positivists are guilty of the original sin of philosophical empiricism: They convert a worthy practical maxim into a philosophical doctrine.

## THE BOUNDS OF BOUNDS

The source of the paradoxes of logical positivist is the attempt to fix hard and fast boundaries of a sort—the bounds of sense. It is important to understand, in my view, that this attempt follows a classical philosophical pattern. The bounds of sense are, in function and results, a replica in new jargon of the old bounds of knowledge, which are themselves an instance of the Holy Grail of metaphysics, the bounds of thought. Far from doing away with metaphysics, as they promised, the logical positivists found a new way to keep it going.

*The Bounds of Thought.* Metaphysics has always been a pure thinking which arrives at knowledge. It does so by circumscribing thought, by finding the edge of thinking, where thinking becomes being. The problem, as philosophers like Hegel and Wittgenstein acknowledged, was that thinking the bounds of thought means thinking the unthinkable. Mysticism is the attempt to find the edge of thought (or expression), to indicate in some way the 'that' which can never be made the 'what' of thought.

*The Bounds of Knowledge.* Unhappy with the vagaries of metaphysics' unthinkable thoughts, philosophers sought secure employment in defining the bounds of knowledge. Although there are plenty of bounds to our knowledge—for example, we lack the technology to explore the other side of the galaxy—philosophers wished to consider only the universal bounds of all possible knowledge. Particular bounds, after all, would most likely fall one by one with the progress of human knowledge. But the universal bounds of all possible knowledge are nothing other than the bounds of thought. If knowledge is possible, it is conceivable, so only what is inconceivable lies beyond its bounds. Not surprisingly, the knowledge binders recreated the original paradox: They denied the possibility of knowing what they *ipso facto* claimed to know.

*The Bounds of Sense.* Bounds of sense to the rescue! Okay, so there are no bounds of thought or knowledge, said the logical positivists, but there are bounds of sense.

Philosophy can still be a universal science if it limits itself to questions about what can and cannot be expressed sensibly. But the bounds of sense are the bounds of what can be expressed, and the bounds of what can be expressed are the bounds of thought. The same old paradox appeared: The sense binders were forced to give some sense to that which they claimed had no sense.

The conception of the bounds of sense, as we saw with the early Wittgenstein, originated in a philosophy of logic. For this reason, perhaps, the early analytic philosophers sometimes blurred an important distinction between grammar and logic. The logical positivists wanted their bounds of sense to behave like walls of logic: absolute barriers beyond which none could venture. They lost track of the simple fact that rules of grammar, like definitions, syntax, and so forth are not binding in the same way that a logical inference is. They are binding, of course, if within a limited social space and time one wishes to be understood clearly and quickly. But they cannot in principle exclude meanings, since they are themselves arbitrary. One can always define a new term, change grammar, or even adopt a new language. If something can be thought, it can be expressed. If it cannot be expressed, it cannot be thought. There are no bounds of sense.

## RE-KANTED?

Who was the greatest philosopher of bounds? Kant. Was logical positivism so much more Kant? The early Wittgenstein's conception of the bounds of sense was perhaps more Kantian than that of the logical positivists. The latter simply wanted to trash everything on the other side of sense. For them it was all unscientific nonsense. Wittgenstein, on the other hand, believed that things of the highest value lay beyond the bounds of sense. It all comes down to the Indeterminacy Principle. When thinking what cannot be thought, or saying what cannot be said, philosophy engages in an activity whose results cannot be determined in advance—whose determination is inevitably the work of extraneous factors, like mood, disposition, and upbringing.

## HELP WANTED (?): CLARIFIERS

What remains for philosophy, according to the logical positivists, is the activity of clarification. (There is here more than an echo of Socrates and his quest for definitions and claims of ignorance.) Clarifying what? According the logical positivists, philosophy can assist in the progress of human knowledge by serving modern science. The most obvious applications would be in psychology and neurology, though all fields are meant to be included. It should help scientists define their terms and think clearly about what they should investigate. This is, of course, something of a comedown: Formally the queen of the sciences, philosophy becomes their conceptual custodian, perhaps merely a parasite.

Yet even this minimalist project is of dubious merit. First, as indicated by the discussion of the apparently nonsensical verification principle, even logical positivism needs to clean up its own act. Second, it is doubtful that by the time a philosopher masters the subject and clarifies its own confusions and disputes, he or she really has the time and energy to master and then clarify a field of science. (For in order to clarify their concepts for them, a philosopher would presumably have to be about as familiar with the discipline as the scientist himself.) Third, why can't the scientists do this sort of clarification by themselves? At the end of the day, clarification has no peculiar methods or content: It means simply thinking clearly. Granted, many advances in science have come from a rethinking of terms and definitions (for example, Einstein's theory of special relativity and the concept of 'simultaneity'); but this rethinking could have been and, in all cases that come to mind, was in fact performed by a clever scientist, not a trained philosopher.

Finally, and most damaging, it is not unlikely that any philosophical concepts, even if in service of the logical positivist project of clarification, would lead to a dogmatism, to an obscurity in thinking which could actually hinder scientific advance. Empirical evidence suggests that this may well be the case. The famous physicist Ernst Mach, for example, might have been even more famous had he not drawn the conclusion on the basis of the positivist principles that the terms "atom" and so forth were nonsense. A similar philosophical bias afflicted psychologists around mid-century. For them, unobservable mental states were just as nonsensical as was the "atom" for Mach; they maintained adamantly that mental phenomena had no more meaning than observable inputs and outputs, i.e., physical behaviors. It seems now that things are not so simple.

## THE END OF LOGIC

The logical positivist experience was in some ways a letdown for the Logical Program. From the sophisticated (though questionable) philosophies of logic earlier in the century, the logical positivists drifted into a bleak conventionalist account of logic. The focus on sense and nonsense suggested that logic was no longer first philosophy. Indeed the logical positivists cleared the way for the next ground-churning episode in analytic philosophy, the replacement of the Logical Program with the Language Program.

## THE LABORATORY OF LANA CITY, PH.D.

After visiting Drs. D. A. Sein and M. H. Denken, I came to the laboratory of Dr. Lana City. She looked somewhat superior when I mentioned my previous visits. "Oh, yes, we're a little different, you see. We're doing pure analysis. I think they do a lot of metaphysics. I myself used to work on the mind–body problem, but now I'm into basic research." I was not quite sure what the "pure analysis" analyzed, but I kept my ignorant mouth shut. So began the tour.

On the first table was an array of reassuringly familiar scientific instruments: a microscope, a telescope, a camera, and a few optical lenses. "This is one of many specific analyses of individual concepts," she explained. "In this case, we are analyzing the concept of 'seeing.' " As she spoke, a young lab assistant sat down and peered through the telescope, which, as far as I could tell, was pointing at the wall. He scribbled something in his notepad.

"I see," I said, nodding sagely (or so I hoped). "Any conclusions yet?"

"Well, yes," she smiled proudly, "our results thus far indicate that seeing is believing."

On the next table was a more unusual, even frightening, machine. On one side of the machine stood a stack of books. An assistant fed books to the machine one at a time. With loud ripping and crunching sounds, the machine spit out things into two piles. One, the larger pile, consisted of small shreds of paper, apparently ripped out of the books. The other pile was what was left of the books, their cover, and a few pages, or rather, parts of pages.

"We've nicknamed this 'The Critic,' " she began. "Really, it's a Sense Processor. It scans each line of a book and tests it against the Verification Principle. If the line turns out to be nonsense, we slice it out of the book—" she made a triumphant chopping gesture with her hand through the air "—and that leaves us with the sensible parts of the book only."

I felt uneasy, perhaps wondering if the machine might detect the nonsense in my speech, and cut my tongue out. I asked quietly, "Have you thought of any applications for this device?"

"You bet," she enthused. "We're mainly interested in the philosophical applications, you know, sorting out the history of philosophy. But the potential is limitless. Think of it. We could take over the textbook market. What school wouldn't want our *sensored* versions of the classics? Business executives could use it to prune the reports from their subordinates. Ordinary people could use it to weed out their junk mail."

"Sounds promising," I said weakly. I had been reading the titles of some of the books that had already been "processed." Hegel was reduced to an empty cover. Kant had enough material left for an introduction. The collected works of Shakespeare looked like it consisted of about one play. As we walked away, I thought I saw an assistant feed a Bible into the machine.

In the general hubbub, I thought I had been hearing a familiar voice. It turned out to be the queen of England, on a television screen. She held a copy of Plato's *Republic* in her hands and appeared to be giving some kind of commentary on it. She was saying something like, "Now, Socrates says to Thrasymachus, 'You are a very naughty person.' We shall tell you what justice is, and why the Royal Family ought to be so very philosophical."

"Is it live?" I asked incredulously.

"You bet," replied Dr. City. "She's alive and kicking. We've got a satellite transmission all the way from London, England. It was a real *coup* to get her to participate in this experiment."

"What experiment is that?" I asked while trying to figure out what the tabloids might pay for a freelance piece.

"Sure, let me give you some background," she replied. "Of course, you know that philosophers have for a long time been trying to create a kind of pure or perfect language, you know, so that logical relationships would become transparent. If we could just translate everything—like important texts from the history of philosophy—into this language, everything would become quite clear. Do you follow?"

"Uh huh," I nodded, "So you think maybe the queen's . . ."

"Exactly. We're working on the hypothesis that this metalanguage already exists, and that it is in fact the queen's English." The Doctor turned to me and whispered, "Personally, I'm a little skeptical about this experiment. But I thought we might as well give the old lady a shot. She needs a bit of cheering up."

Trying to recover my skills as an investigative reporter, I took the initiative and said, "You said that you were engaged in a kind of *pure* analysis."

"That's right."

"Can you explain to me exactly what you meant, and how these experiments are relevant to that?"

"You got it," she said with characteristic self-confidence. "Take a look over here," she said as she led me to yet another table. "Everything leads up to this. This is where we are doing the purest research. What we're trying to discover here is the meaning of meaning. It's kind of like analyzing pure analysis. If we're successful, then we'll have the key to all meaning. Everything will be preanalyzed."

On the table were two clipboard notepads. Two attendants went rushing back and forth between the pads. One was scribbling something down each time on the second pad, the other reading both pads with a puzzled look on his face.

"We are taking a random series of expressions," she explained, "and then our first assistant here," she pointed to the one with the pen, "is writing down the meaning of these expressions on the second pad. Our second assistant's job is to analyze the relationship between the expression and its meaning, mainly looking for any differences, so that we can be clear on what meaning does, or what it means."

"I see," said I. "May I take a closer look?"

"Of course."

I picked up the first notepad, and saw the first two expressions: "Snow is white," and "The dog ate the cat." I picked up the second notepad, which read, to my horror, "Snow is white," and "The dog ate the cat."

"But Dr. City," I protested, "According to this, the meaning of 'Snow is white' is that 'Snow is white.' So what are you analyzing?"

She looked at me sternly, and said, "No one said this was going to be easy."

Feeling at the same time chastised and awed by her immense professional qualifications and self-assurance, I decided that I would never be able to understand what she and her team were up to. I wished them all the best, and went on my way. Next on my list of appointments was a certain Dr. Skull Features, working in a new and exciting field of research called "phrenology."

# The Language Program

# The Later Wittgenstein

## Seriously Intractable

Wittgenstein was more honest than most philosophers. When he concluded that he had solved all the problems of philosophy and that these problems were not particularly important anyway, at the ripe old age of thirty, he acted as logic required: He stopped doing philosophy. When he returned to philosophical investigations ten years later, he staked out a position for which few philosophers have the courage: He opposed his own earlier work.

In some contemporary versions of the history of philosophy, the later Wittgenstein opposed more than just his own earlier work. His later work marks a fundamental turning point in the history of philosophy. All philosophy hitherto, it seems, was mired in confusions in and about language. The later Wittgenstein exposes these confusions, and so does away with the whole tradition of Western metaphysics.

This version of events is radically untrue, or so I will argue. The insight behind the later Wittgenstein's work does indeed have considerable purchase on all previous philosophy. In this respect, however, it is no different, and certainly not superior to, the work of countless earlier philosophers, who also offered critiques of philosophy motivated by the same insight. Kant, Hegel, and Nietzsche may serve as examples, though others would also be appropriate. Insofar as the later Wittgenstein offers a new teaching, usually thought to be something to do with the use and abuse of language, his contribution is just another example of metaphysical illusion, or precisely what he and the other philosophers sought to critique.

## TWO WITTGENSTEINS?

The early Wittgenstein, epitomized in the *Tractatus*, expresses himself in seemingly rigorous, systematic form. The later Wittgenstein, represented by the *Philo-*

*sophical Investigations*, written in the 1940s and published in 1953, two years after his death, eschews systematicity, and favors a decentralized, fragmentary, aphoristic approach in philosophy. The early Wittgenstein sets out to discover the fundamental and eternal structures of logic, language, and reality. The later Wittgenstein rejects the idea of such a project, and offers instead what he takes to be tactical illuminations, isolated comparisons and contrasts designed to eliminate specific confusions and obscurities.

The division seems obvious, although scholars no doubt could refine it by finding three, four, or five Wittgensteins spanning the time between the usual two. Even so, I will argue, this is fundamentally the wrong way to divide Wittgenstein. From a philosophical perspective, the early and later Wittgensteins are essentially the same. Both, however, are divided against themselves, in roughly parallel ways. On the one hand, I contend, there is a mystical/metaphysical Wittgenstein, on the other hand a critical one. The former, in both early and later incarnations, conceives of projects which are instances of the traditional, mystical project of philosophy. The latter, again in both phases, offers a critical perspective which allows one to rise above the limitations of this project, and keep open a philosophical disposition toward thought. Not coincidentally, the division is the same that may be said to afflict Kant, or, for that matter, Socrates.

In the later Wittgenstein the idea of language replaces the idea of logic as the source of both insight and illusion. This change, however, is less relevant for understanding Wittgenstein than it is for understanding other philosophers, for whom the later Wittgenstein would mark the "advance" from the Logical Program to the Language Program of analytic philosophy.

## METAPHILOSOPHY

Although Wittgenstein's *practice* of philosophy changes dramatically from the logically ordered propositions of the *Tractatus* to the disjointed paragraphs of the *Investigations*, the *concept* of philosophy he offers within those works is in essential respects the same. In both cases, philosophy is conceived as a pure activity barred from advancing propositions, theses, or doctrines. It serves merely to elucidate and clarify the propositions which arise elsewhere. It lays things out on the table, without judgment, so that all may see and judge for themselves. Its chief task is negative, to eliminate philosophical confusions and illusions so that one may see the world aright. It sets up warning signs at the bounds of sense so that others, especially other philosophers, might not wreck themselves on the shoals of nonsense. It is a self-dissolving activity. For the early Wittgenstein, philosophy is a ladder to be kicked away; for the later Wittgenstein, it is a therapy to be discontinued once the cure is effected.

The underlying continuity in Wittgenstein's metaphilosophy provides the basis for a critique of his later philosophy. The idea of philosophy as a "pure" activity is, in my view, vacuous. Insofar as it makes sense, it says that philosophy is nothing more than the project of thinking clearly. It is a noble and worthy practical maxim converted into an empty and valueless effort at doing nothing in particular. The idea acquires substance only by surreptitiously polluting this vacuous basis with philosophical doctrines. (Indeed, any meaningful, nonvacuous activity—in the sense of a conscious, goal-directed activity—must presuppose something about the world within which it takes place.) In the early Wittgenstein, those doctrines belong chiefly to the philosophy of logic. In the later Wittgenstein, they are part of the philosophy of language. In form and function, however, they are the same.

Let's elucidate it this way. Clarifying confusions in language is fine. It amounts to insisting on clear, critical thinking. In the later Wittgenstein, strangely, the confusions of greatest concern are those which have to do with the words "language," "proposition," "rule," and so forth. Why the linguistic focus, given that Wittgenstein himself points out that these are words just like any other? Because there is an essential ambiguity in any attempt to present Wittgenstein's own project: It is, on the one hand, a clarification of concepts *in* language and, on the other hand, a clarification of concepts *about* language. In the former case, the "in language" adds nothing; the project is simply one of seeing clearly how things stand, of not letting the words get in the way. The latter case, by assuming an underlying, alternative philosophy of language, provides the basis for a nonvacuous concept of philosophy as clarification.

Any attempt to criticize the later Wittgenstein encounters a traditional problem. Criticizing Hegel on internal terms, as I suggested a while back, is virtually impossible. Criticism must take as its object some doctrine. By identifying his philosophy with the dialectical method, however, Hegel ensures that no such doctrine can be regarded as the definitive statement of his philosophy and that any such critique is itself a further manifestation of the truth of the dialectic. Criticizing the later Wittgenstein produces a similar difficulty. Wittgenstein insists that he is advancing no doctrines, and further claims the very notion of clarification—the analog of 'critique' in this instance—as a part of his own philosophy. It is for this reason, perhaps, that the otherwise quite different afflictions of Hegelianism and Wittgensteinianism share this feature, that they are usually terminal. As with Hegel, our only hope is to examine how and to what extent the proposed method (or activity) is free from doctrine. To the extent that it is, it turns out, it is empty, and to the extent that it is not, it is indeed open to critique.

## PHILOSOPHY OF LANGUAGE

Since the vacuous aspect of the idea of philosophy as activity has by its nature nothing specific to Wittgenstein, let us turn to the "substantive" aspect, his underlying philosophy of language. The following document of mysterious origin outlines the later Wittgenstein's philosophy of language and in a strange way makes clear its identity in form and function with the early Wittgenstein's philosophy of logic.

# TRACTATUS LINGUISTICO-PHILOSOPHICUS

1 The world is everything you can talk about.

2 Language is a rule-following activity.

2.1 Meaning is use.

2.11 The meaning of a word is not to be found in the thing it supposedly represents, or in an abstract definition. One must look at how the word is used in context.

2.111 For example, "tea" may not mean "a brown liquid" but "Honey, would you put the kettle on and make me a cup of tea?"

2.112 For example, the verb "to know" will have many different meanings, or uses, which may or may not resemble each other in a variety of ways.

2.2 Understanding is not a mental process.

2.21 The grammar of "to understand" is very close to that of "to be able." If we say that someone understands something, we mean that he is able to make use of it, he knows how it works.

2.22 We fall victim to philosophical prejudice when we imagine that words like "understand" and "know" and "reading" imply the existence of hidden mental entities and processes.

2.3 To understand a language means to be a master of a technique.

2.4 The technique of language consists in applying the rules of that language.

2.41 Obeying a rule is practice. It is something done regularly, repeatedly, blindly, perhaps out of habit.

2.42 Rules are not what they appear to be.

2.421 Rules may guide behavior precisely only where context makes clear the way in which a rule is to be understood.

2.43 Rules are by their nature public.

3 A set of language rules together with their relevant context is a language-game.

3.01 It is not possible to define what we mean here by games, but we can offer examples of lots of different kinds of games: Monopoly, catch, solitaire, ring around the rosie. They bear only a "family resemblance" to one another, as games.

3.02 So stop asking me for a definition.

3.1 The language-game includes the full context within which linguistic utterances have meaning.

3.11 The idea of context here goes well beyond words and sentences. It includes behaviors, the physical environment, and anything that is important to the situation within which language is used.

3.2 There must be a certain regularity to the games; otherwise we would not know how to play.

3.3 The language-game is the smallest unit within which words may be said to have definite meanings.

3.31 Thus, it is no use trying to come up with elementary propositions, or "simples." Words and propositions have a stability of meaning only insofar as they appear within the recurring context of a language-game.

3.311 The declarative proposition, which says "This is how things stand," and with which logicians have been primarily concerned, is just one of many ways of using words and language. Consider also telling jokes; acting, and so on.

3.32 Augustine was wrong when he said he learned to speak by being shown objects and then told their names.

3.321 Naming is just one, probably not very important, language game.

4 A complete set of language-games constitutes the grammar of a language.

4.1 The rules and language-games which constitute grammar are essentially customs, practices, or institutions.

4.12 A grammar is inherently public.

4.121 It would not be possible for one person one time to obey a rule or play a game; the rules are given in the grammar of a language.

4.122 A "private language," in which an individual uses a language referring to his own sensations in a manner unintelligible to others, is not possible. The idea reflects an inadequate appreciation of the role of rules, practice, and context in language.

4.2 Grammar has no meaning in itself, but is the structure of meaning. It is the framework of our world.

4.3 What lies outside grammar, cannot be said.

5 Grammar is the structure of meaning for a given form of life.

5.1 In order for language to work, we must have not only agreement in definitions, but agreement in judgments as well.

5.12 These judgments are not within life, but within the form of life, and so are beyond judgment.

5.2 There is no point in going beyond the form of life for explanations. This is where we hit bedrock.

6 Philosophy is pretty much a waste of time.

6.1 It is impossible to advance theses in philosophy.

6.11 Inasmuch as philosophy puts forward nontrivial theses, it is a futile attempt to go beyond grammar, or to find meaning in pure form.

6.111 The problems with which philosophy has concerned itself are only pseudo-problems, and result from misunderstandings about the nature of language.

6.112 The cloud of philosophy can be condensed to a drop of grammar.

6.2 At best, philosophy is clarification.

6.21 A good philosopher is like a grammatical policeman. He blows the whistle when others try to step beyond the bounds of sense.

6.3 Everything I have written above is nonsense, and should discarded once it is understood.

6.31 I have offered objects of comparison with which to understand language, intended to illuminate by their differences as well as their similarities.

**WITTGENSTEIN: FRUIT PLAYING LANGUAGE GAMES**

6.4  There are some things which cannot be said. They can only be *shown*.

6.41  Ethics is still out of bounds. It is transcendental.

6.42  You will notice I have also written nothing of consequence about politics, history, and art.

6.43  The mystical lies in accepting what *is, that* it is. It is accepting the form of life.

7  What we cannot speak about we must pass over in silence.

## WHERE'S THE BEEF?

Yes, it does read remarkably like the *Tractatus* **Logico**-*Philosophicus*. What is essential in Wittgenstein's early work is the *role* he intends "logic" to play. This role is preserved in the later Wittgenstein's work in the concepts of 'grammar' and 'form of life'. This is the "beef" in both the early and later philosophies. Here is how that role may be characterized:

*1. To provide a "hard core" of meaning in language,* that is, a stable and sure source of meaning of what we say. To be sure, the later Wittgenstein rejects individual words and propositions as such a source on grounds that their meanings may be vague, fluid, dependent on context, and based on conventional practice. Nonetheless, the project of philosophy as clarification requires, and he does indeed locate, a fixed and stable core of meaning beneath these superficial vagaries: "grammar." A word or sentence may vary in meaning, but grammar determines precisely what it will mean in a given context. Thus, Wittgenstein elevates context and practice to a stable and sure 'form of life'. It is a "top down" approach as opposed to the earlier, "bottom up" approach of building everything on elementary propositions, but the consequences are the same.

*2. To ensure that there is a specifiable boundary between sense and nonsense.* In the early work, that which does not conform to the logical structure of language is nonsense. In the later work, that which violates the rules of grammar is nonsense. In the final analysis, it really doesn't matter what justification Wittgenstein uses for dividing propositions along the bounds of sense; what does matter is that he believes he can so divide them, in advance, with the help of his special brand of philosophy.

*3. To categorize philosophy as an attempt to transgress the bounds of sense.* Whether on account of logic or grammar, philosophical propositions are not false, but nonsensical. They claim more than the structure of language permits. Indeed, they typically confuse this structure of language (logic or grammar) with something real and substantial. Philosophical propositions attempt to derive a content from the pure form of language, and in doing so show themselves to be nonsense. Early and later, Wittgenstein is consistent in that he extends this judgment on philosophy to his own work. His own philosophy, once understood, should be discarded as nonsense. It is an attempt to *show* what cannot be *said*.

*4. To secure a place for the world of value free from philosophical intrusions.* This is what really counts. For both the early and the later Wittgenstein, philosophy is worse than a nuisance: It is a diabolical threat to happiness. It must be solved, silenced, or just stymied. Its greasy, probing fingers must be kept away from what we love—our sense of purity, of duty, of beauty, of value. These valuables are therefore locked away on the other side of logic and/or language. Or, they are locked into our form of life, and thus out of bounds for philosophical speculation.

What is going on here? It's no secret. What we have here is the familiar attempt to deduce a content from pure form. The idea is that language is the form of our world. It is our spectacles. And now, from an analysis of this form, we are to arrive at some basic truths about the world, a content. It is as though, by looking hard enough at our spectacles, we will determine what will be seen through them. In other words, language defines what is possible. It is the structure of what is possible. It is this structure and no other. No other is possible. Therefore, it is actual. The possible is the actual—the Holy Grail of philosophy.

---

*In the Monastery.* New and silly questions for the philosophers:

1. *Is a private language possible?*

2. *What does it mean to follow a rule?*

3. *How can we be sure that rules will always apply?*

4. *What is the meaning of meaning?*

---

## WHY PHILOSOPHERS SHOULD NOT IGNORE THE HISTORY OF PHILOSOPHY

As far as the later Wittgenstein was concerned, there was only one philosopher worth refuting: the early Wittgenstein. As far as the early Wittgenstein was concerned, there were Frege, Russell, a bit of Schopenhauer, and before that eons of ignorance. Alas, these were not judgments illuminated by any extensive knowledge of the history of philosophy. Which permits us to introduce a new corollary of Santayana's theory about history: *philosophers who ignore the history of philosophy are bound to repeat it.*

Some of the circles to which Wittgenstein's thinking leads were anticipated by some of his more historically aware predecessors. For example, as a result of his intensive study of earlier philosophy, Hegel understood the problematic about limits or bounds (of any sort) and therefore reconceived his own philosophy as a method of continual transgression of limits. Nietzsche, through his study of Plato and the early Greeks, identified the otherworldly dynamic of philosophical mysticism, and tried to reconceive of things as pure appearances, with no limiting reality.

Hegel and Nietzsche, however, ended up in circles of their own. Perhaps their difficulties might even have been resolved with a Wittgensteinian insight or two. All of which suggests yet another Santayanan corollary: *philosophers who do not ignore the history of philosophy are bound to repeat it anyway.*

## PHILOSOPHY AS THERAPY

Let us return to the Wittgensteinian concept of philosophy as an activity, specifically in the form of his later concept of philosophy as a kind of therapy. The idea is that (bad) philosophy is a condition in which one is tormented by questions arising out of confusions in and/or about language, and that (good) philosophy clarifies the confusions and so cures the illness. A therapy (or collection of therapies), however, is defined by more than its result, the elimination of the offending condition. A lobotomy might cure an individual's philosophical afflictions, but it is presumably not the same as the treatment prescribed by Wittgenstein. A therapy is made up of a specific body of techniques, a set of methods, rules, past findings, presumptions, and so forth.

In considering the specific techniques that would make up any version of the later Wittgenstein's course of therapy, however, it becomes apparent that those which do not rely on the philosophy of language outlined above in what I have dubbed the *Tractatus Linguistico-Philosophicus* are nothing more than what can be expressed in a word: analysis. Those which do rely on that philosophy of language necessarily bear with them the ills of philosophy.

In the end, the only techniques unique to *philosophical* clarification are those which have to do with clarifying the confusions of philosophy. This is true not only because the good, clarifying philosopher has the advantage of familiarity with vocabulary, turns of thought, and so forth, but also because the clarification of anything other than philosophical confusions would not require any philosophical basis, and so would not support a unique project of clarification. So it comes about that Wittgensteinian philosophy-as-therapy is, as a critic once put it, a disease which mistakes itself for its cure.

The ideal of a "pure" activity, considered in most general terms, is nothing new in philosophy. The ancient Greeks, too, imagined philosophy as an activity, pure contemplation, without much concern about exactly what was to be contemplated. Philosophy has often been conceived essentially as a practice, a way of life, and not a body of knowledge. The ideal of pure activity is something which in Kantian language could be expressed as "purposiveness without purpose." It is the ideal of a way of life which requires no external goals, which generates its values internally, which is self-sufficient. In short, it is a form of mysticism. Perhaps the difference between the ancient Greeks and Wittgenstein is, as Nietzsche might have observed, that while the Greeks happily affirmed the idiosyncrasy and isolation of their chosen way of life, Wittgenstein adopted the more modern tone of pessimism and self-alienation, according to which his chosen practice took the form of a complaint.

## THE CULT OF WITTGENSTEIN

In the long term, Wittgenstein's appeal has rested less on his philosophical work than on his personality. Perhaps no philosopher better illustrates Nietzsche's claim that the philosophy *is* the personality. During his lifetime and especially in the decades since his death, a cult has arisen around Wittgenstein. The followers belong chiefly to the young, the philosophically minded, and other impressionable groups.

---

From *The Psychoanalyst's Handbook on Philosophers*

**NoG**. *Definition*. Nonconformist Genius. A NoG is entitled to pursue an unconventional career, oppose the received wisdom in both the academic world and in society at large, and otherwise behave in unusual ways. His behavior is believed to conform to a higher authority—reason, for example, or his own aesthetic sensibilities. The conception is essentially Romantic, and usually expresses a perceived deficiency in its adherent (whoever conceives of the NoG as NoG, whether himself or his followers).

**PAPA**. *Definition*. Paternal Anti-Paternal Agent. A PAPA is typically a NoG. His nonconformism is a form of anti-establishmentarianism. The PAPA thus serves as an expression of the adolescent's rebellion against authority/the father. Hence the AP—Anti-Paternal. In providing a very strong guiding hand of his own, however, the PAPA fulfills the adolescent's need for a substitute father figure. Hence the PA—Paternal Agent (placed on the outside, since that's nicer than APPA or PAAP).

---

Wittgenstein is the paradigmatic PAPA. Though clearly outside of and opposed to the "normal" forms of social and academic authority, Wittgenstein did and still does exert a considerable sway over the members of his cult and the professional industry that has sprouted up around it. Those who followed the living Wittgenstein often found their careers completely redirected at their master's whim. (He usually ordered them to stop doing philosophy and start doing something useful, like practicing medicine.) Worshipers of the dead Wittgenstein have a somewhat easier time of it. Some make a decent living as professional philosophers, posing as rebels; others simply strive to achieve the self-assurance and individuality they perceive in their master.

The cure to cultism remains, as always, a combination of introspection on the part of the cultist and biographical fact concerning the cult figure. The latter may support the following general observation: *Philosophers are often very screwed-up individuals.*

## The Catcher in the Philosophy Faculty

*I am in a field. Children—I mean, philosophers—are playing with each other among the tall shafts of rye. I am their protector. When they come too near the edge of the field, and attempt to advance controversial theses in philosophy, I gently catch them before they fall. With malice toward none, I guide them back to the safety of their tautologies. There they cannot hurt themselves or anyone else. I have suffered the torment; I have suffered it for them. I am the Catcher in the Philosophy Faculty.*

From *The Psychoanalyst's Handbook on Philosophers*

**Father Substitution in Philosophy.** Walking through the modern campus one is likely to bump into many great philosophers. On most campuses one may find several Wittgensteins, Nietzsches, Heideggers, Platos, Hegels, and perhaps the odd Schopenhauer or Descartes. One finds also that it is impossible to refute any of the arguments of these philosophers, as the principle of the eternal defensibility of any philosophy predicts, since their living heirs can always extend the defense indefinitely. Whence the psychological conditions which give rise to this mode of operation? An answer is to be found in the career path of most modern philosophers. Herewith an illustrative example:

Undergraduate essay: "Wittgenstein on the Problem of Mind"

(Age: 21. Accepted for graduate work in modern philosophy.)

Doctoral thesis: *Wittgenstein on the Problem of Other Minds*

(Age: 30. Appointed assistant professor in contemporary Anglo-Austrian philosophy.)

First book: *Wittgenstein on the Problem of Other Minds*

Second book: *Wittgenstein on the Problem of Other Philosophers*

(Age: 38. Appointed to tenured professorship in Fundamental Viennese Ontology.)

Third book: *The World as Wittgenstein Created It*

Fourth book: *My Philosophy*, by Wittgenstein

# Ordinary and Extraordinary Language People

Under the influence of the later Wittgenstein, the school of so-called ordinary language philosophy dominated British philosophy in the early post-World War II period. Members of the school took the view that everyday language contained more wisdom than the high-falutin' verbiage of philosophy. They believed that it was the proper business of philosophy to analyze language in its common applications and limit philosophical speculation to what could be derived therefrom.

## CATEGORY MISTAKES AND CONCEPTUAL GEOGRAPHIES

As early as 1930 or so, Gilbert Ryle (1900–1976) began philosophizing in a way that emphasized close attention to proper linguistic usage. He argued that many erroneous philosophical doctrines could be attributed to "category mistakes." His classic, rather donnish example of a category mistake is that of the tourist who wanders around Oxford and asks, Where is the university? Since Oxford University consists of colleges, each of which consists of a few buildings and the odd people running around inside them, the university is in no one place. It "exists," like most such institutions, only in the minds and ongoing practices of its members. So, the question places Oxford University in the wrong category, and so admits of no sensible answer. In his most successful book, *The Concept of Mind* (1949), Ryle argues that most philosophies of mind, especially Cartesian dualism, rest on category mistakes. For example, they tend to think of 'mind' as a different kind of 'matter' under the category of 'material substance'. Ryle argues that mental language, i.e., claims about what people are thinking and so on, can be analyzed into complex statements about behavior.

If there is a positive project which comes out of Ryle's work, it must be what he called "mapping out conceptual geographies." It should be possible to avoid category mistakes, the story goes, by tracing the categorial affiliations of our major concepts. Unfortunately, Ryle never completed or even attempted such a universal project. Like most philosophical critics, he limited his analyses of concepts to those which had been previously abused by other philosophers.

## SPEECH-ACTS

The central figure of the ordinary language movement was J. L. Austin (1911–1960), author of *How to Do Things with Words* (1962). He had a strong personal affinity with G. E. Moore, whom he perceived as a fellow champion of common sense. He was viscerally opposed to philosophical theories, and favored close attention to the details of language. For Austin, it seems, ordinary language held a fascination. He believed that important truths could be found even in its most banal workings.

Wittgenstein had already pointed out that philosophers grant unwarranted privilege to declarative propositions—e.g., "it is raining," "snow is white"—in their thinking about language. They ignore or marginalize the performative aspect of language, i.e., the ways in which individuals use words in order to get things done. Consider the utterance, "I do take thee to be my lawful wedded husband." It makes no sense to consider such an utterance a true or false description of a state of affairs. It is an action. Austin took up the notion that language and action form a seamless whole of communication. He identified the "speech-act" as the basic element of communication, and set about to analyze the kinds of speech-acts which make up our fabric of communication. Kinds of speech-acts include, for example, making excuses, making promises, and ordering dessert.

The focus on speech-acts created an especially important role for the concept of 'intention'. The utterance "How are you?" for example, is rarely what its form would indicate, a question about a state of affairs, but is rather the expression of an individual's desire to open a conversation in good will, or something like that. Its intended meaning, what Austin would call its "illocutionary force," has to be explained with reference to the intentions of the speaker within the given context. So, any theory that would claim to analyze communication in the form of speech-acts finds itself also trying to account for types of intentions, and the forms of action to which those intentions may give rise. The fancy word "intentionality" derives from this context. It means most generally the capacity of having intentions. (This includes the capacity of having beliefs, desires, and fears—in short, attitudes toward propositions—and so is pretty close to what is normally meant by "consciousness.")

## WHY SO ORDINARY?

Ordinary language philosophy came under fire for some apparently extraordinary presuppositions about the nature of language. The new philosophy seemed to imply that ordinary language was a fixed and given structure of meaning. As many observed, however, it is quite ordinary for language to evolve. It is also quite ordinary for a language to branch off into specialized forms which, though they retain some link to the mother tongue, also have valid standards of their own. It does not seem implausible that even the analysis of ordinary language should change ordinary language, or at least form a specialized branch of its own.

## EXTRAORDINARY LANGUAGE PEOPLE: THE THEORETICAL TURN

While Austin and his coterie of Oxford dons may have been content to wander among the endless particulars of ordinary language, others sensed that the project could not go on without some sort of universal theory. Philosophy, especially in its academic form, will always favor theory. Its ultimate aim is and always has been the theory that can explain everything. So, "linguistic philosophy" gave way to "philosophy of language." From the 1950s through the 1980s a wide range of variously incompatible schools and theories about language arose. Although the inquiries which motivated the new theorists varied according to their theories, the general sorts of questions they investigated were something like these: What does it mean to understand the meaning of a word or sentence? How is a language speaker able to formulate and understand a potentially infinite number of sentences like this one? What is the meaning of meaning? The most sought-after theory, the Holy Grail of the new philosophy, was a theory of meaning.

For some, like Donald Davidson (*Inquiries into Truth and Interpretation*, 1984), the theory of meaning was to be one in a group—including theories of truth, interpretation, mind, and action—which would together make up a broader project of philosophical anthropology. For the true believers, like Michael Dummett (*Frege's Philosophy of Language*, 1973), a "full-blooded" theory of meaning was to be the long-sought champion of philosophy, the Atlas on which all solutions to philosophical problems would rest. John Searle (*Speech Acts: An Essay in the Philosophy of Language*, 1970), among others, took up the specific task of discovering a grand theory of speech-acts.

How did speech-act theory find itself swinging on this ancient pendulum between empiricism and rationalism? I would suggest it has to do with the core concept of intentionality. Within this concept and its role in speech-act theory are embedded some very traditional philosophical problems about freedom, determinism, and consciousness. To put the matter schematically: Austin's attempt to classify speech-acts was really an effort to discover the "forms" of freedom. It was an attempt to prescribe all possible (speech-)actions. Despite the meticulous cataloging of many natural forms of communication, he was unable to bring the project to a close for the simple reason that intentional action is always free to do what it likes. There is no inherent or internal limit to freedom. The theoreticians sensed this. They thought that they could resolve the problems in a Spinozan way, at the purely conceptual level. Speech-act theory, in its philosophical form, was merely an expression of the hope for an understanding that would overcome subjectivity, unite activity with passivity, and lay out all the possibilities of life in advance.

## SuperStar News Exclusive!
## TOP PHILS TURNING INTO DICTIONARIES!!

Top philosophers in several countries are suffering from a mystery illness which makes them want to *turn themselves into dictionaries!* A senior philosophical official who refused to be named, described, denoted, or referred to in any way revealed yesterday that the top docs are *sick* of the old problems in metaphysics. They think previous philosophy was just *confusions* about the meanings of words. The only way forward they say is to get clear about linguistic usages.

He pointed out that the new philosopher-dictionaries are *not at all* like the old *Webster's* or *Oxford English Dictionary*. They don't define just words. They define whole sentences, speech-acts, and even language-games!

In some cases it is hard to tell that the disease is present. Unlike the wandering ancient Greek philosophers, today's philosophers have endured years of confinement in poorly lit libraries. They are dry, brittle, and pasty pale creatures, so it is easy to mistake them for dictionaries anyway!

Many philosophers are finding the transformation difficult. "There are so many words in a dictionary," one said,

"and while we've been used to producing torrents of words, we usually use the same ones lots of times, instead of lots of different ones. Besides," he said, "there are lots of really nasty language-games in the world. I'd call them language-pranks." Others complain that their students don't recognize them any more, and scribble obscene notes to each other in their margins.

The biggest problem the philosophers face though, is that the old words like "metaphysics," "ethics," and "language" are still in the dictionary! Plus they've had to include speech-acts like "proofs of the existence of God." So it looks like the old philosophy is following them into their new books. Some of the new dictionaries are starting to fight among themselves about the correct definitions of these terms.

We advise our readers to take a good look through their bookshelves at home. If you hear ruffling pages and whispered arguments, you may have some philosophers on the shelf. The best cure is to bring them out into the sunlight. That usually causes them to wither away.

# The Tenure Sutra

Many thousands of years ago, sometime in the late twentieth century, when the castes were first given their holy form, when they were not yet called the Tenureds and the Untenurables, a young prince discovered the true meaning of our noble system. He changed his name to Chair, and preached his new gospel far and wide. His first disciple, who called himself T. A., wrote down the Master's words for the benefit of future generations.

*Thus have I heard, from the lips of our Master, the Great Chair. When the Master was living at the Great University of Thought (GUT), he gathered his disciples from among the Teacher-Slaves and said to them:*

*Ye are many. But the Tenureds are few. Ye who would rise to the blessed state of Holy Tenureship, listen carefully, and I shall reveal The Sixfold Path to Tenure. Verily, I say unto thee, only the few have ears to hear me. Perhaps I speak only to one. The many who cannot hear can only know a superficial life, without inner peace, status, or job security.*

*To Thee who have ears I say: Thou shalt attain the Nirvana known to the Tenureds. In this state of exalted bliss, of oneness with the Nothing, thou shalt no longer feel the pressure of selfish desires, nor the need to work. Thou shalt attain perfect happiness in the life of pure contemplation. For thou shalt learn to contemplate Nothing.*

## The Sixfold Path

**First,** *thou shalt purge thyself of undesirable and unnecessary personal characteristics, as these will distract thyself and others and perhaps arouse jealousy. A sense of humor, for example, is undesirable. An ability to teach is unnecessary.*

**Second,** *thou shalt join one of the Holy Tribes, and worship at the Shrine of its Holy Doctrine. Verily, a One without Tribe is no One. And thou shalt swear eternal vigilance against all Enemies of the Tribe.*

**Third,** *thou shalt choose a personal Master from among the Elders of one's Holy Tribe. The Master will guide and protect thee, his Teacher-Slave, on the Path to Tenure.*

**Fourth,** *thou shalt find a small insect, larger than a mite, smaller than a fruit fly, and make this insect the object of all thy labor and attention. In time, thou shalt become one with this insect.*

**Fifth,** *thou shalt learn the Seven Arguments, and be able to repeat them backwards or in any order:*

Argument from Authority. *Those with Tenure are right. Those without are wrong. Those with more Tenure are more right than those with less.*

Argument from Length of Argument. *Those who have published more are more right. Those who have published less are less right. Those who have not published at all are wrong.*

Argument from Footnotes. *The publication with the most footnotes is the most right. That with the least is the least right. A publication with no footnotes is wrong.*

Argument from Vocabulary. *Speech or writing which may be understood by ordinary people is not specialized. It does not belong to our discipline. It is wrong.*

Argument from Size of Subject. *The smaller the subject-matter, the more likely it is to be right. Anything larger than the leg hairs of a small insect is almost certainly wrong.*

Argument from the Professional Circle. *We are specialists in our discipline. Therefore, our discipline is whatever we do.*

Argument from the Classics. *If it is written by one of the living, it is trite or silly. If it is written in a Classic it is fundamentally true or profoundly false.*

**Sixth,** *once thou hast chosen a Tribe, a Master, and an Insect, and thou hast learnt the Seven Arguments, thou shalt participate in the ritual slaying of trees and spilling of ink. Thou shalt be responsible for the deaths of at least two large Oak trees and enough ink to drown a small insect one thousand times over.*

*This is the Sixfold Path to Tenure. There is no other path than the Sixfold Path.*

Thus spake the Chair.

## WAITING FOR GENERAL THEORY

(Scene 1: A group of philosophers of language are gathered at a bus stop. They seem to be waiting for someone, a certain General Theory.)

SEARLE[1]: Once one has a General Theory of speech acts—a theory which Austin did not live long enough to develop himself. . . .

PUTNAM[2]: A general and precise Theory . . . is not to be expected until one has a general and precise model of a language user; and that is still a long way off . . .

DUMMETT[3]: . . . the Theory of meaning is the fundamental part of philosophy which underlies all others. . . . No doubt, once we have a workable account of what it is, in general, to know the meaning of a word or expression . . .

PUTNAM[4]: Utopia is a long way off . . .

DAVIDSON[5]: Once we have a Theory [of truth], producing the required

---

1. John Searle, "Reiterating the Differences: A Reply to Derrida," in *Glyph*, Vol. 2 (Baltimore: Johns Hopkins, 1977), p. 205, cited in Jacques Derrida, *Limited Inc.* (Evanston, Ill.: Northwestern University Press, 1988), p. 91.

2. Hilary Putnam, "Is Semantics Possible?" *Naming, Necessity, and Natural Kinds*, ed. Stephen P. Schwartz (Ithaca, N.Y.: Cornell, 1977), p. 118.

3. Michael Dummett, *Frege: Philosophy of Language*, 2nd ed. (Cambridge, Mass.: Harvard University Press, 1981), pp. 669, 106.

4. Putnam, "Is Semantics Possible?" p. 118.

5. Donald Davidson, *Inquiries into Truth and Interpretation* (Oxford: Clarendon Press, 1984), p. 61.

proof [of how the truth-value of the sentence depends on the meanings of its words] is easy enough; the process could be mechanized.

STEWART: Once upon a time . . .

(Scene 2: The philosophers continue to describe how they imagine General Theory in considerable detail.)

DUMMETT: A Theory of meaning must, in General . . .

PUTNAM[6]: Traditional semantic theory leaves out two contributions to the determination of reference—the contribution of society and the contribution of the real world; a Better semantic Theory must encompass both.

DAVIDSON[7]: We want a Theory that is simple and clear . . .

STEWART: Look, guys, maybe he just isn't going to show. It's late already—the late twentieth century. Let's go home.

SEARLE: Wait! I'm Rediscovering the Mind. [*Curtain falls.*]

## To Mean or Not to Mean: Whether 'tis Nobler to Be a Native Speaker

At least since Leibniz dreamt of his *characteristica universalis*, philosophers have been seeking a perfect language, one so perspicuous in its representations that meanings would never be in doubt, and disputes could be resolved with simple accounting exercises. Let us see how the great philosophers of the analytic tradition fare as each attempts to translate a snippet of Shakespeare into what we may take to be his own idiom of truth.

### *Shakespeare, Hamlet, Act II, Scene 2*

HAMLET: . . . you are a fishmonger.
POLONIUS: Not I, my lord.
HAMLET: Then I would you were so honest a man.
POLONIUS: Honest, my lord!
HAMLET: Ay, sir; to be honest, as this world goes, is to be one man pick'd out of ten thousand.

### *Frege*

HAMLET: $\vdash$—F(you)
POLONIUS: $\vdash$⊤—F(I)
HAMLET: $\vdash_x$⊤— H(x) and $\vdash$——W(F[you])
           └— F(x)

F = "is a fishmonger"

H = "is honest"; W = "has the property of being wished it were true by Hamlet"

---

6. Putnam, "Is Semantics Possible?" p. 132.
7. Davidson, *Inquiries into Truth and Interpretation*, p. 214.

POLONIUS: H(x)!

HAMLET: ⊢ₓ⌐ I(x)                    I = "is one man picked out of
          ⌊ H(x)                          ten thousand"

Explanation of symbols:

F(x)     An expression is split up into a variable part and an invariable part. The latter is the function, and the former is its argument.

⊢——      The horizontal stroke indicates that the following symbols form a whole, an idea which is a possible content of judgment. The vertical stroke at the start affirms that what follows is indeed a judgment.

⊢ᵥ——     The small vertical stroke indicates negation.

⊢ₓ——     The following judgment is true for any argument.

⊢⌐⌊      It is not possible to affirm the bottom judgment and deny the top.

## RUSSELL

HAMLET: The propositional function "x is a fishmonger and x is you" is not always false.

POLONIUS: The propositional function "x refers to the current speaker and x affirms what the previous speaker said a moment ago and x is me at this moment in time" is false.

HAMLET: The propositional function "If x is a fishmonger then 'x is honest' is true" is always true, and I wish it were not true that it is always false of x that "x is honest and x is my present interlocutor and y is you and y is identical with x."

POLONIUS: Huh?

HAMLET: Affirmative. Let M be the class of all men and H the class of all honest men. Let x be the number of members of M and y the number of members of H. Then x = y • 10,000.

## LOGICAL POSITIVIST

HAMLET: The sense-data I experience from the space-time coordinates I perceive your body to occupy are similar to those I experience when those who say "fishmonger" and point to themselves are present.

POLONIUS: The sense-data I experience from the space-time coordinates I perceive my body to occupy are *not* similar to those I experience when those who say "fishmonger" and point to themselves are present.

HAMLET: The sense-data I experience when those who say "fishmonger" and point to themselves are present frequently occur together with the sense-data of honest behavior, which are sense-data of behavior involving statements about intentions which accurately predict sense-data associated with future behavior. It is therefore likely that the sense-data from the space-time coordinates I perceive your body to occupy involving statements of intention will not accurately predict sense-data associated with your future behavior. I would be better able to predict sense-data associated with your future behavior if the sense-data I experienced from the space-time coordinates I perceive your body to occupy were similar to those I experience when those who say "fishmonger" and point to themselves are present.

POLONIUS: I have not experienced the sense-data of honest behavior.

HAMLET: "The sense-data of honest behavior occur in only one per ten thousand experiences involving humanoid figures."

(The last line is in quotes because, strictly speaking, it is nonsense, since there is no way Hamlet could ever get to know ten thousand people sufficiently well to verify their honesty.)

## WITTGENSTEIN (LATER)

HAMLET: . . . you are a fishmonger.

POLONIUS: Not I, my lord.

HAMLET: Then I would you were so honest a man.

POLONIUS: Honest, my lord!

HAMLET: Ay, sir; to be honest, as this world goes, is to be one man pick'd out of ten thousand.

(It's their own language game. Let them play it.)

## ORDINARY LANGUAGE PHILOSOPHER

HAMLET: Hey, you're the guy from the grocery store, the one who works at the seafood counter!

POLONIUS: No, I'm not.

HAMLET: Too bad. That guy is pretty honest.

POLONIUS: Are you trying to tell me something?

HAMLET: Yeah, not many people are honest around here.

## TRUTH-CONDITIONED SEMANTICIST

HAMLET: The False.

POLONIUS: The True.

HAMLET: The True.

POLONIUS: The False.

HAMLET: The True.

# The Mind Program

## Mind Fills the Gap

From the perspective of the twenty-fifth century, aboard the Federation Starship *Enterprise* perhaps, twentieth-century knowledge will in no field seem so barbaric as in the sciences concerning mental phenomena. While our electronic and mechanical technologies will seem respectable, if clumsy, our understanding of our own minds and brains will smell like medieval alchemistry does to us. From the twentieth century looking forward, this means that the sciences of the mental are where the action is. Here are the frontiers of knowledge. It is an exciting time to be a researcher, perhaps even to be a philosopher of mind.

The philosophy of mind has always been a member of the inner circle of subdisciplines by means of which analytic philosophy has divided the world into timeless investigative projects. Russell wrote extensively on the analysis of mind. The logical positivists understood a form of behaviorism in mental matters to be an important payoff of their work. The philosophers of language often built their theories with a particular philosophy of mind in view. Sometime in the 1980s, however, the philosophy of mind surpassed the other subdisciplines as the favored candidate for the first philosophy of analytic philosophy. Its adherents claimed, with the absence of irony common to analytic philosophers, that theirs was true occupation of philosophy, and the basis for any of the subsidiary investigations in its other subdisciplines.

Why should the philosophy of mind suddenly experience a renaissance? Why bring back dusty nonentities like Descartes's *cogito*? Why risk another Hegelianism? The answer is as plain as the laboratory next door. Neuroscience is just beginning to get a grip on the extraordinarily complex structure of the human brain. Though they have not yet delivered much, the new fields of artificial intelligence and cognitive psychology are promising. Evolutionary theory has kicked in a few stimulating hypotheses about human mental development, and ethnology has produced interesting insights into human behavior. In short, the sciences of the mind are in an infantile state. Like physics in the seventeenth century, the social sciences in the nineteenth century, or linguistics just a few decades ago, they are generating just enough knowledge to tease and tantalize philosophical speculators, but not enough to shut them up. Recent philosophy of mind is a case of science fanaticism.

What claim do philosophers have to mind? Why should philosophy have a different role here than it does with respect to biology or knitting? In fact, there is no good reason why philosophers should have anything of particular interest to say about the nature of mental phenomena. What is (or should be) of interest on matters of mind are the facts and the theories which bring them together, and these are the property of those who look for the first and confirm the second, namely, the scientists. There is, however, a bad reason why philosophers may stake a claim to mind. Even more so than the common run of humankind, philosophers have harbored extraordinary prejudices about the mind. Descartes, to cite just one example, invested the belief in mind as substance with heavy theological baggage. Many other philosophers have maintained that knowledge about the mind is somehow very different from any other kind of knowledge. These prejudices are at once the basis for any project which calls itself the philosophy of mind and the objects of the critiques which motivate much philosophy of mind as well. In other words, philosophers barged into the world of mind without a ticket, and their only legitimate mission now that they're in is to destroy each other and beat a retreat.

As the various sciences of the mind mature, philosophy will be forced to give ground. As a rule, philosophers can hold territory only so long as there is little evidence with which to be concerned. As the evidence accumulates, philosophers of mind will find themselves working as historians: They will survey old, unsubstantiated theories of mind, usually put forward by dead philosophers, so as to prevent their interference with the progress of research. They may become popularizers of science: They will relate the most recent discoveries to the ensemble of human knowledge and wisdom on the question of what it all means. Some of those who call themselves philosophers may even make a contribution to science. Philosophers, after all, are clever people, and in the anarchic environment of the contemporary sciences of the mind their generalist approach and critical skills may result in fresh insights. At that point, however, they would probably no longer be working as philosophers. None of this should be cause for anxiety. It is all part of a recurring historical cycle. It once took a philosopher to speculate on the bizarre phenomena of electricity; now it's just the cable guy.

Even if there is no rational project for a philosophy of mind, there may still be pressing questions that seem to have no other home. Will our self-image as free, thinking beings disintegrate under the pressure of new knowledge about neurons and psychochemistry? Does our self-esteem suffer in the knowledge that it might one day be possible for a computer to write sonnets, feel the pang of lost love, experience the mystery of a clear blue sky, and discover dialectical reason? One may wish to employ a few philosophers, if only to preserve the meaning of life from the onslaught of cold technology. It is worth remembering, though, that at one time many people thought that without the belief that the earth was at the center of the universe our civilization would crumble, and that even today a few cling to the idea that the fact of biological evolution is untrue. Where knowledge is incompatible with faith, after all, is where faith depends on ignorance. Better, perhaps, to look on the bright side: More knowledge enriches our possibilities. And trust our wisdom to make the right choices. Maybe in the twenty-fifth century the ways in which even ordinary people think of themselves will be more truthful and valuable than what will appear to them the simplistic and superstitious vocabulary we now use in describing our beliefs, moods, and desires.

# The Poor Man's Dialectic
# or Ground-Churning?

Is the history of analytic philosophy redeemable? I suggested above that the history of analytic philosophy is a poor man's dialectic, that is, a gradual but continuous and determined purgation of illusion, culminating in a recognition of ignorance. Now I think it may well be a case of churning the earth, that is, just one damned illusion after another.

*Logical Illusions for Empirical Illusions.* Analytic philosophy arose out of the empiricist tradition of philosophy, but soon denied itself the avail to philosophical empiricism. Frege struck the first blow in his attack on psychologism. The logical positivists put the new logic of Frege, Russell, and Wittgenstein in service of what remained of empiricism, but failed. In his *From a Logical Point of View* (1953), Harvard philosopher W. V. D. Quine delivered the final blow in his attack on the "two dogmas of empiricism": the dogma of the distinction between analytic and synthetic judgments, and the dogma that sense data may be taken as direct evidence for all empirically significant propositions. The Wittgensteinian hullabaloo about private languages was also an attack on philosophical empiricism, and its attendant preconceptions about language and mind. Looking on the bright side, the general principle of empiricism remains as strong as ever in the analytic tradition, even while its use as the foundation of a philosophical project is no longer taken seriously.

The logicians, however, expected too much out of their critique. It did not follow from the fact that psychological doctrines about the mental character of all ideas were incoherent that ideas necessarily exist in an abstract, Platonic world. In their quest for a purely logical knowledge, the logicians violated the basic insight of empiricism and so recreated in their own form the fallacies of psychologism.

*Language for Logic.* The illusion that logic is the structure of the world is no more grievous than the illusion that language is the study of the world. In both cases there is the false hope for a land of unconditioned knowledge, a universal science for philosophy. The linguistic philosophers, beginning with the logical positivists, were simply unable to understand the basic insights achieved by the logicians.

*Mind for Language.* In "On the Very Idea of a Conceptual Scheme," reprinted in *Inquiries into Truth and Interpretation,* Davidson identified the "third dogma" as the "dogma of scheme and content." Running through empiricist and language philosophy was the idea that the mind operates with a structure or scheme of meanings—a language or a conceptual scheme—which is different from and prior to the content of experience. In a rather self-destructive way, for a philosopher of language, Davidson concluded that "there is no such thing as languages," at least, not as intended by his fellow philosophers. Indeed, the failure of any theory of meaning to account fully for intentionality reflects this recognition that the analysis of the nature of language cannot provide the sort of universal science that philosophy seeks.

However, that that which disrupts the structure of language—intentionality—should have a philosophically analyzable structure of its own is a false hope. The philosophy of mind shifts the location of the mysterious structure whose analysis is the object of philosophy, but fails to eliminate the paradoxical and illusory character of that structure.

*Empirical Illusions for Mind.* The process here is not yet complete. Eventually, however, philosophers will recognize that the questions that trouble the so-called philosophy of mind will reduce to questions of fact, open to empirical investigations, or mere signals of discontent motivated by ancient prejudices.

Prediction: In the first years of the coming century, as the philosophy of mind cedes even more territory to the sciences of mind, it will end up favoring a kind of psychologism. Analytic philosophy will take its last stand on the insistence that somewhere at the base of all empirical knowledge there is this funny, ineliminable element of subjectivity that belongs to mind. But this is precisely the position whose overthrow was the originary act of analytic philosophy, at the beginning of the present century. A hundred years of churning, and we find ourselves standing on the same piece of earth.

All of this demonstrates a principle that should be familiar to anyone with experience in large corporations or government:

---

**The Make-Work Principle.** So long as you pay people to do something, they'll find something to do.

---

DEPARTMENT OF ANALYTIC PHILOSOPHY

DEPARTMENT OF ANALYTIC PHILOSOPHY

BULLETIN BOARD

**Wanted**

Refuted or Alive

**—The Skeptic—**

**Reward: Hereditary Tenure**

No known name or address. Charged with refusing to believe anything, except that what we believe is false. Armed with bad arguments and dangerous to know. Cannot be perceived.

   A.k.a. "the foil" and "the justification for professional philosophy."

PERSONAL ADS

**SOLIPSIST** seeks company

**CONSCIOUSNESS** in search of itself. Are you there?

**SWEM/AD**—Single White European Male Academic Department—seeks reason for being, meaning in life. Experienced and mature, but innocent and hopeful. All dressed up and nowhere to go. Can you help me? Will provide material comforts for the one who can show me the way.

Lost & Found

**FOUND** A private language argument. Write to: SSSS, c/o The Mind

**FOUND** The bounds of sense. Contact: Jabberwadlyebahbah

**LOST** The argument from design. Please call: God

## The School of Outrageous Counterfactuals

"Suppose that there are fifty-nine other universes exactly identical to our own in all respects save one. Each has a planet earth, an identical history, a person with your name who does what you are doing now, reading book. But each universe has its own unique name for ice cream . . ."

"Imagine that people got pregnant in this way: little spores fall from the sky, and when they land on someone's belly button, whether male or female, he or she gets pregnant. The implications for . . ."

"Suppose that future technology allows us to graft the frontal lobes of a human brain onto a microwave oven. Now let's consider two cases: one where the *left* lobe is used, the other where the *right* lobe is used . . ."

Such are the marvelous conjectures your correspondent overheard from students on a recent visit to the newly created School of Outrageous Counterfactuals. Dr. W. Hatif, the school's founder, explained the school's mission in this way. "Success in modern analytic philosophy belongs to those who can think up the most imaginative and outrageous counterfactuals with which to illustrate their points."

"So, you are providing an auxiliary service to the philosophical community," I ventured.

"Oh, no," he corrected me. "It's much more than that. We think we're at the forefront of philosophy. We see the development of outrageous counterfactuals as the ultimate outcome of the history of Western philosophy. You see, philosophy has always relied on imaginative illustrations, but we believe that the points behind the illustrations are less relevant, perhaps not relevant at all. What matters is the illustration, the counterfactual example. That's what people want!"

As I wandered around some more I heard: "Imagine a Twin Earth in which there was no philosophy, no School of Outrageous Counterfactuals. . . ."

## News Flash: Philosophers' Publication Problems Threaten World Survival

The level of anxiety in philosophy faculties seems to be increasing as at no time since the existentialists held tenure. A job which is enormously stressful even in ordinary times has been made worse by the worldwide paper shortage. Philosophers who need to publish vital results are finding their work delayed by months and even years. Some say that the impact on world culture, politics, and the general happiness could be profound.

Professor Ann Steich, a leading philosopher of ethics, is particularly concerned about the moral state of the world. She is working on a book that will "establish the nature of good and evil, and conclusively resolve the MacIntosh dilemma." (Professor A. MacIntosh has already published his argument that the history of thought has brought the world to the brink of a moral osterizer, which may soon blend our values into an amoral mush.) Steich's worry is that if her manuscript is held up at the press, the world may lose its sense of values, and succumb to a disastrous nihilism. "People may become unable to find any meaning in their lives," she warns. Other experts in the related field of political philosophy express similar anxieties concerning the legitimacy of existing regimes, and are predicting anything up to global revolution.

A noted philosopher of science, Chuck Windar, has recorded his concerns about future progress in the biological sciences. He has some important manuscripts on the philosophy of microbiology "just sitting on publishers' desks around the world." He describes them as "efforts in conceptual clarification, focusing primarily on the nature of the 'Micro', and how small it has to be." He believes that contemporary research into the life of the amoeba will be held up as scientists become confused about what fits in the definition of their specialty.

An anonymous philosopher of ordinary language, working on emergency utterances, has also cried for help. Her unpublished work situates the meaning of these utterances within a theory of meaning based on truth conditions. "It's the man in the street I worry about," she says, "especially the man crossing the street. Without a clear understanding of the truth-conditional meaning of utterances like 'watch out!' and 'run!' and 'arrrggghh', a person can easily get run over." Our philosopher is spending her weekends "hanging around intersections" in order to make sure nothing happens until her seminal work is published.

Perhaps most worrying of all is the testimony of Herr Doktor Feedman, a leader in the relatively new field called alimentology, or "the philosophy of food." He claims he has cooked up "the solutions to centuries-old problems concerning the nature of eating." For want of paper to print his work, he laments, "we may soon find ourselves unable to eat. We might all perish." It was not clear to whom the "we" referred.

## Top Ten Most Boring Philosophy Books

10. Aristotle's *Physics*. Lots of concepts, not a single fact.

9. Aquinas's *Commentary on Aristotle*. Still no facts.

8. Locke's *Essay Concerning Human Understanding*, etc. Okay, so there are objects, senses, and the mind, and words stand for objects in the mind. We get the picture. Why go on for another five hundred pages?

7. Quine's *Word and Object*. Shoot the damn translator, and that stupid rabbit. And stop quibbling.

6. Hegel's *Philosophy of Nature*. A compendium of early-nineteenth-century misunderstandings about early-nineteenth-century science.

5. Frege's *Begriffschrift*. A new way of playing with letters of the alphabet and other funny symbols.

4. Russell's *Principia Mathematica*. Read by two people, one of whom fell into terminal sleep.

3. Husserl, *Logical Investigation*. Eddy looks for a permanent conceptual distinction, and never finds it.

2. Plato's *Laws*. Its three readers formed a society, then committed group suicide.

1. Heidegger, *passim*. Basis for BBC documentaries on peasant life in the Black Forest.

## ANTI-SYMPOSIUM: PHILOSOPHERS TO AVOID AT A DINNER PARTY

1. **Heidegger.** He will start by trying to ask a question but will never finish. "How are you? *(I'm fi—)* We are on the way to a questioning. Let us wander through the forest in search of the clearing which discloses the meaning of this question. *(I-uh—)* How is it with the 'you'? *(I—could you—)* How is it with the 'how'? *(please—)* What is the Being of the beings which 'are' you? *(Would you pl—)* Let us think this question of Being. What is Being? *(ME; now, PASS THE BUTTER)* What is the 'is'? . . ."

2. **Wittgenstein.** He will pass over the whole dinner in a sullen silence, until he tastes the dessert, which will seem horribly botched to his refined Viennese palate, at which point he will turn livid and launch unstoppable tirades about the ghastliness of modern life; the ubiquity of philistines, like you; the evils of philosophy; etc.

3. **Analytic philosophers in general.** When it is discovered that you have nothing of interest to say about modal logics in formal semantic theories for non-quantifier languages, or whatever their specialty is, you will be reduced to talking about the weather, house prices, and the ventilation system in the library. Boring.

4. **Plato.** He'll be a fine companion during dinner, but afterwards will write up a dialogue in which your views are thoroughly distorted and refuted.

# THE END OF PHILOSOPHY

## AT LAST

At long last our history comes to an end, as it must, not because it has finally arrived at its destination, but because we have to draw the line somewhere. It would have been reassuring if we could have ended the history of philosophy in a meaningful way. Even if it would have been too much to expect that the truth about everything would at last have been found, at least we might have hoped that the search would have led through some logical sequence of twists and turns before finally ending in ignominy. In the end, however, we have not really advanced from our beginning, and the logic of our philosophy is no more evolved than that of, say, the Presocratics. Three millennia have brought us no closer to the end of philosophy; we are, at best, closer to an understanding of philosophy's need for an end.

---

### A Pointless Parable

*Three philosophical hikers and their Sherpa guide decided to climb the highest mountain in the world. It was an undiscovered mountain so high that from its peak it was expected that one would be able to view the entire world. So they set out on their climb one sunny day. Several millennia later, they finally arrived at the peak. They swung their eyes around, and then looked at each other perplexed. They could survey the entire world, but their altitude was so great that everything below blended into a solid, undifferentiated mass of gray. They could see everything at once, but nothing in particular.*

*The first hiker, who was partial to Eastern philosophies, exclaimed: "We have*

---

461

*mastered everything and achieved the ultimate Nothingness. We no longer exist."*
*He sat down and closed his eyes.*

*The second hiker, who was schooled in Continental philosophy, lamented: "Our long tradition of metaphysical mountain climbing has led us to an encounter with nihilism. We must undermine the foundations of this mountain, and only then we will be able to see everything." He took out a shovel and began to dig.*

*The third, an analytic philosopher by training, said, "We're just not high enough. Fortunately, we have developed some new technologies to take us higher." He looked around for a ladder.*

*The Sherpa, under the impression that his customers were dissatisfied, said, a little defensively, "Sorry, no refunds."*

## THE QUESTIONABLE CAST

At the very least it would have been reassuring to reflect on the relative permanence of the cast of characters that comprises the traditional histories of philosophy. Such a reassurance is not to be had, however, except at some expense to the facts. Greatness, as we have seen, does not invariably follow from the internal logic of a philosopher's doctrines. It arises more often from a confluence of style, circumstances, and chance, and does not always last. To be sure, there is nothing incomprehensible here—just something that exceeds authorial intentions, and escapes the logical framework of a philosophical narrative. In the history of philosophy, character is destiny, but only retrospect, in virtue of the defiantly complex, inevitably historical, all-too-human art of the making of a classic.

### The Making of a Classic

*"It is a detestable piece of human excrement,"* said the author's conscience.

*"It is a futile attempt at an impossible goal,"* said the author to a friend.

*"It is a successful attempt to get out of housework,"* said the spouse.

*"It is a niche-product for the benefit of a small and disturbed audience,"* said the publisher.

*"It is the advocate of a one-sided point of view,"* said the reviewer.

*"It is an innovative approach to contemporary issues,"* said the reviewer a few years later.

*"It is a contribution to the conversation of our times,"* said the historian.

> *"It is a landmark in the history of culture,"* said the historian a few centuries later.
>
> *"It is the spirit of its time expressed and transcended,"* said the philosophical historian.
>
> *"It is one of the supreme achievements of humanity,"* said the blurb on the back of the latest reprint edition.

## THE IMMODESTY OF MY PREDECESSORS

> In this enquiry I have made completeness my chief aim, and I venture to assert that there is not a single metaphysical problem which has not been solved, or for the solution of which the key has not been supplied.
>
> Immanuel Kant[1]

> I therefore believe myself to have found, on all essential points, the final solution of the problems [of philosophy].
>
> Ludwig Wittgenstein[2]

> In the end I would rather have been a Basel professor than God; but I did not dare to push my private egoism so far as to forego on its account the creation of the world.
>
> What is disagreeable and compels my modesty is that, in the end, I am every name in history.
>
> Friedrich Nietzsche[3]

I do not fault my predecessors so much for their immodesty. Anyone who aims to deliver the promised results of philosophy must consider it pretentious to forego pronouncing on the truth about everything, or possibly even creating the world as we know it. Philosophy can be a meaningful project only if the end of philosophy, the solution of all problems, can be grasped, or at least foreseen. It is not the humility of philosophers which is in question here, then, but perhaps their *faith*. I believe that they are untrue to the faith that inspires all philosophy, the faith of all reasonable people as well as all philosophers that, in the end, there is nothing that cannot be understood. Driven by doubt and insecurity, or possibly excessive ambition, philosophers have exchanged this faith for the supposed demonstration that everything has been understood. They have confused the insight that all problems can be solved with the dogma that there is a single solution to all problems. Their apparent immodesty is really a false modesty, for they assume that philosophy must be more than the creation of their own mere attitude or disposition, and that it must have some foundation in the things themselves.

---

1. Preface to the first edition of *The Critique of Pure Reason*, p. xiii.

2. Preface to *Tractatus Logico-Philosophicus* (London: Routledge & Kegan Paul, 1961), p. 4.

3. In a letter written to Professor Jakob Burckhardt, Nietzsche's old friend and mentor (January 6, 1889), Nietzsche's last written words before descending into eleven years of silent madness. Friedrich Nietzsche, *Werke*, ed. Karl Schlechta (Frankfurt: Ulistein, 1969), Vol. III, p. 1352.

# The Future of Philosophy

Having pretended omniscience about the history of philosophy, I could not plausibly refrain from judgment about the future of philosophy. Yet I'm afraid I don't have much to say. I believe that I have shown that there is no internal logic to the history of philosophy. Why should the future be any different? There is no logic to philosophy, whether retrospective or prospective. The idea of the future of philosophy seems to me as empty as the idea of the history of philosophy.

## A THOUGHT EXPERIMENT

What's next in the future of humankind? Well, things might go on pretty much as before—except our cars will go faster, or they won't use wheels anymore, and we will be eating tasty protein substitutes. Let's suppose, though, for philosophy's sake, that things really do change. Suppose that over the next few centuries bioengineering skills improve to the extent that humans can graft artificial devices into their bodies in order to aid cognitive functions. Suppose that in a few thousand years the species learns to control genes so well that it not only tinkers at the margins, shaping better noses or favoring higher intelligence, but is able to produce entirely new creatures, superhumans who can better take advantage of bioengineering potential. Suppose that some eons later these machine-beings decide that in order to save on postage they might as well merge together, into one giant biomechanical individual. Suppose that this new being acquires a kind of immortality, inasmuch as it can always replace parts that go bad. Suppose that with all that time on its many hands it eventually discovers just about everything there is to know about how the universe works. Maybe it even has the opportunity to change the course of things on a cosmic scale, to jump-start a new Big Bang in order to forestall some possible collapse or disintegration of the universe.

464

So what happens to philosophy? If philosophy is the industry of conceptual schemes, then surely our three millennia will count as a single, primitive period. The concepts of self, world, God, and all the rest with which philosophers have been obsessed to date would have to be refined considerably, if not thrown out altogether. The whole three thousand years would be dismissed as early mammalian thought, or something like that. There would, for a change, be real change in the history of philosophy.

On the other hand, is such a future really inconceivable within our supposed philosophy? Improbable and fantastic maybe—but *prima facie* not inconceivable, it would seem, for it has just been conceived. With some modest effort, philosophy's concepts can be extended indefinitely into the future. Anything may be possible, it is true, but anything which is possible is also in principle conceivable. It is our convictions, not our concepts, which seem to be at stake. And it is quite possible that our convictions are wrong, and therefore not philosophical.

So what? Does this mean that philosophy will never change?

# Matthew

## The Last Philosopher

> **Autobiofact.** I gave up on philosophy a few years
> ago. Sometime just after getting a doctoral degree
> and before entering a professional career, I came
> upon what I thought was the answer to one of the
> ancient questions of philosophy. What is the good
> life? Not the life of philosophy. My reasoning took
> the honorable form of a syllogism: philosophy is a
> waste of time; a waste of time is not the good life;
> philosophy is not the good life. So, I dismissed
> philosophy from my life as a youthful aberration. Or
> so I thought.

What have I accomplished? Is this book just an excuse to sacrifice more trees? All right, then, let me rephrase the question: What have I submitted that is new and worthy of your consideration?

I would not say that there is much that is original in the interpretations and the criticisms I have offered of individual philosophers. For the most part, I have borrowed shamelessly. (Some of the best sources for criticism, by the way, are a philosopher's own contemporaries and immediate successors. Maybe it's because they aren't yet blinded by the glory of greatness.)

There is also not much new in the idea of criticizing the whole idea of philosophy. As I have shown, a number of philosophers have explicitly dismissed the whole previous history as unsubstantiated metaphysical speculation, confusions about language, mere scholasticism, and so on. My criticisms of philosophy are simply approximations of what has already been said by philosophers such as

Hume, Kant, Nietzsche, and Wittgenstein. And maybe all philosophers have made such a gesture at least implicitly.

Come to think of it, there really is nothing new, at least not entirely new, that can be said in philosophy. I believe that I have offered a new collection or synthesis of some of the old views. I have assembled the critiques in a way that makes plain some aspects of the general pattern of the history of philosophy. I think I have provided a more general understanding of the failure of philosophy than is available from other philosophers who have made their critiques of previous philosophy explicit. It is as important to recognize the overarching failures as it is to take note of the threads of truth that weave in and out of the history of philosophy. Even so, this understanding should serve more as general clue for remembering something simple and obvious than an original claim about the way things are. It might be useful as a way of eliminating certain contemporary prejudices and dogmas.

One of the dogmas with which I have been concerned is the very idea that there is such a thing as a history of rationality, or Western thought, or something like that. Another has been the idea that there is some special task for philosophy. These dogmas, or myths, are the sustaining ideology of the modern institutional form of philosophy. I hope I have pulled together enough of the history to do away with these modern myths.

I have opposed a traditional view of the history of philosophy, and recast the logic of the story at a number of levels. For the sake of students facing exams, I summarize my findings in the following handy truth table.

| THE TRADITIONAL STORY | THE TRUTH ABOUT EVERYTHING |
|---|---|
| ***Origin Myths*** | |
| The Presocratics became the fathers of Western thought when they invented rationality and created the first, primitive philosophies. | 1. Rationality was never "invented." |
| | 2. Those thinkers identified as Presocratics have in common their attempt to reexpress fundamentally mythological concerns—cosmo-babble—in a new idiom. Their precursors were Eastern mystics, and their work essentially mythopoeic. |
| | 3. Rationality, according to any reasonable criteria, can be more readily discovered in the work of the physicians of the time than the Presocratic physicist-philosophers. |
| | 4. The complex whole of Presocratic philosophies not only anticipates but actually instantiates all of the major dynamics of the subsequent history of philosophy not, however, because their work was "original" in terms of influence or foundations, but because philosophy by its nature is a circular enterprise. |

| | |
|---|---|
| The Sophists were a bunch of naughty men who almost spoiled the purity of Greek thought. | 1. As a group, the Sophists were considerably more reasonable in their ideas and practice than the traditional superstars of the history of Greek philosophy (the Presocratics, Socrates, Plato, etc.).<br>2. The Sophists were considerably more "Greek" than the official philosophers such as Plato, who were outcasts at least in their own minds. |
| Socrates became the father of Western philosophy by inventing critical reason in the form of the dialectic and introducing it into ethical discussions. | 1. Socrates did not invent critical reason. Actually, he was quite unreasonable.<br>2. The dialectical method is just asking decent questions. Anything more is mystification, paradoxophilia.<br>3. Anthropological and ethical concerns were not new with Socrates.<br>4. Socrates' interest in ethics was merely his way of advocating a particular and bizarre ethics of his own, an idiosyncratic view of the good life. |
| Plato created Western metaphysical thought by inventing idealism. | 1. What can I say? Who but a few loons ever really believed in Plato's Forms?<br>2. Plato was a Pythagorean mystic. His thought is better characterized as irrationalism than rationalism.<br>3. What's all this about "Western metaphysical thought"? |

### Boundary Myths

| | |
|---|---|
| Eastern philosophy is very different from Western philosophy. Eastern philosophy is essentially religious mysticism, Western philosophy is scientific rationalism. | Wrong. Western philosophy, especially in its "rationalist" forms, is essentially mystical. There is no better way to understand the largest part of Western philosophy than to understand the ways of mysticism, East or West. Eastern philosophy, on the other hand, is hardly monolithic, and includes, if with less emphasis, all the significant philosophical perspectives on rationality, science, and so on, traditionally associated with "Western thought." |
| Medieval philosophy is for fat monks. Modern Western philosophy has emancipated itself from theology. | 1. Medieval thought already encompasses whatever empiricist insights philosophy can have (which isn't saying much).<br>2. Modern Western philosophy is essentially theology. |

### Foundation Myths

| | |
|---|---|
| Descartes became the father of modern philosophy by inventing the project of epistemology, emphasizing the importance of a scientific method in philosophy and elsewhere, and creating the metaphysical concept of the subject. | He did no such things.<br>His "first philosophy," as distinct from his scientific work, was an attempt to provide a new home for theological concerns within the context of the new science. His arguments are a lucid but unso- |

phisticated representation of medieval theology. It is absurd to say that Descartes invented the concept of the self. His "method," insofar as it formed part of his philosophy, was not scientific, but mystical, an attempt to find a method which would produce its own results.

| | |
|---|---|
| Empiricism is the foundation of empirical science.<br><br>Hobbes and Bacon, together with Descartes, became the fathers of modern scientific rationality by providing the philosophical foundations of science. | 1. Empirically speaking, not true. The early modern philosophers were science fanaticists, who were inspired by prospects of science to create new forms of philosophical theologies. Scientific advances were perfectly possible without their philosophies, and did in fact occur for the most part without any regard for them.<br>2. Empiricism is the foundation of its own brand of mysticism, if of anything at all. |

### Revolutionary Myths

| | |
|---|---|
| Kant created modern philosophy by throwing out the traditional metaphysics, replacing it with a critical philosophy, and making of the faculties of the knowing subject philosophy's central concern. | 1. Kant did not throw out the old metaphysical philosophy, but simply found a new way to express it. He revived the project of scholastic theology on behalf of the modern university.<br>2. The critical philosophy is either pure analysis, i.e., plain thinking, or a metaphysics, according to which critique mysteriously produces unconditioned knowledge about the world.<br>3. Kant's conclusions about the centrality of the knowing subject, insofar as they are supported by argument and fact, are a set of truisms from which nothing of consequence can follow. |
| Hegel historicized philosophy. | He did, but only by philosophizing history. He did not create the historical sense, but used it in order to recreate a brand of metaphysics. |
| Schopenhauer, Kierkegaard, and Nietzsche were the first to reject the entire history of philosophy and take a stand on behalf of personal, existential truth. | 1. 'The personal' had long been a part of philosophy.<br>2. They produced philosophies very much in the 'impersonal' mode of the tradition.<br>3. Nietzsche, at least, was not an irrationalist, but a kind of enlightenment philosopher. |
| Heidegger, Foucault, Derrida, and the other continental trendies are out to overthrow the Western metaphysical tradition. | There is no such tradition, in the sense of something constitutive of Western thought. There is, however, a tradition of saying foolish things, sometimes known as metaphysics, and of this their project of overthrowing metaphysics is very much a part. |

| | |
|---|---|
| Modern Western thought is besotted with the idea of metaphysical subjectivity, of which it ought to be purged. | Insofar as such an idea is widespread among Westerners, it is the simple, indispensable, universal, and eternal idea that seeing is believing. The "problem," if there is one, is the very idea that such an idea could be "foundational" for all Western thought, and the inference that there must be some alternative possible foundation. |
| Analytic philosophy is an entirely new kind of philosophy, originating out of late-nineteenth-century developments in logic and mathematics. | It's the same old scholastic-theological drivel dressed up in new symbols. The philosophy of language is metaphysics for secular academics; the philosophy of mind is the latest fodder for sci-ence-fanaticism. |
| The later Wittgenstein overthrew the whole tradition of metaphysical thought by showing that philosophy was based on confusions in and about language. | Sure. So did Heidegger, Nietzsche, Kant, and all the rest. Wittgenstein recreated the whole tradition by being its latest overthrower, by basing this "overthrow" on a claim to find in something purely formal (i.e., language) content of significance. |

**Professional Myths**

| | |
|---|---|
| Philosophy is the special, second-order investigation of all phenomena, and includes epistemology (the study of knowledge), ontology (the study of being), ethics (the study of the good), and a number of other important-sounding disciplines. | It includes neither those pseudo-disciplines nor witchcraft (the study of spells and incantations), astrology (how the stars affect you), and alimentology (the study of food consumption). |
| Philosophers are wiser than the rest of us. | Who knows? |
| Philosophy is a serious activity. | Philosophy can be fun! |

## MORE OF THE SAME?

You're boiling over, I know. You've been dying to turn the tables and say: *Look, Matthew, you've been a very foolish and naughty boy. If what you want is to champion free thought, you defeat your own purpose by attacking the great thinkers of history. What's more, you're just another philosopher, and a rotten one to boot! You suffer from an Aristotle complex, in a major way. You have implemented a slash-and-burn, scorched-earth, take-no-prisoners policy toward philosophers. You fault them for seeking a unity in all things, and yet all you have done is reduce everything to one, too. Your idea of the Holy Grail is your own Holy Grail. It is your universal key to past, present, and future. You are the latest (but definitely not the greatest) "overthrower" of the Western metaphysical tradition. What's more, you have engaged in pathetic self-justification for what you are doing. You have excused any insanity by placing philosophy beyond sanity. You have excused lack of professionalism by defining philosophy as an amateur activity. You have set up your own criteria for success and then (surprise) fulfilled them. You have conveniently left open only one possibility for philosophy, namely, the critique of all other philosophy in a satirical history of philosophy. Even now, you are internalizing your own critique, building your paranoid defenses through auto-critique. You are hyperreflexive. Worse, you're a paradoxophiliac!*

My first impulse, of course, is to run and hide. It wasn't me, honest! I am one thing, my book is another. Suitably chastened, I return to offer a meek defense. I want to address three points: I have abused the great; I have repeated the disreputable error of claiming to know the truth about everything; and I have made my own project inevitable, the only true philosophy.

I have been unkind to the great philosophers. But don't get too worked up. Reprints of Descartes will be selling long after the last copy of my book has rotted off the shelf. And a few potshots from me aren't much compared to the slings and arrows of other outraged philosophers. Have I been *unfair* to the great philosophers? Given the constraints of space I have tried hard not to be. I have no intention of basing the criticism of any great philosopher on my own mere authority, which wouldn't be very effective anyway, since I have none. I have appealed to fact and to reason, or so I hope, and, all right, the odd bit of humor. The alternative, to forgive these so-called powerhouses of philosophy out of kindness on matters of fact and reason, is clearly unacceptable. In this think I would have the support of most of these great minds (provided they can forgive me a few harmless jokes, nothing personal). Have I damaged the cause of free thinking by assaulting the great defenders of thought? I don't think so. I'm not so sure that the greats in their present form do all that much good for thought. Insofar as they are just an excuse for students to memorize a list of silly doctrines so that they can regurgitate it on exams, maybe we could do without them. I suggest we let the greats defend themselves, and may the best man or woman win.

Is the Holy Grail of philosophy my own Holy Grail? Am I just another— yikes!—totalizing philosopher? Am I just another self-important overthrower? I could point out that, if so, this is not necessarily self-inconsistent. Of course, you would have to throw me out with the rest of the philosophers, but presumably not before having accepted my chief arguments. But things are not so dramatic. I have only claimed to find the truth about philosophy, not the truth about everything. At best, I have merely tested a series of philosophical systems against their intentions to represent the truth about everything and have found them wanting. The claim that there is no truth about everything, if true, must have a basis in some banal logic, and need not appear weighty or apocalyptic. Nor does it follow that Western thought has been informed by some dubious or perhaps evil presuppositions. Philosophy is not thought, or so I have argued, and its errors are just plain bad thinking. Philosophy just dissolves. As I said in the introduction, this is a book for those who love to think. It is not likely to satisfy those who want a philosophical system, or anything like that.

Have I made my own project inevitable, the only possible way of philosophizing? It looks pretty suspicious, I have to admit. But what I have intended to show is not that my own way of doing philosophy, as it's done in this book, is the *only* legitimate project for philosophy, but that it has *just as much* right to the title of philosophy as anything else that has hitherto gone under that name. In doing philosophy, it simply is not possible to stop short of the truth about everything. But, if you believe my conclusions about philosophy, there could be no single, correct way of doing philosophy, for the simple reason that the idea that philosophy as a project is erroneous. Even with respect to the history of philosophy itself, I have only covered what is philosophical, in a certain sense; I have mostly ignored the historical, biographical, cultural, and intellectual dimensions of the story. Everything other than pure philosophy—which really means *everything*—remains untouched. What remains, I think, is not to do philosophy, but to do things in a philosophical way. So far as that goes, I haven't even begun to explore the possibilities. Everything remains open.

Now I think not just that there are many other things I could have done, but that this could have been done better, too. The only sense of inevitability I have about the whole thing is of a plain and ordinary kind, what any writer feels when he knows that his work is finished: not because the thing is perfect, but because there is nothing more that he can do.

# PROPOSALS

Having been so unremittingly destructive, I am surely obliged to offer some constructive suggestions about how philosophy ought to proceed. I'm afraid, however, that I have no very good idea on how best to take the next step in the search for the truth about everything. So I have no truly philosophical proposal to make. I can, however, offer some advice having to do with the worldly manifestations of present philosophical activity. My first proposal, detailed below, concerns the institutional framework within which virtually all that calls itself philosophy is practiced today. My second proposal has to do with public relations, or what sort of findings philosophy should present to the general public.

## INSTITUTIONAL PROPOSALS

The brute fact is that virtually all of what passes today for philosophy is practiced within the modern university. The primary denotation of the word "philosophy" now may well be the institutional structure, the academic department, within which philosophy itself presumably takes place. So, I address my first proposals to the institution.

Academic philosophy departments will do better in promoting the general happiness, in my view, once they become clear on their primary mission. The primary mission of a philosophy faculty is to teach. Research, the production of new truths, ought to be pursued only in service of education. Which brings up a point about which academic philosophers are often unclear: Their job is to teach their students *how* to think, not *what* to think. To be sure, even that mission requires some research, to preserve and enhance the heritage of critical thinking. Critical thinking itself, however, is no great mystery and involves no specialized techniques, though it is nonetheless not ubiquitous in the still-to-be-educated masses of humankind.

With this general statement of mission in mind, I propose the following.

## (1) ABOLISH THE PH.D. IN ITS PRESENT FORM

*Limit time spent* in immediate postgraduate studies to a maximum of three years. The current average time to complete a philosophy Ph.D. is a billion years, after which the average student spends another gadzillion years in the limbo of post-doctoral fellowships, temporary lectureships, and the like. Such a system is bound to produce economically captive, hyperspecialized bores.

*Curtail the length* of dissertations to something like a long essay. More extensive work should be postponed until later in one's career. Lengthy tomes on serious subjects written before one's thirtieth year, as Plato might have observed, are usually worthless. Why not wait until the individual has something to say? The objective of learning the scholarly arts could be achieved with shorter, less time-consuming works. Perhaps save the title of "doctor" as a reward for the mature works produced toward the middle of one's career.

*Ban the publication of dissertations.* Assistant professors typically make their first books out of microwaved leftovers from doctoral theses. The result is hyperspecialization and many bad books. Force them to work on something else when they finish their degrees.

*Down with feudalism.* Graduate students in the later stages of their thesis work are the serfs of the modern university. A system of economic and professional bondage forces them to carry the bulk of the teaching load while receiving the minimum of compensation. Once they complete their servitude, they are too old and impoverished to have any option but to join the ranks of the oppressive professor-lords. The system is a disservice to students as well as teachers.

*Encourage extracurricular activities.* Make aspiring philosophers spend a few years in the Peace Corps, or working for living. Let them grow up. It certainly won't do them any harm.

*Hire without Ph.D.s.* Not every good teacher of philosophy need have gone through specialized training. Some will have built a base of valuable experience elsewhere. Many a Ph.D., conversely, will have no experience worth a damn and be a rotten teacher to boot. The Ph.D. in its present form is a membership purchased by economic indentureship in an exclusive guild whose function is to restrict the natural activity of the marketplace.

## (2) Make philosophy a segment of an undergraduate major, not a major itself

Philosophy on its own is sterile. Thought needs material, critique needs an object. Philosophy should therefore be combined with other subjects to form possible undergraduate majors. As at Oxford University, for example, it may be combined with Politics and Economics. It could also be matched with History, Literary Studies, Religion, Art History, Creative Writing, and the like. It may be combined with the sciences and mathematics, but not in the form of the philosophy of science or mathematics, pointlessly scholastic activities which are liable to confuse the budding scientist or mathematician.

## (3) Abolish tenure

The only rationale for tenure is that it protects the freedom of expression of professors. Such an extraordinary protection would be justified if social conditions were such that the openness of the marketplace of ideas could not otherwise be maintained. Circumstances in most Western countries are no longer such as to justify tenure. Absent the rationale, tenure is merely an excuse for economic exploitation, inefficiency, and laziness. Instead of keeping the marketplace open, tenure restricts it by redirecting resources from the new and promising to the old, privileged, and immutable. It also induces odd and disturbing behavior among those who aspire to tenure. Professors have jobs, their job is to teach, and it deserves no more or less security than any other comparable job.

## (4) Publish and perish

By abolishing tenure, we would, one hopes, eliminate the publish-or-perish syndrome which afflicts those who seek tenure. Of course, we would want to avoid a situation in which, in abolishing tenure, all professors suffer from said syndrome. To that end I propose:

*A two-year moratorium* on philosophical publication (to commence sometime after the publication of this book). The general public will never know the difference, and the specialists will have time to take a breather, smell the roses, catch up on other reading, and try out something new.

*A new ethos.* Censorship and other artificial restriction on publications will never work as long-term solutions. What is required is a whole new way of acting and valuing. A new ethos is called for, one that would induce a positive kind of self-censorship. Philosophers would publish only on the condition that they had something new, interesting, and important to say. They would summarize and compress their findings so as to limit the number of times in which they would make a claim on the world's attention. According to the new ethos, a philosopher's professional value and self-esteem would no longer be linked to his or her corpus of publications. The abilities to teach, to inspire, to discuss, and so forth would be decisive.

## POPULAR PROPOSAL

Everyone has a set of general beliefs, and most people at any one time (and throughout history) have shared a certain subset of such beliefs. We sometimes call such sets "philosophies," though that may be an abuse of language. What may count as philosophy is the activity of keeping these initial beliefs, or dispositions, on track, open to the truth about things, free from self-inflicted confusions. Philosophy often marshals reminders with the strategic purpose of keeping the popular mind open and critical. Here I propose a few such reminders, all platitudinous maxims, renewed attention to which might help guard against some of the popular preconceptions of our time. Given that my target is vast, amorphous, and not self-consistent, one should expect no more than generalities and pontifications.

There are those today who preach that we are all victims of a certain, inherited way of thinking; that the history of Western philosophy has conditioned our thought, belabored us with prejudicial conceptual schemes, made us into immoral monsters, divided us into incompatible and uncommunicating groups. They preach that the individual is a selfish illusion, that only the group is real, and that we must break the code of our thought if we are to achieve salvation.

Against these preachers of falsehood I say:

*You are what you think.* You alone are responsible for what you think. No one, no history, no language, no unconscious can take your place. There is nothing more or less to you than what you can think of yourself. Nothing is hidden. Thousands of years of thought and culture are not there to trap you into fixed ways of thinking, but to liberate your thought. That is our only real heritage in philosophy.

*You can make things better.* If you *think*, if you see how things stand, you can see how to change them. It won't always work according to plan, but sometimes it does. Reason is your friend. Things can get better. We can do better. (This is not just an American ideology. Shame on those who say otherwise.)

*Philosophy holds no mystery.* There may be mystery in the world, if you like, but none in philosophy. There is no great secret reserved for the philosophically initiated. No secret fabric of thought, whether cultural, historical, or metaphysical. No explanation to end all explanations. No "what it is" which is identical with a "that it is." No single answer to all the problems of the world. Philosophy is at best the home for a few unanswered questions. So far as philosophical knowledge is concerned, it's not *what* you know, but *how* you know, and for that there is no need for more than a few, sensible maxims.

In sum, I say only: Think! Be responsible! Be good! Be true to yourself. Become what you are.

# Index